Peter Norton's®

Computing
Fundamentals

Fifth Edition

McGraw Hill **Glencoe**

New York, New York   Columbus, Ohio   Chicago, Illinois   Peoria, Illinois   Woodland Hills, California

Glencoe/McGraw-Hill

A Division of The McGraw·Hill Companies

Peter Norton's® Computing Fundamentals, Fifth Edition

Send all inquiries to:

Glencoe/McGraw-Hill
21600 Oxnard St., Suite 500
Woodland Hills, CA 91367-4906

ISBN: 0-07-830960-3 (P)
ISBN: 0-07-845448-4 (C)

3 4 5 6 7 8 9   027   06 05 04 03 (P)
2 3 4 5 6 7 8 9   027   06 05 04 03 (C)

Between the time that Web site information is gathered and published, it is not unusual for some sites to have closed. URLs will be updated in reprints when possible.

About Peter Norton

Acclaimed computer software entrepreneur Peter Norton is active in civic and philanthropic affairs. He serves on the boards of several scholastic and cultural institutions and currently devotes much of his time to philanthropy.

Raised in Seattle, Washington, Mr. Norton made his mark in the computer industry as a programmer and businessman. *Norton Utilities*™, *Norton AntiVirus*™, and other utility programs are installed on millions of computers worldwide. He is also a best-selling author of computer books.

Mr. Norton sold his PC-software business to Symantec Corporation in 1990 but continues to write and speak on computers, helping millions of people better understand information technology. He and his family currently reside in Santa Monica, California.

Editorial Consultant

Tim Huddleston

Academic Reviewers

Teresa Beatty
ECPI College of Technology

Robert Caruso
Santa Rosa Junior College

Glenda Chagaris
Carteret Community College

James T. Davis
Gulf Coast Community College

Rhonda Davis
Isothermal Community College

J. Timothy Dunigan
West Virginia University

Lynn Dee Eason
Sault College

Terry A. Felke
William Rainey Harper College

J. Patrick Fenton
West Valley College

Mary Hanson
Northwest Technical College

Patrick A. T. Kelly
Mount Royal College

Alex Morgan
West Valley College

Cindi A. Nadelman
Naugatuck Valley Community College

Mava F. Norton
Lee University

Wilson E. "Bill" Stroud
Joliet Junior College

Technical Reviewers

Bill Brandon
Emmett Dulaney
Molly E. Holzschlag

Acknowledgments

Others who contributed to the content and development of this project: Beth Anderson, Emmett Dulaney, Jeff Durham, Molly Holzschlag, Cynthia Karrasch, Kate Mueller, Hurix Systems Private Limited, Tata Interactive Systems, and Setting Pace.

Special thanks goes to the individuals at Glencoe/McGraw-Hill whose dedication and hard work made this project possible.

Foreword to the Student

Why Study Computer Technology?

The computer is a truly amazing machine. Few tools can help you perform so many different tasks. Whether you want to track an investment, publish a newsletter, design a building, or practice landing an F14 on the deck of an aircraft carrier, you can use a computer to do it. Equally amazing is the fact that the computer has taken on a role in nearly every aspect of our lives. Consider the following examples:

◆ Tiny embedded computers control our alarm clocks, entertainment centers, and home appliances.

◆ Today's automobiles could not even start—let alone run efficiently—without embedded computer systems.

◆ In the United States, more than half of all homes now have at least one personal computer, and the majority of those computers are connected to the Internet.

◆ An estimated ten million people now work from home—instead of commuting to a traditional workplace—thanks to PC and networking technologies.

◆ People use e-mail for personal communications nearly ten times as often as ordinary mail, and nearly five times more often than the telephone.

◆ Routine, daily tasks, such as banking at automated teller machines, talking over digital telephone networks, and paying for groceries with the help of computerized cashiers, are affected by computer technologies.

Here are just a few personal benefits you can enjoy by developing a mastery of computer technology:

◆ **Improved Employment Prospects.** Computer-related skills are essential in many careers—not just computer programming. Whether you plan a career in automotive mechanics, nursing, journalism, or archaeology, having computer skills will make you more marketable to prospective employers.

◆ **Skills That Span Different Aspects of Life.** Many people find their computer skills valuable regardless of the setting—at home, work, school, or play. Your knowledge of computers will be useful in many places other than your work.

◆ **Greater Self-Sufficiency.** Those people who truly understand computers know that computers are tools—nothing more or less. We do not give up control of our lives to computer systems; rather, we use computer systems to suit our needs. By knowing how to use computers, you can actually be more self-sufficient, whether you use computers for research, communications, or time-management.

◆ **A Foundation of Knowledge for a Lifetime of Learning.** Basic computing principles have not changed over the past few years, and they will be valid well into the future. By mastering fundamental concepts and terminology, you will develop a strong base that will support your learning for years to come.

Regardless of your reasons for taking this course, you have made a wise decision. The knowledge and skills you gain should pay dividends in the future, as computers become even more common at home and at work.

VISUAL ESSAY: COMPUTERS IN OUR LIVES

A Millions of people use handheld computers to manage their schedules, send e-mail and faxes, create documents, and more.

B Using 3-D CAD tools, designers can create photorealistic three-dimensional renderings of a finished building's interior and exterior. These capabilities enable the designer and client to visualize the completed project before the first shovel of dirt has been turned.

C Factories use computerized robotic arms to do physical work that is hazardous or highly repetitive.

D Computers have become a creative tool for musicians. The Musical Instrument Digital Interface (MIDI) allows different electronic instruments to be connected to one another, as well as to computers.

E The military is often at the forefront of technology. This man is using an Airborne Warning and Aircraft Control (AWAC) system to track the in-flight progress of missiles and jets. The military also uses computers to keep track of one of the largest payroll and human-resource management systems in the world.

F Perhaps no area of science has benefited more from computer technology—or contributed more to its growth—than the space program.

G Many movies and television productions now use motion-capture technology to enable computer-generated characters to move realistically. Special sensors are attached to an actor, who moves in a tightly choreographed way. Movements are recorded by a computer. The data then can be assigned to the corresponding parts of a digital character's body, so that its movements exactly mimic the actor's movements.

Brief Table of Contents

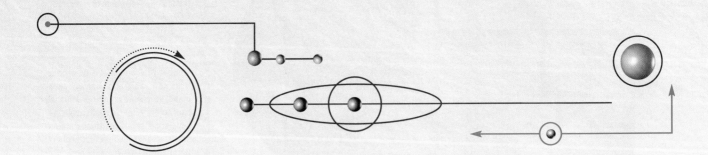

Table of Contents

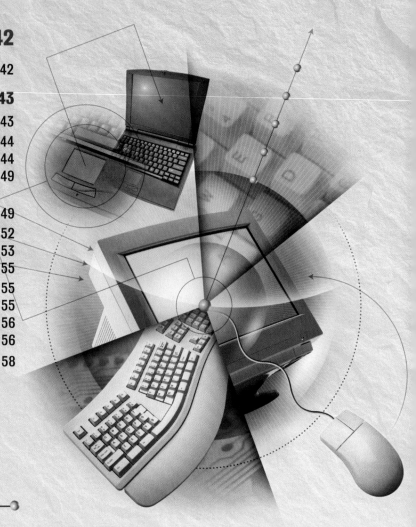

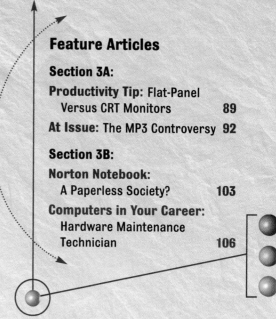

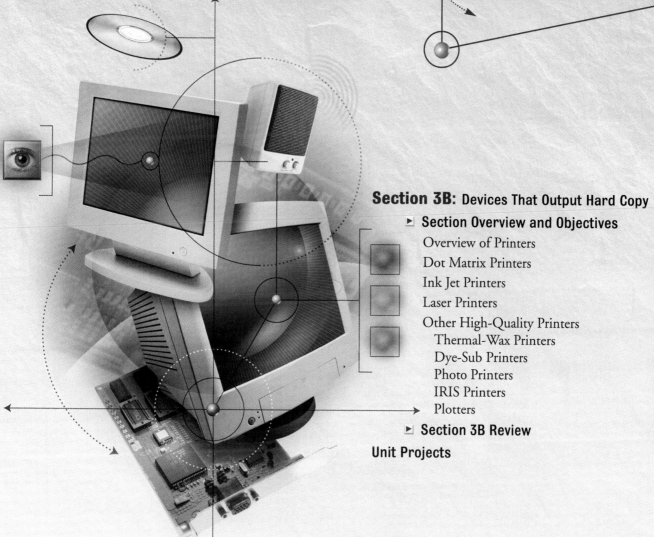

Unit 4: Processing Data 112

Unit 6: The Operating System and User Interface 188

Feature Articles

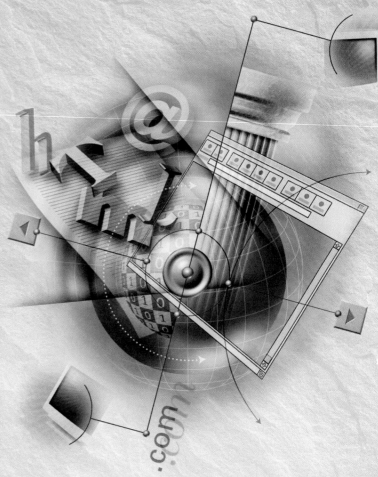

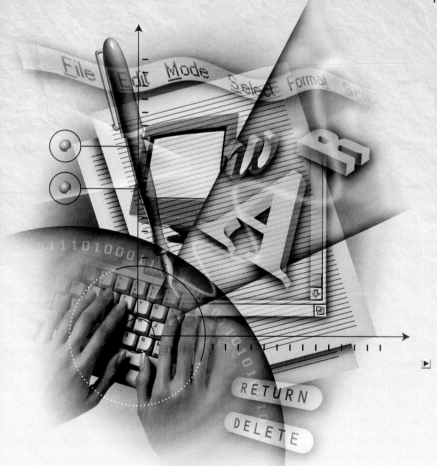

Feature Articles

Section 8A:

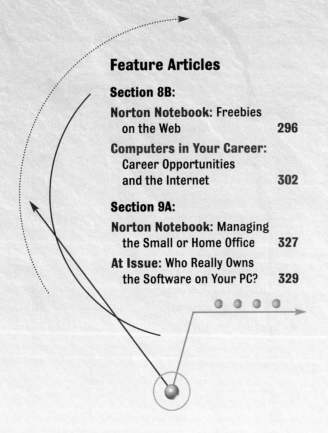

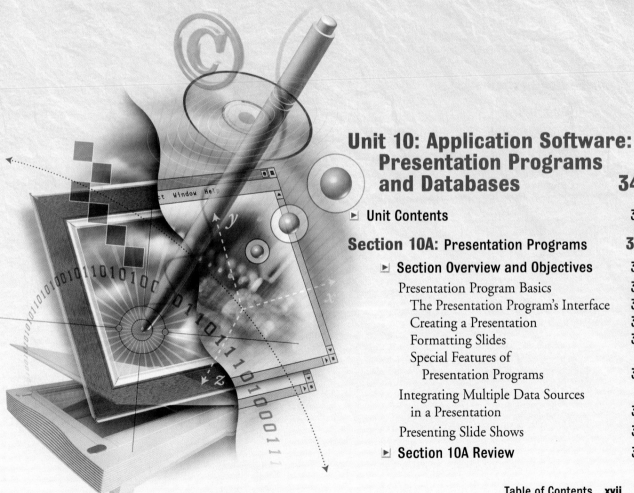

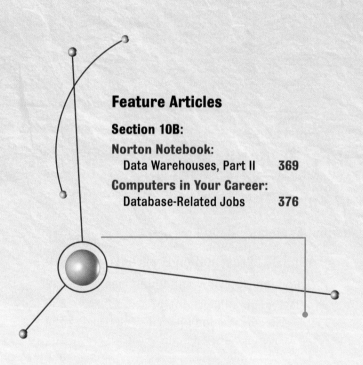

Unit 11: Graphics and Multimedia   **388**

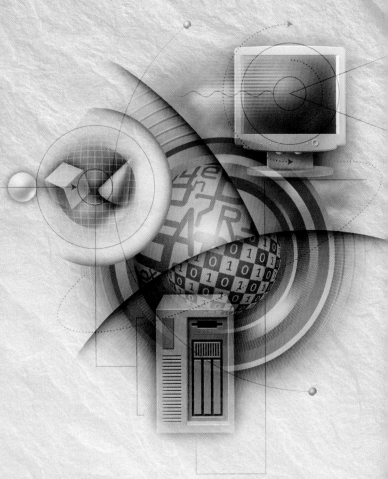

Unit 12: Development of Information Systems 430

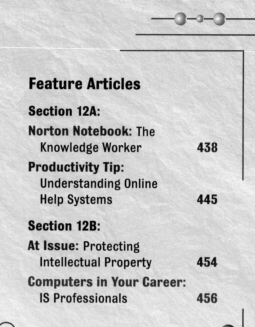

Feature Articles

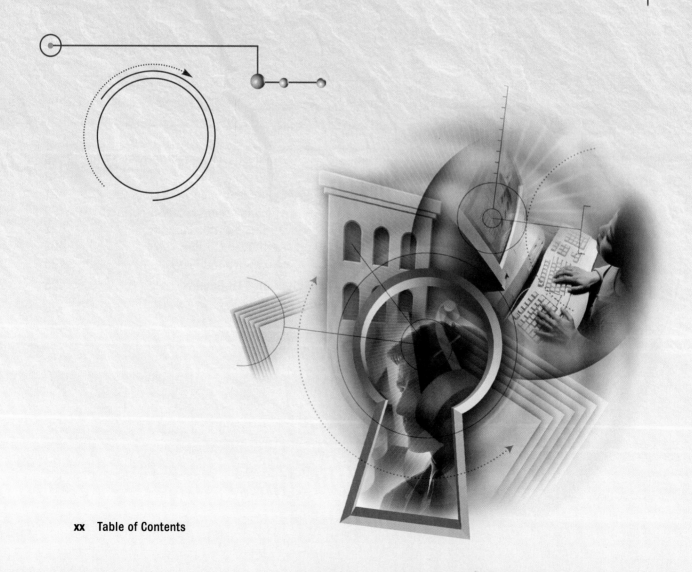

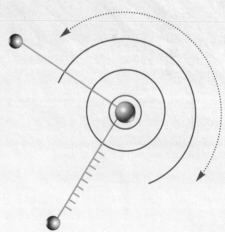

Appendices   462

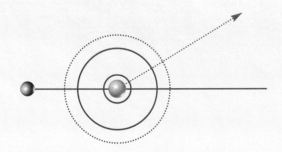

Feature Articles

Prerequisites

What You Should Know Before Using This Book

This book assumes that you have never used a computer before or that your computer experience has been very limited. If this is so, you may need to learn some basic computer skills before proceeding with this course. This Prerequisites section introduces basic skills, using illustrations to help you recognize and remember the hardware or software involved in each skill. Some of these skills are covered in greater detail in other units of this book. In such cases, you will find references that point you to more information.

Equipment Required for This Book's Exercises

- An IBM-compatible personal computer
- A two-button mouse
- An Internet connection
- A keyboard
- Windows 95 or higher
- A Web browser

TURNING THE COMPUTER ON AND OFF

As simple as it may sound, there is a right way to turn a computer's power on and off. If you perform either of these tasks incorrectly, you may damage the computer's components or cause problems for the operating system, programs, or data files.

Turning On the Computer

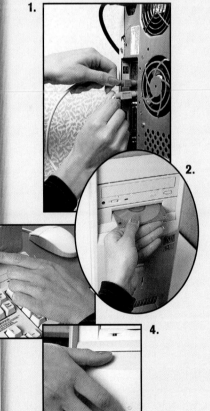

1. Before turning on your computer, make sure that all the necessary cables (such as those for the mouse, keyboard, and printer) are connected to the system unit. Also, make sure that the system's power cords are connected to an appropriate power source.

2. Make sure that there are no diskettes in the computer's diskette drive, unless you must boot the system from a diskette. (The term *booting* means starting the computer.) If you must boot the system from a diskette, ask your instructor for specific directions.

3. Find the On/Off switch on each attached device (the monitor, the printer, etc.), and place it in the ON position. A device's power switch may not be on the front panel. Check the sides and back to find the On/Off switch if the switch is not located on the front panel.

4. Find the On/Off switch on the computer's system unit—its main box into which all other components are plugged—and place it in the ON position.

   Most computers take a minute or two to start. Your computer may display messages during the start-up process. If one of these messages prompts you to perform an action (such as providing a network user ID and password), ask your instructor for directions. After the computer has started, the Windows desktop will appear on your screen.

Turning Off the Computer

For more information on Windows and other operating systems, see Unit 6, "The Operating System and User Interface."

1.

In Windows-based systems, it is critical that you shut down properly, as described here. Windows creates many temporary files on your computer's hard disk when it is running. By shutting down properly, you give Windows the chance to erase those temporary files and do other "housekeeping" tasks. If you simply turn off your computer while Windows or other programs are running, you can cause harm to your system.

Note: The figures show the shut-down process in Windows 98. The process, menus, and dialog boxes are the same in all versions of Windows except Windows XP, as noted in the following instructions.

1. Remove any disks from the diskette and CD-ROM drive, and make sure that all data is saved and all running programs are closed. (For help with saving data and closing programs, ask your instructor.)

2. Using your mouse pointer, click the Start button, which is located on the taskbar. The Start menu will appear. On the Start menu, click Shut Down. (If you use Windows XP, click the Turn Off Computer option.) The Shut Down Windows dialog box will appear. (In Windows XP, the Turn Off Computer dialog box will appear.)

The background is called the desktop.

Icons are pictures that represent programs, files, disks, and other resources on your computer.

You use the mouse pointer to access resources by clicking icons and commands.

Taskbar

Click the Start button to open the Start menu.

Click Shut Down to turn off the computer.

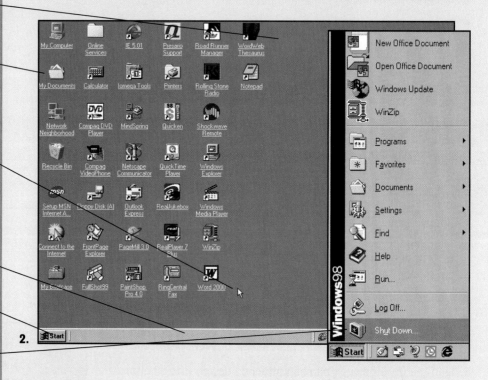

2.

3. Click Shut Down or Turn Off, depending on which version of Windows you use. Click the OK button, if necessary.

Windows will begin the shut-down process. Windows may display a message telling you that it is shutting down. Then it may display the message, "It is now safe to turn off your computer." When this message appears, turn off the power to your system unit, monitor, and printer.

In some newer computers, the system unit will power down automatically after Windows shuts down. If your computer provides this feature, you need to turn off only your monitor and other devices.

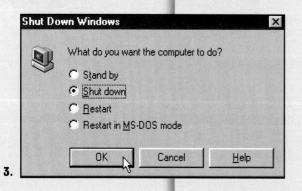

3.

USING THE KEYBOARD

A. If you know how to type, then you can easily use a computer keyboard. The keyboard contains all the alphanumeric keys found on a typewriter, plus some keys that perform special functions.

B. In Windows, the Enter key performs two primary functions. First, it lets you create paragraph ("hard") returns in application programs, such as word processors. Second, when a dialog box is open, pressing Enter is like clicking the OK button. This accepts your input and closes the dialog box.

C. The Shift, Ctrl (control), and Alt (alternate) keys are called modifier keys. You use them in combination with other keys to issue commands. In many programs, for example, pressing Ctrl+S (hold the Ctrl key down while pressing the S key) saves the open document to disk. Used with all the alphanumeric and function keys, the modifier keys let you issue hundreds of commands.

D. In Windows programs, the Esc (escape) key performs one universal function. That is, you can use it to cancel a command before it executes. When a dialog box is open, pressing Esc is like clicking the Cancel button. This action closes the dialog box and ignores any changes you made in the dialog box.

E. Depending on the program you are using, the function keys may serve a variety of purposes, or none at all. Function keys generally provide shortcuts to program features or commands. In many Windows programs, for example, you can press F1 to launch the online help system.

F. In any Windows application, a blinking bar—called the cursor or the insertion point—shows you where the next character will appear as you type. You can use the cursor-movement keys to move the cursor to different positions. As their arrows indicate, these keys let you move the cursor up, down, left, and right.

G. The Delete key erases characters to the right of the cursor. The Backspace key erases characters to the left of the cursor. In many applications, the Home and End keys let you move the cursor to the beginning or end of a line, or farther when used with a modifier key. Page Up and Page Down let you scroll quickly through a document, moving back or ahead one screen at a time.

The keyboard is covered in detail in Section 2A, "Standard Input Devices."

B.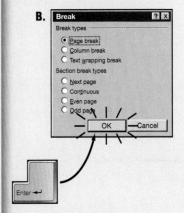

C.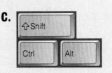

D.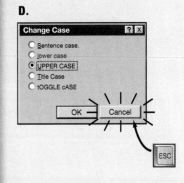

F. I am what I am. | — Cursor (or insertion point)

Cursor-movement keys

G.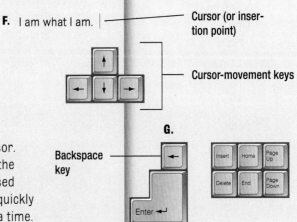

Backspace key

USING THE MOUSE

The mouse makes your computer easy to use. In fact, Windows and Windows-based programs are mouse-oriented, meaning their features and commands are designed for use with a mouse.

The mouse is covered in greater detail in Section 2A, "Standard Input Devices."

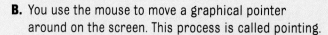

B.

A. This book assumes that you are using a standard two-button mouse. Usually, the mouse's left button is the primary button. You press ("click") it to select commands and perform other tasks. The right button opens special "shortcut menus," the contents of which vary according to the program you are using.

B. You use the mouse to move a graphical pointer around on the screen. This process is called pointing.

C. The pointer is controlled by the mouse's motions across your desktop's surface. When you push the mouse forward (away from you), the pointer moves up on the screen. When you pull the mouse backward (toward you), the pointer moves down. When you move the mouse to the left or right, or diagonally, the pointer moves to the left, right, or diagonally on the screen.

C.

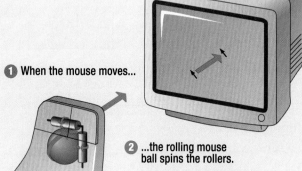

1 When the mouse moves...

2 ...the rolling mouse ball spins the rollers.

3 The information from the spinning rollers is sent to the system software, which controls the pointer.

D. To click an object, such as an icon, point to it on the screen, then quickly press and release the left mouse button one time. Generally, clicking an object selects it, or tells Windows that you want to do something with the object.

E. To double-click an object, point to it on the screen, then quickly press and release the left mouse button twice. Generally, double-clicking an object selects and activates the object. For example, when you double-click a program's icon on the desktop, the program launches so you can use it.

F. To right-click an object, point to it on the screen, then quickly press and release the right mouse button one time. Generally, right-clicking an object opens a shortcut menu that provides options for working with the object.

G. You can use the mouse to move objects around on the screen. For example, you can move an icon to a different location on the Windows desktop. This procedure often is called drag-and-drop editing. To drag an object, point to it, press and hold down the left mouse button, drag the object to the desired location, and then release the mouse button.

"click"

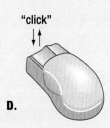

D.

"click click"

E.

"click"

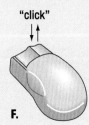

F.

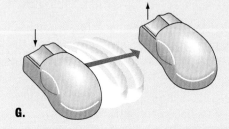

G.

Peter Norton's®

Computing Fundamentals

Fifth Edition

UNIT 1

The Amazing Computer

UNIT CONTENTS

This unit contains the following sections:

The Interactive Browser Edition CD-ROM provides additional labs and activities to apply concepts from this unit.

Introduction to Computer Systems

OVERVIEW:
Dissecting the Ultimate Machine

Have you ever watched an incredible scene in a movie, or have you seen a drawing that looked so realistic you thought it was a photograph? Afterward, were you amazed to learn that the scene or drawing had been generated by using a computer? If so, you are certainly not alone. We are surprised endlessly by the feats accomplished with the help of computers, and we marvel at their complexity. For this reason, many people assume that computers must be difficult to understand and difficult to use. Most of us do not realize, however, that computers are basically simple devices, and all computers have a great deal in common. Most computers— from the largest to the smallest—operate on the same fundamental principles. They are all fabricated from the same basic types of components, and they all need instructions to make them run.

As a first step toward understanding and learning to use computers, this section gives you a peek at these fascinating machines. You will learn about the types of hardware that all computer systems use, as well as the types of software that make them run. You also will see that without a user—someone like you— a computer system is not really complete.

OBJECTIVES

- List the four parts of a computer system.
- Identify four types of computer hardware.
- List four units of measure for computer memory and storage.
- Provide two examples of input and output devices.
- Name and describe three types of storage devices.
- Differentiate the two main categories of computer software.
- List at least four specific types of application software.
- Describe the five key categories of computers in use today.

THE PARTS OF A COMPUTER SYSTEM

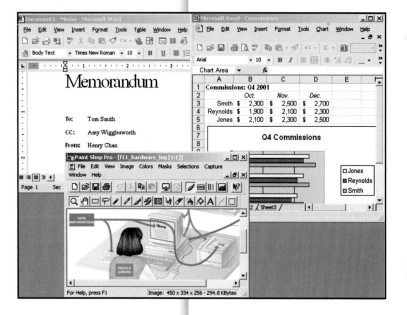

Figure 1A.1
The computer system

In basic terms, a **computer** is an electronic device that processes data, converting it into information that is useful to people. Any computer—regardless of its type—is controlled by programmed instructions, which give the machine a purpose and tell it what to do.

Computers come in many varieties, from the tiny computers built into household appliances to the astounding supercomputers that have helped scientists map the human genome. In this book, you will focus primarily on personal computers (PCs), which individuals use in countless ways. But no matter how big it is or how it is used, every computer is part of a system. A complete **computer system** consists of four parts: hardware, software, one or more users, and data (see Figure 1A.1).

Hardware

The physical devices that make up the computer are called **hardware.** Hardware is any part of the computer you can touch. A computer's hardware consists of interconnected electronic devices that you can use to control the computer's operation, input, and output. (The generic term **device** refers to any piece of hardware.)

Software

Software is a set of instructions that makes the computer perform tasks. In other words, software tells the computer what to do. Some programs exist primarily for the computer's use, helping it perform tasks and manage its own resources. Other types of programs exist for the user, enabling him or her to perform tasks such as creating documents. (The term **program** refers to any piece of software.)

Users

People are the computer operators, also known as **users.** It can be argued that some computer systems are complete without a person's involvement; however, no computer is totally autonomous. Even if a computer can do its job without a person sitting in front of it, people still design, build, program, and repair computer systems. This lack of autonomy is especially true of personal computer systems, which are designed specifically for use by people, and which are the focus of this book.

Data

Data consists of individual facts or bits of information, which by themselves may not make much sense to a person. The computer

Figure 1A.2
This memo, budget worksheet, and drawing are all examples of information stored in a computer as files.

reads and stores data of all kinds—whether words, numbers, images, or sounds—in the form of numbers. Consequently, computerized data is **digital,** meaning that it has been reduced to digits, or numbers. (You will learn more about this later in the book.) Following instructions from the software and the user, the computer manipulates data by performing calculations, doing comparisons, or arranging the bits of information so they make sense to the user.

Within the computer, data is organized into **files.** A file is simply a set of data that has been given a name. A file that the user can open and use is often called a **document.** Although many people think of documents simply as text, a computer document can include many kinds of data (see Figure 1A.2). For example, a computer document can be a text file (such as a letter), a group of numbers (such as a budget), a video clip (which includes images and sounds), or any combination of these items. Programs arc organized into files as well; these files contain the instructions and data that a program needs in order to run and perform tasks.

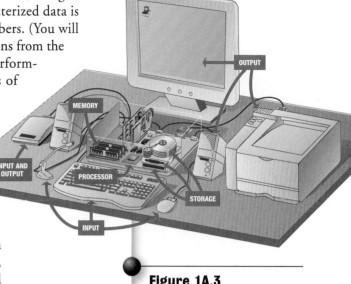

Figure 1A.3
Types of hardware devices

LOOKING INSIDE THE MACHINE

The computer itself—the hardware—has many parts, but the critical components fall into one of four categories (see Figure 1A.3):

1. Processor   **3.** Input and output devices

2. Memory   **4.** Storage

While any type of computer system contains these four types of hardware, this book focuses on these types as they relate to the personal computer, or PC.

NORTON
ONLINE

Visit **www.norton.glencoe.com** for more information on **computer hardware.**

The Processor

The procedure that transforms raw data into useful information is called **processing.** To perform this transformation, the computer uses two components: the processor and memory.

The **processor** is like the brain of the computer; it organizes and carries out instructions that come from either the user or the software. In a personal computer, the processor usually consists of one or more **microprocessors** (sometimes called chips), which are slivers of silicon or other material etched with many tiny electronic circuits. To process data or complete an instruction from a user or a program, the computer passes electricity through the circuits.

As shown in Figure 1A.4, the microprocessor is plugged into the computer's motherboard. The **motherboard** is a

Figure 1A.4
Processing devices

Motherboard

Circuit board

The microprocessor is inside this plastic case.

rigid rectangular card containing the circuitry that connects the processor to the other hardware. The motherboard is an example of a **circuit board.** In most personal computers, many internal devices—such as video cards, sound cards, disk controllers, and other devices—are housed on their own smaller circuit boards, which attach to the motherboard. In many newer computers, these devices are mounted directly onto the motherboard. Newer microprocessors are large and complex enough to require their own dedicated circuit boards, which plug into a special slot in the motherboard. (Older microprocessors were single chips.) You can think of the motherboard as the master circuit board in a computer.

A personal computer's processor is usually a single chip or a set of chips contained on a circuit board. In some powerful computers, the processor consists of many chips and the circuit boards on which they are mounted. In either case, the term **central processing unit (CPU)** refers to a computer's processor (see Figures 1A.5 and 1A.6). People often refer to computer systems by the type of CPU they contain. A "Pentium 4" system, for example, uses a Pentium 4 microprocessor as its CPU.

Memory

Memory is like an electronic scratch pad inside the computer. When you launch a program, it is loaded into and run from memory. Data used by the program is also loaded into memory for fast access. As new data is entered into the computer, it is also stored in memory—but only temporarily. The most common type of memory is called **random access memory,** or **RAM** (see Figures 1A.6 and 1A.7).

Figure 1A.5

The CPUs of modern personal computers are small, considering the amount of processing power they provide. The early microprocessors were not much larger than a thumbnail. Processors such as Intel's Pentium III are considerably larger, requiring their own circuit board.

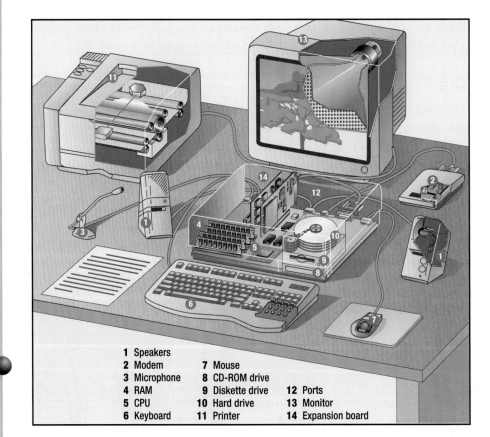

1	Speakers				
2	Modem	7	Mouse		
3	Microphone	8	CD-ROM drive		
4	RAM	9	Diskette drive	12	Ports
5	CPU	10	Hard drive	13	Monitor
6	Keyboard	11	Printer	14	Expansion board

Figure 1A.6

Most personal computer systems include the types of hardware components shown here.

As a result, the term *memory* is commonly used to mean RAM. Data is both written to and read from this memory. (For this reason, RAM is also sometimes called *read/write memory*.)

Perhaps the most important thing to remember about RAM is that it is volatile, so it needs a constant supply of power. When you turn off a computer, everything in RAM disappears. Thus, you should save your data files to a storage device frequently.

One of the most important factors affecting the speed and power of a computer is the amount of RAM it has. Generally, the more RAM a computer has, the more it can do and the faster it can perform certain tasks. The most common measurement unit for describing a computer's memory is the **byte**—the amount of memory it takes to store a single character, such as a letter of the alphabet or a numeral. When referring to a computer's memory, the numbers are often so large that it is helpful to use terms such as **kilobyte (KB), megabyte (MB), gigabyte (GB),** and **terabyte (TB)** to describe the values (see Table 1A.1).

Today's personal computers commonly have at least 128 million bytes of random access memory (or 128 MB). Many newer systems feature 256 MB or more.

Computers use other types of memory, too. Examples are read-only memory (ROM), which permanently stores instructions that the computer needs to operate; flash memory, like the kind used in digital cameras to store images; and cache memory, which helps the CPU retrieve data and instructions more quickly. You will learn about these and other important kinds of memory later.

Table 1A.1	Units of Measure for Computer Memory and Storage			
Unit	**Abbreviation**	**Pronounced**	**Approximate Value (bytes)**	**Actual Value (bytes)**
Kilobyte	KB	KILL-uh-bite	1,000	1,024
Megabyte	MB	MEHG-uh-bite	1,000,000 (1 million)	1,048,576
Gigabyte	GB	GIG-uh-bite	1,000,000,000 (1 billion)	1,073,741,824
Terabyte	TB	TERR-uh-bite	1,000,000,000,000 (1 trillion)	1,099,511,627,776

Input and Output Devices

A computer would be useless if you could not interact with it because the machine could not receive instructions or deliver the results of its work. **Input devices** accept data and instructions from the user or from another computer system (such as a computer on the Internet). **Output devices** return processed data to the user or to another computer system.

Input Devices

The most common input device is the **keyboard,** which accepts letters, numbers, and commands from the user. Another important type of input device is the **mouse,** which lets you select options from on-screen menus. You use a mouse by moving it across a flat surface and pressing its buttons. Nearly every computer sold today

NORTON
ONLINE

Visit **www.norton.glencoe.com** for more information on **input and output devices.**

Microphone   Keyboard   Mouse

Figure 1A.8
The keyboard, mouse, and microphone are common input devices. Many new computers are equipped with these three devices.

includes a mouse. Other popular input devices are **trackballs, touchpads, joysticks, scanners, digital cameras,** and **microphones.** Figure 1A.8 shows a personal computer with a keyboard, mouse, and microphone.

The mouse, trackball, and touchpad enable you to draw or point on the screen. The joystick is especially well suited for playing fast-moving video games. A scanner can copy a printed page of text or a graphic into the computer's memory, eliminating the time-consuming step of typing text or creating an image from scratch. Digital cameras record live images that can be viewed and edited on the computer. A microphone or CD player attached to the computer enables you to add the sound of a voice or a music selection.

Output Devices

The function of an output device is to present processed data to the user. The most common output devices are the **monitor** and the **printer.** The computer sends output to the monitor (the display screen) when the user needs only to see the output. It sends output to the printer when the user requests a paper copy—also called a hard copy—of a document. Just as computers can accept sound as input, they can use stereo speakers or headphones as output devices to produce sound. Figure 1A.9 shows a PC with a monitor, printer, and speakers.

Some types of hardware can act as both input and output devices. A **touch screen,** for example, is a type of monitor that displays text or icons you can touch. When you touch the screen, special sensors detect the touch and the computer calculates the point on the screen where you placed your finger. Depending on the location of the touch, the computer determines what information to display or what action to take next.

Communications devices are the most common types of devices that can perform both input and output. These devices connect one computer to another—a process known as networking. The most common kinds of communication devices

Monitor   Printer

Speakers

Figure 1A.9
The monitor, printer, and speakers are common output devices. Many new computers are equipped with a monitor and speakers. A printer, which is usually an extra cost, can be added to the computer system.

are modems, which enable computers to communicate through telephone lines or cable television systems, and network interface cards (NICs), which let users connect a group of computers to share data and devices.

Storage

Visit **www.norton.glencoe.com** for more information on **storage**.

A computer can function with only processing, memory, input, and output devices. To be really useful, however, a computer also needs a place to keep program files and related data when they are not in use. The purpose of **storage** is to hold data permanently.

You may think of storage as an electronic file cabinet and RAM as an electronic worktable. When you need to work with a program or a set of data, the computer locates it in the file cabinet and puts a copy on the table. After you have finished working with the program or data, you put it back into the file cabinet. The changes you make to data while working on it replace the original data in the file cabinet (unless you store it in a different place).

Novice computer users often confuse storage with memory. Although the functions of storage and memory are similar, they work in different ways. There are three major distinctions between storage and memory:

A. There is more room in storage than in memory, just as there is more room in a file cabinet than there is on a tabletop.

B. Contents are retained in storage when the computer is turned off, whereas the programs or the data you put into memory disappear when you shut down the computer.

C. Storage is very slow compared to memory, but it is much cheaper than memory.

There are many types of storage devices, including **tape drives, optical drives,** and **removable hard drives.** However, the most common storage medium is the **magnetic disk.** A disk is a round, flat object that spins around its center. **Read/write heads,** which are similar to the heads of a tape recorder or VCR, are used to read data from the disk or write data onto the disk.

The device that holds a disk is called a **disk drive.** Some disks are built into the drive and are not meant to be removed; other kinds of drives enable you to remove and replace disks (see Figure 1A.10). Most personal computers have at least one nonremovable **hard disk** (or **hard drive**). In addition, there is also a **diskette drive,**

Figure 1A.10
Standard PCs have a built-in hard disk and a diskette drive.

The hard disk is built into the computer's case.

Diskettes can be inserted into and removed from the diskette drive.

which allows you to use removable **diskettes** (or **floppy disks**). The hard disk serves as the computer's primary filing cabinet because it can store far more data than a diskette can contain. Diskettes are used to load new programs or data onto the hard disk, to trade data with other users, and to make backup copies of the data on the hard disk. (Note, however, that some kinds of computers do not have built-in disks or disk drives at all. They use other types of devices for storage or rely on another computer to store their data. You will learn more about these kinds of computers later in this unit.)

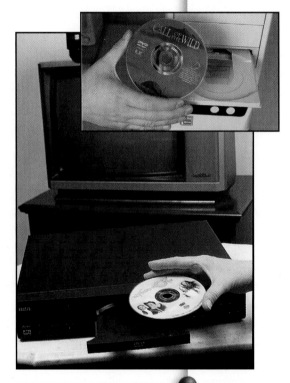

The **CD-ROM drive** is another common type of storage device (see Figure 1A.11). **Compact disks (CDs)** are a type of optical storage device, identical to audio CDs. Until recently, a standard CD could store about 74 minutes of audio or 650 MB of data. A newer breed of CDs can hold 80 minutes of audio or 700 MB of data. The type used in computers is called **Compact Disk-Read-Only Memory (CD-ROM).** As the name implies, you cannot change the information on the disk, just as you cannot record over an audio CD.

If you purchase a **CD-Recordable (CD-R)** drive, you have the option of creating your own CDs. A CD-R drive can write data to and read data from a compact disk. To create your own compact disks, you must use special CD-R disks, which can be written on only once, or **CD-ReWritable (CD-RW)** disks, which can be written to multiple times, like a floppy disk.

An increasingly popular data storage technology is the **Digital Video Disk (DVD),** which is revolutionizing home entertainment. Using sophisticated compression technologies, a single DVD (which is the same size as a standard compact disk) can store an entire full-length movie. DVDs can hold a minimum of 4.7 GB of data and as much as 17 GB.

Figure 1A.12
DVD players are now standard on many PCs and are found in many home entertainment centers.

DVDs require a special player (see Figure 1A.12). Many DVD players, however, can play audio, data, and DVD disks, freeing the user from purchasing different players for each type of disk. DVD drives are now standard equipment on many new personal computers. Users not only install programs and data from their standard CDs, but they also can watch movies on their personal computers by using a DVD.

☑ **Self Check**

NORTON
ONLINE

Visit www.norton.glencoe.com for more information on **disks**.

Complete each statement by filling in the blank(s).

1. A(n) _processor_ is an electronic device that processes data.

2. There is more room in storage than in _memory_ in a computer.

3. A device that holds a disk is called a(n) _disk drive_ .

At Issue

The Importance of Computer Literacy

Today, computers are no longer specialized tools used only by scientists or engineers. They do not hum behind sealed, glass walls in climate-controlled environments. Computer systems are everywhere—in places you cannot see or would not expect to find them. They are a fact of life, a common thread that ties together our education, work, and home life.

With computers touching nearly every facet of our lives, the issue of computer literacy becomes important. But what is computer literacy, and why is it so crucial? Why should you spend your time and energy studying books like this one and becoming "computer literate"?

Someday—perhaps sooner than you think—you may not be able to imagine living without computer skills. Consider the fact that computers are an essential part of business today, whether you are a secretary or a surgeon, a journalist or a pilot. Just as we depend on cars for transportation to work each day, we rely on computers as tools to help us in our work.

You can benefit from computer literacy in many ways. Consider the following:

Computers are becoming increasingly important tools in all types of workplaces, from offices to factories.

◆ **Increased Employability.** If you have basic computer knowledge along with specific job skills, you will be considered more trainable in and adaptable to the computerized work environment by potential employers.

◆ **Greater Earnings Potential.** As you increase your computer skills, you become a more valuable worker, especially if you focus on high-tech skills such as programming, network administration, or hardware maintenance. However, you do not have to become a computer expert to increase your earnings potential. Skills that involve application of the computer to specific tasks (such as desktop publishing or database management) are highly valued.

◆ **Greater Access to Resources.** Computers are incredible learning tools, especially when you have access to data on CDs or the Internet. You can use a PC to access vast knowledge bases on almost any topic, search archives of information dating back decades, and even take online courses for credit.

◆ **Greater Control of Assets.** Using the power of the Internet and only a little knowledge of computers, you can manage your personal finances and indulge your interests in ways that were not possible just a few years ago. Online banking and investing give you control of every dollar you earn. Online shopping makes it easier than ever to spend your money, too. New technologies enable you to monitor your entire household via a personal computer: You can adjust your air conditioner or alarm clock, start your coffee maker or sprinklers, and activate your alarm system.

Because of the growth of computer technologies, we now live in an information society—where information is considered to be an extremely valuable commodity. Those who control important information, or who simply know how to access and use it, are key players in the information-based economy. Computer literacy and skills are essential for success in this society, not only in our working lives but also in the way we learn, manage our finances, and improve our standard of living.

Visit **www.norton.glencoe.com** for more information on **operating systems.**

VISUAL ESSAY: SOFTWARE BRINGS THE MACHINE TO LIFE

The ingredient that enables a computer to perform a specific task is software, which consists of electronic instructions. You will recall that a set of instructions that drives a computer to perform specific tasks is called a program. When a computer uses a particular program, it is said to be **running** or **executing** that program.

Most software falls into two major categories: **system software** and **application software.** One major type of system software, the **operating system,** tells the computer how to use its own components. Examples of operating systems include Windows, the Macintosh Operating System, UNIX, and Linux. Another type of system software, called a network operating system, allows computers to communicate and share data across a network. A third type of system software, called a utility, makes the computer system easier to use or to perform highly specialized functions.

Application software tells the computer how to accomplish specific tasks, such as word processing or drawing, for the user. Some of the major categories of these applications include the following:

◆ Word processing software for creating text-based documents, such as newsletters or brochures

◆ Spreadsheets for creating numeric-based documents, such as budgets or balance sheets

◆ Database management software for building and manipulating large sets of data

◆ Presentation programs for creating and presenting electronic slide shows

◆ Graphics programs for designing illustrations or manipulating photographs, movies, or animation

◆ Multimedia authoring applications for building digital movies that incorporate sound, video, animation, and interactive features

◆ Entertainment and education software packages, many of which are interactive multimedia events

◆ Web design tools, Web browsers, and other Internet applications, such as newsreaders and e-mail programs

◆ Games, some of which are for a single player, and many of which can be played by several people over a network or the Internet

A Windows is just one example of a computer operating system. An operating system is essential for any computer, because it acts as an interpreter between the hardware and application programs. When an application wants the hardware to do something, it communicates through the operating system. Similarly, when you want the hardware to do something (such as copying or printing a file), your request is handled by the operating system.

A

B Word processing software is designed for creating documents that consist primarily of text. New word processors also let you include graphics and sounds in your documents, and they provide sophisticated layout features that enable you to create brochures, newsletters, business documents, Web pages, and more.

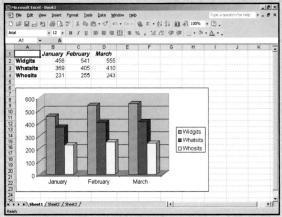

C Spreadsheet programs are designed to work with numbers and are used in business to create budgets, payrolls, and analytical documents. Your document can contain text, numbers, and formulas for calculating numbers. Spreadsheet programs also let you create colorful charts from your data or convert your data into Web pages.

D This screen shows a database of products sold by a company. Database management software makes it easy to reorganize data. For example, you can rearrange this list by product names or by categories. Large companies and government agencies use enormous databases containing millions of lines of information about people, products, and more.

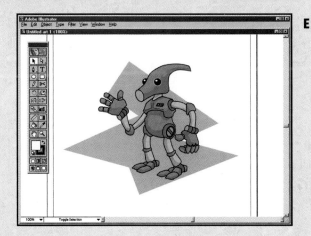

E Graphics software lets you create and edit images of all types. Some graphics programs are specially designed to work with electronic photographs, while others excel at manipulating line drawings or text. Such programs are essential in document design, Web site design, multimedia authoring, and game and movie production.

F

Presentation software is most often used for creating sales presentations, although it can be effective for any type of electronic slide show. Today's presentation programs can create slide shows for viewing in a Web browser, from a Web server or a network.

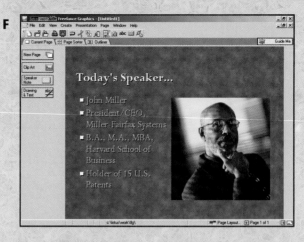

G

Using a Web-page design program, you can create colorful documents for publication on the World Wide Web. These programs enable you to add different fonts, graphics, and hyperlinks to your Web pages.

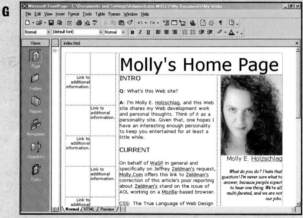

H

Web browsers quickly have become one of the most commonly used—and important—types of application software. Using a Web browser and an Internet connection, you can view documents (called "Web pages") from around the world.

I

There are hundreds of utility programs available for personal computers. This one helps you manage your hard disk to get the most from it.

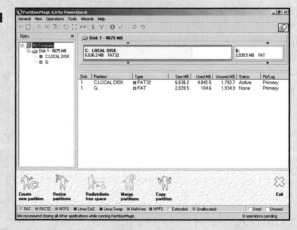

VISUAL ESSAY: THE SHAPES OF COMPUTERS TODAY

Computers come in many different sizes and ranges of power, and different types of computer systems have varying capabilities. Basically, today's computer systems fall into one of the following categories:

◆ Supercomputers

◆ Mainframe computers

◆ Minicomputers

◆ Workstations

◆ Microcomputers, or personal computers

All of these computers can be connected to form networks of computers, but each individual computer, whether or not it is on a network, falls into one of these five categories. As you will see, some of these categories—especially microcomputers—can be divided into subcategories, some of which are growing rapidly enough to become major categories in their own right.

A

B

C

A Supercomputers are the most powerful computers made, and physically, they are some of the largest. These systems can process huge amounts of data, and the fastest supercomputers can perform more than 1 trillion calculations per second. Some supercomputers—such as the Cray T3E system—can house thousands of processors. Supercomputers are used in the mapping of the human genome, forecasting weather, and modeling complex processes like nuclear fission.

B **Mainframe** computers are used in large organizations where many people need access to the same data. In a traditional mainframe environment, each user accesses the mainframe's resources through a device called a **terminal.** There are two kinds of terminals. A dumb terminal does not have its own CPU or storage devices; it is simply an **input/output (I/O) device** that functions as a window into a computer located somewhere else. An intelligent terminal can perform some processing operations, but it usually does not have any storage.

C First released in the 1960s, **minicomputers** got their name because of their small size compared to other computers of the day. The capabilities of a minicomputer are somewhere between mainframes and personal computers. (For this reason, minicomputers increasingly are being called midrange computers.) Although some "minis" are designed for a single user, the most powerful minicomputers can serve the input and output needs of hundreds of users at a time. This is the HP 3000 minicomputer.

Workstations—like the Sun Blade 100—are specialized, single-user computers with many of the features of a personal computer but with the processing power of a minicomputer. These powerful machines are popular among scientists, engineers, and animators who need a great deal of number-crunching power.

D

The terms **microcomputer** and **personal computer (PC)** are interchangeable, and refer to a type of computer system that was designed for use by a single person. Two common designs for PCs are shown here. The more traditional desktop model features a horizontally oriented system unit, on top of which many users place the monitor. Vertically oriented tower models have become the more popular style of desktop system.

E

Notebook computers, as their name implies, approximate the shape of an 8.5- by 11-inch notebook and can fit inside a briefcase easily. Also called **laptop computers,** they can operate on alternating (plug-in) current or special batteries. Notebooks are fully functional microcomputers; the people who use them need the power of a full-size PC wherever they go.

F

Some notebook systems are designed to be plugged into a **docking station** (also called an expansion base or a port replicator), which may include a large monitor, a full-size keyboard and mouse, or other devices such as an additional hard drive or backup tape unit. Docking stations also provide additional ports that enable the notebook computer to be connected to different devices in the same manner as a desktop system.

G

H

Handheld personal computers—also called **palmtop computers**—are computing devices small enough to fit in your hand. A popular type of handheld computer is the **personal digital assistant (PDA)**. PDAs like this Compaq iPac are no larger than a small appointment book, and are normally used for special applications, such as taking notes, displaying telephone numbers and addresses, and keeping track of dates or agendas.

I

Some new cellular phones, like the Nokia 9290 Communicator, double as miniature PCs. Advanced cellular devices combine digital cell-phone service with e-mail capabilities. Such phones enable the user to check and send e-mail and faxes over the phone. They offer features not normally found on a phone, such as personal organizers or access to the Web. Some models even break in half to reveal a miniature keyboard.

J

The **tablet PC**—like this model, created by Microsoft—is the newest development in portable, full-featured computers. Tablet PCs offer all the functionality of a notebook PC, but they are lighter and can accept input from an electronic pen or the user's voice.

PRODUCTIVITY Tip

Choosing the Right Tool for the Job

Buying a computer is a lot like buying a car because there are so many models and options from which to choose! Before deciding which computer is best for you, identify the type of work for which you want to use the computer.

Depending on your job, you may need to use a computer on a limited basis. A handheld system is great if you want to:

◆ **Manage Your Schedule on a Daily or Hourly Basis.** Handheld computers are popular for their calendar and schedule-management capabilities, which enable you to set appointments, track projects, and record special events.

◆ **Manage a List of Contacts.** If you need to stay in touch with many people and travel frequently, personal digital assistants provide several contact-management features.

◆ **Make Notes on the Fly.** Some PDAs feature small keyboards, which are handy for tapping out quick notes. Others feature pens, which enable the user to "write" on the display screen. Many newer handheld systems also provide a built-in microphone, so you can record notes digitally.

Portable computers enable you to work almost anywhere.

◆ **Send Faxes and E-Mail.** Most popular handheld PCs have fax and e-mail capabilities and a port that lets them exchange data with a PC.

If your job requires you to travel but you still need a full-featured computer, you may consider using a laptop or notebook computer. This option is the best choice if you want to:

◆ **Carry Your Data With You.** If you need to take presentations on the road or keep up with daily work while traveling, portable PCs are ideal. Laptop systems offer nearly as much RAM and storage capacity as desktop models. Many portables have built-in CD-ROM drives; others accept plug-in CD-ROM and hard drives, which can greatly increase their capacity.

◆ **Be Able to Work Anywhere.** Portable PCs run on either rechargeable batteries or standard current.

◆ **Communicate and Share Data From Any Location.** Most portable computers have built-in modems or slots for plugging in a modem.

If you work in one place and need to perform various tasks, a desktop computer is the best choice. Choose a desktop computer if you want to:

◆ **Work With Graphics-Intensive or Desktop Publishing Applications.** Complex graphics and page-layout programs require a great deal of system resources, and a desktop system's large monitor reduces eye fatigue. Desktop models also can accept many different types of pointing devices that can make graphics work easier.

◆ **Design or Use Multimedia Products.** Even though many portable computers have multimedia features, you can get the most for your money with a desktop system. Large screens make multimedia programs easier to see, and stereo-style speakers optimize sound quality.

◆ **Set Up Complex Hardware Configurations.** A desktop computer can support many peripherals—including printers, sound and video sources, and various external devices—at the same time. If you want to swap video or audio cards easily, increase RAM, or perform other configuration tasks, a desktop system will provide many options.

18

SUMMARY

- A computer is an electronic device used to process data, converting it into information that is useful to people.

- A complete computer system includes hardware, software, data, and users.

- Hardware consists of electronic devices, the parts you can see.

- Software, also known as programs, consists of organized sets of instructions for controlling the computer.

- Data consists of text, numbers, sounds, and images that the computer can manipulate.

- The hardware, or physical components, of a computer consists of a processor, memory, input and output (I/O) devices, and storage.

- The processing function is divided between the processor and memory.

- The processor, or CPU, organizes and carries out instructions from the user or a program.

- Memory holds data and program instructions as the CPU works with them.

- The most common units of measure for memory are the byte, kilobyte, megabyte, gigabyte, and terabyte.

- The role of input is to provide data from the user or another source.

- The function of output is to present processed data to the user or to another computer.

- Communications devices perform both input and output functions, allowing computers to share information.

- Storage devices permanently hold data and programs.

- The operating system tells the computer how to interact with the user and how to use the hardware devices attached to the computer.

- Application software tells the computer how to accomplish tasks the user requires.

- Supercomputers are the most powerful computers in terms of processing.

- Mainframe computers handle massive amounts of input, output, and storage for multiple users.

- Minicomputers are smaller than mainframes, but larger than microcomputers. They often support multiple users.

- Workstations are powerful single-user computers that are used by engineers, scientists, and graphic artists.

- Microcomputers are more commonly known as personal computers. Desktop computers are the most common type of personal computer.

- Notebook computers (laptops) are used by people who need portable computing power outside the office or away from home.

- Handheld personal computers are the smallest computing devices. They lack the power of a desktop or notebook PC, but they offer specialized features for users who need only limited functions and small size.

KEY TERMS

application software, *12*
byte, *7*
CD-Recordable (CD-R), *10*
CD-ReWritable (CD-RW), *10*
CD-ROM drive, *10*
central processing
    unit (CPU), *6*
circuit board, *6*
communications device, *8*
compact disk (CD), *10*
compact disk-read-only
    memory (CD-ROM), *10*
computer system, *4*
computer, *4*
data, *4*
device, *4*
digital, *5*
digital camera, *8*
Digital Video Disk
    (DVD), *10*
disk drive, *9*

diskette drive, *9*
diskette, *10*
docking station, *16*
document, *5*
execute, *12*
file, *5*
floppy disk, *10*
gigabyte (GB), *7*
handheld personal
    computer, *17*
hard disk, *9*
hard drive, *9*
hardware, *4*
input device, *7*
input/output device, *15*
joystick, *8*
keyboard, *7*
kilobyte (KB), *7*
laptop computer, *16*
magnetic disk, *9*
mainframe, *15*

megabyte (MB), *7*
memory, *6*
microcomputer, *16*
microphone, *8*
microprocessor, *5*
minicomputer, *15*
monitor, *8*
motherboard, *5*
mouse, *7*
notebook computer, *16*
operating system, *12*
optical drive, *9*
output device, *7*
palmtop computer, *17*
personal computer
    (PC), *16*
personal digital
    assistant (PDA), *17*
printer, *8*
processing, *5*
processor, *5*

program, *4*
random access
    memory (RAM), *6*
read/write head, *9*
removable hard drive, *9*
run, *12*
scanner, *8*
software, *4*
storage, *9*
supercomputer, *15*
system software, *12*
tablet PC, *17*
tape drive, *9*
terabyte (TB), *7*
terminal, *15*
touch screen, *8*
touchpad, *8*
trackball, *8*
user, *4*
workstation, *16*

KEY TERM QUIZ

Complete each statement by writing one of the terms listed under Key Terms in each blank.

1. The term _comp system_ refers to the combination of hardware, software, data, and people.

2. A(n) _file_ is a set of data or program instructions that has been given a name.

3. A(n) _Disk drive_ is a device that holds a disk.

4. Electronic instructions that tell the computer's hardware what to do are known as _software_.

5. The generic term _device_ refers to a piece of hardware.

SECTION QUIZ

True/False

Answer the following questions by circling True or False.

True   False   **1.** A complete computer system has two parts: hardware and software.

True   False   **2.** In a personal computer, the processor consists of one or more microprocessors.

True   False   **3.** The keyboard and monitor are examples of output devices.

True   False   **4.** Workstations are specialized, single-user computers with many features of a PC and the power of a minicomputer.

True   False   **5.** Mainframe computers are now obsolete.

Multiple Choice

Circle the word or phrase that best completes each statement.

1. The most common type of computer memory is called _____ .
   A. storage   **B.** RAM   C. neither A nor B

2. A _____ can perform both input and output functions.
   A. trackball   B. microphone   **C.** communications device

3. One major type of system software is called _____ .
   A. operating system software   B. utility software   C. application software

4. The _____ is the most powerful kind of computer.
   A. mainframe   **B.** supercomputer   C. personal digital assistant

5. A _____ is an example of a handheld computer.
   A. personal digital assistant   B. thin client   C. neither A nor B

REVIEW QUESTIONS

In your own words, briefly answer the following questions.

1. List the four key components of a computer system.

2. List the three major distinctions between storage and memory.

3. Name the two major categories of software.

4. What are the five values used to describe a computer's memory or storage capacity?

5. What are the five main categories of computers?

SECTION LABS

Complete the following exercises as directed by your instructor.

1. What type of computer system do you use in class or in the lab? How much can you tell about the system by looking at it? List as much information as you can about the computer. Is it a desktop or tower model? What brand is it? What type of processor does it have? What are the model and serial numbers? What external devices does it have? Is it connected to a network or printer?

2. What kind of software is installed on your computer? To find out, all you have to do is turn on your computer. After it starts, you should see a collection of icons—small pictures that represent the programs and other resources on your computer. List the icons that appear on your screen and the names of the software programs they represent.

Introduction to the Internet

OBJECTIVES

- List two reasons for the Internet's creation.
- Identify three ways in which people commonly use the Internet.
- Use a Web browser to navigate the World Wide Web.
- Successfully search for content on the Web, using standard search tools.

OVERVIEW: What Is the Internet?

It seems impossible to make it through a day without hearing a reference to the Internet. This is true for a good reason: The Internet has become much more than a collection of telephone lines and computers. It has exploded into a powerful force that reaches into our very way of life, changing the way we work, play, study, express our ideas, and spend money.

As you will learn in this section and in later units, the Internet connects thousands of individual networks, extending around the world. Through the Internet, a computer on one network can communicate with virtually any other computer on any other network. Using these global connections, people can use their computers to exchange messages, to communicate in real time, to share data and programs, and to access limitless stores of information.

The Internet, in fact, has become so important that its use is considered an essential part of computer use. In other words, mastering the Internet is one of the first things you should do, if you want to get the most from your computing experience. In this section, you will get a brief overview of the Internet's history, learn how people use the Internet, and learn to use a browser to navigate and search the World Wide Web.

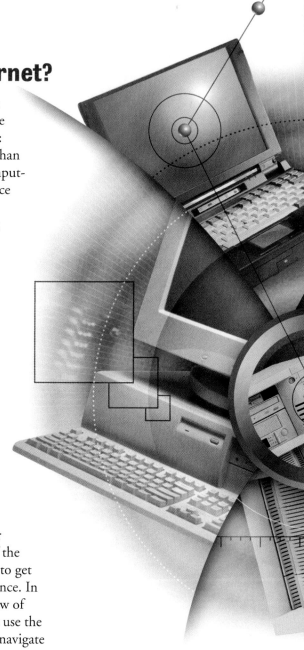

THE INTERNET: THEN AND NOW

No introduction to the Internet is complete without a short review of its history. Even though today's Internet bears little resemblance to its forebear of 30-plus years ago, it still functions in basically the same way. As you will see in the next few pages, the Internet has evolved into something different than the special-purpose, restricted-use network its planners envisioned originally.

Visit **www.norton.glencoe.com** for more information on the **history of the Internet.**

The Beginning: A "Network of Networks"

The seeds of the Internet were planted in 1969, when the Advanced Research Projects Agency (ARPA) of the U.S. Department of Defense began connecting computers at different universities and defense contractors (see Figure 1B.1). The resulting network was called **ARPANET.** The goal of this early project was to create a large computer network with multiple paths—in the form of telephone lines—that could survive a nuclear attack or other disaster. If one part of the network were destroyed, other parts of the network would remain functional because data could continue to flow through the surviving lines. ARPA also wanted users in remote locations to be able to share scarce computing resources.

At first, ARPANET was basically a large network serving only a handful of users, but it expanded rapidly. Initially, the network included four primary host computers. A **host** is like a network server, providing services to other computers that connect to it. ARPANET's host computers (like those on today's Internet) provided file transfer and communications services and gave connected systems access to the network's high-speed data lines. The system grew quickly and spread widely as the number of hosts grew.

Figure 1B.1
Before it became known as the Internet, ARPA's network served universities, defense contractors, and a few government agencies.

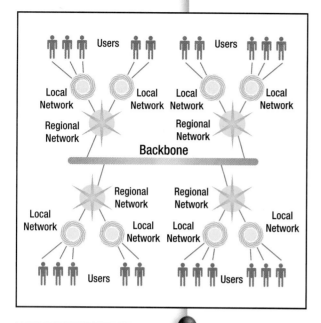

The network jumped across the Atlantic to Norway and England in 1973, and it never stopped growing. In the mid-1980s, another federal agency, the National Science Foundation (NSF), joined the project after the Defense Department dropped its funding. NSF established five "supercomputing centers" that were available to anyone who wanted to use them for academic research purposes.

The NSF expected the supercomputers' users to use ARPANET to obtain access, but the agency quickly discovered that the existing network could not handle the load. In response, the NSF created a new, higher capacity network, called **NSFnet,** to complement the older and by then overloaded ARPANET. The link between ARPANET, NSFnet, and other networks was called the **Internet.** (The process of connecting separate networks is called **internetworking.** A collection of "networked networks" is described as being internetworked, which is where the Internet—a worldwide network of networks—gets its name.)

Figure 1B.2

At its heart, the Internet uses high-speed data lines, called backbones, to carry huge volumes of traffic. Regional and local networks connect to these backbones, enabling any user on any network to exchange data with any other user on any other network.

NSFnet made Internet connections widely available for academic research, but the NSF did not permit users to conduct private business over the system. Therefore, several private telecommunications companies built their own network backbones that functioned in much the same manner as NSFnet. Like a tree's trunk or an animal's spine, a network **backbone** is the central structure that connects other elements of the network (see Figure 1B.2). These private portions of the Internet were not limited by NSFnet's "appropriate use" restrictions, so it became possible to use the Internet to distribute business and commercial information.

The original ARPANET was shut down in 1990, and government funding for NSFnet was discontinued in 1995, but the commercial Internet backbone services have easily replaced them. By the mid-1990s, interest in the Internet began to expand dramatically. The system that had been created as a tool for surviving a nuclear war found its way into businesses and homes. Now, advertisements for movies are far more common online than collaborations on physics research.

Figure 1B.3

Today, the Internet is available to anyone who can use a computer, as long as the computer has a working Internet connection.

Today: Still Growing

Today, the Internet connects thousands of networks and hundreds of millions of users around the world. It is a huge, cooperative community with no central ownership. This lack of ownership is an important feature of the Internet, because it means that no single person or group controls the network. Although there are several organizations (such as The Internet Society and the World Wide Web Consortium) that propose standards for Internet-related technologies and guidelines for its appropriate use, these organizations almost universally support the Internet's openness and lack of centralized control.

As a result, the Internet is open to anyone who can access it (see Figure 1B.3). If you can use a computer and if the computer is connected to the Internet, you are free not only to use the resources posted by others, but to create resources of your own; that is, you can publish

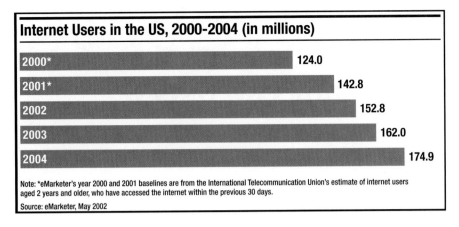

Internet Users in the US, 2000-2004 (in millions)

Year	Users
2000*	124.0
2001*	142.8
2002	152.8
2003	162.0
2004	174.9

Note: *eMarketer's year 2000 and 2001 baselines are from the International Telecommunication Union's estimate of internet users aged 2 years and older, who have accessed the internet within the previous 30 days.

Source: eMarketer, May 2002

Figure 1B.4
The number of Internet users is expected to continue its dramatic increase for the foreseeable future.

documents on the World Wide Web, exchange e-mail messages, and perform many other tasks.

This openness has attracted millions of users to the Internet. As of this writing, it was estimated that nearly one-half billion people had access to the Internet in the year 2001. The number of actual users continues to climb dramatically, as shown in Figure 1B.4.

Self Check

Complete each statement by writing a term in the blank(s).

1. The Internet is sometimes called a _____ of networks.

2. The network that eventually became the Internet was originally called _____ .

3. _____ controls the Internet.

USING YOUR BROWSER AND THE WORLD WIDE WEB

Throughout this book, you will find many Internet-related discussions, as well as exercises and review questions that require you to use the World Wide Web ("the Web"). The Web enables users to view specially formatted documents, called Web pages, which can contain text, graphics, and multimedia objects (such as video, audio, or animations). Web pages also can display navigational tools to help you move around within a Web page, to move from one page to another within a Web site, or to move among different sites. (You will learn about the Web in greater detail in Unit 8, "The Internet and Online Resources.")

To access the Web, you need a special software program called a Web browser. The two most popular Web browsers are Microsoft Internet Explorer and Netscape Navigator. There are, however, many other browsers, each with its own unique features and capabilities. Web browsers provide tools that let you navigate the Web, moving from one page to another as easily as you can flip through the pages of a magazine.

This section shows you the basic steps required for using a browser and navigating the Web. You should complete the following steps and become familiar with your browser before going any further in this book.

NORTON ONLINE

Visit **www.norton.glencoe.com** for more information on **Web browsers**.

Norton Notebook

REFERENCE BOOKS GO ONLINE

Being a student once meant owning a shelf filled with reference books. Today, however, even in many homes where you cannot find a dictionary, you can find at least one PC and an Internet connection. And thus ends the need for many kinds of printed reference manuals. Reference books have gone online.

Although using an online encyclopedia or dictionary is not always as convenient as grabbing a book from a shelf, the online version offers two distinct advantages:

◆ **Up-to-Date Information.** Online references can be updated quickly and frequently, and the best ones are kept up-to-date by their owners.

◆ **Depth and Variety.** Printed reference books suffer from page-count and page-size limitations, so they can provide only so much information on a given topic. This limitation doesn't apply to online references.

An overview of some references you can find on the Internet includes the following:

◆ **Encyclopedias.** In recent years, several popular printed encyclopedias have become available on CD-ROM. These products provide a lot of value, and most are filled with links to the Web (so you can find more and updated information), but they still have their limitations. Web-based encyclopedias, however, are rapidly gaining popularity. Sites such as Microsoft's Encarta and Encarta Deluxe (**http://encarta.msn.com/**), Britannica Online (**http://www.britannica.com/**), and Encyclopedia.com (**http://www.encyclopedia.com/**) provide all the articles you would expect to find, along with graphics, audio and video, links to relevant sites, search tools, and more. Note, however, that not all online encyclopedias are free or completely free. Some require you to register or to pay a subscription fee for some services.

◆ **Dictionaries.** Online dictionaries are better illustrated, are more detailed, and offer a variety of tools compared to their printed counterparts. You can find online editions of standard printed dictionaries, such as Webster's (**http://www. m-w.com/**) and the Cambridge Dictionaries Online (**http://dictionary.cambridge.org/**), as well as lexicons available only online, such as OneLook

Anyone with an Internet connection can access an up-to-date dictionary or encyclopedia online.

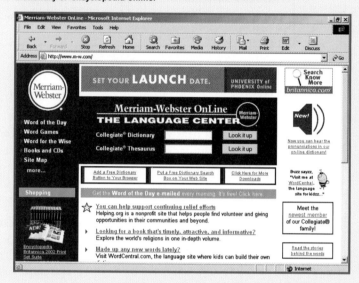

Dictionaries (**http://www.onelook.com/**) and The Alternative Dictionaries (**www.notam.uio.no/~hcholm/altlang/**).

◆ **Thesauri.** The Internet is a great place to check your word choices. Online thesauri provide synonyms, antonyms, and homonyms in addition to definitions and pronunciations. Some allow you to look up phrases, as well as single words. The king of the thesaurus world, Roget's, is available at **www.thesaurus.com/,** but others are also worth a look, including The Wordsmyth Dictionary/Thesaurus (**www.wordsmyth.net/**), Lexical FreeNet (**www. link.cs.cmu.edu/lexfn/**), and Phrase Finder (**www.shu.ac.uk/web-admin/phrases/go.html**).

Of course, plenty of specialized reference guides are also on the Web, covering subjects from computer technology to law, and economics to particle physics. If you need to find a specialty reference online, visit your favorite search engine (such as Yahoo! or Lycos) and look for a Reference link, which should lead to more information about online reference materials. Otherwise, you can search on the term that describes your field of study (such as particle physics). If you do not get the results you need, search on multiple terms, such as law AND reference guide.

Launching Your Browser

Your Web browser is an application program that is stored on your computer's disk. You must launch the program before you can view any Web pages. You may need to connect to the Internet before launching the browser. (If so, ask your instructor for directions on connecting to the Internet.) Once you have established a connection, launch your browser by following these steps:

1. Click the Start button on the Windows taskbar. The Start menu opens.

2. Point to Programs (or All Programs) to open the Programs menu. When the Programs menu opens, find the name of your browser and click it, as shown in Figure 1B.5.

   Your browser will open on your screen, as shown in Figure 1B.6. The browser shown here is Microsoft Internet Explorer. If you are using a different browser (or a different version of Internet Explorer), you will notice that your screen looks different.

   Depending on how your browser is configured, a Web page may open in the browser window as soon as you launch the program. This page is called the start page. You can set the browser to open any page (either from a Web site or from your computer's disk) when it launches. In Figure 1B.6, the Microsoft Network (MSN) home page is the start page.

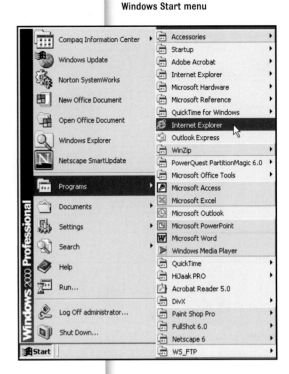

Figure 1B.5
Launching a Web browser from the Windows Start menu

Navigating the Web

Navigating the Web means moving from one Web page to another or from one Web site to another. A Web page is a document formatted with Hypertext Markup Language (HTML) tags. A Web site is a collection of related Web pages.

Using URLs

Every Web page has a unique address, called a uniform resource locator, or URL (pronounced as spelled: U-R-L). Here is an example of a URL:

http://www.glencoe.com/

You will learn about URLs in detail in Unit 8. For now, you just need to know that URLs are the key to navigating the Web.

When you provide a URL for the browser, the browser loads that URL's page onto your PC. You can specify a URL in several ways. For example, you can type the URL in the browser's Address box, or you can click a hyperlink that is linked to that URL, or you can store the URL in your browser's Favorites or Bookmarks list.

Figure 1B.6
The Internet Explorer browser

Figure 1B.7

Navigating the Web by typing a URL

Type a URL here, then press Enter.

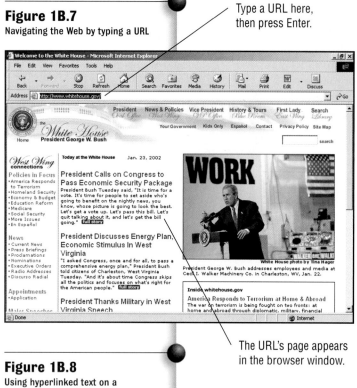

The URL's page appears in the browser window.

Figure 1B.8

Using hyperlinked text on a Web page

If you click the hyperlinked text, the browser will open the page with the URL shown on the status bar.

The mouse pointer is resting on hyperlinked text.

Hyperlinked graphics act as navigation tools.

Figure 1B.9

Using hyperlinked graphics on a Web page

For example, suppose you want to visit the White House Web site. To do this, you can click in the Address box, type **http://www.whitehouse.gov/** and then press Enter. The home page of the White House Web site appears in the browser window (see Figure 1B.7).

Using Hyperlinks

A hyperlink is simply a part of the Web page that is linked to a URL. When text has a hyperlink assigned to it, you can click it and "jump" from your present location to the URL specified by the hyperlink. Hyperlinked text looks different from normal text in a Web page: It is usually underlined, but it can be formatted in any number of ways (see Figure 1B.8).

Many Web pages also provide hyperlinked pictures or graphical buttons—called navigation tools—that direct you to different pages, making it easier to find the information you need (see Figure 1B.9). When your mouse pointer touches hyperlinked text or a navigation tool, it turns into a hand pointer, and the hyperlink's URL appears in the browser's status bar.

Using the Browser's Navigation Tools

Web browsers offer a variety of tools to help you move around the Web. These tools can save you the trouble of typing URLs or searching for links, and they allow you to quickly go back to pages that you have already visited.

The Back and Forward buttons return you to recently viewed pages, similar to flipping through a magazine (see Figure 1B.10). The Back button returns you to the previously opened Web page. After using the Back button, you can click Forward to move forward again, returning to the last page you opened before you clicked the Back button.

Most browsers allow you to "bookmark" Web pages that you visit frequently. Instead of typing the page's URL, you simply select the page's title from your list of bookmarks. Depending on the browser you use, your bookmarks may be stored in a list called Bookmarks, Favorites, or something similar (see Figure 1B.11). Simply select a bookmark from that list, and the browser returns to that page.

When you type URLs into the Address bar, your browser saves them, creating a history list for the current session (see Figure 1B.12). You can choose a URL from this list and return to a previously opened page without having to use the Back button or any other tools.

To close your browser, open the File menu and choose Close. You also can close the browser by clicking the Close button on the title bar. It may be necessary to close your Internet connection, too.

Getting Help With Your Browser

Although most browsers are easy to use, you may need help at some point. Newer browsers provide comprehensive Help systems, which can answer many of your questions about browsing and the World Wide Web.

Open the browser's Help menu, and then choose Contents. (Depending on your browser, this option may be called Help Contents, Contents and Index, or something similar.)

Figure 1B.10
The Back and Forward buttons in Internet Explorer

The opened list of bookmarks

You can organize your bookmarks into groups called folders.

Click a bookmark to jump directly to that page.

Figure 1B.11
Selecting a bookmark from Internet Explorer's Favorites list

Figure 1B.12
Selecting a Web page's URL from the History list

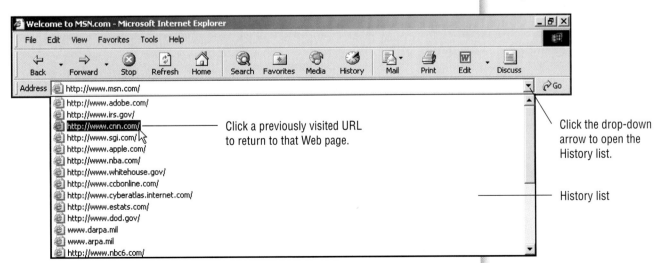

Click a previously visited URL to return to that Web page.

Click the drop-down arrow to open the History list.

History list

A Help window appears, listing all the topics for which help or information is available (see Figure 1B.13). Look through the list of topics and choose the one that matches your interest. When you are done, click the Close button on the window's title bar.

SEARCHING THE WEB

It is not always easy to find what you want on the Web. That is because there are tens of millions of unique Web sites, which include hundreds of millions of unique pages! This section explains the basics of Web search tools and their use. The two most basic and commonly used Web-based search tools are the following:

Figure 1B.13

Internet Explorer's Help window

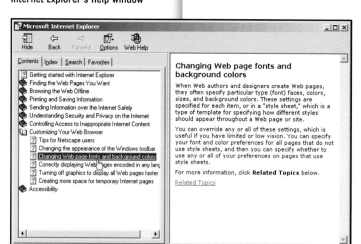

◆ **Directories.** A **directory** enables you to search for information by selecting categories of subject matter. The directory separates subjects into general categories (such as "companies"), which are broken into increasingly specific subcategories (such as "companies—construction—contractors—builders and designers"). After you select a category or subcategory, the directory displays a list of Web sites that provide content related to that subject. For example, the LookSmart directory at **http://www.looksmart.com/** is shown in Figure 1B.14.

◆ **Search Engines.** A **search engine** lets you search for information by typing one or more words. The engine then displays a list of Web pages that contain information related to your words. (This type of look-up is called a **keyword** search.) Any search engine lets you conduct a search based on a single word. Most also let you search for multiple words, such as "scanner AND printer." A growing number of engines also let you use "plain English" phrases or questions as the basis for your search, such as "movies starring Cary Grant" or "How do cells divide?" The Excite search engine at **http://www.excite.com/** is shown in Figure 1B.15.

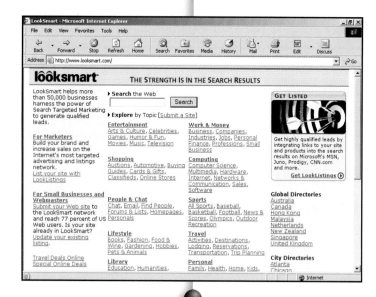

Figure 1B.14

The LookSmart home page. You can use the site's directory to search for Web sites relating to many topics.

Both types of search tools are commonly called search engines. While this terminology is not technically correct, the differences between the two types are blurring, because most Web-based search tools provide both directories and keyword search engines. In fact, looking at both Figures 1B.14 and 1B.15, you will see a box for performing keyword searches and a list of categories for performing directory-style searches in both.

Using a Directory

Suppose you want to find some Web sites that provide information about the latest digital cameras. Perhaps you want to buy a camera, or you just want to read about the technology before deciding whether to buy one. In the following exercise, you will use the LookSmart directory to find Web sites that provide "buyers guide" information.

1. Launch your Web browser.

2. In the Location/Address bar, type **http://www.looksmart.com/** and press Enter. The LookSmart home page opens in your browser window.

3. Under Computing, click the Hardware category. A new page appears, displaying a list of subcategories under the Hardware category.

4. Click the Peripherals subcategory; then click Digital Cameras; then click Buyers Guides (see Figure 1B.16); then click General Guides. After you click the last subcategory (General Guides), a new page appears listing sites that provide information about buying digital cameras (see Figure 1B.17).

5. Browse through the list of Web sites, and click one. The new site opens in your browser window. After reviewing it, you can use your browser's Back button to navigate back to the list of buyers guides to choose another Web site.

Sites listed in a directory generally will provide valuable, relevant information. This is because, before adding a site to its list, a directory reviews the site's content. Sites that offer poor content may

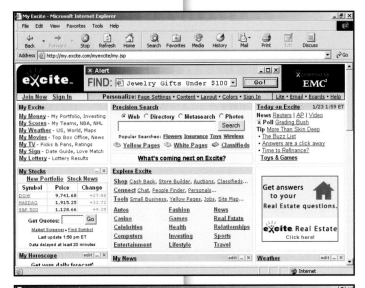

Figure 1B.15
Using the Excite search engine, you can search for information by using a word, a phrase, or a question.

Figure 1B.16
Selecting categories and subcategories of topics in the LookSmart directory

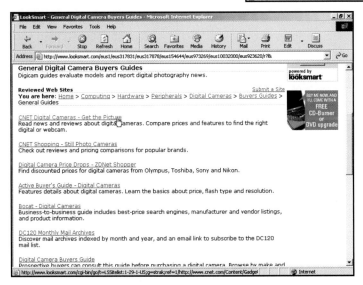

Figure 1B.17
After you select the final subcategory, LookSmart displays a list of Web sites that provide information related to your topic.

not be included in the list. For this reason, Web sites listed in a directory are considered to be "prescreened." Also, because the list of suggested sites has been reviewed already, you are unlikely to find a site listed multiple times within the same topic category. This is a big advantage over search engines, which are notorious for listing the same sites multiple times.

Using a Search Engine

Suppose you want to find some information about ink jet printers. You know there are many different types of printers that are available at a wide range of prices. You also know that you want a printer that prints in color, rather than in black and white only. In the following exercise, you will use a search engine to help you find the information you need.

1. Launch your Web browser.

2. In the Location/Address bar, type **http://www.lycos.com/** and press Enter. The Lycos home page opens in your browser window, as shown in Figure 1B.18. (Lycos is just one example of a Web search engine.)

3. In the Search text box, type **"ink jet printer"** (include the quotation marks) and click the Go button. A new page appears, listing Web pages that contain information relating to ink jet printers. Note, however, that the list includes thousands of pages (see Figure 1B.19). Unlike most directories, search engines generally do not "screen" other Web sites for quality of content. Rather, they assume a Web site is relevant to your needs if it contains terms that match the keywords you provide.

4. To narrow the search results, you must provide more specific search criteria. Click in the Search text box, and type **"color ink jet printer"** (again, including the quotation marks); then click the Go button. Another page appears, listing a new selection of Web sites that match your keywords. Note that this list is shorter than the original one, by several thousand matches.

5. Scroll through the list, and notice if it contains any duplicate entries. How many of the suggested pages actually seem irrelevant to your search criteria? Duplicate and useless entries are two significant problems users encounter when working with search engines.

Figure 1B.18
The Lycos home page features a directory (on the left side of the window) and tools for performing keyword searches in the upper right corner.

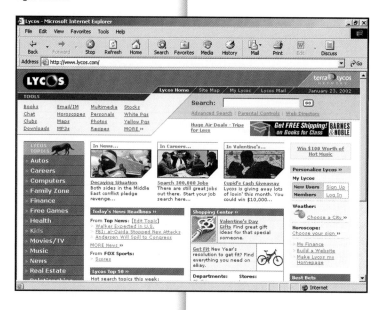

This search produced over 26,000 matches.

Figure 1B.19
Search engines commonly produce thousands (even hundreds of thousands) of matches, depending on your search criteria. To narrow your list of results, you need to provide more specific keywords.

Fortunately, most search engines provide other tools to help you search more accurately and find Web pages that are more relevant to your interests. These include Boolean operators and advanced search tools.

Using Boolean Operators in Your Searches

Most search engines allow you to use special words, called **Boolean operators,** to modify your search criteria. Boolean operators are named after George Boole, a 19th century British mathematician.

There are three basic Boolean operators you can use in searching: AND, OR, and NOT. To use an operator, simply include it in the text box where you type your keywords. The following table shows simple examples of keyword searches that include the operators, and it explains how the operator affects each search.

Operator	Search Criteria	Effect
AND	printer AND color	The search engine looks only for pages that include both terms and ignores pages that include only one of them.
OR	printer OR color	The search engine looks for pages that include either or both of the terms.
NOT	printer NOT color	The search engine looks for pages that include the term *printer*, which do not also include the term *color*. The engine ignores any pages that include both terms.

Some search engines also support a fourth operator, NEAR. This operator determines the proximity, or closeness, of your specified keywords. For example, you may specify "printer NEAR color," with a closeness of 10 words. This tells the search engine to look for pages that include both terms, where the terms are no more than 10 words apart.

A good way to determine whether you need to use operators is to phrase your interest in the form of a sentence, and then use the important parts of the sentence as your keywords along with the appropriate operators. Here are some examples:

Interest	Search
I need information about cancer in children.	cancer AND children
I need information about dogs.	dog OR canine
I need information about acoustic guitars, but not electric guitars.	guitar NOT electric

A few (but not all) search engines will let you use multiple operators and set the order in which they are used. Suppose, for example, that you want to find information about cancer in dogs. You might set up your search criteria like this:

> (dog OR canine) AND cancer

This tells the engine to look for pages that include either "dog," "canine," or both, and then to search those pages for ones that also include "cancer."

A few search engines accept symbols to represent operators. For example, you may be able to use a plus sign (+) to represent the AND operator, and a minus sign (−) to represent NOT.

Many search engines use implied Boolean logic by default, meaning you may not need to include an operator in some searches. For example, if you type the following search criteria:

dog canine

some search engines will assume that you want to find pages that include either term (using the OR operator by default), and others will assume you want pages that include both terms (using the AND operator by default).

When dealing with implied logic, remember that each search engine operates in a slightly different way. For example, in some engines, you should use quotation marks when searching for a phrase or when you want all words to be included, as in:

"ink jet printer"

Without the quotation marks, some engines will return pages that include the word "ink," others that include "jet," and others that include "printer," as well as pages that include all three.

The best way to determine how any search engine works is to study its Help-related pages (see Figure 1B.20). The Help section will tell you whether or how you can use operators with that particular engine.

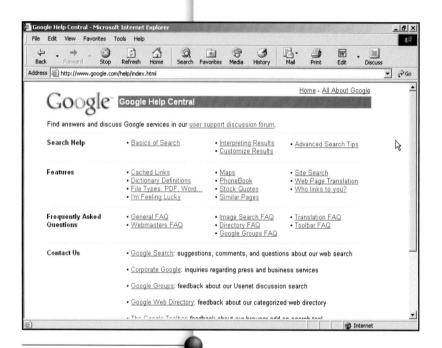

Figure 1B.20
The Help links at the Google search engine site. This Help section provides a basic overview of Google and how it conducts searches. You also can find information about Google's support for Boolean operators, basic and advanced search techniques, and more. The Help section is the best place to start when working with a search engine for the first time.

Using Advanced Search Options

To overcome the problems of duplicate and irrelevant results, many search engines provide a set of advanced search options, sometimes called advanced tools. It is important to remember that each engine's advanced tool set is somewhat different from the tool set of another, but they all have the same goal of helping you refine your search criteria to get the best results.

In some engines, advanced search options include support for phrase-based searching or Boolean operators, as already discussed. In other engines, an advanced search provides you with customized tools. At Excite, for example, if you select the Advanced Search link, you can work in a special form to structure your search criteria. The form lets you specify multiple words and phrases; then you decide whether each one "must," "must not," or "should be" included in the results. The form also provides tools that let you filter adult-oriented content (such as pornographic Web sites) from your results and search for information in a different language or from a given country.

As mentioned earlier, the best way to learn about a specific search engine's advanced options is to study its Help section and then to practice using the tools. After you learn to use an engine's advanced options, you may never want to conduct a search without them.

Using a Metasearch Engine

In addition to the tools described in the preceding sections, a new breed of Web-based search engine is also gaining popularity. These sites, called **metasearch engines,** use multiple search engines simultaneously to look up sites that match your keywords, phrase, or question (see Figure 1B.21). Examples of metasearch engines include Dogpile (**www.dogpile.com/**), Mamma (**www.mamma.com/**), and The BigHub (**www.thebighub.com/**). Metasearch engines are helpful if you are not certain which keywords to use, or if you want to get a very long list of Web sites that meet your search criteria.

Figure 1B.21
Metasearch engines such as Mamma let you decide which search engines to use. You can select all the available engines in the list, if you like.

Site-Specific Search Tools

Many high-volume Web sites feature built-in search tools of their own. These site-specific search tools enable you to look for information on the Web site you are currently visiting.

Suppose, for example, you are visiting the Microsoft Web site and want to find information about Flight Simulator, which is a popular Microsoft game. Instead of jumping from one page to another looking for information, you can click in the Search box, type the words **Flight Simulator,** and click the Go button. The site's search engine displays a list of pages on the Microsoft site that are related to Flight Simulator.

Some site-specific search tools also let you search outside that particular site. At ZDNet's site (**http://www.zdnet.com/**), for example, you can type one or more keywords in the Search box, and then decide whether you want to search only the ZDNet site or the entire Web for related information, before you click the Go button (see Figure 1B.22).

Figure 1B.22
You can search only the ZDNet site or the entire Web.

COMPUTERS
in your career

Computer Knowledge Opens Doors

Although there are still many professions that do not rely on computers, these professions are becoming fewer all the time. Because computers do not necessarily have to take the form of a PC, there is a good chance that your career path will bring you in contact with some type of computer. Whether it is a supercomputer or a bar code reader, an automated machining tool or a telephone switchboard, many of the tools in today's workplace use computer technology in some way.

Thus, it is important to have a basic understanding of computer technology, which is what this book is about. Regardless of your career choice, you can benefit from having some knowledge of computer hardware and software, and how these components function together. Even if your job does not require you to work directly with a computer, this knowledge may help you to envision new ways of using computers in your work, resulting in a more productive work environment. Your knowledge also can lead to career advancement opportunities.

If you think this case is being overstated, and that computers are not being used that much, consider this: Computers are popping up in places and professions that may seem unlikely. The following list presents some examples:

◆ **Restaurant and Grocery Store Managers.** Restaurants, grocery stores, and retail outlet managers use computer systems of all kinds—from handheld units to mainframes—to monitor inventories, track transactions, and manage product pricing. Store managers frequently use portable devices to check stock levels and to change prices. These devices can be networked with a single store's computer system or a chain's wide area network.

◆ **Courier Dispatchers.** Courier services of all types use computerized terminals to help dispatchers schedule deliveries, locate pickup and drop-off points, generate invoices, and track the location of packages. Such systems are used by cross-town delivery services and by national carriers such as Federal Express.

◆ **Construction Managers.** Construction managers and estimators use specialized software to analyze construction documents and to calculate the amount of materials and time required to complete a job. These computerized tools—which often read information directly from disk files provided by the architect—help contractors manage costs and make competitive bids. On the job site, construction workers use computerized measuring devices and laser beams to calculate precise measurements quickly. Field managers and laborers alike routinely use portable computers to check plans and other construction documents or to manage inventories of materials.

◆ **Automotive Mechanics.** Automotive mechanics and technicians use computer systems to measure vehicle performance, diagnose mechanical problems, and determine maintenance or repair strategies. These systems are sometimes networked to regional or national databases of automotive information.

Each of the following units in this textbook features a discussion of computers in the professional world. Each discussion, which focuses on the type of technology introduced in that unit, is designed to help you understand how that particular technology is used in one or more professions.

SUMMARY

- The Internet was created for the U.S. Department of Defense as a tool for communications. Today, the Internet is a global network of interconnected networks.

- The Internet carries messages, documents, programs, and data files that contain every imaginable kind of information for businesses, educational institutions, government agencies, and individuals.

- Today, nearly one-half billion people have access to the Internet, and the number of users continues to grow.

- One of the services available through the Internet is the World Wide Web (or Web). To access the Web, you need an Internet connection and a Web browser.

- Navigating the Web means moving from one Web page or Web site to another.

- Web pages can contain navigational tools, in the form of hyperlinks, which help the user move from page to page.

- Most Web browsers allow the user to navigate the Web in various ways by using toolbar buttons, hyperlinks, bookmarks, and a history list.

- Web browsers, like other application programs, feature online Help systems.

- To search for content on the Web, you can use a directory, a search engine, or a metasearch engine.

- A directory is a categorized list of links. Users can find the information they need by selecting categories and subcategories of topics.

- A search engine lets users search for content by using keywords. The engine lists any Web sites it finds that match the keywords.

- Users can refine their Web searches by using tools such as Boolean operators or advanced search tools.

- Metasearch engines use multiple search engines simultaneously to look up sites that match your keywords, phrase, or question.

KEY TERMS

ARPANET, *23*

backbone, *24*

Boolean operator, *33*

directory, *30*

host, *23*

Internet, *24*

internetworking, *24*

keyword, *30*

metasearch engine, *35*

NSFnet, *24*

search engine, *30*

KEY TERM QUIZ

Complete each statement by writing one of the terms listed under Key Terms in each blank.

1. AND, OR, and NOT are examples of _____ .

2. On the Internet, a(n) _____ computer works like a network server computer.

3. A(n) _____ uses multiple search engines simultaneously to look up sites that match your keywords, phrase, or question.

4. The process of connecting separate networks together is called _____ .

5. A(n) _____ helps you find content on the Web by allowing you to choose categories and subcategories of topics.

SECTION QUIZ

True/False

Answer the following questions by circling True or False.

True	False	1. The Internet was first known as ARCNet.
True	False	2. A network backbone is the central structure that connects other elements of the network together.
True	False	3. The Internet is governed by a group called The Internet Society.
True	False	4. To access the World Wide Web, you need a special software program called a Web browser.
True	False	5. A hyperlink is a part of a Web page that is linked to a URL.

Multiple Choice

Circle the word or phrase that best completes each statement.

1. Construction of the network now known as the Internet began in _____ .
   A. 1959 **B.** 1969 **C.** 1979

2. The Internet is open to _____ .
   A. members **B.** government agencies **C.** anyone who can access it

3. Web pages can contain _____ .
   A. text and graphics **B.** audio and video content **C.** both A and B

4. Every Web page has a unique address, called a _____ .
   A. hyperlink **B.** uniform resource locator **C.** navigation tool

5. When you use a search engine, you specify one or more _____ .
   A. keywords **B.** operators **C.** URLs

REVIEW QUESTIONS

In your own words, briefly answer the following questions.

1. What is an Internet host?

2. Why is the Internet sometimes described as a "network of networks"?

3. What happens when you provide a URL for your Web browser?

4. List three ways you can specify a URL in your Web browser.

5. What is a bookmark in a Web browser, and what do bookmarks allow you to do?

SECTION LABS

Complete the following exercises as directed by your instructor.

1. Practice using your browser. Launch your browser and practice navigating the Web. Try using URLs based on the names of people or companies you want to learn more about. For example, if you type **http://www.cheerios.com/** in your Address box, what happens? Make up five different URLs from company, product, or individual names and see where they lead your browser. As you visit different sites, look for hyperlinked text and graphics; click them and see where they lead.

2. Search, search, search. Pick a topic and search the Web for information about it. Pick a keyword to use in your search, then visit three search engines and use each of them to conduct a search using your chosen keyword. Use Yahoo (**http://www.yahoo.com/**), AltaVista (**http://www.altavista.com/**), and Google (**http://www.google.com/**) for your searches. Do the results differ from one search engine to another?

UNIT PROJECTS

UNIT LABS

Complete the following exercises using a computer in your classroom, lab, or home.

1. **Explore your disk.** Once you are familiar with your computer's hardware, it is time to see the folders and files that reside on its hard disk. To see what is on your disk, take these steps:

   A. Minimize or close all running program windows, so you can see the Windows desktop.

   B. On the desktop, double-click the My Computer icon. The My Computer window opens, listing all the disks on your computer.

   C. Double-click the icon labeled "LOCAL DISK (C:)" to open a window displaying that disk's contents.

   D. Double-click at least five of the folders and review the contents of each one. Can you tell which files are data files and which are program files?

   E. When you finish exploring your disk, close all open windows.

2. **Get some help.** If you do not know how to perform a task on your computer, turn to its online help system for answers and assistance. Browse your operating system's help system to learn more about your computer.

   A. Click the Start button on the Windows taskbar to open the Start menu.

   B. On the Start menu, click Help (or Help and Support). The Windows Help window opens.

   C. Click Index to see an alphabetical list of all the terms covered by the help system. To see the help information associated with a term, click the term, then click Display.

   D. Review the Help information for at least three more topics.

   E. Close the Help window by clicking the Close button (with an X on it) in the upper right corner of the window.

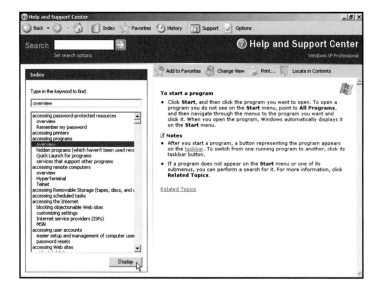

3. **Learn more about browsers.** There are many different Web browsers available, and you may decide you like one of the lesser-known browsers better than the most popular ones. The following Web sites can provide information about browsers:

   • Microsoft. Visit **http://www.microsoft.com/windows/ie/default.asp** for information about Microsoft Internet Explorer.

   • Netscape. Visit **http://browsers.netscape.com/browsers/main.tmpl** for information about Netscape Navigator.

- Opera Software. Visit **http://www.opera.com/** for information about Opera.

- Ubvision. Visit **http://www.ultrabrowser.com/** for information about UltraBrowser.

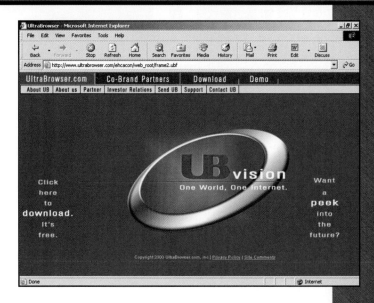

DISCUSSION QUESTIONS

As directed by your instructor, discuss the following questions in class or in groups.

1. Home computers are used more extensively than ever for tasks such as banking, investing, shopping, and communicating. Do you see this trend as having a positive or a negative impact on our society and economy? Do you plan to use a computer in these ways? Why or why not?

2. Describe your experience with computers so far. Have you worked with (or played with) computers before? If so, why? Has your past experience with computers influenced your decision to study them?

RESEARCH AND REPORT

Using your own choice of resources (such as the Internet, books, magazines, and newspaper articles), research and write a short paper discussing one of the following topics:

■ The world's smallest computer

■ The use of supercomputers in mapping the human genome

■ The birth of the World Wide Web

When you are finished, proofread and print your paper, and give it to your instructor.

 ## ETHICAL ISSUES

Computer skills can make a difference in a person's employability. With this thought in mind, discuss the following questions in class.

1. A factory is buying computerized systems and robots to handle many tasks, meaning fewer laborers will be needed. The company needs people to run the new equipment, but it wants to hire new workers who already have computer skills. Is the company obligated to keep the workers with no computer skills and to train them to use the equipment? Are workers obligated to learn these new skills if they want to keep their jobs?

2. You are a skilled drafter with 15 years of experience. You have always done your drafting work using traditional methods (using pen and paper). Now you want to move to a different city and have sent resumes to several drafting firms there. You learn, however, that none of those firms will consider you for employment because you have no experience drafting on a computer. Is this fair? Why or why not? What would you do?

UNIT **2**

Interacting With Your Computer

UNIT CONTENTS

This unit contains the following sections:

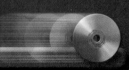

The Interactive Browser Edition CD-ROM provides additional labs and activities to apply concepts from this unit.

SECTION 2A

Standard Input Devices

OVERVIEW:
The Keyboard and the Mouse

If the CPU is the computer's brain, then the input devices are its eyes and ears. From the user's point of view, input devices are just as important as the CPU—more so, in fact. After you have purchased and set up the computer, you may take the CPU for granted, because you interact directly with input devices and only indirectly with the CPU. Your ability to use input devices is critical to your overall success with the whole system.

An input device does exactly what its name suggests: it enables you to input information and commands into the computer. The most commonly used input devices are the keyboard and the mouse. In fact, if you buy a new personal computer today, it will include a keyboard and a mouse, unless you specify otherwise. As you will see, many other types of input devices are available, including variations of the mouse and specialized "alternative" input devices, such as microphones and scanners.

This section introduces you to the keyboard and the mouse. You will learn the importance of these devices, the way the computer accepts input from them, and the many tasks they enable you to perform on your PC.

OBJECTIVES

- Identify the five key groups on a standard computer keyboard.
- Name six special-purpose keys found on all standard computer keyboards.
- List the five steps a computer follows when accepting input from a keyboard.
- Describe the purpose of a mouse and the role it plays in computing.
- Identify the five essential techniques for using a mouse.
- Identify three common variants of the mouse.

THE KEYBOARD

The keyboard was one of the first peripherals to be used with computers, and it is still the primary input device for entering text and numbers. A standard keyboard includes about 100 keys; each key sends a different signal to the CPU.

If you have not used a computer keyboard or a typewriter, you will learn quickly that you can use a computer much more effectively if you know how to type. The skill of typing, or **keyboarding,** is the ability to enter text and numbers with skill and accuracy. Certainly, you can use a computer without having good typing skills. Some people claim that when computers can interpret handwriting and speech with 100 percent accuracy, typing will become unnecessary. But for now and the foreseeable future, keyboarding remains the most common way to enter text and other data into a computer.

The Standard Keyboard Layout

Keyboards for personal computers come in many styles. The various models differ in size, shape, and feel, but except for a few special-purpose keys, most keyboards are laid out almost identically. Among IBM-compatible computers, the most common keyboard layout is the IBM Enhanced Keyboard. It has 101 keys arranged in five groups, as shown in Figure 2A.1.

The Alphanumeric Keys

The **alphanumeric keys**—the parts of the keyboard that look like a typewriter—are arranged the same way on almost every keyboard. Sometimes this common arrangement is called the QWERTY (pronounced KWER-tee) layout because the first six keys on the top row of letters are *Q, W, E, R, T,* and *Y.*

Figure 2A.1
Most IBM-compatible PCs use a keyboard like this one.

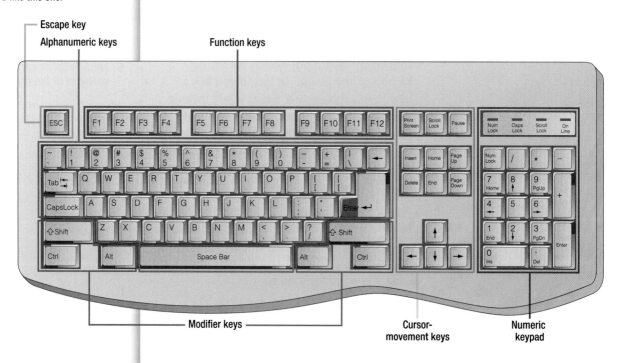

Along with the keys that produce letters and numbers, the alphanumeric key group includes four keys that have specific functions. The Tab, Caps Lock, Backspace, and Enter keys are described in Figure 2A.2.

Figure 2A.2
Functions of the Tab, Caps Lock, Backspace, and Enter keys

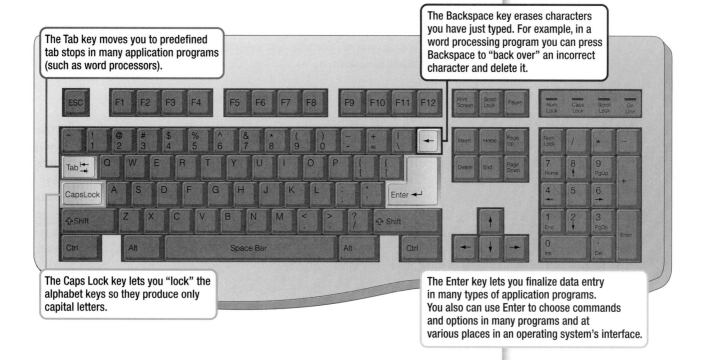

The Tab key moves you to predefined tab stops in many application programs (such as word processors).

The Backspace key erases characters you have just typed. For example, in a word processing program you can press Backspace to "back over" an incorrect character and delete it.

The Caps Lock key lets you "lock" the alphabet keys so they produce only capital letters.

The Enter key lets you finalize data entry in many types of application programs. You also can use Enter to choose commands and options in many programs and at various places in an operating system's interface.

The Modifier Keys

A keyboard's **modifier keys** are so named because they modify the input of other keys. In other words, if you hold down a modifier key while pressing another key, then you are changing the key's input in some way. Modifier keys are extremely useful, because they give all other keys multiple capabilities. Figure 2A.3 describes the modifier keys and their uses.

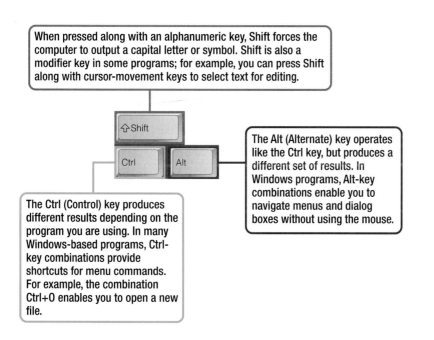

When pressed along with an alphanumeric key, Shift forces the computer to output a capital letter or symbol. Shift is also a modifier key in some programs; for example, you can press Shift along with cursor-movement keys to select text for editing.

The Alt (Alternate) key operates like the Ctrl key, but produces a different set of results. In Windows programs, Alt-key combinations enable you to navigate menus and dialog boxes without using the mouse.

The Ctrl (Control) key produces different results depending on the program you are using. In many Windows-based programs, Ctrl-key combinations provide shortcuts for menu commands. For example, the combination Ctrl+O enables you to open a new file.

Figure 2A.3
Functions of the Shift, Ctrl, and Alt keys

The Numeric Keypad

The **numeric keypad** is usually located on the right side of the keyboard, as shown in Figure 2A.1. The numeric keypad looks like an adding machine, with its ten digits and mathematical operators (+, -, *, and /). The numeric keypad also features a Num Lock key, which works like the Caps Lock key in the alphanumeric key group: The Num Lock key forces the numeric keys to input numbers. When Num Lock is deactivated, the numeric keypad's keys perform cursor-movement control and other functions.

The Function Keys

The fourth part of the keyboard consists of the **function keys.** These keys (labeled *F1, F2,* and so on, as shown in Figure 2A.1) are usually arranged in a row along the top of the keyboard. They allow you to input commands without typing long strings of characters or navigating menus or dialog boxes. Each function key's purpose depends on the program you are using. For example, in most programs, F1 is the help key. When you press it, a special window appears to display information about the program you are using. Most IBM-compatible keyboards have 12 function keys. Many programs use function keys along with modifier keys to give the function keys more capabilities.

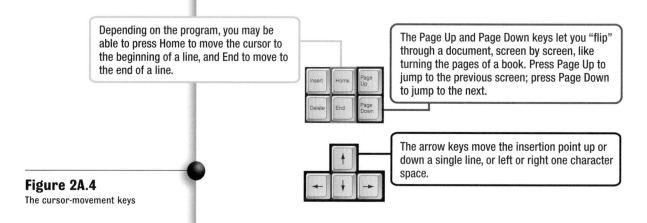

Depending on the program, you may be able to press Home to move the cursor to the beginning of a line, and End to move to the end of a line.

The Page Up and Page Down keys let you "flip" through a document, screen by screen, like turning the pages of a book. Press Page Up to jump to the previous screen; press Page Down to jump to the next.

The arrow keys move the insertion point up or down a single line, or left or right one character space.

Figure 2A.4
The cursor-movement keys

The Cursor-Movement Keys

The fifth part of the keyboard is the set of **cursor-movement keys,** which let you move around the screen without using a mouse. In many programs and operating systems, a mark on the screen indicates where the characters you type will be entered. This mark, called the **cursor** or **insertion point,** appears on the screen as a blinking vertical line, a small box, or some other symbol to show your place in a document or command line. Figure 2A.4 describes the cursor-movement keys, and Figure 2A.5 shows an insertion point in a document window.

Figure 2A.5
The cursor, or insertion point, shows where the next letter typed will appear.

Now is the time for all good men to |

The cursor, or insertion point, in a document

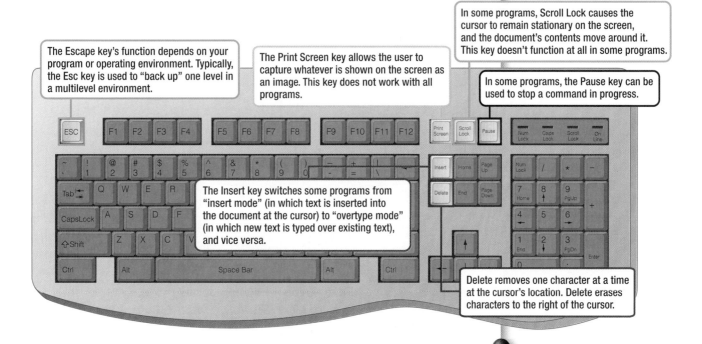

The Escape key's function depends on your program or operating environment. Typically, the Esc key is used to "back up" one level in a multilevel environment.

The Print Screen key allows the user to capture whatever is shown on the screen as an image. This key does not work with all programs.

In some programs, Scroll Lock causes the cursor to remain stationary on the screen, and the document's contents move around it. This key doesn't function at all in some programs.

In some programs, the Pause key can be used to stop a command in progress.

The Insert key switches some programs from "insert mode" (in which text is inserted into the document at the cursor) to "overtype mode" (in which new text is typed over existing text), and vice versa.

Delete removes one character at a time at the cursor's location. Delete erases characters to the right of the cursor.

Figure 2A.6
Special-purpose keys on most standard keyboards

Special-Purpose Keys

In addition to the five groups of keys described earlier, all IBM-compatible keyboards feature six special-purpose keys, each of which performs a specialized function. Figure 2A.6 describes these special-purpose keys.

Since 1996, nearly all IBM-compatible keyboards include two additional special-purpose keys designed to work with Windows operating systems (see Figure 2A.7).

◆ **Start.** This key, which features the Windows logo (and is sometimes called the Windows logo key), opens the Windows Start menu on most computers. Pressing this key performs the same function as clicking the Start button on the Windows taskbar.

◆ **Shortcut.** This key, which features an image of a menu, opens an on-screen shortcut menu in Windows-based application programs.

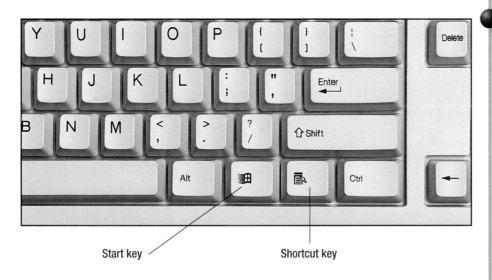

Start key   Shortcut key

Figure 2A.7
The Start key and the Shortcut key appear frequently on the newer keyboards that are sold with Windows-based computers.

These buttons give you quick access to the Internet, and they can be programmed to perform specific tasks.

NORTON
ONLINE

Visit **www.norton.glencoe.com** for more information on **different types of keyboards**.

One of the latest trends in keyboard technology is the addition of Internet and multimedia controls (see Figure 2A.8). Microsoft's Internet keyboards, for example, feature a row of buttons at the top of the unit. You can program these buttons to perform any number of tasks, including launching a Web browser, checking e-mail, and starting your most frequently used programs. Several keyboard manufacturers also have added multimedia buttons that let you control the computer's CD-ROM or DVD drive and adjust the speaker volume.

As more people shop online, computer manufacturers are adding keyboard-based tools to make the shopping experience easier. For example, Compaq's Internet Smart Credit Card keyboard features a built-in credit card reader (see Figure 2A.9). Instead of typing your credit card information when shopping online, you can simply insert your credit card into the reader, and the data is transmitted for you. This feature requires a "smart credit card," which encrypts the user's information on a small chip.

This slot accepts a smart credit card.

Figure 2A.9

This keyboard can read data directly from your smart credit card without you having to type it.

Ergonomic and Specialty Keyboards

Many variations have been made to the standard keyboard, primarily for users' comfort and to reduce repetitive stress injuries. People who type for extended periods of time are susceptible to wrist and hand fatigue and strain. Ergonomically designed keyboards can help reduce those problems.

Figure 2A.10
Ergonomically designed keyboards can make keyboarding more comfortable while reducing repetitive stress injuries to the wrists and the hands.

Ergonomically designed keyboards enable the user's hands to remain positioned correctly on the keyboard while reducing bending and strain. As shown in Figure 2A.10, an ergonomic keyboard may be curved in some way, or its keys may be arranged in two separate sections so that the user's hands are placed comfortably on the keyboard. (Ergonomics, correct posture and hand position, and specially designed input devices are covered in detail in Unit 14, "Living With Computers.")

HOW THE COMPUTER ACCEPTS INPUT FROM THE KEYBOARD

You might think the keyboard simply sends the letter of a pressed key to the computer—after all, that is what appears to happen. Actually, the process of accepting input from the keyboard is more complex, as shown in Figure 2A.11.

A tiny computer chip, called the **keyboard controller,** notes that a key has been pressed. The keyboard controller places a code into part of its memory, called the **keyboard buffer,** to indicate which key was pressed. (A buffer is a temporary storage area that holds data until it can be processed.) This code is called the key's **scan code.** The keyboard controller then signals the computer's system software that something has happened at the keyboard.

The signal the keyboard sends to the computer is a special kind of message called an **interrupt request.** The keyboard controller sends an interrupt request to the system software when it receives a complete keystroke. For example, if you type the letter *r*, the controller immediately issues an interrupt request. If you hold down the Shift key before typing the letter *R*, the controller waits until the whole key combination has been entered.

When the system software receives an interrupt request, it evaluates the request to determine the appropriate response. When a keystroke has occurred, the system reads the memory location in the keyboard buffer that contains the scan code of the key that was pressed. It then passes the key's scan code to the CPU.

The keyboard buffer can store many keystrokes at one time. This capability is necessary, because some time elapses between the pressing of a key and the computer's reading of that key from the keyboard buffer. With the keystrokes stored in a buffer, the program can react to them when it is convenient.

Figure 2A.11

How input is received from the keyboard

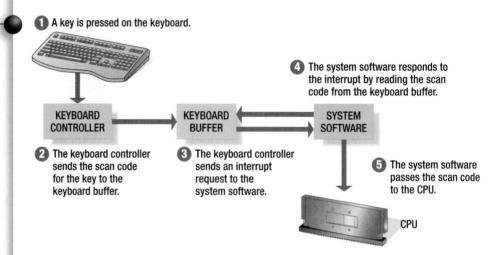

1 A key is pressed on the keyboard.

4 The system software responds to the interrupt by reading the scan code from the keyboard buffer.

| KEYBOARD CONTROLLER | → | KEYBOARD BUFFER | ← | SYSTEM SOFTWARE |

2 The keyboard controller sends the scan code for the key to the keyboard buffer.

3 The keyboard controller sends an interrupt request to the system software.

5 The system software passes the scan code to the CPU.

CPU

In many newer systems, the keyboard controller handles input from the computer's mouse and stores settings for both the keyboard and the mouse. One keyboard setting, the **repeat rate,** determines how long you must hold down an alphanumeric key before the keyboard will repeat the character and how rapidly the character is retyped while you press the key. You can set the repeat rate to suit your typing speed. (You will learn how to check your keyboard's repeat rate in the lab exercises at the end of this unit.)

Self Check

Answer the following questions by filling in the blank(s).

1. The __QWERTY__ keyboard layout is so called because of the location of the first six keys in the top row of letter keys.

2. The __Shift__ key works as part of the alphanumeric keys but also functions as a modifier key.

3. When you press a key on the keyboard, a(n) __scan code__ tells the computer which key was pressed.

PRODUCTIVITY Tip

Working Faster With Keyboard Shortcuts

In the 1980s, as programmers began packing more features into PC software, they also developed ways for users to issue an ever-increasing number of commands. Software packages came with long lists of commands, all of which had to be entered at the keyboard. (This was before the mouse came into common use.) As a result, the computer keyboard rapidly became a valuable tool.

Programmers began devising keyboard shortcuts that allow users to issue commands quickly by typing a short combination of keystrokes. Keyboard shortcuts involve using a modifier key (such as Alt or Ctrl) along with one or more alphanumeric or function keys. To print a document in many applications, for example, the user can press Ctrl + P.

Function keys also became important. The F1 key, for example, became the universal way to access online help. IBM-compatible computer keyboards originally had ten function keys; eventually, the number of function keys was expanded to twelve.

Another common type of keyboard shortcut involves pressing the Alt key to access a program's menu system. When running any Windows program, you can press Alt to activate the menu bar, and then press a highlighted letter in a menu's name to open that menu.

Still, a keyboard can hold only so many keys, and the lists of keyboard shortcuts became unmanageable. A single program could use dozens of "hotkeys," as these shortcuts were called. If you used several programs, you had to learn different shortcuts for each program. Finally, the Common User Access (CUA) standard led to the standardization of many commonly used hotkeys across different programs and environments. With this standard for commonly used hotkeys, users have fewer hotkeys to remember.

Despite such standards, pointing devices (such as the mouse) came along none too soon for hotkey-weary computer users. Microsoft Windows and the Macintosh operating system gained popularity because of their easy-to-use, mouse-oriented graphical interfaces. Even DOS-based programs began using toolbars, pull-down menus, and dialog boxes. By operating the mouse, users

The following table lists some of the shortcut keys available in Microsoft Word.

Press	To
Ctrl + Shift + Spacebar	Create a nonbreaking space
Ctrl + Hyphen	Create a nonbreaking hyphen
Ctrl + B	Make letters bold
Ctrl + I	Make letters italic
Ctrl + U	Make letters underline
Ctrl + Shift + <	Decrease font size
Ctrl + Shift + >	Increase font size
Ctrl + Q	Remove paragraph formatting
Ctrl + Spacebar	Remove character formatting
Ctrl + C	Copy the selected text or object
Ctrl + X	Cut the selected text or object
Ctrl + V	Paste text or an object
Ctrl + Z	Undo the last action
Ctrl + Y	Redo the last action

could make selections visually from menus and dialog boxes. Emphasis rapidly began shifting away from the keyboard to the screen; today, many users of popular programs probably do not know what each function key does!

Pointing, however, can slow you down. As menus and dialog boxes become increasingly crowded, commands can be hard to find, and their locations can be as difficult to remember as keyboard shortcuts. Many computer users are overcoming these problems by using a combination of keyboard shortcuts and a pointing device. You use one hand to issue many basic shortcuts (such as Ctrl + P and Ctrl + S) or to launch macros. A macro is a series of commands that a program memorizes for you. Macros enable you to issue an entire set of commands in just a few keystrokes. These techniques minimize keystrokes and leave a hand free to use a pointing device.

Mouse

THE MOUSE

A personal computer that was purchased in the early 1980s probably included a keyboard as the only input device. Today, most new PCs include a **pointing device** as standard equipment, as shown in Figure 2A.12. If the computer is a desktop or tower model, the pointing device is usually a mouse. A mouse is an input device that rolls around on a flat surface (usually on a desk or keyboard tray) and controls the pointer. The **pointer** (also called the *mouse pointer*) is an on-screen object—usually an arrow—that is used to select text; access menus; and interact with programs, files, or data that appear on the screen. Figure 2A.13 shows an example of a pointer in a program window.

Figure 2A.12
Most modern personal computers are equipped with a mouse.

Most mice are mechanical; they contain a small rubber ball that protrudes through a hole in the bottom of the mouse's case. The ball rolls inside the case when you move the mouse around on a flat surface. Inside the mouse, rollers and sensors send signals to the computer, telling it the distance, direction, and speed of the ball's motions. The computer uses this data to position the mouse pointer on the screen.

Another type of mouse is the **optical mouse.** This nonmechanical mouse emits a beam of light from its underside; it uses the light's reflection to judge the distance, direction, and speed of its travel.

Figure 2A.13
An example of a pointer

The mouse offers several benefits. For example, the mouse lets you quickly position the cursor anywhere on the screen, without using the cursor-movement keys. You simply move the pointer to the on-screen position you want and press the mouse button; the cursor appears at that location.

Instead of forcing you to type or issue commands from the keyboard, the mouse and mouse-based operating systems let you choose commands from easy-to-use menus and dialog boxes (see Figure 2A.14). The result is a much more intuitive way to use computers. Instead of remembering obscure command names, users can figure out rather easily where commands and options are located.

Figure 2A.14
Using the mouse to issue a command from a menu.

Click a menu's name to open the menu.

Click a command to issue it.

If you use a drawing program, you can use the mouse to create graphics such as lines, curves, and freehand shapes on the screen. The mouse has helped establish the computer as a versatile tool for graphic designers, starting what has since become a revolution in the graphic design field.

VISUAL ESSAY: USING THE MOUSE

You use a mouse to point to a location on the screen, a process called **pointing**. Everything you do with a mouse is accomplished by combining pointing with other techniques, such as clicking, double-clicking, dragging, and right-clicking.

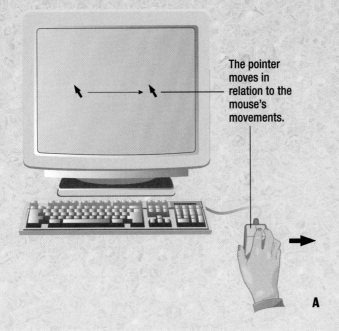

The pointer moves in relation to the mouse's movements.

A

A

Pointing means pushing the mouse across your desk; on the screen, the pointer moves in relation to the mouse. Push the mouse forward, and the pointer moves up. Push the mouse to the left, and the pointer moves to the left. To point to an object or location on the screen, you simply use the mouse to place the pointer on top of the object or location.

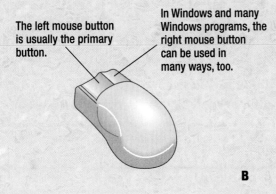

The left mouse button is usually the primary button.

In Windows and many Windows programs, the right mouse button can be used in many ways, too.

B

B

The mice that come with IBM-compatible computers usually have two buttons, but techniques such as clicking, double-clicking, and dragging are usually carried out with the left mouse button. (In multi-button mice, one button must be designated as the "primary" button; it is referred to as the mouse button.)

"click"

C

C

Clicking an item with the mouse means moving the pointer to the item on the screen and pressing and releasing the mouse button once.

Double-clicking an item means pointing to the item with the mouse pointer and then pressing and releasing the mouse button twice in rapid succession.

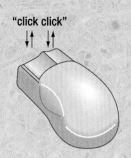

"click click"

D

Dragging an item means positioning the mouse pointer over the item, pressing the mouse button, and holding it down as you move the mouse. As you move the pointer, the item is "dragged" along with it. You then can drop the item in a new position on the screen. This technique is called **drag-and-drop editing**, or just **drag and drop**.

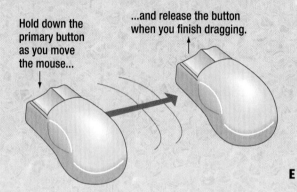

Hold down the primary button as you move the mouse...

...and release the button when you finish dragging.

E

Windows and many Windows programs support **right-clicking**, which means pointing to an item on the screen, then pressing and releasing the right mouse button. Right-clicking usually opens a shortcut menu, which contains commands and options that pertain to the item you are pointing to.

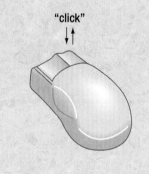

"click"

F

A fairly recent enhancement is the **wheel mouse.** A wheel mouse has a small wheel nestled among its buttons. You can use the wheel for various purposes, one of which is scrolling through long documents. Note that not all applications and operating systems support the use of the wheel.

You can use this wheel to scroll through a document on the screen.

G

Mouse Button Configurations

The mouse usually sits to the right of the keyboard (for right-handed people), and the user maneuvers the mouse with the right hand, pressing the left button with the right forefinger. For this reason, the left mouse button is sometimes called the primary mouse button.

If you are left-handed, you can configure the right mouse button as the primary button (as shown in Figure 2A.15). This configuration lets you place the mouse to the left of the keyboard, control the mouse with your left hand, and use your left forefinger for most mouse actions.

VARIANTS OF THE MOUSE

Although the mouse is a handy tool, some people do not like using a mouse or have difficulty maneuvering one. For others, a mouse requires too much desktop space—a real problem when you are not working at a desk!

For these reasons and others, hardware makers have developed various input devices that duplicate the mouse's functionality but interact with the user in different ways. The primary goals of these "mouse variants" are to provide ease of use while taking up less space than a mouse. They all remain stationary, and they can even be built into the keyboard.

The Trackball

A trackball is a pointing device that works like an upside-down mouse. You rest your thumb on an exposed ball and your fingers on the buttons. To move the pointer around the screen, you roll the ball with your thumb. Because you do not move the whole device, a trackball requires less space than a mouse. Trackballs gained popularity with the advent of laptop computers, which typically are used on laps or on small work surfaces that have no room for a mouse.

Trackballs come in different models, as shown in Figure 2A.16. Some trackballs are large and heavy, with a ball about the same size as a cue ball. Others are much smaller. Most trackballs feature two buttons, although three-button models are also available. Trackball units also are available in right- and left-handed models.

Figure 2A.15
Most operating systems provide tools for configuring mouse buttons.

Figure 2A.16
Trackballs come in many different shapes and sizes.

The Trackpad

The **trackpad** (also called a touchpad) is a stationary pointing device that many people find less tiring to use than a mouse or trackball. The movement of a finger across a small touch surface is translated into pointer movement on the computer screen. The touch-sensitive surface may be only 1.5 or 2 inches square, so the finger never has to move far. The trackpad's size also makes it suitable for a notebook computer. Some notebook models feature a built-in trackpad, rather than a mouse or trackball (see Figure 2A.17).

Like mice, trackpads usually are separate from the keyboard in desktop computers and are attached to the computer through a cord. Some special keyboards feature built-in trackpads. This feature keeps the pad handy and frees a port that would otherwise be used by the trackpad.

Trackpads include two or three buttons that perform the same functions as mouse buttons. Some trackpads are also "strike sensitive," meaning you can tap the pad with your fingertip instead of using its buttons.

Trackpad

Figure 2A.17
Some notebook computers and desktop keyboards feature a built-in trackpad.

Pointers in the Keyboard

Several computer manufacturers now offer another space-saving pointing device. A small joystick is positioned near the middle of the keyboard, typically between the G and H keys. The joystick is controlled with either forefinger, and it controls the movement of the pointer on screen. Because users do not have to take their hands off the keyboard to use this device, they can save a great deal of time and effort. Two buttons that perform the same function as mouse buttons are just beneath the spacebar; they are pressed with the thumb. Because the joystick occupies so little space, the device is built into many different laptop models. This type of pointing device also is available on some models of desktop computer keyboards.

Several generic terms have emerged for this device; many manufacturers refer to it as an **integrated pointing device,** while others call it a 3-D point stick. On the IBM ThinkPad line of notebook computers, the pointing device is called the **TrackPoint** (see Figure 2A.18).

TrackPoint

Figure 2A.18
IBM's ThinkPad comes with the TrackPoint pointing device.

At Issue

Equal-Opportunity Computing

Innovations in operating systems, software applications, and hardware are making computers increasingly accessible to persons with disabilities. These technological improvements span a broad range—from general system settings that can make a PC more user-friendly to disability-specific hardware that can help a user overcome a physical challenge.

Resetting the System

Newer operating systems provide several accessibility settings that are easy to configure. While these settings cannot make a keyboard or mouse accessible to someone with a significant mobility impairment, they can make the computer a little easier to use for persons who can use a keyboard and/or a mouse. These settings include:

◆ **Sticky Keys.** For users who have trouble pressing two keys at one time, a "sticky keys" option allows the user to activate any modifier key by pressing it once and releasing it. The key stays active until it is pressed again.

◆ **Filter Keys.** If a person cannot release a key quickly after pressing it, this option tells the computer to ignore repeated key strokes.

◆ **Mouse Keys.** In newer versions of Windows, the user can set the keyboard's cursor-movement keys to control the mouse pointer.

◆ **SerialKey Device Support.** Input devices that support the SerialKey standard can provide alternative access to the features of a keyboard or mouse.

Recent versions of operating systems also provide various alarm methods. Hearing-impaired users can set their PCs for displaying visual alerts instead of sounding audible alerts.

Special Hardware and Software

Many kinds of help are available through specialized input devices, output devices, and software. Some of the major accessibility products can be categorized as follows:

◆ **Keyboard Alternatives.** This category includes software programs that enable users to input data with fewer keystrokes, as well as devices that replace traditional keyboards entirely.

◆ **Breath-Enabled Devices.** A breath-enabled device can perform many types of input, such as opening menus and choosing commands. By inhaling (sipping) and blowing (puffing) through a tube, the user can control different system functions.

◆ **Speech Recognition.** A speech-recognition system includes a microphone and special software that can recognize certain words and phrases. With this type of system, a user can issue commands, navigate menu systems, and dictate text for the PC to type by "talking" to the computer.

◆ **Braille Input and Output Devices.** Braille note-takers, keyboards, displays, and printers (also called embossers) are all available. Specialized software can convert standard PC keyboards to Braille input devices.

◆ **Screen Readers.** Using speech-synthesis technology, a screen reader can "read" the computer screen's contents to the user. These systems convert text to audio output for blind or visually impaired users.

The Accessibility Options dialog box lets Windows 2000 users set various accessibility options.

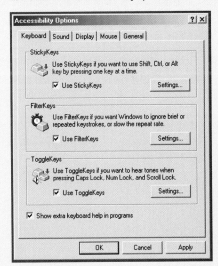

57

SUMMARY

■ A standard computer keyboard has about 100 keys; each key sends a different signal to the CPU.

■ Most keyboards follow a similar layout, with their keys arranged in five groups. Those groups include alphanumeric keys, the numeric keypad, function keys, modifier keys, and cursor-movement keys.

■ Ergonomically designed keyboards are available to help users prevent repetitive stress injuries to the wrists and hands.

■ When you press a key, the keyboard controller places a code in the keyboard buffer to indicate which key was pressed. The keyboard sends the computer an interrupt request, which tells the CPU to accept the keystroke.

■ The mouse is a pointing device that lets you control the position of a graphical pointer on the screen without using the keyboard.

■ Using the mouse involves five techniques: pointing, clicking, double-clicking, dragging, and right-clicking.

■ A trackball is like a mouse turned upside-down. It provides the functionality of a mouse, but it takes less space on the desktop.

■ A trackpad is a touch-sensitive pad that provides the same functionality as a mouse. To use a trackpad, you glide your finger across its surface.

■ Many notebook computers provide a joystick-like pointing device that is built into the keyboard. You control the pointer by moving the joystick. On IBM systems, this device is called a TrackPoint. Generically, it is called an integrated pointing device.

KEY TERMS

alphanumeric key, 44	insertion point, 46	pointing, 53
clicking, 53	integrated pointing device, 56	pointer, 52
cursor, 46	interrupt request, 49	pointing device, 52
cursor-movement key, 46	keyboard buffer, 49	repeat rate, 50
double-clicking, 54	keyboard controller, 49	right-clicking, 54
dragging, 54	keyboarding, 44	scan code, 49
drag-and-drop editing	modifier key, 45	trackpad, 56
(drag and drop), 54	numeric keypad, 46	TrackPoint, 56
function key, 46	optical mouse, 52	wheel mouse, 54

KEY TERM QUIZ

Complete each statement by writing one of the terms listed under Key Terms in each blank.

1. IBM-compatible PCs have 10 or 12 _____ keys. *function*

2. In addition to pointing, the four primary mouse techniques are _*pointing*_, *clicking*, _*double clicking*_, and _*right-clicking*_

3. In many programs, an on-screen symbol called a(n) _*cursor*_ or a(n) _*insertion point*_ shows you where you are in a document.

4. You use a mouse (or one of its variants) to position a(n) _*pointer*_ on the screen.

5. A(n) _____ lets you control the pointer by sliding your finger across a touch-sensitive pad. *track pad*

SECTION QUIZ

True/False

Answer the following questions by circling True or False.

True	*(False)*	1. A standard keyboard has 88 keys.
(True)	False	2. The keyboard keys labeled F1, F2, and so on, are called function keys.
(True)	False	3. The Delete key erases characters to the right of the cursor.
(True)	False	4. The Start and Shortcut keys perform special functions in the Windows operating system.
True	*(False)*	5. On a two-button mouse, you usually click, double-click, and drag by using the right mouse button.

Multiple Choice

Circle the word or phrase that best completes each statement.

1. On standard keyboards, keys usually are arranged in _____ groups.
   A. three   **(B.** five)   **C.** eight

2. On a PC keyboard, the modifier keys include _____ .
   A. Alt, Delete, and Insert   **(B.** Shift, Ctrl, and Alt)   **C.** Backspace, Esc, and Command

3. As you type, the system stores _____ in the keyboard buffer.
   A. interrupt requests   **(B.** scan codes)   **C.** neither A nor B

4. A _____ works like an upside-down mouse.
   (A. trackball)   **B.** trackpad   **C.** joystick

5. The term _____ is another term for integrated pointing device.
   A. trackpad   **B.** mouse   **(C.** TrackPoint)

REVIEW QUESTIONS

In your own words, briefly answer the following questions.

1. Most standard keyboards include five major groups of keys. List them.
   Alphanumeric, Modifier, Numeric, Functions, cursor-movement Keys
2. Why are most standard keyboards called QWERTY keyboards?
   The letters are the 1st 6 keys on the top row
3. What does the Ctrl key do?
   Provides short cuts when used in combination w/other Keys
4. What is an optical mouse?
   no trackball - uses light reflection
5. Some trackpads are "strike-sensitive." What does this mean?
   When you "tap" on it, it acts as the left mouse click.

SECTION LABS

Complete the following exercises as directed by your instructor.

1. Test your typing skills in Notepad. Click the Start button, point to Programs (or All Programs), click Accessories, and then click Notepad to open the Notepad text editing program. Notepad opens in a window. Have a classmate time you as you type a paragraph of text. The paragraph should be at least five lines long and should make sense. (For example, you could type a paragraph of text from any page in this book.) Do not stop to correct mistakes; keep typing until you are finished typing the selection.

2. Inspect your system's mouse settings. (Do not change any settings without your instructor's permission.) Use the following steps:
   A. As indicated by your instructor, open the Control Panel window. (The way you do this will depend on your version of Windows.)
   B. Double-click the Mouse icon to open the Mouse Properties dialog box. Click the tabs in this dialog box and inspect your settings.
   C. Experiment with the Pointer Speed and Show Pointer Trails tools. When you are finished, click Cancel.

Alternative Input Devices

OVERVIEW:
Options for Every Need and Preference

Although the keyboard and mouse are the input devices that people use most often, there are many other ways to input data into a computer. Sometimes the tool is simply a matter of choice. Some users just prefer the feel of a trackball over a mouse. In many cases, however, an ordinary input device may not be appropriate. For example, using a keyboard or mouse in a dusty factory or warehouse could cause damage to the equipment if the keyboard or mouse became clogged with dirt. And if cashiers manually inputted product codes and prices, it would slow down the check-out process in grocery and retail stores. Thus, optical scanning devices often are used to speed the process and to reduce the risk of input errors.

Alternative input devices are important parts of some special-purpose computers. Tapping a handheld computer's screen with a pen is a much faster way to input commands than typing on a miniature keyboard. On the other hand, a specialized device can give new purpose to a standard system. If you want to play action-packed games on your home PC, for example, you will have more fun if you use a joystick or game controller than a standard keyboard or mouse.

This section examines several categories of alternative input devices and discusses the special uses of each. You may be surprised at how often you see these devices, and you may decide that an alternative device will be your primary means of interacting with your computer.

OBJECTIVES

- List two reasons why some people prefer alternative methods of input over a standard keyboard or mouse.
- List three categories of alternative input devices.
- List two types of optical input devices and describe their uses.
- Describe the uses for speech-recognition systems.
- Identify two types of video input devices and their uses.

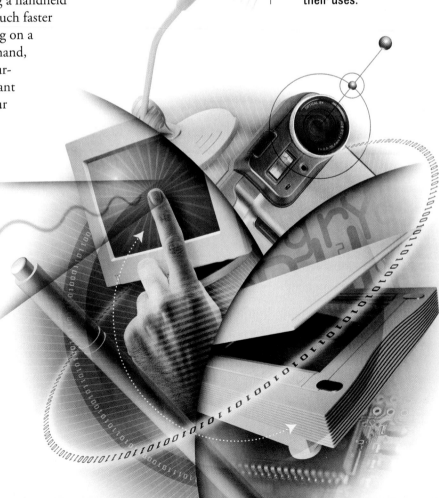

Figure 2B.1
To interact with a pen-based computer, you can use the pen to point, tap, drag, draw, and even write on the device's screen.

Figure 2B.2
Many handheld computers allow the user to input data (such as notes, appointments, or phone numbers) by writing directly on the screen with the unit's pen.

Figure 2B.3
When you receive a package via UPS, you may sign your name on a pen-based computer that stores a digital image of your signature.

DEVICES FOR THE HAND

Most input devices are designed to be used by hand. Even specialized devices like touch screens enable the user to interact with the system by using his or her fingertips. Unlike keyboards and mice, many of these input devices are highly intuitive and easy to use, even without special skills or training.

Pens

Pen-based systems—including many personal digital assistants and other types of handheld computers—use a **pen** for data input (see Figure 2B.1). This device is sometimes called a **stylus.** You hold the pen in your hand and write on a special pad or directly on the screen. You can also use the pen as a pointing device, like a mouse, to select commands by tapping the screen.

You might think that pen-based systems would be a handy way to enter text into a computer for word processing. In reality, developers have had a great deal of trouble perfecting the technology so that it deciphers people's handwriting with 100 percent reliability. Because handwriting recognition is so complex, pen-based computers generally are not used to enter large amounts of text, although they are used frequently for taking notes and creating short messages (see Figure 2B.2).

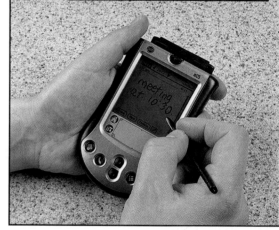

Pen-based computers are used more commonly for data collection, where the touch of a pen might select a reply box or mark a box to indicate a part that must be ordered or a service that has been requested. Another common use is for inputting signatures or messages that are stored and transmitted as a graphic image, such as a fax. When delivery-service drivers make deliveries, they often have recipients sign their names on such a computer-based pad (see Figure 2B.3). As handwriting-recognition technology becomes more reliable, pen-based systems undoubtedly will become more common.

Touch Screens

Touch screens accept input by allowing the user to place a fingertip directly on the computer screen, usually to make a selection from a menu of choices. Most touch-screen computers use sensors on the screen's surface to detect the touch of a finger. There are several different touch screen technologies in use. Most systems work by placing one or more clear, electrically charged layers over the monitor's surface and running electrical current through them. When you touch the screen, sensors determine the touch's location by detecting a change in the electrical current. Many touch screens use infrared detectors to sense the user's touch; others use strain gauges that "feel" the user's touch by detecting pressure.

Figure 2B.4
This student is using a touch-screen system to get information at a public-information kiosk.

A new type of touch screen technology uses acoustical waves to determine touch points on the screen. This system works by transmitting acoustic (sound) waves across the screen's surface. When you touch the screen, sensors detect the location where the waves have been disturbed.

Touch screens work well in environments where dirt or weather would render keyboards and pointing devices useless, and where a simple, intuitive interface is important. They are well suited for simple applications, such as automated teller machines or public information kiosks (see Figure 2B.4). Touch screens have become common in fast-food restaurants, department stores, drugstores, and supermarkets, where they are used for all kinds of purposes, from creating personalized greeting cards to selling lottery tickets.

Game Controllers

You may not think of a **game controller** as an input device, but it is. Personal computers are widely used as gaming platforms, challenging long-time video game units like the Sony PlayStation and others (see Figure 2B.5). Because PCs offer higher graphics resolution than standard televisions, many gamers believe a well equipped PC provides a better game-playing experience. If your computer is connected to the Internet, you can play games with people around the world.

Figure 2B.5
With their fast processors and high-quality graphics, PCs are great for playing games.

A game controller can be considered an input device because a computer game is a program, much like a word processor. A game controller accepts input from the user. As computer games become more detailed and elaborate, more specialized game controllers are being developed to take advantage of their features.

Visit **www.norton.glencoe.com** for more information on **touch screens**.

Figure 2B.6
Several kinds of game control devices are available, some of which are quite sophisticated. Some controllers even provide tactile feedback, such as vibrations or pulses, to help players "feel" the action in the game.

Figure 2B.7
To enter prices and product information into a cash register, a cashier passes groceries over a flatbed bar code reader. The reader projects a web of laser beams onto the package's bar code and measures the pattern of the reflected light.

NORTON
ONLINE

Visit www.norton.glencoe.com for more information on **game controllers.**

Figure 2B.8
Courier services, like Federal Express, use handheld bar code readers to track packages all the way to their destination.

Game controllers generally fall into two broad categories: game pads and joysticks (see Figure 2B.6). **Joysticks** have been around for a long time, and they can be used with applications other than games. (Some joystick users actually prefer using a joystick rather than a mouse with some business applications.) Joysticks enable the user to "fly" or "drive" through a game, directing a vehicle or character. They are popular in racing and flying games. A variant of the joystick is the racing game controller, which includes an actual steering wheel; some racing game controllers even include foot pedals and gearshifts.

If you have ever used a video gaming system, you are familiar with game pads. A **game pad** is a small, flat device that usually provides two sets of controls—one for each hand. These devices, which are extremely flexible, are used to control many game systems. If you do not have a joystick, you can use a game pad to control most racing and flying games. (Many computer games still provide support for a mouse or a keyboard, so a dedicated game controller usually is not required.)

OPTICAL INPUT DEVICES

For a long time, futurists and computer scientists have had the goal of enabling computers to "see." Computers may never see in the same way that humans do, but new technologies allow computers to use light as a source of input. These tools fall into the category of optical input devices.

Bar Code Readers

Bar code readers are one of the most widely used input devices. The most common type of bar code reader is the flatbed model, which is commonly found in supermarkets and department stores (see Figure 2B.7). Workers for delivery services, such as Federal Express, also use handheld bar code readers in the field to identify packages (see Figure 2B.8).

These devices read **bar codes,** which are patterns of printed bars that appear on product packaging. The bar codes identify the product and provide other information about it, such as its price.

The bar code reader emits a beam of light—frequently a laser beam—that is reflected by the bar code image. A light-sensitive detector identifies the bar code image by recognizing special bars at both ends of the image. These special bars are different, so the reader can tell whether the bar code has been read right-side up or upside down.

After the detector has identified the bar code, it converts the individual bar patterns into numeric digits. The reader converts the printed bars into a code the computer can understand (see Figure 2B.9). The reader then feeds the data into the computer, as though the number had been typed on a keyboard.

Image Scanners and Optical Character Recognition (OCR)

The bar code reader is a special type of image scanner. **Image scanners** (also called scanners) convert any printed image into electronic form by shining light onto the image and sensing the intensity of the light's reflection at every point. Figure 2B.10 illustrates the scanning process.

Color scanners use filters to separate the components of color into the primary additive colors (red, green, and blue) at each point. Red, green, and blue are known as primary additive colors because they can be combined to create any other color. Processes that describe color in this manner are said to use RGB color.

Figure 2B.9
Manufacturers use bar codes to identify millions of unique products.

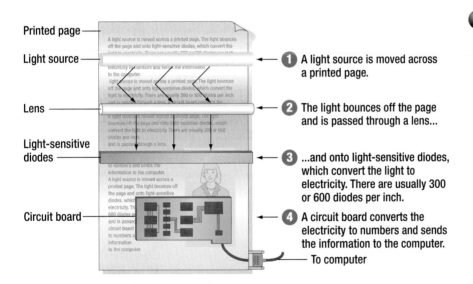

Printed page
Light source
Lens
Light-sensitive diodes
Circuit board

Figure 2B.10
How an image is scanned

1. A light source is moved across a printed page.

2. The light bounces off the page and is passed through a lens...

3. ...and onto light-sensitive diodes, which convert the light to electricity. There are usually 300 or 600 diodes per inch.

4. A circuit board converts the electricity to numbers and sends the information to the computer.

To computer

The image scanner is useful, because it translates printed images into an electronic format that can be stored in a computer's memory. Then you can use software to organize or manipulate the electronic image. For example, if you scan a photo, you can use a graphics program, such as Adobe Photoshop, to increase the contrast or adjust the colors. If you have scanned a text document, you might want to use **optical character recognition (OCR)** software to translate the image into text that you can edit. When a scanner first creates an image from a page, the image is stored in the computer's memory as a bitmap. A bitmap is a grid of dots, each dot

NORTON ONLINE

Visit **www.norton.glencoe.com** for more information on **scanning** and **OCR**.

Figure 2B.11

These are a few of the ways that a lowercase *g* can appear in print.

g **g** g g **g g g** g ǵ

g g g **g** **g** g g **g** g

g g g ℊ **g** g g ℊ g

g g *g* **g** g g **g** g **g**

g **g** g **g** ɡ g **g** **g** ℨ

g ℊ g g **g** g **g** ℊ **g**

represented by one or more bits. The job of OCR software is to translate that array of dots into text that the computer can interpret as letters and numbers.

To translate bitmaps into text, the OCR software looks at each character and tries to match the character with its own assumptions about how the letters should look. Because it is difficult to make a computer recognize an unlimited number of typefaces and fonts, OCR software is extremely complex and not always 100 percent reliable. Figure 2B.11 shows a few of the many ways the letter *g* can appear on a printed page.

Despite the complexity of the task, OCR software has become quite advanced. Today, many programs can decipher a page of text received by a fax machine. In fact, computers with fax modems can use OCR software to convert faxes directly into text that can be edited with a word processor.

Scanners come in a range of sizes from handheld models to flatbed scanners that sit on a desktop (see Figure 2B.12). Handheld scanners are more portable, but they typically require multiple passes to scan a single page, because they are not as wide as letter-size paper. Flatbed scanners offer higher-quality reproduction than do handheld scanners and can scan a page in a single pass. (Multiple scans are sometimes required for color images, however.) To use a flatbed scanner, you place the printed image on a piece of glass, similar to the way you place a page on a photocopier. In some medium-sized scanners, you feed the sheet to be scanned through the scanner, similar to the way you feed a page through a fax machine.

Figure 2B.12

Large-format flatbed scanners produce high-resolution, digitized versions of documents. Graphic artists prefer this type of scanner, because it yields the highest-quality scans of photographs and other images.

Complete each statement by filling in the blank(s).

1. ___Pen based___ are often used for taking notes or creating short messages.

2. Game controllers generally fall into the categories of ___Joystick___ and ___gamepad___ .

3. ___OCR___ software can translate a scanned image of a text document into text that can be edited.

AUDIOVISUAL INPUT DEVICES

Today, many new PCs are equipped with complete multimedia capabilities. New computers have features that enable them to record audio and video input and play it back.

Microphones and Speech Recognition

Now that sound capabilities are standard in computers, microphones are becoming increasingly important as input devices to record speech. Spoken input is used often in multimedia, especially when the presentation can benefit from narration. Most PCs now have phone-dialing capabilities. If you have a microphone and speakers (or a headset microphone with an earphone), you can use your PC to make telephone calls.

Microphones also make the PC useful for audio and videoconferencing over the Internet. For this type of sound input, you need a microphone and a sound card that translates the analog signal (that is, sound waves) from the microphone into digital codes the computer can store and process. This process is called **digitizing.** Sound cards also can translate digital sounds back into analog signals that can then be sent to the speakers.

Using simple audio recording software that is built into your computer's operating system, you can use a microphone to record your voice and create files on disk (see Figure 2B.13). You can embed these files in documents, use them in Web pages, or e-mail them to other people.

There is also a demand for translating spoken words into text, much as there is a demand for translating handwriting into text. Translating voice to text is a capability known as **speech recognition** (or **voice recognition**). With it, you can dictate to the computer instead of typing, and you can control the computer with simple commands, such as "Open" or "Cancel."

NORTON ONLINE

Visit **www.norton.glencoe.com** for more information on **microphones and speech-recognition technologies.**

Figure 2B.13
Your PC may enable you to record spoken messages with a microphone and a sound card.

Norton Notebook

A BRIEF HISTORY OF THE MOUSE

As recently as 15 years ago, most people saw no future for the mouse. Many computer experts regarded it as a toy or a gimmick with no real value. Only a few people regarded the mouse as being ahead of its time. Today, we can hardly imagine using a computer without one. The device literally changed the face of computing—indeed, the entire computing industry—by changing the way people interacted with their computers.

The Stuff of Legends?

As simple and unassuming as it looks, the mouse is actually surrounded by myth. Many experienced computer users believe that Apple Computer, Inc. created the mouse. Even though Apple was the first company to distribute the mouse as a standard component with personal computers, Apple did not conceive the tailed input device.

Doug Engelbart, inventor of the mouse

The mouse's history actually goes back to the early 1960s when a group of scientists and engineers at the Stanford Research Institute (SRI) in California were charged with the task to develop ways to "augment human intellect." Specifically, Doug Engelbart's group was looking for ways to use computer systems to help people solve complex problems.

In his vision of this problem-solving system, Engelbart saw the need for a device that would enable the computer user to input data more efficiently than could be done using other standard input devices of the time, such as keyboards, light pens, and joysticks. With funding from NASA, Engelbart's team developed a series of simple tests to determine which input device would enable users to move a cursor around the screen in the least amount of time and with the least effort. Engelbart and a fellow scientist, Bill English, created a simple wooden gadget that became a prototype for the mouse we know today.

The first mouse was a small wooden box. Rather than the hard rubber ball used in modern mice, Engelbart's mouse actually used two small wheels that were placed perpendicular to one another on the mouse's underside. With this device, the user could move the mouse only up and down or side to side (moving diagonally was a problem), but the prototype worked well.

On to Fame, With a Side-Trip to Obscurity

The mouse was not noticed immediately by industry titans. In fact, few people—including leaders at SRI—saw the mouse's value. Many people did not see much of a future for computers in general, except for military and large business uses.

This lack of vision, however, did not stop (or even slow) the visionary Engelbart. Throughout his career, he has described or developed technology that was considered to be ahead of its time. His discoveries and inventions in the fields of networking, hypertext, user interface technologies, and other computing disciplines continue to affect everyday computer users. Although inventing the mouse did not make him rich, it helped launch one of the most brilliant and innovative careers in the history of computing science.

Speech-recognition software takes the smallest individual sounds in a language, called phonemes, and translates them into text or commands. Although the English language uses only about forty phonemes, reliable translation is difficult. For example, some English words sound the same but have different meanings (*two* versus *too,* for example). The challenge for speech-recognition software is to deduce a sound's meaning correctly from its context and to distinguish meaningful sounds from background noise.

Speech-recognition software has been used in commercial applications for years, but traditionally, it has been extremely costly. It is also difficult to develop and use. Low-cost commercial versions of speech-recognition software are now available, and they promise to be a real benefit to users who cannot type or have difficulty using a keyboard.

Newer generation speech-recognition programs are much more reliable than the packages that were available a few years ago. Some packages can recognize accurately 80 to 90 percent of spoken words by using large stored vocabularies, or words they can recognize. The user may need to "train" the software to recognize speech patterns or the pronunciation of some words, but this procedure is relatively simple. Another enhancement to speech-recognition programs is their ability to recognize continuous speech. Older systems required the user to pause between words, which improved accuracy but greatly slowed the data-entry process.

Speech-recognition programs usually require the use of a noise-canceling microphone (a microphone that filters out background noise). Most commercial packages come with a microphone (see Figure 2B.14).

Video Input

With the growth of multimedia and the Internet, computer users are adding video input capabilities to their systems in great numbers. Applications such as video-conferencing enable people to use full-motion video images, which are captured by a **PC video camera,** and transmit them to a limited number of recipients on a network or to the world on the Internet. Videos are commonly used in presentations and on Web pages where the viewer can start, stop, and control various aspects of the playback.

The video cameras used with computers digitize images by breaking them into individual pixels. (A pixel is one or more dots that express a portion of an image.) Each pixel's color and other characteristics are stored as digital code. This code is then compressed (video images can be very large) so that it can be stored on disk or transmitted over a network.

Many PC video cameras attach to the top of the PC screen, enabling the user to "capture" images of himself or herself while working at the computer. This arrangement is handy for videoconferencing, in which multiple users see and talk to one another in real time over a network or Internet connection (see Figure 2B.15).

Using a **video capture card,** the user also can connect other video devices, such as VCRs and camcorders, to the PC. This enables the user to transfer images from the video equipment to the PC, and vice versa. Affordable video capture cards enable home users to edit their videotapes like professionals. Newer versions of the Windows operating system (specifically Windows 98, 2000, and later) offer support for cable-television hookups so that you can connect your PC to your building's television cable system.

Figure 2B.15

PC video cameras enable you to conduct video phone calls. Many PCs feature built-in software that transforms a conventional telephone call into a two-way video phone call.

Digital Cameras

Digital cameras work much like PC video cameras, except that digital cameras are portable, handheld devices that capture still images (see Figure 2B.16). Whereas normal film cameras capture images on a specially coated film, digital cameras capture images electronically. The digital camera digitizes the image, compresses it, and stores it on a special disk or memory card. The user can then copy the information to a PC, where the image can be edited, copied, printed, embedded in a document, or transmitted to another user.

Figure 2B.16

Although most digital cameras look like traditional film cameras, they work very differently.

Most digital cameras can store dozens of high-resolution images at a time, and most cameras accept additional memory that increases their capacity even further. Moving digital images from a digital camera to a computer is a simple process that uses standard cables, disks, or even infrared networking capabilities. A wide range of digital cameras is available, from inexpensive home-use models (with prices starting at just over $100) to professional versions costing several thousand dollars.

Digital cameras have become standard equipment for designers of all kinds. In the field of Web page design, for example, digital cameras enable designers to shoot a subject and quickly load the images onto their computers. This process saves the step of acquiring existing photographs or developing and printing film-based photos—which then must be scanned into the computer. Designers can update a Web site's images quickly and regularly using digital cameras.

Graphic designers can edit and enhance digital photographs in innumerable ways, using photo-manipulation software (see Figure 2B.17). For example, a landscape designer can use a digital camera to take a picture of a house, and then use landscape design software to modify the image to show how the house might appear with different landscaping.

Visit **www.norton.glencoe.com** for more information on **digital cameras**.

Figure 2B.17
Using photo-manipulation software, a photographer can edit a digital photograph in many different ways.

COMPUTERS
in your career

Computer Scientists

In many ways, the job title "computer scientist" represents the pinnacle of the computing industry. In other words, if you are a computer scientist, you cannot go much higher up the ladder—at least in terms of technical expertise, if not in terms of pay. If you are serious about your computer-related studies and are curious about many different aspects of computers, then you may want to consider becoming a computer scientist.

Of course, the process will not be easy. Computer scientists must master a broad range of subjects, including mathematics, programming languages, networking, and more. For this reason, computer scientists often pursue advanced degrees and spend years gaining work experience in many different positions.

Computer scientists require a wide range of knowledge, because they are the ultimate problem-solvers in the computing world. They spend much of their time studying and analyzing problems, then working out solutions to those problems. Solutions may involve creating a new type of computer system, a new piece of hardware, or a new type of software program. Computer scientists often work on creating new programming languages or modifying existing ones for a special purpose.

Computer scientists work in government, private industry, and academia. Depending on his or her work environment, the scientist may need to know a lot of nontechnical information, too. For example, scientists working for an automobile manufacturer need to have a good understanding of that specific business and its needs. This knowledge helps the scientist to understand the business' problems and to more intelligently create solutions to those problems. The same is true whether the scientist works for NASA, the Department of Defense, or a big university.

Depending on the specific discipline they choose, computer scientists may enter the workforce with starting salaries in the $45,000–$50,000 range. Of course, salaries vary widely with experience, location, and industry. Scientists working for large corporations, for example, can count on earning more than those working in the field of education.

In many fields, computer scientists are expected to continue their education almost constantly. This can include field work, research, classroom time, and other kinds of work. Many computer scientists publish exhaustive papers and journal articles on technologies and new innovations; in fact, some schools and employers insist that their computer scientists regularly publish papers or articles.

According to the Bureau of Labor Statistics, there are more than 1.5 million computer scientists now working in the United States. The demand for qualified computer scientists will continue to grow in the future as people become more and more dependent on computer systems for their livelihood.

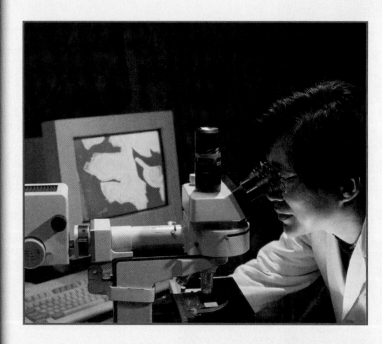

SUMMARY

- With a pen-based system, you use a pen (also called a stylus) to write on a special pad or directly on the screen.

- Pen-based computers are handy for writing notes or selecting options from menus, but they are not well suited for inputting long text documents, because handwriting-recognition technology has not yet achieved 100 percent reliability.

- Touch-screen systems accept input directly through the monitor. Touch-screen systems are useful for selecting options from menus, but they are not useful for inputting text or other types of data in large quantities.

- A game controller is a special input device that accepts the user's input for playing a game. The two primary types of game controllers are joysticks and game pads.

- Bar code readers, such as those used in grocery stores, can read bar codes, translate them into numbers, and input the numbers into a computer system.

- Image scanners convert printed images into digitized formats that can be stored and manipulated on computers.

- An image scanner equipped with OCR software can translate a page of text into a string of character codes in the computer's memory.

- Microphones can accept auditory input. Using speech-recognition software, you can use your microphone as an input device for dictating text, navigating programs, and choosing commands.

- To use a microphone or other audio devices for input, you must install a sound card on your computer.

- A sound card takes analog sound signals and digitizes them. A sound card also can convert digital sound signals to analog form.

- PC video cameras and digital cameras can digitize full-motion and still images, which can be stored and edited on a PC or transmitted over a LAN or the Internet.

KEY TERMS

bar code, *64*

bar code reader, *64*

digital camera, *70*

digitizing, *67*

game controller, *63*

game pad, *64*

image scanner, *65*

joystick, *64*

optical character

    recognition (OCR), *65*

PC video camera, *69*

pen, *62*

speech recognition, *67*

stylus, *62*

video capture card, *70*

voice recognition, *67*

KEY TERM QUIZ

Complete each statement by writing one of the terms listed under Key Terms in each blank.

1. _Digitizing_ is the process that PC video cameras use to break images into individual pixels.

2. Using _voice recognition_ software, you can issue simple commands to dictate text to the computer, instead of typing the text.

3. A(n) _barcode_ is a series of lines that can be used to store information about a product.

4. _Joystick_ and _game pad_ are two popular types of game controllers.

5. Many handheld computing devices let you input data by touching the screen with a(n) _pen or stylus_.

SECTION QUIZ

True/False

Answer the following questions by circling True or False.

True   ~~False~~   1. Because handwriting-recognition technology is 100 percent reliable, pen-based input devices are ideal for inputting large amounts of text.

True   ~~False~~   2. A game controller is not really an input device.

~~True~~   False   3. Bar code readers use laser beams to convert patterns of printed bars into codes the computer can understand.

~~True~~   False   4. If you scan a text document into your computer, you can use optical character recognition software to convert the scanned image into text that can be edited.

True   ~~False~~   5. All speech-recognition programs require you to pause between words as you talk.

Multiple Choice

Circle the word or phrase that best completes each statement.

1. For a bar code reader to read a bar code correctly, the code must be positioned _____ .
   A. right-side up   **B.** upside down   **C.** neither A nor B

2. When a sound card translates signals from a microphone into codes the computer can use, it uses a process called _____ .
   A. scanning   **B.** digitizing   **C.** inputting

3. Translating voice to text is a capability known as _____ .
   A. speech recognition   **B.** voice recognition   **C.** both A and B

4. PC video cameras digitize images by breaking them into individual _____ .
   A. pixels   **B.** bar codes   **C.** waves

5. Using a _____ , you can connect devices such as a VCR or camcorder to your PC.
   A. WebTV   **B.** sound card   **C.** video capture card

REVIEW QUESTIONS

In your own words, briefly answer the following questions.

1. Why is a game controller considered a true input device?

2. What is a bar code?

3. How does a bar code reader recognize a bar code?

4. What does OCR software do?

5. A sound card performs two basic functions. What are they?

SECTION LABS

Complete the following exercises as directed by your instructor.

1. If your computer has a microphone and sound card, complete the following steps to record a message and play it back:
   A. Click the Start button to open the Start menu; then click Programs (or All Programs), Accessories, Entertainment, and Sound Recorder.
   B. When the Sound Recorder program opens, click the record button and speak into your computer's microphone; then click the Stop button.
   C. Click Play to hear your message.
   D. Close the program by clicking the Close button (with an **X** on it) in the upper-right corner of the window. If Windows prompts you to save the file, click No.

UNIT PROJECTS

UNIT LABS

Complete the following exercises using a computer in your classroom, lab, or home.

1. **Check Your Keyboard's Repeat Rate.** In this exercise, check your keyboard's repeat settings, but do not change any settings without your instructor's permission.

A. Click the Start button on the Windows taskbar.

B. Open the Control Panel window. Double-click the Keyboard icon in the Control Panel dialog box.

C. Click the tabs at the top of the Keyboard Properties dialog box, and inspect the current settings.

D. Click the Speed tab. Drag the Repeat delay and Repeat rate indicators all the way to the right, then to the left, and then in different combinations. Test the repeat rate at each setting by clicking in the test box and then holding down an alphanumeric key.

E. Drag the Cursor blink rate indicator to the right and left. How fast do you want your cursor to blink?

F. Click Cancel to close the dialog box without making changes. Close the Control Panel window.

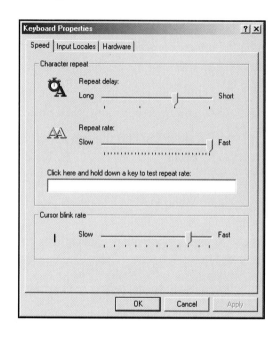

2. **Mouse Practice.** Take the following steps:

A. Click the Start button on the Windows taskbar to open the Start menu.

B. Click Programs (or All Programs), then Accessories, then WordPad. The WordPad program will open in its own window. Notice the blinking insertion point in the window.

C. Type: **Now is the time for all good men to come to the aid of their country.**

D. Using your mouse, click in different parts of the sentence. The insertion point moves wherever you click.

E. Double-click the word *good* to select it.

F. Right-click the selected word. A shortcut menu appears.

G. Choose the Cut option. The highlighted word disappears from your screen.

H. Click in front of the word *country* to place the insertion point; right-click again. When the shortcut menu appears, choose Paste. The word *good* reappears.

I. Double-click the word *good* again to select it. Now click on the selected word and drag it to the left while holding down the mouse button. (A little mark appears on the mouse pointer, indicating that you are dragging something.) When the mouse pointer arrives in front of the word *men,* release the mouse button. The word *good* is returned to its original place.

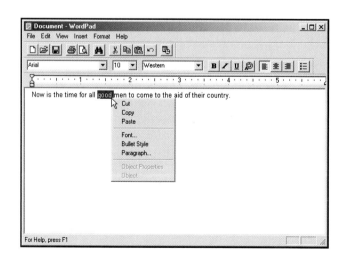

J. Continue practicing your mouse techniques. When you are finished, close the WordPad program by clicking the Close button (the button marked with an **X**) in the upper-right corner of the window. The program will ask if you want to save the changes to your document; choose No.

DISCUSSION QUESTIONS

As directed by your instructor, discuss the following questions in class or in groups.

1. Despite the rapid advancements being made with handwriting-recognition software, do you think that the keyboard will continue to be the preferred input device for generating text? Which alternative—speech recognition or handwriting recognition—do you think has a better chance of ultimately replacing the keyboard as the primary means of input?

2. Suppose that you are responsible for computerizing a gourmet restaurant's order-entry system. What type of input devices do you think would work best for waiters to input orders to the kitchen?

RESEARCH AND REPORT

Using your own choice of resources (such as the Internet, books, magazines, and newspaper articles), research and write a short paper discussing one of the following topics:

- The availability and use of screen reading technologies for computer users who are sight impaired
- The kind of information stored in a product's bar code
- The DVORAK keyboard (an alternative to the standard QWERTY keyboard)

When you are finished, proofread and print your paper, and give it to your instructor.

 **ETHICAL ISSUES** A computer's input devices make it useful to people. With this thought in mind, discuss the following questions in class.

1. Currently, commercially available PCs are configured for use by persons without physical impairments or disabilities that would prevent them from using a computer. If a person with a physical impairment wants to use a computer, he or she may need to purchase special equipment or software. Do you think this is fair? Should every PC be accessible to everyone, whether they have physical impairments or not? If you believe this should be the case, how would you make computers accessible to everyone?

2. You have applied for a job as a reporter for a newspaper. Your journalistic skills are excellent. You are not a touch typist, however, and your typing speed is very slow. For this reason, the managing editor is reluctant to hire you at the position's advertised salary. How would you react to this situation? Is the editor right? Should keyboarding skills be a requirement for such a job? Would you be willing to learn to type or accept the job at a lower salary? Be prepared to defend your position.

UNIT 3

Output Devices

UNIT CONTENTS

This unit contains the following sections:

Section 3A: Monitors and Sound Systems

Section 3B: Devices That Output Hard Copy

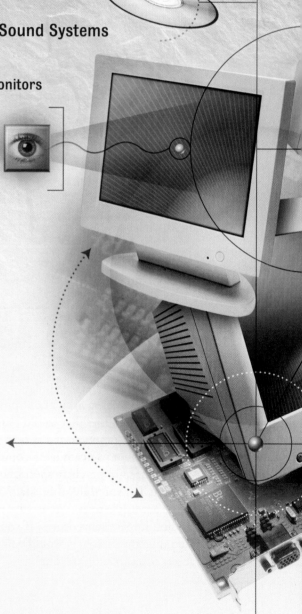

The Interactive Browser Edition CD-ROM provides additional labs and activities to apply concepts from this unit.

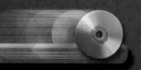

Monitors and Sound Systems

OVERVIEW:
Reaching Our Senses
With Sight and Sound

In the beginning, computing was anything but a feast for the senses. The earliest computers were little more than gigantic calculators controlled by large panels of switches, dials, and buttons. Today, nearly every computer features some kind of visual display, but display screens were uncommon until the 1960s.

Now, computers can communicate information to you in several ways, but the most exciting types of output are those that appeal to the senses. It is one thing to read text on a printed page, but it is very different to see a document take shape before your eyes. It can be very exciting to watch moving, three-dimensional images on a large, colorful screen while listening to sounds in stereo.

Modern display and sound systems make the computing experience a more inviting one. Because of these sophisticated output technologies, computers are easier to use, data is easier to manage, and information is easier to access. These technologies enable us to play games and watch movies, experience multimedia events, and use the PC as a communications tool.

This section introduces you to monitors and sound systems. You will learn about the different types of monitors commonly used with computers and how they work. You also will learn some important criteria for judging a monitor's performance. This lesson also shows you how computers can output sounds.

OBJECTIVES

- List the two most commonly used types of computer monitors.
- Explain how a CRT monitor displays images.
- Identify two types of flat-panel monitors and explain their differences.
- List four characteristics you should consider when comparing monitors.
- Explain how a computer outputs sound.

MONITORS

On most personal computer systems, the keyboard is the most commonly used input device, and the monitor is the most commonly used output device. As you use your computer—whether you are typing a letter, copying files, or surfing the Internet—hardly a moment goes by when you are not looking at your monitor. In fact, people often form an opinion about a computer just by looking at the monitor. They want to see whether the image is crisp and clear and how well graphics are displayed on the monitor.

Two important hardware devices determine the quality of the image you see on any monitor: the monitor itself and the video controller. In the following sections, you will learn about both of these devices in detail and find out how they work together to display text and graphics.

Two basic types of monitors are used with PCs (see Figure 3A.1). The first is the typical monitor that you see on a desktop computer; it looks a lot like a television screen and works the same way. This type of monitor uses a large vacuum tube, called a **cathode ray tube (CRT).** The second type, known as a **flat-panel display,** is used primarily with portable computers, but it is becoming an increasingly popular feature with desktop computers.

Figure 3A.1
The most common types of monitors used with personal computers

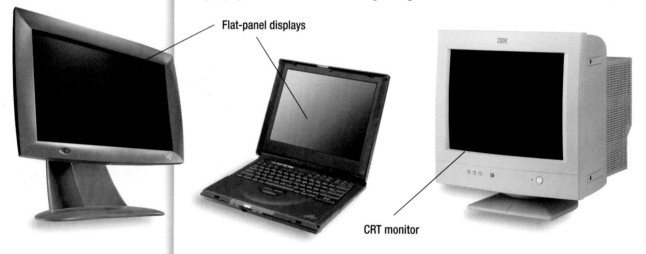

Flat-panel displays

CRT monitor

All monitors can be categorized by the way they display colors:

◆ **Monochrome monitors** display only one color (such as green, amber, or white) against a contrasting background, which is usually black. These monitors are used for text-only displays where the user does not need to see color graphics (see Figure 3A.2).

◆ **Grayscale monitors** display varying intensities of gray (from a very light gray to black) against a white or off-white background; they are essentially a type of monochrome monitor. Grayscale flat-panel displays are used in low-end portable systems—especially handheld computers—to keep costs down (see Figure 3A.3).

◆ **Color monitors** can display anywhere from 16 colors to 16 million colors (see Figure 3A.4). Today, most new monitors display in color. Many color monitors can be set to work in monochrome or grayscale mode.

Figure 3A.2
Monochrome monitors usually are used for text-only displays.

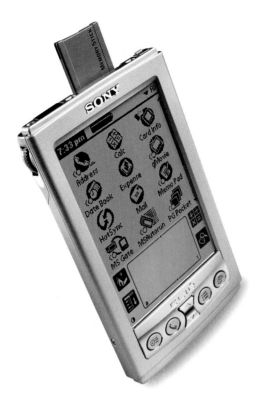

CRT Monitors

Figure 3A.5 shows how a typical CRT monitor works. Near the back of a monochrome or grayscale monitor housing is an electron gun. The gun shoots a beam of electrons through a magnetic coil, which aims the beam at the front of the monitor. The back of the monitor's screen is coated with phosphors, chemicals that glow when they are struck by the electron beam. The screen's phosphor coating is organized into a grid of dots. The smallest number of phosphor dots that the gun can focus on is called a **pixel,** a contraction of the term *pic*ture *el*ement. Each pixel has a unique address, which the computer uses to locate the pixel and control its appearance. Modern monochrome and grayscale monitors can focus on pixels as small as a single phosphor dot.

1. Electron guns shoot streams of electrons toward the screen.

2. Magnetic yoke guides the streams of electrons across and down the screen.

3. Phosphor dots on the back of the screen glow when the electron beams hit them.

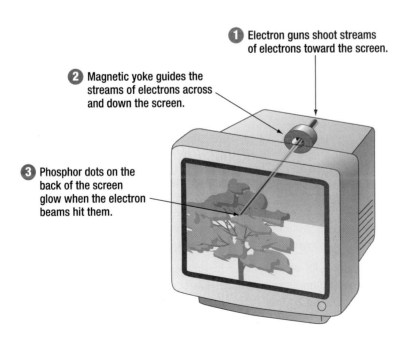

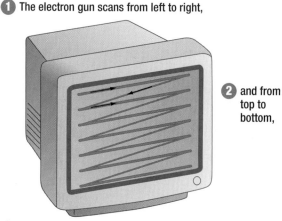

1 The electron gun scans from left to right,

2 and from top to bottom,

3 refreshing every phosphor dot in a zig-zag pattern.

Actually, the electron gun does not focus on just one spot and shoot electrons at it. It systematically aims at every pixel on the screen, starting at the top left corner and scanning to the right edge. Then it drops down a tiny distance and scans another line, as shown in Figure 3A.6.

Like human eyes reading the letters on a page, the electron beam follows each line of pixels across the screen until it reaches the bottom of the screen. Then it starts over. As the electron gun scans, the circuitry driving the monitor adjusts the intensity of each beam to determine whether a pixel is on or off or, in the case of grayscale, how brightly each pixel glows.

A color monitor works like a monochrome one, except that there are three electron beams instead of one. The three guns represent the primary additive colors (red, green, and blue), although the beams they emit are colorless. In a color monitor, each pixel includes three phosphors—red, green, and blue—arranged in a triangle. When the beams of each of these guns are combined and focused on a pixel, the phosphors light up. The monitor can display different colors by combining various intensities of the three beams.

A CRT monitor contains a **shadow mask,** which is a fine mesh made of metal, fitted to the shape and size of the screen. The holes in the shadow mask's mesh are used to align the electron beams, to ensure that they strike precisely the correct phosphor dot. In most shadow masks, these holes are arranged in triangles.

Flat-Panel Monitors

CRT monitors have long been the standard for use with desktop computers, because they provide the brightest and clearest picture for relatively low cost. There are two major disadvantages, however, associated with CRT monitors:

◆ Because CRT monitors are big, they take up desktop space and can be difficult to move. By contrast, flat-panel monitors are gaining popularity because of their comparatively light weight.

◆ CRT monitors require a lot of power to run; therefore, they are not practical for use with notebook computers. Instead, notebook computers use flat-panel monitors that are less than 1 inch thick and which can run on battery power, which is built into the computer.

NORTON
ONLINE

Visit **www.norton.glencoe.com** for more information on **flat-panel monitors.**

There are several types of flat-panel monitors, but the most common is the **liquid crystal display (LCD)** monitor (see Figure 3A.7). The LCD monitor creates images with a special kind of liquid crystal that is normally transparent but which, when charged with electricity, becomes opaque. Handheld calculators and digital watches usually use liquid crystal displays.

One disadvantage of LCD monitors is that their images can be difficult to see in bright light. For this reason, laptop computer users often look for shady places to sit when working outdoors or near windows. A bigger disadvantage of LCD monitors, however, is their limited **viewing angle**—that is, the angle from which the display's image can be viewed clearly (see Figure 3A.8). With most CRT monitors, you can see the image clearly even when standing at an angle to the screen. In LCD monitors, however, the viewing angle shrinks; as you increase your angle to the screen, the image becomes fuzzy quickly. In many older flat-panel systems, the user must face the screen nearly straight on to see the image clearly. Technological improvements have extended the viewing angles of flat-panel monitors while causing their prices to increase.

Figure 3A.7

Today, most portable computers and handheld computing devices feature a color LCD monitor. Even very small devices can deliver crisp, sharply detailed images by using the latest advances in LCD technology.

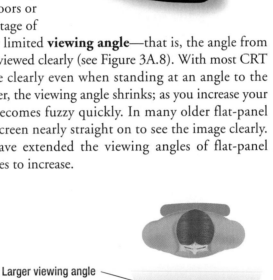

Larger viewing angle

Smaller viewing angle

Figure 3A.8

Flat-panel displays typically have a smaller viewing angle than CRT monitors.

There are two main categories of liquid crystal displays:

◆ **Passive matrix LCD** relies on transistors for each row and each column of pixels, thus creating a grid that defines the location of each pixel. The color displayed by a pixel is determined by the electricity coming from the transistors at the end of the row and the top of the column. Although passive matrix monitors are inexpensive to manufacture, they have a narrow viewing angle. Another disadvantage is that they don't "refresh" the pixels very often. (Refresh rate is described in more detail later in this unit.) If you move the pointer too quickly, it seems to disappear, an effect known as **submarining**. Animated graphics can appear blurry on a passive matrix monitor.

Most passive matrix screens now use **dual-scan LCD** technology, which scans the pixels twice as often. Submarining and blurry graphics are less troublesome than they were before the dual-scan technique was developed.

◆ **Active matrix LCD** technology assigns a transistor to each pixel, and each pixel is turned on and off individually. This enhancement allows the pixels to be refreshed much more rapidly, so submarining is not a problem. Active matrix screens have a wider viewing angle than dual-scan screens. Many active matrix displays use **thin-film transistor (TFT)** technology, which employs as many as four transistors per pixel.

Although flat-panel monitors have been used primarily on portable computers, a new generation of large, high-resolution, flat-panel displays is gaining popularity among users of desktop systems (see Figure 3A.9). These new monitors provide an equal or larger diagonal display area, but they take up less desk space and run cooler than traditional CRT monitors. Flat-panel displays for desktops, however, are expensive.

Figure 3A.9
Flat-panel monitors are becoming an increasingly popular option for desktop computers.

Other Types of Monitors

While CRT and flat-panel monitors are the most frequently used types of displays in PC systems, there are other kinds of monitors. These displays use specialized technologies and have specific uses:

◆ **Paper-White Displays.** This type of monitor is sometimes used by document designers, such as desktop publishing specialists, newspaper or magazine compositors, and other persons who create high-quality printed documents. A paper-white display produces a very high contrast between the monitor's white background and displayed text or graphics, which usually appear in black. An LCD version of the paper-white display is called the page-white display. Page-white displays utilize a special technology, called supertwist, to create higher contrasts.

◆ **Electroluminescent (ELD) Displays.** ELD displays are similar to LCD monitors but use a phosphorescent film held between two sheets of glass. A grid of wires sends current through the film to create an image.

◆ **Plasma/Gas Plasma Displays.** These thin displays are created by sandwiching a special gas (such as neon or xenon) between two sheets of glass. When the gas is electrified via a grid of small electrodes, it glows. By controlling the amount of voltage applied at various points on the grid, each point acts as a pixel to display an image.

NORTON
ONLINE

Visit **www.norton.glencoe.com** for more information on **monitor manufacturers.**

VISUAL ESSAY: COMPARING MONITORS

When you are considering buying a monitor, you may wish to do some comparison shopping before you make your purchase. You want to find a monitor that displays graphics nicely and is easy on your eyes, which will allow you to work longer and more comfortably. A poor monitor will cause eyestrain and headaches and even can cause long-term vision problems.

When you shop for a monitor, first look closely at the display. Look at a screen full of text and examine the crispness of the letters, especially near the corners of the screen. Also, if you are going to work with graphics, display a picture with which you are familiar and see whether the colors look accurate. If possible, spend some time surfing the World Wide Web to display different types of pages.

Even if the monitor looks good (or if you are buying it through the mail), you need to check several specifications. The following are the most important:

- Size
- Resolution
- Refresh rate
- Dot pitch

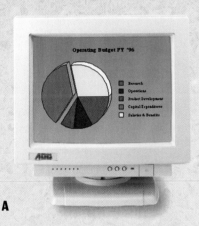
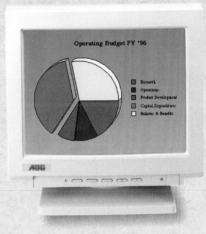

A

A A monitor's size affects how well you can see images. With a larger monitor, you can make the objects on the screen appear bigger, or you can fit more of them on the screen. Monitors are measured diagonally, in inches, across the front of the screen. A 17-inch monitor measures 17 inches from the lower left to the upper right corner. The actual viewing area, however, is smaller than the monitor's overall size. On a 17-inch monitor, the viewing area is a little over 15 inches. As a rule of thumb, buy the largest monitor you can afford.

B A monitor's **resolution** is determined by the number of pixels on the screen, expressed as a matrix. For example, a resolution of 640 × 480 means that there are 640 pixels horizontally across the screen and 480 pixels vertically down the screen. Because the actual resolution is determined by the video controller—not by the monitor itself—most monitors can operate at several different resolutions. This illustration shows pixel grids that allow for five resolution settings: (a) 640 × 480, (b) 800 × 600, (c) 1024 × 768, (d) 1152 × 864, and (e) 1280 × 1024.

B

C There are various standards for monitor resolution. The **Video Graphics Array (VGA)** standard is 640 × 480 pixels. The **Super VGA (SVGA)** standard expanded the resolutions to 800 × 600 and 1024 × 768. Today, nearly any color monitor can be set to even higher resolutions. Higher settings are not always better, however, because they can cause objects on the screen to appear too small, resulting in eye-strain and squinting. Compare these two images, taken from a 17-inch monitor. The first image is displayed at 640 × 480 resolution; the second image shows the same screen at 1280 × 1024.

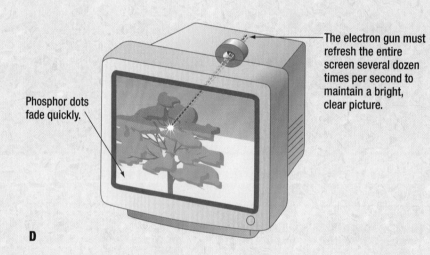

D A monitor's **refresh rate** is the number of times per second that the electron guns scan every pixel on the screen. Refresh rate is important because phosphor dots fade quickly after the electron gun passes over them. If the screen is not refreshed often enough, it appears to flicker, and flicker is one of the main causes of eyestrain. Refresh rate is measured in Hertz (Hz), or in cycles per second; a refresh rate of 72 Hz or higher should not cause eyestrain. Note that some monitors have different refresh rates for different resolutions. Make sure the refresh rate is adequate for the resolution you will be using.

The electron gun must refresh the entire screen several dozen times per second to maintain a bright, clear picture.

Phosphor dots fade quickly.

D

E The last critical specification of a color monitor is the **dot pitch,** the distance between the phosphor dots that make up a single pixel. In a color monitor, each pixel includes three dots—one red, one green, and one blue. If these dots are not close enough together, the images on the screen will not be crisp. In general, when you are looking for a color monitor, look for a dot pitch no greater than 0.28 millimeter.

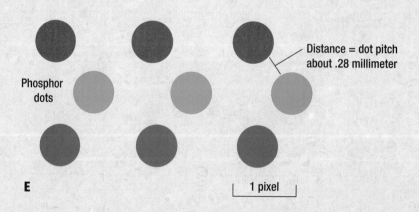

Distance = dot pitch about .28 millimeter

Phosphor dots

E

1 pixel

86

Unit 3

THE VIDEO CONTROLLER

The quality of the images that a monitor can display is defined as much by the **video controller** as by the monitor itself. As shown in Figure 3A.10, the video controller is an intermediary device between the CPU and the monitor. It contains the video-dedicated memory and other circuitry necessary to send information to the monitor for display on the screen. It consists of a circuit board, usually referred to simply as a card (the terms *video card* and *video controller* have the same meaning), which is attached to the computer's motherboard. Within the monitor's constraints, the controller's processing power determines the refresh rate, resolution, and number of colors that can be displayed.

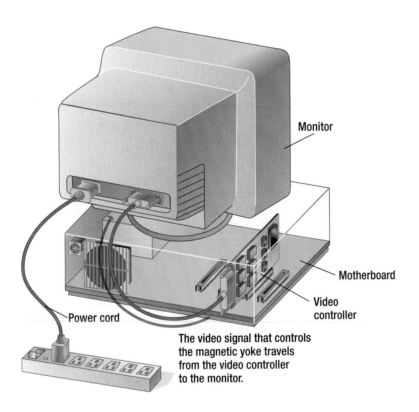

Monitor

Motherboard

Video controller

Power cord

The video signal that controls the magnetic yoke travels from the video controller to the monitor.

Figure 3A.10
The video controller connects the CPU, via the data bus on the motherboard, to the monitor.

In the early days of personal computing, PC screens displayed only text characters, which were usually in only one color. These displays took little processing power, because there were only 256 possible characters and 2,000 text positions on the screen. Rendering each screen required only 4,000 bytes of data. Today, however, computers are required to display colors and graphics at high resolutions. These displays require the CPU to send information to the video controller about every pixel on the screen. At a minimum resolution of 640×480, there are 307,200 pixels to control. Most users run their monitors at 256 colors, so each pixel requires one byte of information. Thus, the computer must send 307,200 bytes to the monitor for each screen. The screen changes constantly as you work—the screen is updated many times each second, whether anything on the screen actually changes or not.

If the user wants more colors or a higher resolution, the amount of data can be much higher. For example, for "high color" (24 bits, or 3 bytes, per pixel will render millions of colors) at a resolution of 1024×768, the computer must send 2,359,296 bytes to the monitor for each screen.

The result of these processing demands is that video controllers have increased dramatically in power and importance. Today's video controllers feature their own built-in microprocessors (see Figure 3A.11), which frees the CPU from the burden of making the millions of calculations required for displaying graphics. The speed of the video controller's chip determines the speed at which the monitor can be refreshed.

Video controllers also feature their own built-in **video RAM,** or **VRAM** (which is separate from the RAM that is connected to the CPU). VRAM is dual-ported, meaning that it can send a screen full of data to the monitor and at the same time receive the next screen full of data from the CPU. Today's most sophisticated video controllers—which are fine-tuned for multimedia, video, and 3-D graphics—may have as much as 64 MB of video RAM.

Figure 3A.11
Today's video controllers feature sophisticated circuitry to meet the demands of animation, 3-D graphics, and full-motion video.

Self Check

Complete each statement by filling in the blank(s).

1. Monochrome monitors are used for text-only displays where the user does not need to view color graphics.

2. In a monitor, a(n) Electron Gun aims a beam of electrons at the front of the monitor.

3. A disadvantage of LCD monitors is their limited Viewing angle

PRODUCTIVITY Tip

Flat-Panel Versus CRT Monitors

Whether you are shopping to equip a future office or to buy a home computer, you have quite a few monitor options to choose from. Basically, you can pick from two categories of desktop monitors: CRTs and flat-panel displays. Of course, you will get an LCD monitor if you buy a laptop system, but do not forget that most laptops have a port for connecting a desktop monitor. Both types of desktop monitors offer advantages and disadvantages.

In Some Ways, They Are All the Same

Flat-panel technology has made some big leaps in the last few years. Flat-panel monitors used to be small, low-resolution devices found mostly on portable systems; they now rival CRT monitors feature for feature. Whatever type of monitor you buy, make sure it meets your requirements in each of these areas: size, refresh rate, resolution, and dot pitch.

But In Other Ways, They Are Not

While all monitors may be created equal (or fairly equal) in terms of the resolutions and colors they can display, there are significant differences you need to consider:

◆ **Desktop Space Requirements.** Obviously, this is the criterion in which CRT monitors cannot match flat-panels. A typical CRT monitor with a 15.8-inch viewable area stands about 19 inches high (including the base) and is about 16 inches wide and 19 inches deep. A typical flat-panel monitor with a 15-inch viewable area stands about 18 inches high (including the base) and is about 16 inches wide, but it is only about 10 inches deep—4 inches without the base. Many flat-panel monitors can be hung on a wall or mounted on a swing-arm stand, further reducing their desktop space requirements.

◆ **Viewable Area.** CRT monitors offer viewable areas ranging from just over 13 inches to more than 22 inches. Flat-panels for the desktop range from about 14 inches to more than 18 inches, but larger viewing areas are being developed all the time.

◆ **Viewing Angle.** CRT monitors are usually hands-down winners in this category, but flat-panel systems are catching up. If you usually do not need to look at the monitor from an angle, and if you do not

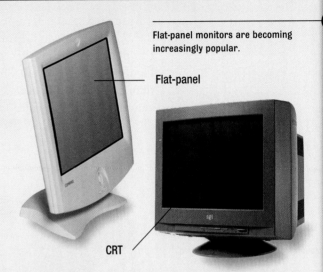

Flat-panel monitors are becoming increasingly popular.

Flat-panel

CRT

typically have several people looking at the monitor at one time, the flat-panel's restricted viewing angle should not be a problem.

◆ **Screen Curvature.** CRT screens are flatter than they once were, and some higher-end models are almost completely flat. With most moderately priced CRTs, however, some curvature of the screen is normal and can easily be seen. If you use a computer for long periods, you will notice this curvature can cause minor distortions in the picture that may lead to eyestrain. Because LCD monitors are flat, they do not pose this problem.

◆ **Power Consumption.** Flat-panel systems win in this category. CRT monitors consume a great deal of electricity to keep the screen refreshed. Conversely, LCD systems are energy efficient because of their tiny transistors. As an added benefit, flat-panel displays run cooler than CRTs.

◆ **Radiation Emissions.** CRT monitors emit low-level radiation. This radiation is not thought to be harmful, but it is there just the same. LCD monitors do not emit radiation.

◆ **Cost.** This category is usually the tie-breaker for shoppers who cannot decide between a flat-panel and CRT monitor. Despite their many advantages, flat-panel displays are generally much more expensive than CRT monitors. Flat-panel prices are steadily coming down, however.

Visit **www.norton.glencoe.com** for more information on **digital light projectors**.

DIGITAL LIGHT PROJECTORS

Portable computers have all but replaced old-fashioned slide projectors and overhead projectors as the source of presentations. Instead of using 35-millimeter photographic slides or 8.5- by 11-inch overhead transparencies, more and more people are using software to create colorful slide shows and animated presentations. These images can be shown directly from the computer's disk and displayed on the PC's screen or projected on a wall or large screen.

To get these presentations onto the "big screen," **digital light projectors** are becoming increasingly common. A digital light projector plugs into one of the computer's ports and then projects the video output onto an external surface (see Figure 3A.12). These small devices weigh only a few pounds and can display more than 16 million colors at resolutions up to 1024 × 768. Some projectors can be converted from still-video (slide) mode to full-video (animation) mode in order to display output from a VCR or DVD drive.

Figure 3A.12
Digital light projectors make it easy to deliver a presentation directly from a computer, so it can be viewed by a group of people.

Most projectors use LCD technology to create images. (For this reason, these devices are commonly called *LCD projectors.*) Like most types of light projectors, LCD projectors require the room to be darkened. They display blurry images in less-than-optimal lighting conditions.

Newer models use **digital light processing (DLP)** technology to project brighter, crisper images. DLP devices use a special microchip, called a digital micromirror device, which actually uses mirrors to control the image display. Unlike LCD-based projectors, DLP units can display clear images in normal lighting conditions.

SOUND SYSTEMS

Microphones are now important input devices, and speakers and their associated technology are key output systems (see Figure 3A.13). Today, when you buy a multimedia PC, you receive a machine that includes a CD-ROM (or DVD) drive, a high-quality video controller with plenty of video RAM, speakers, and a sound card.

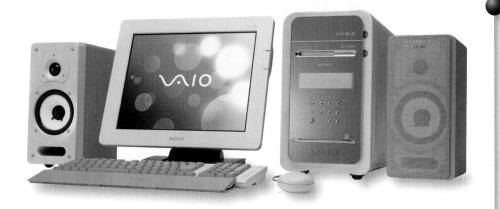

Figure 3A.13
Speakers are common features on today's multimedia PCs. Top-of-the-line PC audio systems include premium sound cards and tweeters, midrange speakers, and subwoofers for sound quality that rivals home stereo systems.

The speakers attached to these systems are similar to those you connect to a stereo. The only difference is that they are usually smaller, and they contain their own small amplifiers. Otherwise, they do the same thing any speaker does: They transfer a constantly changing electric current to a magnet, which pushes the speaker cone back and forth. The moving speaker cone creates pressure vibrations in the air—in other words, sound (see Figure 3A.14).

The more complicated part of the sound output system is in the sound card. The **sound card** translates digital sounds into the electric current that is sent to the speakers. Sound is defined as air pressure varying over time. To digitize sound, the waves are converted to an electric current that is measured thousands of times per second and recorded as a series of numbers. When the sound is played back, the sound card reverses this process, translating the numbers into electric current that is sent to the speakers. The magnet moves back and forth with the changing current, creating vibrations.

With the appropriate software, you can do much more than simply record and play back digitized sound. Sound editing programs provide a miniature sound studio, allowing you to view the sound wave and edit it. In the editing, you can cut bits of sound, copy them, and amplify the parts you want to hear more loudly; cut out static; and create many exotic audio effects.

NORTON
ONLINE

Visit **www.norton.glencoe.com** for more information on **PC audio technology.**

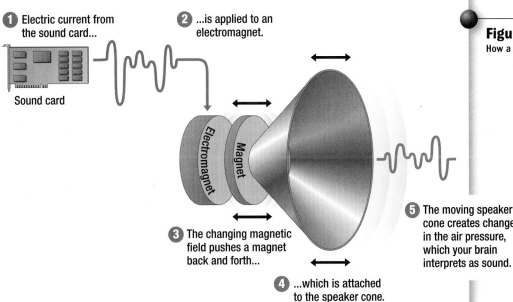

1 Electric current from the sound card...

2 ...is applied to an electromagnet.

Sound card

3 The changing magnetic field pushes a magnet back and forth...

4 ...which is attached to the speaker cone.

5 The moving speaker cone creates changes in the air pressure, which your brain interprets as sound.

Figure 3A.14
How a speaker creates sound

At Issue

The MP3 Controversy

MP3 (MPEG Layer 3) is an audio-compression standard that can compress digitized music to one-tenth its original size. A song that requires 10 MB of uncompressed storage space can be reduced to about 1 MB. With MP3, the compression takes place with virtually no loss in sound quality.

After coming into the public consciousness in 1998, MP3 quickly gained favor among computer users, who have used the technology to digitize and compress millions of songs, then exchange them over the Internet. This practice led to the creation of Web-based systems that allowed users to copy MP3 files directly from one another's hard disks over the Internet. MP3 swapping became so popular that it was perceived as a threat to the entire music industry; in fact, the industry blamed slumping sales on the MP3 phenomenon.

How MP3 Works

To compress a digitally recorded song in MP3 format, you need a special software program, called a "ripper." After copying digitized music (from your computer's CD-ROM drive, for example) onto your hard drive, you can use the ripper software to compress the music. The result is an MP3-format file, the size of which is much smaller than the original.

To play back an MP3 file from your computer, you need MP3 playback software. Some players act as a plug-in to your Web browser, and some can run as a stand-alone program. If you store MP3 songs on your computer's disk, you can use these players to play them back for you in jukebox-fashion. If you prefer, you can carry your MP3 recordings with you

and play them back on a tiny player. These tiny devices cost from $100 to $400 and can store an hour or more of MP3 music.

Upsides and Downsides

The promise of MP3 is vast. The technology is enabling unknown artists to distribute and promote their music for free over the Internet. It also provides a new way for record companies and music resellers to provide free samples to customers in hopes of selling complete albums. The compression technology also may be applied to video data and software, as well as to digitized audio.

MP3, however, makes it too easy to compress and distribute music. As a result, millions of copyrighted songs have been recorded in MP3 format and distributed illegally on the Internet. The practice reached its peak in 2001, through a Web-based service called Napster. Napster (and several similar services) allowed music fans to copy MP3 files directly from one another's computers over the Internet.

Why is the practice illegal? Simply put, if a musical piece has been published, then it is copyrighted, and a person or company owns the rights to it. Technically, a copyrighted piece can not be copied and distributed legally unless the copier or distributor has permission from—and pays a fee to—the music's owner.

That is why the music industry filed a flurry of lawsuits in 2000 and 2001 in an effort to shut down Napster and force its owners to pay millions of dollars in damages. The recording industry eventually won, forcing Napster to stop supporting the swapping of published music. But other services continued, and many fans continue to privately swap MP3 files via e-mail, newsgroups, and Web sites.

If you decide to download music over the Internet in MP3 format, be sure to download it from a site that provides the service legally. These sites provide copyright information about the music, along with information on how to purchase the music on CD or in some other format. Also, never distribute recorded music over the Internet or in any format; this practice could get you into trouble.

RealJukebox is just one example of a media player that can record, organize, and play back MP3 files.

SUMMARY

- Computer monitors are roughly divided into two categories: CRT and flat-panel displays.

- Monitors also can be categorized by the number of colors they display. Monitors are usually monochrome, grayscale, or color.

- A CRT monitor works with one or more electron guns that systematically aim a beam of electrons at every pixel on the screen.

- Most LCD displays are either active matrix or passive matrix.

- When purchasing a monitor, you should consider its size, resolution, refresh rate, and dot pitch.

- The video controller is an interface between the monitor and the CPU. The video controller determines many aspects of a monitor's performance; for example, the video controller lets you select a resolution or set the number of colors to display.

- The video controller contains its own on-board processor and memory, called video RAM.

- A digital light projector is a portable light projector that connects to a PC. This type of projector is rapidly replacing traditional slide projectors and overhead projectors as a means for displaying presentations.

- Many digital light projectors provide the same resolutions and color levels as high-quality monitors, but they project images on a large screen.

- The newest projectors use digital light processing to project bright, crisp images. A DLP projector uses a special microchip that contains tiny mirrors to produce images.

- Multimedia PCs generally come with sound systems, which include a sound card, speakers, a CD-ROM or DVD drive, and a video controller.

- The sound card translates digital signals into analog signals that drive the speakers.

KEY TERMS

active matrix LCD, *84*
cathode ray tube (CRT), *80*
color monitor, *80*
digital light processing (DLP), *90*
digital light projector, *90*
dot pitch, *86*
dual-scan LCD, *83*
flat-panel display, *80*

grayscale monitor, *80*
liquid crystal display (LCD), *83*
monochrome monitor, *80*
passive matrix LCD, *83*
pixel, *81*
refresh rate, *86*
resolution, *85*
shadow mask, *82*

sound card, *91*
submarine, *83*
Super VGA (SVGA), *86*
thin-film transistor (TFT), *84*
video controller, *87*
Video Graphics Array (VGA), *86*
video RAM (VRAM), *88*
viewing angle, *83*

KEY TERM QUIZ

Complete each statement by writing one of the terms listed under Key Terms in each blank.

1. A(n) _____ monitor displays only one color, usually against a black background.

2. The term _____ is a contraction of the term *picture element*.

3. All CRT monitors use _____ with holes in them to align the beams from the electron gun.

4. A(n) _____ matrix LCD monitor assigns one transistor to each pixel.

5. A monitor's _____ is determined by the numbers of pixels on the screen, expressed as a matrix.

SECTION QUIZ

True/False

Answer the following questions by circling True or False.

True   False   **1.** A cathode ray tube monitor looks and works much like a television screen.

True   False   **2.** A CRT monitor uses a gun to shoot pixels at the front of the screen.

True   False   **3.** LCD monitors typically offer a wider viewing angle than do CRT monitors.

True   False   **4.** Flat-panel displays are used only with notebook computers.

True   False   **5.** Some digital light projectors can display 16 million colors at resolutions up to 1024 × 768.

Multiple Choice

Circle the word or phrase that best completes each statement.

1. _____ monitors are most commonly used with desktop computers.
   A. Flat-panel display   **B.** Cathode ray tube (CRT)   **C.** Neither A nor B

2. A(n) _____ LCD relies on transistors for each row and each column of pixels.
   A. active matrix   **B.** passive matrix   **C.** flat-panel

3. The _____ of flat-panel monitors is limited, compared to CRT monitors.
   A. resolution   **B.** viewing angle   **C.** dot pitch

4. A video controller contains a _____ , which frees the CPU from making the calculations required for the display of graphics.
   A. cable   **B.** video RAM   **C.** microprocessor

5. Sound can be defined as _____ .
   A. multimedia   **B.** electric current   **C.** air pressure varying over time

REVIEW QUESTIONS

In your own words, briefly answer the following questions.

1. There are two basic types of monitors used with PCs. List them.

2. How does a color CRT monitor produce images on the screen?

3. What is the most common type of flat-panel monitor?

4. How does a dual-scan LCD monitor produce a clearer image than an ordinary passive matrix monitor?

5. You should consider four factors when comparing monitors. List them.

SECTION LABS

Complete the following exercises as directed by your instructor.

1. Examine your computer's video setup. First, look at the monitor attached to your computer. What brand is it? What model? What other information can you get from the monitor by examining its exterior? (Remember to look at the back.) Next, measure your monitor. What is the diagonal measurement of the monitor's case? What is the viewing area, measured diagonally? If you are connected to the Internet, go to the manufacturer's Web site and find your monitor. Write down the resolution and refresh rate.

2. If your PC has speakers attached to it, you can easily check or change the speaker volume. Move the mouse pointer to the Windows taskbar. Look for a speaker icon and click it. A small volume control will appear on the screen. You can use the mouse to drag the volume control up or down to change the volume setting, or you can select the Mute checkbox to silence the sound system entirely. Click anywhere outside the volume control to close it.

Devices That Output Hard Copy

OBJECTIVES

- List the three most commonly used types of printers.
- List the four criteria you should consider when evaluating printers.
- Describe how a dot matrix printer creates an image on a page.
- Explain how a laser printer creates an image on a page.
- Explain how an ink jet printer creates an image on a page.
- List four types of high-quality printing devices commonly used in business.

OVERVIEW:
Putting Digital Content in Your Hands

Most computer users can't imagine working without a printer. Monitors and sound systems let you see and hear your work, but printers give you something you can touch, carry, and share with others. Printed documents are essential in most workplaces, where people must share reports, budgets, memos, and other types of information.

Over the past decade, the variety of available printing devices has exploded; however, three types of printers have become the most popular: dot matrix, ink jet, and laser. Within those three groups, consumers have hundreds of options, ranging widely in price and features. Several other types of special printing devices are available for users with special needs, such as large-format printouts or images with extremely accurate color and high resolution.

This section introduces you to the basics of hard-copy output devices. You will learn about the most common types of printers and see how each creates an image on paper. You will learn the criteria for evaluating different printers and examine some of the specialized printing devices designed for professional use.

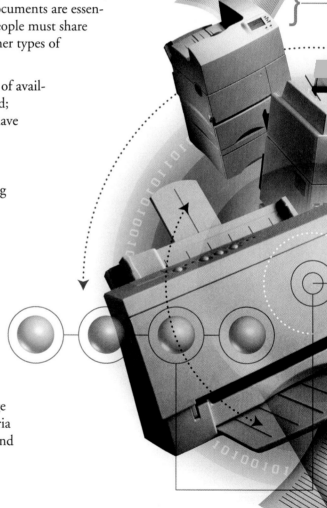

OVERVIEW OF PRINTERS

Besides the monitor, the other important output device is the printer. Generally, printers fall into two categories: impact and nonimpact. An **impact printer** creates an image by using pins or hammers to press an inked ribbon against the paper. A simple example of an impact printer is a typewriter, which uses small hammers to strike the ribbon. Each hammer is embossed with the shape of a letter, number, or symbol; that shape is transferred through the inked ribbon onto the paper, resulting in a printed character.

Although it is seldom done today, many modern electric typewriters can be connected to a PC and used as a letter-quality printer (see Figure 3B.1). As a printer, however, even a good typewriter is slow and limited in the kinds of images it can produce. The most common type of impact printer is the dot matrix printer (see Figure 3B.2). Other types of impact printers are line printers, band printers and daisy wheel printers (although this last type is nearly obsolete).

Visit **www.norton.glencoe.com** for more information on **evaluating printers**.

Figure 3B.1
Although they are much slower than normal printers, many electronic typewriters can be connected to a PC and used to print documents, such as letters or memos. This arrangement works well when the user does not need many different fonts or printing options or to print a high volume of documents.

Figure 3B.2
Many people think dot matrix printers are obsolete, but these printers are still widely sold and used. They are inexpensive compared to other kinds of printers, and while they are not well suited to printing graphics, good dot matrix printers can produce high-quality text documents. Like other types of impact printers, dot matrix printers can be used with carbon-copy and other kinds of copy forms.

Nonimpact printers use other means to create an image. Ink jet printers, for example, use tiny nozzles to spray droplets of ink onto the page. Laser printers work like photocopiers, using heat to bond microscopic particles of dry toner to specific parts of the page (see Figure 3B.3).

In the early years of computing, dot matrix printers were the most commonly used printing devices. They are not as prevalent now, although dot matrix printers are still popular in business and academic settings because they are relatively fast and inexpensive to operate, and they do a good job of printing text and simple graphics. Ink jet printers now offer much higher quality for about the same price, and they have become more popular than dot matrix printers in homes and small businesses. Laser printers are also popular in homes and businesses, but they are more expensive to buy and operate than either ink jet or dot matrix devices.

Figure 3B.3

Laser printers produce the highest-quality text and graphics output. Laser printers, which can be as large as photocopiers, are commonly found in business settings where many people need to print documents. Sophisticated high-volume laser printers are often connected to networks and handle printing tasks for large workgroups.

When you are ready to buy a printer, you must consider how you plan to use the printer. Do you need to print only text, or are graphics capabilities also important? Do you need to print in color? Will you need to print a wide variety of fonts in many sizes? How quickly do you want your documents to be printed?

When evaluating printers, four additional criteria are important:

◆ **Image Quality.** Image quality, also known as print resolution, usually is measured in **dots per inch (dpi).** The more dots per inch a printer can produce, the higher its image quality. For example, most medium-quality ink jet and laser printers can print 300 or 600 dots per inch, which is fine for most daily business applications. If a printer's resolution is 600 dpi, this means it can print 600 columns of dots and 600 rows of dots in each square inch of the page, a total of 360,000 dots ($600 \times 600 = 360,000$) per inch, as shown in Figure 3B.4. Professional-quality printers, used for creating colorful presentations, posters, or renderings, offer resolutions of 1800 dpi or even higher.

◆ **Speed.** Printer speed is measured in the number of **pages per minute (ppm)** the device can print. (The speed of dot matrix printers is measured differently, as you will learn later.) Most printers have different ppm ratings for text and graphics, because graphics generally take longer to print. As print speed goes up, so does cost. Most consumer-level laser printers offer print speeds of 6 or 8 ppm, but high-volume professional laser printers can exceed 50 ppm.

Figure 3B.4

The image quality of laser and ink jet printers is measured in dots per inch.

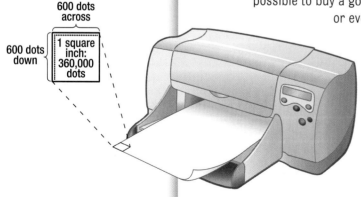

600 dots across

600 dots down

1 square inch: 360,000 dots

◆ **Initial Cost.** The cost of new printers has fallen dramatically in recent years, while their capabilities and speed have improved just as spectacularly. It is possible to buy a good-quality ink jet printer for personal use for $100 or even less; low-end laser printers can be found for $250 or less. Professional-quality, high-output systems can range in price from $1,000 to tens of thousands of dollars. Color printers always cost more than black-and-white printers.

◆ **Cost of Operation.** The cost of ink or toner and maintenance varies with the type of printer (see Figure 3B.5). Many different types of printer paper are available, too, and the choice can affect the cost of operation. Low-quality recycled paper, for example, is fine for printing draft-quality documents and costs less than a penny per sheet. Glossy, thick photo-quality stock, used for printing photographs, can cost several dollars per sheet, depending on size.

DOT MATRIX PRINTERS

Dot matrix printers are commonly used in workplaces where physical impact with the paper is important, such as when the user is printing to carbon-copy or pressure-sensitive forms. These printers can produce sheets of plain text very quickly. They also are used to print very wide sheets, as data processing departments often use when generating large reports with wide columns of information.

A dot matrix printer creates an image by using a mechanism called a **print head,** which contains a cluster (or *matrix*) of short pins arranged in one or more columns. On receiving instructions from the PC, the printer can push any of the pins out in any combination. By pushing out pins in various combinations, the print head can create alphanumeric characters (see Figures 3B.6 and 3B.7).

When pushed out from the cluster, the protruding pins' ends strike a ribbon, which is held in place between the print head and the paper. When the pins strike the ribbon, they press ink from the ribbon onto a piece of paper.

The more pins that a print head contains, the higher the printer's resolution. The lowest resolution dot matrix printers have only nine pins; the highest resolution printers have twenty-four pins.

The speed of dot matrix printers is measured in **characters per second (cps).** The slowest dot matrix printers create 50 to 70 cps; the fastest print more than 500 cps.

Figure 3B.5
For all their speed and convenience, high-volume printers can be costly to maintain. Toner cartridges for high-quality laser printers can cost more than $100 apiece.

Figure 3B.6
A dot matrix printer forms a character by creating a series of dots.

Visit **www.norton.glencoe.com** for more information on **dot matrix printers.**

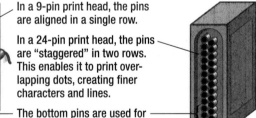

In a 9-pin print head, the pins are aligned in a single row.

In a 24-pin print head, the pins are "staggered" in two rows. This enables it to print overlapping dots, creating finer characters and lines.

The bottom pins are used for the portions of lowercase letters that extend below the line, such as *g* or *q*.

PRINT HEAD

PRINT HEAD

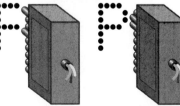

Direction of print head

Figure 3B.7
How a dot matrix printer creates an image

Figure 3B.8
Line printers use a special wide print head to print an entire line of text at one time.

Although dot matrix printers are not commonly used in homes, they are still widely used in business, as are other types of impact printers:

◆ **Line Printers.** This special type of impact printer works like a dot matrix printer but uses a special wide print head that can print an entire line of text at one time (see Figure 3B.8). Line printers do not offer high resolutions but are incredibly fast; the fastest can print 3,000 lines of text per minute.

◆ **Band Printers.** A band printer features a rotating band embossed with alphanumeric characters. To print a character, the machine rotates the band to the desired character, then a small hammer taps the band, pressing the character against a ribbon. Although this sounds like a slow process, band printers are very fast and very robust. Depending on the character set used, a good-quality band printer can generate 2,000 lines of text per minute.

◆ **Daisy Wheel Printers.** This type of printer is nearly obsolete, but it can still be found where older systems are used. These printers use a spinning wheel with characters embossed around its edge. A hammer strikes the wheel from behind, pressing a character against a ribbon. Daisy wheel printers can create clean text, but they cannot print graphics. They are also very slow in comparison to other printers.

INK JET PRINTERS

Ink jet printers create an image directly on the paper by spraying ink through tiny nozzles (see Figure 3B.9). The popularity of ink jet printers jumped around 1990 when the speed and quality improved and prices plummeted.

Figure 3B.9
How an ink jet printer creates an image

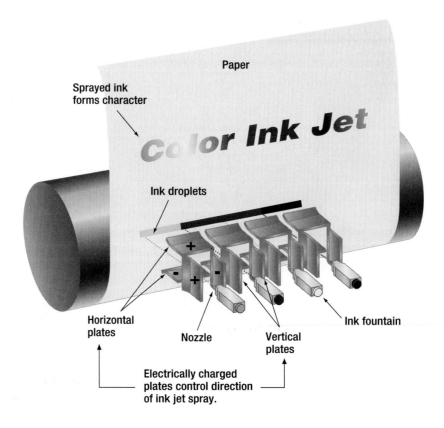

Paper

Sprayed ink forms character

Ink droplets

Horizontal plates

Nozzle

Vertical plates

Ink fountain

Electrically charged plates control direction of ink jet spray.

Today, good ink jet printers are available for as little as $100. These models typically attain print resolutions of at least 360 dots per inch. These same models can print from two to four pages per minute (only slightly slower than the slowest laser printers).

Compared to laser printers, the operating cost of an ink jet printer is relatively low. Expensive maintenance is rare, and the only part that needs routine replacement is the ink cartridge, which ranges in price from $20 to $35. Many ink jet printers use one cartridge for color printing and a separate black-only cartridge for black-and-white printing. This feature saves money by reserving colored ink only for color printing.

Color ink jet printers have four ink nozzles: cyan (blue), magenta (red), yellow, and black. For this reason, they are sometimes referred to as CMYK printers, or as using the CMYK color process. These four colors are used in almost all color printing because it is possible to combine them to create any color. Notice that the colors are different from the primary additive colors (red, green, and blue) used in monitors. Printed color is the result of light bouncing off the paper, not color transmitted directly from a light source. Consequently, cyan, magenta, yellow, and black are sometimes called subtractive colors, and color printing is sometimes called four-color printing. When used with special printing paper, many ink jet printers can produce photo-quality images. For this reason, they often are used to print pictures taken with a digital camera.

Ink jet printers are combined with other technologies to create complete, all-in-one office machines (see Figure 3B.10). Manufacturers such as Hewlett-Packard, Canon, and others offer combination printers, copiers, fax machines, and scanners based on ink jet technology. A basic all-in-one unit with black-and-white printing can be purchased for less than $500. High-resolution color systems are considerably more expensive.

Figure 3B.10
Ink jet technology is the basis for many "all-in-one" office machines like this one, which includes a printer, copier, scanner, and fax.

LASER PRINTERS

Laser printers are more expensive than ink jet printers, their print quality is higher, and most are faster. As their name implies, a laser is at the heart of these printers. A CPU and memory are built into the printer to interpret the data that it receives from the computer and to control the laser. The result is a complicated piece of equipment that uses technology similar to that in photocopiers. Figure 3B.11 shows how a laser printer works. The quality and speed of laser printers make them ideal for office environments, where several users can easily share the same printer via a LAN.

Just as the electron gun in a monitor can target any pixel, the laser in a laser printer can aim at any point on a drum, creating an electrical charge. **Toner,** which is composed of tiny particles of oppositely charged ink, sticks to the drum in the places the laser has charged. Then, with pressure and heat, the toner is transferred off the drum onto the paper. The amount of memory that laser printers contain determines the speed at which documents are printed.

NORTON ONLINE

Visit **www.norton.glencoe.com** for more information on **laser printers**.

A color laser printer works like a single-color model, except that the process is repeated four times, and a different toner color is used for each pass. The four colors used are the same as in the color ink jet printers: cyan, magenta, yellow, and black.

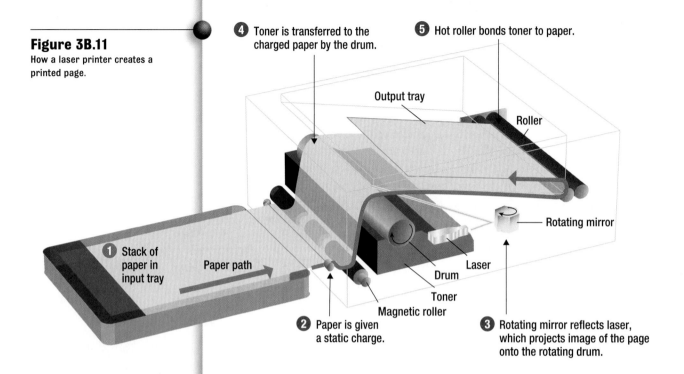

Figure 3B.11
How a laser printer creates a printed page.

④ Toner is transferred to the charged paper by the drum.

⑤ Hot roller bonds toner to paper.

Output tray

Roller

Rotating mirror

① Stack of paper in input tray

Paper path

Laser

Drum

Toner

Magnetic roller

② Paper is given a static charge.

③ Rotating mirror reflects laser, which projects image of the page onto the rotating drum.

Single-color (black) laser printers typically can produce between four and 16 pages of text a minute. If you are printing graphics, the output can be a great deal slower. The most common laser printers have resolutions of 300 or 600 dpi, both horizontally and vertically, but some high-end models have resolutions of 1,200 or 1,800 dpi. The printing industry stipulates a resolution of at least 1,200 dpi for top-quality professional printing. It is difficult to detect the difference between text printed at 600 dpi and at 1,200 dpi; the higher resolution is most noticeable in graphics reproduction such as photographs and artwork.

Laser printers start at about $150, and the price increases dramatically along with speed and resolution. Color laser printers are considerably more expensive than single-color printers. In addition, laser printers require new toner cartridges after a few thousand pages, and toner cartridges can cost anywhere from $40 to $200.

✓

Complete the following statements by filling in the blank(s).

1. Image quality is also known as _print resolution_ when discussing printers.

2. In a dot matrix printer, a(n) _print head_ contains a cluster (or matrix) of pins.

3. _Daisy wheel_ printers are nearly obsolete.

Norton Notebook

A PAPERLESS SOCIETY?

In the mid-1980s, as businesses and schools began connecting their computers in greater numbers, people began to see the advantages of sharing information over networks. By accessing data on a centralized server or sharing files by electronic mail, users found they could greatly reduce their reliance on printed documents.

Experts envisioned a paperless society: a world where documents are created, distributed, and read on computer systems. They imagined a world where people gathered all their information online and shared written communications across networks. At least, experts thought, we can achieve a paperless office: work environments where printed documents were no longer used.

Why Do We Print So Much?

In 1985, when the notion of the paperless office entered public debate, Xerox Corporation estimated that American businesses produced nearly 1.5 trillion paper documents a year. Although it cost only a few cents per page to create printed documents, the accumulated cost of billions of pages was astronomical.

That was nearly 20 years ago. Today, the flood of paper has hardly been reduced. In fact, in many homes and offices, people are printing more documents (and throwing away more of them) than ever before. Ironically, this trend is a direct result of the computer systems that were supposed to *reduce* the demand for printed documents. By making it so easy to print documents, computers have actually increased our reliance on paper.

The paperless society has yet to materialize, and most experts now believe it never will. Here is why:

◆ **Printers and Paper Are Cheap and Plentiful.** Ink jet printers cost as little as $100. Many new computer systems include a printer, making it an irresistible option. A box of printer paper can be purchased for about $20.

◆ **People Simply Prefer Paper Documents.** Although portable computers are increasingly affordable, they do not necessarily make reading and writing easier. Most people find paper documents more comfortable to use, lighter, and easier on the eyes.

◆ **Not Everyone Has a Computer.** More than 40 percent of Americans still do not have computers in their homes. Many have no intention of ever buying one. For these people, the demand for printed documents will not decrease.

◆ **Paper Provides Security.** Even in businesses where documents are generated and distributed electronically, many people still print them and file them. This practice is rooted in an ongoing distrust of computers. A paper copy makes the distrustful computer user feel more secure.

Despite the reasons for printing documents, computer users should consider the negative effects of producing so many hard copies: deforestation, solid waste that gluts landfills, and wasted electricity.

What Can You Do?

Computer users should use paper and energy responsibly. This practice requires thought and discipline, but it can actually make your work life easier and less expensive—saving you time, storage space, and money. Here are three simple steps you can take:

◆ **Think Before You Print.** Do you really need a hard copy? Are people asking for a hard copy when an e-mail attachment would work just as well? If you plan to stick the printout in a file cabinet, add it to a stack of papers, or throw it out, you may not need to print it.

◆ **Archive on Disk.** If you are concerned that your electronic documents will be lost or altered, back them up and store them on removable media such as a floppy disk. Kept in a safe place, the electronic copy will not change, and it will always be accessible.

◆ **Encourage Others to Print Wisely.** When someone brings you a printed document, ask him or her to send it by e-mail or to give it to you on disk next time. These practices can actually be faster than waiting for a printout.

Each year, millions of tons of office paper are discarded.

OTHER HIGH-QUALITY PRINTERS

Although most offices and homes use ink jet or laser printers, other types of printers are used for special purposes. These printers often are used by publishers and small print shops to create high-quality output, especially color output. The last type discussed in this section, the plotter, is designed specifically for printing large-format construction and engineering documents.

Thermal-Wax Printers

Thermal-wax printers are used primarily for presentation graphics and handouts. They create bold colors and have a low per-page cost for pages with heavy color requirements. The process provides vivid colors, because the inks do not bleed into each other or soak the specially coated paper. Thermal-wax printers operate with a ribbon coated with panels of colored wax that melts and adheres to plain paper as colored dots when passed over a focused heat source.

Dye-Sub Printers

Desktop publishers and graphic artists get realistic quality and color for photo images using **dye-sub** (for **dye-sublimation**) **printers** (see Figure 3B.12). In dye-sublimation technology, a ribbon containing panels of color is moved across a focused heat source capable of subtle temperature variations. The heated dyes evaporate from the ribbon and diffuse on specially coated paper or another material, where they form areas of different colors. The variations in color are related to the intensity of the heat applied. Dye-sub printers create extremely sharp images, but they are slow and costly. The special paper they require can make the per-page cost as high as $3 to $4.

Photo Printers

With digital cameras and scanners becoming increasingly popular, users want to be able to print the images they create or scan. While the average color ink jet or laser printer can handle this job satisfactorily, many people are investing in special **photo printers** (see Figure 3B.13). Many photo printers use inkjet technology, but a few use dye-sublimation technology. The best photo printers can create images that look nearly as good as a photograph printed using traditional methods.

Photo printers work slowly; some can take two to four minutes to create a printout. Several models create prints no larger than a standard 4- by 6-inch snapshot, although newer photo printers can produce 8- by 10-inch or even 11- by 14-inch prints. Many photo printers can print multiple images on a single sheet of paper.

Because they spray so much ink on the paper, it can take several minutes for a printout to dry, so smearing can be a problem. Still, these printers give digital photography enthusiasts a way to print and display their photos in hard-copy form. Photo printers range in price from $200 to more than $500, and the cost per print ranges from fifty cents to a dollar (several times more expensive than traditional film processing).

Figure 3B.12

Dye-sublimation printers come in a wide range of sizes and are used to print all kinds of high-resolution color documents, such as photographs, presentation graphics, posters, and t-shirts.

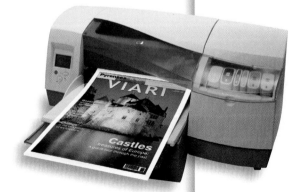

Figure 3B.13

Photo printers make it easy to print hard copies of images taken on a digital camera.

One advantage of the newest photo printers is that they do not need a computer. Devices like the Epson Stylus Photo 785EPX, for example, feature slots for memory cards used by many digital cameras. Instead of connecting the printer to a computer, the user can simply remove the memory card from the camera and plug it into the printer. Some photo printers can connect to a camera by a cable or even by an infrared connection.

IRIS Printers

IRIS printers are used by print shops to produce high-resolution presentation graphics and color proofs that resemble full-color offset printed images. The IRIS is a high-tech form of ink jet printing in which individual sheets of paper are mounted onto a drum. The nozzles on the ink jet printing head pass from one end of the spinning drum to the other, spraying tiny drops of colored ink to form the image. This type of printer can produce an image with a resolution of 1,800 dpi.

Plotters

A **plotter** is a special kind of output device. It is like a printer because it produces images on paper, but the plotter typically is used to print large-format images, such as construction or engineering drawings created in a CAD system.

Early plotters were bulky, mechanical devices that used robotic arms, which literally drew the image on a piece of paper. Table plotters (or flatbed plotters) use two robotic arms, each of which holds a set of colored ink pens, felt pens, or pencils. The two arms work in concert, operating at right angles as they draw on a stationary piece of paper. In addition to being complex and large (some are almost as big as a billiard table), table plotters are notoriously slow; a large, complicated drawing can take several hours to print.

A variation on the table plotter is the roller plotter (also known as the drum plotter) which uses only one drawing arm but moves the paper instead of holding it flat and stationary (see Figure 3B.14). The drawing arm moves side to side as the paper is rolled back and forth through the roller. Working together, the arm and roller can draw perfect circles and other geometric shapes, as well as lines of different weights and colors.

In recent years, mechanical plotters have been displaced by thermal, electrostatic, and ink jet plotters, as well as large-format dye-sub printers. These devices, which also produce large-size drawings, are faster and cheaper to use than their mechanical counterparts. They also can produce full-color renderings as well as geometric line drawings, making them more useful than standard mechanical plotters (see Figure 3B.15).

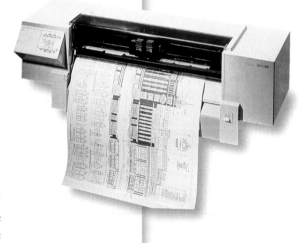

Figure 3B.14
A roller plotter uses a robotic arm to draw with colored pens on oversized paper. Here, an architectural drawing is being printed.

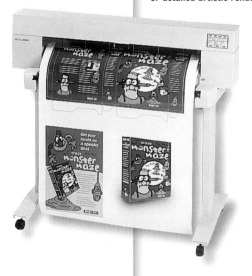

Figure 3B.15
Like desktop ink jet printers, an ink jet plotter uses a spray system to create either simple line drawings or detailed artistic renderings.

COMPUTERS
in your career

Hardware Maintenance Technician

Walk into nearly any office, factory, or other workplace today, and you will find one common element: computer hardware. Most workplaces now use computer equipment—including desktop PCs, laptops, network servers, routers, hubs, printers, modems, cabling systems, and peripherals of all types. And as the old saying goes, "the more parts something has, the more likely it is to break down." That is why there is a continued strong demand for qualified PC hardware maintenance technicians. (This position goes by several names, including PC technician, hardware technician, PC technology specialist, and break/fix technician.)

What Does a Hardware Maintenance Technician Do?

The hardware maintenance technician's job title answers this question. In most settings, this technician is responsible for the following kinds of tasks:

◆ Installing and configuring new computer hardware

◆ Installing peripherals

◆ Upgrading computers (installing updated cards, memory, drives, etc.)

◆ Dealing with network-related hardware issues

◆ Troubleshooting and repairing hardware of all types

Skills and Educational Requirements

The exact skills and educational requirements for a hardware maintenance technician's job depend on the organization. In a small company, the technician may need only basic PC troubleshooting experience and a certificate that proves some training in electronics or computer maintenance. This kind of training or certification is available through many two-year colleges, vocational schools, and technical training schools.

In a demanding corporate environment, however, the requirements may be more rigorous, including several years of similar work experience, a degree in electronics or computer science, and certification in operating system or networking software. To obtain these qualifications, a person may need a four-year college degree, as well as significant technical training and testing for certification.

In any case, the hardware maintenance technician must be able to show that he or she has experience and/or training in the specific types of systems and software used by the organization. Beyond that, a qualified technician shows an aptitude for learning and an eagerness to master any proprietary, legacy, or unusual systems that the organization chooses to operate.

Entry-level technicians can earn starting salaries in the range of $20,000 to $25,000; however, pay scales can increase quickly with experience, especially if an employer needs a technician with specialized skills. Experienced technicians can earn $50,000 a year or more. Many technicians, however, work on an hourly basis and earn between $25 and $50 per hour. In some cases, however, technicians can command wages as high as $75 or $100 per hour, depending on the demands of a specific job.

For more information on the qualifications you need to become a hardware maintenance technician, talk to a computer science instructor at your school or to someone in your school's placement office. Otherwise, seek guidance from a local IT professional, who may be able to put you in touch with working hardware maintenance technicians.

SUMMARY

- Printers fall into two general categories: impact and nonimpact.

- Impact printers create an image on paper by using a device to strike an inked ribbon, pressing ink from the ribbon onto the paper. Nonimpact printers use various methods to place ink (or another colored substance) on the page.

- When evaluating printers for purchase, you should consider four criteria: image quality, speed, initial cost, and cost of operation.

- A dot matrix printer is an impact printer. A dot matrix printer uses a print head, which contains a cluster of pins. The printer can push the pins out in rapid sequence to form patterns. The pins are used to press an inked ribbon against paper, creating an image.

- The speed of dot matrix printers is measured in characters per second. The fastest ones can print 500 characters each second.

- An ink jet printer is an example of a nonimpact printer. It creates an image by spraying tiny droplets of ink onto the paper.

- Ink jet printers are inexpensive for both color and black printing, have low operating costs, and offer quality and speed comparable to low-end laser printers.

- Laser printers are nonimpact printers. They use heat and pressure to bond tiny particles of toner (a dry ink) to paper.

- Laser printers produce higher-quality print and are fast and convenient to use, but they are also more expensive than ink jet printers. Laser printers are available in both color and black, and the highest end laser printers provide resolutions of 1,200 dpi and greater.

- Thermal-wax, dye-sublimation, and IRIS printers are used primarily by print shops and publishers to create high-quality color images.

- Snapshot printers are specialized printers used to print color photographs taken with digital cameras.

- Plotters create large-format images, usually for architectural or engineering purposes, using mechanical drawing arms, ink jet technology, or thermal printing technology.

KEY TERMS

characters per second (cps), *99*
dot matrix printer, *99*
dots per inch (dpi), *98*
dye-sublimation (dye-sub)
   printer, *104*
impact printer, *97*

ink jet printer, *100*
IRIS printer, *105*
laser printer, *101*
nonimpact printer, *98*
pages per minute (ppm), *98*
photo printer, *104*

plotter, *105*
print head, *99*
thermal-wax printer, *104*
toner, *101*

KEY TERM QUIZ

Complete each statement by writing one of the terms listed under Key Terms in each blank.

1. _____ is composed of charged particles of ink that bond to the paper in a laser printer.

2. A dot matrix printer is an example of a(n) _____ printer.

3. A(n) _____ printer is designed to print digital photographs.

4. A(n) _____ printer uses heat to diffuse special dyes from a ribbon onto the paper.

5. _____ are used to create large-format images, such as construction drawings.

SECTION QUIZ

True/False

Answer the following questions by circling True or False.

True   False   1. The two categories of printers are impact and nonimpact.

True   False   2. Printer speed is measured in dots per inch (dpi).

True   False   3. A dot matrix printer works by pushing pins against an inked ribbon, thus creating a series of dots on the paper.

True   False   4. An ink jet printer is an example of an impact printer.

True   False   5. Dye-sublimation is another term for laser printing.

Multiple Choice

Circle the word or phrase that best completes each statement.

1. The speed of dot matrix printers is measured in _____ .
   A. dots per inch (dpi)　　B. characters per second (cps)　　C. pages per minute (ppm)

2. A laser printer creates an image by placing _____ at specific points on the page.
   A. toner　　　　　　　　B. electric charges　　　　　　C. neither A nor B

3. A(n) _____ printer is a high-resolution printer that uses a variation on ink jet technology.
   A. ink jet　　　　　　　B. photo　　　　　　　　　　C. IRIS

4. A(n) _____ printer is a high-tech version of an ink jet printer, capable of printing at resolutions of 1,800 dpi.
   A. dot matrix　　　　　B. plotter　　　　　　　　　C. IRIS

5. _____ are ideal for creating large-format drawings, like those required by architects and engineers.
   A. Dot matrix printers　　B. Plotters　　　　　　　　C. Photo printers

REVIEW QUESTIONS

In your own words, briefly answer the following questions.

1. You should consider four factors when evaluating printers. List them.

2. What units of measure are used to determine the speed of a dot matrix printer and a laser printer?

3. Color ink jet printers use four colors of ink. List them.

4. What is the difference between an impact printer and a nonimpact printer?

5. Why are plotters special output devices?

SECTION LABS

Complete the following exercises as directed by your instructor.

1. Find out what type of printer is connected to your computer. Open your PC's Printers window as directed by your instructor. If a printer is connected to your system, it will appear in this window. Right-click the printer's icon to open a shortcut menu. Then choose Properties to open the Properties dialog box for the printer. Write down the data in the dialog box. Do not make any changes in the dialog box, but leave it open for the next exercise.

2. With your printer's Properties dialog box open, click the General tab. Near the bottom of the tab, click the button labeled Print Test Page. A new dialog box appears, asking you to confirm that your printer produced a test page. If your printer produces a test page, click Yes (or OK). If not, click No (or Troubleshoot) and ask your instructor for assistance. When you are finished, Click Cancel to close the dialog box. Close all open windows.

UNIT PROJECTS

UNIT LABS

Complete the following exercises using a computer in your classroom, lab, or home.

1. **Change Your Color Settings.** By experimenting with your PC's color settings, you can determine the settings that work best for you. For example, if you do not plan to browse the World Wide Web or use multimedia products, you probably do not need to use the system's highest color settings; if you do, you need to make sure your monitor's settings are up to the task, or you will not get the most from your computing experiences. Before you take the following steps, close any running programs, and make sure there is no disk in your system's floppy disk drive.

   A. Open the Control Panel window, as directed by your instructor.

   B. Double-click the Display icon. The Display Properties dialog box opens.

   C. Click the Settings tab. Note the setting in the Colors box, and write it down. (In Windows XP, this box is named Color quality.)

   D. Click the Colors drop-down list arrow, and choose the lowest color setting. Then click Apply. Follow any instructions that appear on your screen. (Your computer may restart.)

   E. Open a program or two, and look at the screen. How does it look? Note your impressions.

   F. Repeat steps A to E, this time choosing the highest color setting. Again, note your impressions.

   G. Repeat steps A to E, and select the system's original color setting.

2. **What Is Your Resolution?** Like the color setting, your system's screen resolution can affect the quality of your computing experience. If your resolution is set too high, text and icons may be too small to view comfortably, and you may strain your eyes. If the resolution is too low, you will spend extra time navigating to parts of your applications that do not fit on the screen. Try different settings to find what works best for you.

   A. Open the Control Panel window.

   B. Double-click the Display icon. The Display Properties dialog box opens.

   C. Click the Settings tab. Note the current setting in the Screen area (or screen resolution) box, and write it down.

   D. Click the Screen area slider control, and drag it to the lowest setting. Then click Apply. Follow any instructions that appear on your screen. (Your computer may restart.)

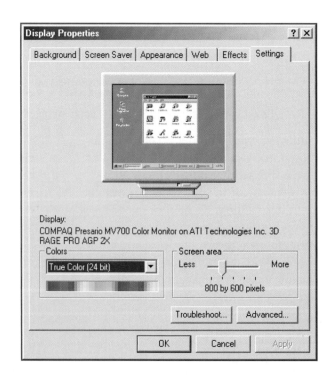

E. Open a program or two, and look at the screen. How does it look? Note your impressions.

F. Repeat steps A to E, this time choosing the highest setting. Again, note your impressions.

G. Repeat steps A to E, and select the system's original resolution setting.

DISCUSSION QUESTIONS

As directed by your instructor, discuss the following questions in class or in groups.

1. When you think about the two most frequently used output devices for computers (monitors and printers), why will color technology for printers become more commonplace, more affordable, and more necessary to many users?

2. Think about your career plans. What types of output devices will be essential to your work?

RESEARCH AND REPORT

Using your own choice of resources (such as the Internet, books, magazines, and newspaper articles), research and write a short paper discussing one of the following topics.

■ Trends in monitor sizes, features, and prices

■ The most popular type of printer among home users

■ An in-depth discussion of dye-sublimation technology and its uses

When you are finished, proofread and print your paper, and give it to your instructor.

 **ETHICAL ISSUES** We may think we cannot use a computer unless it has a full array of output devices, but is this true? With this thought in mind, discuss the following questions in class.

1. The number of unneeded printouts is growing every year. This practice wastes paper, electricity, storage space, and natural resources. It also contributes to pollution and landfill use. If you could do one thing to reduce the practice of unnecessary printing, what would it be? Would you restrict paper use in offices? Would you ration paper? Would you take printers away from certain types of workers? Would you forbid the printing of certain types of documents (such as e-mail messages)? Are such radical actions needed? If you do not agree, what types of actions would you support?

2. Because PCs provide an ever-increasing variety of multimedia options, people are spending more and more time at their computers. Much of this time is spent playing games, downloading music from the Internet, Web surfing, and so on. In fact, recent studies indicate that many computer users are addicted to the Internet or to game playing. Do these facts bother you? Why or why not? Do you worry that you spend too much time at your computer? What would you do to help a friend or coworker if you thought he or she was devoting too much time to the computer?

UNIT

4

Processing Data

UNIT CONTENTS

This unit contains the following sections:

The Interactive Browser Edition CD-ROM provides additional labs and activities to apply concepts from this unit.

Transforming Data Into Information

OVERVIEW:
The Difference Between Data and Information

It often seems as though computers must understand us, because we understand the information they produce. However, computers cannot understand anything. Computers recognize two distinct physical states produced by electricity, magnetic polarity, or reflected light. Essentially, they understand whether a switch is on or off. In fact, the CPU, which acts like the "brain" of the computer, consists of several million tiny electronic on/off switches, called **transistors.** A computer appears to understand information only because it operates at such phenomenal speeds, grouping its individual on/off switches into patterns that become meaningful to us.

In the world of computing, *data* is the term used to describe the information represented by groups of on/off switches. Although the words *data* and *information* often are used interchangeably, there is an important distinction between the two. In the strictest sense, data consists of the raw numbers that computers organize to produce information.

You can think of data as facts out of context, like the individual letters on this page. Taken individually, most of them do not have meaning. Grouped together, however, the data convey specific meanings. Just as a theater's marquee can combine thousands of lights to spell the name of the current show, a computer can group meaningless data into useful information, such as spreadsheets, graphs, and reports.

OBJECTIVES

- List two reasons why computers use the binary number system.
- List the two main parts of the CPU, and explain how they work together.
- Explain the difference between RAM and ROM.
- Identify two RAM technologies used in PCs.
- List three hardware factors that affect processing speed.

113

HOW COMPUTERS REPRESENT DATA

To a computer, everything is a number. Numbers are numbers; letters and punctuation marks are numbers; sounds and pictures are numbers. Even the computer's own instructions are numbers. When you see letters of the alphabet on a computer screen, you are seeing just one of the computer's ways of representing numbers. For example, consider this sentence: *Here are some words.* It may look like a string of alphabetic characters to you, but to a computer it looks like the string of ones and zeros shown in Figure 4A.1.

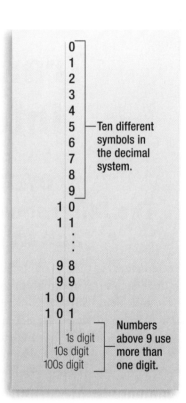

H	0100 1000
e	0110 0101
r	0111 0010
e	0110 0101
	0010 0000
a	0110 0001
r	0111 0010
e	0110 0101
	0010 0000
s	0111 0011
o	0110 1111
m	0110 1101
e	0110 0101
	0010 0000
w	0111 0111
o	0110 1111
r	0111 0010
d	0110 0100
s	0111 0011
.	0010 1110

0
1
2
3
4
5 — Ten different
6   symbols in
7   the decimal
8   system.
9
1 0
1 1
: :
9 8
9 9
1 0 0
1 0 1

1s digit
10s digit
100s digit

Numbers above 9 use more than one digit.

Figure 4A.1

These 1s and 0s represent a sentence in the binary number system. The decimal system uses ten symbols and multiple digits for the numbers 9 and higher.

Computer data looks especially strange because people normally use base 10 to represent numbers. The **decimal number system** (*deci* means "10" in Latin) is called base 10 because ten symbols are available: 0, 1, 2, 3, 4, 5, 6, 7, 8, and 9. When you need to represent a number greater than 9, you use two symbols together, as in 9 + 1 = 10. Each symbol in a number is called a digit, so 10 is a two-digit number.

In a computer, however, all data is represented by the state of the computer's electronic switches. A switch has only two possible states—on and off—so it can represent only two numeric values. To a computer, when a switch is off, it represents a 0; when a switch is on, it represents a 1 (see Figure 4A.2). Because there are only two values, computers are said to function in base 2, which also is known as the **binary number system** (*bi* means "2" in Latin).

When a computer needs to represent a quantity greater than 1, it does the same thing you do when you need to represent a quantity greater than 9: It uses two (or more) digits. To familiarize yourself with the binary system, look at Table 4A.1.

Figure 4A.2

In a computer, data is represented by the state of electronic switches. If a switch is on, it represents a 1. If a switch is off, it represents a 0.

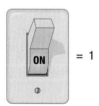

= 1

= 0

Bits and Bytes

When referring to computerized data, the value represented by each switch's state—whether the switch is turned on or off—is called a **bit** (a combination of *binary digit*). A bit is the smallest possible unit of data a computer can recognize or use. To represent anything meaningful (in other words, to convey information), the computer uses bits in groups.

A group of eight bits is called a byte (see Figure 4A.3). With 1 byte, the computer can represent one of 256 different symbols or characters, because the eight 1s and 0s in a byte can be combined in 256 different ways.

Table 4A.1	Counting in Base 10 and Base 2	
Base 10		**Base 2**
0		0
1		1
2		10
3		11
4		100
5		101
6		110
7		111
8		1000
9		1001
10		1010

The byte is an extremely important unit, because there are enough different 8-bit combinations to represent all the characters on the keyboard, including all the letters (uppercase and lowercase), numbers, punctuation marks, and other symbols. If you look back at Figure 4A.1, you will notice that each of the characters (or letters) in the sentence *Here are some words.* is represented by 1 byte (8 bits) of data.

1 bit

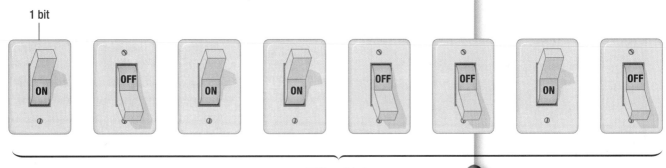

8 bits = 1 byte

Figure 4A.3
One byte is composed of eight bits.

Text Codes

Early programmers realized that they needed a standard **text code** that was agreeable to all of them. In this system, binary numbers represented the letters of the alphabet, punctuation marks, and other symbols. This standard code system would enable any programmer or program to use the same combinations of numbers to represent the same individual pieces of data. Three of the most popular text code systems invented include the following:

◆ **EBCDIC.** EBCDIC (pronounced EB-si-dic) stands for Extended Binary Coded Decimal Interchange Code. EBCDIC is an 8-bit code that defines 256 symbols. EBCDIC is still used in IBM mainframe and midrange systems, but it is rarely encountered in personal computers.

◆ **ASCII.** ASCII (pronounced AS-key) stands for the American Standard Code for Information Interchange. Today, the ASCII character set is by far the most commonly used in computers of all types. Table 4A.2 shows the first 127 ASCII codes. ASCII is an 8-bit code that specifies characters up to only 127, so there are many variations that specify different character sets for codes 128 through 255.

◆ **Unicode.** The **Unicode Worldwide Character Standard** provides two bytes—16 bits—to represent each letter, number, or symbol. With 2 bytes, enough Unicode codes can be created to represent more than 65,536 different characters or symbols. This total is enough for every unique character and symbol in the world, including the vast Chinese, Korean, and Japanese character sets and those found in known classical and historical texts. One major advantage that Unicode has over other text code systems is its compatibility with ASCII codes. The first 256 codes in Unicode are identical to the 256 codes used by ASCII systems. Unicode then extends far beyond the standard ASCII character set.

HOW COMPUTERS PROCESS DATA

Two components handle processing in a computer: the central processing unit, or CPU, and the memory. Both are located on the computer's motherboard (see Figure 4A.4), the circuit board that connects the CPU to the other hardware devices.

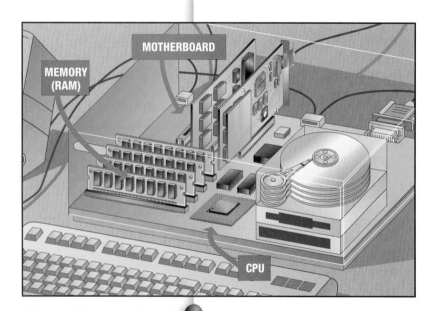

Figure 4A.4
Processing devices

The CPU

The CPU is the "brain" of the computer, the place where data is manipulated. In large computer systems, such as super-computers and mainframes, processing tasks may be handled by multiple processing chips. (Some powerful computer systems use hundreds or even thousands of separate processing units.) In the average microcomputer, the entire CPU is a single unit, called a microprocessor.

Most microprocessors are single chips mounted on a piece of plastic with metal wires attached to it. Some newer microprocessors include multiple chips and are encased in their own cover, which fits into a special socket on the motherboard. Regardless of its construction, every CPU has at least two basic parts: the control unit and the arithmetic logic unit.

The Control Unit

All the computer's resources are managed from the **control unit.** Think of the control unit as a traffic cop directing the flow of data through the CPU, as well as to and from other devices. The control unit is the logical hub of the computer (see Figure 4A.5).

Table 4A.2 ASCII Codes

ASCII Code	Decimal Equivalent	Character	ASCII Code	Decimal Equivalent	Character	ASCII Code	Decimal Equivalent	Character
0000 0000	0	Null prompt	0010 1011	43	+	0101 0110	86	V
0000 0001	1	Start of heading	0010 1100	44	,	0101 0111	87	W
0000 0010	2	Start of text	0010 1101	45	-	0101 1000	88	X
0000 0011	3	End of text	0010 1110	46	.	0101 1001	89	Y
0000 0100	4	End of transmit	0010 1111	47	/	0101 1010	90	Z
0000 0101	5	Enquiry	0011 0000	48	0	0101 1011	91	[
0000 0110	6	Acknowledge	0011 0001	49	1	0101 1100	92	\
0000 0111	7	Audible bell	0011 0010	50	2	0101 1101	93	]
0000 1000	8	Backspace	0011 0011	51	3	0101 1110	94	^
0000 1001	9	Horizontal tab	0011 0100	52	4	0101 1111	95	_
0000 1010	10	Line feed	0011 0101	53	5	0110 0000	96	`
0000 1011	11	Vertical tab	0011 0110	54	6	0110 0001	97	a
0000 1100	12	Form feed	0011 0111	55	7	0110 0010	98	b
0000 1101	13	Carriage return	0011 1000	56	8	0110 0011	99	c
0000 1110	14	Shift out	0011 1001	57	9	0110 0100	100	d
0000 1111	15	Shift in	0011 1010	58	:	0110 0101	101	e
0001 0000	16	Data link escape	0011 1011	59	;	0110 0110	102	f
0001 0001	17	Device control 1	0011 1100	60	<	0110 0111	103	g
0001 0010	18	Device control 2	0011 1101	61	=	0110 1000	104	h
0001 0011	19	Device control 3	0011 1110	62	>	0110 1001	105	i
0001 0100	20	Device control 4	0011 1111	63	?	0110 1010	106	j
0001 0101	21	Neg. acknowledge	0100 0000	64	@	0110 1011	107	k
0001 0110	22	Synchronous idle	0100 0001	65	A	0110 1100	108	l
0001 0111	23	End trans. block	0100 0010	66	B	0110 1101	109	m
0001 1000	24	Cancel	0100 0011	67	C	0110 1110	110	n
0001 1001	25	End of medium	0100 0100	68	D	0110 1111	111	o
0001 1010	26	Substitution	0100 0101	69	E	0111 0000	112	p
0001 1011	27	Escape	0100 0110	70	F	0111 0001	113	q
0001 1100	28	File separator	0100 0111	71	G	0111 0010	114	r
0001 1101	29	Group separator	0100 1000	72	H	0111 0011	115	s
0001 1110	30	Record separator	0100 1001	73	I	0111 0100	116	t
0001 1111	31	Unit separator	0100 1010	74	J	0111 0101	117	u
0010 0000	32	Blank space	0100 1011	75	K	0111 0110	118	v
0010 0001	33	!	0100 1100	76	L	0111 0111	119	w
0010 0010	34	"	0100 1101	77	M	0111 1000	120	x
0010 0011	35	#	0100 1110	78	N	0111 1001	121	y
0010 0100	36	$	0100 1111	79	O	0111 1010	122	z
0010 0101	37	%	0101 0000	80	P	0111 1011	123	{
0010 0110	38	&	0101 0001	81	Q	0111 1100	124	|
0010 0111	39	'	0101 0010	82	R	0111 1101	125	}
0010 1000	40	(	0101 0011	83	S	0111 1110	126	~
0010 1001	41	)	0101 0100	84	T	0111 1111	127	Delete or rubout
0010 1010	42	*	0101 0101	85	U			

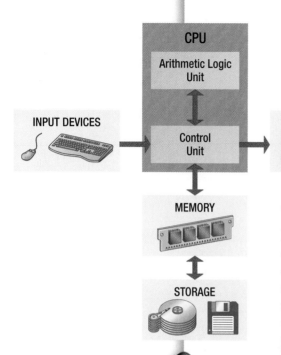

CPU

Arithmetic Logic
Unit

INPUT DEVICES

Control
Unit

OUTPUT DEVICES

MEMORY

STORAGE

Figure 4A.5
All the data that flows through the computer is directed by the control unit in the CPU.

The CPU's instructions for carrying out commands are built into the control unit. The instructions, or **instruction set,** list all the operations that the CPU can perform. Each instruction in the instruction set is expressed in **microcode**—a series of basic directions that tells the CPU how to execute more complex operations.

The Arithmetic Logic Unit

Because all computer data is stored as numbers, much of the processing that takes place involves comparing numbers or carrying out mathematical operations. In addition to establishing ordered sequences and changing those sequences, the computer can perform two types of operations: arithmetic operations and logical operations. **Arithmetic operations** include addition, subtraction, multiplication, and division. **Logical operations** include comparisons, such as determining whether one number is equal to, greater than, or less than another number. Also, every logical operation has an opposite. For example, in addition to "equal to" there is "not equal to." Table 4A.3 shows the symbols for all the arithmetic and logical operations.

Remember that some of the logical operations can be done on text data. For example, when you want to search for a word in a document, the CPU carries out a rapid succession of "equals" operations to find a match for the sequence of ASCII codes that make up the word for which you are searching.

Table 4A.3	Operations Performed by the Arithmetic Logic Unit	
Arithmetic Operations		**Logical Operations**
$+$	add	$=, \neq$ equal to, not equal to
$-$	subtract	$>, \not>$ greater than, not greater than
$\times$	multiply	$<, \not<$ less than, not less than
$\div$	divide	$\geqq, \not\geqq$ greater than or equal to, not greater than or equal to
$\wedge$	raise by a power	$\leqq, \not\leqq$ less than or equal to, not less than or equal to

Many instructions carried out by the control unit involve simply moving data from one place to another—from memory to storage, from memory to the printer, and so forth. When the control unit encounters an instruction that involves arithmetic or logic, however, it passes that instruction to the second component of the CPU— the **arithmetic logic unit,** or **ALU.** The ALU actually performs the arithmetic and logical operations described earlier.

The ALU includes a group of **registers**—high-speed memory locations built directly into the CPU that are used to hold the data currently being processed. For example, the control unit might load two numbers from memory into the registers in the ALU. Then it might tell the ALU to divide the two numbers (an arithmetic operation) or to see whether the numbers are equal (a logical operation).

Machine Cycles

Each time the CPU executes an instruction, it takes a series of steps. The completed series of steps is called a **machine cycle.** A machine cycle itself can be broken down into two smaller cycles: the **instruction cycle** and the **execution cycle.** At the beginning of the machine cycle (that is, during the instruction cycle), the CPU takes two steps:

1. **Fetching.** Before the CPU can execute an instruction, the control unit must retrieve (or **fetch**) a command or data from the computer's memory.

2. **Decoding.** Before a command can be executed, the control unit must break down (or **decode**) the command into instructions that correspond to those in the CPU's instruction set.

At this point, the CPU is ready to begin the execution cycle:

1. **Executing.** When the command is **executed,** the CPU carries out the instructions in order by converting them into microcode.

2. **Storing.** The CPU may be required to **store** the results of an instruction in memory (but this condition is not always required).

Depending on the type of processor in use, a machine cycle may include other steps. For example, some processors employ multiple decoders when translating instructions to microcode; other processors skip this step. Some processors retire the instructions after they have been executed, and collect the results in the proper order. This step may be needed if the processor can execute instructions out of order.

Although the process is complex, the computer can accomplish it at an incredible speed, translating millions of instructions every second. In fact, CPU performance is often measured in **millions of instructions per second (MIPS).**

Even though most microprocessors execute instructions rapidly, newer ones can perform even faster by using a process called **pipelining** (or pipeline processing). In pipelining, the control unit begins a new machine cycle—that is, it begins executing a new instruction—before the current cycle is completed. Executions are performed in stages; when the first instruction completes the "fetching" stage, it moves to the "decode" stage, and a new instruction is fetched. Using this technique, some microprocessors can execute up to six instructions simultaneously.

Memory

The CPU contains the basic instructions needed to operate the computer, but it cannot store entire programs or large sets of data permanently. The CPU needs to have millions (or even billions, in some computers) of bytes of space where it can quickly read or write programs and data while they are being used. This area is called memory, and it consists of chips either on the motherboard or on a small circuit board attached to the motherboard. This electronic memory allows the CPU to store and retrieve data quickly.

NORTON
ONLINE

Visit **www.norton.glencoe.com** for more information on **computer memory.**

There are two types of built-in memory: permanent and nonpermanent (see Figure 4A.6). Some memory chips retain the data they hold, even when the computer is turned off. This type of permanent memory is called **nonvolatile.** Other chips—in fact, most of the memory in a microcomputer—lose their contents when the computer's power is shut off. This type of nonpermanent memory is called **volatile.**

ROM

Nonvolatile chips always hold the same data; the data in them cannot be changed except through a special process that overwrites the data. In fact, putting data permanently into this kind of memory is called "burning in the data," and it is usually done at the factory. During normal use, the data in these chips is only read and used—not changed—so the memory is called read-only memory (ROM).

One important reason a computer needs ROM is that it must know what to do when the power is first turned on. Among other things, ROM contains a set of start-up instructions, which ensures that the rest of memory is functioning properly, checks for hardware devices, and checks for an operating system on the computer's disk drives.

RAM

Memory that can be instantly changed is called read-write memory or random-access memory (RAM). When people talk about computer memory in connection with microcomputers, they usually mean the RAM. RAM's job is to hold programs and data while they are in use. Physically, RAM consists of chips on a small circuit board (see Figure 4A.7).

A computer does not have to search its entire memory each time it needs to find data, because the CPU uses a memory address to store and retrieve each piece of data (see Figure 4A.8). A **memory address** is a number that indicates a location on the memory chips, just as a post office box number indicates a slot into which mail is placed. Memory addresses start at zero and go up to one less than the number of bytes of memory in the computer.

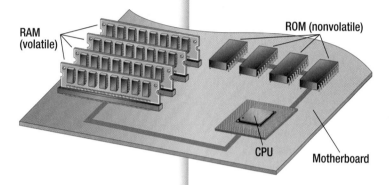

Figure 4A.6
The CPU is attached to two kinds of memory: RAM, which is volatile, and ROM, which is nonvolatile.

RAM (volatile)

ROM (nonvolatile)

CPU

Motherboard

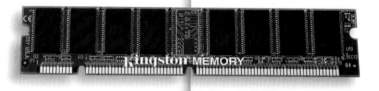

Figure 4A.7
In personal computers, RAM chips normally are mounted on a small circuit board, which plugs into the motherboard.

Figure 4A.8
To request a byte of data, the CPU sends a memory address to RAM.

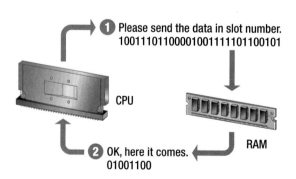

❶ Please send the data in slot number.
100111011000010011111101100101

CPU

RAM

❷ OK, here it comes.
01001100

RAM is not used just in conjunction with the computer's CPU. RAM can be found in various places in a computer system. For example, most newer video and sound cards have their own built-in RAM (see Figure 4A.9), as do many types of printers.

Several types of RAM are used in personal computers:

◆ **Dynamic RAM (DRAM).** **Dynamic RAM (DRAM)** gets its name from the fact that it must be refreshed frequently. (The term *refreshing* means recharging the RAM chips with electricity.) DRAM chips must be recharged many times each second, or they will lose their contents. Standard DRAM supports data transfer rates of about 60 nanoseconds. (A nanosecond is one-billionth of a second.) This may seem very fast, and it is, but other types of RAM are actually much faster than standard DRAM.

◆ **DRAM Variations.** **Synchronous DRAM (SDRAM)** operates faster than standard DRAM because it runs "in synch" with the computer's system clock. By running at the same speed, the CPU and SDRAM can move data much more efficiently than is possible with standard DRAM. (You will learn about the system clock later in this unit.) **Rambus Dynamic RAM (RDRAM)** and **Double Data Rate SDRAM (DDR SDRAM)** are both newer and faster variations on DRAM, and they are commonly used in today's newer computer systems (see Figure 4A.10).

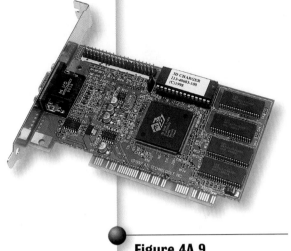

Figure 4A.9
Memory chips can be found in many parts of a computer system, such as this video card.

Dell | Home Desktops

Dimension™ 2100 Desktop

Affordable Desktop Solution
- Intel® Celeron® Processor at 1.10GHz
- 128MB shared³⁰ SDRAM at 100MHz
- 40GB⁸ Value Hard Drive
- 17" (15.9" v.i.s., .27dp) E771 Monitor
- Integrated Intel® 3D® AGP Graphics
- 48x Max CD-ROM Drive
- SB Live! 1024V Digital Sound Card
- Harman Kardon® HK-195 Speakers
- 56K⁸ PCI Data Fax Modem for Windows®
- Windows® XP Home Edition; Works Suite 2002
- 6 Months of DellNet™ by MSN® Included¹⁰
- 1-Yr Limited Warranty,² 1-Yr At-Home Service,⁴ 1-Yr 24x7 Phone Support

$799 Ask us about no payments for 90 days for qualified customers
E-VALUE Code: 01026-500307c

Dimension™ 4400 Desktop

This system has 128 MB of RAM.

Figure 4A.10
Checking the type of RAM in an ad for a new computer

◆ **Static RAM (SRAM).** **Static RAM (SRAM)** does not need to be refreshed as often as DRAM and can hold its contents longer. SRAM is considerably faster than DRAM, but it is also more expensive. For this reason, SRAM is usually used only for special purposes and not as a computer's primary RAM.

Self Check ✓

Complete each statement by filling in the blank(s).

1. A computer's CPU consists of millions of tiny switches called _transistors_ .

2. Base 2 is another name for the _binary # system_ .

3. _Unicode_ can represent more than 65,536 different characters or symbols.

NORTON ONLINE

Visit **www.norton.glencoe.com** for more information on **RAM technologies.**

At Issue

How Much Information Is Too Much?

People receive so much information through e-mail, cell phones, pagers, and the Web (not to mention television and other "traditional" sources) that dealing with it all can be difficult.

The problem of information overload (or "infoglut," as it's sometimes called) is less a result of technology than of human nature. The manner in which people deal with the information they receive often depends on their personal habits and tendencies. While television, PCs, and the Internet may be conduits for information, handling infoglut is manageable if you master your habits and keep a healthy perspective on the information that flows your way each day.

Understanding the Symptoms

You know that you need a certain amount of groceries each week. If you buy more groceries than you need, you shouldn't blame the supermarket for carrying so many items! Similarly, you gather information from many sources, including the Internet. If you spend too much time surfing the Web or reading e-mail, you shouldn't blame the Internet for causing you to run short of time. We all consume information, just as we consume groceries; however, it pays to be a smart consumer.

To cure infoglut, start by examining your own behavior. By answering the following questions; you may figure out whether you are addicted to receiving too much information:

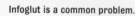
Infoglut is a common problem.

- Do you feel obligated to read or listen to all the information you receive?

- Do you believe that all information is important?

- Do you search for more information than you need?

- Do you assume that other people always want to see the information you receive?

- Do you have trouble getting rid of information you don't need?

- Do you use e-mail instead of talking face to face, even when the other person is nearby?

- Do you feel overwhelmed (even victimized) by all the information you receive, yet powerless to solve the problem?

If you answer "yes" to any of these questions, then you should evaluate your habits as an information consumer.

Dealing With the Problem

If you are an "infoglutton," you can solve the problem by setting some simple rules:

- **Set priorities for information.** Decide what information is important, and give it priority. Save the other information to read when you have free time, or discard it.

- **Set time limits.** Many infoglut sufferers are slaves to their e-mail and voice mail, checking it several times a day. Set aside one or two blocks of time during the day for using e-mail.

- **Be selective.** Focus on the information you need or are most interested in; let the rest go by.

- **Share only items of interest that need to be shared.** Resist the urge to make multiple copies of a magazine article to share with coworkers. Similarly, forward e-mail messages and Web pages to friends and colleagues only when it is necessary.

- **Avoid using technology as a substitute for personal communication.** Some people view an e-mail message as impersonal. Face-to-face contact or a phone call is more appropriate when the message is very important or cannot be explained in a few words.

- **Delete items that you do not need to keep.** Develop a filing system for storing important items you need to keep. Get rid of everything else.

FACTORS AFFECTING PROCESSING SPEED

A CPU's design determines its basic speed, but other factors can make chips already designed for speed work even faster. You already have been introduced to some of these, such as the CPU's registers and memory. In this section, you will see how other factors—such as the cache memory, the clock speed, and the data bus—affect a computer's speed. Figure 4A.11 shows how these components might be arranged on the computer's motherboard.

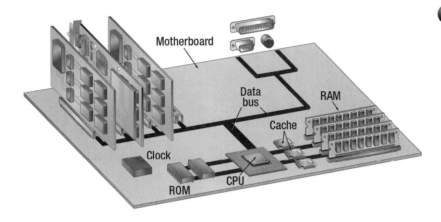

Figure 4A.11
Devices affecting processing speed

Registers

The registers in the first PCs could hold two bytes—16 bits—each. Most CPUs sold today, for both PCs and Macintosh computers, have 32-bit registers. Many newer PCs, as well as minicomputers and high-end workstations, have 64-bit registers.

The size of the registers, which sometimes is called the **word size,** indicates the amount of data with which the computer can work at any given time. The bigger the word size, the more quickly the computer can process a set of data. Occasionally, you will hear people refer to "32-bit processors," or "64-bit processors," or even "64-bit computers." This terminology refers to the size of the registers in the processor. If all other factors are kept equal, a CPU with 32-bit registers can process data twice as fast as one with 16-bit registers.

Memory and Computing Power

The amount of RAM in a computer can have a profound effect on the computer's power. More RAM means the computer can use bigger, more powerful programs, and those programs can access bigger data files.

More RAM also can make the computer run faster. The computer does not necessarily have to load an entire program into memory to run it. However, the greater the amount of the program that fits into memory, the faster the program runs. To run Windows, for example, the computer usually does not need to load all its files into memory to run properly; it loads only the most essential parts into memory.

When the computer needs access to other parts of a program or data on the disk, it can unload, or **swap out,** nonessential parts from RAM to the hard disk. Then the computer can load, or **swap in,** the program code or data it needs. While this is an effective method for managing a limited amount of memory, the computer's system performance is slower because the CPU, memory, and disk are

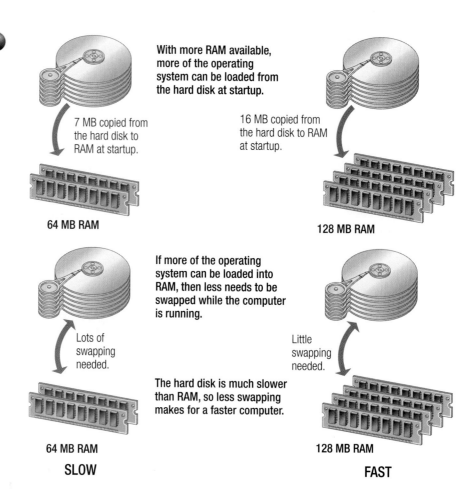

With more RAM available, more of the operating system can be loaded from the hard disk at startup.

7 MB copied from the hard disk to RAM at startup.

16 MB copied from the hard disk to RAM at startup.

64 MB RAM

128 MB RAM

If more of the operating system can be loaded into RAM, then less needs to be swapped while the computer is running.

Lots of swapping needed.

Little swapping needed.

The hard disk is much slower than RAM, so less swapping makes for a faster computer.

64 MB RAM
SLOW

128 MB RAM
FAST

continuously occupied with the swapping process. As shown in Figure 4A.12, if your PC has 128 MB of RAM (or more), you will notice a dramatic difference in how fast Windows runs, because the CPU will need to swap program instructions between RAM and the hard disk much less often.

If you purchase a new computer system, it probably will come with at least 128 MB of RAM, although 256 MB is rapidly becoming the standard minimum for PCs. If you already own a PC and decide that it needs more RAM, usually you can purchase additional RAM, open up your computer, and plug it in.

In today's computers, RAM chips usually are grouped together on small circuit boards called **single in-line memory modules (SIMMs)** or **dual in-line memory modules (DIMMs),** both of which are shown in Figure 4A.13. The primary difference between SIMMs and DIMMs is the arrangement of the pins along one edge, which connect them to the computer's motherboard. Rambus DRAM comes in its own type of circuit board, called a **Rambus in-line memory module (RIMM).** The cost of upgrading the memory of a computer has actually gone down, so upgrading RAM is often the most cost-effective way to boost your PC's performance.

Figure 4A.13
On the top is a SIMM; on the bottom is a DIMM.

The Computer's Internal Clock

Every microcomputer has a **system clock,** but keeping the time of day is not the clock's primary purpose. Like most modern wristwatches, the clock is driven by a quartz crystal. When electricity is applied, the molecules in the crystal vibrate millions of times per second, at a rate that never changes. The speed of the vibrations is determined by the thickness of the crystal. The computer uses the vibrations of the quartz in the system clock to time its processing operations.

Over the years, system clocks have become steadily faster. For example, the first PC operated at 4.77 megahertz. **Hertz (Hz)** is a measure of cycles per second. **Megahertz (MHz)** means "millions of cycles per second." **Gigahertz (GHz)** means "billions of cycles per second."

The computer's operating speed is tied to the speed of the system clock. For example, if a computer's **clock speed** is 800 MHz, it "ticks" 800 million times per second. A **clock cycle** is a single tick, or the time it takes to turn a transistor off and back on again. A processor can execute an instruction in a given number of clock cycles. As the system's clock speed increases, so does the number of instructions it can carry out each second.

Clock speeds of 1 GHz and higher are now common, and processor speeds are increasing rapidly. At the time this book was written, processor speeds had eclipsed 2 GHz.

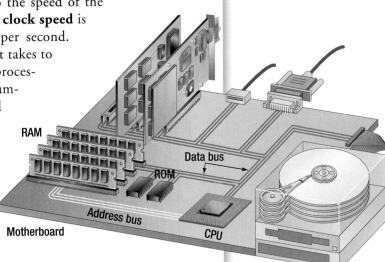

Figure 4A.14
The system bus includes an address bus and a data bus. The address bus leads from the CPU to RAM. The data bus connects the CPU to memory, and to all the storage, input/output, and communications devices that are attached to the motherboard.

RAM

Data bus

ROM

Address bus

Motherboard

CPU

Disk drives

The Bus

A **bus** is a path between the components of a computer. There are two main buses in a computer: the internal (or system) bus and the external (or expansion) bus. The system bus resides on the motherboard and connects the CPU to other devices that reside on the motherboard. An expansion bus connects external devices, such as the keyboard, mouse, modem, printer, and so on, to the CPU. Cables from disk drives and other internal devices are plugged into the bus. The system bus has two parts: the data bus and the address bus (see Figure 4A.14).

The Data Bus

The **data bus** is an electrical path that connects the CPU, memory, and the other hardware devices on the motherboard. Actually, the bus is a group of parallel wires. The number of wires in the bus affects the speed at which data can travel between hardware components, just as the number of lanes on a highway affects how long it takes people to reach their destinations. Because each wire can transfer 1 bit of data at a time, an 8-wire bus can move 8 bits at a time, which is a full byte (see Figure 4A.15). A 16-bit bus can transfer 2 bytes, and a 32-bit bus can transfer 4 bytes at a time. Newer model computers have a 64-bit data bus, which transfers 8 bytes at a time.

Like the processor, the bus' speed is measured in megahertz (MHz) because it has its own clock speed. As you would imagine, the faster a bus' clock speed, the faster it can transfer data between parts of the computer. The majority of today's PCs have a bus speed of either 100 MHz or 133 MHz, but higher speeds are becoming more common.

Figure 4A.15
With a wider bus, the computer can move more data in the same amount of time, or the same amount of data in less time.

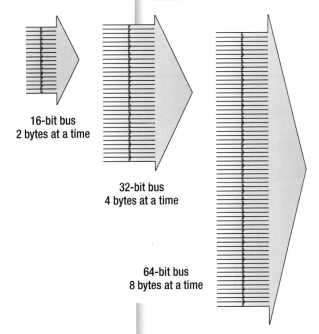

16-bit bus
2 bytes at a time

32-bit bus
4 bytes at a time

64-bit bus
8 bytes at a time

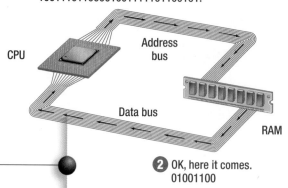

① Please send the data in slot number
1001110110000100111110110010 1.

CPU

Address
bus

Data bus

RAM

② OK, here it comes.
01001100

Figure 4A.16

Requests for data are sent from the CPU to RAM along the address bus. The request consists of a memory address. The data comes back to the CPU via the data bus.

NORTON
ONLINE

Visit **www.norton.glencoe.com** for more information on **bus technologies**.

The Address Bus

The **address bus** is a set of wires similar to the data bus (see Figure 4A.16). The address bus connects only the CPU and RAM and carries only memory addresses. (Remember, each byte in RAM is associated with a number, which is its memory address.)

Bus Types

PC buses are designed to match the capabilities of the devices attached to them. When CPUs could send and receive only 1 byte of data at a time, there was no point in connecting them to a bus that could move more data. As microprocessor technology improved, however, chips were built that could send and receive more data at once, and improved bus designs created wider paths through which the data could flow. Common bus technologies include:

◆ The **Industry Standard Architecture (ISA) bus** is a 16-bit data bus. After its release in the mid-1980s, ISA became the de facto industry standard, and it is still used in many computers to attach slower devices (such as modems and input devices) to the CPU.

◆ **Local bus** technology was developed to attach faster devices to the CPU. A local bus is an internal system bus that runs between components on the motherboard. Most system buses use some type of local bus technology today and are coupled with one or more kinds of expansion bus.

◆ The **Peripheral Component Interconnect (PCI) bus** is a type of local bus designed by Intel to make it easier to integrate new data types, such as audio, video, and graphics.

◆ The **Accelerated Graphics Port (AGP) bus** incorporates a special architecture that allows the video card to access the system's RAM directly, greatly increasing the speed of graphics performance. The AGP standard has led to the development of many types of accelerated video cards that support 3-D and full-motion video. While AGP improves graphics performance, it cannot be used with all PCs. The system must use a chip set that supports the AGP standard. Most new computers feature AGP graphics capabilities in addition to a PCI system bus and an expansion bus.

◆ Two relatively new bus technologies—**Universal Serial Bus (USB)** and **IEEE 1394 (FireWire)**—not only provide fast data transfer speeds, they also eliminate the need for expansion slots and boards. Most new PCs and Macintosh computers feature at least one USB port, and each USB port can support 127 different devices. FireWire ports were once found only on Macintosh computers, but they are now increasingly common in IBM-compatible PCs. If you have USB- or FireWire-compliant devices such as keyboards, mice, printers, and modems, you can plug them all into a single USB port.

Traditionally, the performance of computer buses was measured by the number of bits they could transfer at one time. Hence, the newest 64-bit buses are typically considered the fastest available. However, buses now are also being measured according to their **data transfer rates**—the amount of data they can transfer in a second. This type of performance usually is measured in **megabits per second (Mbps)** or **megabytes per second (MBps).**

For example, the newest version of USB supports a data transfer rate of 480 Mbps. An IEEE 1394 bus has a data transfer rate of 400 Mbps. AGP buses are typically rated at 266 MBps, but they can support data transfer rates of more than 1 GBps. PCI buses offer data transfer rates of 133 MBps.

Cache Memory

Moving data between RAM and the CPU's registers is one of the most time-consuming operations a CPU must perform, simply because RAM, is much slower than the CPU. A partial solution to this problem is to include a cache memory in the CPU. **Cache** (pronounced *cash*) **memory** is similar to RAM, except that it is extremely fast compared to normal memory, and it is used in a different way.

Figure 4A.17 shows how cache memory works with the CPU and RAM. When a program is running and the CPU needs to read data or program instructions from RAM, the CPU checks first to see whether the data is in cache memory. If the data is not there, the CPU reads the data from RAM into its registers, but it also loads a copy of the data into cache memory. The next time the CPU needs that same data, it finds it in the cache memory and saves the time needed to load the data from RAM.

Since the late 1980s, most PC CPUs have cache memory built into them. This CPU-resident cache is often called **Level-1 (L1) cache.** Today, many CPUs have as much as 256 KB built in.

In addition to the cache memory built into the CPU, cache is also added to the motherboard. This motherboard-resident cache is often called **Level-2 (L2) cache.** Many PCs being sold today have 512 KB or 1024 KB of motherboard cache memory; higher-end systems can have as much as 2 MB of L2 cache.

Visit www.norton.glencoe.com for more information on **cache memory**.

Figure 4A.17
The cache speeds processing by storing frequently used data or instructions in its high-speed memory. External (Level-2) cache is shown here, but most computers also have memory circuitry built directly into the CPU.

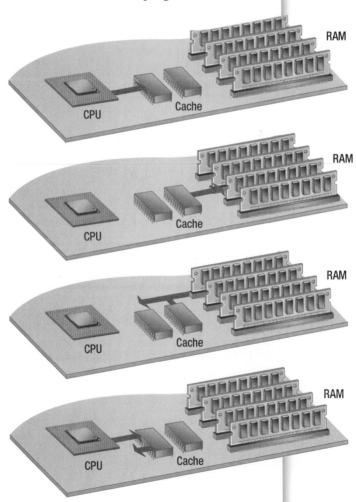

PRODUCTIVITY Tip

Do You Need More RAM?

You have probably heard it a hundred times: RAM upgrades are cheap, easy, and fast—a great way to improve your PC's performance. But is it really as simple and inexpensive as the experts keep saying?

Well, yes and no. A lot of factors determine how costly or difficult a RAM upgrade will be, and other factors determine whether it will even do you any good. But make no mistake about it: If your computer is running slower than you like, adding RAM may give it some pep. If your PC is relatively new, you may want to consider installing more RAM before trading up to a new system. The performance boost could make you want to keep that old PC a while longer.

If your PC is more than a couple of years old, and if you are becoming increasingly unhappy with its performance, then perhaps it is time to think about a memory upgrade. If that sounds like an overly simplistic approach to making the decision, ask yourself the following questions:

◆ Does your PC have less than 128 MB of RAM?

◆ Do you typically run more than one application at a time?

◆ Are you using a newer version of Windows, such as Windows Me, 2000, or XP?

◆ Does the system noticeably slow down during a long computing session, especially if you launch and close multiple programs or use the Internet?

A RAM upgrade may be the fastest, cheapest, and easiest way to improve your PC's performance.

◆ Do you need to reboot frequently?

◆ Do you ever see "insufficient memory" messages when you try to run a program or load a file?

◆ Does your hard disk light seem to flicker most of the time?

If you can answer "yes" to more than one of those questions, then a RAM upgrade may be a good idea.

The decision to upgrade does not require a degree in computer science, and you do not need to do much math. You should base your decision to upgrade on your satisfaction with the computer's performance. You should compare the cost and probable benefits of a RAM upgrade with the expense of a more thorough upgrade (such as replacing a processor, motherboard, and hard disk) or simply buying a new system.

Deciding to upgrade RAM offers two big advantages. First, it is less expensive than just about any other kind of upgrade you can do. Second, even if the upgrade does not improve your computer's performance a lot, it probably will not hurt anything, either.

You should not expect a RAM upgrade to speed up your system the way a new processor would. In fact, experts say that there is no reason to put more than 512 MB of RAM in most personal computers. Depending on the types of applications that are run, additional memory may not even be used, because Windows allocates a certain amount of memory for itself and for each running application.

On the other hand, if your PC is short on RAM, it will not be able to run current software products very efficiently. For example, the practical minimum for a PC running Windows 98 or Me is now considered to be 64 MB, and for running Windows 2000 or XP, the minimum is 128 MB. These requirements will give the PC enough memory to load essential operating system components and a couple of applications. Beyond that, however, the system has to rely on the hard disk as a source of "virtual memory," requiring the hard disk and RAM to spend time swapping data back and forth as it is needed. This process greatly reduces performance.

Realistically, the only way to answer this question is to do the upgrade. Chances are probable that you will notice at least some improvement in your system's behavior.

SUMMARY

- Computer data is reduced to binary numbers because computer processing is performed by transistors that have only two possible states: on and off.

- The binary number system works the same way as the decimal system, except that it has only two available symbols (0 and 1) rather than ten (0, 1, 2, 3, 4, 5, 6, 7, 8, and 9).

- A single unit of data is called a bit; 8 bits make up 1 byte.

- In the most common text-code set, ASCII, each character consists of 1 byte of data. In the Unicode text-code set, each character consists of 2 bytes of data.

- A microcomputer's processing takes place in the central processing unit, the two main parts of which are the control unit and the arithmetic logic unit (ALU).

- Within the CPU, program instructions are retrieved and translated with the help of an internal instruction set and the accompanying microcode.

- The CPU follows a set of steps for each instruction it carries out. This set of steps is called the machine cycle. By using a technique called pipelining, many CPUs can process more than one instruction at a time.

- The actual manipulation of data takes place in the ALU, which is connected to registers that hold data and program instructions while they are being processed.

- Random-access memory (RAM) is volatile (or temporary). Programs and data can be written to and erased from RAM as needed.

- Read-only memory (ROM) is nonvolatile (or permanent). It holds instructions that run the computer when the power is first turned on.

- The CPU accesses each location in memory by using a unique number, called the memory address.

- The size of the registers, also called word size, determines the amount of data with which the computer can work at one time.

- The amount of RAM can affect speed because the CPU can keep more of the active program and data in memory, which is faster than storage on disk.

- The computer's system clock sets the pace for the CPU by using a vibrating quartz crystal. The faster the clock, the more instructions the CPU can process per second.

- The system bus has two parts—the data bus and the address bus—both of which are located on the motherboard.

- The width of the data bus determines how many bits can be transmitted at a time between the CPU and other devices.

- Peripheral devices can be connected to the CPU by way of an expansion bus.

- Cache memory is a type of high-speed memory that contains the most recent data and instructions that have been loaded by the CPU. The amount of cache memory has a tremendous impact on the computer's speed.

KEY TERMS

Accelerated Graphics Port (AGP) bus, *126*
address bus, *126*
arithmetic logic unit (ALU), *118*
arithmetic operation, *118*
ASCII, *116*
binary number system, *114*
bit, *115*
bus, *125*
cache memory, *127*
clock cycle, *125*
clock speed, *125*
control unit, *116*
data bus, *125*
data transfer rate, *127*
decimal number system, *114*
decode, *119*
Double Data Rate SDRAM (DDR SDRAM), *121*
dual in-line memory module (DIMM), *124*
dynamic RAM (DRAM), *121*
EBCDIC, *115*

execute, *119*
execution cycle, *119*
fetch, *119*
Gigahertz (GHz), *125*
Hertz (Hz), *125*
IEEE 1394 (FireWire), *126*
Industry Standard Architecture (ISA) bus, *126*
instruction cycle, *119*
instruction set, *118*
Level-1 (L1) cache, *127*
Level-2 (L2) cache, *127*
local bus, *126*
logical operation, *118*
machine cycle, *119*
megabits per second (Mbps), *127*
megabytes per second (MBps), *127*
Megahertz (MHz), *125*
memory address, *120*
microcode, *118*
millions of instructions per second (MIPS), *119*
nonvolatile, *120*

Peripheral Component Interconnect (PCI) bus, *126*
pipelining, *119*
Rambus Dynamic RAM (RDRAM), *121*
Rambus in-line memory module (RIMM), *124*
register, *119*
single in-line memory module (SIMM), *124*
Static RAM (SRAM), *121*
store, *119*
swap in, *123*
swap out, *123*
synchronous DRAM (SDRAM), *121*
system clock, *124*
text code, *115*
transistor, *113*
Unicode Worldwide Character Standard, *116*
Universal Serial Bus (USB), *126*
volatile, *120*
word size, *123*

KEY TERM QUIZ

Complete each statement by writing one of the terms listed under Key Terms in each blank.

1. People use the _____ number system, but computers use the _____ number system.

2. The term _bit_ is a combination of the words *binary digit*.

3. The most widely used text code system among personal computers is _ASCII_ .

4. A processor's built-in instructions are stored as _microcode_

5. _cache_ are high-speed memory locations built directly into the CPU, which hold data while it is being processed.

SECTION QUIZ

True/False

Answer the following questions by circling True or False.

True   (False)   1. The only things a computer can understand are yes and no. *off on*

True   (False)   2. Base 2 is another name for the decimal number system. *binary*

True   (False)   3. Unicode is by far the most commonly used text code system. *ASCII*

(True)   False   4. The CPU's control unit contains a list of all the operations that the CPU can perform.

(True)   False   5. Static RAM is considerably faster than dynamic RAM.

Multiple Choice

Circle the word or phrase that best completes each statement.

1. The _Unicode_ standard promises to provide enough characters to cover all the world's languages.
   A. ASCII   **B.** Unicode   **C.** RAM

2. _____ may be built directly into a CPU or placed on the motherboard.
   A. RAM   **B.** Cache memory   **C.** Neither A nor B

3. The CPU uses a _____ to store and retrieve each piece of data in memory.
   A. control unit   **B.** cache   **C.** memory address

4. The computer can move data and instructions between storage and memory, as needed, in a process called _____ .
   A. swapping   **B.** volatility   **C.** pipelining

5. A bus's _____ is measured in Mbps or MBps.
   A. clock speed   **B.** daisy chain   **C.** data transfer rate

REVIEW QUESTIONS

In your own words, briefly answer the following questions.

1. What is the difference between data and information?

2. How many characters or symbols can be represented by one 8-bit byte?

3. What is meant by "word size"?

4. What is the difference between arithmetic operations and logical operations?

5. What is a data bus?

SECTION LABS

Complete the following exercises as directed by your instructor.

1. Using the list of ASCII characters in Table 4A.2, compose a sentence using ASCII text codes. Make sure the sentence includes at least six words, and make it a complete sentence. (Be sure to include blank spaces, and use punctuation.) Swap your ASCII sentence with a classmate, then translate his or her sentence into alphabetical characters. Time yourself. How long did it take you to translate the sentence? What does this tell you about the speed of a computer's processor?

2. See how much RAM your computer has. Open the Control Panel. In the Control Panel window, double-click the System icon. In the System Properties window, click the General tab. General information about your system should appear on this tab. Note the amount of RAM. Close the System Properties window, then close Control Panel.

CPUs Used in Personal Computers

OBJECTIVES

- Name the two best-known families of CPUs.
- Differentiate the processors used in Macintosh and IBM-compatible PCs.
- Define the terms CISC and RISC.
- Identify one advantage of using multiple processors in a computer.
- Identify four connections used to attach devices to a PC.

OVERVIEW:
The Race for the Desktop

How fast is fast enough? How powerful does a computer need to be? We may never know the ultimate answer to these questions, because when it comes to computer performance, the bar continues to be raised.

Software developers and users constantly make greater demands of computers, requiring them to perform an ever-higher number of tasks. Processor developers respond with chips of ever-increasing speed and power. Chip makers such as Intel, Motorola, Advanced Micro Devices (AMD), and others keep proving that there seems to be no end to the potential power of the personal computer.

This section looks at the processors most commonly found in personal computers and describes some of their most important features and distinguishing characteristics. You will learn how these CPUs are typically differentiated from one another and see how their performance is measured. You also will learn some of the ways you can extend the power of your PC's processor to other components by using its expansion capabilities.

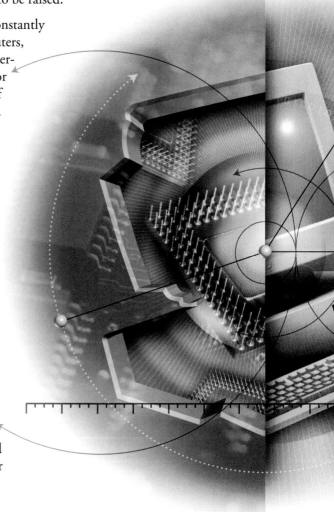

A LOOK INSIDE THE PROCESSOR

You already have seen how a PC processes and moves data. For most people, the great mystery of the PC is what takes place inside its circuitry. How can this box of chips, wires, and other parts—most of which don't even move—do its work?

A processor's performance—even its ability to function—is dictated by its internal design, or **architecture.** A chip's architecture determines where its parts are located and connected, how it connects with other parts of the computer, and much more. It also determines the path that electricity (in the form of moving electrons) takes as it moves through the processor, turning its transistors on and off. There are many different chip architectures in use today, and each family of PC processors is based on its own unique architecture.

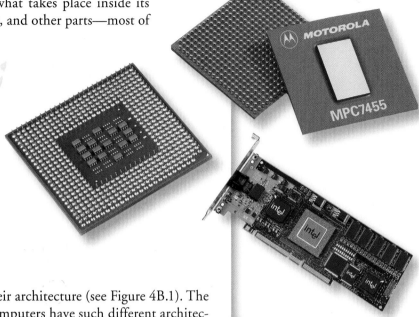

In fact, processors are differentiated by their architecture (see Figure 4B.1). The processors of IBM PCs and Macintosh computers have such different architectures, for example, that they cannot even run the same software; operating systems and software must be written to run on each processor's specific architecture, to meet its requirements.

Figure 4B.1
Different processors have different architectures. In some cases, architectures are so different that processors cannot run the same software. For this reason, software must be written especially for IBM-compatible PCs, Macintosh computers, and workstations.

A processor's architecture determines how many transistors it has, and therefore the processor's power (see Figure 4B.2). Simply stated, the more transistors in a processor, the more powerful it is. The earliest microprocessors had a few thousand transistors. The processors in today's PCs contain tens of millions. In the most powerful workstation and server computers, a processor may contain hundreds of millions of transistors. When a computer is configured to use multiple processors, it ultimately can contain billions of transistors.

Figure 4B.2
Transistors are a key ingredient in any processor. The more transistors available, the more powerful the processor.

Chip designers are constantly looking for ways to squeeze more transistors into their processors, while keeping the processor itself as small as possible. (Tiny processors are what make small computers like PDAs and laptops possible.) A processor chip is made of silicon or some other semiconductive material; the transistors themselves and the connections between them are actually etched into the chip's surface.

One way to get more transistors into a chip is to produce the chip in layers; each layer has its own set of transistors and connections. Another way is to reduce the amount of space between the etched transistors and connections. At the time of this writing, that amount of space

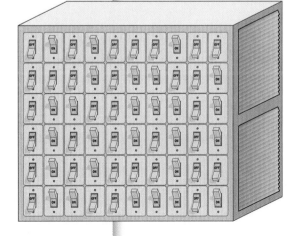

had been reduced to 0.13 microns in some processors. (A **micron** is one-millionth of a meter.) In fact, designers worry that they soon may not be able to squeeze more transistors into a chip because at these tolerances, electrons can actually jump from one transistor to another. When that happens, chip circuitry malfunctions.

A processor includes many other features that affect its performance. For example, a processor's performance is affected by the number of bits of data it can process at any one time. Currently, nearly all standard PC processors move data in 32-bit chunks; they are called "32-bit processors." Within the next few years, however, a new generation of desktop PC processors will handle 64 bits of data. (High-end workstations and many minicomputer systems have used 64-bit processors for about a decade.)

MICROCOMPUTER PROCESSORS

For two decades after the birth of the personal computer, the biggest player in the PC CPU market was Intel Corporation. This dominance began to change in 1998, when several leading computer makers began offering lower-priced systems using chips made by American Micro Devices (AMD) and other chip manufacturers. These microprocessors were comparable in many respects to chips made by Intel, but they typically offered less performance at a lower price. That situation changed, however, as AMD made rapid advances in its products' capabilities. Today, Intel and AMD chips compete head to head, not only in performance, but also in price.

Meanwhile, Motorola continues making the processors used in Macintosh computers, and many other companies make specialized processors for workstations, minicomputers, mainframe systems, and handheld computing devices. These processors are all very different (at least, in terms of their architectures) from the processors described in the following sections, which are used in IBM-compatible PCs.

As you read the following sections, remember that performance specifications and features can change rapidly. Chip manufacturers make constant improvements to their products; as a result, the most popular PC processors now operate at speeds higher than 2 GHz, and they continue to be faster every month. By continuously refining chip designs and manufacturing processes, chip makers are always finding ways to add more transistors to chips.

Intel Processors

Intel is historically the leading provider of chips for PCs. In 1971, Intel invented the microprocessor—the so-called computer on a chip—with the 4004 model (see Figure 4B.3). This invention led to the first microcomputers that began appearing in 1975. Even so, Intel's success in this market was not guaranteed until 1981, when IBM released the first IBM PC, which was based on an Intel microprocessor.

A list of current Intel chips (see Figure 4B.4), along with their clock speeds and numbers of transistors, is shown in Table 4B.1.

In 2000, Intel released the Itanium processor, a 64-bit chip designed for use in high-end workstations and network servers. Itanium processors run at speeds of 800 MHz and higher and can utilize far more RAM than Pentium, Xeon, or Celeron chips can.

Visit **www.norton.glencoe.com** for more information on **Intel's line of products.**

Figure 4B.3
Intel's first microprocessor, the 4004

Figure 4B.4
The Pentium 4, Celeron, Itanium, Pentium III Xeon, and Pentium III processors

Table 4B.1	Intel Processors Used in Today's Personal Computers	
Model	**Clock Speed**	**Number of Transistors**
Pentium 4	1.4 GHz and up	42–55 million
Pentium III Xeon	700 MHz and up	42–55 million
Pentium III	650 MHz and up	28–44 million
Celeron	500 MHz and up	28–44 million

Figure 4B.5
The Athlon and Duron processors

Advanced Micro Devices (AMD) Processors

In 1998, **Advanced Micro Devices (AMD)** emerged as a primary competitor to Intel's dominance in the IBM-compatible PC market. Until that time, AMD processors typically were found in lower-performance, low-priced home and small business computers that sold for less than $1,000. With the release of the K6 and Athlon processor series, AMD proved that it could compete, feature for feature, with many of Intel's best-selling products. AMD even began a new race for the fastest PC processor.

A list of current AMD chips (see Figure 4B.5), along with their clock speeds and numbers of transistors, is shown in Table 4B.2.

Table 4B.2	AMD Processors Used in Today's Personal Computers	
Model	**Clock Speed**	**Number of Transistors**
Athlon	1.0 GHz and up	37 million
Duron	600 MHz and up	25 million

Motorola Processors

Motorola is another major manufacturer of microprocessors for small computers. As mentioned earlier, Apple's Macintosh computers use Motorola processors. Other computer manufacturers, including workstation manufacturers such as Sun Microsystems, also have relied heavily on Motorola chips. Motorola processors were an early favorite among companies that built larger, UNIX-based computers.

Today, Motorola offers two families of processor chips that are used in Macintosh computers. The first is known as the $680x0$ family. This family of processors has almost completely been replaced by a new type of processor, which was developed by Motorola, Apple, and IBM. This new processor, called the PowerPC processor, is the basis for all new computers made by Apple. The PowerPC processor comes in two models, the G3 and the G4 (see Figure 4B.6).

Figure 4B.6
The PowerPC processors

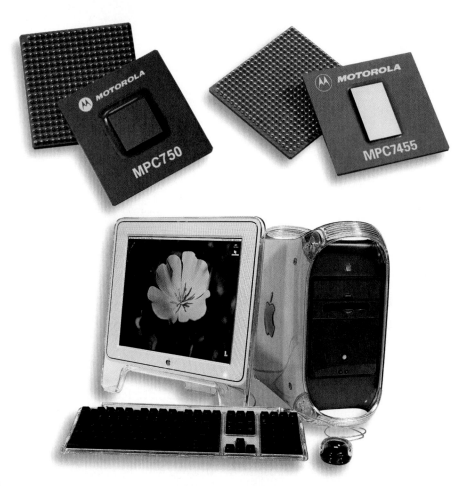

Self Check

Complete each statement by filling in the blank(s).

1. Intel invented the _microprocessor_.

2. The Athlon and Duron processors are made by _AMD_.

3. Macintosh computers use processors made by _Motorola_.

Norton Notebook

WHAT *IS* A COMPUTER CHIP?

Throughout this book (and in any other information you read about computers), you see references to chips. Processors reside on chips, as do memory and other types of computer circuitry. But what does this mean? What is a computer chip?

To understand how chips work, you have to think small . . . very, very small. That's because the transistors, circuits, and connections that exist on a computer chip are so tiny that their dimensions are sometimes measured in terms of atoms rather than millimeters or inches.

Most computer chips are created on very thin wafers, which are made of nearly pure silicon. (Silicon is a mineral that is purified and refined for use in chips. It is used in many other products, too.) Some chips may be made from other materials, such as various types of plastic, but the chips commonly found in personal computers are silicon-based.

The Making of a Chip

Transistors and circuits exist as tiny channels on the surface of a chip, which means they must be carved out of the silicon. To do this, chip manufacturers use a process called photolithography to physically etch out the tiny grooves and notches that make up the chip's circuits. In the first step of this process, the silicon wafer's surface is covered with a gooey substance called photoresist, which is sensitive to certain types of light.

Next, a glass pattern (called a mask) is placed over the wafer. This pattern is marked with the precise lines where each transistor and circuit will lie on the chip's surface. The manufacturer then shines ultraviolet light through the pattern; the pattern's dark lines "mask" the silicon wafer from the light, protecting it. The exposed photoresist reacts to the light that touches it, softening the silicon beneath it. The exposed silicon is washed away, leaving a pattern of fine tracings on its surface.

The manufacturer then coats the wafer's surface with ions. This coating changes the way the silicon conducts electricity, making it more efficient at moving electrons through its circuits. (Moving electrons represent the binary 1s and 0s that make up data for the computer.) Because electrons are so small, the chip's circuitry can be very fine.

In the next step of the process, atoms of metal (such as aluminum or copper) are placed in the etched channels on the wafer's surface. These connections will conduct electrons as they move through the chip.

So Many Transistors, So Little Space

Today's manufacturing processes are so precise that they can squeeze millions of transistors onto a single chip that is not much larger than a person's thumbnail. One way to achieve this is by etching the chip's surface in separate layers, literally stacking sets of circuits on top of one another.

Another way is to place those circuits closer and closer together. Currently, chip makers can place transistors so close that they are separated by less than a micron. (A micron is one-millionth of a meter.) Production technologies are constantly being refined. Today's popular PC processors contain tens of millions of transistors; in a few years, there may be as many as one billion transistors on a single processor chip.

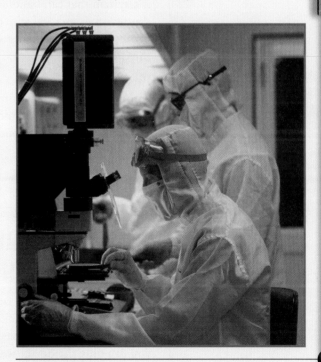

Chip designs are constantly evolving, making processors ever faster and more powerful.

RISC PROCESSORS

The processors in IBM-compatible PCs are **complex instruction set computing (CISC)** processors. The instruction sets for these CPUs are large, typically containing 200 to 300 instructions.

Another theory in microprocessor design holds that if the instruction set for the CPU is kept small and simple, each instruction will execute in much less time, allowing the processor to complete more instructions during a given period. CPUs designed according to this theory are called **reduced instruction set computing (RISC)** processors. RISC instruction sets are considerably smaller than those used by CISC processors. The RISC design, which is used in the PowerPC processor but was first implemented in the mid-1980s, results in a faster and less expensive processor. Because of the way the Pentium and its spin-offs process instructions, they are called RISC-like, but their architecture is still based on complex instruction set computing.

Figure 4B.7
This AlphaServer 1200 system is a RISC-based enterprise server. Some of the most powerful network servers and workstations are based on RISC technology.

RISC technology has been the engine of mainframe systems, minicomputers, and many types of high-end workstations for years (see Figure 4B.7). The PowerPC and G3/G4 processors reflected a major move on the part of industry giants toward using RISC technology in desktop and notebook computers.

PARALLEL PROCESSING

An emerging school of thought on producing faster PCs is to build them with more than one processor. This type of system uses **parallel processing;** that is, the system harnesses multiple processors that share the processing workload. The result is a system that can handle a much greater flow of data, complete more tasks in a shorter time, and deal with the demands of many input and output devices. Parallel processing also is called **multiprocessing (MP)** or **symmetric multiprocessing (SMP).**

Visit **www.norton.glencoe.com** for more information on **RISC processors.**

Parallel processing is not a new idea in the minicomputer, mainframe, and supercomputer arenas. Manufacturers have developed computers with hundreds and even thousands of microprocessors—systems known as **massively parallel processing (MPP)** computers.

At the other end of the spectrum, multiple-processor versions of PCs are available today; they are commonly used as network servers, Internet host computers, and stand-alone workstations.

EXTENDING THE PROCESSOR'S POWER TO OTHER DEVICES

You already have learned that all the components of a computer tie into the computer's CPU by way of the bus. When you need to add a new piece of hardware to your computer, you need to know how to connect it to the bus. In some cases, you can plug the device into an existing socket, or port, on the back of the computer. Most computers have several types of ports, each with different capabilities and uses. Older computers feature only three or four distinct types of ports, but new systems provide a wide array of specialized ports. When a port is not available, you must install a circuit board that includes the port you need.

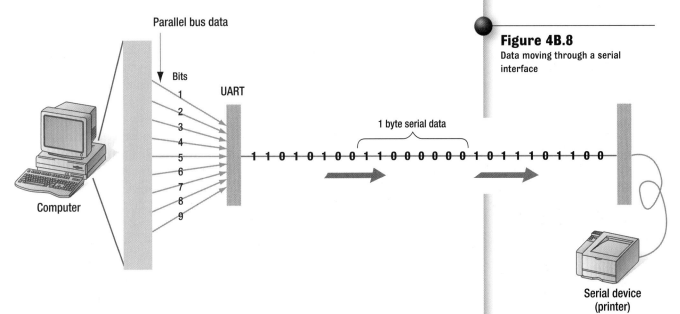

Parallel bus data

Bits
1
2
3
4
5
6
7
8
9

UART

Computer

1 byte serial data

1 1 0 1 0 1 0 0 1 1 0 0 0 0 0 0 1 0 1 1 1 0 1 1 0 0

Serial device
(printer)

Figure 4B.8
Data moving through a serial
interface

Serial and Parallel Ports

A PC's internal components communicate through the data bus, which consists of parallel wires. Similarly, a **parallel interface** is a connection of eight or more wires through which data bits can flow simultaneously. Most computer buses transfer 32 bits simultaneously. However, the standard parallel interface for external devices, like printers, usually transfers eight bits (one byte) at a time over eight separate wires.

With a **serial interface,** data bits are transmitted one at a time through a single wire (however, the interface includes additional wires for the bits that control the flow of data). Inside the computer, a chip called a **universal asynchronous receiver-transmitter (UART)** converts parallel data from the bus into serial data that flows through a serial cable. Figure 4B.8 shows how data flows through a 9-pin serial interface.

As you would expect, a parallel interface can handle a higher volume of data than a serial interface, because more than one bit can be transmitted through a parallel interface simultaneously. Figure 4B.9 shows how data moves through a parallel interface.

Specialized Expansion Ports

In addition to the standard collection of expansion ports, many PCs include specialized ports. These ports allow the connection of special devices, which extends the computer's bus in unique ways.

Figure 4B.9
Data moving through a parallel
interface

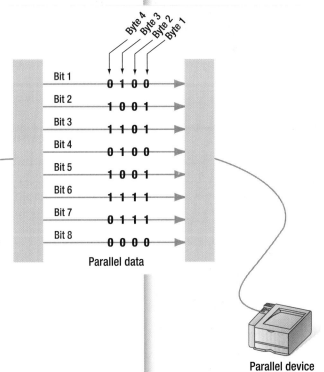

Byte 4 Byte 3 Byte 2 Byte 1

Bit 1   0 1 0 0
Bit 2   1 0 0 1
Bit 3   1 1 0 1
Bit 4   0 1 0 0
Bit 5   1 0 0 1
Bit 6   1 1 1 1
Bit 7   0 1 1 1
Bit 8   0 0 0 0

Parallel data

Computer

Parallel device
(printer)

SCSI

The **Small Computer System Interface** (**SCSI,** pronounced *scuzzy*) takes a different approach from standard parallel or serial ports. Instead of forcing the user to plug multiple cards into the computer's expansion slots, a single SCSI adapter extends the bus outside the computer by way of a cable. Thus, SCSI is like an extension cord for the data bus. Like plugging one extension cord into another to lengthen a circuit, you can plug one SCSI device into another to form a chain, as shown in Figure 4B.10. When devices are connected together this way and plugged into a single port, they are called a "daisy chain." Many devices use the SCSI interface. Fast, high-end hard disk drives often have SCSI interfaces, as do scanners, tape drives, and optical storage devices such as CD-ROM drives.

Figure 4B.10
SCSI peripherals daisy-chained together

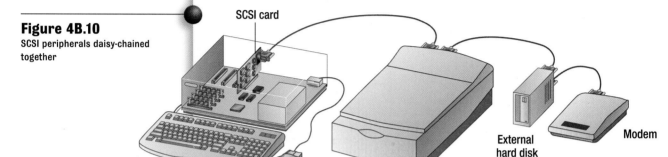

SCSI card

External hard disk

Modem

Scanner

High-performance, business-class PCs feature a built-in SCSI adapter and port. However, most home computers do not include a SCSI adapter. To provide a PC with a SCSI port, you need to insert a SCSI adapter board into one of the PC's available expansion slots.

USB

The **Universal Serial Bus** (**USB**) standard is rapidly gaining popularity for PCs— both IBM-compatible and Macintosh systems. Because the USB standard allows 127 devices to be connected to the bus via a single port, many experts believe that USB will emerge as the single bus standard of the future. Today, most new computers feature at least one or two USB ports.

IEEE 1394 (FireWire)

Like the USB standard, the **IEEE 1394** (**FireWire**) standard extends the computer's bus to many peripheral devices through a single port. Because IEEE 1394-compliant technology is so expensive, however, it is not expected to become the dominant bus technology, although it may gain wide acceptance as a standard for plugging video and other high-data-throughput devices to the system bus.

Musical Instrument Digital Interface (MIDI)

The **Musical Instrument Digital Interface** (**MIDI**) has been in use since the early 1980s, when a group of musical instrument manufacturers developed the technology to enable electronic instruments to communicate. Since then, MIDI has been adapted to the personal computer. Many sound cards are MIDI-compliant and feature a special MIDI port. Using a MIDI port, you can plug a wide variety of musical instruments and other MIDI-controlled devices into the computer. MIDI systems are widely used in recording and performing music to control settings for electronic synthesizers, drum machines, light systems, amplification, and more.

Expansion Slots and Boards

PCs are designed so that users can adapt, or **configure,** the machines to their own particular needs. PC motherboards have two or more empty **expansion slots,** which are extensions of the computer's bus that provide a way to add new components to the computer. The slots accept **expansion boards,** also called **cards, adapters,** or sometimes just **boards.** Figure 4B.11 shows a PC expansion board being installed. The board is being attached to the motherboard—the main system board to which the CPU, memory, and other components are attached.

Adapters that serve input and output purposes provide a port to which devices can be attached; adapters then act as translators between the bus and the device itself. Some adapters also do a significant amount of data processing.

Figure 4B.11
An expansion board being inserted into an expansion slot

PC Cards

Another type of expansion card is the **PC Card.** It is a small device about the size of a credit card (see Figure 4B.12). This device was designed initially for use in notebook computers and other computers that are too small to accept a standard expansion card. A PC Card fits into a slot on the back or side of the notebook computer. PC Card adapters also are available for desktop computers, enabling them to accept PC Cards. Even some types of digital cameras accept PC Cards that store digital photographs. PC Cards are used for a wide variety of purposes and can house modems, network cards, memory, and even fully functioning hard disk drives.

There are three categories of PC Card technologies: Type I, Type II, and Type III. The different types typically are defined by purpose. For example, Type I cards usually contain memory, Type II cards are used for network adapters, and Type III cards usually house tiny hard drives. Type I PC Cards are the thinnest available, and they have the fewest uses. Type III cards are the thickest, and they enable developers to fit disk storage devices into the card-size shell. Some PC Card adapters can hold multiple cards, greatly expanding the capabilities of the small computer.

Figure 4B.12
Small PC Card devices provide memory, storage, communications, and other capabilities.

Plug and Play

With the introduction of Windows 95, Intel-based PCs began supporting the **Plug and Play** standard, making it easier to install hardware via an existing port or expansion slot. Using hardware that complies with Windows' Plug and Play standard, the operating system can detect a new component automatically, check for existing driver programs that will run the new device, and load necessary files. In some cases, Windows will prompt you to install the needed files from a disk. This process may require restarting the system for the new hardware's settings to take effect. Still, this process is much simpler than the one required prior to Plug and Play technology, which usually forced the user to manually resolve conflicts between the new hardware and other components.

VISUAL ESSAY: STANDARD COMPUTER PORTS

A

A 9-pin serial port is provided for an external communication device (such as a modem) or an input device (such as a mouse). Some types of printers and other devices also can use this type of port.

B

A 25-pin parallel port typically is used by a printer, but it also can be used by backup devices, such as tape drives, Zip drives, and others.

C

These small ports are devoted specifically to the keyboard and the mouse. Most newer systems use a 6-pin "mini-DIN" connector for these devices, although some systems use a larger, 5-pin DIN plug.

D

Most PCs feature a special 15-pin port for the monitor.

E

Multimedia PCs include a built-in sound card that provides single-pin miniplugs, such as an input jack, for a microphone, or a stereo output jack for a set of speakers or headphones. Other plugs are dedicated audio line input and output jacks for devices such as tape decks or CD players.

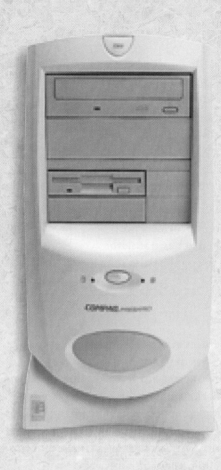

F. Telephone & modem

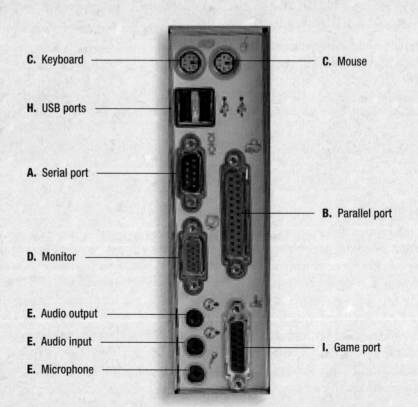

C. Keyboard
C. Mouse

H. USB ports

A. Serial port

B. Parallel port

D. Monitor

E. Audio output

E. Audio input

I. Game port

E. Microphone

G. Network interface

F

If the PC includes a built-in modem card, the card provides two standard phone line (RJ-11) plugs. One plug is for the modem line; the other enables you to plug a telephone directly into the PC.

G

Most business-class computers and many home computers feature built-in network interface cards that enable the computer to be connected to a network. In home computers, this card enables the user to create a home network or to connect to a cable modem system. The type of plug used depends on the networking protocols supported by the card.

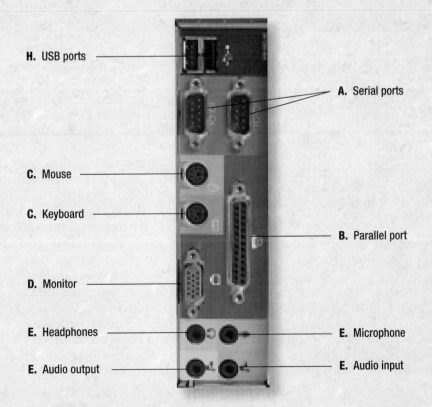

H. USB ports

A. Serial ports

C. Mouse

C. Keyboard

B. Parallel port

D. Monitor

E. Headphones

E. Microphone

E. Audio output

E. Audio input

H

All new Macintosh computers and a growing number of IBM-compatible PCs feature one or more universal serial bus (USB) ports. As many as 127 USB-compliant devices can be connected to a single USB port. These devices include printers, keyboards, mice, video devices, and other peripherals.

I

Many newer PCs include a dedicated port for game controllers, such as a joystick.

COMPUTERS in your career

Computer Sales Professional

Thinking about a career in sales? If so, you should consider a position in the computer hardware, software, or services market. Depending on the type of sales you pursue, the rewards can be enormous. Despite what you may be thinking, a degree in computer science is not always required for a career in computer-related sales.

Computer sales professionals sell a wide variety of products and services. Here are just a few:

◆ **PC hardware sales.** This field includes personal computers—desktops, portables, network servers, network computers (NCs), and handheld computers. You may sell to individual end users; small, medium, and large businesses; government agencies or schools; or to a variety of other organizations.

◆ **Network sales.** Although it may be impossible to find an organization that is not networked, opportunities abound in the networking sales field. Organizations are constantly upgrading and expanding their existing networks, looking for hardware and software solutions that will enable them to store and transmit data faster and more efficiently.

◆ **Telecommunications sales.** Telecommunications and computer technologies go hand in hand. Markets are expanding for wireless systems; systems that can transmit voice and data simultaneously; and phone systems that can connect to networks, enabling users to bring up a caller's data instantly.

◆ **Internet services sales.** The Internet is now an entire industry unto itself. Thousands of companies have sprung up, selling Internet services of all types, including Web hosting; Web site management; design; advertising; security; e-commerce; consulting; software and content development; and many others.

◆ **Software sales.** This industry extends beyond sales of operating systems and word processors; enterprise software includes massive database systems, network management software, data-mining tools, and other powerful and expensive packages.

◆ **Professional services sales.** "Professional services" is a catch-all term that covers nearly every type of computer or network-related service, including system analysis and design; installation and configuration; programming and development; systems management; break-fix; help desk services; and software support.

A career in computer sales can be very rewarding. Sales professionals are paid in many different ways, under many different compensation programs. Any compensation plan might include a straight salary, commissions, bonuses, profit sharing, stock options, and other rewards. Many retail salespeople earn base salaries of $20,000 to $30,000, plus bonuses and commissions. The most sucessful corporate sales representatives earn literally millions of dollars. Computer sales can mean long hours, hard work, and endless negotiating. It also requires an understanding of the products, services, and prices offered by your company and your competitors. Computer sales is extremely competive, especially when dealing with large corporate clients who purchase millions of dollars worth of products and services in a single order.

SUMMARY

- A processor's architecture, or internal design, dictates its function and performance.

- A key to a processor's performance is the number of transistors it contains. Chip designers constantly look for new ways to place more transistors on microprocessor chips. Today's PC processors contain tens of millions of processors.

- Intel manufactured the processors used in the first IBM personal computers. Today, Intel's most popular PC processors are the Pentium 4, Pentium III Xeon, Pentium III, and Celeron. A newer Intel processor, the Itanium, is a 64-bit processor used in high-performance workstations and network servers.

- Advanced Micro Devices (AMD), which initially made lower-performance processors for low-cost PCs, now manufactures high-performance processors that compete directly with Intel. AMD's most popular PC processors are the Athlon and Duron.

- Motorola manufactures processors used in Apple's Macintosh computers; its most popular processors are in the PowerPC family. Motorola also makes processors for other types of computing devices, such as minicomputers and workstations.

- Most of the processors used in personal computers are based on complex instruction set computing (CISC) technology. PowerPC processors, and processors used in many other types of computers, are based on reduced instruction set computing (RISC) technology. Because they contain a smaller instruction set, RISC processors can run faster than CISC processors.

- A parallel processing system harnesses the power of multiple processors in a single system, enabling them to share processing tasks. In a massively parallel processor (MPP) system, many processors are used. Some MPP systems use thousands of processors at one time.

- External devices, such as those used for input and output, are connected to the system by ports on the back or front of the computer.

- Most computers come with a serial port and a parallel port. A serial port transmits one bit of data at a time; a parallel port transmits one byte (eight bits) of data at a time.

- If the computer does not have the right type of port for an external device (or if all the existing ports are in use), an expansion board can be installed into one of the PC's empty expansion slots.

- Bus technologies such as Small Computer System Interface (SCSI), Universal Serial Bus (USB), and IEEE 1394 enable the user to connect many devices through a single port.

KEY TERMS

adapter, *141*
Advanced Micro Devices (AMD), *135*
architecture, *133*
board, *141*
card, *141*
complex instruction set computing (CISC), *138*
configure, *141*
expansion board, *141*
expansion slot, *141*
IEEE 1394 (FireWire), *140*
Intel, *134*
massively parallel processing (MPP), *138*
micron, *134*

Motorola, *136*
multiprocessing (MP), *138*
Musical Instrument Digital Interface (MIDI), *140*
parallel interface, *139*
parallel processing, *138*
PC Card, *141*
Plug and Play, *141*
reduced instruction set computing (RISC), *138*
serial interface, *139*
Small Computer System Interface (SCSI), *140*
symmetric multiprocessing (SMP), *138*
universal asynchronous receiver-transmitter (UART), *139*
Universal Serial Bus (USB), *140*

KEY TERM QUIZ

Complete each statement by writing one of the terms listed under Key Terms in each blank.

1. A processor's internal design is called its _architecture_

2. _Intel_ and _AMD_ are the leading manufacturers of processors for IBM-compatible personal computers.

3. The _USB_ and _SCSI_ buses provide fast data transfer speeds and eliminate the need for expansion slots and boards.

4. With a(n) _serial_ interface, data bits are transmitted one at a time through a single wire.

5. The _MIDI_ enables electronic musical instruments and computers to communicate with one another.

SECTION QUIZ

True/False

Answer the following questions by circling True or False.

True   ~~False~~   1. The Athlon processor is manufactured by Intel. *AmD*

~~True~~   ~~False~~   2. Today's fastest PC processors contain more than one billion transistors. *9.5 million a millimeter*

True   ~~False~~   3. A micron is one millionth of an inch.

~~True~~   False   4. Because it uses eight wires to transmit data, a parallel interface can transmit eight bits of data at one time.

~~True~~   False   5. Parallel processing uses multiple processors to share the workload.

Multiple Choice

Circle the word or phrase that best completes each statement.

1. A computer system that uses multiple processors is said to use _____ technology.
   A. parallel processing   **B.** RISC **C.** neither A nor B

2. FireWire is another name for the _____ interface.
   A. parallel **B.** IEEE 1394   **C.** MIDI

3. The _____ processor is used in Apple's Macintosh computers.
   A. Celeron **B.** Athlon **C.** PowerPC

4. The more _____ a processor has, the more powerful it is.
   A. microns **B.** transistors   **C.** connections

5. The instruction set for a _____ processor usually contains 200 to 300 instructions.
   A. CISC **B.** SMP **C.** RISC

REVIEW QUESTIONS

In your own words, briefly answer the following questions.

1. Describe the purpose of expansion slots in a PC.

2. What is the primary difference between a RISC processor and a CISC processor?

3. Describe two ways designers place more transistors in processor chips.

4. What are the advantages of parallel processing?

5. What is the purpose of the UART?

SECTION LABS

Complete the following exercises as directed by your instructor.

1. To view information about your computer's components, follow these steps:
   A. Open the Control Panel window. (The steps for opening the Control Panel vary, depending on the version of Windows you use. If you need help, ask your instructor.) In the Control Panel window, double-click the System icon.
   B. In the System Properties dialog box, open the Device Manager window to view the list of categories of devices attached to your system. If a category is preceded by a plus sign (+), click this symbol to display all the devices in that category.
   C. To read about a device, right-click its name; then click Properties. A dialog box will appear, displaying information about the selected device. *Warning:* Do not make any changes.
   D. Review the properties for your system's disk drives, ports, and system devices.
   E. Close any open windows or dialog boxes; then close the Control Panel window.

UNIT PROJECTS

Complete the following exercises using a computer in your classroom, lab, or home.

1. **Plug It In.** With your instructor observing, turn your computer and monitor off and unplug them from their power source. Then take these steps:

   A. Move to the back of the computer and inspect all the cables plugged into it. Which devices are connected to the PC and by which cables? Which port is connected to each device? Make a chart of these connections.

   B. Unplug each connection. After everyone has unplugged the devices for the computers, switch places with someone and reconnect all the devices to the computer. Does the other student's system have the same connections as yours? If not, can you reconnect all its devices correctly?

   C. Return to your PC. Use your chart to see whether your system has been reconnected correctly. If not, correct any connecting errors. When you are sure all devices are plugged into the right ports, reconnect the PC and monitor to the power source. Turn the PC on, and make sure everything is working correctly.

2. **Watch Those Files Grow.** The concept of bits and bytes may seem unimportant until you begin creating files on your computer. Then you can begin to understand how much memory and storage space your files take up (in bytes, of course). Create a file in Notepad, save it to disk, and take the following steps to add to the file to see how it grows:

   A. Launch Notepad. The steps to launch the program vary, depending on which version of Windows you use. If you need help, ask your instructor for directions.

   B. Type two or three short paragraphs of text. When you are done, click the File menu, and then click the Save As command.

   C. In the Save As dialog box, choose a drive and folder in which to save the new file, and give the file a short name you can remember easily, such as SIZE-TEST.TXT.

   D. With Notepad running, launch Windows Explorer. If you need help, ask your instructor for directions.

   E. Navigate to the drive and folder in which you saved your Notepad file. When you find the file, look for its size in the Size column, and write down the size. Close the Explorer window.

   F. Return to the Notepad window, and add two or three more paragraphs of text. Then click the File menu, and click the Save command to resave the file under the same name.

   G. Reopen Windows Explorer and look at the file's size again. Has it changed? By how much?

3. Pick the Perfect Processor. For this exercise, imagine you are planning to buy a new PC. Set a budget for yourself; then use the following links to decide which processor meets your needs best, based on your budget:

   Intel—**http://www.intel.com/**

   AMD—**http://www.amd.com/**

   Apple—**http://www.apple.com/**

   Motorola—**http://www.motorola.com/**

DISCUSSION QUESTIONS

As directed by your instructor, discuss the following questions in class or in groups.

1. Do you see any benefits to Unicode's widespread implementation?

2. Why is the CPU commonly referred to as the computer's "brain"? Do you think it is a good idea to use this term to describe the CPU? Why?

RESEARCH AND REPORT

Using your own choice of resources (such as the Internet, books, magazines, and newspaper articles), research and write a short paper discussing one of the following topics:

■ The history of the Pentium family of processors

■ The uses of parallel processing computer systems in business

■ The USB and FireWire bus standards, and their impact on computers

When you are finished, proofread and print your paper, and give it to your instructor.

ETHICAL ISSUES

Computers are becoming more powerful all the time. Many people see this capability as a source of limitless benefits, but others view it as a threat. With this thought in mind, discuss the following questions in class.

1. As technology improves, processing becomes faster. It can be argued that computer technology has made Americans less patient than they were a decade ago. Do you agree? If so, do you see it as a benefit of our technological progress or as a drawback? Should we restrain our urge to increase the pace of life? Be prepared to explain your position.

2. Computers are not only getting faster, but they also are becoming exponentially more powerful all the time. For example, many think that in the next decade artificial intelligence will be developed to the point that computers can begin reasoning—weighing facts, solving problems, perhaps even making decisions. Will people relinquish even a tiny bit of control to computers? If so, what kinds of decisions will we allow them to make for us? What risks do we run by enabling computers to become "smart" enough to solve problems or, ultimately, to think?

UNIT 5

Storing Information in a Computer

UNIT CONTENTS

This unit contains the following sections:

The Interactive Browser Edition CD-ROM provides additional labs and activities to apply concepts from this unit.

Types of Storage Devices

OVERVIEW:
An Ever-Increasing Need

If you ask several people to list the four most important features in a computer, you will probably receive the same answer from most people:

- A fast processor
- Lots of random access memory (RAM)
- Plenty of storage space
- Multiple storage options

As you have already seen, PCs are getting faster every year, and the newest generation of PCs offers more RAM than ever before. Likewise, PC storage systems are constantly being expanded. The newest home PCs feature storage capacities once found only in the most sophisticated business-class systems. Users can choose from a constantly changing array of storage options to complement their systems' built-in storage devices.

This section examines the primary types of storage found in today's personal computers. You'll learn how each type of storage device stores and manages data.

OBJECTIVES

- List five types of magnetic storage devices.
- Name the four areas that are created on a magnetic disk.
- Explain how data is stored on the surface of a magnetic disk.
- List seven types of optical storage devices.
- Explain how data is stored on the surface of an optical disk.
- List and describe three types of emerging storage technologies.

VISUAL ESSAY: CATEGORIZING STORAGE DEVICES

The purpose of storage devices is to hold data—even when the computer is turned off—so the data can be used whenever it is needed. Storage involves two processes:

◆ Writing data—or recording data on the surface of a disk or tape—where it is stored for later use.

◆ Reading data—or retrieving the data from the surface of a disk or tape—and then transferring it into the computer's memory.

The physical materials on which data is stored are called **storage media.** The hardware components that write data to, and read it from, storage media are called **storage devices.** For example, a diskette is a storage medium (*medium* is the singular form of *media*), whereas a diskette drive is a storage device.

The two main categories of storage technology used today are **magnetic storage** and **optical storage.** Although most storage devices and media employ one technology or the other, some use both. Table 5A.1 lists the primary types of magnetic and optical storage media used in today's PCs.

Table 5A.1	Common Storage Media in PCs
Magnetic Storage	**Optical Storage**
Diskettes	Compact Disk Read-Only Memory (CD-ROM)
Hard disks	CD-Recordable (CD-R)/CD-ReWritable (CD-RW)
High-capacity floppy disks	Digital Video Disk Read-Only Memory (DVD-ROM)
Disk cartridges	DVD Recordable (DVD-R)/DVD ReWritable (DVD-RW)
Magnetic tape	PhotoCD

A Every new PC comes with a diskette drive and a hard disk drive. Most new PCs also have a CD-ROM or DVD-ROM drive; for a little more expense, many consumers replace the optical drive with a CD-R, CD-RW, DVD-R, or DVD-RW drive so they can record data, music, and video to an optical disk. A built-in drive for removable, high-capacity floppy disks is another common feature in new PCs.

B Floppy disks are common storage media, although they provide limited storage capacities. Floppies are popular because they are extremely portable and inexpensive.

C A hard disk is standard equipment on a personal computer. Because a standard hard disk is built into the system unit (and is called an internal device), you cannot see it. Most PCs feature an indicator light that blinks when the hard disk is accessed.

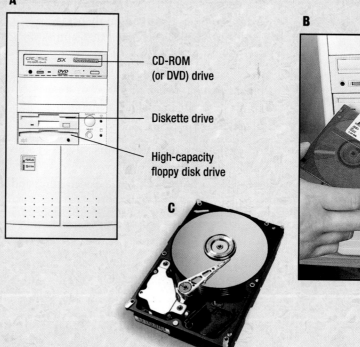

A

CD-ROM (or DVD) drive

Diskette drive

High-capacity floppy disk drive

C

B

D

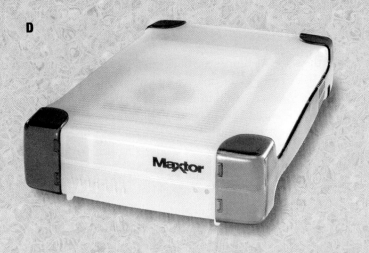

D Not all hard drives are internal. External hard drives can be connected to one of the computer's ports. This drive, made by Maxtor Corp., can be plugged into the PC's FireWire port.

E

E The Iomega Zip system is an example of a high-capacity floppy disk. These disks store data in quantities of 100 MB and 250 MB. All high-capacity floppy disks require a drive made especially for their use.

F

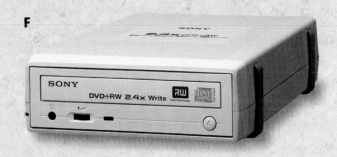

F New DVD-RW drives, like this one from Sony Corp., are the cutting edge in optical storage technology for the PC. These drives can play any type of audio or video optical disk, and they can record audio/video or computer data to CD-R, CD-RW, DVD-R, and DVD-RW disks.

G

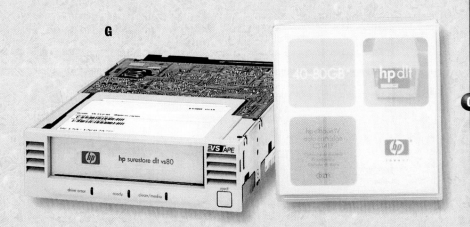

G An example of an external tape drive is made by Hewlett-Packard. Although tape drives are considered to be add-ons, many tape drives can be inserted into one of the system unit's drive bays, making them an integral part of the system.

Floppy Disk

Surfaces are covered with special magnetic coating.

Hard Disk

Tape

Figure 5A.1
Although they look different, hard disks, diskettes, high-capacity floppy disks, and tapes all have a magnetic coating on their surface. This coating enables each medium to store data.

MAGNETIC STORAGE DEVICES

Because they all use the same medium (the material on which the data is stored), diskette drives, hard disk drives, high-capacity floppy disk drives, and tape drives use similar techniques for writing and reading data. The surfaces of diskettes, hard disks, high-capacity floppy disks, and magnetic tape are coated with a magnetically sensitive material, such as iron oxide, that reacts to a magnetic field (see Figure 5A.1).

Diskettes contain a single thin disk, usually made of plastic. This disk is flexible, which is why diskettes are often called floppy disks. A diskette stores data on both sides of its disk (numbered as side 0 and side 1), and each side has its own read/write head. Most high-capacity floppy disks contain a single disk, too, but their formatting enables them to store much more data than a normal floppy disk, as you will see later. Hard disks usually contain multiple disks, which are called platters because they are made of a rigid material such as aluminum.

How Data is Stored on a Disk

You may remember from science projects that one magnet can be used to make another. For example, you can make a magnet by taking an iron bar and stroking it in one direction with a magnet. The iron bar becomes a magnet itself, because its iron molecules align themselves in one direction. Thus, the iron bar becomes **polarized;** that is, its ends have opposite magnetic polarity (see Figure 5A.2).

Magnetic storage devices use a similar principle to store data. Just as a transistor can represent binary data as "on" or "off," the orientation of a magnetic field can be used to represent data. A magnet has one important advantage over a transistor: It can represent "on" and "off" without a continual source of electricity.

Figure 5A.2
How an electromagnet creates a field on a magnetic surface

Another way to make a magnet is to wrap a wire coil around an iron bar and send an electric current through the coil. This produces an electromagnet.

If you reverse the direction of the current, the polarity of the magnet also reverses.

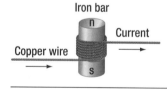

If you place the electromagnet against a magnetic surface, such as the coating of a diskette...

...the electromagnet's pole induces a magnetic field on the diskette's surface.

The surfaces of disks and magnetic tapes are coated with millions of tiny iron particles so that data can be stored on them. Each of these particles can act as a magnet, taking on a magnetic field when subjected to an electromagnet. The read/write heads of a magnetic disk or tape drive contain electromagnets that generate magnetic fields in the iron on the storage medium as the head passes over the disk or tape. As shown in Figure 5A.3, the read/write heads record strings of 1s and 0s by alternating the direction of the current in the electromagnets.

To read data from a magnetic surface, the process is reversed. The read/write head passes over the disk or tape while no current is flowing through the electromagnet. Because the storage medium has a magnetic field but the head does not, the storage medium charges the magnet in the head, which causes a small current to flow through the head in one direction or the other, depending on the polarity of the field. The disk or tape drive senses the direction of the flow as the storage medium passes by the head, and the data is sent from the read/write head into memory.

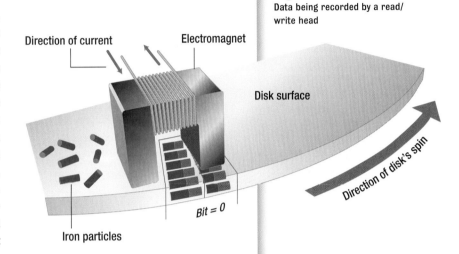

Figure 5A.3
Data being recorded by a read/write head

How Data Is Organized on a Magnetic Disk

Before the computer can use a magnetic disk to store data, the disk's surface must be magnetically mapped, so that the computer can go directly to a specific point on it without searching through data. The process of mapping a disk is called **formatting** or **initializing.** (Actually, when you purchase new diskettes or high-capacity floppy disks, they should be formatted already.)

You may find it helpful to reformat diskettes from time to time, because the process ensures that all existing data is deleted from the disk. During the formatting process, you can determine whether the disk's surface has faulty spots, and you can copy important system files to the disk. You can format a floppy disk by using operating system commands, as shown in Figure 5A.4.

Figure 5A.4
Formatting a diskette and a Zip high-capacity floppy disk

Hard disks also must be formatted, so the computer can locate data on them. When you buy a computer, its hard disk has been formatted correctly already and probably contains some programs and data. You can format your hard disk, if necessary, but the process is different from formatting a floppy disk.

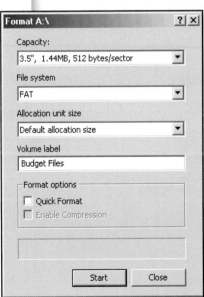

Tracks and Sectors

When you format a magnetic disk, the disk drive creates a set of concentric rings, called **tracks,** on each side of the disk. The number of tracks required depends on the type of disk. Most high-density diskettes have 80 tracks on each side of the disk. (You will learn more about disk densities later in this unit.) A hard disk may have several hundred tracks on each side of each platter. Each track is a separate circle, like the circles on a bull's-eye target. The tracks are numbered from the outermost circle to the innermost, starting with zero, as shown in Figure 5A.5.

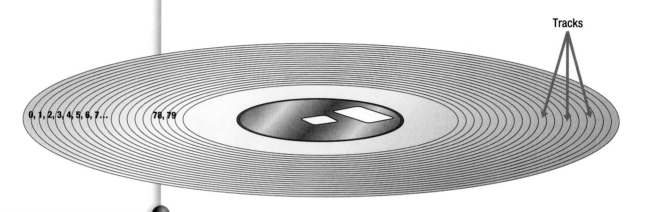

Figure 5A.5
Tracks are concentric circles numbered from the outside in.

Each track on a disk also is split into smaller parts. Imagine slicing a disk the way you cut a pie. As shown in Figure 5A.6, each slice would cut across all the disk's tracks, resulting in short segments, or **sectors.** In both diskettes and hard disks, a sector can store up to 512 bytes (0.5 KB). All the sectors on the disk are numbered in one long sequence, so that the computer can access each small area on the disk with a unique number. This scheme simplifies what would be a set of two-dimensional coordinates into a single numeric address.

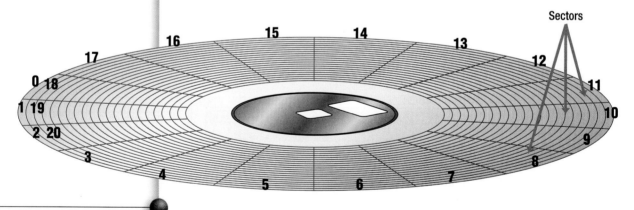

Figure 5A.6
Sectors on a disk, each with a unique number

If a diskette has 80 tracks on each side, and each track contains 18 sectors, then the disk has 1,440 sectors (80 × 18) per side, for a total of 2,880 sectors. This configuration is true regardless of the length of the track. The diskette's outermost track is longer than the innermost track, but each track is still divided into the same number of sectors. Regardless of physical size, all of a diskette's sectors hold the same number of bytes; that is, the shortest, innermost sectors hold the same amount of data as the longest, outermost sectors.

Of course, a diskette's allocation of sectors per track is somewhat wasteful, because the longer outer tracks could theoretically store more data than the shorter inner tracks. For this reason, most hard disks allocate more sectors to the longer tracks on the disk's surface. As you move toward the hard disk's center, each subsequent track has fewer sectors. This arrangement takes advantage of the hard disk's potential capacity and enables a typical hard disk to store data more efficiently than a floppy disk. Because many hard disks allocate sectors in this manner, their sectors-per-track specification is often given as an average. Such hard disks are described as having "an average of *x* sectors per track."

As you will learn in Unit 6, "The Operating System and User Interface," the computer's operating system (sometimes with the aid of utility programs) is responsible for managing all disk operations in a computer. It is up to the operating system to determine the precise locations where files are stored on the surface of a disk.

Clusters

Because files are not usually a size that is an even multiple of 512 bytes, some sectors contain unused space after the end of the file. In addition, the Windows operating system allocates a group of sectors, called a **cluster,** to each file stored on a disk. Cluster sizes vary, depending on the size and type of the disk, but they can range from 4 sectors for diskettes to 64 sectors for some hard disks. A small file that contains only 50 bytes will use only a portion of the first sector of a cluster assigned to it, leaving the remainder of the first sector and the remainder of the cluster allocated but unused.

A sector is the smallest unit with which any disk drive (diskette drive or hard drive) can work. Each bit and byte within a sector can have different values, but the drive can read or write only whole sectors at a time. If the computer needs to change just 1 byte out of 512, it must rewrite the entire sector.

How the Operating System Finds Data on a Disk

A computer's operating system can locate data on a disk because each track and sector is labeled, and the location of all data is kept in a special log on the disk. The labeling of tracks and sectors is called **logical formatting.** (This type of formatting also is called **low-level formatting** or **soft formatting.**) A commonly used logical format performed by Windows creates four disk areas (see Figure 5A.7):

◆ **The master boot record:** The **master boot record** is a program that runs when you first start the computer. This program determines whether the disk has the basic components that are necessary to run the operating system successfully. If the program determines that the required files are present and the disk has a valid format, it transfers control to one of the operating system programs that continues the process of starting up. This process is called **booting**—because the boot program makes the computer "pull itself

Visit **www.norton.glencoe.com** for more information on **formatting disks.**

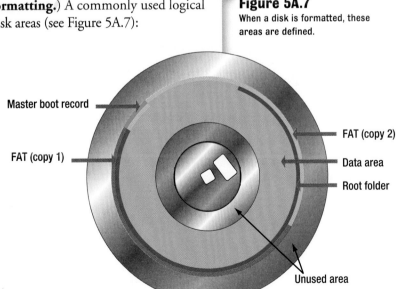

Figure 5A.7
When a disk is formatted, these areas are defined.

Master boot record

FAT (copy 1)

FAT (copy 2)

Data area

Root folder

Unused area

The folder named C: is the root; it contains all other folders on this disk.

up by its own bootstraps." The boot record also describes other disk characteristics, such as the number of bytes per sector and the number of sectors per track—information that the operating system needs to access the data area of the disk.

Folders can contain other folders and individual files.

The selected folder contains these files.

♦ **The file allocation table:** The **file allocation table (FAT)** is a log that records the location of each file and the status of each sector. When you write a file to a disk, the operating system checks the FAT for an open area, stores the file, and then identifies the file and its location in the FAT.

♦ **The root folder:** Users do not see the information listed in the FAT, but they often use the information. A **folder,** also called a **directory,** is a tool for organizing files on a disk. Folders can contain files or other folders, so it is possible to set up a hierarchical system of folders on your computer, just as you have folders within other folders in a file cabinet. The top folder on any disk is known as the root. (Experienced computer users may refer to this folder as the **root folder** or **root directory.**) When you use the operating system to view the contents of a folder, the operating system lists specific information about each file in the folder, such as the file's name, its size, the time and date that it was created or last modified, and so on. Figure 5A.8 shows a typical folder listing on a Windows 2000 system.

♦ **The data area:** The part of the disk that remains free after the boot sector, FAT, and root folder have been created is called the **data area,** because that is where the data files (or program files) are actually stored.

MOTOR READ/WRITE HEAD DRIVE SPINDLE

Diskette drive

EJECT BUTTON

METAL SHUTTER

DISKETTE

DRIVE LIGHT

Plastic diskette with magnetic coating

Diskettes (Floppy Disks)

Figure 5A.9 shows a diskette and a diskette drive. The drive includes a motor that rotates the disk on a spindle and read/write heads that can move to any spot on the disk's surface as the disk spins. The heads can skip from one spot to another on the disk's surface without having to scan through all of the data in between.

Diskettes spin at about 300 revolutions per minute. Therefore, the longest it can take to position a point on the diskette under the read/write heads is the amount of time required for one revolution—about 0.2 second. The farthest the heads have to move is from the center of the diskette to the outside edge (or vice versa). The heads can move from the center to the outside edge in even less time—about 0.17 second. Because both operations (rotating the diskette and moving the heads from the center to the outside edge) take place simultaneously, the maximum time to position the heads over a given location on the diskette—known as the maximum access time—remains the greater of the two times, or 0.2 second (see Figure 5A.10).

Visit **www.norton.glencoe.com** for more information on **diskettes (floppy disks)**.

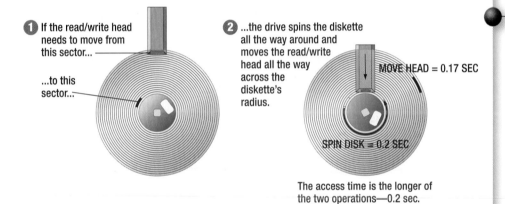

1 If the read/write head needs to move from this sector...

...to this sector...

2 ...the drive spins the diskette all the way around and moves the read/write head all the way across the diskette's radius.

MOVE HEAD = 0.17 SEC

SPIN DISK = 0.2 SEC

The access time is the longer of the two operations—0.2 sec.

Figure 5A.10
How maximum access time is determined for a diskette drive

The maximum access time for diskettes can be even longer, however, because diskettes do not spin when they are not being used. It can take about 0.5 second to rotate the disk from a dead stop.

A 3.5-inch diskette, shown in Figure 5A.11, is encased in a hard plastic shell with a sliding shutter. When the disk is inserted into the drive, the shutter slides back to expose the disk's surface to the read/write head.

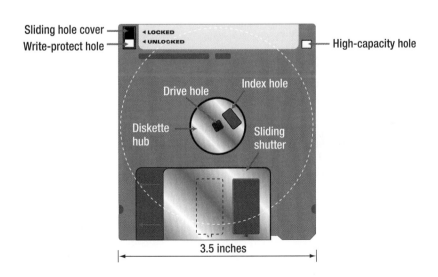

Sliding hole cover
Write-protect hole

◄ LOCKED
◄ UNLOCKED

High-capacity hole

Drive hole

Index hole

Diskette hub

Sliding shutter

3.5 inches

Figure 5A.11
A 3.5-inch diskette

Today's 3.5-inch diskettes are available in two densities, as shown in Table 5A.2. The **density** of the disk is a measure of its capacity—that is, how much data the disk can store. Early versions of diskettes were double density (DD). As diskette media improved, storage capacities increased; the double-density diskettes have been almost completely replaced by high-density (HD) diskettes, which provide significantly more storage.

Table 5A.2	Formatting Specifications for 3.5-Inch Floppy Disks*						
Density	Tracks	Sectors/ Track	Sectors	Bytes/ Sector	Total Bytes	Bytes Expressed In KB	MB
Double	80	9	1440	512	737,280	720	.7
High	80	18	1880	512	1,474,560	1440	1.44

*These formats and capacities are for 3.5-inch diskettes used with IBM-compatible PCs only.

Hard Disks

Much of what you have learned about diskettes and diskette drives applies to hard disks as well. Like diskettes, hard disks store data in tracks divided into sectors. Physically, however, hard disks look quite different from diskettes.

A hard disk includes one or more platters mounted on a central spindle, like a stack of rigid diskettes. Each platter is covered with a magnetic coating, and the entire unit is encased in a sealed chamber. Unlike diskettes, where the disk and drive are separate, the hard disk and drive are a single unit. It includes the hard disk, the motor that spins the platters, and a set of read/write heads (see Figure 5A.12). Because you cannot remove the disk from its drive (unless it is a removable or external hard disk), the terms *hard disk* and *hard drive* are used interchangeably.

Hard disks offer a wide range of capacities. The smallest hard disks available today can store several hundred megabytes; the largest store 80 GB or even more. Most entry-level consumer PCs now come with hard disks of at least 10 GB, but minimum capacities are continually increasing. At the time this text was written, home and business-class PCs could easily be found with hard disk capabilities of 20 GB and greater.

The hard disks found in most PCs spin at a speed of 3,600, 7,200, or 10,000 rpm, whereas very high-performance disks found in workstations and servers can spin as fast as 15,000 rpm. (Compare these figures to a diskette's spin rate of 300 rpm.) The speed at which the disk spins is a major factor in the overall performance of the drive.

Figure 5A.12
Parts of a hard disk

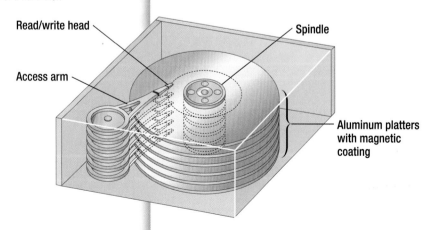

Read/write head

Access arm

Spindle

Aluminum platters with magnetic coating

The hard disk's high rotational speed allows more data to be recorded on the disk's surface. As you may recall, waving a magnet past an electric coil like the one in a drive's read/write head causes a current to flow through the coil. The faster you wave the magnet and the closer the magnet is to the coil, the larger the current it generates in the coil. Therefore, a disk that spins faster can use smaller magnetic charges to make current flow in the read/write head. The drive's heads also can use a lower-intensity current to record data on the disk.

Hard disks pack data more closely together than floppy disks can, but they also hold more data, because they usually include multiple platters stacked one on top of another. To the computer system, this configuration means that the disk has more than two sides; sides 0, 1, 2, 3, 4, and so on. Larger-capacity hard disk drives may use twelve or more platters, but both sides of every platter are not always used.

With hard disks, the number of sides that the disk uses is specified by the number of read/write heads. For example, a particular hard disk drive might have six disk platters (that is, twelve sides) but only eleven heads, indicating that one side is not used to store data. Often, the unused side is the bottom side of the bottom disk, as shown in Figure 5A.13.

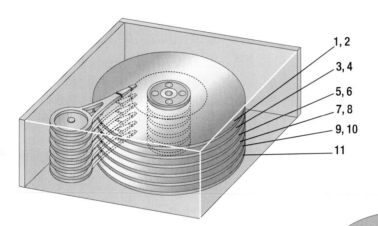

1, 2
3, 4
5, 6
7, 8
9, 10
11

Figure 5A.13
Read/write heads on each side of each platter, except the bottom side of the bottom platter

Because hard disks are actually a stack of platters, the term **cylinder** is used to refer to the same track across all the disk sides, as shown in Figure 5A.14. For example, track 0 (the outermost track) on every disk is cylinder 0.

Like diskettes, hard disks generally store 512 bytes of data in a sector, but because of their higher tolerances, hard disks can have more sectors per track—54, 63, or even more sectors per track are not uncommon.

In spite of all the capacity and speed advantages, hard disks have one major drawback. To achieve optimum performance, the read/write head must be extremely close to the surface of the disk without actually touching the disk. In fact, the read/write heads fly so close to the surface of the disk that if a human hair, a dust particle, or even a fingerprint were placed on the disk, it would bridge the gap between the head and the disk and cause the head to crash. A **head crash,** in which the head touches the disk, can destroy the data stored in the area of the crash.

A cylinder consists of a vertical stack of tracks, one track on each side of each platter.

Figure 5A.14
A cylinder on a hard disk's platters

Figure 5A.15

The distance between a hard disk's read/write head and the disk's surface compared to the size and/or width of possible contaminants

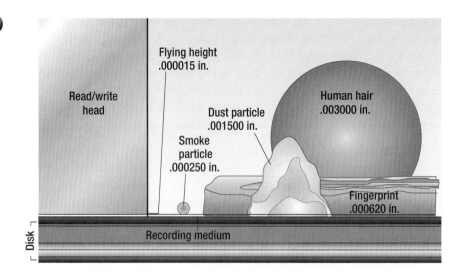

A severe head crash not only damages the surface of the disk, but it also can destroy a read/write head. Figure 5A.15 shows the height at which a hard disk head floats compared to the sizes of dust particles, fingerprints, and the width of a hair.

Removable High-Capacity Magnetic Disks

Removable high-capacity disks and drives attempt to combine the speed and capacity of a hard disk with the portability of a diskette. This category includes many different types of devices. Choosing the best type is usually a matter of balancing your needs for speed, storage capacity, compatibility in different computers, and price.

◆ **High-Capacity Floppy Disks.** Many computer users are adding **high-capacity floppy disk** drives to their systems. These disks, which are about the same size as a 3.5-inch diskette, have a much greater capacity than a standard diskette. In fact, many computer manufacturers now offer high-capacity floppy disk drives on their systems. The drive may be offered in addition to a standard diskette drive, but some of these specialty drives can read both standard and high-capacity floppy disks. Popular high-capacity floppy disks include Zip disks (made by Iomega Corp.), SuperDisks (made by Imation Corp.), and HiFD disks (made by Sony Corp.).

◆ **Hot-Swappable Hard Disks.** At the high end in terms of both price and performance are **hot-swappable hard disks.** These disks are sometimes used on high-end workstations or servers that require large amounts of storage. They allow the user to remove (swap out) a hard disk and insert (swap in) another while the computer is still on (hot). Hot-swappable hard disks are like removable versions of normal hard disks. The removable box includes the disk, drive, and read/write heads in a sealed container.

◆ **Disk Cartridges.** **Disk cartridges** work a bit like a diskette, with a disk in a plastic case that is inserted into or removed from the drive. Iomega Corp. makes two popular disk cartridge systems: the Jaz disk (available in 1 GB and 2 GB capacities) and the Peerless disk (available in 10 GB and 20 GB capacities), as shown in Figure 5A.16.

Figure 5A.16

Iomega's Peerless disk cartridge system is an external peripheral that can connect to a PC via a USB or FireWire port. Peerless disks come in capacities of 10 GB and 20 GB.

Tape Drives

Tape drives read and write data to the surface of a tape the same way an audiocassette recorder does. The difference is that a computer tape drive writes digital data rather than analog data—discrete 1s and 0s rather than the finely graduated signals created by sounds in an audio recorder.

The best use of tape storage is for data that you do not use often, such as backup copies of your hard disk (which you will need only if your hard drive malfunctions or you accidentally delete a valuable file). Because a tape is a long strip of magnetic material, the tape drive has to write data to it serially—one byte after another. Serial access is inherently slower than the direct access provided by media such as disks. When you want to access a specific set of data on a tape, the drive has to scan through all the data you do not need to get to the data you want. The result is a slow access time. In fact, the access time varies, depending on the speed of the drive, the length of the tape, and the position on the tape to which the head wrote the data originally.

With capacities as high as 100 GB, 200 GB, and higher, tape offers an inexpensive way to store a lot of data on a single cassette (see Figure 5A.17).

Figure 5A.17
New generation tape drives feature data capacities of 200 GB and higher, and they can transfer several megabytes of data per second.

PC Cards

A PC Card is a small device about the same size as a credit card. For years, PC Cards have been used to add features, such as memory, modems, and network adapters to portable and desktop computers alike. To use a PC Card, your computer needs a special adapter, into which the card slides.

PC Card technologies are categorized as Type I, Type II, and Type III. Type I is the thinnest type of PC Card, while Type III is the thickest. Type II and Type III PC Cards can be used to house miniature hard disks (see Figure 5A.18). These cards are a very convenient way to expand the storage capacity of a laptop PC or an older desktop system, or to transport large files between computers.

Figure 5A.18
This Kingston Datapak Type II PC Card hard disk has a capacity of 2 GB.

Self Check

Complete each statement by filling in the blank(s).

1. The physical materials on which data is stored are called _storage media_.

2. The read/write heads of a disk drive or tape drive contain _electromagnets_.

3. Some operating systems allocate a group of sectors, called a(n) _cluster_, to each file they store on a disk.

PRODUCTIVITY Tip

Insurance for Your Data

Backing up your data simply means making a copy of it, separate from the original version on your computer's hard disk. You can back up the entire disk, programs and all, or you can back up your data files. If your original data is lost, you can restore the backup copy, then resume your work with no more than a minor inconvenience. Here are some tips to help you start a regular backup routine.

Choose Your Medium

The most popular backup medium is the floppy disk, but you may need dozens of them to back up all your data files. A tape drive, removable hard disk, disk cartridge, CD-RW, or DVD-RW drive may be a perfect choice if the medium provides enough storage space to back up your entire disk. When choosing your own backup medium, the first rule is to make sure it can store everything you need. It also should enable you to restore backed-up data and programs with little effort. You can find medium-capacity tape drives and Zip or Jaz drives for as little as $100 to $300. Prices increase with speed and capacity. Large-capacity disk cartridges, such as Iomega's Peerless system, start at around $350 for the drive;

Online backup services such as @Backup can back up your system's hard drive over an Internet connection, on any schedule.

10 GB Peerless disks cost about $150, while 20 GB disks cost about $200.

Remote backup services are a growing trend. For a fee, such a service can connect to your computer remotely (via an Internet or dial-up connection) and back up your data to their servers. You can restore data remotely from such a system.

Make Sure You Have the Right Software

For backing up your entire hard disk to a high-capacity device, use the file-transfer software that came with the device. Your operating system also may have a built-in backup utility that works with several devices. The critical issue when choosing backup software is that it should enable you to organize your backups, perform partial backups, and restore selected files when needed.

Set a Schedule and Stick to It

Your first backup should be a full backup—everything on your hard disk—and it should be repeated once a week. Beyond that, you can do a series of partial backups—either incremental (files that have changed since the last partial backup) or differential (files that have changed since the last full backup).

Keep Your Backups Safe

Be sure to keep your disks or tapes in a safe place. Experts suggest keeping them somewhere away from the computer. If your computer is damaged or stolen, your backups will not suffer the same fate. Some organizations routinely ship their media to a distant location, such as a home office or a commercial warehouse, or store them in weather- and fireproof vaults. Home users may want to keep their backups in a fireproof box. Companies often keep three or more full sets of backups, all at different sites. Such prudence may seem extreme, but when crucial records are at stake, backups of files are vital to the welfare of a business.

OPTICAL STORAGE DEVICES

The most popular alternatives to magnetic storage systems are optical systems. The most widely used type of optical storage medium is the compact disk (CD), which can be read by nearly every type of optical storage device. However, several variations on the CD have emerged in the past few years, each with unique features. With those innovations, the storage capacity of "standard" CDs has increased a bit, while the emergence of the digital video disk (DVD) and its variants are taking storage capacities to a much higher level.

Since the mid-1990s, nearly all new PCs have been sold with a built-in CD-ROM drive. However, consumers are buying more and more systems with DVD-ROM drives, or with drives that can write data to compact disks or digital video disks. All these devices fall into the category of optical storage, because they store data on a reflective surface so it can be read by a beam of laser light. A laser uses a concentrated, narrow beam of light, focused and directed with lenses, prisms, and mirrors.

Figure 5A.19

Real Networks, Inc. makes a variety of programs that let you record and play music on your PC. Here, the RealOne Player is being used to play the contents of an audio CD.

CD-ROM

The familiar audio compact disk is a popular medium for storing music. In the computer world, however, the medium is called *compact disk-read-only memory (CD-ROM)*. CD-ROM uses the same technology used to produce music CDs. In fact, if your computer has a CD-ROM drive, a sound card, and speakers, you can play audio CDs on your PC (see Figure 5A.19).

A CD-ROM drive reads digital data (whether computer data or audio) from a spinning disk by focusing a laser on the disk's surface. Some areas of the disk reflect the laser light into a sensor, and other areas scatter the light. A spot that reflects the laser beam into the sensor is interpreted as a 1, and the absence of a reflection is interpreted as a 0.

Data is laid out on a CD-ROM disk in a long, continuous spiral that starts at the outer edge and winds inward to the center. Data is stored in the form of **lands**, which are flat areas on the metal surface, and **pits**, which are depressions or

NORTON
ONLINE

Visit **www.norton.glencoe.com** for more information on **optical storage devices**.

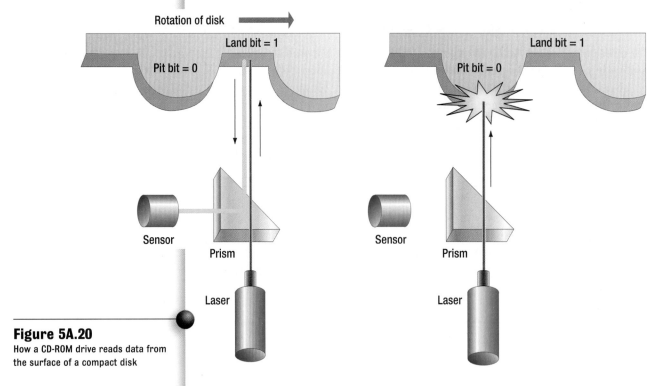

Figure 5A.20

How a CD-ROM drive reads data from the surface of a compact disk

hollows. As Figure 5A.20 shows, a land reflects the laser light into the sensor (indicating a data bit of 1), and a pit scatters the light (indicating a data bit of 0). On a full CD-ROM, the spiral of data stretches almost three miles long! A standard compact disk can store 650 MB of data, or about 70 minutes of audio. A newer generation of compact disks, however, can hold 700 MB of data or 80 minutes of audio.

Compared to hard disk drives, CD-ROM drives are quite slow, in part because the laser reads pits and lands one bit at a time. Another reason has to do with the changing rotational speed of the disk. Like a track on a magnetic disk, the track of an optical disk is split into sectors. However, the sectors are laid out differently than they are on magnetic disks (see Figure 5A.21).

Figure 5A.21

How sectors are laid out on a compact disk versus a magnetic disk

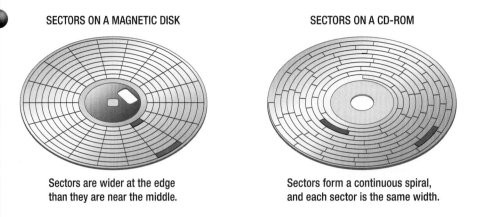

SECTORS ON A MAGNETIC DISK

Sectors are wider at the edge than they are near the middle.

SECTORS ON A CD-ROM

Sectors form a continuous spiral, and each sector is the same width.

The sectors near the middle of the CD wrap farther around the disk than those near the edge. For the drive to read each sector in the same amount of time, it must spin the disk faster when reading sectors near the middle and slower when reading sectors near the edge. Changing the speed of rotation takes time—enough to seriously impair the overall performance of the CD-ROM drive.

The first CD-ROM drives read data at 150 KBps (kilobytes per second) and were known as *single-speed* drives. Today, a CD-ROM drive's speed is expressed as a multiple of the original drive's speed—2x, 4x, 8x, and so on. A 2x drive reads data at a rate of 300 KBps (2 x 150). At the time this book was published, the fastest available CD-ROM drive was listed at a speed of 75x, meaning it can read data at a rate of 11,250 KBps (or slightly more than 11 MBps).

DVD-ROM

Many of today's new PCs feature a built-in digital video disk read-only memory (DVD-ROM) drive rather than a standard CD-ROM drive. DVD-ROM is a high-density medium capable of storing a full-length movie on a single disk the size of a CD. DVD-ROM achieves such high storage capacities by using both sides of the disk, by using special data-compression technologies, and by using extremely small tracks for storing data. (Standard compact disks store data on only one side of the disk.)

The latest generation of DVD-ROM disks actually uses layers of data tracks, effectively doubling their capacity. The device's laser beam can read data from the first layer, and then look through it to read data from the second layer.

DVDs look like CDs (see Figure 5A.22). DVD-ROM drives can play ordinary CD-ROM disks. A slightly different player, the DVD movie player, connects to your television and plays movies like a VCR (see Figure 5A.23). The DVD movie player also will play audio CDs.

Each side of a standard DVD-ROM disk can hold up to 4.7 GB. Therefore, these two-sided disks can contain as much as 9.4 GB of data. Dual-layer DVD-ROM disks can hold 17 GB of data.

Figure 5A.22
If your PC features a DVD drive, you can watch movies in DVD format on your computer's screen.

DVD-ROM drive

Figure 5A.23
DVD-ROM movie players can read video, audio, and data from DVD and CD disks. In PC systems, built-in DVD-ROM drives look just like standard CD-ROM drives.

Recordable Optical Technologies

For years, it was not possible for consumers to write data onto compact disks without investing in very expensive hardware. Despite the cost, the early "CD burners" were slow, difficult to use, and notorious for producing faulty disks. Today, however, consumers can easily create their own compact disks using inexpensive, simple hardware and software. The latest innovations in consumer-grade optical technologies allow home users to create their own DVDs, filled with audio and video, music, or computer data.

Here are some popular "writable" CD and DVD technologies:

◆ **CD-Recordable.** A CD-Recordable (CD-R) drive allows you to create your own data or audio disks that can be read by any CD-ROM drive. Most CD-R disks can be played in audio CD players, too. After information has been written to part of the special recordable disk (called a CD-R disk), that information cannot be changed. With most CD-R drives, however, you can continue to record information to other parts of the disk until it is full.

Figure 5A.24
With a CD-RW drive, you can record, erase, and re-record data on special compact disks.

◆ **CD-ReWritable (CD-RW).** Using a CD-ReWritable (CD-RW) drive, as shown in Figure 5A.24, you can write data onto special rewritable compact disks (called CD-RW disks), then overwrite it with new data. In other words, you can change the contents of a CD-RW disk in the same manner as a floppy disk. CD-RW disks have the same capacity as standard compact disks, and most can be overwritten up to 100 times. CD-RW disks, however, will not play on every CD-ROM drive, and most CD-RW disks cannot store audio data.

◆ **PhotoCD.** Kodak developed the **PhotoCD** system to store digitized photographs on a recordable compact disk. Many film developing stores have PhotoCD drives that can record your photos on a CD. You can then put the PhotoCD in your computer's CD-ROM drive (assuming that it supports PhotoCD, and most do) and view the images on your computer. You also can paste them into other documents (see Figure 5A.25). With a PhotoCD, you can continue to add images until the disk is full. After an image has been written to the disk, however, it cannot be erased or changed.

Figure 5A.25
After your pictures have been processed and stored on a PhotoCD, you can see them on your computer screen and copy them into documents.

◆ **DVD-Recordable (DVD-R).** After PC makers began adding DVD-ROM drives to computers, it did not take long for user demand to build for a recordable DVD system. The first to emerge is called **DVD-Recordable (DVD-R).** Like CD-R, a DVD-R system lets you record data onto a special recordable digital video disk, using a special drive. Once you record data onto a DVD-R disk, you cannot change it.

◆ **DVD-RAM.** The newest optical technology to reach consumers, sophisticated **DVD-RAM** drives let you record, erase, and re-record data on a special disk. Using video editing software, you can record your own digitized videos onto a DVD-RAM disk, then play them back in any DVD player. (However, special encoding makes it impossible to copy movies from commercial DVD onto a DVD-RAM disk.) DVD-RAM drives can read DVDs, DVD-R disks, CD-R disks, CD-RW disks, and standard CDs.

EMERGING STORAGE TECHNOLOGIES

In response to demands for storage devices with greater capacity and speed, developers seemed to focus their efforts on improving existing technologies instead of creating new ones. As a result, we now have PC hard disks approaching one terabyte, which spin many times faster than they once did. CD-ROM and DVD-ROM devices seem to have reached their maximum capacities, but that could change with innovations yet to be made.

Future PCs, however, may incorporate a new set of storage technologies. Whether these ultra-high-capacity, super-fast storage systems replace standard storage devices—or merely supplement them—remains to be seen. For now, the computer world is watching emerging technologies, such as the following, with anticipation:

◆ **FMD-ROM.** A new type of optical technology, **fluorescent multi-layer disk, read-only memory (FMD-ROM)** uses special fluorescent material in the reflective surface of the disk. FMD-ROM disks can contain ten or more data layers (compared to two layers in the highest-capacity DVD-ROM disks). A single FMD-ROM disk can store up to 140 GB of data. FMD-ROM drives can read standard CD-ROM and DVD-ROM disks.

◆ **Smart Cards.** Although it looks like an ordinary credit card, a **smart card** is a device with extraordinary potential (see Figure 5A.26). Smart cards contain a small chip that stores data. Using a special device, called a **smart card reader,** the user can read data from the card, add new data, or revise existing data. Some smart cards—called **intelligent smart cards**—also contain their own tiny microprocessor, and they function like a computer. Although they have not come into widespread use yet, smart cards are finding many purposes. For example, large hotels now issue guests a smart card instead of a key; the card not only allows guests to access their room, but it also allows them to charge other services and expenses to the card as well. Someday smart cards may be used to store digital cash that can be used to make purchases in stores or online (as long as the user has a reader connected to the PC). Smart cards could store a person's entire medical history, or they could be used as a source of secure identification. As their storage capacity increases, smart cards may be used someday the same way PC Card storage devices are used today.

Figure 5A.26

Smart cards may replace credit cards and drivers' licenses someday, or they may be used as a form of portable storage for computer data.

◆ **Holographic memory.** Its name sounds futuristic, but **holographic memory** could revolutionize data storage for decades to come. Holographic memory uses the power of lasers, like CD-ROM and DVD-ROM devices do; but instead of storing data on the surface of a spinning platter, a holographic memory system uses the internal structure of a crystalline or synthetic cube for storage. Theoretically, a holographic memory system could store 1 TB of data in a crystal the size of a sugar cube. Holographic memory systems were first conceived in the 1960s, and development on them was slow until recently. While no one can predict accurately when (or even if) these mass storage systems will be integrated into consumer- or business-class PCs, their potential is exciting.

NORTON
ONLINE

Visit **www.norton.glencoe.com** for more information on **emerging storage technologies.**

Norton Notebook

DATA WAREHOUSES, PART I

For years, companies have gathered and managed vast amounts of data of every imaginable kind. Because data truly is the lifeblood of a corporation, you can think of the corporation's data storage system as its heart. The bigger and stronger that system is, the more information it can handle, and the more effectively it will operate.

Large and medium-size companies are taking new approaches to storing and managing their huge collections of data. On the storage side of the equation is the data warehouse—a massive collection of corporate information, often stored in gigabytes or terabytes of data. Setting up a data warehouse is much more complicated than simply dumping all kinds of data into one storage place. Companies must consider several factors, such as the following, before investing in a data warehousing structure:

◆ **Storage Space.** One of the most popular mass-storage schemes is based on a redundant array of independent disks (RAID). RAID is a storage system that links any number of disk drives so that they act as a single disk. In this system, information is written to two or more disks simultaneously to improve speed and reliability, and to ensure that data is available to users at all times. Large-scale RAID systems offer up many terabytes of storage and incredibly fast access and data transfer times.

◆ **Processing Scheme.** Generally, two technologies are used to control data warehouses: symmetrical

multiprocessing (SMP) or massively parallel processing (MPP). Using special RAID controllers, such systems can rapidly collect data, check it for errors, and retrieve a backup copy of the data if necessary.

◆ **Backup Strategy.** RAID's capabilities are based on three basic techniques: (1) mirroring, (2) striping, and (3) striping-with-parity. In a mirrored system, data is written to two or more disks simultaneously, providing a complete copy of all the information on a drive in the event one drive should fail. Striping provides the user with a speedy response by spreading data across several disks. Striping alone, however, does not provide backup if one of the disks in an array fails. Striping-with-parity provides the speed of striping with the reliability of mirroring; in this scenario, the system stores parity information that can be used to reconstruct data if a disk drive fails.

◆ **Speed.** Newer data-warehousing systems not only incorporate huge disk drives, but some interconnect the drives with fiber-optic lines rather than standard wire-based buses. Fiber-optic lines use beams of pulsing light to transmit data; they operate many times faster than standard data-bus technologies.

Huge data warehouses can supply the data requirements for tens of thousands of users in a large organization. They also are used to store and support thousands or millions of transactions per day on active Web sites, such as the popular electronic auction and retail Web sites.

Having a place to store lots of data, however, leads to another question: How do you find what you need in all that data? The answer is a process called data mining, and it is explained in Part II of this discussion, in Unit 10.

In a simple RAID array like this, data is written to two or more disks at once, resulting in multiple copies. This protects the data in case one disk fails. In more sophisticated RAID configurations, data from a single file is spread over multiple disks, and duplicates are made. Error-checking is also provided in such arrays.

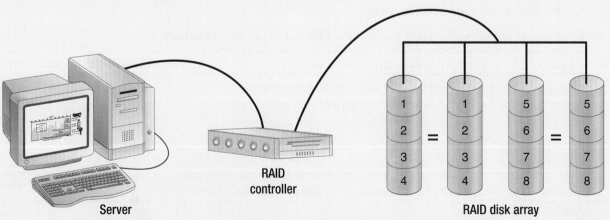

Server

RAID controller

RAID disk array

SUMMARY

- Storage devices can be categorized as magnetic or optical.

- The most common magnetic storage devices are diskettes, hard disks, high-capacity floppy disks, disk cartridges, and magnetic tape.

- The primary types of optical storage are compact disk-read-only memory (CD-ROM), digital video disk read-only memory (DVD-ROM), CD-Recordable (CD-R), CD-ReWritable (CD-RW), DVD-Recordable (DVD-R), DVD-RAM, and PhotoCD.

- Magnetic storage devices work by polarizing tiny pieces of iron on the magnetic medium. Read/write heads contain electromagnets that create magnetic charges on the medium.

- Before a magnetic disk can be used, it must be formatted—a process that maps the disk's surface and creates tracks and sectors where data can be stored.

- When a disk is formatted, the operating system creates four distinct areas on its surface: the boot sector, FAT, root folder, and data area.

- Hard disks can store more data than diskettes because of their higher-quality media, faster rotational speed, and the tiny distance between the read/write head and the disk's surface.

- Removable hard disks combine high capacity with the convenience of diskettes.

- High-capacity floppy disks are becoming a popular add-on for many computers. They offer capacities up to 250 MB and the same portability as standard floppy disks.

- Data cartridges are like small, removable hard disks, and they can store up to 20 GB.

- Magnetic tape systems offer slow data access; because of their large capacities and low cost, they are a popular backup medium.

- CD-ROM uses the same technology as a music CD does: A laser reads lands and pits on the surface of the disk.

- Standard CD-ROM disks can store up to 650 MB, although newer disks can hold 700 MB. Once data is written to the disk, it cannot be changed.

- DVD-ROM technology is a variation on the standard CD-ROM. DVDs offer capacities up to 17 GB.

- Other popular variations on the CD-ROM are CD-Recordable, CD-ReWritable, and PhotoCD. Popular variations of DVD-ROM are DVD-Recordable and DVD-RAM.

KEY TERMS

boot, *157*
cluster, *157*
cylinder, *161*
data area, *158*
density, *160*
directory, *158*
disk cartridge, *162*
DVD-RAM, *168*
DVD-Recordable (DVD-R), *168*
file allocation table (FAT), *158*
fluorescent multi-layer disk,
    read-only memory (FMD-ROM), *169*
folder, *158*
format, *155*
head crash, *161*
high-capacity floppy disk, *162*
holographic memory, *169*
hot-swappable hard disk, *162*
initialize, *155*

intelligent smart card, *169*
land, *165*
logical format, *157*
low-level format, *157*
magnetic storage, *152*
master boot record, *157*
optical storage, *152*
PhotoCD, *168*
pit, *165*
polarize, *154*
root directory, *158*
root folder, *158*
sector, *156*
smart card reader, *169*
smart card, *169*
soft format, *157*
storage device, *152*
storage media, *152*
track, *156*

KEY TERM QUIZ

Complete each statement by writing one of the terms listed under Key Terms in each blank.

1. When an iron bar is ~~polarized~~ , its ends have opposite magnetic polarity.

2. When formatting a magnetic disk, the disk drive creates a set of concentric rings, called ~~tracks~~ on its surface.

3. The process of labeling tracks and sectors is called _____ , _____ , or _____ .

4. A disk's ~~FAT~~ records the location of each file and the status of each sector.

5. A disk's ~~density~~ is a measure of its capacity.

SECTION QUIZ

True/False

Answer the following questions by circling True or False.

True False
1. The hardware components that write data to storage media are called storage devices.

True False
2. Writing data means recording data on the surface of a disk.

True **False**
3. The process of mapping a disk's surface is called ~~organizing~~ data. *formatting a initializing*

True False
4. A cluster is a group of sectors.

True **False**
5. The top folder on any disk is known as the master boot sector. *root*

Multiple Choice

Circle the word or phrase that best completes each statement.

1. A _____ is an example of a magnetic storage device.
   A. hard disk drive   **B.** PhotoCD drive   **C.** neither A nor B

2. Diskettes spin at about _____ revolutions per minute.
   A. 150   **B.** 300   **C.** 600

3. The _____ is a small program that runs when you start the computer.
   A. file allocation table   **B.** master boot record   **C.** sector

4. Using a _____ drive, you can record, erase, and re-record data to a DVD.
   A. DVD-ROM   **B.** DVD-R   **C.** DVD-RAM

5. A(n) _____ hard disk can be inserted and removed while the computer is running.
   A. cartridge   **B.** optical   **C.** hot-swappable

REVIEW QUESTIONS

In your own words, briefly answer the following questions.

1. List five types of magnetic storage devices.

2. List seven types of optical storage devices.

3. Describe how a magnetic disk's read/write head can pass data to and from the surface of a disk.

4. What is the purpose of a magnetic disk's file allocation table (FAT)?

5. Describe the function of lands and pits on the surface of a compact disk.

SECTION LABS

Complete the following exercises as directed by your instructor.

1. Format a blank floppy disk:
   A. Make sure the disk's write-protect tab is closed. Place the disk in the diskette drive.
   B. Launch Windows Explorer. (The steps to launch Windows Explorer depend on the version of Windows you use. Ask your instructor for specific directions.)
   C. Right-click the floppy disk icon in the left pane. Click Format on the shortcut menu.
   D. In the Format dialog box, choose a capacity for the disk. Click the "Quick (erase)" option. Make sure the "Display summary when finished" option is checked. Click Start.
   E. Click Close twice. Remove the disk from the drive. Leave the Explorer window open.

2. Explore the contents of your hard disk. In the Explorer window's left pane, click the system's hard disk icon labeled (C:). Look at the status bar at the bottom of the window. How many "objects" (folders) are stored on the hard disk? How much free space is available? Click several folders, and review their contents in the right pane. When finished, close the Explorer window.

Measuring and Improving Drive Performance

OBJECTIVES

- Explain the importance of understanding drive performance.
- Define the term *average access time* and describe how it is measured.
- Explain why file compression is a factor in drive performance.
- Define the term *data transfer rate* and describe how it is measured.
- Explain two steps you can take to optimize the performance of your computer's hard disk.
- Identify four drive interface standards commonly used in PCs.

OVERVIEW: The Need for Speed

An important factor in measuring overall system performance is the speed at which the computer's disk drives operate. Measures of drive performance generally are applied to the computer's hard disk, but they also can be applied to other types of drives.

When evaluating the performance of common storage devices, you need to be aware of two common measures: the average access time and the data transfer rate. For random-access devices (all the storage devices discussed, with the exception of magnetic tapes), you generally want a low access time and a high data transfer rate. With tape drives, all you really need to worry about is convenience and capacity.

These performance factors can be important when you are buying a new computer or upgrading your current system. You want to make sure that your drives operate at a speed that complements your processor's capabilities. You also want to make sure that the drive uses an interface that is compatible with any other devices you may add to the computer.

AVERAGE ACCESS TIME

For a storage device, **average access time** (or **seek time**) is the amount of time the device takes to move its read or read/write heads to any spot on the medium. It is important that the measurement be an average, because access times can vary greatly, depending on how far the heads need to move. To measure the access time of a drive effectively, you must test many reads of randomly chosen sectors—a method that approximates the actual read instructions a disk drive would receive under normal circumstances.

Average access time is an important measure of performance for storage devices and memory. Even though memory chips have no moving read/write head, it is still critical to know how fast a memory system can locate a piece of data on a chip. For storage devices, access times are measured in **milliseconds (ms),** or one-thousandths of a second. For memory devices, access times are measured in **nanoseconds (ns),** or one-billionths of a second.

In a disk drive, access time depends on a combination of two factors: the speed at which a disk spins (revolutions per minute, or rpm) and the time it takes to move the heads from one track to another. For example, the longest amount of time needed for a diskette drive's read/write head to access any point is about 0.2 second, which is the amount of time needed for the disk to complete one revolution at 300 rpm. The maximum access time for diskettes, therefore, is 0.2 second, or 200 milliseconds. The average access time is about one-half the maximum, or 100 milliseconds.

Average access times for hard drives can vary, but most good drives work at rates of 6 to 12 milliseconds, many times faster than diskette drives. Some very high-performance hard disks have access times as fast as 4 or 5 milliseconds.

At 80 to 800 ms, access times for CD-ROM drives tend to be quite slow by hard disk drive standards, but tape drives have the longest average access times of any storage device. Depending on the type of drive and format used, tape drives can take from a few seconds to a few minutes to find a specific piece of data on the tape's surface.

The easiest way to determine the average access time for a device is to check the manufacturer's specifications. You should be able to find the specifications for a device in its packaging or documentation, or you may be able to get them from the manufacturer's Web site (see Figure 5B.1). Popular computer-related magazines—such as *PC Magazine, Computer Shopper,* and others—regularly test new drives to measure various performance factors.

Figure 5B.1
Like many storage device manufacturers, Seagate Technology, Inc. provides product specifications on its Web site. This page shows the specifications for several of Seagate's hard disks.

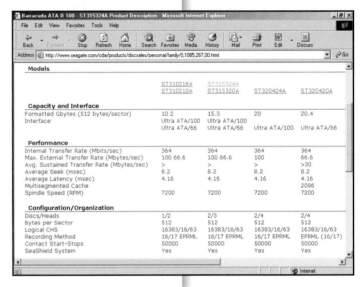

FILE COMPRESSION

Even with the large storage devices available, many users still find themselves pushing the limits of what they can store on their PCs. One solution to this storage problem, besides upgrading to larger devices, is to compress data. **File compression,** or **data compression,** is the technology for shrinking the size of a file, thereby freeing up space for more data and programs to reside on the disk.

Compressing files will not necessarily improve a disk's performance; that is, compressing files will not reduce a disk's access time. However, file compression can enable you to store more data on a disk, effectively increasing the disk's capacity.

File compression is performed by software that squeezes data into smaller chunks by removing information that is not vital to the file or data. When the file is returned to its original state, this data is reinserted so that the original data is reproduced exactly as it was before compression.

Some favorite compression programs for PCs include PKZIP and WinZip. StuffIT is a favorite compression utility among Macintosh enthusiasts.

Most file-compression utilities are useful for compressing one or more files to reduce their storage requirements. When you use a utility like WinZip, the program actually shrinks the selected files and then saves them together inside a new file, with its own name. The resulting file is called an **archive file** because it stores the compressed files inside it. Archive files commonly are used for exactly that purpose—archiving unneeded data files.

Figure 5B.2 shows an example of a file compression utility at work. Depending on the circumstances (the compression software used, the data file's native program, and other factors), the user may need to **extract** the compressed files manually (that is, return them to their uncompressed state) before using them. Most file compression utilities enable the user to create self-extracting archive files—files that can extract themselves automatically.

Figure 5B.2
The WinZip file compression utility at work

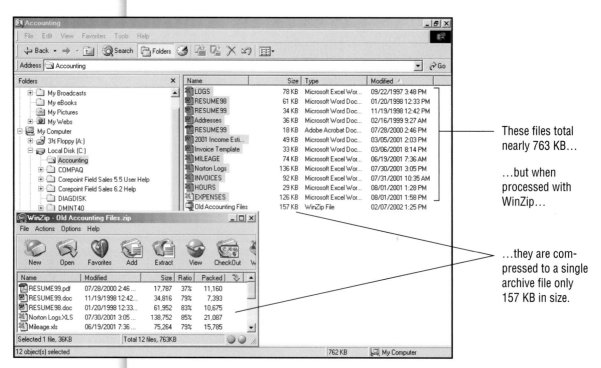

These files total nearly 763 KB...

...but when processed with WinZip...

...they are compressed to a single archive file only 157 KB in size.

Utilities like WinZip, PKZIP, or StuffIT generally are not used to compress the contents of an entire hard disk. Because such files must be expanded manually, a lot of effort would be required to compress a disk's contents, select and expand files when you want to use them, and then recompress them. For this reason, programs such as DriveSpace are helpful. (DriveSpace is built into some versions of Windows, and you can purchase commercial utilities that perform full-disk compression.)

DriveSpace effectively doubles the storage capacity of a hard disk by compressing all its contents. You can use your programs and data in compressed form without expanding them manually; DriveSpace handles those tasks for you. Full-disk compression schemes are not without risks, however. For example, a disk may perform more slowly because of all the compressing and expanding that occurs in the background, and the likelihood of data errors increases.

NORTON ONLINE

Visit www.norton.glencoe.com for more information on **data transfer rate**.

DATA TRANSFER RATE

The other important statistic for measuring drive performance is the speed at which it can transfer data—that is, the amount of time it takes for one device to transfer data to another device. Speeds are expressed as a rate, or as some amount of data per unit of time. When measuring any device's **data transfer rate** (also called **throughput**), time is measured in seconds, but units of data may be measured in bytes, KB, MB, or GB. Figure 5B.3 illustrates data transfer rate.

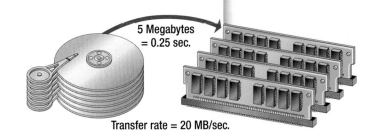
5 Megabytes = 0.25 sec.

Transfer rate = 20 MB/sec.

Figure 5B.3
Data transfer rate is the time required to move a specific amount of data (for example, 20 MB) from one device to another, such as from the hard disk to memory.

As is the case with access times, data transfer rates can vary greatly from one device to another. Speeds for hard disks are generally high, from about 15 MBps for low-end home systems to 80 MBps and higher for the faster drives designed for high-performance workstations and servers. When buying a hard disk, the data transfer rate is at least as important a factor as the access time.

CD-ROMs and diskettes are the slowest storage devices. CD-ROMs range from 300 KBps for a double-speed player, to 900 KBps for a 6x drive, to even higher speeds, with the data transfer rate corresponding to the drive's speed. Diskette drives average about 45 KBps. Removable hard disks range from about 1.25 MBps up into the hard disk range.

Some drive manufacturers and dealers advertise their drives' data transfer rates in units of megabytes per second (MBps); others express them in megabits per second (Mbps). When shopping, note if the rate specified is "MBps" or "Mbps."

Self Check ☑

Complete each statement by filling in the blank(s).

1. For storage devices, access times are measured in _____ .

2. _____ is the technology for shrinking the size of a file.

3. Throughput is another term for _____ .

At Issue

Is It Too Easy To Make Copies?

If computers are useful for anything, it is for copying data. Whether the data is a letter you typed in a word processing program or a song you converted to an MP3 file, it can be easily copied and recopied.

There are some obvious advantages to managing data in digital form and using computers to copy it. First, the process is easy. Once the file is on disk, you can duplicate it on other disks, e-mail it to someone, transfer it over the Internet, rename it, and perform lots of tasks with it. You can easily rename a copied file, and then change it, so the original file remains unchanged.

Second, the quality of digital data does not degrade as it is copied. No matter how often a file is duplicated, it never changes or gets "fuzzy."

In spite of these advantages, however, is it possible that computers make it too easy to copy data? Many ethicists ponder this question, for a few good reasons:

◆ **Waste.** If you spend some time examining the contents of your own computer's disks, you will probably find lots of files you do not need. Many of these unneeded files will be duplicates. Many programs and operating systems also create duplicates of files, usually without notifying the user. These duplicates sometimes are removed from the disk when a program closes, but sometimes they are left behind, taking up disk space. When the number of unnecessary files builds up, a disk's performance can decrease, because it must keep track of all those files and search through them when looking for needed data.

Unneeded files also can contribute to disk fragmentation. This happens when a disk cannot store a file in contiguous sectors and has to "fragment" the file, storing pieces of it on different areas of the disk. The more fragmented a disk's surface becomes, the slower it performs.

◆ **Piracy.** As you will see in Unit 14, "Living with Computers," software piracy is one of the most common problems plaguing the computer industry, and it causes billions of dollars in lost revenues. One reason software piracy is so commonplace is that programs are easy to duplicate. For example, if you have a CD-R drive, you can easily make copies of programs on a CD.

◆ **Copyright infringement.** Many publishers place original, copyrighted files on the Internet as a way to publicize their work. These files can be photographs, illustrations, videos, animations, text excerpts, or audio. Once a file is placed on the Internet, however, it is a simple matter for someone to download it, make copies of it, and distribute it. This type of copying can infringe on the owner's copyright if the users are expected to pay for the file, or if someone copies a file and then uses it in his or her own work or for commercial purposes.

Industry experts are trying to develop systems to protect files from being copied. These efforts may reduce piracy or copyright infringement. Until such copy prevention systems are foolproof, however, unscrupulous copying will continue.

The Internet is filled with copyrighted images, which should not be copied or redistributed. But even though copying copyrighted material is a violation of the copyright law, it is a common practice which often results in lost revenues for the copyright owners.

Matthew Broderick, Jennifer Jason Leigh
PHOTO BY J. RUDOLPH

OPTIMIZING DISK PERFORMANCE

NORTON
ONLINE

Visit **www.norton.glencoe.com** for more information on **optimizing disk performance.**

Over time, a PC's performance can slow down. This is especially true with older systems, but even newer PCs can suffer from occasional performance downturns. The computer may act sluggish in general, or it may slow down when performing specific tasks, such as loading or saving documents.

When a PC slows down in this manner, some disk maintenance may fix the problem. Any PC that gets used a lot should get routine disk maintenance, or **disk optimization.** Using your operating system's built-in tools or other utilities, you can keep your computer's hard disk and other magnetic disks running the best they can.

Cleaning Up Unneeded Files

If your system has been in service for a while (even just a few months), there is a good chance that hundreds of unneeded files are cluttering up your hard disk. Windows accumulates all sorts of files during normal operations. Some of these files are meant to be stored only temporarily, but Windows does not always clean them out. If you ever shut down your computer improperly, Windows does not have a chance to delete these files, and they will stay put until you clear them out yourself.

These files, called **temporary (temp) files,** are used by Windows to store various versions of documents in progress, files being sent to the printer, automatic backup files, and more. Windows usually stores these files with the file-name extension .tmp in various locations on your disk. A hard disk also can become cluttered by temporary Internet files, which are saved by your Web browser.

Over time, a normal PC can accumulate hundreds of temporary files stored in different locations. These files can really slow down your system, because the hard disk has to deal with the unneeded files when it is looking for data or for space to store new files.

Newer versions of Windows feature a built-in utility called Disk Cleanup (see Figure 5B.4). Disk Cleanup and other disk-cleaning utilities can quickly find and identify temporary files and remove them from your disk. The process takes only a few minutes, and it can free hundreds of megabytes of wasted space on an average hard disk. Most computer users should clean the temporary files off their hard disks at least once a week.

If your hard disk contains programs that you do not plan to use, you can remove them—a process called **uninstalling.** To remove a program, start by checking its group in the Programs menu. If you see an "Uninstall" option, click it, and the program will uninstall itself. If you use a recent

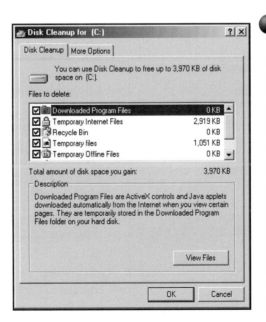

Figure 5B.4
This is the Disk Cleanup utility in Windows 2000. It lets you choose the kinds of files you want to delete, then locates and removes them from the disk. This user's hard disk contains nearly 3 MB of temporary Internet files and more than 1 MB of other temporary files. The cleanup process takes only a few seconds, and it will recover nearly 4 MB of disk space.

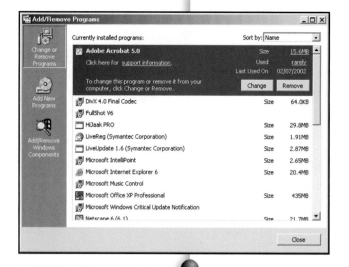

Figure 5B.5

This is the Add/Remove Programs utility in Windows 2000. This window lets you select a program on your hard disk and remove it. The utility tells you how much disk space you will recover by removing a program.

Figure 5B.6

The disk scanning utility in Windows 2000 attempts to fix disk errors and recover lost data.

Figure 5B.7

The Disk Defragmenter utility in Windows 2000 can show you what percentage of the disk's surface is covered with fragmented files. It then can piece the files back together, storing them in contiguous sectors. This can greatly improve your disk's performance.

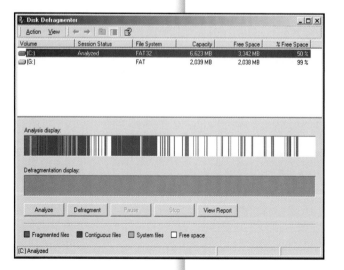

version of Windows, you also can use its Add/Remove Programs utility (see Figure 5B.5). There are a number of commercial software products that can uninstall programs from your system, too.

Scanning a Disk for Errors

Another way to optimize disk performance is to scan the disk for errors, fix the errors, and possibly recover data that has been lost or corrupted because of a disk error. A disk error can be a bad spot on the disk's physical surface, or it can be a piece of data that cannot be accounted for in the FAT. Scanning a disk can be time-consuming, but scanning may be able to fix problems and improve performance. Several versions of Windows have a built-in disk-scanning utility (see Figure 5B.6), but you also can buy very sophisticated disk scanners.

Defragmenting a Disk

On the surface of a magnetic disk, **fragmentation** occurs when a file is stored in pieces on different sectors on the disk's surface. As you create, modify, copy, and delete files (and install and uninstall programs) over time, many files can become fragmented. Although your operating system keeps track of each fragment, a greatly fragmented disk can slow system performance, because it can take longer to find and load all the pieces of files as they are needed.

Windows has a built-in defragmentation utility, called Disk Defragmenter (see Figure 5B.7). You can use this utility—or one of several commercial utilities—to ensure that your files are stored efficiently. After the initial defragmentation, you may notice a big performance improvement.

DRIVE-INTERFACE STANDARDS

Visit **www.norton.glencoe.com** for more information on **drive-interface standards**.

Another important factor in determining how quickly a drive can read and write data is the type of controller that the drive uses. Just as a video monitor requires a controller to act as an interface between the CPU and the display screen, storage devices also need a controller to act as an intermediary between the drive and the CPU. A **disk controller** connects the disk drive to the computer's bus, enabling the drive to exchange data with other devices.

Currently, most personal computers use one of two drive-interface standards: EIDE or SCSI. A lot of confusion has surrounded drive-interface standards, because competing developers have introduced many variations of and names for these technologies. If you buy a PC today, it almost certainly will feature one of these two drive interfaces. If you plan to purchase a drive for an existing PC, be sure that the new drive is compatible with the computer's drive interface.

Enhanced Integrated Drive Electronics (EIDE)

Enhanced integrated drive electronics (EIDE) is an enhanced version of an older drive-interface standard, called integrated drive electronics (IDE). While the IDE standard still exists and is the basis for several drive interfaces, the standard is known by many different names, and EIDE is widely regarded as the catch-all term for drive interfaces based on this standard.

As a result, most new computer systems use the EIDE drive-interface standard, or one like it. The latest version of EIDE supports data transfer rates of 66 MBps. The EIDE standard's variants go by names such as Fast IDE, ATA, Fast ATA, ATA-2, ATA-3, ATA-4, Ultra ATA, and ATA66. Each offers somewhat different features and performance.

Small Computer System Interface (SCSI)

The history of the small computer system interface (SCSI) goes back to the 1970s. SCSI originally was developed as a way to connect third-party peripheral devices to mainframe computers—specifically, IBM mainframe computers. SCSI went through many transformations before the American National Standards Institute (ANSI) established a definition for the interface in 1986. Since then, the definition of SCSI has continued to evolve into SCSI-2, Wide SCSI, Fast SCSI, Fast Wide SCSI, Ultra SCSI, SCSI-3 (also known as Ultra-Wide SCSI), Ultra 2 SCSI, and Wide Ultra 2 SCSI.

SCSI allows even higher data transfer rates than are possible with EIDE. The Wide Ultra 2 SCSI interface, for example, supports a data transfer rate of 80 MBps. Because of its speed, flexibility, and high throughput rates, the SCSI drive interface standard usually is found in higher-end business systems, servers, and workstations (see Figure 5B.8).

Figure 5B.8
SCSI drive interfaces often are found in high-performance desktop computers, workstations, and network servers.

COMPUTERS
in your career

Computer Training Specialists

As long as computers keep evolving and new software programs are developed, people will need help learning to use them. This is the domain of the computer training specialist.

Many companies have full-time trainers, who help employees master computer hardware and software. Trainers can be especially important in a company that uses its own proprietary software, or that relies on unusual applications with special uses. Trainers are critical in companies that have a large workforce and high employee turnover rates, because new workers must master their skills and become productive quickly.

There is also a growing demand for freelance computer training specialists who have a broad general knowledge of hardware and software. Many small- and medium-sized companies, for example, contract freelance trainers a few times each year to teach workers about standard productivity applications (such as word processors or spreadsheet programs) or operating systems. A qualified freelance trainer can find consistent, high-paying contract work with a variety of clients.

In many environments, a trainer works in a classroom or lab setting, similar to one found in a school. In these settings, each student sits at a computer, and the trainer leads the class through its tasks. Increasingly, however, trainers work one-on-one with individual workers—not only to teach them how to use a program, but also to teach them how to master advanced features, work toward a certification, or troubleshoot problems.

A successful trainer needs a strong background in general computer hardware and software. This means that a trainer should have a solid understanding of how a computer system functions and have a mastery of current operating systems and common application software.

Often, trainers must get additional instruction or certification if they want to teach others to use certain programs. Companies such as Microsoft and Oracle, for example, offer trainer-certification programs that ensure employers that a trainer has mastered certain products and is qualified to teach others how to use them.

The pay scale for computer training specialists covers a wide range. Freelance trainers, for instance, may charge an hourly rate (ranging from $25 to $50, or higher), which goes up with the complexity of the programs being taught. The annual salary for full-time trainers can start out in the $18,000 to $30,000 range, but it can go up with experience and expertise. Top-level trainers (who teach other trainers and develop training courses or materials) can earn $50,000 per year or more.

SUMMARY

- In storage devices, the average access time is the time it takes a read/write head to move to a spot on the storage medium.

- Diskette drives offer an average access time of 100 milliseconds. Hard drives are many times faster.

- Tape drives provide the slowest average access times of all magnetic storage devices; optical devices are also much slower than hard disks.

- File compression technology is used to shrink the size of files so that they take up less disk space.

- By using compression utilities, you can shrink multiple files into a single archive file. Utilities such as Windows' DriveSpace enable you to compress the entire contents of your hard disk.

- The data transfer rate is a measure of how long it takes a given amount of data to travel from one device to another. Hard disks offer the fastest data transfer rates of any storage device.

- You can optimize the performance of a PC's hard disk by cleaning off unneeded files, scanning the disk for errors, and defragmenting the disk.

- All PCs use a disk controller as an interface between a disk drive and the CPU. Two drive-interface standards—EIDE and SCSI—are commonly used today.

KEY TERMS

archive file, *176*
average access time, *175*
data compression, *176*
data transfer rate, *177*
disk controller, *181*
disk optimization, *179*
enhanced integrated drive electronics (EIDE), *181*
extract, *176*

file compression, *176*
fragmentation, *180*
millisecond (ms), *175*
nanosecond (ns), *175*
seek time, *175*
temporary (temp) files, *179*
throughput, *177*
uninstall, *179*

KEY TERM QUIZ

Complete each statement by writing one of the terms listed under Key Terms in each blank.

1. _____ is another term for data transfer rate.

2. Using _____ , you can fit more data onto a magnetic disk.

3. A(n) _____ connects a disk drive to the computer's bus.

4. To remove a program from your computer, you can _____ it.

5. Routine disk maintenance, which can improve a disk's performance, is called _____ .

SECTION QUIZ

True/False

Answer the following questions by circling True or False.

True   False   **1.** To measure the access time of a drive, you must test the way the drive reads data from a single sector.

True   False   **2.** One purpose of file compression technology is to create free space on a disk.

True   False   **3.** Data transfer rates should not vary from one device to another.

True   False   **4.** EIDE and SCSI are two common drive-interface standards used in PCs.

True   False   **5.** One way to improve a hard disk's performance is to remove temporary files that may no longer be needed.

Multiple Choice

Circle the word or phrase that best completes each statement.

1. The amount of time a storage device takes to position its head over any spot on the medium is called _____ .
   A. average access time   B. seek time   C. both A and B

2. For storage devices, access times are measured in _____ .
   A. nanoseconds   B. milliseconds   C. seconds

3. Some file compression utilities can shrink a group of files and save them together in a new file called a(n) _____ .
   A. data file   B. extraction file   C. archive file

4. _____ is when pieces of a file are scattered across the surface of a disk.
   A. Fragmentation   B. Optimization   C. Compression

5. The term MBps stands for _____ .
   A. megabits per second   B. megabytes per second   C. neither A nor B

REVIEW QUESTIONS

In your own words, briefly answer the following questions.

1. What is the primary use of file-compression utilities, such as WinZip?

2. What do the terms EIDE and SCSI stand for?

3. What is data transfer rate?

4. How is average access time measured for storage and memory devices?

5. List three tasks you can perform that can improve the performance of a computer's hard disk.

SECTION LABS

Complete the following exercises as directed by your instructor.

1. Learn what kind of hard disk controllers are installed in your computer.
   A. Open the Control Panel window, as directed by your instructor.
   B. Double-click the System icon to open the System Properties dialog box.
   C. Click the Device Manager tab. Click the plus sign (+) in front of Hard Disk Controllers. (Note: Depending on which version of Windows you use, you may need to access the Device Manager in a different way. Ask your instructor for specific directions.)
   D. Click to highlight an item listed under Hard Disk Controllers, then click the Properties button. Write down the data for the selected controller, and then click Cancel.
   E. Repeat step D for each item listed under Hard Disk Controllers. When you are finished, click Cancel to close the System Properties dialog box. Then close the Control Panel dialog box.

UNIT LABS

Complete the following exercises using a computer in your classroom, lab, or home.

1. **Find Your Optimization Tools.** If you use Windows 98 or a later version, you can use the operating system's built-in disk optimization tools to remove unneeded files from a disk, to defragment a disk, and to scan a disk for errors.

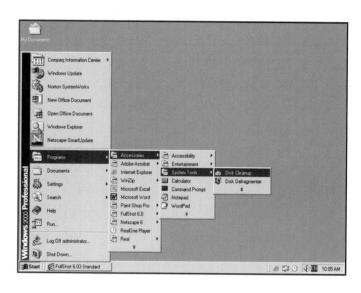

To use Disk Cleanup in Windows 98, Me, 2000, or XP:

A. Click the Start button, open the Programs menu, click Accessories, click System Tools, and then click Disk Cleanup.

B. When the Select Drive dialog box appears, click the drop-down arrow and select your primary hard disk. (This should be drive C:. If you are not sure which drive to select, ask your instructor for assistance.

C. Click OK.

D. In the Disk Cleanup for dialog box, select all the check boxes in the *Files to delete* list.

E. If you want to see any of the files before deleting them, click the type of files you want to see, and then click the View Files button. Close any windows that open to return to the Disk Cleanup for dialog box.

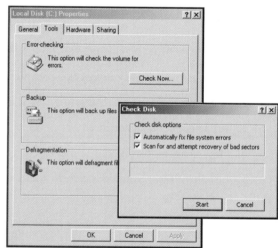

F. Click OK in the Disk Cleanup for dialog box.

G. Windows may display a message box, asking if you are sure you want to delete the files. If so, click the Yes button.

To scan your disk for errors:

In Windows 98 or Me:

A. Click the Start button, click Programs, click Accessories, click System Tools, and then click ScanDisk.

B. When the ScanDisk dialog box opens, select your computer's primary disk drive. (This should be drive C:. If you are not sure which drive to choose, ask your instructor for help.)

C. Set other options in the ScanDisk dialog box, as directed by your instructor. Then, click Start.

D. Watch as Windows scans the disk for errors.

E. Click the Cancel button when your instructor tells you to. Then click Close to close the ScanDisk dialog box.

If you use Windows 2000 or XP:

A. Launch either Windows Explorer or My Computer, depending on your preference.

B. When the Windows Explorer or My Computer window opens, select your computer's primary disk drive. (This should be drive C:. If you are not sure which drive to choose, ask your instructor for help.

C. Right-click the selected drive's icon. When the shortcut menu appears, click Properties.

D. When the Properties dialog box appears, click the Tools tab. Under Error-checking, click the Check Now button.

E. When the Check Disk dialog box appears, set options as directed by your instructor, and then click Start.

F. Watch as Windows performs the scan. The actions Windows takes will depend on the options you selected in step E. When the scan is complete, close all open dialog boxes, then close the Windows Explorer or My Computer window.

DISCUSSION QUESTIONS

As directed by your instructor, discuss these questions in class or in groups.

1. Why do you think a basic truth in computing is that one never has enough storage space? As hard disks get larger, do you think we will reach a point where the standard desktop computer has more than enough storage space for the average user's needs? Have we reached that point already?

2. Suppose that your class is actually one department within a medium-size company. You need to adopt a backup system for the department's data. As a group, what factors should you consider in making this decision? What backup technologies should you consider? What type of backup schedule should you follow?

RESEARCH AND REPORT

Using your own choice of resources (such as the Internet, books, magazines, and newspaper articles), research and write a short paper discussing one of the following topics.

■ The growth in capacity of PC storage devices, from the 1980s to the present

■ The consequences of compressing an entire hard disk's contents, using a utility such as DriveSpace

■ Holographic memory and its potential uses

When you are finished, proofread and print your paper, and give it to your instructor.

 **ETHICAL ISSUES** Many storage device options are available. These choices are beneficial for many users, but they also can be drawbacks for software companies, music publishers, and others. With this thought in mind, discuss the following questions in class:

1. If you had a CD-R or CD-RW drive, would you make illegal copies of software programs and swap them with friends? Why or why not? Defend your answer.

2. Many companies store huge amounts of information about their customers. Should they be free to share or sell that information? Why or why not? Support your answer.

UNIT 6

The Operating System and User Interface

UNIT CONTENTS

This unit contains the following sections:

The Interactive Browser Edition CD-ROM provides additional labs and activities to apply concepts from this unit.

Operating System Basics

OVERVIEW:
The Role of the Operating System

An operating system (OS) is a software program, but it is different from word processing programs, spreadsheets, and all the other software programs on your computer. As you may recall from Unit 1, the OS is an example of system software—software that controls the system's hardware, and which interacts with the user and application software. In short, the operating system is the computer's master control program. The OS provides you with the tools (commands) that enable you to interact with the PC. When you issue a command, the OS translates it into code that the machine can use. The OS ensures that the results of your actions are displayed on screen, printed, and so on. The operating system also acts as the primary controlling mechanism for the computer's hardware.

The operating system performs the following functions:

► Provides the instructions to display the on-screen elements with which you interact. Collectively, these elements are known as the user interface.

► Loads programs (such as word processing and spreadsheet programs) into the computer's memory so that you can use them.

► Coordinates how programs work with the CPU, RAM, keyboard, mouse, printer, and other hardware, as well as with other software.

► Manages the way information is stored on and retrieved from disks.

The functioning of the OS can be extended by adding utility software.

OBJECTIVES

● List the four primary functions of an operating system.

● Identify four components found in most graphical user interfaces.

● Describe the operating system's role in running software programs.

● Explain how the operating system enables users to manage files.

● List three ways the operating system manages the computer's hardware.

● Name five types of utilities that enhance an operating system's capabilities.

OPEN

SAVE

PRINT

COPY

PASTE

VISUAL ESSAY: THE USER INTERFACE

When you work directly with an operating system, you see and use a set of items on the screen. Taken together, these items are called the **user interface.** Most current operating systems, including all versions of Windows, the Macintosh operating system, OS/2, and some versions of UNIX and Linux, provide a **graphical user interface (GUI,** pronounced GOO-ee). Graphical user interfaces are so called because you use a mouse (or some other pointing device) to point at graphical objects—such as windows, menus, icons, buttons, and other tools—on the screen. These graphical tools all represent different types of commands; the GUI enables you to issue commands to the computer by using visual objects instead of typing commands. This is one of the key advantages of the graphical user interface: It frees you from memorizing and typing text commands.

A

This screen shows the **desktop** displayed by Windows XP Professional. The desktop is the main interface to the computer. The pictures—called **icons**—represent resources on the PC or network, such as programs, folders, files, and printers. Using your mouse or other pointing device, you can **choose** (or **activate**) an icon, telling Windows you want to use the resource that the icon represents. For example, you can choose the Internet Explorer icon to launch that program. The items that appear on the desktop depend on the contents of the computer's disks and the resources it can access. For this reason and others, any two Windows desktops may look different.

The background is called the desktop.

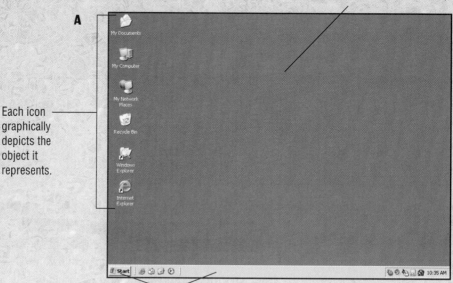

A

Each icon graphically depicts the object it represents.

The taskbar and Start button are unique to Windows.

B

The **taskbar** appears at the bottom of the Windows desktop; it lets you launch and manage programs. The **Start button** is a permanent feature of the taskbar; click it to open the **Start menu.** The Start menu gives you access to all the programs and resources on your computer. When you start a program in Windows, a button for it appears on the taskbar.

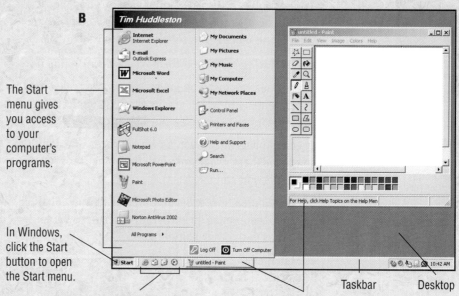

B

The Start menu gives you access to your computer's programs.

In Windows, click the Start button to open the Start menu.

You can launch programs by clicking icons you added to the taskbar.

If a program is running, a button appears on the taskbar.

Taskbar   Desktop

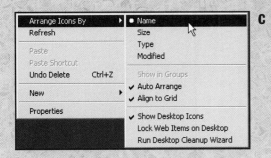

C

C

When you right-click many objects in Windows, a small menu appears, containing the most common commands associated with that object. This type of menu may be called a **shortcut menu** or a **context menu**. The screen shot shows the shortcut menu that appears when you right-click the desktop in Windows XP Professional.

The title bar identifies the window's contents.

The Minimize, Maximize, and Close buttons let you hide or resize the window, or close it altogether.

The menu bar provides lists of commands and options for this program.

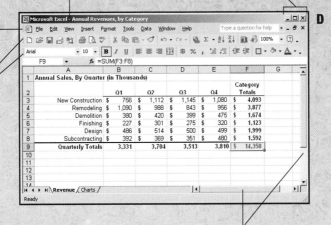

D

When you launch a program, it is loaded into memory and begins to run. A running program may take up the whole screen, or it may appear in a rectangular frame, called a **window**. A different window appears for each resource you want to use. This illustration shows Microsoft Excel 2002 running in a window. Some tools, such as the tools shown here, appear in nearly every window you open. In the Windows GUI, programs share many of the same features, so you see a familiar interface, no matter what program you are using.

Toolbars contain buttons, which let you issue commands quickly.

Scroll bars let you view parts of the program or file that do not fit in the window.

E

Lotus 1-2-3 is the active program. Its window is on top, and its title bar and taskbar button are highlighted.

Graphical operating systems let you have multiple programs and resources running at the same time, but you can work in only one window at a time. The window that is currently in use is called the **active window**; its title bar appears in color, and its taskbar button appears highlighted. Unless all open windows are arranged side by side, the active window will appear on top of any inactive windows. You must select the window you want to use before you can access its contents, either by clicking in it or by clicking its taskbar button. The process of moving from one open window to another is called **task switching**.

Netscape Navigator is in the background. Its title bar is grayed out, and its taskbar button is not highlighted. When an item is grayed out, it is not available for selection.

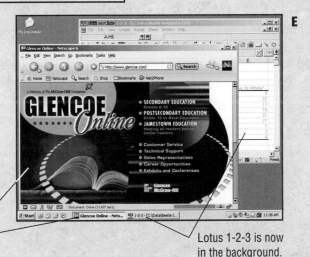

E

Netscape Navigator is now the active program.

Lotus 1-2-3 is now in the background.

You initiate many tasks by clicking icons and toolbar buttons, but you also can perform tasks by choosing commands from lists called **menus**. In most program windows, you open menus from a horizontal list called the **menu bar**. As shown in this illustration, many programs feature a File menu, which typically contains commands for opening, closing, saving, and printing files. To execute or run one of the menu commands, you click it. In many cases, you can issue menu commands by using keyboard shortcuts instead of the mouse.

You can open a menu by clicking its name on the menu bar.

The underlined F indicates that you can press Alt+F to open the File menu, instead of clicking.

With the File menu open, you can press P to execute the Print command.

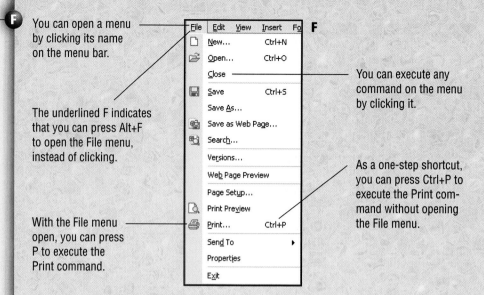

You can execute any command on the menu by clicking it.

As a one-step shortcut, you can press Ctrl+P to execute the Print command without opening the File menu.

Dialog boxes are special-purpose windows that appear when you need to tell a program (or the operating system) what to do next. A dialog box is so named because it conducts a "dialog" with you as it seeks the information it needs to perform a task. This illustration shows a typical dialog box and describes some of the most common dialog box features.

Click a tab to display different "pages" of the dialog box.

Option buttons let you select one option from a set of choices.

The Help button provides information about the tools in the dialog box.

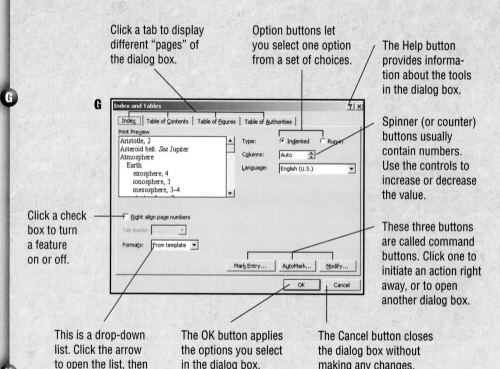

Spinner (or counter) buttons usually contain numbers. Use the controls to increase or decrease the value.

Click a check box to turn a feature on or off.

These three buttons are called command buttons. Click one to initiate an action right away, or to open another dialog box.

This is a drop-down list. Click the arrow to open the list, then make a selection.

The OK button applies the options you select in the dialog box.

The Cancel button closes the dialog box without making any changes.

Some older operating systems (such as MS-DOS) and some current versions of UNIX and Linux feature a **command-line interface**, which uses typewritten commands—rather than graphical objects—to execute tasks. Users interact with a command-line interface by typing strings of characters at a **prompt** on the screen. In DOS, the prompt usually includes the identification for the active disk drive (a letter followed by a colon), a backslash (\), and a greater-than symbol, as in C:\>. This illustration shows the DOS prompt, which is still available in Windows for those who want to run DOS programs or to work with DOS keyboard commands.

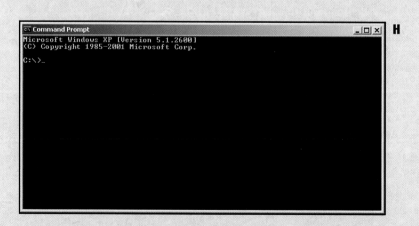

PRODUCTIVITY Tip

Do-It-Yourself Tech Support

If you want to learn a new feature or need help solving a problem, the answers may be on your hard disk or the Internet.

Using Local Online Help

Most commercial operating systems and applications include an online help system that is installed on your computer with the software. New-generation help systems include descriptions, tips, audio/video demonstrations, hyperlinks, and links to Internet-based resources.

To find help on your hard disk, open the help system and look for answers. To get help with the Windows XP operating system, for example, click the Start button, and choose Help and Support from the Start menu. In any Windows application, click the Help menu, and choose Contents or Help Topics. A Help window appears, providing tools that let you search for help in different ways. Remember the following tips:

◆ **Be Patient.** You may not find your answer immediately. Be prepared to try again.

◆ **Learn Different Search Options.** Most Windows-based help systems provide different options for finding help. For example, you may be able to browse a list of help topics that are organized by category. Or you may be able to search the help system for topics that contain certain terms or phrases. Some Help systems let you type questions in plain English. If you need help printing a document, for example, you can type the question, "How do I print a document?"

◆ **Think of the Problem in Different Ways.** For example, if you want help with setting up an Internet connection, the terms "Internet", "connection", "modem", and "Internet account" may bring up the right answers.

◆ **Use Bookmarks and Annotations.** Most help systems let you bookmark specific help topics, so you can find them again quickly. You also can add your own notes to specific topics.

Using Remote Online Help

Many software makers provide help resources that you can access over the Internet.

A program's help system is often the last place users turn for help. It should be the first place you look.

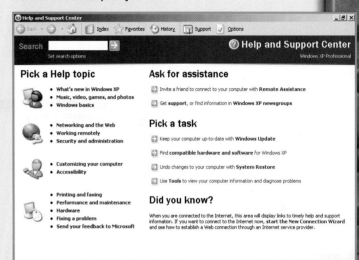

◆ **Web-Based Technical Support.** Many software companies have a "Support" or "Help" link on their Web site's home page.

◆ **FAQs.** Most software companies have Web sites with lists of Frequently Asked Questions (FAQs).

◆ **E-Mail Help.** At the company's Web site, you may find an option that lets you describe a problem and submit a request for help. A support technician will investigate the problem, or an automated system will send you a list of possible solutions.

◆ **Knowledge Bases.** A knowledge base is a sophisticated database containing detailed information about specific topics. To use a knowledge base, you type a term or phrase or describe a problem. After your text is matched against a database, you are presented with a list of possible solutions.

◆ **Newsgroups.** Large software companies sponsor newsgroups on the Internet. Using your newsreader, you can access these newsgroups, post questions for other users to answer, or participate in discussions about specific products and technical issues.

Before you use any remote online help resource, read all the information the company provides about it. Look for notices about fees, registration, and proof of product ownership.

Complete each statement by filling in the blank(s).

1. In Windows, the ___desktop___ is the main interface to the computer.
2. In Windows, clicking the ___start button___ opens the Start menu.
3. The process of moving from one open window to another is called ___task switching___.

Visit **www.norton.glencoe.com** for more information on **data sharing**.

RUNNING PROGRAMS

The operating system provides a consistent interface between programs and the user. It is also the interface between those programs and other computer resources such as memory, a printer, or another program. Programmers write computer programs with built-in instructions—called **system calls**—that request services from the operating system. (They are known as "calls" because the program has to call on the operating system to provide some information or service.)

For example, when you want your word processing program to retrieve a file, you use the Open dialog box to list the files in the folder that you specify (see Figure 6A.1). To provide the list, the program calls on the operating system. The OS goes through the same process to build a list of files, whether it receives its instructions from you (via the desktop) or from an application. The difference is that when the request comes from an application, the operating system sends the results of its work to the application, rather than to the desktop.

Figure 6A.1
The Open dialog box in Microsoft Word, a word processing program

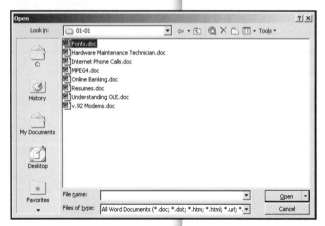

Some other services that an operating system provides to programs, in addition to listing files, include:

◆ Saving the contents of files to a disk.

◆ Reading the contents of a file from disk into memory.

◆ Sending a document to the printer, and activating the printer.

◆ Providing resources that let you copy or move data from one document to another, or from one program to another.

◆ Allocating RAM among the programs that are running.

◆ Recognizing keystrokes or mouse clicks, and displaying characters or graphics on the screen.

Sharing Information

Many types of applications let you move chunks of data from one place to another. For example, you may want to copy a chart from a spreadsheet program and place the copy in a document in a word processing program (see Figure 6A.2).

Many operating systems accomplish this feat with a feature known as the **Clipboard.** The Clipboard is a temporary holding space (in the computer's memory) for data that is being copied or moved. The Clipboard is available for use by applications running under the operating system. For example, if you want to

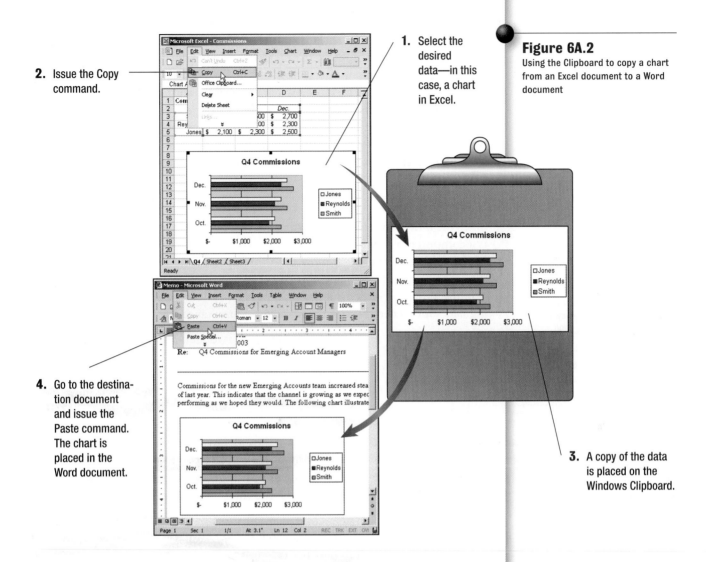

2. Issue the Copy command.

1. Select the desired data—in this case, a chart in Excel.

4. Go to the destination document and issue the Paste command. The chart is placed in the Word document.

3. A copy of the data is placed on the Windows Clipboard.

move a paragraph in a document in a word processor, select the paragraph, and then choose the **Cut command**; the data is removed from the document and placed on the Clipboard. (If you want to leave the original data in place, you can use the **Copy command**: A copy is made of the data, and it is stored on the Clipboard, but it is not removed from the document.) After placing the insertion point in the document where you want to place the paragraph, you choose the **Paste command**; the data on the Clipboard is placed into the document.

The Clipboard also can be used to move data from one document to another. For example, you can copy an address from one letter to another, and thereby avoid rekeying the address. The real versatility of the Clipboard, however, stems from the fact that it is actually a part of the operating system; it is not a particular application. As a result, you can use the Clipboard to move data from one program to another.

The versatility of the Clipboard has been extended further with a feature known in Windows as **OLE,** which stands for **Object Linking and Embedding.** A simple cut and paste between applications results in object embedding. The data, which is known as an "object" in programming terms, is embedded in a new type of document. It retains the formatting that was applied to it in the original application, but its relationship with the original file is destroyed; that is, it is simply part of the new file.

Object linking adds another layer to the relationship: The data that is copied to and from the Clipboard retains a link to the original document, so that a change in the original document also appears in the linked data. For example, suppose that the spreadsheet and memo shown in Figure 6A.2 are generated quarterly. They always contain the same chart updated with the most recent numbers. With object linking, when the numbers in the spreadsheet are changed, the chart in the report will automatically reflect the new figures. Of course, object linking is not automatic; you need to use special commands in your applications to create the link.

Multitasking

Since the mid-1990s, all PC operating systems have been able to multitask, which is a computer's version of being able to "walk and chew gum at the same time." **Multitasking** means much more than the capability to load multiple programs into memory; it means being able to perform two or more procedures—such as printing a multiple-paged document, sending e-mail over the Internet, and accepting data input when the user types a letter—simultaneously (see Figure 6A.3).

Figure 6A.3

Multitasking lets you do more than one task at a time. Here the computer is printing a document, while the user downloads a file from the Internet. This figure shows multitasking in Windows 2000.

Software engineers use two methods to develop multitasking operating systems. The first requires cooperation between the operating system and application programs. Programs that are currently running will periodically check the operating system to see whether any other programs need the CPU. If any do, the running program will relinquish control of the CPU to the next program. This method is called **cooperative multitasking,** and it is used to allow activities such as printing while the user continues to type or use the mouse to input more data.

The second method is called **preemptive multitasking.** With this method, the operating system maintains a list of programs that are running and assigns a priority to each program in the list. The operating system can intervene and modify a program's priority status by rearranging the priority list. With preemptive multitasking, the operating system can preempt the program that is running and reassign the time to a higher priority task at any time. Preemptive multitasking thus has the advantage of being able to carry out higher-priority programs faster than lower-priority programs.

MANAGING FILES

The files that the operating system works with may be program or data files. Most programs come with any number—possibly thousands—of files. When you use programs, you often create your own data files, such as word processing documents, and store them on a disk under names that you assign to them. The operating system tracks all these files so that it can copy any one of them into RAM at a moment's notice.

To accomplish this feat, the operating system maintains a list of the contents of a disk on the disk itself. The operating system updates the information in the file allocation table (FAT) any time a file is created, moved, renamed, or deleted. In addition, the operating system keeps track of different disks or disk drives by assigning names to them. On IBM and compatible computers, diskette drives are assigned

NORTON

ONLINE

Visit **www.norton.glencoe.com** for more information on **multitasking**.

the letters A and B, and hard disk drives are designated as the C drive and up. CD-ROM drives have the first available letter following the hard drives—often the letter D. Non-Microsoft operating systems use slightly different schemes for keeping track of disks and their contents, but each scheme accomplishes the same task.

When there are hundreds of files on a disk, finding the one you want can be time-consuming. To find files quickly, you can organize them using folders. Figure 6A.4 shows a list of a folder on a hard disk, as shown in the Windows Explorer utility. Notice how file names are accompanied by the file sizes in bytes and the date and time when the files were last modified.

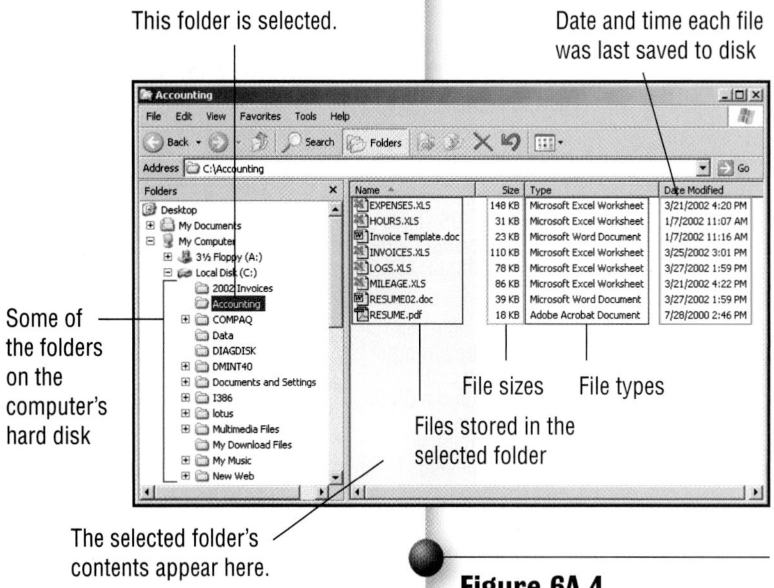

This folder is selected.

Date and time each file was last saved to disk

Some of the folders on the computer's hard disk

File sizes   File types

Files stored in the selected folder

The selected folder's contents appear here.

Figure 6A.4
Some of the folders and files on a typical hard disk, viewed in Windows Explorer

Also notice that there are several folders in the list. Folders can contain other folders, so you can create a structured system known as a **hierarchical file system.** Figure 6A.5 illustrates an example of a hierarchical file system.

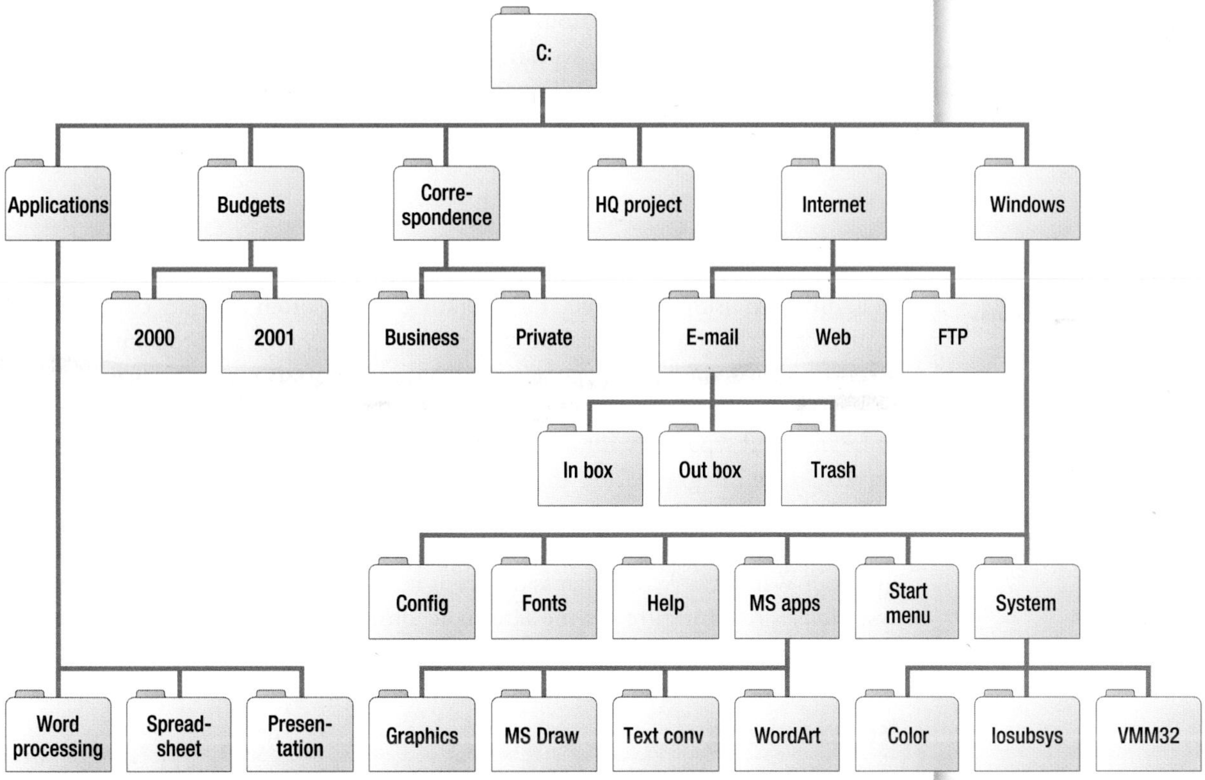

Figure 6A.5
A hierarchical file system

MANAGING HARDWARE

When programs run, they need to use the computer's memory, monitor, disk drives, and other devices, such as a printer. The operating system is the intermediary between programs and hardware. In a computer network, the operating system also mediates between your computer and other devices on the network.

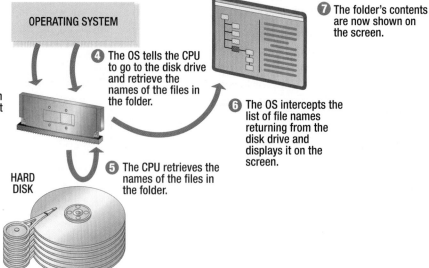

① When you click on a folder, the OS interprets the action as a command to list the files in that folder.

② The OS sends an interrupt request to the CPU.

③ When possible, the CPU pauses any other processing and checks with the OS to see what new processing job is being requested.

④ The OS tells the CPU to go to the disk drive and retrieve the names of the files in the folder.

⑤ The CPU retrieves the names of the files in the folder.

⑥ The OS intercepts the list of file names returning from the disk drive and displays it on the screen.

⑦ The folder's contents are now shown on the screen.

OPERATING SYSTEM

HARD DISK

Figure 6A.6

How the operating system communicates with the CPU

Visit **www.norton.glencoe.com** for more information on **drivers**.

Processing Interrupts

The operating system responds to requests to use memory and other devices, keeps track of which programs have access to which devices, and coordinates everything the hardware does so that various activities do not overlap and cause the computer to become confused and stop working. The operating system uses interrupt requests (IRQs) to help the CPU coordinate processes. For example, if you tell the operating system to list the files in a folder, it sends an interrupt request to the computer's CPU (see Figure 6A.6).

Drivers

In addition to using interrupts, the operating system often provides complete programs for working with special devices, such as printers. These programs are called **drivers** because they allow the operating system and other programs to activate and use—that is, "drive"—the hardware device. When DOS reigned, drivers had to be installed separately for each program used. With today's operating systems, drivers are an integral part of the operating system. Most of the software you buy will work with your printer, monitor, and other equipment without requiring you to install any special drivers. For example, many modems use the same unified driver in Windows 9x. All that is different is the setup information the operating system uses to configure the modem to accommodate the specific capabilities of each modem.

Networking

Besides providing interrupt requests and drivers for working with individual devices, the operating system also can allow you to work with multiple computers on a network. On a network, usually each person has a separate PC with its own operating system. The network server also has its own operating system, which manages the flow of data on the file server and around the network. As operating systems continue to evolve, networking will become a more integral part of all operating systems.

VISUAL ESSAY: UTILITY SOFTWARE

Operating systems are designed to let you do most of the tasks you normally would want to do with a computer, such as managing files, loading programs, printing documents, and so on. But software developers are constantly creating new programs—called **utilities**—that enhance or extend the operating system's capabilities, or which simply offer new features not provided by the operating system itself. There are thousands of different utility programs, and you can find many of them for free on the Internet.

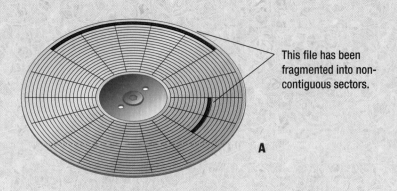

This file has been fragmented into non-contiguous sectors.

A

A

If a file is too large to be saved in a single sector on a disk, it must be broken into pieces. Each piece is saved in a separate sector. Ideally, the pieces will be stored in contiguous sectors, but this is not always possible, because enough contiguous sectors may not be available. In this case, the pieces are stored in noncontiguous sectors. When this happens to a large number of files, the disk is said to be fragmented. Fragmentation slows disk performance, because the OS must spend time looking for pieces of files stored in various places.

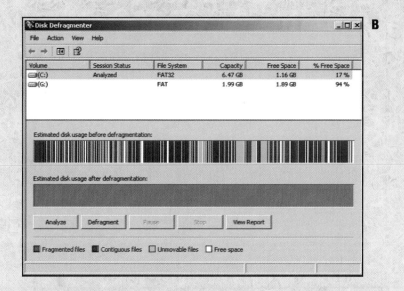

B

B

To make sure your computer is using its disk space optimally, you need to defragment the disk once in a while. To do this, you can use a special utility called a **disk defragmenter.** This type of tool rearranges fragmented pieces of data so that your files are stored in contiguous sectors. Windows 95 and later versions feature a built-in utility named Disk Defragmenter, as shown here in Windows XP. But you also can purchase sophisticated defragmenters, such as the defragmenter included in Norton Utilities, which can do a better job of storing files and claiming unused disk space.

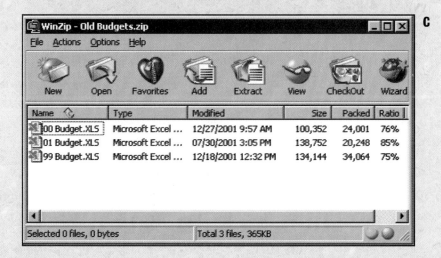

C

C

You can use a **data compression utility** (also called a **file compression utility**) to reduce the size of files so that they consume less disk space. Utilities such as WinZip, StuffIT, and others use special algorithms to search files for unnecessary bits, which are stripped out. The process can significantly shrink some types of files. In this collection of compressed files, the files have shrunk by more than 70 percent.

A **backup utility** can help you copy large groups of files from your hard disk to another storage medium, such as tape or a CD-R disk. Many newer operating systems feature built-in backup utilities, but feature-rich backup software is available from other sources. These utilities not only help you transfer files to a backup medium, they also help organize the files, update backups, and restore backups to disk in case of data loss.

Many different programs fall under the category of **disk management utilities,** and they perform many different kinds of tasks. Some, like PartitionMagic (shown here), allow you to divide a hard disk into multiple partitions, so one large disk can work like several smaller ones. Other disk management utilities specialize in keeping your computer's hard disk healthy by constantly checking its surface for errors or bad spots that can corrupt data. Others called **antivirus utilities** can examine a disk or RAM for hidden viruses (parasitic programs that can delete or scramble files or replicate themselves until the host disk is full).

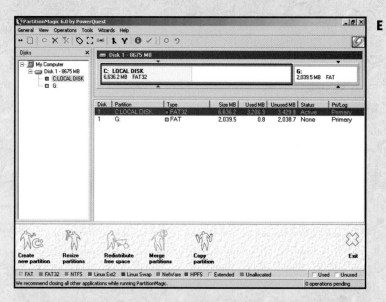

Screen savers are popular utilities, although they serve little purpose other than to hide what would otherwise be displayed on the screen. A screen saver automatically appears when the system has gone unused for a specified period of time. Screen savers display a constantly moving image on the screen and were originally created to prevent constantly displayed images from "burning" into the monitor.

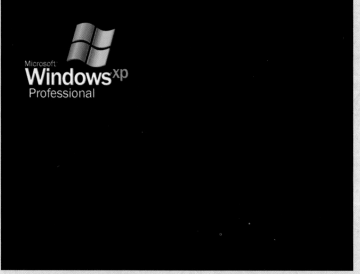

Norton Notebook

CHANGING YOUR PC'S OPERATING SYSTEM

The operating system market has expanded over the past few years, freeing PC users to choose different operating systems. Users no longer feel locked into the OS provided by the PC's manufacturer.

Any newer model PC (if it has sufficient resources) can run almost any currently available operating system. For example, if you have a Pentium II-class or later computer with 128 MB of RAM and a large hard disk, you do not necessarily need to run Windows 9x. Instead, you can use Windows NT or 2000, OS/2, Linux, and some versions of UNIX (but not the Mac OS). You might even be able to run Windows XP. If you have a Macintosh, you also may be able to run some versions of UNIX or Linux (but not Windows).

Consider Your Needs First

Consider your need for a new operating system. Do you need a different OS to use a specific application? Is the OS used in your workplace or school, or do you need to be OS-compliant with a workgroup? Do you plan to develop or test applications that run on a specific operating system? Or will a different operating system allow better performance from your computer? If you answer yes to any of these questions, a new OS may be a good idea.

Compatibility Is a Must

Before installing an OS, make sure that your hardware is completely compatible with it. If you have any doubts, check with the manufacturers of your computer and any devices attached to it. Check with the operating system's developer to see if a "hardware compatibility list" is available; it may be found on the developer's Web site. This document may answer all your hardware-related questions. If you suspect a problem, weigh the costs of replacing the hardware against installing a new OS.

If your hardware is compatible, make sure you have adequate resources for the new OS. Having adequate resources can be a problem for some operating systems, such as Windows 2000 and XP, which consume a great deal of system resources. Make sure your PC has enough power, memory, and storage, not just for the OS, but also for your applications and data.

Next, make a list of all the applications you use or plan to use, and make sure they will run under the new OS. Be sure to include your utilities, Internet tools, and

others. You may need to upgrade or replace some or all of your software to accommodate the new OS. Again, weigh this cost against the need for a new OS.

Taking the Big Step

Before you install anything, take these precautions:

◆ **Back Up Your Hard Disk.** If you plan to install the OS on your existing hard disk, make a complete backup beforehand. If the installation goes wrong, you can restore the disk to its previous state. Before you back up, test the disk for errors (by using ScanDisk or a similar utility), defragment the drive, and run a full virus scan.

◆ **Decide Whether to Reformat.** You may want to reformat the disk completely before installing a new OS. Reformatting erases everything related to the previous operating system, and it may make installation easier. If you do not know how to format a hard disk, look in your current operating system's help system and follow the directions closely.

◆ **Call for Help if You Need It.** If you have never installed a new OS, you may not be prepared for all the pitfalls involved. If the upgrade is essential, then it is worth doing right, so get help from an experienced user or a computer technician before you start. Most computer manufacturers have extensive customer service support, but be prepared to wait some time before talking to a "real" person. If your questions are answered, then it is worth the wait.

Many operating systems, such as Windows 2000 and XP, walk you through the upgrade process. They can even tell you if your existing hardware and software are compatible with the new OS.

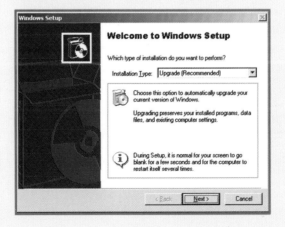

SUMMARY

- Most modern operating systems feature a graphical user interface (GUI). You control a GUI-based system by pointing and clicking graphical objects on the screen. In a GUI, all objects and resources appear on a background called the desktop.

- You access programs and other resources in rectangular frames called windows. Applications running under the same operating system use many of the same features, so you see a familiar interface no matter what program you are using.

- Some older operating systems use a command-line interface, which the user controls by typing commands at a prompt.

- The operating system manages all the other programs that run on the PC, and it provides services such as file management, memory management, and printing to those programs.

- Some operating systems enable programs to share information. This lets you create data in one program and use it again in other programs.

- Modern operating systems support multitasking, which is the capability of running multiple processes at the same time.

- The operating system keeps track of all the files on each disk. To track each file's location, the OS maintains a running list of information on each file in a table that is usually called the file allocation table (FAT).

- You can make your own file management easier by creating a hierarchical file system that includes folders and subfolders organized in a logical order.

- The OS uses interrupt requests (IRQs) to maintain organized communication with the CPU and other hardware.

- Each hardware device is controlled by another piece of software, called a driver, which allows the OS to activate and use the device.

- The operating system also provides some of the software needed to link computers together and form a network.

- A utility is a program that extends or enhances the operating system's capability. It may add a new capability to the operating system. The most popular types of utility programs include disk defragmenters, data compression programs, backup utilities, antivirus programs, disk managers, and screen savers.

KEY TERMS

activate, *190*
active window, *191*
antivirus utility, *200*
backup utility, *200*
choose, *190*
Clipboard, *194*
command-line interface, *192*
context menu, *191*
cooperative multitasking, *196*
Copy command, *195*
Cut command, *195*
data compression utility, *199*
desktop, *190*
dialog boxes, *192*
disk defragmenter, *199*
disk management utility, *200*
driver, *198*
file compression utility, *199*
graphical user interface (GUI), *190*

hierarchical file system, *197*
icon, *190*
menu bar, *192*
menu, *192*
multitasking, *196*
Object Linking and Embedding (OLE), *195*
Paste command, *195*
preemptive multitasking, *196*
prompt, *192*
screen saver, *200*
shortcut menu, *191*
Start button, *190*
Start menu, *190*
system call, *194*
task switching, *191*
taskbar, *190*
user interface, *190*
utility, *199*
window, *191*

KEY TERM QUIZ

Complete each statement by writing one of the terms listed under Key Terms in each blank.

1. In a graphical user interface, _icon_ represent resources on the computer, such as files, programs, or printers.

2. _multitasking_ means the ability to perform two or more tasks at the same time.

3. You interact with a command-line interface by typing strings of characters at a(n) _prompt_.

4. The _Clipboard_ is a temporary storage space for data that is being copied or moved.

5. Data compression programs are examples of _utilities_.

SECTION QUIZ

True/False

Answer the following questions by circling True or False.

True	False	1. Graphical user interfaces are so called because you point at graphical objects on the screen.
True	False	2. You interact with icons by using the keyboard.
True	False	3. All windows are unique, because none share the same features.
True	False	4. Many programs allow you to choose menu commands by using either the mouse or keyboard shortcuts.
True	False	5. The operating system is responsible for allocating RAM among the programs that are running.

Multiple Choice

Circle the word or phrase that best completes each statement.

1. In a GUI, the window that is currently in use is called the _____ window.
   A. active
   B. biggest
   C. framed

2. Graphical operating systems often let you choose commands from lists called _____ .
   A. command lines
   B. menus
   C. neither A nor B

3. DOS and some versions of UNIX are examples of _____ interfaces.
   A. old-fashioned
   B. GUI
   C. command-line

4. To remove data from one document and place it in another, you can use the _____ and _____ commands.
   A. Cut, Paste
   B. Copy, Paste
   C. File, Open

5. The term _____ describes one type of multitasking.
   A. simultaneous
   B. preemptive
   C. neither A nor B

REVIEW QUESTIONS

In your own words, briefly answer the following questions.

1. What are the four primary functions that an operating system performs?

2. What is the primary tool you use to interact with a graphical user interface?

3. In later versions of the Windows operating system, what happens when you right-click many parts of the desktop?

4. What is the function of windows in a GUI?

5. Why is task switching a necessary feature of a multitasking operating system?

SECTION LABS

Complete the following exercises as directed by your instructor.

1. Use your online help system to learn more about Windows. Click the Start button, then choose Help (or Help and Support) from the Start menu. Explore the Help window to learn more about the tools provided by the Help system in your particular version of the operating system. (The exact features vary from one version of Windows to another.) When you are comfortable with the Help window, use any method you prefer to search for information on these topics: **operating system, GUI, command, dialog box, menu,** and **multitasking.** When you are finished, close the Help window.

2. Practice using the DOS command prompt:
   A. Click the Start button.
   B. If you use Windows 9x or 2000, point to Programs, then click the MS-DOS prompt on the Programs menu. If you use Windows XP, point to All Programs, point to Accessories, and then click Command Prompt. Either way, the command prompt appears in a new window.
   C. At the prompt, type **DIR** and press Enter. Review the results. Then type the **VER** command, press Enter, and review the results. Close the window.

PC Operating Systems

OVERVIEW:
A Brief Historical Perspective

The personal computer has come a long way in a relatively short time, and much of the progress is due to the continuing advancements in operating systems. Over the past twenty years, the evolution in operating systems has made PCs easier to use and understand, more flexible, and more reliable. Today, in addition to the operating systems that consume hundreds of megabytes of disk space on personal computers, miniaturized operating systems fit onto tiny portable digital assistants (PDAs) and even cellular telephones.

Many early computers ran under operating systems, such as CP/M, which are no longer used. As PCs came into common usage in homes and businesses, the vast majority of them ran DOS—a much maligned, command-line-based operating system that still is present to one extent or another in most versions of Windows. Now, as in the past, many PCs run under some version of UNIX, which is one of the richest and most enduring operating systems.

Users have several choices when it comes to operating systems, although the choice is not always easy. The vast majority of new PCs are sold with some version of Windows installed, but many users (especially in business) are choosing to run UNIX or Linux.

This section introduces you to the primary operating systems used on personal computers and describes the basic features of each. The operating systems are discussed chronologically, in order of their appearance on the desktop. You will learn how operating systems have evolved over the past two decades.

OBJECTIVES

- List all the major PC operating systems.
- Explain why DOS is no longer the dominant OS for personal computers.
- List two advances that made the Macintosh OS popular.
- Differentiate between the terms *operating environment* and *operating system*.
- List and differentiate the various versions of Windows.

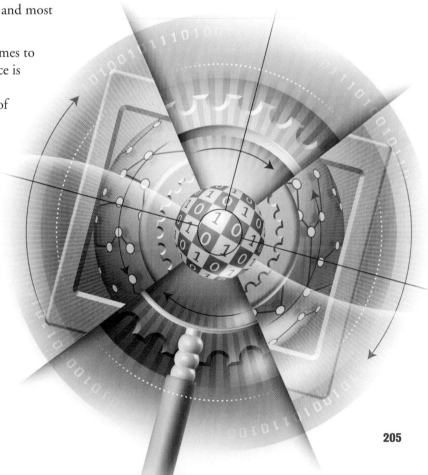

```
linex2> ls
Mail/         News/         brian/         mail/
Mailboxes/    ShopCart.dat  james.pl       public_html/
linex2> cd mail
linex2> ls
saved-messages    sent-mail        sent-mail-feb-1996
linex2> cd ..
linex2> ls
Mail/         News/         brian/         mail/
Mailboxes/    ShopCart.dat  james.pl       public_html/
linex2> ps
  PID TT STAT  TIME COMMAND
 3023 p8 S     0:00 -csh (csh)
linex2> ftp
ftp> open ftp.netscape.com
Connected to ftp20.netscape.com.
220 ftp20 FTP server (Version wu-2.4(17) Tue Feb 20 09:08:35 PST 1996) ready.
Name (ftp.netscape.com:swankman): anonymous
331 Guest login ok, send your complete e-mail address as password.
Password:
230-Welcome to the Netscape Communications Corporation FTP server.
230-
230-If you have any odd problems, try logging in with a minus sign (-)
230-as the first character of your password.  This will turn off a feature
230-that may be confusing your ftp client program.
230-
230-Please send any questions, comments, or problem reports about
230-this server to ftp@netscape.com.
230-
230-***********  October 13, 1995  ***********
230-Private ftp is now only on ftp1.netscape.com.  Anonymous is supported on
230-ftp 2 through 8.  If you are accessing a named account please use ftp1.
230-
230 Guest login ok, access restrictions apply.
ftp> bye
221 Goodbye.
linex2> 
```

Figure 6B.1

The UNIX command-line interface—Most versions of UNIX are case-sensitive: They can differentiate between upper- and lowercase letters typed at the command prompt.

Visit www.norton.glencoe.com for more information on UNIX.

UNIX

UNIX (pronounced YOO-niks) is older than all the other PC operating systems, and in many ways, it served as a model for them. Initially developed by Bell Labs in the 1970s, UNIX was geared toward uses in telecommunications systems.

Instead of marketing UNIX as a commercial product, Bell Labs distributed the operating system's underlying source code and allowed users to modify it. As a result, dozens (if not hundreds) of different versions of UNIX began springing up, especially at universities, where UNIX was widely used as a teaching and research tool by programmers and computer scientists. Today, there are two major "families" of UNIX—one developed and promoted by AT&T (called System V), and the other from Berkeley University (known as BSD UNIX). Many specific versions of UNIX exist, including A/UX for the Mac, AIX for IBM high-end workstations, Solaris for Sun Microsystems workstations, SCO UNIX, XENIX, and others.

From nearly the beginning, UNIX was an incredibly powerful and flexible operating system that could run on a single computer or on a network. It provides preemptive multitasking, which makes efficient use of the computer's resources, especially when meeting the demands of many users or applications. UNIX allows multiple users to work from more than one keyboard and monitor attached to a single CPU, like a mainframe with terminals. UNIX also supports multiprocessor systems—a PC with more than one CPU working at a time.

UNIX runs on many types of computers, including supercomputers, notebook PCs, and everything in between, including mainframes and minicomputers. Because of its ability to work with so many kinds of hardware, UNIX remains a very popular operating system for Internet host computers. Thanks to its power and its appeal to engineers and other users of CAD and CAM software, UNIX has been popular for RISC workstations such as those from Sun Microsystems, Hewlett-Packard, and Silicon Graphics.

UNIX is not for the faint of heart because of its command-line interface and cryptic instructions, plus the fact that it requires many commands to do even simple tasks (see Figure 6B.1). In an attempt to make UNIX more user-friendly, developers have created windows-based GUIs for UNIX, such as MOTIF and OpenLook, which are based on a windowing standard called X-Windows. Nonetheless, UNIX never really caught on as a consumer operating system. It eventually gave way to DOS, Windows, and the Mac OS, which generally have been perceived as easier to learn and use.

In the business world, UNIX remains a popular operating system, especially among organizations that manage large databases shared by hundreds or thousands of users. Many types of specialized database-specific software programs have been developed for the UNIX platform; they are deeply entrenched in industries such as insurance, medicine, banking, and manufacturing. UNIX is also widely used on Web servers, especially those that support online transactions and make heavy use of databases.

DOS

Microsoft's **MS-DOS** (which stands for Microsoft Disk Operating System), along with IBM's PC-DOS (Personal Computer Disk Operating System), was once the most common of all the PC operating systems. An overwhelming volume of software that ran under DOS was available, and a large installed base of PCs ran DOS.

DOS was developed in the 1970s and distributed on some of the earliest commercial PCs. In the 1980s, DOS became the operating system for the huge market of IBM and IBM-compatible computers, making it the dominant operating system for more than a decade. Throughout the 1980s and early 1990s, virtually every new consumer PC (and most business PCs) ran DOS.

Among the strengths of DOS were its reliability and stability. On a properly configured system, DOS and DOS programs ran well; crashes and lockups were rare. Most users needed to learn only a small set of commands. Although the DOS prompt was not an elegant interface, it was not very difficult to use once you mastered the commands you used most frequently. Eventually, however, DOS became mouse-compatible; although the OS itself remained primarily a command-line interface, many DOS-based applications adopted features now common to windowed operating systems, such as pull-down menus and dialog boxes.

DOS was adequate for the IBM-compatible PCs of the early 1980s. However, its limitations became more noticeable as PCs became more powerful, as illustrated by the following:

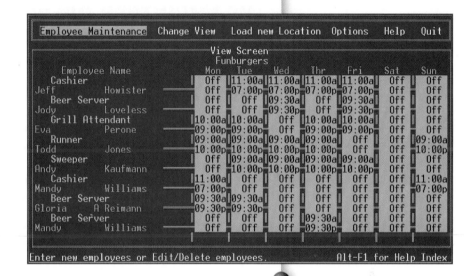

Figure 6B.2

An application running under DOS: DOS-based programs were often as difficult to use as the operating system itself, requiring users to memorize dozens of cryptic key combinations to issue commands.

◆ DOS could load only one application into memory at a time. To work with a second program, the user had to close the first—a process that often hindered productivity.

◆ DOS supported only one user and a single processor.

◆ Because DOS did not dictate how an application's interface must look or function, developers created a wide variety of program-specific interfaces (see Figure 6B.2 for an example). Some applications appeared as nearly blank, text-only screens; to issue commands, you had to memorize keystrokes or use function keys. Others attempted to use primitive menu systems, which proved difficult for DOS users who did not have a mouse. Keyboard templates and "cheat sheets" were commonly distributed with DOS-based applications to help users remember the many special keystroke combinations required to issue commands.

◆ Initially, DOS was designed to recognize only 640 KB of RAM; therefore, it could not handle large amounts of RAM. Users with more RAM had to use utilities to access memory beyond the 640 KB limit. Eventually, DOS was able to handle 1 MB of RAM without the aid of utilities.

◆ DOS was designed for 8-bit and 16-bit CPUs; it could not take advantage of the 32-bit architecture of newer microprocessors. In other words, DOS forced higher-performance computers to work at speeds below their capacity.

◆ Hardware was difficult to install and configure under DOS, because each device required a unique driver. Often, different DOS applications used different drivers for the same device.

◆ DOS file names were limited to eight characters, plus a three-character "extension" following a period, as in the name WORDPROC.DOC. Windows 95 remedied this situation by allowing file names up to 256 characters long. The UNIX and Macintosh operating systems, however, had already supported long file names for years.

◆ Finally, many people found the DOS command-line interface more difficult to learn and use than a well-designed GUI. When Windows came along, most users were all too happy to stop typing commands and start clicking icons.

THE MACINTOSH OPERATING SYSTEM

The Macintosh is a purely graphical machine. It brought the first truly graphical user interface to consumers (see Figure 6B.3). In its early days (mid-1980s), the Macintosh's integration of hardware and operating system, along with its GUI, made it popular among users who did not want to deal with the DOS command-line interface. Another advantage of the Macintosh was that all its applications looked alike and functioned similarly, making them easier to learn than DOS applications, most of which had their own unique "look and feel." Now that GUIs have become the standard, it is difficult to appreciate the significance of this big breakthrough.

The **Macintosh operating system** (or the **Mac OS**) was also ahead of Windows with many other features, such as built-in network support and Plug and Play hardware support. The Mac OS also provides multitasking and allows data sharing across different applications. Such features quickly made even die-hard DOS enthusiasts envious and led Microsoft to develop the Windows operating environment for the IBM-compatible market.

Figure 6B.3

Before the advent of Windows, the Mac OS enabled users to run multiple applications in a graphical user interface.

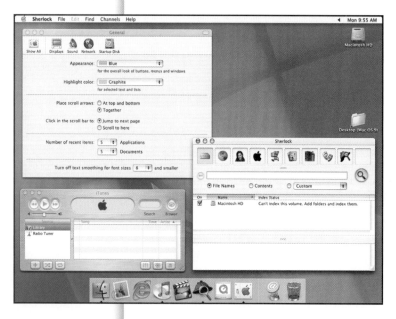

The fact that the Mac OS works only on Macintosh computers and compatible hardware has long been considered one of the operating system's biggest drawbacks. Similarly, DOS and all the varieties of Windows work only on IBM-compatible computers (although they can be run on PowerPC computers with a special dedicated section of the hard drive). Still, the Mac remains the first choice of many publishers, multimedia developers, graphic artists, and schools.

WINDOWS 3.X

In the mid-1980s, Microsoft accepted the popularity of the Macintosh computer and users' desire for a GUI. Microsoft's solution was **Windows,** a GUI that ran on top of DOS, replacing the command-line interface with a point-and-click system. Windows was not originally an operating system; it was an **operating environment,** another term for an interface that disguises the underlying operating system.

The first version of Windows did not work or sell very well, and the second version also was not a success. Not until Microsoft released Windows 3.0 in 1990 did the product really take off.

Windows 3.0—and its successor, Windows 3.1—were reasonably stable and succeeded in providing a GUI, as shown in Figure 6B.4, and the capability to load more than one program into memory at a time. Users also could run their old DOS programs under Windows, either in full-screen mode (so the screen looked like a plain DOS system) or within a window.

Despite its success and the capabilities it added to DOS computers, early versions of Windows did little else to overcome the built-in limitations of DOS. For example, users still had to deal with DOS memory-use limitations, although Windows made it easier to access 1 MB of memory. Plug and Play capabilities were not intro-

Figure 6B.4

The interface for Windows 3.x had a lot in common with the Macintosh OS. Users could work with files and programs by clicking desktop icons to open windows.

duced until later versions of Windows, so users still had to install drivers and configure each piece of hardware manually. Because it attempted to force DOS to support multitasking, Windows was fairly unstable; it became known for crashing and locking up when the system's resources reached their limits. Although Windows featured a memory-protection scheme that reserved blocks of memory space and CPU time for individual processes, the system was not reliable, and Windows users frequently lost data to crashes.

Windows for Workgroups (also known as Windows 3.11) was an important step for the Windows line of operating systems, because it was network-enabled. In other words, two computers running Windows for Workgroups could be networked together, without the need to purchase a separate network operating system, like Novell NetWare.

From time to time, you may see the term **Windows 3.x.** This term is used when referring to more than one member of the Windows 3 family. Although these early versions of Windows marked important steps in the development of operating systems, like DOS, they are now considered obsolete. You would have a difficult time finding many organizations (or many individuals) still using DOS-based or Windows 3.x systems.

OS/2 WARP

Although they are now rivals, IBM and Microsoft once were allies. In 1982, both companies recognized the need to take advantage of the capabilities of new, more powerful CPUs. They joined forces to develop **OS/2 Warp** (originally called just OS/2), a multitasking, GUI-based operating system for Intel microprocessors (see Figure 6B.5).

Unlike Windows 3.*x,* OS/2 was a true operating system, not an operating environment that ran on top of DOS. OS/2 provided networking support, true multitasking and multiuser support, and other features that made it superior to

Figure 6B.5
The OS/2 Warp interface

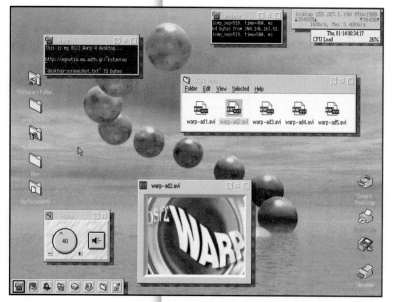

DOS as an operating system for Intel-based PCs. OS/2 enabled users to run OS/2-specific applications, as well as programs written for DOS and Windows 3.*x.* OS/2 became the first operating system to provide built-in speech recognition technology, and it could run on a wide range of hardware platforms, from PCs to multiprocessor systems with up to 64 processors.

Despite its advanced features and power, OS/2 never caught on with consumers, although it developed a modest following among enterprise users. It never rivaled Windows or UNIX in terms of sales. As this text was being written, IBM announced that it would not develop any future versions of OS/2.

WINDOWS NT

Microsoft released **Windows NT,** a 32-bit operating system for PCs, in 1993. Windows NT (New Technology) was originally designed as the successor to DOS, but by the time it was ready for release, it had become too large to run on most PCs in use at the time. As a result, Microsoft repositioned Windows NT to be a high-end operating system for powerful workstations and network servers. (After releasing Windows NT, Microsoft went back to the drawing board to create a more consumer-oriented version of Windows to replace DOS on home and office PCs. Windows 95, which is discussed later, was the result.)

At the time of its release, Windows NT addressed the market for the 32-bit, networked workstations that used some of the most powerful CPUs on the market. Because these computers fell into two primary categories, Microsoft separated Windows NT into two products:

◆ **Windows NT Workstation.** Although **Windows NT Workstation** looked almost identical to consumer versions of Windows (see Figure 6B.6), its underlying operating system was almost completely different. Windows NT Workstation was designed to take better advantage of the most powerful PCs of its time; it also ran on a broad range of CPUs, including Intel, Alpha, PowerPC, and other RISC-based processors. As its name implied, Windows NT Workstation typically was used on individual, stand-alone PCs that may or may not have been part of

NORTON
ONLINE

Visit **www.norton.glencoe.com** for more information on **OS/2 Warp.**

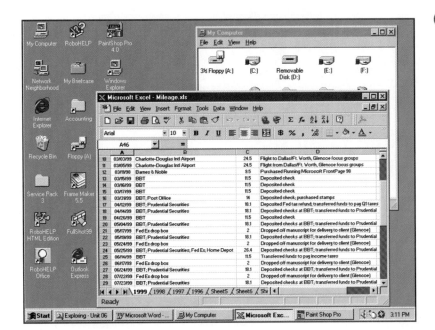

a network. While Windows NT Workstation supported networking and could be used to run peer-to-peer networks, it generally was not used on network servers. "Power users" made up a large part of the market for Windows NT Workstation. As a result, it could be (and still is) found in such varied places as architectural firms, audio and video production studios, and graphics studios.

◆ **Windows NT Server. Windows NT Server** incorporated all the features of Windows NT Workstation, but it also had other capabilities. Microsoft worked to fine-tune Windows NT Server so it would function as an operating system for file and print servers and on other systems that provide services for other computers on the LAN or Internet. Windows NT Server offered expanded security features for grouping and authenticating users and controlling their access to network resources. Windows NT Server supported the use of many hard disks, working together to store huge amounts of data; in some systems of this type, the same data is written to multiple disks, so it is preserved in case one disk fails. All these features made it possible for Windows NT Server to ensure disk and data security, even in the event of a catastrophic failure of a hard disk.

In late 2001, Microsoft announced that it would stop selling and supporting Windows NT—a move meant to encourage users to adopt newer versions of Windows: Windows 2000 and Windows XP.

Self Check

Complete each statement by filling in the blank(s).

1. MOTIF and OpenLook are examples of _GUI (windows)_ for UNIX.

2. The _MAC-OS_ brought the first truly graphical user interface to consumers.

3. Windows 3.x is called a(n) _operating environment_, because it is not a true operating system.

The Operating System and User Interface   **211**

At Issue

When Is an Operating System Not an Operating System?

In recent years, debate has raged regarding the power of operating systems—and, specifically, about the numbers and types of features that they now contain.

At the heart of this debate are some complex questions: When is an operating system no longer just an operating system? Do today's operating systems have more features than they need? Does an OS have certain features that give the product's maker an unfair advantage in the marketplace, making it more difficult for other software makers to sell their products?

The debate which focuses intensely on Microsoft Windows, took on a new urgency with the release of Windows 98. Critics complained even more loudly when subsequent versions of Windows were released; they claim that Microsoft has hurt other software developers by insisting on incorporating certain features into the operating system. In its own defense, Microsoft says that it continually adds features to Windows in an effort to innovate, create a more compelling product, increase user satisfaction, and address the concerns of its customers.

No matter which side you take in the debate, there is no questioning the fact that PC operating systems are not what they used to be. Consider that Windows XP includes a raft of programs that have little to do with the basic OS tasks you learned about earlier. Along with tools for managing your files, programs, and other resources, Windows provides a media player, a Web browser, an e-mail and news program, chat software, an image editor, and other "accessory" programs. Windows has long featured built-in utilities for disk defragmenting, disk scanning, networking, and more.

These features make Windows powerful and convenient for users, but they raise another issue: If these features are built into the operating system, why should anyone buy similar programs from other software companies? For instance, if the Internet Explorer Web browser is built into the operating system, why would consumers want to buy and install another browser, such as Netscape Navigator? The same question applies to the other utilities and accessory programs that are built into Windows: Does their presence in the operating system reduce the demand for similar products from other companies?

While those issues will continue to be discussed by industry experts and the court system, the central question remains: Are such "accessory" programs necessary in an operating system? Before you answer that question, consider another one: If you had the choice of buying Windows without all those built-in extras, would you?

With its array of built-in Internet tools, media player, graphics-editing program, and other features, Windows is more than a simple operating system. Many critics see this as a problem.

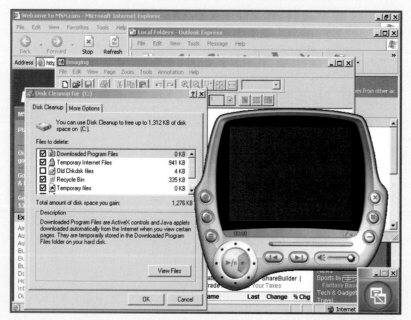

WINDOWS 9X

In 1995, Microsoft released **Windows 95,** a complete operating system and a successor to DOS for desktop computers. Windows 95 was a 32-bit, preemptive multitasking operating system with a revised GUI. All the strengths of Windows 95, which followed the Windows 3.*x* series, had already existed in other operating systems—most notably the Macintosh and Windows NT.

The greatest marketing strength of Windows 95 was the fact that it continued to include older, 16-bit code that enabled it to run programs that originally had been designed to run under DOS and Windows 3.*x* (see Figure 6B.7). If a company had already invested in many such programs, it could continue to use its familiar programs while migrating to the new operating system.

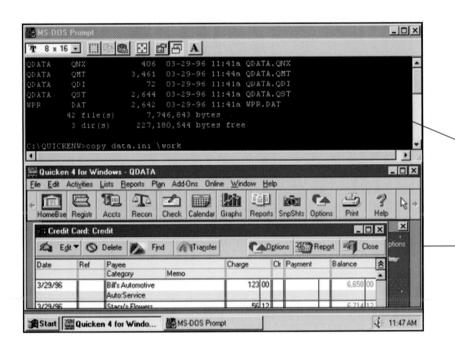

Figure 6B.7
Windows 95 was designed primarily to run 32-bit applications, but it could run older 16-bit applications designed for Windows 3.*x* and DOS.

DOS, running in a window

A 16-bit application written for Windows 3.*x*

Windows 95 had several other attractions as well. First, for programs designed with 32-bit processing, the operating system could exchange information with printers, networks, and files in 32-bit pieces instead of 16-bit pieces (as in Windows 3.*x* and DOS). For information moving around in the computer, the effect was like doubling the number of lanes on an expressway.

Windows 95 offered preemptive multitasking rather than the less efficient cooperative multitasking used by Windows 3.1 and the Macintosh. This meant that, if one program failed, you still had access to all the other programs in memory. In most cases, you did not have to restart the computer to work with those programs, as was usually required with earlier versions of Windows.

Windows 95 also had an improved graphical interface. Windows Explorer, for example, was an improvement on earlier Microsoft operating systems for working with files. One of the more significant additions to Windows 95 was the Start button, which gave users a whole new way to access system components and applications. Windows 95 also supported file names up to 256 characters, with blank spaces and other punctuation marks—freedoms that had not been available on DOS-based PCs.

NORTON ONLINE

Visit **www.norton.glencoe.com** for more information on **Windows.**

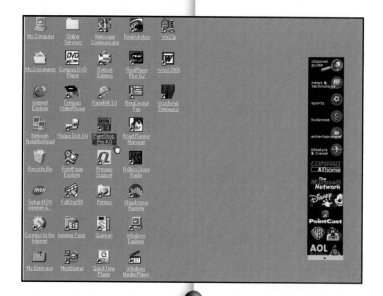

Figure 6B.8

The Windows 98 Active Desktop lets the operating system function like a Web browser.

In addition, Windows 95 offered the Plug and Play standard for connecting new hardware. Another Windows 95 asset was compatibility with networking software such as NetWare and Microsoft Windows NT Server. With networks, you could simply identify the network operating system when you installed Windows 95, and Windows 95 would be compatible with it.

Many experts considered **Windows 98** to be an update to Windows 95 rather than a major Windows operating system upgrade. In other words, the differences from Windows 95 to Windows 98 are not as significant as the differences from Windows 3.x to Windows 95. However, one key change in Windows 98 was the inclusion of the Internet Explorer Web browser. A new feature, called the Active Desktop, let users browse the Internet and local computer in a similar manner (see Figure 6B.8). Active Desktop enabled users to integrate Internet resources such as stock tickers and news information services directly on the Windows desktop.

In 2000, Microsoft released **Windows Me** (Millennium Edition), the last member of the Windows 9x family of consumer-grade operating systems. Windows Me offered several notable enhancements over its predecessors, such as improved multimedia capabilities, built-in support for digital video editing, and enhanced Internet features. But like Windows 95 and 98, Me still contained a lot of 16-bit code that supported old DOS and Windows 3.x applications. As a result, Windows Me was not much more stable or robust than Windows 95 or 98, and it was subject to frequent crashes.

You may see the term **Windows 9x.** This term is used when referring to more than one member of the Windows 95, 98, and Me family. Although these versions of Windows are considered obsolete by many experts in the computer industry, they are still widely used, especially by consumers with older PCs. Today, Windows 9x is only rarely offered as an option on new PCs.

LINUX

Between the release of Windows 95 and Windows 98, the computer world's attention focused on another new operating system, called **Linux.** In fact, Linux (LIH-nuhks) is a new version of UNIX that was developed by a worldwide cooperative of programmers; it is freely distributed by various sources.

Even though Linux is considered a "freeware" operating system, industry experts have been impressed by its power, capabilities, and rich feature set. Like UNIX, Linux is a full 32-bit, multitasking operating system that supports multiple users and multiple processors. Also like UNIX, Linux can run on nearly any computer and can support almost any type of application. Linux uses a command-line interface, but windows-based GUIs are available.

The big difference with Linux is its price. Anyone can get a free copy of Linux on the Internet, and disk-based copies are often inserted in popular computer books and magazines. Commercial versions of Linux, which are very inexpensive

NORTON
ONLINE

Visit **www.norton.glencoe.com** for more information on **Linux.**

when compared to the cost of other powerful operating systems, also are available from a variety of vendors. For all these reasons, Linux has become a popular OS in certain circles. Students and teachers have flocked to Linux not just for its technical advances, but to participate in the global community that has built up around the operating system. This community invites Linux users and developers to contribute modifications and enhancements, and it freely shares information about Linux and Linux-related issues.

Figure 6B.9 shows the version of Linux released by Red Hat, with the KDE Desktop environment. Red Hat has grown into one of the most popular Linux releases, complete with its own community of followers, as well as their own Linux certification program, known as the Red Hat Certified Engineer (RHCE) program.

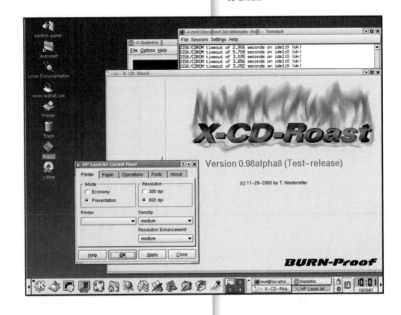

Figure 6B.9
Although Linux is typically considered to be a server platform, an increasing number of software companies are porting their applications to Linux.

WINDOWS 2000

Released in 2000, **Windows 2000** combined the user-friendly interface and features of Windows 98 with the file system, networking, power, and stability of Windows NT, plus some new and improved features. This combination of features made Windows 2000 the most powerful and easy-to-use Windows released to that point, and it brought a unified look and feel to all Windows-based computers (see Figure 6B.10).

Microsoft developed four versions of Windows 2000:

◆ **Professional.** This version is found primarily on PCs in offices and small businesses. (Note that Microsoft did not release a version of Windows 2000 specifically for home or casual users.) It includes support for symmetric multi-processing (SMP) with up to two processors.

◆ **Server Standard Edition.** This version is fine-tuned for use as a network server for the average business, with SMP support for up to two processors.

◆ **Advanced Server.** This is a more powerful version of the server edition. It includes support for SMP with up to four processors, and support for more RAM. Another important feature is print server clustering. With clustering, Windows 2000 can group print servers to provide alternate printers if one print server fails.

◆ **Data Center Server.** This version is the most powerful of the server editions, optimized for use as a large-scale application server, such as a database server. It includes the Advanced Server features, plus support for SMP with up to 32 processors.

Figure 6B.10
The Windows 2000 desktop

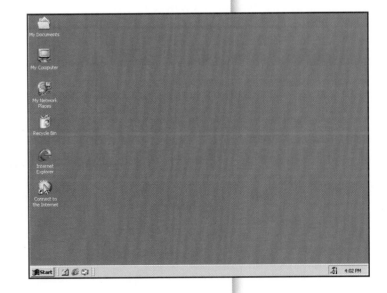

WINDOWS XP

Windows XP is the latest in the Windows suite of operating system families (see Figure 6B.11). Released in October 2001, Windows XP is available in two different editions, the Home edition and the Professional edition. With Windows XP, Microsoft consolidated its consumer-grade and enterprise operating systems into one environment. For home users, this means added security and an operating system that is far less likely to stall or crash than Windows 9*x*. Here are some of the features that have been upgraded in Windows XP:

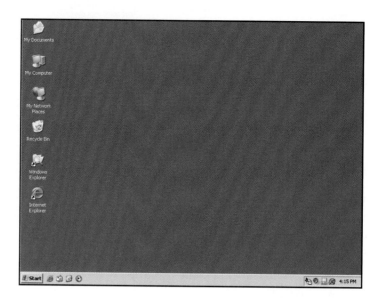

◆ **Digital Media Support.** Through the use of Windows Media Player 8, users of XP can take advantage of digital broadcast support, as well as video and audio rendering for multimedia projects.

◆ **Advanced Networking and Communications.** Windows XP takes advantage of Universal Plug and Play support, which enables the PC to find and use hardware connected via a network, without forcing the user to configure the system or install drivers. It also makes use of Internet Connection Sharing, which allows users to connect multiple computers to the Internet via a single connection.

◆ **Advanced Mobile Computing.** Through the use of features like Automatic Configuration, you can connect an XP-based laptop to a desktop PC without needing to know different types of network settings. XP's IrComm modem support lets you use a cellular telephone to connect to the Internet.

WINDOWS .NET

The suite of **Windows .NET Enterprise Server** operating systems is the latest addition to the server-based Windows OS family. The .NET Enterprise Server suite consists of several different servers that perform specialized tasks and which are designed for use in business-class network servers. The different types of server operating systems in the .NET framework include the following:

◆ **Application Center.** This is the center of the system for Web-based applications.

- **BizTalk Server.** It allows for building business processes and linking different business components together.
- **Commerce Server.** This is the server that is used to create and maintain e-commerce infrastructures.
- **Exchange Server.** Exchange server is the e-mail and collaboration server that takes care of e-mail and messaging routing and processes.
- **Internet Security and Acceleration Server.** This component provides for Internet connectivity.
- **Mobile Information Server.** It allows mobile users to take advantage of all the network options and resources available to desktop systems.
- **SharePoint Portal Server.** It allows for the setup and maintenance of intranet sites.
- **SQL Server.** This is a powerful Web-based database server package.

EMBEDDED OPERATING SYSTEMS

An **embedded operating system** is one that is built into the circuitry of an electronic device, unlike a PC's operating system, which resides on a magnetic disk. Embedded operating systems typically are found in devices such as PDAs, like the Palm Pilot or the Compaq iPaq. Three of the most popular embedded operating systems include the following:

- **Palm OS.** The Palm OS is the standard operating system for the Palm brand, as well as other proprietary handheld devices (see Figure 6B.12). The Palm OS is one of the more popular options for handheld devices. As a result, users have a large degree of choice in terms of software and hardware options that can be used with this embedded system.

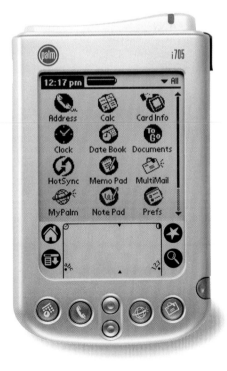

Figure 6B.12
Like many other handheld computing devices, the Palm line of personal digital assistants uses the Palm OS.

- **Windows CE.** Windows CE is the Microsoft version of an embedded system that is used on handhelds and other portable devices. Windows CE looks like other versions of Windows, and it offers some of the same functionality. It also allows for the use of smaller versions of Microsoft Word, Excel, and Outlook.

- **Pocket PC OS.** The Pocket PC OS is a specific type of operating system that Microsoft developed to use on smaller versions of handheld computers. These devices are targeted at the business and corporate market, rather than consumers. The latest version gives users the ability to securely access data from a business network via a handheld device, and it gives system administrators the ability to manage and control a PC or server via a wireless network connection.

NORTON
ONLINE

Visit **www.norton.glencoe.com** for more information on **embedded operating systems**.

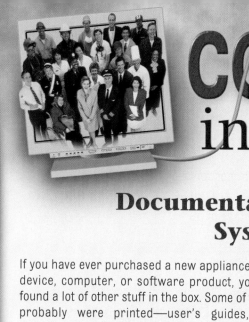

COMPUTERS
in your career

Documentation and Online Help
System Designers

If you have ever purchased a new appliance, electronic device, computer, or software product, you probably found a lot of other stuff in the box. Some of those items probably were printed—user's guides, assembly instructions, and other manuals.

This printed information can take many different forms: a single sheet, a brochure, a complete book, or a set of books. This kind of information is called *documentation*. It is a common accessory to many products, especially computer hardware and software.

Documentation does not come just on paper, either. Most software programs feature an electronic help system, which may supplement or even take the place of printed documentation. Today, many companies make documentation for their products available on their Web sites, where they can update it as often as necessary.

All product documentation has one thing in common: Someone has to research, write, edit, design, and publish it.

Many products, like this software program, include printed documentation to help users master its features and troubleshoot problems.

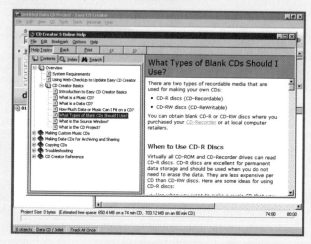

Today, nearly all software products provide online help—sometimes instead of printed documentation.

◆ *Technical writers* are the backbone of any documentation team. Skilled at writing and editing, they work with the product's designers to master the product's use; then they use this knowledge to write instructions for users. Using standard word processing software or sophisticated desktop publishing programs, they create the needed documents from scratch, and then prepare them for the next step in the process, which may be editing, proofreading, indexing, layout, or publishing.

◆ *Technical illustrators* create the graphic components that appear in documentation. The illustrator may use paint, draw, or photo-manipulation software to prepare the artwork that will appear in the documentation.

◆ *Page designers* and *page layout technicians* take the manuscript and illustrations and use desktop publishing software to prepare a professional-looking document that is ready for printing. They also may add special elements to the documentation, such as a table of contents or index.

◆ *Online help architects* use software tools to compile hundreds or thousands of individual documents (each one dealing with a specific topic) and link them together into a seamless online help system. Help architects often must write content for their help systems, create navigation schemes, and set up the many links that let users jump from one help topic to another.

SUMMARY

- UNIX was the first multi-user, multiprocessor, multitasking operating system available for use on PCs.

- DOS was a single-user OS that supported limited amounts of memory and featured a command-line interface.

- The Macintosh operating system supports the graphical capabilities of Macintosh computers. The Mac OS brought the first truly graphical user interface to consumers.

- Early versions of Windows (through Windows 3.*x*) brought a graphical user interface and multitasking capabilities to PCs that ran DOS. Windows 3.*x* is an operating environment, rather than a true operating system.

- IBM's OS/2 Warp was the first true GUI-based operating system for Intel-based PCs. OS/2 is a multitasking operating system that provides support for networking and multiple users.

- Windows NT originally was meant as a replacement for DOS, but it was too resource-intensive to work on most PCs when it was released. Microsoft issued two versions of the operating system—Windows NT Workstation and Windows NT Server.

- Windows 95 was Microsoft's first true GUI-based, 32-bit operating system for Intel PCs. It supported multitasking, and it could run older programs that were written for DOS and Windows 3.*x*.

- Windows 98 and Windows Me offered some improvements to Windows 95, but they still were prone to frequent crashing.

- Linux is a version of UNIX, and it is available for free or at a low cost from various sources. It is a powerful 32-bit OS that supports multitasking, multiple users, networking, and virtually any application.

- Windows 2000 includes the same interface and features of Windows 98, with the file system, networking, power, and stability of Windows NT. Microsoft released several versions of Windows 2000, each targeting a specific user or computing environment.

- Windows XP was released in 2001, and it marked the end of Microsoft's consumer-grade operating systems. This means that all computer users, including casual and home users, can have an operating system with enhanced security, networking support, and stability.

- Microsoft's Windows.NET Enterprise server operating systems are a new breed of enterprise-level operating systems, which were designed to meet the needs of different businesses. A variety of .NET operating systems are available to support Web-based applications, large databases, e-commerce servers, and more.

- Embedded operating systems, such as the Palm OS and Microsoft's Pocket PC operating system, are miniaturized OSes designed to run on small computing devices, such as handheld computers.

KEY TERMS

embedded operating system, *217*
Linux, *214*
Macintosh operating system (Mac OS), *208*
MS-DOS, *207*
operating environment, *209*
OS/2 Warp, *210*
UNIX, *206*
Windows 2000, *215*
Windows 3.*x*, *209*
Windows 95, *213*

Windows 98, *214*
Windows 9*x*, *214*
Windows Me, *214*
Windows .NET Enterprise Server, *216*
Windows NT Server, *211*
Windows NT, *210*
Windows NT Workstation, *210*
Windows XP, *216*
Windows, *209*

KEY TERM QUIZ

Complete each statement by writing one of the terms listed under Key Terms in each blank.

1. _UNIX_ is older than all the other PC operating systems.

2. Throughout the 1980s and early 1990s, virtually every new consumer PC ran the _DOS_ operating system.

3. _3.X_ is the term that refers to Windows versions 3.0, 3.1, and 3.11.

4. A new version of UNIX, called _Linux_ , can be acquired easily, at no cost.

5. A(n) _____ is designed to run on small computing devices, such as personal digital assistants.
Embedded OS

SECTION QUIZ

True/False

Answer the following questions by circling True or False.

True ~~False~~   1. UNIX is an 8-bit, single-user OS for older mainframe computers.

True ~~False~~   2. DOS features a graphical user interface that makes heavy use of icons and menus.

~~True~~ False   3. Windows 3.*x* allowed users to continue running their old DOS-based programs.

True ~~False~~   4. Windows 95 was popular because it featured cooperative multitasking.

~~True~~ False   5. The Palm OS is an example of an embedded operating system.

Multiple Choice

Circle the word or phrase that best completes each statement.

1. Initially, the _____ operating system was geared toward uses in telecommunications systems.
   A. Linux   B. UNIX   C. MS-DOS

2. IBM sells the _____ operating system for use on Intel-based computers.
   A. OS/2 Warp   B. UNIX   C. neither A nor B

3. Unlike Windows 3.*x*, _____ ran on a broad range of CPUs, including Intel, Alpha, and others.
   A. Windows 9*x*   B. Windows Me   C. Windows NT Workstation

4. With _____ , Microsoft consolidated its consumer-grade and enterprise operating systems into one environment.
   A. Windows XP   B. Windows 2000 Server   C. Windows CE

5. _____ is an example of an embedded operating system.
   A. Windows XP   B. Windows CE   C. Windows Me

REVIEW QUESTIONS

In your own words, briefly answer the following questions.

1. Why is UNIX a very popular operating system for Internet host computers?

2. What does "MS-DOS" stand for?

3. Why did the Macintosh operating system become popular?

4. For home computer users, what are the two key advantages of using Windows XP, rather than Windows 9*x?*

5. What is an embedded operating system?

SECTION LABS

Complete the following exercises as directed by your instructor.

1. Use your operating system's tools to find files on your computer's hard disk. Note that the following steps apply if you are using Windows XP. If you use a different version of Windows or a different operating system than Windows, ask your instructor for directions:
   A. Click the Start button, then click Search. The Search Results window opens.
   B. Click All files and folders.
   C. Click in the All or part of the file name text box, and type *.txt. This tells Windows to search for all files with the file-name extension *txt.*
   D. From the Look in drop-down list, select your computer's hard disk (typically C:).
   E. Click Search. Windows conducts the search and displays the results in the right-hand pane of the Search Results window.
   F. Repeat the search, specifying *.html, *.doc, and *.gif as your search criteria. When you are finished, close the Search Results window.

UNIT PROJECTS

UNIT LABS

Complete the following exercises using a computer in your classroom, lab, or home.

1. **Create a File System.** Suppose that you work for a soft drink company. Your manager has asked you to create a business proposal for a new product—a fun, caffeine-free soda for kids under the age of 8. The proposal will be about 50 pages in length and will include several supporting documents, such as reports, memos, budgets, customer lists, research on the product's safety, focus group results, taste tests, and so on. These documents will be created in several forms, including word processing documents, spreadsheet files, databases, presentations, and so on.

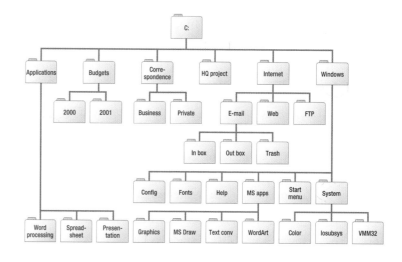

Your first task is to create a file system on your computer's hard disk where you can store and manage all these files. Using a piece of paper, design a set of folders (and subfolders, if needed) to store all the files in a logical manner. Be prepared to share your file system with the class and to discuss the logic behind your file system.

2. **Get the Latest on Windows XP.** If you do not have Windows XP yet, chances are good that you will be using it in the future. Get a jump on the OS by finding the latest information about it on the Web.

   Visit the following Web sites for more information:

   - Microsoft Corp. Visit Microsoft's main Windows XP page at **http://www.microsoft. com/windowsxp/default.asp**

   - PC Magazine. For a series of articles and reviews about Windows XP, visit **http://www.pcmag.com/winxp**

   - CNET. For articles, reviews, and technical information about Windows XP, visit **http://www.cnet.com/,** click the Operating Systems link, then click the Windows XP link to reach CNET's Windows XP Superguide.

3. **Learn More About Linux.** If you are curious about Linux (or UNIX in general), or want to install Linux on your system, you can find everything you need on the Internet. Visit the following Web sites for more information on Linux and learn where you can get a free copy. (*Note:* Do not download any files from the Internet without your instructor's permission.)

   - Linux Online. Hosted by Linux.Org, this site provides a comprehensive array of resources. Visit **http://www.linux.org**

- The Linux Gazette. An online newsletter for Linux users of all levels can be found at **http://www.linuxgazette.com/**
- Linux Planet. For articles, reviews, technical information, and links to Linux resources, visit **http://www.linuxplanet.com/**

DISCUSSION QUESTIONS

As directed by your instructor, discuss the following questions in class or in groups.

1. Discuss the benefits of using the object linking and embedding (OLE) capabilities of newer operating systems. Can you think of a task where OLE would be helpful? What types of documents can someone create using OLE? Give examples.

2. What does multitasking mean to the average computer user?

RESEARCH AND REPORT

Using your own choice of resources (such as the Internet, books, magazines, and newspaper articles), research and write a short paper discussing one of the following topics:

- The benefits of using a command-line interface, rather than a graphical user interface
- The story behind the creation of the Linux operating system
- The uses for file compression programs, and the methods such programs use to compress data

When you are finished, proofread and print your paper, and give it to your instructor.

ETHICAL ISSUES

Many people believe that operating systems have more features and capabilities than they really need. With this thought in mind, discuss the following questions in class:

1. The Windows Update feature has been part of the Windows operating system since the release of Windows 98. This tool enables the operating system to notify the user when updated features are available for downloading on the Internet. Some observers think that future operating systems will be able to update themselves automatically, without first notifying the user. How do you feel about this possibility? What dangers could it pose to users?

2. Many observers believe that by including so many features (such as disk defragmenters, file management tools, and Internet applications) in its operating systems, Microsoft has taken market share away from other companies that might develop and sell such tools to Windows users. Do you agree with this criticism, or do you feel that an operating system should include such "extras"?

Computing *Keynotes*

Buying Your First Computer

Buying your first computer can be just as challenging as buying your first car—and nearly as expensive! Look at a few magazine or television advertisements, and you will quickly see that there are hundreds of models and features from which to choose. Sifting through all those options can be time-consuming and frustrating, and you may never feel certain that you are making the right choice or getting the best price. But if you take the right approach, you will find that buying a PC is not so difficult. In fact, it can be an enjoyable process.

When you are shopping for a computer, keep this important tip in mind: Technology changes quickly. Almost as soon as you start using your new computer, you will learn that it will become obsolete. This is because manufacturers constantly change the PCs they sell by adding new features and making new options available. But you cannot let that stop you from buying a PC; if you wait for the "perfect" PC to come along, you may never buy one! Instead, you need to choose features and options that you know you can live with for a while. (Most PCs remain in use about three years.)

With so many choices to make, what is the best way to buy a new PC? Very simply, the best thing you can do is plan ahead, understand your needs, and do your homework. This kind of preparation will help you find a PC that best meets your needs, at a price you can afford. That is what this Computing Keynote is all about: helping you decide what you need *before* you start shopping.

As overwhelming as computer shopping might be, there is plenty of good news. The best news is that there are lots of good deals to be found. Sales and special deals are everywhere you look, and as the newest PC models appear, sellers slash prices on "yesterday's" computers (which are still perfectly capable machines) to make room for new systems.

Many popular magazines feature advertisements for computers.

Today's PC versus yesterday's PC: much higher performance at much lower prices.

And even though they can be expensive, today's computers are a better value than ever. In the early 1980s, the original IBM-PC featured a 4.77 MHz processor, no hard disk, 16 KB of RAM, a monochrome monitor, and a price tag of nearly $2,500. Today, you can easily find a PC with a 1 GHz (or faster) processor, a 40 GB hard disk, 256 MB of RAM, and a color monitor for less than $1,000. And the new machine will include features such as a CD-RW drive, a modem, a sound card, speakers, a microphone, and other options that were not available a decade ago.

The hardest questions to answer when buying a computer are these: How do you decide which of the many options are best for you? How do you decide how much you should pay for them?

THINK BEFORE YOU SHOP

If you have never purchased a PC before, you probably are eager to get started. After all, you have a lot of looking around to do in order to get the best deal! But before you hit the malls or go online, you need to make some decisions. That way, you will have a good idea of what you need, which may help you avoid looking at models or options that are not right for you.

So grab a pen and a piece of paper, and answer some basic questions. The answers will help you decide what type of computer will best meet your needs.

1. **What will you use your computer for?** This is the most important question you can answer before buying a computer. Will you use a PC primarily for Internet surfing and word processing, or do you plan to develop programs? The more demanding your tasks are, the more powerful your computer should be. Be realistic: Don't add "programming" or "database development" to your list unless you really plan to do those things. Use the following checklist to determine which activities you will use your computer for.

   If your list includes a lot of tasks, or if you plan to work on a few demanding tasks, then you need a more powerful system. This means you will need the fastest processor, greatest amount of memory, and largest hard disk you can afford.

2. **What features or capabilities are most important to you?** If you want to use a PC mostly for game playing and listing to music, then good graphics and audio capabilities may be more important to you than some other options. On the other hand, if you want to work with video, then a large hard disk and plenty of RAM may be most important to you.

Before you shop, list the ways you plan to use your computer. Then list the options you really need.

Task	Yes	No
Internet/e-mail/chatting	☐	☐
Word Processing	☐	☐
Spreadsheet	☐	☐
Database management	☐	☐
Presentations	☐	☐
Listening to or editing audio	☐	☐
Watching or editing video	☐	☐
Creating or editing graphics	☐	☐
Working with digital photos	☐	☐
Web design	☐	☐
Programming	☐	☐
Computer-aided design	☐	☐
Playing games	☐	☐

If you can decide which features you need and do not need, you are more likely to buy a system that is just right for you.

3. What features can you live without?
If you do not plan to watch DVD videos or record CDs on your system, then you probably shouldn't pay for a DVD player or CD-R/CD-RW drive. If you don't plan to install lots of software or hoard thousands of audio files, then you can save money by getting a 20 GB hard disk instead of a 40 GB disk. If you do not plan to connect the computer to a network, then do not pay for a network interface card (although you do need one if you plan to connect to the Internet through a cable modem or DSL connection). By omitting features you do not need, you can save dollars that can be applied to purchase features you do need.

Use the checklist on page 227 to help you decide which options you need and don't need. When you are ready to shop, use the list to help you compare options in the systems you consider buying.

4. How much money can you afford to spend? The answer to this question, of course, determines how much PC you can buy. But do not be disappointed if you cannot afford the biggest, fastest, most power-packed PC in the store. Depending on your needs, you may be able to buy a system that is just right for you, for less than you imagined.

Nearly every PC maker offers a line of home computers for $1,000 or less. Many of these machines feature 1 GHz processors, 128 MB or 256 MB of SDRAM, high-capacity hard drives, and more. And remember: You don't have to buy everything at once. For example, if you already have a monitor, use it instead of buying a new one. The same applies to speakers, a printer, and other peripheral devices. If you already have a computer, you may get by just fine by buying a new system unit alone, saving hundreds of dollars in the process.

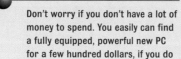

Don't worry if you don't have a lot of money to spend. You easily can find a fully equipped, powerful new PC for a few hundred dollars, if you do your homework.

Option	Yes	No	Details
Processor	√	☐	Type: _____ Speed: _____ MHz/GHz
RAM	√	☐	Type: _____ Amount: _____
Hard disk	√	☐	Type: _____ Capacity: _____ Spin Rate: _____ Avg. Access Time: _____
Optical drive	√	☐	Type: _____ Read Speed: _____ Write Speed: _____
High-capacity floppy disk drive	☐	☐	Type: _____ Capacity: _____
Modem	☐	☐	Type: _____ Speed: _____
Keyboard	√	☐	Type: _____ Special Features: _____
Pointing Device	√	☐	Type: _____ Special Features: _____
Video Card	√	☐	Type: _____ Amount of VRAM: _____
Sound Card	☐	☐	Type: _____
Speakers	☐	☐	Type: _____
Microphone	☐	☐	Type: _____
Video Camera	☐	☐	Type: _____
USB Ports	☐	☐	Number: _____
IEEE 1394 Ports	☐	☐	Number: _____
Special Ports (MIDI, TV In/Out, Audio In/Out, Etc.)	☐	☐	Number: _____ Type(s): _____
Operating System	√	☐	Type: _____ Version: _____
Antivirus software	☐	☐	Type: _____ Version: _____
Warranty	☐	☐	Type: _____ Duration: _____

This checklist will help you decide what options you need and don't need before you begin computer shopping. Items that are checked come standard on almost all computers.

DO SOME HOMEWORK

Once you figure out why you want to use a PC and what basic features are most important, it's time to start learning about the different options that are available from most PC makers.

To learn the latest information on processors, visit the Web sites of the leading makers of CPUs.

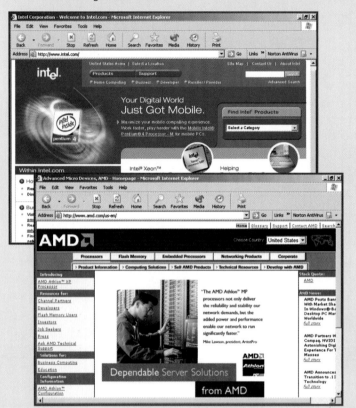

Check Out Processors

Today's PCs are based on processors from two manufacturers—Intel and AMD—and you can learn the differences between their products by visiting their Web sites at **http://www.intel.com/** and **http://www.amd.com/**.

You may have your heart set on the newest, fastest processor for your system, meaning either the Pentium 4 (made by Intel) or the Athlon (from AMD). But because these are also the most expensive processors available—and because you may not actually need all the power they offer—they may not be the right choice for you. For example, if you plan to use your new PC mainly for Web surfing and word processing, you can save hundreds of dollars by buying a PC that features a slower Pentium III or Celeron processor (from Intel), or a Duron processor (from AMD). However, if you plan to work with graphics, digital photos, CAD, or some other sophisticated type of software, you should get the most powerful processor you can afford.

Visiting the CPU makers' Web sites will give you some good basic information on each processor's performance. You can get even more detailed information by visiting some of the many Web sites that regularly review processors, such as:

Computer Shopper—**http://www.computershopper.com/**

MSN Technology—**http://tech.msn.com/**

PC Magazine—**http://www.pcmag.com/**

PC World—**http://www.pcworld.com/**

Know Your RAM Needs

If you can afford it, make sure that your new PC has at least 256 MB of RAM (this amount is standard on many new PCs, but not always); that should give you enough memory to run Windows and several applications at the same time. If the manufacturer gives you the option of installing faster RDRAM or DDR-SDRAM, and if you can afford it, take the option. Your system will perform better.

To best determine how much RAM you will actually need, check the system requirements for the operating system and application programs you plan to use. You can find this information on the side of the program's package or on the manufacturer's Web site. The more programs you plan to run simultaneously, the more RAM you need.

Know your Storage Needs

Many new PCs come with enormous hard disks; it is easy to find models with 40 GB and larger drives. Of course, too little storage capacity will become a problem later on, forcing you to upgrade your system. On the other hand, too much storage capacity is simply a waste. Why pay for storage space you may never use?

As with RAM requirements, your operating system and application programs have specific storage requirements, which should be listed on the package. Check the package or the manufacturer's Web site to see how much disk space you will need for your operating system and applications. Double that amount and you will have a safe *minimum* requirement for your PC's storage. Be sure to allow room for programs you may install in the future, for your data files, and for the many temporary files that Windows creates as it runs.

TALKING TURKEY

Now that you know what you need (and don't need), it is time to start shopping. You can buy a computer in at least three ways; the method you choose depends on your comfort level:

If you want personalized guidance as you shop, a computer or electronics store can be a good place to start.

◆ **At a store.** If you live in or near a large town, you probably have access to stores that carry PCs, software, and peripherals. It is a good idea to visit some of these stores so you can get a close-up look at different types of systems. While you are there, find out what kinds of services the store offers, what types of special deals it offers, and what brands and models of systems it sells.

Buying through a local computer store, office supply store, or electronics store has some advantages. For example, you can develop a relationship with the store personnel, which is important if you have problems later on. But there are downsides, too. If you work with a pushy salesperson, you may wind up paying for options you do not need or—worse—buying a PC that is not right for you.

◆ **By phone.** Many major PC makers offer toll-free numbers, where sales representatives can help you configure a PC and give you an exact price. If you decide to shop by phone, you need to have a credit card handy, along with a list of the options you want.

If you shop online, you can use a "configurator," like this one at the Compaq Web site, to select the exact options you want and see how they affect the system's price.

◆ **Online.** Nearly every PC maker has a Web site that offers secure online shopping. A bonus of online shopping is the availability of "configurators"—tools that let you select options for your system, then show how each option affects the total price. PC makers frequently offer "Internet-only" specials, which are not available if you order by phone or buy from a store. You will need a credit card to shop online; otherwise, you may have to call the vendor and arrange to pay by check or money order.

UNIT 7

Networks and Data Communications

UNIT CONTENTS

This unit contains the following sections:

Section 7A: Networking Basics

➤ The Uses of a Network
➤ How Networks Are Structured
➤ Visual Essay: Network Topologies, Media, and Hardware
➤ Network Technologies
➤ Network Software

Section 7B: Networking the Home, the Office, and the Globe

➤ Data Communications with Standard Telephone Lines and Modems
➤ Using Digital Telephone Lines
➤ Networks in the Home

The Interactive Browser Edition CD-ROM provides additional labs and activities to apply concepts from this unit.

Networking Basics

OVERVIEW:
Sharing Data Anywhere, Anytime

When PCs first appeared in businesses, software programs were designed for a single user. There were few obvious advantages to connecting PCs, and the technology was not adequate for doing so. As computers spread throughout business, and as developers began offering complex software designed for multiple users, many organizations quickly learned the importance of connecting PCs. Data communications—the electronic transfer of information between computers—became a major focus of the computer industry. Networking technology has become the most explosive area of growth in the entire computer industry. The demand for larger, faster, higher-capacity networks has increased as businesses have realized the value of networking their computer systems.

Networks come in many varieties. When most people think of a network, they imagine several computers in a single location sharing documents and devices, such as printers. But a network can include all the computers and devices in a department, a building, or multiple buildings spread over a wide geographic area, such as a city or even a country. By interconnecting many individual networks into a massive single network, people around the world can share information as though they were across the hall from one another. The information they share can be much more than text documents. Many networks carry voice, audio, and video traffic, enabling videoconferencing and types of collaboration that were not possible just a few years ago.

SECTION OBJECTIVES

- List the four benefits of using a network.
- Differentiate between LANs and WANs.
- Identify at least three common network topologies.
- Name four common network media.
- List at least four examples of network operating system software.

Visit **www.norton.glencoe.com** for more information on **networks**.

THE USES OF A NETWORK

A **network** is a set of technologies (including hardware, software, and cabling or some other means) that can be used to connect computers together, enabling them to communicate, exchange information, and share resources in real time. You should think of a network as a set, or group, of technologies, because nearly all networks require hardware, software, and media—such as wires—to connect computer systems together. Networks allow many users to access shared data and programs instantly. When data and programs are stored on a network and can be shared, individual users do not need to keep separate copies of the data and programs on their own computers.

Today, fewer organizations use a centralized system, such as a mainframe and terminals, for data communication. Meanwhile, many businesses and schools have switched from centralized computing systems to PC-based networks (see Figure 7A.1). Although you can think of a mainframe system and its terminals as a network, such a system does not allow the same degree of flexibility as networks that are made of PCs.

Networks provide many benefits. Four of the most important benefits include the following:

◆ They allow many users to access programs and data at the same time.

◆ They allow users to share peripheral devices, such as printers and scanners.

◆ They make personal communications easier.

◆ They make it easy for users and administrators to back up important data files.

The following sections examine each of these advantages in more detail.

Simultaneous Access

At any given moment in any business, several workers may need to use the same data at the same time. A good example is a company's quarterly sales report, which needs to be viewed and updated by several managers. Without a network that allows workers to share files, separate copies of data have to be stored on different disks by each worker who accesses the data. When data is updated on one computer, data on the other computers becomes outdated. It becomes difficult to determine which data is the most current.

Businesses can solve this problem by storing data that must be accessible to more than one person on a **network server** (or just **server**), which is a central computer with a large storage device and other resources that all users can share. Organizations use all types of computer systems as network servers, from large mainframes down to desktop PCs. A server usually has greater storage capacity and memory than the individual PCs on the users' desks, but this is not always the case.

If the server stores data files for users to access, it is commonly called a **file server.** The business can store a single copy of a data file on the server, which employees can access whenever they want (see Figure 7A.2). Then, if one user makes a change to

Figure 7A.1
Most offices have a PC on nearly every desk. The computers are connected to form a network.

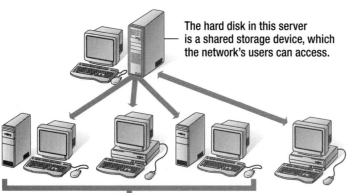

The hard disk in this server is a shared storage device, which the network's users can access.

To protect the shared data, these users can access the files but cannot make changes to them. This type of access privilege is called "read-only" access.

This user can open the files, make changes to them, and save the changes on the server. All users see the changes that this user makes to the shared data. This type of access privilege is called "read/write" access.

Figure 7A.2
Users can share data stored on a central file server.

the file, other users will see the change when they use the file, and no one needs to figure out who has the latest copy of the data.

When files are shared on a network and available to many people, the organization needs to protect the data's integrity. This means making sure that only the right people can view or edit the data. Managers must determine which users should be allowed to update specific files, and which users should be allowed only to view specific files. To protect data, managers usually allow users to have two basic types of access to it:

◆ **Read-Only.** Some users are entitled only to read data that is stored on a shared device. This type of access is called **read-only access** because users can read data, but they cannot make changes to the files. Such protection prevents unauthorized users from making unwanted changes to the data. This type of protection, however, is not always foolproof. Depending on the type of file, a user may be able to open the file, then save it to another disk with a different file name. This removes the read-only status from the second file, enabling the user to modify it, although the original file remains unchanged.

◆ **Read/Write.** Some users may be allowed to open shared files from the network server and to make changes to those files. Because these users can save changes to the shared files, they have **read/write access.** When such users make changes to the files, the updated data can be viewed by all users. But this strategy has some pitfalls. For example, suppose two different users want to make changes to the same file at the same time. To protect the file's integrity, and to make sure that all users know that a file is in use, administrators can set up a priority system that allows only one user at a time to work with the file; if another user attempts to open the file while it is in use, the system notifies him or her that the file is unavailable. The system may allow the second user to open the file in read-only mode, which means that the file cannot be changed until the first user has closed the file. In settings where many users need access to many of the same files (as is the case in software development companies), managers can set up complex version-control systems to ensure that no one ever uses an outdated version of a file and that all modifications are incorporated into the right version of the file.

NORTON
ONLINE

Visit **www.norton.glencoe.com** for more information on **servers.**

To enable users to read and write files, network managers can assign different types of access rights to each user. There are various levels of access rights, and each one gives users a unique set of privileges. If a user has **write access** to certain files, he or she can open, change, and save those files but may not be able to delete or move the files. With **supervisor access,** however, the user can perform any task on the files, including copying, moving, and deleting. Network managers can assign specific access rights to each user on the network on a per-drive, per-folder, or per-file basis. Newer network file server systems, such as the Windows 2000 Server, allow managers to assign specific sets of access rights—called policies—to individuals or groups based on their job descriptions and duties.

In addition to using many of the same data files, most office workers also use the same programs. In an environment where PCs are not networked, a separate copy of each program must be installed on every computer. This setup can be costly for two reasons. First, software can be expensive, especially when you must buy many copies. Second, installing and configuring a program on many different computers can take a lot of time and labor, and maintaining many separate installations of a program is an ongoing expense. There are two basic solutions to this problem:

◆ **Site Licenses.** One solution to this problem is to purchase a **site license** for an application. Under a site license, a business buys a single copy (or a few copies) of an application and pays the developer for a license to copy the application onto a specified number of computers. Under a site license, each user has a complete, individual copy of the program running on his or her PC, but the business generally pays less money than it would by purchasing a complete copy of the software for each user.

◆ **Network Versions.** Another solution is to connect users' computers to a central network server and enable users to share a **network version** of a program. In a network version, only one copy of the application is stored on the server, with a minimum number of supporting files copied to each user's PC. When workers need to use a program, they simply load it from the server into the RAM of their own desktop computers, as shown in Figure 7A.3. In some networks, and with certain types of programs, the user's computer handles all the processing tasks required by the application, even though the application's core files are stored on the network. In other cases, the network server also handles some or all of the processing tasks. In these cases, the network server may be called an **application server**, because it handles some application processing, as well as storage.

Figure 7A.3
Using a network version of an application

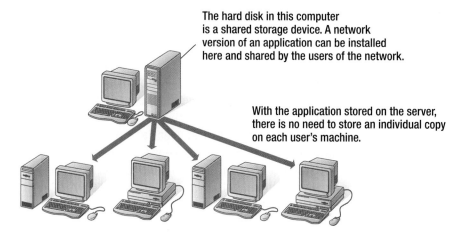

The hard disk in this computer is a shared storage device. A network version of an application can be installed here and shared by the users of the network.

With the application stored on the server, there is no need to store an individual copy on each user's machine.

Despite their advantages, these strategies aren't always less expensive than buying individual copies of a program for each user. Depending on the type of software being used and the number of people using it, licensing can cost about the same, whether the application is installed on each user's computer or run through the network. In some large, busy installations, the cost of the network itself—particularly of providing adequate bandwidth for many users—can cost more than buying many copies of the software. In such cases, the network's real advantage is that it allows the applications to be managed centrally (at the server) instead of on many individual computers. This strategy of centralized software management means that programs can be configured and updated at a single point (the server) rather than at many points (individual users' computers). This plan reduces the time and expense of installing, configuring, and maintaining many different copies of a program on many different computers.

Some software designed for networks is classified as **groupware**. This type of software includes scheduling software, e-mail, and document-management software. Groupware allows multiple users on a network to cooperate on projects. Users can work on the same documents, share their insights, and keep each other abreast of their schedules, so that meetings can be set up easily. Lotus Notes, Microsoft Exchange, and Novell Groupwise are perhaps the best-known examples of groupware.

Shared Peripheral Devices

The ability to share peripheral devices (especially expensive ones, such as high-volume laser printers, which can cost thousands of dollars) is one of the best reasons for a small business to set up a network. Although printers are much cheaper than they were a few years ago, it is still too expensive to provide every worker with his or her own printer. Aside from the cost of buying multiple printers, maintenance contracts and supplies increase the total cost of ownership. When several people can share a printer on a network, printing becomes less expensive and easier to manage.

By using a process called **spooling,** multiple users can send print jobs to a printer at the same time. When users send documents (known as **print jobs**) to a networked printer, each document is stored temporarily on the file server. As the printer finishes printing the current job, the file server sends the next job to the printer, so that it can be printed. To manage many print jobs at one time, the server may store them in a "queue" and give priority to certain jobs, so they are printed before others. For example, the server may be set to print smaller jobs ahead of larger ones or to give printing priority to certain users or workgroups.

Personal Communications

One of the most far-reaching applications of data communications is **electronic mail (e-mail),** a system for exchanging written messages (and increasingly, voice and video messages) through a network. E-mail is like a cross between the postal system and a telephone answering system.

You have probably heard about (or used) e-mail over the Internet. An e-mail system in a company's network works in much the same way. In fact, many companies connect their private networks to the Internet, so workers can send and receive messages across the office network or the Internet. In Unit 8, you will learn more about the Internet and Internet e-mail systems. For now, our discussion focuses on e-mail systems commonly used in private networks.

NORTON
ONLINE

Visit **www.norton.glencoe.com** for
more information on **e-mail**.

In an e-mail system, each user has a unique identifier, called an e-mail address. To send someone an e-mail message, you must use a special e-mail program that works with the network to send and receive messages. You enter the recipient's e-mail address, type the message, then tell the program to send the message to the recipient. The message travels across the network to the server, which usually stores the message and notifies the recipient that a new message has arrived. The recipient uses an e-mail program to get the message from the server. The recipient can save the message, delete it, forward it to someone else, or respond to the sender. Figure 7A.4 shows the process for sending and receiving e-mail.

Figure 7A.4

Sending and receiving e-mail over a typical network.

1 The sender composes an e-mail message and sends it.

2 The message is stored on the server.

3 The server alerts the recipient that there is a message.

4 When the recipient is ready to read the message, the recipient's computer retrieves it from the server.

SERVER

Memo
To: Bob
Meeting Friday, 9:00
See you there,
Sue

Memo

In addition to sending text messages, many e-mail systems allow you to attach data files—such as spreadsheet files or word-processed documents—to a message (see Figure 7A.5). This feature allows people to share files, even when they do not have access to the same storage devices. The use of attachments is a double-edged sword, however. Although it is a convenient way for users to share or exchange files, it also opens the door to viruses—parasitic computer programs that can damage a computer system. For this reason, many organizations take strict precautions to protect themselves against viruses carried by e-mail attachments; in fact, many companies forbid workers to send or receive attached files with e-mail messages. (You will learn more about viruses in Unit 14, "Living with Computers.")

In addition to e-mail, the spread of networking technology is adding to the popularity of teleconferencing and videoconferencing. A **teleconference** is a virtual

Figure 7A.5

Attaching a document to an e-mail message is a simple way to trade files with other people.

The user creates a message in this window.

In this dialog box, the user selects a file to attach to the message.

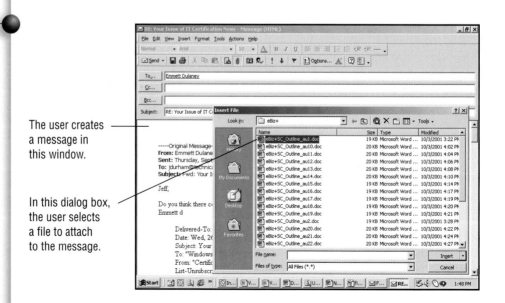

meeting in which a group of people in different locations conduct discussions by typing messages to each other. Each message can be seen by all the other people in the teleconference. Teleconferencing software has become more sophisticated, with features such as a shared scratch pad where diagrams or pictures can be drawn or electronically pasted.

Networking technologies also have boosted the popularity of collaborative software, which allows users to connect with one another over a network or modem connection and see what is happening on other users' computers. This kind of software lets people send messages, exchange files, and sometimes even work on the same document at the same time.

If users have the necessary hardware (a PC video camera, microphone, and speakers) and software, they can see and speak to each other as they meet online, instead of merely typing messages. This process is known as **videoconferencing** (see Figure 7A.6). In a videoconference, the audio and video signals travel across the network's (or Internet's) connections between the participants' computers.

Figure 7A.6
Participating in an online video-conference

Easier Backup

In business, data is extremely valuable, so it is important that employees back up their data. One way to make sure that data is backed up is to keep it on a shared storage device, which employees can access through a network. Often the network manager makes regular backups of the data on the shared storage device (see Figure 7A.7). Managers also can use special software to back up files stored on employees' hard drives from a single, central location. With this method, files do not have to be copied to the server before they can be backed up.

HOW NETWORKS ARE STRUCTURED

If you want to understand the different types of networks and how they operate, you need to know how networks are structured. There are two main types of networks: local area networks (LANs) and wide area networks (WANs). Some networks use servers (server-based networks) and some do not (peer-to-peer networks). These terms will be defined in detail in the following sections.

Local Area Networks (LANs)

A **local area network (LAN)** is a network of computers that are relatively near each other and are connected in a way that enables them to communicate (by a cable, an infrared link, or a small wireless device). A LAN can consist of just two or three

Figure 7A.7
Backup systems like this one can be used to back up a server and individual personal computers on the network.

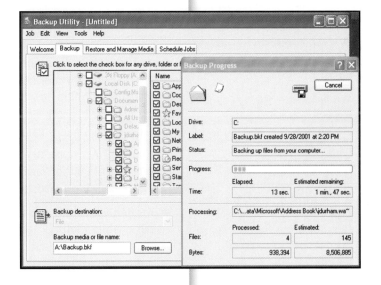

PCs connected together to share resources, or it can include hundreds of computers of different kinds. Any network that exists within a single building, or even a group of adjacent buildings, is considered a LAN.

It often is helpful to connect separate LANs together so that they can communicate and exchange data. In a large company, for example, two departments may have their own separate LANs, but if the departments need to share data, then they can create a link between the two LANs. To understand how this is possible, you need to understand how networks transmit data and how different types of networks can share data.

On a network, data is broken into small pieces—called packets—before being transmitted from one computer to another. A **packet** is a data segment that includes a header, payload, and control elements that are transmitted together (see Figure 7A.8). The receiving computer reconstructs the packets into their original structure.

Figure 7A.8
An e-mail message divided into packets

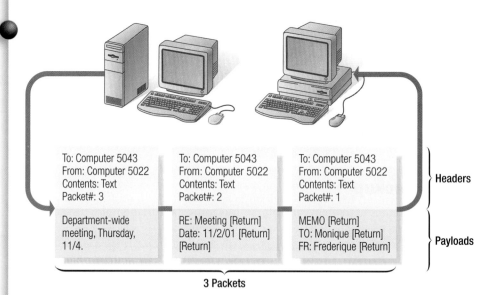

To: Computer 5043	To: Computer 5043	To: Computer 5043	Headers
From: Computer 5022	From: Computer 5022	From: Computer 5022	
Contents: Text	Contents: Text	Contents: Text	
Packet#: 3	Packet#: 2	Packet#: 1	
Department-wide meeting, Thursday, 11/4.	RE: Meeting [Return] Date: 11/2/01 [Return] [Return]	MEMO [Return] TO: Monique [Return] FR: Frederique [Return]	Payloads

3 Packets

The **payload** is the part of the packet that contains the actual data being sent. The **header** contains information about the type of data in the payload, the data's source and destination, and a sequence number that enables the receiving computer to reassemble the data in the proper order. Each LAN is governed by a **protocol,** which is a set of rules and formats for sending and receiving data. A single LAN may utilize more than one protocol. Some of the most common protocols in use today include:

◆ **TCP/IP.** Originally associated with UNIX hosts, TCP/IP is the protocol of the Internet and is required on any computer that must communicate across the Internet. TCP/IP is now the default networking protocol of Windows 2000 and many other operating systems. (You will learn more about TCP/IP in Unit 8, "The Internet and Online Resources.")

◆ **IPX/SPX.** A proprietary protocol of Novell, IPX/SPX has been used in most versions of the NetWare network operating system for networking offices throughout the world. Newer versions of NetWare also support TCP/IP.

◆ **NetBEUI.** A relatively simple protocol that has no real configurable parameters, NetBEUI sends messages to every computer that can receive them. It is an excellent protocol for networking small offices or homes, but it does not expand well into larger environments.

Networking protocols take the form of software, which must be installed on every computer on the network. This software, which is part of each computer's operating system or network operating system, tells the computer exactly how to break up, format, send, receive, and reassemble data. Without such software installed, a computer cannot participate in the network.

If two LANs are built around the same communication rules, then they can be connected with one of three devices:

◆ **Hub.** A **hub** is a simple connection point for different types of devices on a network.

◆ **Bridge.** A **bridge** is a device that looks at the information in each packet header and forwards data that is traveling from one LAN to another.

◆ **Router.** A **router** is a more complicated device that stores the routing information for networks. Like a bridge, a router looks at each packet's header to determine where the packet should go, and then determines a route for the packet to take toward its destination.

If you need to create a connection between different types of networks, you need a **gateway,** which is a computer system that connects two networks and translates information from one to the other. Packets from different types of networks have different kinds of information in their headers, and the information can be in various formats. The gateway can take a packet from one type of network, read its header, and then add a second header that is understood by the second network (see Figure 7A.9).

Figure 7A.9
How a gateway forwards a packet from one type of network to a different type of network

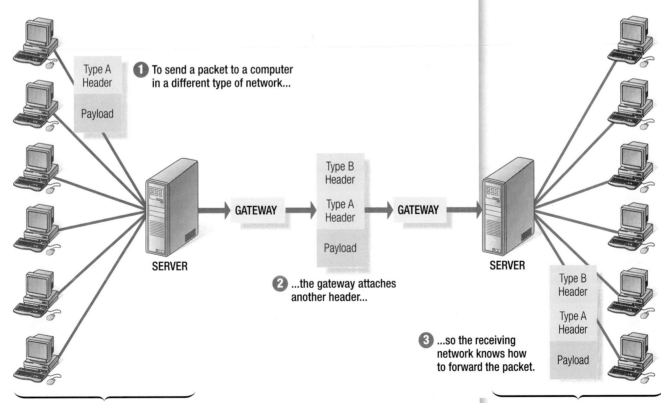

Campus Area Networks (CANs)

A **campus area network (CAN)** follows the same principles as a local area network, only on a larger and more diversified scale. With a CAN, different campus offices and organizations can be linked together. For example, in a typical university setting, a bursar's office might be linked to a registrar's office. In this manner, once a student has paid his or her tuition fees to the bursar, this information is transmitted to the registrar's system so the student can enroll for classes. Some university departments or organizations might be linked to the CAN, even though they already have their own separate LANs.

Metropolitan Area Networks (MANs)

The **metropolitan area network (MAN)** is a relatively new idea. A MAN is a large-scale network that connects multiple corporate LANs together. MANs usually are not owned by a single organization; their communication devices and equipment are usually maintained by a group or single network provider, which sells its networking services to corporate customers. MANs often take the role of a high-speed network that allows for the sharing of regional resources. MANs also can provide a shared connection to other networks using a WAN link.

Wide Area Networks (WANs)

Typically, a **wide area network (WAN)** is two or more LANs connected together, generally across a wide geographical area. For example, a company may have its corporate headquarters and manufacturing plant in one city and its marketing office in another. Each site needs resources, data, and programs locally, but it also needs to share data with the other site. To accomplish this feat of data communication, the company can attach routers connected over public utilities (such as telephone lines) to create a WAN. Note, however, that a WAN does not have to include any LAN systems. For example, two distant mainframe computers can communicate through a WAN, even though neither is part of a local area network.

Geographical distance aside, the chief distinction between a WAN and a LAN is the cost associated with transmitting data. In a LAN, all the pieces of the network usually are owned by the organization that uses them. For instance, if a company connects its networked PCs with cable, it owns the cabling, and it therefore pays a fixed cost to transmit data across the network. To transmit data across great distances, however, WAN-based organizations typically lease many of the components used for data transmission, such as high-speed telephone lines or wireless technologies such as satellites. Figure 7A.10 shows the relationship between LANs, MANs, and WANs.

Server-Based Networks

Terms such as LAN or WAN give you an idea of a network's physical size, but they do not tell you how individual computers on a network, called **nodes,** interact with one another.

Many networks include nodes and a central computer with one or more large hard disks used for shared storage. As you saw earlier, this central computer is known

Figure 7A.10
The use of MANs in their relationship to a WAN and correspondingly connected LANs

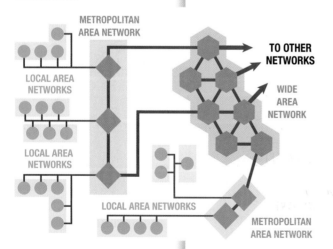

METROPOLITAN AREA NETWORK

LOCAL AREA NETWORKS

LOCAL AREA NETWORKS

LOCAL AREA NETWORKS

TO OTHER NETWORKS

WIDE AREA NETWORK

METROPOLITAN AREA NETWORK

as the file server, network server, application server, or just the server. Files and programs used by more than one user (at different nodes) often are stored on the server.

A **file server network** (see Figure 7A.11) is a fairly simple example of this kind of nodes-and-server network. This arrangement gives each node access to the files on the server, but not necessarily to files on other nodes. When a node needs information from the server, it requests the file containing the information. The server simply stores files and forwards (sends) them to nodes that request them.

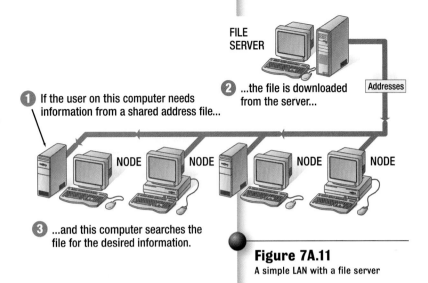

1 If the user on this computer needs information from a shared address file...

2 ...the file is downloaded from the server...

3 ...and this computer searches the file for the desired information.

Figure 7A.11
A simple LAN with a file server

Client/Server Networks

One popular type of server-based network is the **client/server network,** in which individual computers share the processing and storage workload with a central server. This arrangement requires special software for the nodes and the server. It does not, however, require any specific type of network. Client/server software can be used on LANs or WANs, and a single client/server program can be used on a LAN where all the other software is based on a simple file server relationship.

The most common example of client/server computing involves a database that can be accessed by many different computers on the network. The database is stored on the network server, along with a portion of the database management system (DBMS)—the program that allows users to work with the database. The user's computer (which can be called the node, workstation, or client) stores and runs the client portion of the DBMS.

Suppose that two users want information from the database. For example, suppose that the database is a list of customer purchases. The first user needs to know the names of customers in the Wichita area who made purchases of more than $500, and the second user wants a total of purchases made during the month of July. Using their client software to describe the information they need, each user sends a request to the server. The server software searches the database, collects the relevant customer names, and sends them back to the first client. It then searches the database for the information requested by the second user, using some of the same entries. For each user, the client software presents the information in a way that makes sense. Figure 7A.12 illustrates the process.

Client/server software is valuable to large, modern organizations, because it distributes processing and storage workloads among resources efficiently, so users get the information they need faster. Client/server computing is also a

Figure 7A.12
Processing information in a client/server computing model

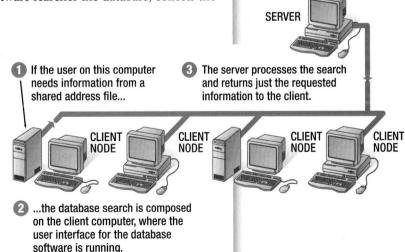

1 If the user on this computer needs information from a shared address file...

3 The server processes the search and returns just the requested information to the client.

2 ...the database search is composed on the client computer, where the user interface for the database software is running.

commonly used model on the Internet. Users typically have client software that provides an easy-to-use interface for interacting with this giant WAN. Other types of processing—such as receiving, storing, and sending e-mail messages—are carried out by remote computers running the server part of the relevant software.

Peer-to-Peer Networks

In a **peer-to-peer network,** (sometimes called a workgroup), all nodes on the network have equal relationships to all others, and all have similar types of software that support the sharing of resources (see Figure 7A.13). In a typical peer-to-peer network, each node has access to at least some of the resources on all other nodes. If they are set up correctly, many multi-user operating systems give users access to files on hard disks and to printers attached to other computers in the network.

Many operating systems—such as Windows 9*x* and later versions and the Macintosh OS—feature built-in support for peer-to-peer networking. This enables users to set up a simple peer-to-peer network, using no other software than their PCs' own operating systems.

Some high-end peer-to-peer networks allow **distributed computing,** which enables users to draw on the processing power of other computers in the network. For example, a user can transfer tasks that take a lot of CPU power—such as creating computer software or rendering a 3-D illustration—to other computers on the network. This leaves the user's machines free for other work.

Figure 7A.13
A peer-to-peer network

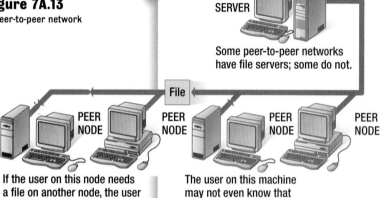

FILE SERVER

Some peer-to-peer networks have file servers; some do not.

File

PEER NODE   PEER NODE   PEER NODE   PEER NODE

If the user on this node needs a file on another node, the user simply copies the file.

The user on this machine may not even know that the file was copied.

Peer-to-peer LANs are commonly set up in small organizations (with fewer than 25 nodes). Peer-to-peer networks are popular in schools, where a network's main benefit is shared storage and printers or enhanced communications.

A peer-to-peer network also can include a network server. In this case, a peer-to-peer LAN is similar to a file server network. The only difference between them is that the peer-to-peer network gives users greater access to the other nodes than a file server network does.

Self Check

Complete each statement by filling in the blank(s).

1. A(n) _Server_ is a central computer that provides storage and other resources that users can share.

2. _Email_ is a system for exchanging written messages over a network.

3. A(n) _Peer to Peer_ is a small network that does not necessarily use a server.

At Issue

Catching "Cyberslackers" On the Job

Imagine that you run a small company, which has 12 employees. To make the workers more productive, you invest in cutting-edge computers, network services, and Internet connections for each of them.

One day, you learn that two of your employees are using their PCs and Internet access a great deal, but not for work-related purposes. One employee, you learn, is using the system to collect pornographic pictures on the Internet and is e-mailing them to friends. The other employee has started her own real estate business on the side and is using your company's computers to run her new business.

Such on-the-job behaviors are called "cyberslacking"—using company computers for personal or recreational purposes instead of work. It is a growing problem in the United States, and many companies are taking a stand against cyberslacking employees. Here's why:

- Some kinds of cyberslacking can lead to lawsuits. If a worker is using the company's computers to distribute pornography, the company can be implicated because it "supported" the person's activities.

- Careless use of the Internet can invite viruses and hacking.

- A company's reputation is put at risk by such activities. How would clients and the community react if you are sued? It could take years to recover and regain trust.

- If the two employees devote just one hour a day to their "hobbies," they are costing 10 hours per week of lost productivity. As the employer, you are paying for those hours, but no work is being done for your company; in fact, you may be paying the cyberslackers to harm your company.

Companies Taking Action

Companies can institute policies against all kinds of computer use. For example, an employer can forbid workers from:

- Visiting Web sites not directly related to their job

- Using the company's e-mail system to send or receive personal messages

- Participating in chat rooms or newsgroups

- Downloading or installing any type of software on a company computer

- Creating or storing certain types of documents on corporate systems

Policies alone, however, may not be enough to protect businesses. For this reason, managers are using sophisticated tools to combat cyberslacking. Such tools include:

- **Web filters.** Filters allow companies to block employee access to certain Web sites.

- **Surveillance software.** This type of software enables managers to review an employee's Internet activities in real time. If the user visits any Web sites, uploads or downloads files, lurks in newsgroups, or joins chat discussions, the software logs the actions.

- **Proxy servers.** This type of software (or hardware/software combination) traps network traffic that is coming from or going to an unauthorized source.

- **Packet sniffers.** Packet sniffers examine all packets being transmitted over a network.

Some employers go so far as to purchase "keystroke capturing" software. When installed on a PC, the program actually captures each keystroke as the user types, then directs the keystroke to a hidden file on the user's disk or network.

Be careful when using an employer's computer. Misusing it can lead to trouble.

243

VISUAL ESSAY: NETWORK TOPOLOGIES, MEDIA, AND HARDWARE

Another important feature of any LAN is its **topology**—the physical or logical layout of the cables and devices that connect the nodes of the network. Regardless of its topology, any network uses some type of media to link its nodes and/or servers together. In network communications, the term media refers to the wires, cables, or other means by which data travels from its source to its destination. Sometimes network media are compared by the amount of data they can carry, a factor commonly referred to as **bandwidth.** Simply stated, the higher a medium's bandwidth, the more data it can transmit at any given time. Bandwidth is expressed in cycles per second (hertz) or in bits per second.

A A **bus topology** network uses one cable; all the nodes and peripheral devices are connected in a series to that cable. A special device, called a **terminator,** is attached at the cable's start and end points to stop network signals, so they do not bounce back down the cable. This topology's main advantage is that it uses the least amount of cabling of any topology. In a bus topology network, however, extra circuitry and software is used to keep data packets from colliding with one another.

B The **star topology** is probably the most common topology. In a star network, a hub is placed in the center of the network; all nodes are connected to the hub and communicate through it. Data packets travel through the hub and are sent to the attached nodes, eventually reaching their destinations. Some hubs—known as intelligent hubs—can monitor traffic and help prevent collisions.

C The **ring topology** connects the network's nodes in a circular chain, with each node connected to the next. The last node connects to the first, completing the ring. Each node examines data as it travels through the ring. If the data—known as a **token**—is not addressed to the node examining it, that node passes it to the next node. There is no danger of collisions, because only one packet of data travels the ring at a time.

D In a **mesh topology,** a cable runs from every computer to every other computer. If you have four computers, you must have twelve cables—three coming from each computer to the other computers. The big advantage to this arrangement is that data can never fail to be delivered.

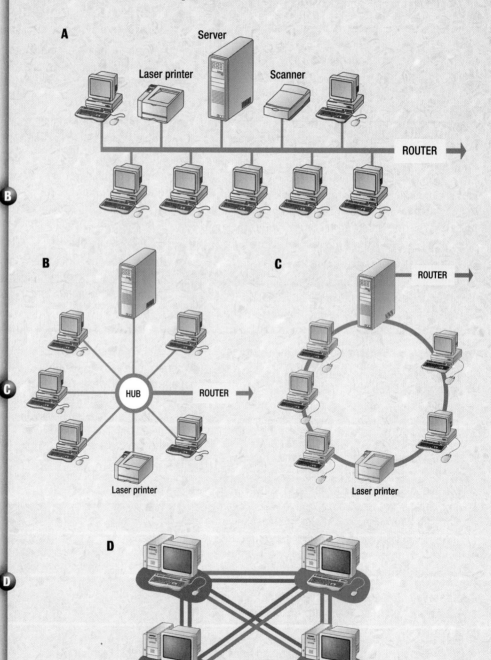

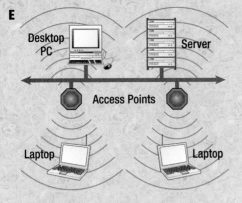

E Desktop PC   Server

Access Points

Laptop   Laptop

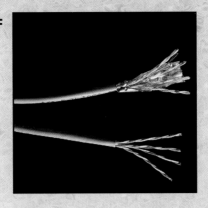

F

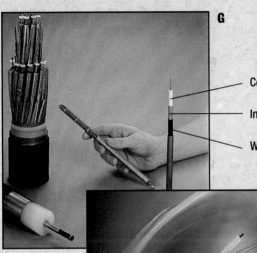

G

Central wire

Insulator

Wire mesh

H

Strands of glass

I

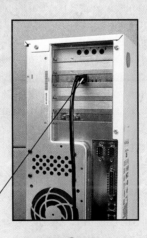

J

The network interface card accepts a network cable, which physically attaches the computer to the network.

E The **wireless topology** has been developed for mobile computing. In a wireless topology, single or multiple machines can connect through a single wireless **access point.**

F **Twisted-pair cable** normally consists of two wires individually insulated in plastic, then twisted around each other and bound together in a layer of plastic.

G Like the cabling used in cable television systems, **coaxial cable** has two conductors. One is a single wire in the center of the cable, and the other is a wire mesh shield that surrounds the first wire, with an insulator between.

H A **fiber-optic cable** is a thin strand of glass that transmits pulsating beams of light, rather than electric current.

I **Wireless networks** use radio or infrared signals for transmitting data.

J Regardless of the wiring and topology used, each computer on the network needs a hardware component to control the flow of data. The device that performs this function is the **network interface card (NIC)**, commonly called a network card.

Networks and Data Communications

NETWORK TECHNOLOGIES

Another critical piece of a network is the type of cabling equipment (also called the network technology) used to create a LAN. Each network technology is designed to work with a certain kind of network topology, and each one has certain standard features. The most common types of network technologies include:

◆ **Ethernet** is the most common network technology in use. The original implementations of Ethernet used coaxial cable and were called 10Base-5 and 10Base-2. The most popular implementation of Ethernet—called 10Base-T— uses a star topology and twisted-pair wires and can achieve transmission speeds up to 10 Mbps. Most new network installations use an Ethernet star topology with either twisted-pair or fiber-optic cables as the medium. With Ethernet, if two nodes transmit data at the same instant, the collision is detected, and the nodes retransmit one at a time.

◆ **Fast Ethernet** (also called 100Base-T) is available using the same media and topology as Ethernet, but it uses different network interface cards to achieve speeds of up to 100 Mbps. Other implementations of Ethernet are pushing transmission speeds even higher.

◆ **Gigabit Ethernet** is the newest addition to Ethernet technology; it evolved from the same 10 Mb Ethernet technology that was created in the 1970s. Capable of transferring 10 Gb of data per second, this Ethernet protocol can allow a network administrator to back up 2 TB (terabytes) of data in about 27 minutes. Gigabit Ethernet also can carry about 900 video signals at once, at about 1.5 MB per second of digital video. With the advanced audio, video, and telephone applications coming into the market every day, it will not be long before the Gigabit Ethernet standard will become the norm for high bandwidth tasks and processes.

◆ **Token Ring** is IBM's network technology. The controlling hardware in a Token Ring network transmits an electronic token—a small set of data—to each node on the network many times each second if the token is not already in use by a specific node. A computer can copy data into the token and set the address where the data should be sent. The token then continues around the ring, and each computer along the way looks at the address until the token reaches the computer with the address that was recorded in the token. The receiving computer then copies the contents of the token and sends an acknowledgment to the sending computer. When the sending computer receives the acknowledgment from the receiving computer, it resets the token's status to "empty" and transmits it to the next computer in the ring. Token Ring networks once operated at either 4 or 16 Mb, but like Ethernet, new technology has pushed the transmission rate up to 100 Mbps.

NETWORK SOFTWARE

Most of the networking terms you have seen so far—with the exception of network protocols—have referred to hardware. As with every other part of the computer system, however, software is needed to control the hardware. The group of programs that manages the resources on the network is often called the **network operating system (NOS).**

Network operating systems can range in size from Windows 95 (which allows you to connect several computers in a peer-to-peer network) to Windows 2000, Windows XP, Novell NetWare, and others. Some of the popular network operating systems include:

Visit **www.norton.glencoe.com** for more information on **network software**.

◆ **Novell NetWare.** One of the earliest and most popular network operating systems in terms of number of installations, NetWare (developed by Novell, Inc.) can be used to run networks with different topologies. NetWare also includes support for various hardware platforms, such as Mac, PC, and UNIX hosts and servers.

◆ **Microsoft Windows NT Server.** Microsoft Windows NT Server provides a graphical, Windows 9x–style user interface. It is ideal for administering small and medium-sized networks. Many companies that have invested in older versions of Microsoft Windows use Windows NT Server as their NOS. Windows NT Server also works with many other network operating systems.

◆ **Microsoft Windows 2000.** Available in four variations (Professional, Server, Advanced Server, and DataCenter), Microsoft Windows 2000 adds an enterprise directory model known as Active Directory. With these features and scalability/expandability, it is ideal for administering small and large networks alike.

◆ **Microsoft XP.** XP is the latest edition of the localized operating system for both the home and small office. Both the Home and the Professional editions are available for purchase. Microsoft XP brings small home/office networking capabilities right into the hands of beginning to intermediate users. In addition, it employs several new multimedia components that allow for advanced audio and video streaming capabilities. Other capabilities—such as mobile computing and stronger security protections—have been implemented, as well.

Figure 7A.14
Windows XP Professional includes networking and other features useful for business and advanced home computing.

◆ **Microsoft .NET Server.** The suite of .NET (pronounced "dot-net") Enterprise servers is the newest component of the Windows network operating systems. The .NET infrastructure consists of several different servers that take care of specified jobs and processes. All together, they make up Microsoft's answer to an enterprise-level solution. The server software packages that make up this enterprise suite are as follows: Application Center, BizTalk Server, Commerce Server, Exchange Server, Internet Security and Acceleration Server, Mobile Information Server, SharePoint Portal Server, and SQL Server.

◆ **Linux.** Linux has garnered a large share of the small business and home market for providing Internet and networking services. An open operating system, it is a cost-effective alternative to other operating systems for sharing files, applications, printers, modems, and Internet services.

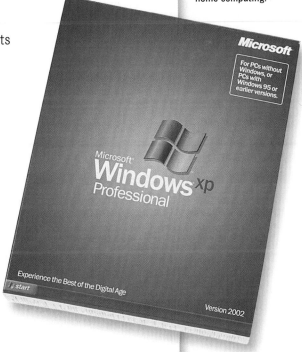

Norton Notebook

FIGHTING HACKERS

It may sound too alarming, but experts say there is a good chance that your home computer has already been visited by hackers via the Internet. In fact, if your home computer has broadband, always-on Internet access through a high-speed connection—such as an ISDN, DSL, or cable modem connection—it is almost certain that hackers have found your system and determined whether it can be invaded. Because these connections are always "on" (meaning your system remains connected to the Internet as long as the power is on), they give hackers plenty of time to find your system on the Internet and look for ways to get inside.

Networking experts say that home PCs have a number of vulnerabilities, which can grant a hacker easy access. These include security holes in Windows itself, as well as Internet applications such as browsers. Further, most users fail to password-protect any part of their systems.

Hackers, Crackers

Malicious hackers (sometimes called "crackers") spend a great deal of time mapping the Internet: that is, trying to identify as many vulnerable computers as they can. To accomplish this, they use a variety of software tools.

At the very least, a hacker or cracker can "ping" your computer to see if it is turned on and connected to the Internet. This is like walking through a neighborhood and trying to open the front door to each house. In pinging, someone sends a message to your computer; if it responds, the sender knows your computer is active and connected to the network. Pinging is usually the first step in the invasion process, and experts say that a typical PC gets pinged several times each week.

Once an invader finds a way to access your system's resources, there may be no limit to the damage that can be done. Files containing important data can be moved, renamed, deleted, or copied. Hackers may try to use your PC's resources without your knowledge.

Keeping Invaders at Bay

If you connect to the Internet through a standard modem and a dial-up connection, and if you stay connected for only short periods, then you may not need to worry about an invader getting into your system. However, if you leave your dial-up connection active for long periods, or if you have a perpetual connection through a high-speed link,

then you should take a serious look at your system's security.

Here are a few basic steps you can take to keep crackers out of your system:

◆ Plug Windows' security holes. This means turning off file and printer sharing, at the very least, unless you need these features to be activated for a LAN or home network connection. To learn more about these features, open the Windows help system and look for information on file sharing and printer sharing.

◆ Use passwords, and manage them effectively. Windows enables you to password-protect a variety of resources. If you use any network features, you should password-protect them and change your passwords frequently. Experts advise that you use long passwords (more than eight characters), and do not use passwords that could be easily guessed. Never use a "blank" password.

◆ Get a personal firewall. As you may recall, a firewall is a hardware and/or software tool that prohibits unauthorized access to a network, especially over the Internet. Personal firewalls are available in a wide range of prices and features, but you can get a good one for about $50. Some are even available for free.

◆ Ask your Internet Service Provider (ISP) for help. Check your ISP's Web site for security-related information. If you still have questions, call the ISP and talk to a technical support person. List your concerns about security and see what kind of answers you get.

If you connect to the Internet through a high-speed connection, a personal firewall is one of your best defenses against hackers.

248

SUMMARY

- A network is a way to connect computers for communication, data exchange, and resource sharing.

- The four main benefits of networking are simultaneous access to programs and data, peripheral sharing, streamlined communications, and easier backups.

- Many networks are built around a central computer called a server, which provides storage and other resources that users can share.

- Networks are categorized in different ways, such as by their size or by the presence or absence of a central server.

- A local area network (LAN) consists of computers that are relatively close to one another. A LAN can have a few PCs or hundreds of them in a single building or several buildings.

- Multiple LANs can be connected to create a much larger network that covers a larger area.

- A wide area network (WAN) results when multiple LANs are connected through public utilities, such as phone lines or microwave systems.

- Many networks are built around a central server. The PCs that connect to the server are called nodes.

- In a file server network, the server provides storage and file-sharing services for the nodes.

- In a client/server network, nodes and the server share the storage and processing tasks.

- A peer-to-peer network is a small network that usually does not include a central server. In a peer-to-peer network, users can share files and resources on all the network's nodes.

- A topology is the physical layout of the cables and devices that connect the nodes of a network. Topologies get their names—such as bus, star, or ring—from the shape of the network they create.

- When used in the context of networks, the term *media* refers to the wires, cables, and other means by which data travels from its source to its destination.

- The most common media for data communications are twisted-pair wire, coaxial cable, fiber-optic cable, and wireless links.

- The performance of network media is measured by the amount of data they can transmit each second. This value is called bandwidth. The higher a network's bandwidth, the more data it can carry.

KEY TERMS

access point, *245*
application server, *234*
bandwidth, *244*
bridge, *239*
bus topology, *244*
campus area network (CAN), *240*
client/server network, *241*
coaxial cable, *245*
distributed computing, *242*
electronic mail (e-mail), *235*
Ethernet, *246*
Fast Ethernet, *246*
fiber-optic cable, *245*
file server network, *241*
file server, *232*
gateway, *239*
Gigabit Ethernet, *246*
groupware, *235*
header, *238*

hub, *239*
local area network (LAN), *237*
mesh topology, *244*
metropolitan area
    network (MAN), *240*
network interface card (NIC), *245*
network operating system (NOS), *246*
network server, *232*
network version, *234*
network, *232*
node, *240*
packet, *238*
payload, *238*
peer-to-peer network, *242*
print job, *235*
protocol, *238*
read/write access, *233*
read-only access, *233*
ring topology, *244*

router, *239*
server, *232*
site license, *234*
spooling, *235*
star topology, *244*
supervisor access, *234*
teleconference, *236*
terminator, *244*
Token Ring, *246*
token, *244*
topology, *244*
twisted-pair cable, *245*
videoconference, *237*
wide area network (WAN), *240*
wireless networks, *245*
wireless topology, *245*
write access, *234*

KEY TERM QUIZ

Complete each statement by writing one of the terms listed under Key Terms in each blank.

1. A(n) __LAN__ is a network of computers that serves users located relatively near each other.

2. If you connect computers together to communicate and exchange information, the result is called a(n) __network__

3. The physical layout of wires and devices that connect the network's nodes is called the network's __topology__

4. The group of programs that manages the resources on a network is known as the __NOS__.

5. The amount of data a network's media can carry is called its __bandwidth__

SECTION QUIZ

True/False

Answer the following questions by circling True or False.

True   False   1. If network users can open shared files, but they cannot make changes to those files, they have read-only access.

True   **False**   2. When a user sends a document to a network printer, the document is called a spool. *print jobs*

True   False   3. On a network, data is transmitted in small groups called packets.

True   False   4. Distributed computing means getting other computers on the network to do some of your processing.

True   **False**   5. The mesh topology is the most commonly used networking topology because of its support for wireless devices.

Multiple Choice

Circle the word or phrase that best completes each statement.

1. _____ is one of the benefits of using a network.
   A. Easier backups   **B.** Peripheral sharing   **C.** Both A and B

2. If a server stores data files for users to access, it is commonly called a(n) _____ .
   A. file server   **B.** application server   **C.** neither A nor B

3. _____ software allows people to communicate over a network connection while seeing and hearing one another.
   A. Teleconferencing   **B.** Videoconferencing   **C.** Network operating system

4. A _____ is a networking device that stores the addressing information of each computer on each of the LANs it connects.
   A. bridge   **B.** router   **C.** server

5. A _____ network places a hub in the center of the network nodes.
   A. bus   **B.** ring   **C.** star

REVIEW QUESTIONS

In your own words, briefly answer the following questions.

1. List the benefits that networks provide to their users.

2. How can a network help a small business save money on printing?

3. How are e-mail messages usually sent and received on a network?

4. What are the four primary types of media used to link networks?

5. List the four most common types of networking technologies.

SECTION LABS

Complete the following exercise as directed by your instructor. (*Note: This exercise assumes you are using Windows Me or Windows 2000. If you have a different version of Windows, ask your instructor for specific directions.*)

1. Explore your network.
   A. On your Windows desktop, double-click the My Network Places icon. The My Network Places window opens. This window lets you access all the computers, folders, files, and devices on the network.
   B. Find the icon named Entire Network and double-click it. What do you see? Because every network is unique, the contents of this window will vary from network to network.
   C. Following your instructor's directions, click icons and open new windows to explore your network. How many network resources can you access?
   D. When you finish exploring, close all open windows.

SECTION 7B

Networking the Home, the Office, and the Globe

OBJECTIVES

- Explain how computer data travels over telephone lines.
- Explain a modem's function.
- List four features you should consider when evaluating modems.
- Differentiate four types of digital telephone services.
- Describe one potential use for a home network.

OVERVIEW:
The Local and Global Reach of Networks

Networks once were used mainly by universities, the military, and large government agencies, but today, networks span the globe and reach into the average home. For many small businesses, networking means connecting several PCs together, so workers can collaborate and share data. Small businesses often set up connections to the Internet, enabling users to browse the World Wide Web and exchange e-mail.

Medium and large businesses typically use networks to connect users for the same reasons as small businesses, but they also may use a large-scale LAN or WAN to connect departments or divisions that may be located in different buildings, regions, or even continents. Many businesses use a direct connection to the Internet to provide Internet access to their users.

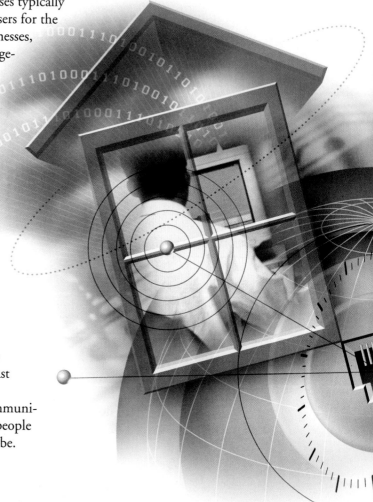

Even a home computer user can be part of a truly global network. A connection to the Internet makes your home computer one of the millions of nodes on the vast Internet network. You can share files, collaborate, communicate, and conference with people on the other side of the globe.

DATA COMMUNICATIONS WITH STANDARD TELEPHONE LINES AND MODEMS

Data communications usually takes place over media (such as cables or wireless links) that are specifically set up for the network, and thus are known as **dedicated media.** The alternative to using dedicated media is to use the telephone system—called the **plain old telephone system (POTS)**—for data communications. This option is possible because the telephone system is really just a giant network owned by the telephone companies.

As we know it, the telephone network is designed to carry the two-way transmission of electronic information, but it is very different from a typical computer network. Remember, the telephone system was originally designed to carry voice messages, which are analog signals. Increasingly, however, telephone lines are being used to send digital data. The reason for this trend is simple. By connecting your computer to the telephone, you can send data to potentially anyone else in the world who has a computer and phone service, and you do not need to set up a network to do it.

However, regular analog phone lines are not very well suited for carrying data (see figure 7B.1). They transmit data at a much, much slower rate than a typical Ethernet network—so slowly, in fact, that standard phone lines are simply impractical for many kinds of data transmissions. Also, computers and analog phone lines cannot work directly with one another; they require special hardware and software to "translate" data between the digital computer and analog phone line. As a result, telephone companies now offer digital lines specifically designed for data communications.

Although digital telephone lines are gaining popularity, millions of homes and businesses still have only analog telephone lines. Attaching a computer to an analog telephone line requires a modem, so it is important to know something about how modems work and what to look for when you buy one.

Figure 7B.1
The telephone system was designed to handle voice transmissions, rather than digital data.

In standard telephone service, a telephone converts the sound of your voice into an electric signal that flows through the telephone wires. The telephone at the other end converts this electric signal back into sound, so that the person you are talking to can hear your voice. Both the sound wave and the telephone signal are analog signals, which are electrical waves that vary continuously with the volume and pitch of the speakers' voices.

A computer's "voice" is digital; that is, it consists of on/off pulses representing 1s and 0s. Therefore, a device called a *modem* (short for *mod*ulator-*dem*odulator) is needed to translate these digital signals into analog signals that can travel over standard telephone lines. In its modulation phase, the modem turns the computer's digital signals into analog signals, which are then transmitted across the phone line. The reverse takes place during its demodulation phase, as the modem receives analog signals from the phone line and converts them into digital signals for the computer. Figure 7B.2 shows how computers communicate through modems and a telephone connection.

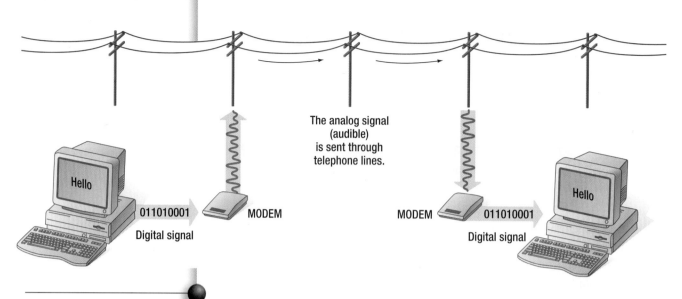

The analog signal (audible) is sent through telephone lines.

Hello

011010001

MODEM

Digital signal

MODEM

011010001

Hello

Digital signal

Figure 7B.2

How modems connect computers through telephone lines

Choosing a Modem

A modem can be a simple circuit board—an expansion card—that plugs into one of the PC's expansion slots, or it can be an external device that plugs into a serial port. Today, nearly every new PC comes with a built-in modem that supports all the latest technologies. If you have an older computer, however, or if you do not have a modem, you may decide to buy a modem to enhance your computer's ability to communicate. Modems are available from many manufacturers; therefore, it is wise to consider your needs before purchasing a modem (see figure 7B.3).

Although most of today's modems are similar in features and capabilities, four basic factors, including the following, should be considered:

◆ **Transmission Speed.** A modem's transmission speed (the rate at which it can send data) is measured in **bits per second (bps).** Today's fastest modems for dial-up connections on standard phone lines have a maximum theoretical transmission speed of 56,000 bits per second (56 Kbps) and are called 56K modems. The 56K modem's speed is due to several factors, such as the modem's use of the V.90 or newer V.92 data communications standards. These standards allow modems to communicate more efficiently over analog phone lines. Note, however, that these modems seldom actually achieve their highest potential transmission rate. Still, if you must use a standard phone line for data communications, a 56K modem will give you the fastest data transmission speeds available for PCs.

Figure 7B.3

Modem shopping can be confusing because there are many different brands and features to consider.

◆ **Data Compression.** Modern modems typically use data compression technologies to shrink the size of data before transmitting it over the telephone line. This method enables the modem to send and receive more data in less time than is possible when dealing with uncompressed data. Many different data compression schemes have been introduced over the years, and the newest modems are compatible with all of them. Today, if you purchase a 56K modem, it will most likely support the older V.42bis and newer V.44 data compression standards.

◆ **Error Correction.** Data moves through the line so quickly that even the smallest amount of static can introduce significant errors. Noise you could not hear if you were using the telephone line for a conversation can wreak havoc with computer data. As a result, modems and communications software use **error-correction protocols** to recover from transmission errors. These protocols enable a modem to detect errors in the data it is receiving and to request that error-ridden data be re-sent from its source.

◆ **Internal Versus External.** An **external modem** is a box that houses the modem's circuitry outside the computer (see Figure 7B.4). It connects to the computer via a serial, USB, or FireWire port, then connects to the telephone system with a standard telephone jack. An **internal modem** is a circuit board that plugs into one of the computer's expansion slots (see Figure 7B.5). An internal modem saves desktop space, but it occupies an expansion slot. Modems also come in the form of a PC Card for use with laptop computers (see Figure 7B.6). Some use standard telephone lines, but others include a cellular phone, which enables completely wireless transmissions.

Many of the latest 56K modems include innovative features that assure the user not only of faster data transmissions, but also better compatibility with telephone services than was available with older modems. For example, some new modems offer an "Internet hold" feature, which is helpful if you use the same line for phone calls and Internet use. With this feature, if you are online and receive a phone call, you can put your Internet session "on hold," answer the call, and then resume your Internet session exactly where you left off. A few modems with this feature also have caller ID, so you can decide whether you want to interrupt your Internet session to talk on the phone.

Most modems used with personal computers also can emulate a fax machine. Called **fax modems,** these devices can exchange faxes with any other fax modem or fax machine. With the proper software, users can convert incoming fax files into files that can be edited with a word processor—something that stand-alone fax machines cannot do.

Uses for a Modem

File transfer is the process of exchanging files between computers, either through telephone lines or a network. If you use your computer to send a file to another person's computer, you are said to be **uploading** the file. If you use your computer to copy a file from a remote computer, you are said to be **downloading** the file. For a file to be transferred from one computer to another through a pair of modems, both computers must use the same file transfer protocol (FTP)—the set of rules or guidelines that dictate the format in which data will be sent. The most common file transfer protocols for modems are called Kermit, Xmodem, Ymodem, Zmodem, and MNP.

Figure 7B.4
On the back of this external modem are connections for attaching it to the computer, a telephone jack, and a telephone.

Figure 7B.5
An internal modem plugs into one of the computer's expansion slots.

Figure 7B.6
This notebook computer is equipped with a modem in the form of a PC Card. The modem comes equipped with a cellular unit, so the user can log into a network without using a telephone line.

PRODUCTIVITY Tip

The Telecommuter's Checklist

Millions of Americans work at home or on the road with the help of computers, telecommunications equipment, and the Internet. These workers are called *telecommuters,* because they work at a remote location, rather than their employer's office.

Many companies encourage employees to work at home, because it can be less expensive to equip a home worker than to pay for on-site office space. Employers can also reduce workplace-related hazards by minimizing the number of workers on site. Another benefit of telecommuting is that many workers are more productive in a home office, where they can dress as they please and have greater control of their daily schedule and work environment.

To be effective in his or her job, the telecommuter must be just as well equipped as someone working in the company's office. The home office must be equipped for creating and processing data, exchanging data with others, and communicating with colleagues and clients. A typical telecommuter's equipment can include:

◆ **A computer.** Because they must be more self-sufficient than their office-based coworkers, telecommuters may need more powerful computers, or at least adequate equipment to complete the necessary tasks. Often, the telecommuter needs to have important programs and data files stored on a local disk, because the off-site worker may not always be able to access all programs and data files he or she needs by remotely logging into the company's network. Because the telecommuter's computer may need to perform additional tasks— such as remotely connecting to other systems, faxing, and printing to a local printer—the more power and storage space the computer system has, the better.

◆ **PC communications.** Although most newer computers have a modem, dial-up connections are too slow and inefficient for many business uses. For this reason, many employers equip telecommuters' PCs with a network card, enabling them to use a cable modem or some other type of high-speed connection. Either way, telecommuters may use the Internet to connect with the office's network and to do other tasks. The Internet connection must be fast enough to meet all these needs.

With the help of PCs and communications equipment, millions of people have found that they can be more productive working at home than at the company's office.

◆ **Phone lines.** Many companies are willing to pay for an additional telephone line for business usage in the telecommuter's home. This line may be for phone and fax communications, or it may serve as a data line for a PC. Either way, a second line is far more efficient than using a single home phone line for all purposes.

◆ **Faxing.** Rather than purchasing a fax machine, which costs more, takes up space, and ties up a phone line, many telecommuters use a scanner instead. Using fax software, they can send and receive faxes directly from their PC; if they need to fax a document with a signature, they can scan the document first, and then fax it. Multi-function "all-in-one" printer/copier/scanner/fax machines are ideal for telecommuters.

◆ **Wireless communications.** A digital phone, pager, or PDA may be even more important than a PC for telecommuters who travel a lot.

◆ **Service accounts.** Telecommuters are often responsible for setting up and maintaining their own accounts for communications and Internet services, especially when their home is in a different city than their employer's office. A conscientious employer will reimburse the worker for reasonable expenses, but the employee may be expected to set up and maintain communication accounts and Internet service.

One of the important functions of the file transfer protocol is to check for errors as a file is sent. Normally, modem communication is **full-duplex,** which means data can travel in both directions at the same time (see Figure 7B.7). Sometimes, however, modem communication can be **half-duplex,** which means that data can be sent in both directions, but in only one direction at a time. In either type of communication, the receiving computer can respond to the sender and verify that the data that was received contained no errors. If there are errors, the computer sending the data retransmits whatever portion is incorrect. Each file transfer protocol uses its own method to check for errors. Some are more efficient than others and, therefore, can transmit data faster.

FULL-DUPLEX TRANSMISSION

Data can be sent in both directions at the same time.

HALF-DUPLEX TRANSMISSION

Data can be sent in both directions but only one direction at a time.

Figure 7B.7
Most modern modem and network connections are full-duplex. However, computers occasionally are connected using half-duplex transmission.

Self Check

Complete each statement by filling in the blank(s).

1. The term *modem* is short for _Modulator-demodulator_

2. A modem's transmission speed is measured in _bps_ .

3. The act of using your computer to send a file to someone else's computer is known as _uploading_ the file.

Figure 7B.8
When sending data, a computer transmits a digital signal to a modem, which transmits an analog signal to the switching station, which transmits a digital signal to another switching station. This process is then reversed until it reaches the receiving computer.

USING DIGITAL TELEPHONE LINES

As you learned earlier, standard telephone lines transmit analog signals, in which sound is translated into an electrical current. As a result, you need a modem to translate data into a form that can be sent over telephone lines. In addition, data has to be compressed in order to travel at more than about 2400 bps over a standard phone line. Data compression has become quite sophisticated, so modems can sometimes transmit data at rates as high as 56 Kbps. Still, when you consider that most networks can transmit data at speeds of at least 10 Mbps (10,000,000 bps), phone lines and modems seem like a poor alternative.

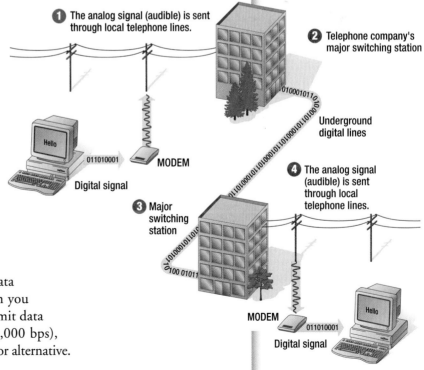

1 The analog signal (audible) is sent through local telephone lines.

2 Telephone company's major switching station

Underground digital lines

Hello

011010001 MODEM

Digital signal

3 Major switching station

4 The analog signal (audible) is sent through local telephone lines.

MODEM 011010001 Hello

Digital signal

The telephone companies recognized this problem several years ago and began the long process of converting an analog system into a digital system. The massive data channels that connect major geographical regions are already digital, but the telephone lines running under or above most city streets are still analog. This combination of digital and analog lines makes for an extremely confusing system, especially when you are transmitting data through a modem (see Figure 7B.8). However, when the telephone companies complete the transition and digital lines are installed to every building, the data transmission system will be a lot simpler.

The transformation from analog to digital lines will affect most users in three simple ways:

◆ You will need a different phone—a digital one that translates your voice into bits, rather than an analog signal.

◆ You will not need a modem to send data. Instead, you will use an adapter that simply reformats the data so that it can travel through the telephone lines.

◆ You will be able to send data much more quickly.

ISDN, T1, and T3

Many different kinds of digital services are offered by the phone companies. Three of the best known are called ISDN, T1, and T3.

ISDN, which stands for **integrated services digital network,** is a system that replaces all analog services with digital services (see Figure 7B.9).

When most people talk about ISDN, they are referring to a particular level of service called BRI (basic rate ISDN). BRI provides three communication channels on one line—two 64 Kbps or 56 Kbps data channels and one 19 Kbps channel that

Figure 7B.9
With local digital telephone lines, data transmissions can remain in a digital format from the sending computer to the receiving computer.

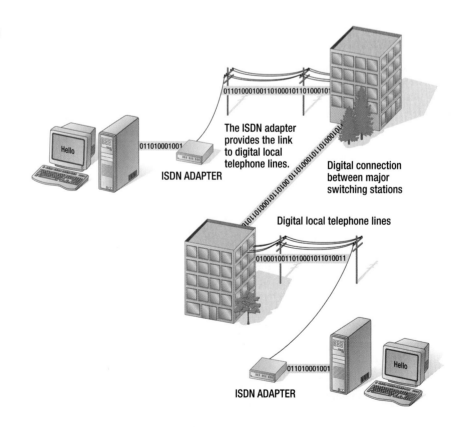

The ISDN adapter provides the link to digital local telephone lines.

ISDN ADAPTER

Digital connection between major switching stations

Digital local telephone lines

ISDN ADAPTER

is used to set up and control calls. The two data channels can carry voice or data, and they can be used simultaneously; thus, you can transmit data and carry on a conversation at the same time on the same line. Also, the channels can be combined so that BRI service can be used to transmit data at rates as high as 128 Kbps without compression.

A higher level of service for ISDN is called primary rate ISDN, or PRI. In the United States, PRI provides twenty-four channels at 64 Kbps each, a total bandwidth of 1.544 Mbps. This level of bandwidth is also known as **T1** service.

Although it is not specified by the ISDN standard, it is also possible to purchase lines from telephone companies that offer even more bandwidth. For example, a **T3** line offers 672 channels of 64 Kbps each (plus control lines) for a total of 44.736 Mbps. Many telephone companies also offer services between the levels of BRI and PRI. Different businesses have all kinds of different needs for bandwidth, so telephone companies try to be as flexible as possible in their offerings.

DSL Technologies

Another type of digital telephone service—called **digital subscriber line (DSL)**—is rapidly outpacing ISDN in some areas of the United States. DSL service is typically less expensive than ISDN service in terms of hardware, setup, and monthly costs. In fact, many local telephone companies are offering only DSL services in their markets, foregoing ISDN altogether.

Visit **www.norton.glencoe.com** for more information on **DSL technology**.

Several types of DSL, including the following, are available in different markets, each offering different capabilities and rates:

◆ Asymmetrical DSL (ADSL)

◆ Rate adaptive DSL (RADSL)

◆ High-bit-rate DSL (HDSL)

◆ ISDN DSL (IDSL)

◆ Symmetric DSL (SDSL)

◆ Very-high-bit-rate DSL (VDSL)

The actual performance you can achieve with DSL depends on the type of DSL service you choose, the distance between the DSL modem and the telephone company's switch, and many other factors.

ATM

DSL, ISDN, T1, and T3 can all be used effectively to set up WANs, as long as the networks are used primarily for transferring the most common types of data—files, e-mail messages, and so on. However, these types of services are not always well suited for transmitting live video and sound. As a result, communications companies offer a service called **ATM,** which stands for **asynchronous transfer mode.**

ATM is a protocol designed by the telecommunications industry as a more efficient way to send voice, video, and computer data over a single network. It was originally conceived as a way to reconcile the needs for these different kinds of data on the telephone system, but the proponents of ATM argue that it can also be implemented on computer LANs and WANs. In fact, ATM is a network protocol, and therefore it is similar to Ethernet and Token Ring.

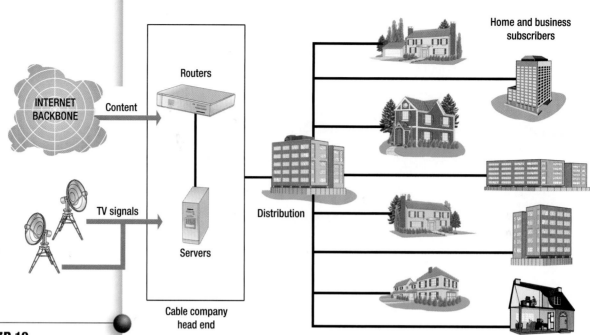

Figure 7B.10
A cable modem system combines a typical cable television network with a wide area network, which is connected to the Internet.

Cable Modem Connections

The cable modem is a technology that enables home computer users to connect to the Internet through their cable TV connection, with higher speeds than those offered by dial-up connections (see Figure 7B.10). However, cable modems also are finding acceptance in small- to medium-sized businesses as an alternative to other technologies, such as DSL and ISDN. Under the best conditions, cable modems can achieve download speeds of about 27 Mbps, a substantial increase over dial-up connections, ISDN, and some varieties of DSL.

In a typical cable network, a head end serves as the primary point where the television signals enter the system, through satellite and standard over-the-air broadcast means. The head end is also where the dedicated Internet connection occurs, connecting the cable TV network to the Internet. From the head end, the network branches out to subscriber locations using combinations of fiber-optic and copper cable, typically terminating at each end-user location as coax cable. Because a transmission often must traverse several miles from the head end to the end user, amplifiers are used to keep the signal strong. The greater the distance from the head end, the more amplifiers that are required.

Figure 7B.11
Millions of homes now have multiple PCs. New technologies enable families to create networks within the home using existing media (such as telephone lines) and existing operating systems (such as Windows).

NETWORKS IN THE HOME

Home networking is becoming more popular as the number of homes with multiple computers increases (see Figure 7B.11), along with the number of people who telecommute. Networks offer essentially the same advantages to home users as to a business. Home networks enable users to share resources such as printers, disks, and backup systems more efficiently, a consideration that often is more important for home users than for business users because of the difference in budgets.

With the introduction of Internet Connection Sharing (ICS) in Windows 98 and Windows 2000, home users can share a single dial-up connection to the Internet among multiple home computers.

In addition to ICS, Windows XP Home Edition makes setup and configuration of a home network simple with its Home Networking feature. It allows for the sharing of home peripherals, such as printers and scanners, as well as the ability to share a single Internet connection. Home networking also is enhanced with the Internet Connection Firewall, which will help protect a home network from the threat of unauthorized access. Figure 7B.12 shows the Windows XP Network Setup Wizard.

Figure 7B.12
The Network Setup Wizard in Windows XP

In the near future, home PCs will gain the ability to communicate with other electric and electronic devices, such as entertainment systems, heating and cooling systems, security systems, and even kitchen appliances.

As the market for home networking has grown, so has the choice of technologies. Like any business, a home can be a good target for standard networks using twisted-pair cable and hubs. This type of network installation requires installation of additional cable, which is not difficult if all the computers share the same room, or if cable can be installed during the home's construction. When only a few computers are involved in the same room, coaxial cable is a quick and easy solution. When computers are located in different rooms, however, adding cable dedicated to networking is not always practical because of cost and difficulty of installation.

Another technology with some success in the home networking market—primarily for implementation in existing structures—is wireless networking. Some solutions use infrared technology, while others use some form of radio transmission. Wireless solutions are most useful in buildings where installing cable is impractical, such as in concrete or masonry structures.

Most home networking requirements are not as extensive as those for a business or large organization. All of the operating systems targeted for the home user, particularly Windows 95/2000 and the Mac operating systems, provide built-in networking capabilities. Beyond the operating system included with the computers, there are generally no other applications required to enable or configure networking in a home network.

COMPUTERS
in your career

Careers in Networking

Two of the most popular (and best-paying) computer-related fields are networking and data communications. Most large organizations have existing networks that must be maintained, repaired, and updated as the company grows or shrinks. When companies merge, networks must be combined to create a seamless interface for the organization. Many times two or more networks that use different topologies, network operating systems, and protocols must be combined into one large network.

As these networks are merged, there must be a limited amount of down time, so employees can continue processing data for the company. People interested in careers relating to networking and data communications must be educated in a wide range of computing and networking topics.

Some careers relating to networking and data communications include the following:

◆ **Network Administrators.** These individuals are responsible for managing a company's network infrastructure. Some of the jobs in this field include designing and implementing networks, setting up and managing users' accounts, installing and updating network software and applications, and backing up the network. To succeed as a network administrator, you should gain experience in the major network operating systems, including Novell NetWare, Windows NT 4.0 Server, and Windows 2000 Server. You also should have experience with major operating systems, such as Windows 2000 and XP Professional, MS-DOS, Apple Macintosh, and UNIX or Linux. You might also consider becoming certified by Novell or Microsoft.

Networking is one of the most rapidly growing fields in the computing industry.

◆ **Information Systems (IS) Managers.** IS managers are responsible for managing a team of information professionals, including network administrators, software developers, project managers, and other staff. Jobs in the IS management field differ according to the needs of the company, but many IS managers maintain project lists, oversee project management, perform database administration, and possibly do some programming. IS managers should possess experience and skills in a wide range of networking and computing areas, including network operating system experience, operating system experience, relational database knowledge, and staff management abilities.

◆ **Data Communications Managers.** These managers are responsible for setting up and maintaining Internet, intranet, and extranet sites. Often, they are also responsible for designing and establishing an organization's telecommuting initiative. This task often requires experience with several technologies, including networking, data communications, remote access software, and Internet technologies. If you are interested in a career in data communications, you should learn as much as you can about these technologies.

SUMMARY

- Networks, and especially home users, commonly transmit data across telephone lines.

- Although telephone companies are offering more digital lines (which are better suited to data transmission), most homes and businesses are still served by analog telephone lines.

- To transfer digital data over analog telephone lines, computers must use modems. When a computer sends data, its modem translates digital data into analog signals for transmission over standard telephone lines. At the receiving end, the computer's modem converts the analog signals back into digital data.

- The most important factors to consider when choosing a modem are its transmission speed, the type of data compression it supports, the type of error correction it uses, and whether it is an internal or external unit.

- Modem transmission speeds are measured in bits per second (bps). Currently, the preferred standard for modems is 56 Kpbs.

- Using digital connections, business and homes can transmit data many times faster than is possible over standard phone lines.

- The most popular digital lines offered by telephone companies include integrated services digital network (ISDN), T1, T3, and DSL. They offer faster data transfer rates and higher bandwidths than standard phone lines.

- Another type of digital service is called ATM (asynchronous transfer mode). ATM is adapted for transmitting high-volume data files, such as audio, video, and multimedia files.

- Many cable companies now offer Internet connections to homes and businesses through the same lines that carry cable television service. Cable modem service can be even faster than ISDN and some types of DSL services.

- New technologies enable homeowners to set up home networks to connect multiple computers and to share devices or an Internet connection. Home networks typically operate on existing media, such as the home's telephone lines or cable wiring.

KEY TERMS

asynchronous transfer
    mode (ATM), *259*
bits per second (bps), *254*
dedicated media, *253*
digital subscriber line (DSL), *259*
download, *255*
error-correction protocol, *255*

external modem, *255*
fax modem, *255*
file transfer, *255*
full-duplex, *257*
half-duplex, *257*
integrated services digital
    network (ISDN), *258*

internal modem, *255*
plain old telephone
    system (POTS), *253*
T1, *259*
T3, *259*
upload, *255*

KEY TERM QUIZ

Complete each statement by writing one of the terms listed under Key Terms in each blank.

1. The process of copying a file from a remote computer onto your computer is called _download_

2. The process of sending a file to another user's computer over a network is called _upload_

3. BRI and PRI are two variations of _ISDN_

4. There are several different versions of _DSL_ service, each offering its own capabilities and rates.

5. _File transfer_ is the process of exchanging files between computers.

SECTION QUIZ

True/False

Answer the following questions by circling True or False.

True   ~~False~~   1. You do not need a modem to connect a computer to an analog telephone line.

~~True~~   False   2. The expression Kbps stands for "thousand bits per second."

~~True~~   False   3. File transfer is possible through a network or telephone lines.

True   ~~False~~   4. Basic Rate ISDN service provides 13 communication channels.

True   ~~False~~   5. Modem communications cannot take place in half-duplex mode.

Multiple Choice

Circle the word or phrase that best completes each statement.

1. You should consider _____ when purchasing a modem.
   A. transmission speed   B. error correction   **C. both A and B**

2. The abbreviation *bps* stands for _____ .
   A. bytes per second   **B. bits per second**   C. bandwidth per second

3. A(n) _____ enables a modem to determine whether data has been corrupted and to request that it be retransmitted.
   A. error-protection protocol   B. file transfer protocol   C. Internet protocol

4. _____ service offers a total of 44.736 Mbps of bandwidth.
   A. ISDN   B. T1   **C. T3**

5. In a cable network, the _____ is where the cable TV network connects to the Internet.
   A. head end   B. switching station   **C. cable modem**

REVIEW QUESTIONS

In your own words, briefly answer the following questions.

1. Why are modems required when two computers need to exchange data over standard telephone lines?

2. What factors should you consider when purchasing a modem?

3. If digital telephone lines completely replace analog lines, how will data communications be simplified?

4. Name three different versions of DSL service.

5. What kind of operating system usually is needed to run a home network?

SECTION LABS

Complete the following exercises as directed by your instructor.

1. Determine what type of modem is in your computer, and view its settings. Open the Control Panel window, then double-click the Modems icon to open the Modems Properties dialog box. If any modems are listed, select them one at a time, and click the Properties button. Review the properties for each modem. Be careful not to change any settings. Close all open windows and dialog boxes.

2. HyperTerminal is a Windows utility that enables your computer to "call" another computer directly and exchange data over a telephone line. Click the Start button, then click Programs, Accessories, Communications, HyperTerminal. When HyperTerminal launches, open the Help menu, and study the Help topics to learn more about the program and its capabilities. When you are finished, close all open windows and dialog boxes.

UNIT PROJECTS

UNIT LABS

Complete the following exercises using a computer in your classroom, lab, or home. (*Note:* These exercises assume you are using Windows Me or Windows 2000, and that your computer is connected to a network. If not, ask your instructor for assistance.)

1. **Learn more about networking in Windows.** Windows provides many networking-related options and services. To learn more about the networking capabilities that are built into your version of Windows, use the Help system to find information. Here's how:

   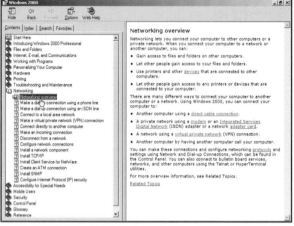

   A. Click the Start button to open the Start menu, then click Help. Depending on which version of Windows you use, a different kind of Help window will appear.

   B. If you use Windows Me, skip to Step C. If you use Windows 2000, click the Show button on the Help window's toolbar to open the left-hand pane of the Help window. Click the Contents tab, then click the Networking link. The category expands, revealing more than a dozen Help topics dealing with networking. Click each topic in the Contents tab, and read the information that appears in the right-hand pane of the Help window.

   C. If you use Window Me, click the Tours and tutorials link at the top of the window. In the list of tutorials, click the Take the Home Networking Tour link. The tour opens in a separate window. Follow the instructions in the window to complete the tour.

   D. When you are finished, close all open windows and dialog boxes.

2. **Want to set up a home network?** If you have more than one computer at home, you may want to set up a home network so they can share a printer, an Internet connection, or other kinds of resources. Creating a home network is a lot easier and cheaper than you might think. The Internet is a good place to learn about all types of home networks, to shop for the hardware and software you need, and to get step-by-step instructions for building your own network. Visit the following sites to learn more:

   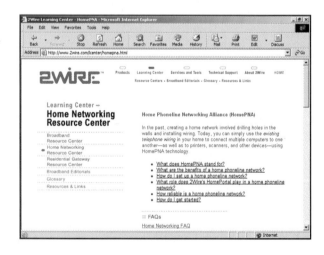

   - 2Wire Learning Center—**http://www.2wire. com/lcenter/homepna.html**

   - About.com's Home Networking Tutorial—**http://compnetworking.about.com/ library/weekly/aa021801a.htm**

   - Actiontec Home Networking Info Center—**http://www. yourhomenetworking.com/**

   - International Engineering Consortium On-Line Education: Home Networking—**http://www.iec.org/online/tutorials/home_net/**

3. **Check out videoconferencing.** Several affordable video-conferencing applications are available, all of which enable you to join online videoconferences on a private network or the Internet. You can learn more about some of these products at these Web sites:

- iVisit—**http://www.ivisit.com/**
- ClearPhone—**http://www.clearphone.com/**
- First Virtual Communications—**http://www.fvc.com/**
- Microsoft—**http://www.microsoft.com/windows/ netmeeting/**

DISCUSSION QUESTIONS

As directed by your instructor, discuss the following questions in class or in groups.

1. Create a list of ways in which companies can save money by setting up a network. Look beyond issues such as printing and sharing programs. Can you imagine other ways to save money by using a network?

2. How practical do you think home networks really are? Do you see a practical use for them, besides playing games or sharing printers? In your opinion, will people really connect their PCs, home appliances, and utilities with a home network someday? Why or why not? Be prepared to support your views.

RESEARCH AND REPORT

Using your own choice of resources (such as the Internet, books, magazines, and newspaper articles), research and write a short paper discussing one of the following topics.

- The growth of telecommuting in American business
- The largest private LAN or WAN in the United States
- Recent advances in modem technology

When you are finished, proofread and print your paper, and give it to your instructor.

 ETHICAL ISSUES Networks give us more freedom in the workplace, but they can be misused. With this in mind, discuss the following in class.

1. Telecommuters enjoy working at home, because it gives them more control over their schedules, while removing the distractions that are part of the workplace. However, some workers abuse their telecommuting privileges because they are no longer under the watch of a supervisor. What are the risks to business of allowing employees to telecommute? At what point is an employee abusing the freedom afforded by telecommuting? In your view, what kinds of activities or behaviors constitute such abuse?

2. It is estimated that most occurrences of hacking are conducted by employees who pilfer data from their employers' networks, and then sell or misuse that information. How far should companies go to prevent such abuse? What kinds of punishments are appropriate?

UNIT **8**

The Internet and Online Resources

UNIT CONTENTS

This unit contains the following sections:

The Interactive Browser Edition CD-ROM provides additional labs and activities to apply concepts from this unit.

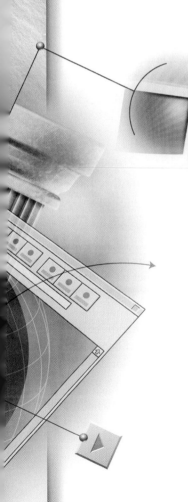

SECTION 8A

Internet Basics

OVERVIEW:
A Growing Influence in Our Lives

By the time it became commonplace in households in the mid-1990s, the Internet had existed for more than 30 years. Relatively few people knew what it was, and even fewer had actually used it. By 1994, when people began "surfing the Internet" in large numbers, its potential was only beginning to be understood. Today, the Internet is a constant in the lives of millions of people around the world, and its reach and usefulness seem almost unlimited.

In fact, the Internet may be one of the most important factors shaping the near future. Its existence already has changed the way many people work, communicate, and do business. The Internet has enabled us to access nearly any kind of information from a PC, and it has freed us from many kinds of chores. It has given us a new place to shop, study, work, and socialize.

As the "information society" moves forward, an understanding of the Internet may become as important as a college degree, depending on the type of career you want to pursue. Certainly, as a tool for personal communication, research, commerce, and entertainment, the Internet is an indispensable asset you should master. If you use it as a business tool, the Internet probably will be as essential to your job as a word processor, spreadsheet, or any other type of computer application.

This unit introduces you to the basic structure and features of the Internet. It shows you how individuals and businesses can connect to the Internet.

OBJECTIVES

- Explain, in basic terms, the importance of TCP/IP to the Internet.
- Describe the basic structure of the Internet.
- List eight major services and features that the Internet provides to its users.
- Identify two key Internet-related features found in many software applications.

HOW THE INTERNET WORKS

The single most important fact to understand about the Internet is that it can potentially link your computer to any other computer. Anyone with access to the Internet can exchange text, data files, and programs with any other user who also is connected to the Internet. For all practical purposes, almost everything that happens across the Internet is a variation of one of these activities. The Internet itself is the pipeline that carries data between computers.

TCP/IP: The Universal Language of the Internet

The Internet works because every computer connected to it uses the same set of rules and procedures (known as protocols) to control the way data is formatted and transmitted between computers. The protocols used by the Internet are called **Transmission Control Protocol/Internet Protocol,** universally abbreviated as **TCP/IP.**

The TCP/IP protocols include the specifications that identify individual computers and that enable computers to exchange data. They also include rules for several categories of application programs, so programs that run on different kinds of computers can talk to one another. For example, someone using a Macintosh computer can exchange data with a UNIX computer on the Internet.

TCP/IP software looks different on different kinds of computers, but it always presents the same appearance to the network. It does not matter if the system at the other end of a connection is a supercomputer, a pocket-size personal communications device, or anything in between; as long as the system recognizes TCP/IP protocols, it can send and receive data through the Internet.

Routing Traffic Across the Internet

Most computers are not connected directly to the Internet. Rather, they are connected to smaller networks that connect to the Internet backbone through gateways. That fact explains why the Internet is called "a network of networks." Figure 8A.1 shows a typical Internet connection.

The core of the Internet is the set of backbone connections that tie the local and regional networks together and the routing scheme that controls the way each piece of data finds its destination. In networking diagrams, the Internet backbone is often portrayed as a big cloud, because the routing details are less important than the fact that the data passes through the Internet between the origin and the destination.

A description of the basic model for most Internet tools follows. A client application on a user's computer requests data through the network from a server. As you learned in Unit 7, a server is a powerful computer—generally containing a large hard disk—that acts as a shared storage resource. In addition to containing stored files, a server also may act

Figure 8A.1
In a typical Internet connection, individual computers connect to a local or regional network, which is connected in turn to the Internet backbone via a gateway.

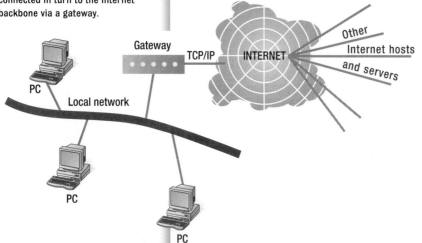

as a gatekeeper for access to programs or data from other computers. The Internet includes many thousands of servers, each with its own unique address. These servers, in tandem with routers and bridges, do the work of storing and transferring data across the network.

Because the Internet creates a potential connection between any two computers, however, the data may be forced to take a long, circuitous route to reach its destination. Suppose, for example, that you request data from a server in another state:

◆ Your request must be broken into packets. (For a detailed explanation of packets, see Section 7A, "Networking Basics.")

◆ The packets are routed through your local network, and possibly through one or more subsequent networks, to the Internet backbone.

◆ After leaving the Internet backbone, the packets then are routed through one or more networks until they reach the appropriate server and are reassembled into the complete request.

◆ Once the destination server receives your request, it begins sending you the requested data, which winds its way back to you—possibly over a different route.

Between the destination server and your PC, the request and data may travel through several different servers, each helping to forward the packets to their final destination.

Addressing Schemes—IP and DNS Addresses

Internet activity can be defined as computers communicating with one another using the common "language" of TCP/IP. Examples include the following:

◆ A client system (such as your home computer) communicating with an Internet server.

◆ An Internet server computer communicating with a client computer.

◆ Two server computers communicating with one another.

◆ Two client computers communicating via one or more servers.

The computer that originates a transaction must identify its intended destination with a unique address. Every computer on the Internet has a four-part numeric address, called the **Internet protocol address (IP address),** which contains routing information that identifies its location. Each of the four parts is a number between 0 and 255, so an IP address looks like this: 205.46.117.104

Computers have no trouble working with long strings of numbers, but humans are not so skilled. Therefore, most computers on the Internet (except those used exclusively for internal routing and switching) also have an address called a **domain name system (DNS) address**—an address that uses words, rather than numbers.

Domains and Subdomains

DNS addresses have two parts: a host name (a name for a computer connected to the Internet) followed by a **domain** that generally identifies the type of institution that uses the address. This type of domain name is often called a **top-level domain.** For example, many companies have a DNS address whose first part is the company name, followed by ".com"—the now-overused marketing gimmick. Table 8A.1 lists the most common types of Internet domains used within the United States.

NORTON
ONLINE

Visit **www.norton.glencoe.com** for more information on **IP addresses, domains, and the domain name system.**

Table 8A.1 Internet Domains

Domain	Type of Organization	Example
.com	Business (commercial)	ibm.com (International Business Machines Corp.)
.edu	Educational	centre.edu (Centre College, Danville, KY)
.gov	Government	whitehouse.gov (The White House)
.mil	Military	navy.mil (The United States Navy)
.net	Gateway or host (or business/commercial)	mindspring.net (Mindspring, a regional Internet service provider)
.org	Other organization (typically nonprofit)	isoc.org (The Internet Society)

Table 8A.2 New Top-Level Domains

Domain	Type of Organization
.info	Informational Web site
.biz	Business related site
.name	Domain registration for individuals

Table 8A.3 Top-Level Domains Under Consideration

Domain	Type of Organization
.aero	Air transport industry
.coop	Cooperatives
.museum	Museums
.pro	Accountants, Lawyers, Physicians

Some large institutions and corporations divide their domain addresses into smaller **subdomains.** For example, a business with many branches might have a subdomain for each office—such as boston.widgets.com and newyork.widgets.com. You also might see some subdomains broken into even smaller subsubdomains, like evolution.genetics.washington.edu.

The Internet Corporation for Assigned Names and Numbers (ICANN) has added three new domains, and as of this writing, several more domains were being considered. Table 8A.2 shows the three newly available top-level domains, which went into effect in May 2001. Table 8A.3 lists some proposed domains that may be added in the future.

MAJOR FEATURES OF THE INTERNET

The Internet has many uses. Electronic mail is an efficient and inexpensive way to send and receive messages and documents around the world within minutes. The World Wide Web is an important advertising medium and a channel for distributing software, documents, and information services. As channels for business research, the databases and other information archives that exist online are often better and more up-to-date than any library. The Internet also has created hundreds of "virtual communities" made up of people who share an interest in a technical discipline, hobby, or political or social movement.

To use any of these services, you need a computer that is connected to the Internet in some way. Most individual users connect their computer's modem to a telephone line (or use a high-speed connection such as ISDN or a cable modem) and set up an account with an **Internet service provider (ISP),** which provides local or regional access to the Internet backbone. Many other users connect to the Internet through a school or business LAN. These methods of connecting to the Internet are discussed later in this unit. The following sections introduce some of the most popular features of the Internet.

The World Wide Web

The **World Wide Web** (the **Web** or **WWW**) was created in 1989 at the European Particle Physics Laboratory in Geneva, Switzerland, as a method for incorporating footnotes, figures, and cross-references into online hypertext documents, using a protocol known as the **hypertext transfer protocol (HTTP)**. A hypertext document is a specially encoded file that uses the **hypertext markup language (HTML)**. This language allows a document's author to embed **hypertext links** (also called **hyperlinks** or just **links**) in the document. HTTP and hypertext links are the foundations of the World Wide Web.

As you read a hypertext document—more commonly called a **Web page**—on screen, you can click a word or picture encoded as a hypertext link and immediately jump to another location within the same document or to a different Web page (see Figure 8A.2). The second page may be located on the same computer as the original page, or anywhere else on the Internet. Because the user does not have to learn separate commands and addresses to jump to a new location, the World Wide Web organizes widely scattered resources into a seamless whole.

Visit **www.norton.glencoe.com** for more information on **HTML and the World Wide Web**.

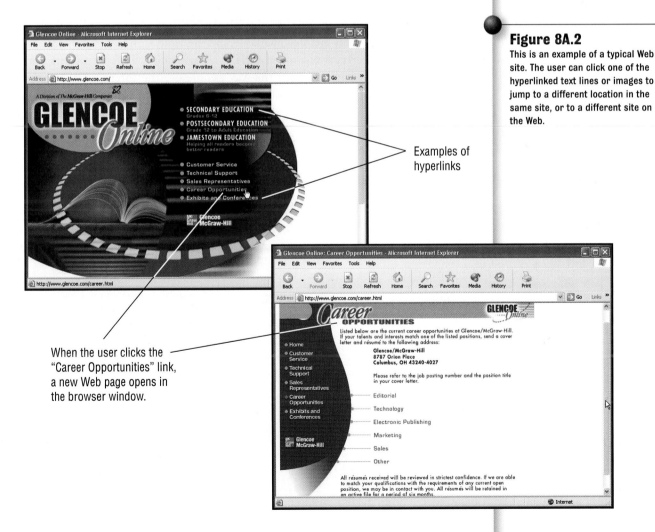

Figure 8A.2
This is an example of a typical Web site. The user can click one of the hyperlinked text lines or images to jump to a different location in the same site, or to a different site on the Web.

Examples of hyperlinks

When the user clicks the "Career Opportunities" link, a new Web page opens in the browser window.

A collection of related Web pages is called a **Web site.** Web sites are housed on **Web servers,** Internet host computers that often store thousands of individual pages. Copying a page onto a server is called **posting** the page, but the process also may be referred to as publishing or uploading. (The term *posting* also is used when other types of documents are placed on Internet host computers, such as posting an article in a newsgroup.)

Web pages are now used to distribute news, interactive educational services, product information and catalogs, highway traffic reports, and live audio and video, among many other items. Interactive Web pages permit readers to consult databases, order products and information, and submit payment with a credit card or other account number.

You may hear the terms *World Wide Web* and *Internet* used interchangeably, as though they are the same. However, the Web is simply a type of service available to persons who can access the Internet's resources.

Web Browsers and HTML Tags

The Web was an interesting but not particularly exciting tool used by scientific researchers—until 1993, when Mosaic, a point-and-click Web browser, was developed at the National Center for Supercomputing Applications (NCSA) at the University of Illinois. A **Web browser** (or **browser**) is a software application designed to find hypertext documents on the Web and then open the documents on the user's computer. A point-and-click browser provides a graphical user interface that enables the user to click graphical objects and hyperlinks. Several text-based Web browsers are also available and are used in non-GUI operating systems, such as in certain versions of UNIX. Mosaic and the Web browsers that have evolved from it have changed the way people use the Internet. Today, the most popular browsers are Microsoft's Internet Explorer and Netscape Navigator (see Figure 8A.3).

Figure 8A.3
Microsoft Internet Explorer and Netscape Navigator

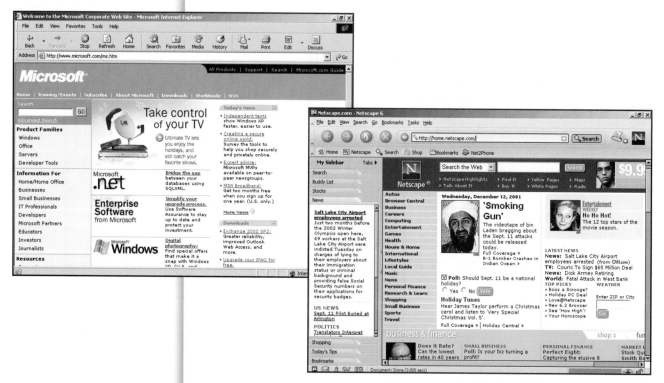

HTTP and URLs

As mentioned, the internal structure of the World Wide Web is built on a set of rules called hypertext transfer protocol (HTTP). HTTP uses Internet addresses in a special format, called a **uniform resource locator (URL).** URLs look like this:

type://address/path/

In a URL, *type* specifies the type of server in which the file is located, *address* is the address of the server, and *path* is the location within the file structure of the server. The path includes the list of folders (or directories) where the desired file is located. Consider one URL for this book's Web site—http://www.glencoe.com/norton/online/—as shown in Figure 8A.4.

If you were looking for a document named Welcome at this Web site, its URL might be the following:

http://www.glencoe.com/norton/online/welcome.html

Note that when a URL ends with a folder name rather than a file, the URL includes a final slash (/). Because URLs lead to specific documents on a server's disk, they can be extremely long; however, every single document on the World Wide Web has its own unique URL (see Figure 8A.5).

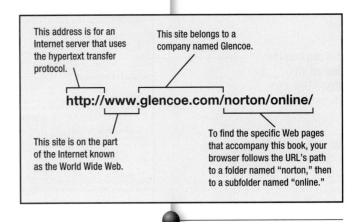

This address is for an Internet server that uses the hypertext transfer protocol.

This site belongs to a company named Glencoe.

http://www.glencoe.com/norton/online/

This site is on the part of the Internet known as the World Wide Web.

To find the specific Web pages that accompany this book, your browser follows the URL's path to a folder named "norton," then to a subfolder named "online."

Figure 8A.4
Parts of a typical URL

Visit **www.norton.glencoe.com** for more information on **HTTP and URLs.**

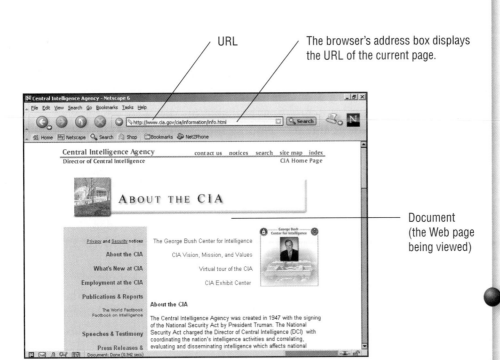

URL

The browser's address box displays the URL of the current page.

Document (the Web page being viewed)

Figure 8A.5
Each Web page has its own unique URL, which directs your browser to the document's location.

As shown in Figure 8A.6, you use URLs to navigate the Web in two ways:

◆ Type the URL for a Web site in the address box of your browser. For example, if you want to visit the Web site of the Internal Revenue Service, click in the browser's address box (to place an insertion point there) and type as follows:

http://www.irs.gov/

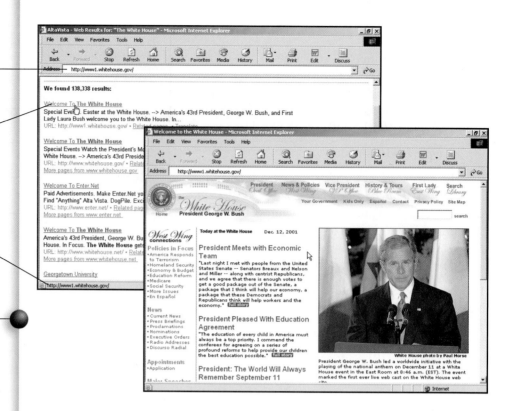

You can type the desired Web page's URL here, then press Enter.

You can click a hyperlink.

When you point to a hyperlink, its URL appears in the browser's status bar.

Figure 8A.6

You can move from one Web page to another by specifying a URL or clicking a hyperlink. Both navigation methods take you to the same place.

◆ Click a hyperlinked word or image, and your browser automatically finds and loads the Web page indicated by the hyperlink. (When you point to a hyperlink, the browser's status bar displays the URL that the link leads to.)

Helper Applications and Multimedia Content

As versatile as they are, Web browsers alone cannot display every type of content—especially multimedia content—now available on the Web. Many Web sites feature audio and video content, including full-motion animation and movies. These large files require special applications in order to be played in real time across the Web. Because these applications help the browser by being "plugged in" at the right moment, they are called **helper applications** or **plug-in applications.**

Figure 8A.7

By streaming audio and video content from the server to the client (the user's PC), multimedia plug-in applications enable you to watch movies and listen to high-quality audio.

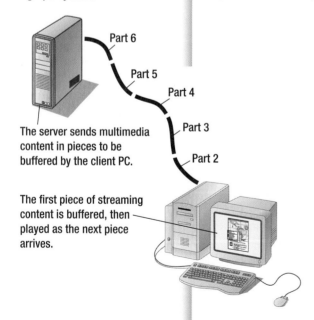

Part 6

Part 5

Part 4

Part 3

Part 2

The server sends multimedia content in pieces to be buffered by the client PC.

The first piece of streaming content is buffered, then played as the next piece arrives.

Plug-ins are used to support several types of content, including **streaming audio** and **streaming video.** Streaming technology works by sending the audio or video content in a continuous stream. The plug-in application receives a portion of the stream and stores it temporarily in a buffer (an area in memory or on disk). After a portion of the stream has been buffered, it is played while the next portion of the stream is stored in the buffer (see Figure 8A.7). This buffer-and-play technique is an effective method for playing a large file quickly without waiting for the entire file to download. Multimedia plug-in applications also use file compression to move the process even faster. Even so, multimedia files can take much longer to download than typical HTML documents.

There is a tremendous array of multimedia content available on the Web. For example, sites like Yahoo! Broadcast (**http://broadcast.yahoo.com/**) and WindowsMedia.com (**http://windowsmedia.com/mg/radio.asp**) provide access to radio stations from around the world, in addition to Internet-only radio. Television channels, such as CNN and The Weather Channel, also deliver their audio and video content over the Web. Using plug-in applications—such as Microsoft's Windows Media Player, Apple's QuickTime Player, or RealNetworks' RealPlayer—you can play any of these sources on your desktop (see Figure 8A.8).

Figure 8A.8
QuickTime Player, Windows Media Player, and other multimedia plug-in applications enable you to enjoy streaming audio and video from different sources.

One of the most commonly used multimedia design tools is made by Macromedia, Inc. This tool—called Flash—enables Web designers to create high-quality animation or video, complete with audio, that plays directly within the browser window. These types of animation do not require the browser to **spawn** (launch) an external application for viewing, as is the case with multimedia types displayed in Windows Media Player, QuickTime, and others. You need the Flash Player plug-in to view many Web sites. It is available from the Macromedia Web site (**http://www.macromedia.com/**).

Self Check

Complete each statement by filling in the blank(s).

1. Every computer on the Internet has a numeric address, called its

   _____ .

2. Hypertext links are also called _____ .

3. The Flash Player is an example of a(n) _____ application.

PRODUCTIVITY Tip

Portals: Your Own Front Door to the Web

A Web portal is a free, personalized start page, hosted by a Web content provider, that you can personalize in several ways. Your personalized portal can provide various content and links that simply cannot be found in typical corporate Web sites. By design, a portal offers two advantages over a typical personal home page:

◆ **Rich, Dynamic Content.** Your portal can include many different types of information and graphics, including news, sports, weather, entertainment news, financial information, multiple search engines, chat room access, e-mail, and more. If you leave your browser open for long periods, you can refresh the page and view any updated content that may have changed since you last checked it.

◆ **Customization.** You can customize a portal page by selecting the types of information you want to view. Many portal sites allow you to view information from specific sources, such as CNN, Time, Slate, the Weather Channel, and others. Some portals even provide streaming multimedia content, such as sound bites, music videos, or news clips. You also can choose the hyperlinks that will appear in your portal, making it easy to jump to other favorite sites. Most portal sites let you change your custom selections whenever you want.

To set up a portal, visit a site that provides portal services; several are listed at the end of this feature. Look for a link such as "Personalize," "My . . . ," or "Make This Your Home Page." Click the link, and a list of instructions and options will appear. Pick the options you want, and follow the directions to save your selections.

Explore several portal sites to find the options you like best. As you customize your portal, remember two points:

◆ The more options you choose, the longer the portal page will take to open in your browser. Be selective.

◆ To save your preferences and use them in the future, your portal will create a cookie and leave it on your computer's disk. A cookie is a small file that contains setting information, and it must reside on your system. Be careful not to delete this cookie, or your portal's settings will be lost. Cookies are not harmful to your system. However, some web sites use cookies to retrieve personal information from your computer and to track your web-browsing activities.

Here are a few Web sites that provide portal services. The Microsoft Network (MSN) is one of several Web sites offering portal services. You can select from a list of options to customize your own portal. Remember, the list is growing and options change constantly, so look at several sites before choosing one.

Microsoft Network—**http://www.msn.com/**

Netscape Netcenter—**http://www.netscape.com/**

Excite—**http://www.excite.com/**

Yahoo—**http://www.yahoo.com/**

Personalizing a portal on the MSN Web site

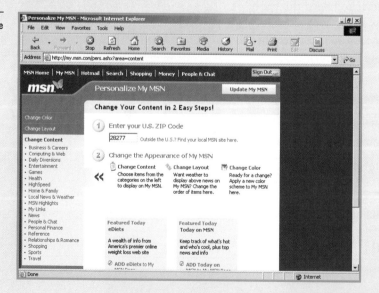

Electronic Mail (E-Mail)

To create, send, and receive e-mail, you need an **e-mail program** (also called an **e-mail client**) and an Internet connection through an ISP or LAN. Most e-mail programs permit users to attach data files and program files to messages. For example, you can send a message to a friend and attach a word processing document or some other file to the message. The recipient then can open and use the document on his or her computer. Popular Internet e-mail programs include Eudora, Microsoft Outlook, and Netscape Messenger, among others.

Visit **www.norton.glencoe.com** for more information on **electronic mail**.

E-Mail Addresses

If you have an account with an ISP or if you are a user on a corporate or school LAN, then you can establish an **e-mail address.** This unique address enables other users to send messages to you and enables you to send messages to others.

As mentioned earlier, DNS addresses and numeric IP addresses identify individual computers on the Internet. Any single computer might have many separate users, however, and each user must have an account on that computer. A user can set up such an account by specifying a unique **user name.** Some of the largest domains, such as America Online (aol.com) may have millions of different users, each with his or her own user name.

When you send a message to a person, rather than to a computer, you must include that person's user name in the address. The standard format is the user name first, separated from the DNS address by an "at" symbol (@). For example, suppose you have a friend named John Smith who works (and has an e-mail account) at a company called Widgets, Inc. If the company's DNS address is widgets.com, then John Smith's e-mail address might be

jsmith@widgets.com

You read this address as "J Smith at widgets dot com." Figure 8A.9 shows how addresses are used in e-mail programs.

When you send an e-mail message, the message is stored on a server until the recipient can retrieve it. This type of server is called a **mail server.** Many mail servers use the **post office protocol (POP)** and are called **POP servers.** Nearly all ISPs and corporate LANs maintain one or more mail servers.

Recipient's address   Sender's address

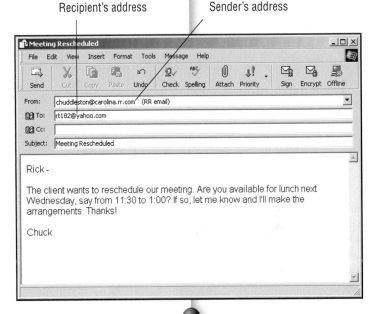

Figure 8A.9
User addresses enable people to send and receive e-mail messages over the Internet.

Listserv Systems

Besides the one-to-one messages that are popular on both the Internet and LAN e-mail systems, Internet e-mail also is used for one-to-many messages, in which the same set of messages goes to a list of many names. One type of mailing list that uses e-mail is an automated list server, or **listserv.** Listserv systems allow users on the list to post their own messages, so the result is an ongoing discussion. Hundreds of mailing-list discussions are in progress all the time on a huge variety of topics.

For example, there are mailing lists for producers of radio drama, makers of apple cider, and members of individual college classes who want to keep up with news from their old classmates.

News

NORTON ONLINE

Visit **www.norton.glencoe.com** for more information on **Internet newsgroups.**

In addition to the messages distributed to mailing lists by e-mail, the Internet also supports a form of public bulletin board called **news.** As of this writing, there were more than 45,000 **newsgroups,** each devoted to discussion of a particular topic. Many of the most widely distributed newsgroups are part of a system called Usenet, but others are targeted to a particular region or to users connected to a specific network or institution, such as a university or a large corporation.

To participate in a newsgroup, users post **articles** (short messages) about the newsgroup's main topic. As users read and respond to one another's articles, they create a **thread** of linked articles. By reading the articles in a thread, you can see the message that initiated the discussion and all the messages that have been posted in response to it.

A **newsreader** program—the client software—obtains articles from a **news server,** a host computer that exchanges articles with other servers through the Internet. Because these servers use the **network news transfer protocol (NNTP),** they are sometimes called **NNTP servers.** To participate in newsgroups, you must run a newsreader program to log on to a server. Most ISPs provide access to a news server as part of an Internet account.

Table 8A.4	Common Usenet Domains
Domain	**Description**
comp	Computer-related topics
sci	Science and technology (except computers)
soc	Social issues and politics
news	Topics related to Usenet
rec	Hobbies, arts, and recreational activities
misc	Topics that do not fit into one of the other domains

The most important alternative topics include the following:

alt	Alternative newsgroups
bionet	Biological sciences
biz	Business topics, including advertisements
clari	News from the Associated Press and Reuters, supplied through a service called Clarinet
K12	Newsgroups for primary and secondary schools

To see articles that have been posted about a specific topic, you can **subscribe** to the newsgroup that addresses that topic. Newsgroups are organized into major categories, called domains, and categorized by individual topics within each domain. There are several major domains within the Usenet structure and many more alternative domains. Table 8A.4 lists the major Usenet domains.

The name of a newsgroup begins with the domain, followed by one or more words that describe the group's topic, such as alt.food. Some topics include separate newsgroups for related subtopics, such as alt.food.chocolate. Newsgroup names can be quite long. As Figure 8A.10 shows, subscribing to a newsgroup is a three-step process. Figure 8A.11 shows a series of articles and responses that make up a thread.

To subscribe, you must download a list of available newsgroups from the server, choose the groups that interest you, and select articles. In most newsreaders, you can choose to reply to an article by posting another article to the newsgroup or by sending a private e-mail message to the person who wrote the original article.

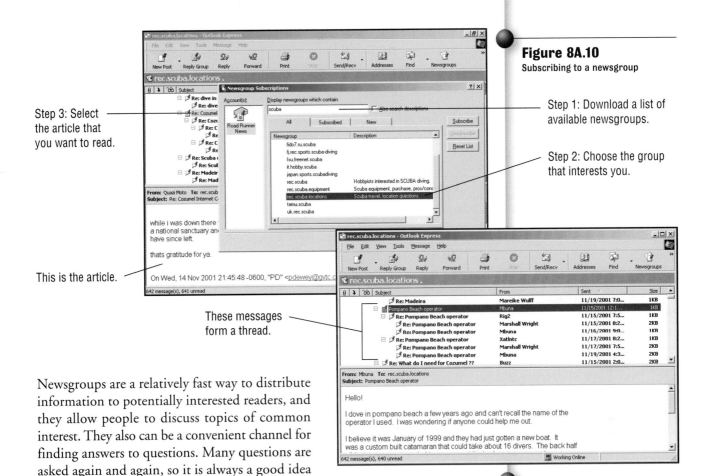

Step 3: Select the article that you want to read.

This is the article.

Figure 8A.10
Subscribing to a newsgroup

Step 1: Download a list of available newsgroups.

Step 2: Choose the group that interests you.

These messages form a thread.

Figure 8A.11
A series of articles and responses create a thread, or ongoing discussion, in a newsgroup.

Newsgroups are a relatively fast way to distribute information to potentially interested readers, and they allow people to discuss topics of common interest. They also can be a convenient channel for finding answers to questions. Many questions are asked again and again, so it is always a good idea to read the articles that other people have posted before you jump in with your own questions. Members of many newsgroups post lists of **frequently asked questions (FAQ)** and their answers every month or two.

Remember that, although newsgroups can be a source of information, there is no fact-checking process for newsgroups. Thus, newsgroups are also one of the biggest sources of misinformation and rumors on the Internet. Be careful about the information you choose as reliable. To combat this problem, some newsgroups are overseen by a moderator—someone who sorts through articles before they are posted and weeds out those that are obviously meant to misinform, spread rumors, or insult someone.

Telnet—Remote Access to Distant Computers

Telnet is the Internet tool for using one computer to access a second computer. Using Telnet, you can send commands that run programs and open data files. The Telnet program is a transparent window between your own computer and a distant host system—a computer that you are logging on to. The host computer is in a different physical place, but it is as if you are sitting in front of it and operating it. A Telnet connection sends input from your keyboard to the host and displays text from the host on your screen.

Connecting to a Telnet host is easy: When you enter the address, the Telnet program sets up a connection. When you see a log-on message from the host, you can send an account name and password to start an operating session. Access to some Telnet hosts is limited to users with permission from the owner of the host, but many other hosts offer access to members of the general Internet public.

NORTON
ONLINE

Visit **www.norton.glencoe.com** for more information on **Telnet**.

Figure 8A.12

A Telnet connection to a library catalog

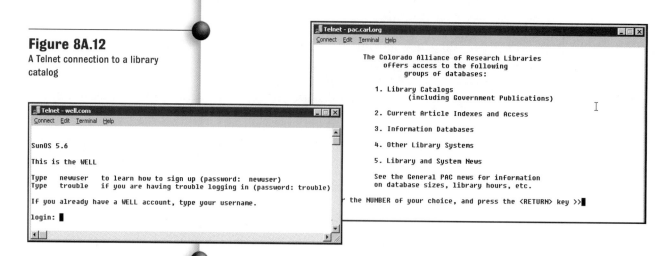

Figure 8A.13

A Telnet connection to an online conference service

NORTON ONLINE

Visit **www.norton.glencoe.com** for more information on **FTP**.

Telnet connections are useful for many purposes. For example, Figure 8A.12 shows a Telnet connection to a library's online catalog. You can obtain information about books in the library's collection over the Internet as easily as you could from the library's own reference room. Another common use for Telnet is to provide access to online conferences that are not part of Usenet, such as the one in Figure 8A.13.

FTP

You can use Telnet to operate a distant computer by remote control through the Internet, but sometimes there is no substitute for having your own copy of a program or data file. **File transfer protocol (FTP)** is the Internet tool used to copy files from one computer to another.

When a user has accounts on more than one computer, FTP can be used to transfer data or programs between them. Public FTP archives will permit anyone to make copies of their files. These **FTP sites** are housed on **FTP servers**—archives often containing thousands of individual programs and files. Anyone can download and use these files by using special **FTP client software** (see Figure 8A.14). Because these public archives usually require visitors to use the word "anonymous" as an account name, they are known as **anonymous FTP archives.**

It is not always necessary to use an FTP client to download files from an FTP site. Web browsers also support FTP. In fact, if you visit a Web site such as Microsoft (www.microsoft.com/) or Macromedia (www.macromedia.com/), you can download programs and data files directly onto your computer through your Web browser. This type of file transfer usually is an FTP operation; it is available through many different Web sites.

Figure 8A.14

Here is a popular FTP client program named WS_FTP LE. It is being used to transfer a file named assist.exe from Microsoft's anonymous FTP site (the remote site) to the user's computer (the local system).

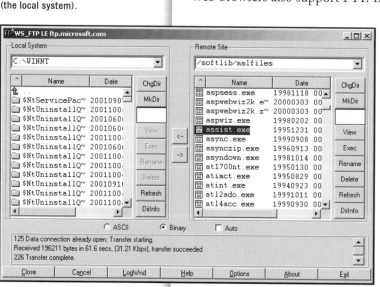

FTP sites provide access to many different types of files. You can find information of all kinds—from weather maps to magazine articles—housed on these systems. Computer hardware and software companies frequently host their own FTP sites, where you can copy program updates, bug solutions, and other types of software.

Although FTP is easy to use, it can be hard to find a file that you want to download. One way to find files is to use Archie, the searchable index of FTP archives maintained by McGill University in Montreal. (Archie is a nickname for archives.) The main Archie server at McGill gathers copies of the directories from more than 1,000 other public FTP archives every month and distributes copies of those directories to dozens of other servers around the world. When a server receives a request for a keyword search, it returns a list of files that match the search criteria and the location of each file. Many FTP client programs provide Archie search tools, and some Web sites enable you to conduct Archie searches through your Web browser (see Figure 8A.15).

Internet Relay Chat (IRC)

Internet relay chat (IRC), or just **chat,** is a popular way for Internet users to communicate in real-time with other users. Real-time communication means communicating with other users in the immediate present. Unlike e-mail, chat does not require a waiting period between the time you send a message and the time the other person or group of people receives the message. IRC is often referred to as the "CB radio" of the Internet because it enables a few or many people to join a discussion.

IRC is a multi-user system where people join channels to talk publicly or privately. **Channels** are discussion groups where chat users convene to discuss a topic. Chat messages are typed on a user's computer and sent to the IRC channel, where all users who have joined that channel receive the message. Users can then read, reply to, or ignore that message or create their own message (see Figure 8A.16).

Chat rooms are also a popular addition to Web sites. Users can participate in chat sessions directly within a Web browser window without installing or running special chat software (see Figure 8A.17).

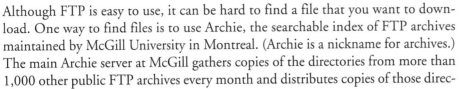

Figure 8A.15
Web sites like this one enable you to use Archie to search for files on the Internet. Here, the user is searching for files related to the keyword hypertext.

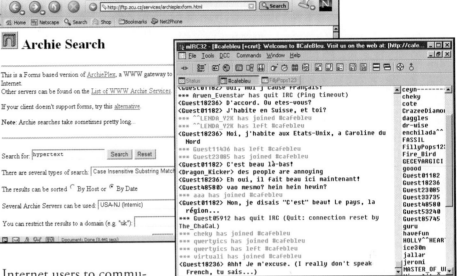

Figure 8A.16
A chat in progress

Figure 8A.17
Many Web sites—including MSN, CNN, and others—provide chat rooms for visitors. At these sites, you can chat without navigating channels or using special chat software.

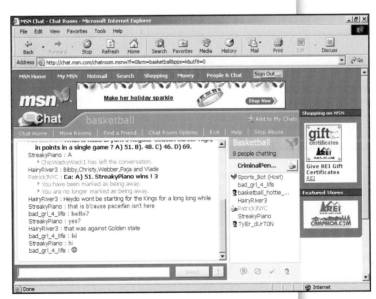

SERVICES RELATED TO THE INTERNET

There are several types of services that provide a range of tools and applications to users of the Internet. While not part of the Internet itself, these applications work with the Internet at some point in order to provide clients with a range of service options.

Figure 8A.18
America Online subscribers can access the Internet and other services through a menu like this one.

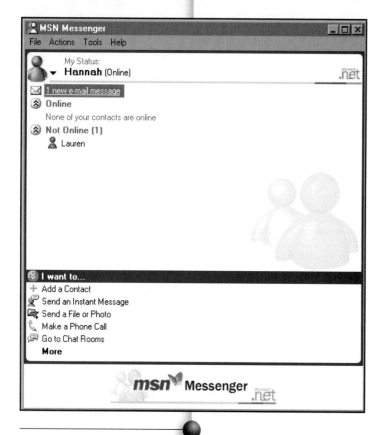

Figure 8A.19
Instant messaging software lets users chat via peer-to-peer connections, using the Internet.

Online Services

An **online service** is a company that offers access, generally on a subscription basis, to e-mail, discussion groups, databases on various subjects (such as weather information, stock quotes, newspaper articles, and so on), and other services ranging from electronic banking and investing to online games. Online services also offer access to the Internet, functioning as an ISP to their subscribers. The most popular online services are America Online (see Figure 8A.18), CompuServe, and Prodigy.

In addition to Internet access, online services offer other features that typical ISPs do not. For example, America Online has become famous for its casual chat rooms, and CompuServe is probably best known for its discussion forums geared to technically oriented users. These activities do not take place on the Internet, where everyone can access them. Rather, these services are provided only for the subscribers of the online services. Discussion groups hosted by online services often are monitored by a **system operator,** or **sysop,** who ensures that participants follow the rules. Users typically pay by the month for a subscription that allows them to use the service for a limited number of hours per month; they may pay by the hour for additional time, if needed. Subscriptions with unlimited hours are also available.

Peer-to-Peer Services

Peer-to-peer (P2P) services are distributed networks that do not require a central server, such as a Web server, to manage the files. Instead, P2P services allow an individual's computer to communicate directly with another individual's computer and even access files on that computer.

An example of P2P services is **instant messaging (IM)** software (see Figure 8A.19). IM software sets up a direct relationship between you and your colleagues and friends. When you use this software, which includes America Online's Instant Messenger, Microsoft's MSN Messenger Service, Yahoo Messenger, or Mirabilis'

ICQ, you can set up "buddy lists" of people with whom you like to chat. When you and a buddy are online at the same time, you can begin a private chat session. Instant messenger applications are popular because they are private, unlike IRC channels, which are open to anyone who wants to join.

Peer-to-peer services are popular, because they allow people to share files of all types directly from the peer connections available via the peer software. Corporations have adopted P2P technology as a quick means of transporting information, without having to have all the information stored in a centralized location.

INTERNET-RELATED FEATURES IN APPLICATION PROGRAMS

To access most of the services on the Internet, you can use stand-alone applications, such as the Web browsers, e-mail clients, and other types of software. However, many productivity applications now feature Internet-related tools. These features enable you to perform two types of tasks:

◆ Retrieve Internet content as though it were a disk on your computer.

◆ Create content to post on the Web or to send as an e-mail message.

Retrieving Content

By creating Internet-aware applications, software designers try to make the Internet as accessible as your computer's hard disk. Applications of this type enable you to access the Web without manually switching to a browser, for example.

Various products take different approaches to this type of content retrieval. In several members of Microsoft's Office suite, for example, a Web toolbar is available. You can use this toolbar to quickly launch your Web browser and visit a specified site. Lotus' SmartSuite features the SmartCenter, which lets you jump from applications directly to Web sites, download files, and more.

Creating Content

Many of today's popular productivity applications feature tools that enable you to convert existing documents into HTML-format files, which frees you from having to learn how to use HTML tags. Three types of these tools are:

◆ **Save As HTML Command.** By using the program's Save As HTML (or save as Web page) command, you can convert an existing document into an HTML file, ready to be posted on a Web server. You then can view your HTML page in your browser. Today's application programs can retain most of the formatting applied to the original document, so the HTML file will resemble the original document.

◆ **Web Templates.** Many applications provide Web templates, which are predesigned Web pages. You can create entire Web sites from templates, which include preselected fonts, backgrounds, color schemes, and more.

◆ **Wizards.** A Web-design wizard is a utility that literally walks you through the process of creating a Web page or site. When you are done, a nearly complete Web page is ready for you to add content (see Figure 8A.20).

Many applications now feature an e-mail command that enables you to export the current document as the body of an e-mail message or as an attachment to a message.

For more information on building Web content, see "Computing Keynotes" on page 308.

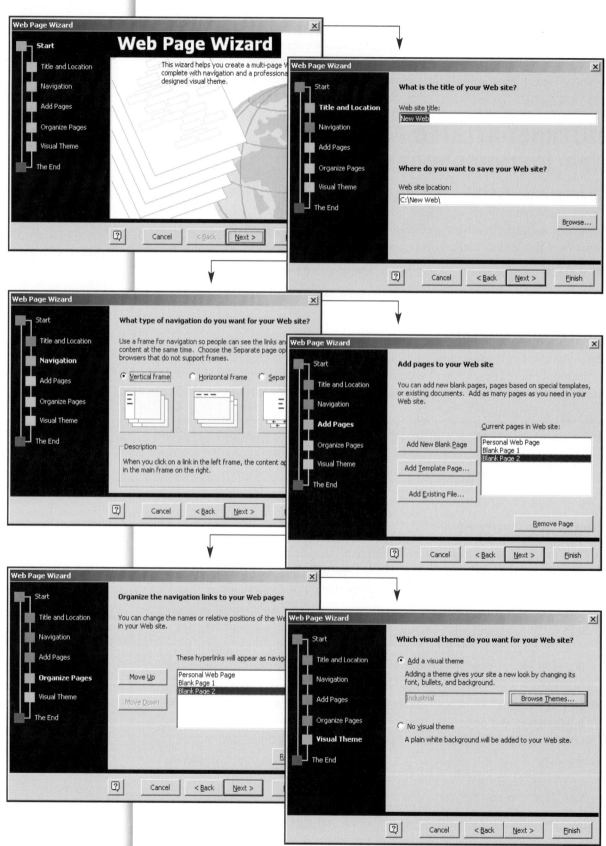

At Issue

Staying Civil Online

Although there is no set of written rules governing behavior on the Internet, the wise user participates in an honor system. On the Internet, appropriate behavior is called netiquette (a combination of *Internet etiquette*). Netiquette is crucial for keeping the Internet a civil place, because the Internet is not policed or run by a single person or group. The basic rules of netiquette are as follows:

1. **Behave As Though You Are Communicating in Person.** When communicating with someone online, act as if you are talking to that person face to face.

2. **Remember That Your Words Are Open to Interpretation.** If you post jokes, sarcasm, or other attempts at humor, do not be surprised if someone is offended. Word your postings clearly and carefully.

3. **Do Not "Shout" Online.** Typing in ALL CAPITAL LETTERS is like shouting and is considered rude.

4. **Do Not "Flame" Other Users.** In "Net-speak," a flame is a posting that contains insults or other derogatory content. Flamers can be shut out of listservs and chat rooms, and other users can block a flamer's messages.

5. **Do Not Send Spam.** Spam is the online equivalent of junk mail—uninvited messages, usually of a commercial nature. Most ISPs have strict spam policies. If you are caught distributing uninvited messages to multiple recipients, your ISP may cancel your account. You'll learn more about spam in Unit 14, "Living with Computers."

6. **Do Not Distribute Copyrighted Material.** Usenet newsgroups and many private Web pages are filled with copyrighted and trademarked text and graphics, posted without the owner's permission. Do not think that text or images are "in the public domain" because you found them on the Internet. Copyrights still apply.

7. **Do Not Be a Coward.** As a general rule, you should never conceal your identity on the Internet. If you choose to use a screen name, do not hide behind it to misbehave.

Always check the rules when you go online. Nearly all ISPs post an appropriate use policy on their Web site that lists guidelines for acceptable behavior on the Internet. This document may be a simple disclaimer, or it may take the form of a FAQ list. If you violate these guidelines and are reported to the ISP, your account may be dropped. Look for a FAQ list before using chat rooms, listservs, message boards, newsgroups, and other Internet services.

Even though you cannot be seen on the Internet, you can still be identified. Conscientious users of e-mail and newsgroups commonly forward flames or inappropriate postings to the poster's ISP. If an ISP collects enough complaints about an account holder, it can cancel that person's account. In cases where libel, copyright infringement, or other potential crimes are involved, the ISP also may turn the poster over to the authorities. In one such case (in December 1999), a Florida teenager posted a threatening chat-room message to a Colorado student. Even though the poster had used an alias to hide his identity, federal agents were able to track him down and arrest him.

Most ISPs provide an appropriate use policy on their Web sites or in their printed documentation. This example is posted on the Web site of EarthLink, a large ISP.

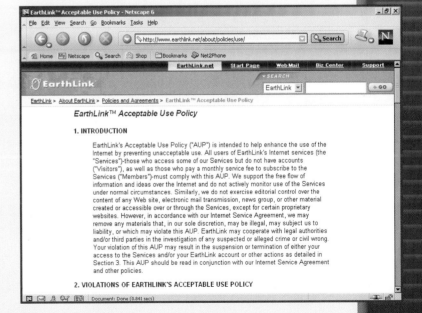

287

SUMMARY

- All computers on the Internet use TCP/IP protocols. Any computer on the Internet potentially can connect to any other computer.

- Individual computers connect to local and regional networks, which are connected through the Internet backbone.

- Every computer on the Internet has a unique numeric IP address, and most also have a DNS address that uses an easily recognizable name.

- The World Wide Web combines text, multimedia content, streaming audio/visual content, and links to other files in hypertext documents.

- Electronic mail systems enable you to exchange messages with any other user anywhere. You also can attach documents or program files to e-mail messages.

- Telnet allows a user to operate a second computer from his or her PC.

- FTP is the Internet tool for copying data and program files from one computer to another.

- News and mailing lists (listservs) are public conferences distributed through the Internet and other electronic networks.

- Chats are public conferences, conducted in real time, through which people join channels to discuss topics of interest.

- In addition to Internet access, online service companies offer other features, such as e-mail, discussion groups, stock quotes, news, and games.

- Using peer-to-peer services via the Internet, users can connect directly to one another's computers to exchange instant messages or files.

- Internet tools and services are commonly added to popular application programs, such as word processors and spreadsheets. Such features enable you either to create content for the Internet or to access content from the Internet.

KEY TERMS

anonymous FTP archive, *282*
article, *280*
channel, *283*
chat, *283*
domain name system
    (DNS) address, *271*
domain, *271*
e-mail address, *279*
e-mail client, *279*
e-mail program, *279*
file transfer protocol (FTP), *282*
frequently asked questions
    (FAQ), *281*
FTP client software, *282*
FTP server, *282*
FTP site, *282*
helper application, *276*
hypertext link (hyperlinks
    or links), *273*
hypertext markup language
    (HTML), *273*

hypertext transfer protocol
    (HTTP), *273*
instant messaging, *284*
Internet protocol address
    (IP address), *271*
Internet relay chat (IRC), *283*
Internet service provider (ISP), *272*
listserv, *279*
mail server, *279*
network news transfer
    protocol (NNTP), *280*
news server, *280*
news, *280*
newsgroup, *280*
newsreader, *280*
NNTP server, *280*
online service, *284*
peer-to-peer (P2P), *284*
plug-in application, *276*
POP server, *279*
post office protocol (POP), *279*

posting, *274*
spawn, *277*
streaming audio, *276*
streaming video, *276*
subdomain, *272*
subscribe, *280*
system operator (sysop), *284*
Telnet, *281*
thread, *280*
top-level domain, *271*
Transmission Control Protocol/
    Internet Protocol (TCP/IP), *270*
uniform resource locator (URL), *275*
user name, *279*
Web browser (browser), *274*
Web page, *273*
Web server, *274*
Web site, *274*
World Wide Web (the Web or
    WWW), *273*

KEY TERM QUIZ

Complete each statement by writing one of the terms listed under Key Terms in each blank.

1. In addition to an IP address, most computers on the Internet also have a(n) _____ .

2. Items such as "com" and "gov" are examples of _____ .

3. A collection of related Web pages is called a(n) _____ .

4. The hypertext transfer protocol uses Internet addresses in a special format, called a(n) _____ .

5. The Internet supports more than 45,000 _____ , each devoted to the discussion of a particular topic.

SECTION QUIZ

True/False

Answer the following questions by circling True or False.

True	False	**1.** The Internet works because every computer connected to it can use a different set of rules and procedures.
True	False	**2.** A computer's IP address is a four-part numeric address that contains routing information and identifies the computer's location.
True	False	**3.** A Web page is an example of a hypertext document.
True	False	**4.** Web browsers can display every type of content available on the Web, especially multimedia content, without help from other applications.
True	False	**5.** As a newsgroup's users read and respond to one another's articles, they create a thread of linked articles.

Multiple Choice

Circle the word or phrase that best completes each statement.

1. The internal structure of the World Wide Web is based on the _____ .
   A. hypertext markup language   **B.** hypertext transfer protocol   **C.** uniform resource locator

2. RealPlayer is an example of a(n) _____ .
   A. Web browser   **B.** HTML editor   **C.** helper application

3. To send and receive e-mail messages, you need a(n) _____ .
   A. e-mail program   **B.** e-mail address   **C.** both A and B

4. To view the articles posted in an Internet newsgroup, you need a program called a(n) _____ .
   A. Web browser   **B.** News browser   **C.** Newsreader

5. The _____ is the Internet tool used to copy files from one computer to another.
   A. World Wide Web (WWW)   **B.** file transfer protocol (FTP)   **C.** Usenet

REVIEW QUESTIONS

In your own words, briefly answer the following questions.

1. What is the difference between a Web page and a Web site?

2. Name the parts of a URL.

3. A potential drawback occurs when you rely on Internet newsgroups as sources of information. Describe the problem.

4. If you use your Web browser to request data that is stored on a Web server in another state, what sort of route might the request and data take while traveling between your PC and the server?

5. What is an online service?

SECTION LABS

Complete the following exercises as directed by your instructor.

1. Determine whether a Web browser is installed on your computer. Search the Programs menu for an application such as Microsoft Internet Explorer or Netscape Navigator. If you find a browser, click its name in the Programs menu to launch the application. Write down what happens after you launch the browser. What appears on the screen?

2. Find out what other types of Internet-related applications are installed on your system. (You may need your instructor's help to complete this exercise.) Check the Programs menu as you did in Section Lab 1. Also, click the Accessories option on the Programs menu, then click Internet Accessories. What other programs are available? Can you find an e-mail program or a newsreader? List the applications and their locations in the menu system. If your instructor permits, launch each application, and see what happens.

Getting Online, Working Online

OVERVIEW:
Joining the Internet Phenomenon

As more businesses and people join the Internet community, they are finding that the Internet is enhancing their work lives. Thanks to communication technologies, many businesspeople now work from home, instead of commuting to an office each day. The World Wide Web is also used at the corporate level to sell products, provide customer services, and support business partnerships among various companies.

This section provides an overview of the options for connecting a computer to the Internet; it also shows you how the Internet (and variations of it, implemented in corporate networks) is affecting the workplace and the way we conduct business transactions.

OBJECTIVES

- List six ways to connect a computer to the Internet.
- Identify three kinds of high-speed data links commonly used to connect individuals and small businesses to the Internet.
- Describe the process of connecting a PC to the Internet through an ISP account.
- List four types of firewalls and explain why businesses use them.
- Define the terms *intranet* and *extranet*.
- Explain what is meant by e-commerce and how it affects consumers and businesses.

ACCESSING THE INTERNET

There are many ways to obtain access to the Internet. The method varies according to the type of computer system being used.

Direct Connection

NORTON
ONLINE

Visit www.norton.glencoe.com for more information on **SLIP and PPP**.

In a direct connection, Internet programs run on the local computer, which uses the TCP/IP protocols to exchange data with another computer through the Internet. Through a serial data communications port, an isolated computer can connect to the Internet. Either a **serial line interface protocol (SLIP)** or a **point-to-point protocol (PPP)** is used to create a direct connection through a telephone line. This type of connection is an option for a stand-alone computer that does not connect to the Internet through an Internet service provider, as discussed later. However, direct connections are uncommon.

Remote Terminal Connection

A **remote terminal connection** to the Internet exchanges commands and data in ASCII text format with a host computer that uses UNIX or a similar operating system. The TCP/IP application programs and protocols all run on the host. Because the command set in UNIX is called a shell, this kind of Internet access is known as a **shell account.** Again, this type of connection works for some types of stand-alone computers, but it is uncommon.

Gateway Connection

Even if a local area network does not use TCP/IP commands and protocols, it may still be able to provide some Internet services, such as e-mail or file transfer. Such networks use gateways that convert commands and data to and from TCP/IP format.

Although it is possible to connect a local network directly to the Internet backbone, it is usually not practical (except for the largest organizations) because of the high cost of a backbone connection. Many businesses and most individual users obtain access through an Internet service provider (ISP), which supplies the backbone connection. ISPs offer several kinds of Internet service, including inexpensive shell accounts; direct TCP/IP connections using SLIP or PPP accounts; and full-time, high-speed access through dedicated data circuits.

Figure 8B.1
If a LAN does not use TCP/IP protocols, it can connect to the Internet through a router and a gateway. However, if a LAN uses TCP/IP protocols, it does not require a gateway to connect to the Internet; only a router is needed.

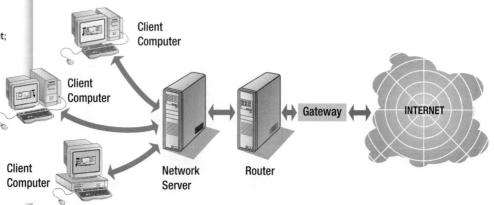

Connecting Through a LAN

If a local area network uses TCP/IP protocols for communication within the network, it is a simple matter to connect to the Internet through a router—another computer that stores and forwards data to other computers on the Internet. If the LAN uses a different kind of local protocol, a gateway converts it to and from TCP/IP (see Figure 8B.1). When a LAN has an Internet connection, that connection extends to every computer on the LAN. This type of connection is commonly used by businesses to provide the LAN's users with Internet access.

Connecting Through a Modem

If no LAN is available, you can connect a single computer to the Internet by using a modem and either a shell account or a SLIP or PPP account. Again, ISPs provide these types of services for home users and businesses who want to connect to the Internet.

Most individual users connect to the Internet by using a telephone line; a 28.8 Kbps, 33.6 Kbps, or 56 Kbps modem; and a SLIP or PPP account. Using settings provided by the ISP, the user can configure the PC's operating system to dial into one of the ISP's server computers, identify itself as the customer's computer, and gain access to Internet services (see Figure 8B.2). Depending on the ISP, the customer's computer may be assigned a permanent IP address (called a "static" address), or its IP address may change each time it logs on to the ISP's server (called a "dynamic" address).

High-Speed Data Links

Modem connections are convenient, but their capacity is limited to the relatively low data-transfer speed of a telephone line. A 56 Kbps modem is fine for text, still images, and low-quality streaming multimedia, but it is not practical for huge digital audio and video files. When many users share an Internet connection through a LAN, the connection between the network and the ISP must be adequate to meet the demands of many users at the same time. Fortunately, dedicated high-speed data circuits are available from telephone companies, cable TV services, and other suppliers. Using fiber optics, microwave, and other technologies, a user can establish an Internet connection at least ten times as fast as a modem link.

ISDN Service

For small businesses and individual users, integrated services digital network (ISDN) is an attractive alternative. ISDN is a digital telephone service that combines voice, data, and control signaling through a single circuit. An ISDN data connection can transfer data at up to 128,000 bits per second (128 Kbps). Most telephone companies offer ISDN at a slightly higher cost than the conventional telephone service that it replaces; costs may become lower over time.

ISDN service operates on standard telephone lines, but it requires a special modem (see Figure 8B.3) and phone service, which add to the cost of the service. Even so, the benefits of ISDN are substantial. For example, you can connect a PC, telephone, and fax into a single ISDN line and use them simultaneously. Many ISPs and local telephone companies that also offer Internet access services support ISDN connections.

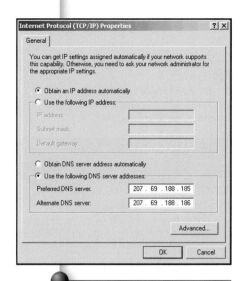

Figure 8B.2

Here, a user configures settings in Windows 2000 Professional for an Internet connection through an ISP. When you set up an ISP account, the ISP should provide you with all the instructions and settings you need. A typical account configuration takes only a few minutes, using tools already in your operating system or ones provided by the ISP.

Figure 8B.3

Many ISDN modems use data compression technologies to double the data transfer rates of a basic ISDN line.

xDSL Services

The abbreviation DSL stands for digital subscriber line, and several versions of DSL technology are available for home and business use. In fact, the abbreviation often begins with an *x* (*x*DSL) because there are various types of DSL service, each providing a different level of service, speed, bandwidth, and distance.

Transmission speeds can vary greatly. They are affected by several factors, including distance, wire and equipment type, service provider capabilities, and others. It also should be noted that different providers may use DSL terms differently, applying different usage standards in delivering DSL services. These variations often create great confusion among customers and cause delays in the acceptance of DSL in some markets.

DSL services are beginning to become widely available. They can be less expensive than ISDN service. DSL is gaining popularity among small businesses that need to connect a LAN to the Internet and provide users with rapid data-transfer rates and continuous service (see figure 8B.4). Due to the widening availability and reasonable cost of DSL services, another growing audience includes individuals who want a high-speed connection in their home. Some DSL services also enable simultaneous data, voice, and fax transmissions on the same line.

Cable Modem Service

Visit **www.norton.glencoe.com** for more information on **ISDN, xDSL,** and **cable modem services.**

Many cable companies now use a portion of their network's bandwidth to offer Internet access through existing cable television connections. Cable modem service took some time to become established, because it required cable systems to set up local Internet servers (to provide access to the Web, e-mail, and news) and to establish connections to the Internet backbone. As the infrastructure grows, however, cable modem services will be available in more cities around the United States.

Cable television systems send data to users over coaxial cable, which can transmit data as much as 100 times faster than common telephone lines. Cable can transmit not only data, but also streaming audio and video simultaneously, at a much higher speed than is possible over standard telephone lines. Because of cable's enhanced bandwidth, Internet data can be transmitted on its own channel, separate from the audio, video, and control signals used for television programming. A user can surf the Internet and watch television at the same time, over the same cable connection, and without the two data streams interfering with one another.

To work with a cable modem (see Figure 8B.5), the user's PC needs a network interface card and access to a cable television outlet (the kind found in many homes). The cable connection is extended to the modem, which is then connected to the network interface card. As a result, the computer becomes part of a wide area network using TCP/IP protocols, and the users share access to the Internet via a dedicated connection.

Cable modem service does not require the use of a standard modem. If the user's PC also has a standard modem installed, it can be used for other purposes, such as faxing. Cable modem service is becoming widespread in homes because of its affordability and ease of use.

CONNECTING A PC TO THE INTERNET

Connecting a desktop computer to the Internet actually involves two separate issues: software and the network connection. The industry has developed a standard interface called Windows Sockets, or **Winsock,** which makes it possible to mix and match application programs from more than one developer and to allow those applications to work with any type of network connection. Figure 8B.6 shows how applications, the Winsock interface, and network drivers fit together.

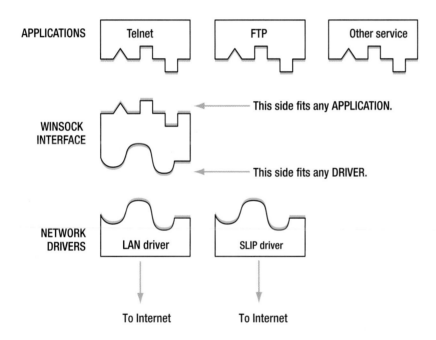

Figure 8B.6
How Winsock provides an interface between applications and networks

Many companies offer suites of Internet access tools. These packages usually contain client programs for e-mail, Telnet, FTP, and other applications, along with a World Wide Web browser and software for connecting to a network using dial-up modem connections, connection through a LAN, or both. In addition, some packages include sign-up utilities that will work with one or more Internet service providers that offer modem access through local telephone numbers in most major metropolitan areas.

Visit **www.norton.glencoe.com** for more information on **Winsock.**

The all-in-one-box approach has several advantages. In most cases, the applications in a suite share a common interface design, so they are easy to learn and use. Because all the applications come from the same source, there is a single point of contact for technical support and product upgrades. If a suite includes an account with a particular ISP, most likely the service provider has worked with the software developer to make sure that there are no incompatibilities between the network and the software.

Norton Notebook

FREEBIES ON THE WEB

If you set up an account with an Internet service provider, you probably will install software, such as a Web browser, an e-mail client, and a newsreader. Many users also install a separate FTP client and Telnet software. A current version of a Web browser is all you need to surf the Web, send and receive e-mail, chat, participate in newsgroup discussions, and more. (In fact, you do not necessarily need an account with an ISP or online service to access these features; you can log on to the Web from a computer at a library or your school's computer center, for example.) Here are a few of the free services you can access through the Web.

E-Mail

By visiting Web sites like Hotmail, Mail.com, Yahoo!, and others, you can set up a free e-mail account. You must register for the account by creating a user name and password; the service creates a complete e-mail address for you, such as yourname@hotmail.com.

You can send and receive e-mail from these sites, and several sites offer other useful personalization features. However, some free Web-based e-mail services will store your messages for only a certain amount of time and then automatically delete them. Some also will cancel your account if you do not use it for a given amount of time. If you use e-mail regularly and you want to access your mail from any browser (without having to log on to your ISP account), then Web-based mail is a good option.

Personal Web Pages

Nearly every ISP provides space on its Web servers where clients can create and post personal Web pages. This service is almost always free. As part of the service, ISPs provide online design tools that make it easy to create a personal Web site.

However, you do not even need an ISP to get a free Web page. Again, Web sites such as the Microsoft Network, America Online, Yahoo!, and many others provide this kind of service. You simply register for the service, select a URL for your site, and post your Web pages. Free design tools are usually available also.

Chat

It is no longer necessary to log on to an IRC chat channel to participate in a chat room discussion, nor do you have to join an online service like AOL or Prodigy to take advantage of their chat rooms. Now you can access chat in real time on the Web.

Many large Web sites, such as CNN, About.com, MSN, and others offer Web communities that are basically chat rooms. At these sites, you can register for a user name and a password and choose from dozens of different communities to join. Web-based communities usually conduct chat sessions right in your browser window, although some communities spawn a separate window to contain the chat.

Many Web sites, including Tripod, offer free personal Web pages and design services.

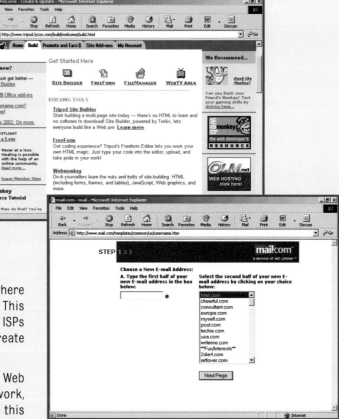

Mail.com is only one source of free e-mail on the World Wide Web.

Complete each statement by filling in the blank(s).

1. A(n) _____ connection to the Internet exchanges commands and data in ASCII text format.

2. The abbreviation DSL stands for _____ .

3. Using a(n) _____ connection, you can surf the Internet and watch television at the same time.

NORTON ONLINE

Visit www.norton.glencoe.com for more information on **firewalls**.

WORKING ON THE INTERNET

Many organizations publish information on the Web, whereas others have employees who pass information to the Internet from the company network or download material from the Internet. This increased use of the Internet and the World Wide Web places networks at greater risk of intrusion by unauthorized users. To protect the data on their networks, companies use special tools to keep spies and hackers from gaining access to their networks via the Internet.

Firewalls

With millions of Internet users able to pass information to and take information from the network, the security of business networks is a major concern. Many businesses set up **firewalls** to control access to their networks by persons using the Internet (see Figure 8B.7). Firewalls block unauthorized entry into a network that is connected to the Internet, allowing outsiders to access public areas but preventing them from exploring private areas of the network.

A firewall system can be hardware, software, or both. A firewall basically works by inspecting the requests and data that pass between the private network and the Internet. If a request or data does not pass the firewall's security inspection, it is stopped from traveling any further. Table 8B.1 lists some of the most common firewall methodologies.

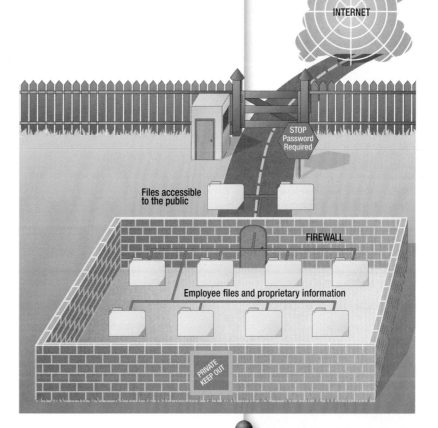

Figure 8B.7
Networks connected to the Internet can use a firewall to prevent unauthorized users from accessing private or proprietary information. In many cases, portions of the network are accessible to the public.

Even if a company does not make any portion of its network available to Internet users, it can allow employees to access the network over the Internet. This capability is important for **telecommuters,** or people who work from home or a remote location, rather than in the office. In these situations, firewalls can ensure that only authorized users can access the network over the Internet (see Figure 8B.8).

Table 8B.1	Common Firewall Methodologies

Method	Description
Proxy server	A proxy server is like a "second server" that hides the actual network server from the Internet. The proxy server examines every packet that enters and leaves the network via the Internet, stopping any data that does not meet security criteria. For example, an administrator can set up a proxy server to block user access to certain types of Web sites.
Packet filter	A packet filter inspects (or filters) each packet of data that enters or leaves the network via a router. The filter uses a set of security rules defined by the organization's network administrator. If any packet does not pass the inspection, it is not allowed to continue.
Application gateway	An application gateway imposes special security restrictions on specific Internet services such as e-mail, FTP, and so on. An application gateway is an effective method for stopping intrusions to private networks.
Circuit gateway	A circuit gateway imposes security restrictions on specific connections, such as a TCP/IP connection between a network server and a remote computer.

NORTON ONLINE

Visit www.norton.glencoe.com for more information on **intranets and extranets**.

Figure 8B.8

Today, many people work at home and use a PC to access their company's network through the Internet. Companies use firewalls, password systems, and other precautions to make sure these connections are secure.

Intranets and Extranets

Before the advent of the World Wide Web, most corporate networks were bland environments that basically supported file sharing and e-mail. However, many newer corporate and academic networks have been configured to resemble the Internet. This setup enables users to work in a Weblike graphical environment, using a Web browser as their interface to corporate data. Two common types of "corporate spin-offs" of the Web are called intranets and extranets. These systems are designed to support data sharing, scheduling, and workgroup activities within an organization.

An **intranet** is a LAN or WAN that uses TCP/IP protocols but belongs exclusively to a corporation, school, or organization. The intranet is accessible only to the organization's workers. If the intranet is connected to the Internet, then it is secured by a firewall to prevent unauthorized users from gaining access to it.

An **extranet** is an intranet that can be accessed by outside users over the Internet. To gain entrance to the extranet's resources, an external user (such as a telecommuter or business partner) typically must log on to the network by providing a valid user ID and password.

Intranets and extranets are popular for several reasons:

◆ Because they use standard TCP/IP protocols, rather than the proprietary protocols used by network operating systems, they are simpler and less expensive to install and configure.

◆ Because they enable users to work in standard (and usually free) Web browsers, they provide a consistent, friendly interface.

◆ Because they function readily with firewalls and other standard Internet security technologies, they provide excellent security against infiltration, viruses, theft, and other problems.

Issues for Business Users and Telecommuters

Whether you use the entire Web in your work or use only your company's network via an Internet connection, you need to consider some issues as you work online. Table 8B.2 lists just three:

Table 8B.2	Business Concerns and the Internet
Issue	**Why It Is a Concern**
Ownership	Many Internet users assume incorrectly that all the data available on the Internet is free and available for use by anyone else. In fact, any piece of text or graphics that you retrieve from the Internet may be covered by trademark or copyright law, making it illegal to reuse it without the owner's consent. This issue is especially important when persons access the Internet over a corporate network, because their employers become involved in cases in which copyrights or trademarks are violated.
Libel	On the Internet, "private" communications (such as e-mail messages) can be quickly forwarded far beyond their intended readership, which amounts to publication. If messages are sent through an employer's network, the employer may become involved if the sender is accused of libel.
Appropriate Use	When using a business network to access the Internet, users must be careful to use network resources appropriately. For example, you should avoid accessing recreational newsgroups over the company's Internet connection or downloading obscene or pornographic images from adult-oriented Web sites.

Employees also need to protect corporate property—such as trade secrets, telephone lists, personnel records, and product specifications—that may be stored on the network (see Figure 8B.9). Suppose, for example, that someone calls you at your office accidentally, intending to call one of your coworkers. To ensure that this person has the correct telephone number, you agree to e-mail your corporate phone directory. This simple favor can become a major headache if the caller turns out to be a telemarketer or recruiter who then starts calling everyone on the list.

Figure 8B.9
Employees should be careful, when sharing data over the Internet, to make sure sensitive business data does not fall into the wrong hands.

COMMERCE ON THE WORLD WIDE WEB

The World Wide Web has become a global vehicle for **electronic commerce (e-commerce),** creating new ways for businesses to interact with one another and their customers. In simple terms, e-commerce means doing business online, and it has become big business, indeed. In fact, the U.S. Department of Commerce estimates that by the year 2005, e-commerce will account for well over a trillion dollars in sales annually.

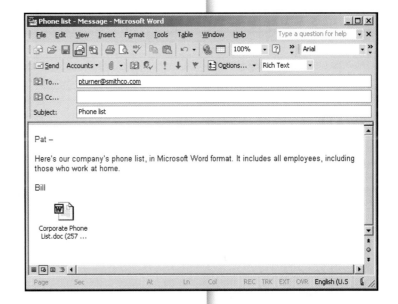

E-Commerce at the Consumer Level

There are tens of thousands of Web sites devoted to e-commerce at the consumer level (see Figure 8B.10). These Web sites are ready to give consumers information about products and services, take orders, receive payments, and provide on-the-spot customer service.

Figure 8B.10
Like many other e-commerce sites that target consumers, amazon.com offers browsing, extensive help systems, secure purchasing, online customer service, and other features.

Using an e-commerce site is like browsing through an online catalog. The more sophisticated sites allow you to search for specific products, look for certain features, and compare prices. They provide an electronic "shopping basket" or "shopping cart" where you can temporarily store information about items you want to buy (see Figure 8B.11). You can select an item, store it in the basket, and continue shopping until you are ready to purchase.

When you are ready to make your purchase, you can pay for it in several ways. Two of the most common payment methods include the following:

◆ **One-Time Credit Card Purchase.** If you do not want to set up an account with the seller, you can provide your personal and credit card information each time you make a purchase.

◆ **Set Up an Online Account.** If you think you will make other purchases from the online vendor, you can set up an account at the Web site (see Figure 8B.12). The vendor stores your personal and credit card information on a secure server, then places a special file (called a **cookie**) on your computer's disk. Later, when you access your account again by typing a user ID and password, the site uses information in the cookie to access your account. Online accounts are required at some vendors' Web sites, such as brokerage sites that provide online investing services.

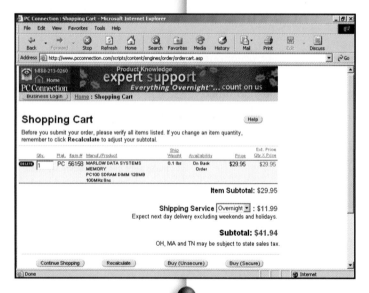

Figure 8B.11
An example of an electronic shopping cart at the PC Connection Web site. This user is preparing to purchase a memory upgrade for a computer. The cart shows the product, model information, price, quantity, in-stock status, shipping charges, and more.

Security

Until 1998, e-commerce was slow to gain acceptance among consumers, who were concerned about security. Many people feared that it was not safe to provide personal or credit card information over the Internet. That fear has almost been eliminated, however, with the advent of security measures and improved public perception.

Reputable e-commerce Web sites (especially those run by well-known companies) use sophisticated measures to ensure that customer information cannot fall into the hands of criminals. One measure is by providing **secure Web pages** where customers can enter personal information, credit card and account numbers, passwords, and other information. When using an e-commerce site, you can determine if the current page is secure in two ways (see Figure 8B.13):

◆ Check the URL. If the page's URL begins with https://, then the page is secure. The letter *s* indicates security measures.

◆ Check Your Browser's Status Bar. If you use Microsoft Internet Explorer or Netscape Navigator, a small padlock symbol will appear in the browser's status bar when a secure Web page is open.

Web masters can provide secure Web sites in several ways. One way is to encode pages using **secure sockets layer (SSL)** technology, which encrypts data. (**Encryption** technology secures data by converting it into a code that is unusable by anyone who does not possess a key to the code.) If a Web page is protected by SSL, its URL will begin with https:// rather than http://. Another way to protect data sent over the Internet is by using the **secure HTTP (S-HTTP)** protocol. Whereas SSL can encode any amount of data, S-HTTP is used to encode individual pieces of data.

Figure 8B.12
Setting up an account at an e-commerce Web site

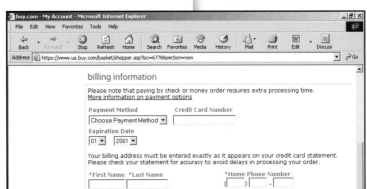

E-Commerce at the Business Level

When viewed beyond the perspective of individual consumer transactions, e-commerce is an entirely different way for companies to conduct business. Using powerful Web sites and online databases, companies not only sell goods to individual customers, but also track inventory, order products, send invoices, and receive payments. Using e-commerce technologies (ranging from LANs to supercomputers), companies are rapidly forming online partnerships to collaborate on product designs, sales and marketing campaigns, and more. Corporate extranets have become an important part of corporate-level e-commerce by giving companies access to vital information on one another's networks.

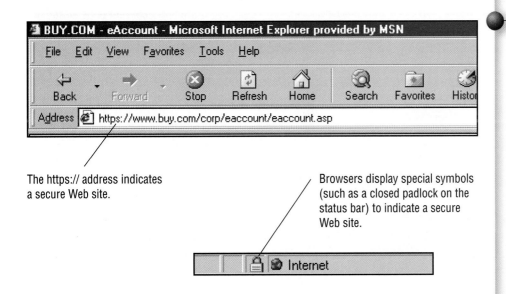

The https:// address indicates a secure Web site.

Browsers display special symbols (such as a closed padlock on the status bar) to indicate a secure Web site.

Figure 8B.13
Verifying a secure Web site

COMPUTERS
in your career

Career Opportunities and the Internet

Many careers are associated with the Internet, including network administrators, information system professionals, and data communications managers. Aside from careers that focus on architecture and administration of the Internet, many other professions require not only a working knowledge of the Internet, but also a mastery of the tools used to create and distribute content across it. Here are a few such careers:

◆ **Web Designers and Web Masters.** Corporate Web, intranet, and extranet sites are developed, designed, and maintained most often by teams of professionals. At the helm of such teams are experienced designers and Web masters. Web designers bring various traditional design skills to the table, such as experience with graphics, text design, and layout. They also are skilled with HTML tools and scripting languages. Web masters often provide more technical skills required for high-level network support. One or both of these leaders also must have management skills to direct and coordinate the efforts of a design team.

◆ **Multimedia Developers.** As more people connect to the Internet, companies face increasing competition to provide highly visual, interactive content that enables them to capture and retain visitors to their Web sites. This need already has increased the demand for multimedia developers who can design content for the Internet, particularly the Web. To become marketable in this field, multimedia developers need a thorough background in multimedia authoring and distribution and expertise in using such products as Macromedia Director, Shockwave, Flash, Adobe LiveMotion, After Effects, and so on. These specialists also benefit from having programming skills and using scripting and programming languages such as JavaScript, ActionScript (Flash), scalable vector graphics (SVG), synchronized multimedia integration language (SMIL), Java, XML, and others that are widely used on the Internet.

◆ **Programmers.** Programmers are finding all sorts of opportunities in Internet development, because Web sites commonly are used to support high-level functions such as interactivity, searches, data mining, and more. To get involved in Internet-related products, these programmers learn a wide variety of languages, including Perl, VisualBasic, Java, C++, and others.

Web site design is often done by teams of people, which may include graphic artists, writers and editors, formatters, researchers, programmers, and professionals with expertise in other disciplines.

◆ **Writers and Editors.** Just as the Internet has changed the way multimedia content is delivered, it also has changed the way books, periodicals, and other printed media are delivered and viewed by consumers. Most publishing housesand newspapers require their writers and editors to work electronically and to deliver manuscript and articles via the Internet or other network. Many writers also must know how to create content for the Internet and must be familiar with HTML. Similarly, editors should know how to work with HTML documents and how to deliver these pages to an Internet site for publication.

SUMMARY

- Users can connect to the Internet through a direct connection, local area network, high-speed data link, and other means.

- Individuals and small businesses access the Internet most commonly by setting up an account with an Internet service provider (ISP) and using a telephone line and modem.

- High-speed data links, such as ISDN and DSL, are more expensive options, but they provide much faster service than standard telephone line connections over a modem.

- Cable modems are quickly becoming a popular high-speed connection method, because they use coaxial cable that is already installed in many homes and businesses.

- The Winsock standard specifies an interface between TCP/IP applications and network connections.

- Internet application suites are available from many suppliers; they combine a full set of applications and drivers in a single package.

- By connecting their networks to the Internet, companies are creating new ways to conduct business and for employees to work. Telecommuters work from remote locations by connecting to the company network via the Internet.

- Businesses that connect their networks to the Internet can use firewalls and other means to prevent unauthorized users from accessing private information.

- Intranets and extranets are internal networks based on TCP/IP, and they support the use of Web browsers.

- The act of conducting business online is called e-commerce.

- At the consumer level, it is possible to buy a wide range of goods and services through Web sites. Many such sites accept different forms of payment online and provide a secure environment for transactions.

- At the corporate level, e-commerce technologies enable companies to form online partnerships, conduct business transactions online, and collaborate on projects.

KEY TERMS

cookie, *300*
electronic commerce
   (e-commerce), *299*
encryption, *301*
extranet, *298*
firewall, *297*

intranet, *298*
point-to-point protocol (PPP), *292*
remote terminal connection, *292*
secure HTTP (S-HTTP), *301*
secure sockets layer (SSL), *301*
secure Web page, *300*

serial line interface
   protocol (SLIP), *292*
shell account, *292*
telecommuters, *297*
Winsock, *295*

KEY TERM QUIZ

Complete each statement by writing one of the terms listed under Key Terms in each blank.

1. The acronym SLIP stands for _____ .

2. The _____ interface makes it possible to mix and match applications programs and allow them to work with any type of network connection.

3. A(n) _____ is someone who works from home or a remote location, rather than the office.

4. A business can set up a(n) _____ to control access to its network by persons using the Internet.

5. Many e-commerce Web sites provide _____ , where customers can enter personal information without fear that it will be stolen.

SECTION QUIZ

True/False

Answer the following questions by circling True or False.

True   False   **1.** Remote terminal connections can be used only with supercomputers.

True   False   **2.** To use ISDN service at home, you must replace your standard telephone lines with special ISDN-only lines.

True   False   **3.** A firewall can control access to a corporate network by someone using the Internet.

True   False   **4.** An intranet can be accessed by anyone over an Internet connection.

True   False   **5.** In simple terms, e-commerce means conducting business online.

Multiple Choice

Circle the word or phrase that best completes each statement.

1. You can set up a direct connection to the Internet over a telephone line by using _____ .
   A. serial line interface protocol   **B.** point-to-point protocol   **C.** either A or B

2. _____ is one type of high-speed data link.
   A. 56 Kbps   **B.** ISDN   **C.** Winsock

3. To work with a cable modem, your PC needs a(n) _____ .
   A. network interface card   **B.** DSL connection   **C.** standard phone line

4. One of the most common ways that consumers pay for online transactions is by using _____ .
   A. cash   **B.** a money order   **C.** a credit card

5. If a Web page's URL includes _____ , the page is secure.
   A. a cookie   **B.** https   **C.** neither A nor B

REVIEW QUESTIONS

In your own words, briefly answer the following questions.

1. How do most individual computer users connect to the Internet?

2. List three technologies people can use to gain high-speed access to the Internet.

3. When a business connects its own network to the Internet, what kind of risk does the business create for itself?

4. In basic terms, what does a firewall do?

5. What is the difference between an intranet and an extranet?

SECTION LABS

Complete the following exercises as directed by your instructor.

1. Determine whether your computer has a modem. (You may need your instructor's assistance to complete this exercise.) Open the Control Panel window. If you see a Modems icon, double-click the icon to open the Modem Properties dialog box. (Depending on which version of Windows you use, this icon may have a different name.)Write down the information about your modem. Close the Modem Properties dialog box.

2. Use the Control Panel window to see whether your PC has a network interface card installed. In Control Panel, double-click the System icon to open the System Properties dialog box. Click the Device Manager tab, then click the plus sign (+) next to Network adapters. (In Windows 2000, you can access the Device Manager through the Hardware tab.) If any adapters are installed, the list expands to show them. Select each adapter in turn, and click Properties to display the Properties dialog box. Write down the information for each adapter, then click Cancel. Close the Control Panel window.

UNIT PROJECTS

UNIT LABS

Complete the following exercises using a computer in your classroom, lab, or home.

1. **Learn More about the Internet.** One of the best places to learn about the Internet is on the Internet. Dozens of authoritative Web sites provide information on the history of the Internet and technical issues, as well as tutorials for using the Web, Internet software, and more. To find more basic information about the Internet, visit these Web sites:

   Webmonkey Guides—**http://www.hotwired. lycos.com/webmonkey/guides/**

   An Overview of the World Wide Web: A New Surfer's Guide—**http://www.imaginarylandscape. com/helpweb/www.oneweb.html**

   Newbie—**http://www.newbie.org/**

   Internet 101—**http://www.internet101.org/**

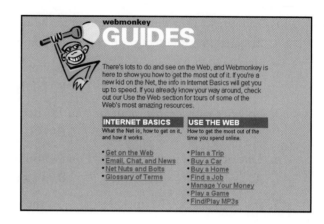

2. **Set Up a Free E-Mail Account.** Even if you don't have an ISP account, you can still use e-mail if you can use a computer with access to the World Wide Web. Visit the following sites to learn more about free e-mail accounts. Pick a provider, then follow the directions on that site to set up an account. Remember to write down your user name and password, then exchange an e-mail message with someone in your class.

   Hotmail—**http://www.hotmail.com/**

   Mail.com—**http://www.mail.com/**

   E-Mail.com—**http://www.email.com/**

   Yahoo!—**http://mail.yahoo.com/**

3. Get a Taste of Telnet. Take the following steps to learn about your Telnet software, which is built right into your Windows operating system. (The following steps assume that you use Windows 98 or Window ME. If you use a different version of Windows or the Telnet program, ask your instructor for assistance.)

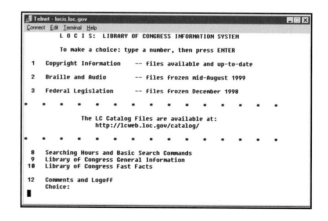

   A. Click the Start button to open the Start menu, then click Programs. In the Programs menu, click the MS-DOS Prompt icon. An MS-DOS Prompt window appears on your desktop. A blinking cursor appears, where you can type commands.

   B. Type **TELNET,** and press Enter. A Telnet window opens on your desktop.

   C. Click Help on the Menu bar to open the Help menu, then click Contents. Review the Help information to learn about your Telnet software. Close the Help window when you are done.

   D. On the menu bar, click Connect to open the Connect menu, then click Remote system. The Connect dialog box opens.

E. In the Host Name box, type **locis.loc.gov** (the Telnet address for the Library of Congress Information System).

F. From the Port drop-down list, select *telnet*. From the Term Type drop-down list, select *vt100*. (Your instructor may direct you to select different options.)

G. Click Connect. If your connection is successful, the Telnet window will change to display the opening screen of the Library of Congress Telnet site. Follow the instructions to log on to the site, and explore. When you are finished, close the Telnet and MS-DOS Prompt windows by clicking the Close buttons on their title bars.

DISCUSSION QUESTIONS

As directed by your instructor, discuss the following questions in class or in groups.

1. Despite the promise that the Internet will perhaps be as universal one day as radio and television, how do you feel about the growing "commercialization" of the Internet? Do you think the motive to use the Internet as a vehicle for profit will have a negative effect on it as a rich source of information?

2. What is your view of the Internet's value to individual people? How important do you think the Internet is in the daily life of average people? For example, could you live without Internet access and enjoy the same quality of life you enjoy today?

RESEARCH AND REPORT

Using your own choice of resources (such as the Internet, books, magazines, and newspaper articles), research and write a short paper discussing one of the following topics:

- The Internet's growth
- The cost and availability of ISDN, DSL, and cable modem services in your area
- The use of firewalls to protect corporate networks

When you are finished, proofread and print your paper, and give it to your instructor.

ETHICAL ISSUES

Despite all the conveniences it offers, the Internet is filled with pitfalls. With this thought in mind, discuss the following questions in class.

1. People can do many things online, and Web designers, Internet marketers, ISPs, and other companies encourage us to use the Internet as much as possible, for any reason. But can Internet use be bad? At what point do we become too dependent on the Internet? At what point does Internet use interfere with our normal routines, instead of enhancing them?

2. Imagine that a large company, such as a bank, discovers that several of its employees are using the company network to download pornography from the Web. These workers also are using the company's e-mail system to exchange images with one another and with people outside the company. In your view, what should the company do about such behavior? Is firing the employees too harsh a punishment? Support your position.

Computing *Keynotes*

Creating Your Own Web Page

If you have been considering creating a Web page, the good news is that it is not very difficult—especially if your goal is simply to create a personal home page or a small, non-e-commerce Web site. Creating and publishing Web content is straightforward; you just need to know what the process entails.

CHOOSING YOUR DESIGN TOOLS

When you set out to create your first Web site, your first challenge is deciding which tools to use. Luckily, there are many Web design programs that let you create a site without mastering HTML or learning a scripting language. If you want to create Web content but prefer to avoid a steep learning curve, these programs offer the easiest route to follow.

To that end, this *Computing Keynote* feature shows you how to create a Web page using Microsoft FrontPage —a popular Web page design program. Because FrontPage is intuitive and easy to use, it is a good choice for the first-time Web designer. It also comes with templates that simplify the page-creation process. If you have Microsoft Office, then you may already have a copy of FrontPage installed on your PC. If not, you can get a trial copy of FrontPage by visiting Microsoft's Web site at **http://www.microsoft.com/frontpage/**.

With the right tools, you can create simple Web pages—such as a list of your favorite links or a basic resume—in a snap.

Visit **http://www.microsoft.com/frontpage/** for more information about FrontPage or to download a trial copy.

If you want to add graphics to your Web page, you will need a graphics-editing program. A professional tool, such as Adobe Photoshop, can be used, or you can choose from a variety of affordable—yet feature-rich—graphics programs. Three low-cost favorites include the following:

◆ Paint Shop Pro, from Jasc, Inc. For more information, visit **http://www.jasc.com/**.

◆ Fireworks, from Macromedia. For more information, visit **http://www.macromedia.com/**.

◆ LiveMotion, from Adobe. For more information, visit **http://www.adobe.com/**.

At press time, a package that included FrontPage and PaintShop Pro—a great software combination for the Web enthusiast—was available from Microsoft.

PLANNING YOUR PAGE OR SITE

Before you design anything, you need to determine what your Web page (or site, if you want to publish several pages) is going to be about. For example, you may want to publish information about yourself or your family. Or you might want to create a page or small site for an organization, such as a synagogue, club, neighborhood association, or community center.

It is important to know your page's main topic before you start. The topic will help you decide what kind of information to prepare, and it also will help you keep the contents focused. Otherwise, visitors will quickly lose interest and leave your site. You need to engage your visitors right away and let them know why they should stay on your site, reading your content and visiting any other pages within the site.

If your site is small, you can draw a basic layout on paper. At this point, you do not need much detail—just an idea of your major topic or topics. Limit your site to one topic per page.

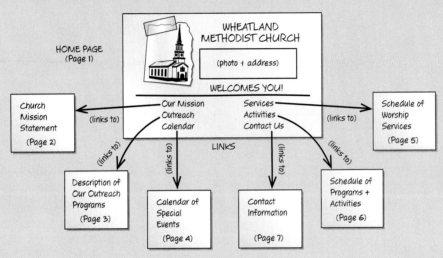

Organizing Text

The next step in planning is to arrange your site's information into sensible categories. Whether you are designing a single page or a site with many pages, you should organize your thoughts in order to help the site's visitors understand what you are trying to do. Get out a piece of paper and start organizing your ideas.

Some common topics for a page's or site's contents may include the following:

- ◆ About You (or your organization)
- ◆ Poems and Stories
- ◆ Resume
- ◆ Photo Album
- ◆ Favorite Links

Be careful here, because many pages suffer from the "Too Much Stuff" syndrome. Clutter can turn visitors off. The best way to avoid this problem is to look carefully at the way you have organized the information you would like to have on your page. Keep written content short and to the point. If you have a lot of written content, such as information about your organization, break up the information by using headers and lists. This practice makes the information more interesting and easier to read.

Planning for Graphical Appeal

Of course, a Web page can have much more than just words on it! You can create your own graphics or find suitable graphics from popular graphic repositories.

Importing Graphics

Graphics—such as scanned drawings or digital photos—can add a touch of your own personality and talent to your pages. To import graphics, you will need a graphics program, as mentioned earlier, as well as the software that came with your scanner and/or digital camera.

If you have a scanner, you can use it to digitize your own snapshots or illustrations. However, you should not scan published images (such as photographs from a magazine), because they are protected by copyright law.

Web sites such as the Paint Shop Pro Resources page (at **http://www.psbook.com/**) can help you learn how to add graphics to your Web site.

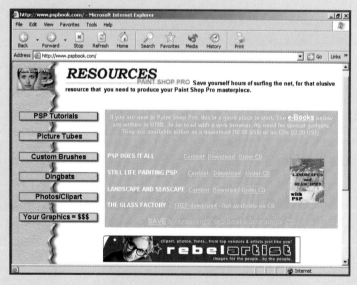

If you want to import photos from your digital camera into your imaging software, you may need to resize them or touch them up to make them more suitable for Web use. Read the documentation that came with your digital camera and your image-editing program to learn about resizing, cropping, changing colors, and dealing with imperfections (such as "red eye" or poor lighting).

Scanning images demands a little more attention. If you scan your work improperly, the results will be disappointing. Follow these tips for successful scanning:

◆ Clean your scanner's surface and the items to be scanned. Check your scanner's documentation for the best way to clean your scanner. To clean photos and art work, use canned air—available at most office and art supply stores—to blast away smudges and dust.

◆ Scan and save your image files at 72 DPI (dots per inch), which is the standard resolution for images on the Web. If your images are fairly detailed or colorful, save them in JPEG (JPG) format; this format works best for photographs. If images do not have a lot of detail or contain only a few colors, save them in GIF format; this format works best for drawings and items such as backgrounds and buttons. You can find resolution settings and file formats in your imaging software.

◆ Use your imaging software to crop and refine the scanned image.

Web graphics should be attractive and download quickly to the visitor's browser. This means keeping your graphics at a reasonable size and resolution. If you do not know how to work with Web graphics, you can learn from many helpful tutorials available online. One good place to start is Internet Eye's Paint Shop Pro Resources page, at **http://the-internet-eye.com/resources/psp.htm**. It provides articles and links to many other graphics-related sites.

Finding Graphics Online

If you want to use clip art, photos, and animations—but you are not an artist—you may find free and inexpensive resources to use for your page by visiting these Web sites:

◆ Barry's Clip Art Server (**http://www.barrysclipart.com/**) serves up a great big help-ing of clip art, animated GIFs, related links, and helpful software.

◆ ArtToday (**http://www.arttoday.com**) is a membership-oriented site that offers clip art, animations, photos, and fonts you can download for a fee. You will find a large amount of free stuff is available, too.

Before you download any kind of image from a Web site (or any other online source), how-ever, be sure to read the licensing or usage agreement that governs its use. Reputable online clip-art services post these agreements on their Web sites, so you cannot miss them. Even free images can have some usage restric-tions; for example, the image's owner may require you to acknowledge the owner or artist on your site or get written permission before you use the graphic.

You will find more information about borrow-ing images, text, and HTML code from other Web sites in the section titled "Web Content and Intellectual Property Rights," at the end of this *Computing Keynote*.

Look for license or usage agreements before you download an image from a clip art service. This agreement appears on Barry's Clip Art Server.

> **Use Of Barrys Clipart Server Images**
>
> Feel free to use Barrys Clipart Server content in personal/ non profit projects to create webpages, T-shirts, posters, book covers, art, advertising, newsletters, presentations, and logos... you name it!
>
> There are no per-image costs, royalties or extra payments for Barrys Clipart Server content when you follow the Usage Guidelines below.
>
> Terms of Use | Consent to Terms | Denial of Responsibility
>
> **Usage Guidelines**
>
> Many font, photo, clipart and web art images (the "Content") contained herein are either licensed from or owned by third-party sources. In utilizing this site you are permitted to use, modify, and publish the content subject to the following restrictions.
>
> You are permitted to use the Content, including online use and multimedia applications, as long as all of the following conditions are met:
>
> o   the images are incorporated for viewing purposes only
> o   the images do not comprise a large portion of the content of the application
> o   no permission is given by you to download and save the images for any reason
>
> You are **not** permitted to...
>
> o   ...redistribute the Content as stock photography, clipart, web art or multimedia
> o   ...use any of the photo or clipart images for any commercial purposes
> o   ...create obscene or scandalous works, as defined by the Federal Government at the time the work is created, using the Content or any modification of the Content

BUILDING YOUR SITE

So you have gathered your tools, organized your ideas, and gotten up to speed with Web graphics. Now it is time to roll up your sleeves and start building your Web site.

Start by launching FrontPage. To do this, open the Start menu, and then open the Programs menu (or the All Programs menu, if you use Windows XP). When you launch FrontPage, it creates a folder on your PC called My Webs. This folder contains a subfolder called Images. Before going any further, open Windows Explorer or My Computer and move all your images into the Images subfolder.

Now it is time to actually create a site, step by step.

Selecting a Template

Since your goal is to create a site right away, you will work with a template and modify it to suit your needs. Follow these steps to select the template in FrontPage:

1. Open the File menu, click New, then click Page. The New dialog box opens; the General tab displays several types of page layouts.

2. Select *one column body with sidebars* and click OK. The layout appears in FrontPage.

Using a FrontPage template to create an attractive home page

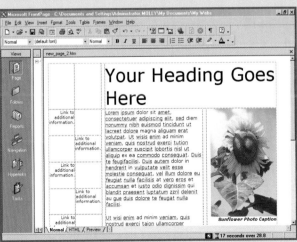

311

3. Open the File menu, and click Save As. The Save As dialog box appears. Here, you need to do two things:

A. Click the Change button next to the Page title. When the Set Page Title dialog box appears, give the page a suitable title, such as Molly's Home Page. Click OK to return to the Save As dialog box.

B. Give the file a name, then click Save. The dialog box closes, and FrontPage saves the file in the My Webs folder.

Saving your first Web page, with a file name and a title

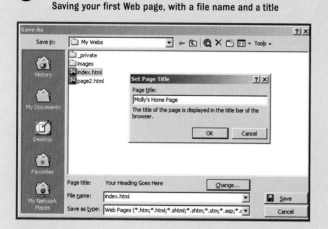

Adding an Image

Next, replace the placeholder image (on the right side of the page) with one of your own images:

1. Click the existing image, and then right-click it. When the shortcut menu opens, click Cut. The image disappears from the template. Leave the cursor where it is.

2. Open the Insert menu, click Picture, and then click From File. The Picture dialog box appears. Since you saved your graphics to the Images subfolder, open that subfolder by double-clicking it.

3. When the Images subfolder opens, select the image you want to use by clicking it. Click OK. The picture is now inserted into your design.

Adding an image to a Web page

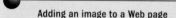

4. To change the picture caption, select the old text (by dragging across it with the mouse pointer), and type your own caption in its place.

Modifying a Heading and Adding Content

Now you are ready to fill in all the template's text areas with your custom information:

1. To modify the heading, select it and type your new heading.

2. To add content to the main section, find the text you would like to use, and then copy and paste it right over the placeholder text. Or you can delete the placeholder text and type your own text in its place.

3. Continue replacing the placeholder text until you're happy with the results. You can modify font styles and sizes by using FrontPage's tools. Use these features carefully; using too many fonts and sizes makes reading difficult.

The template with a new image, heading, and content in place

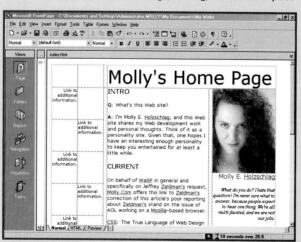

Adding Pages and Linking to Them

Links are the most important part of a Web page. Luckily, the template you are using allows for a number of links. If you want to add other pages to your site—and the page you created earlier is the site's main page—then you probably will want to add lines of text to this page and format them as hyperlinks that lead to the other pages. Here is the procedure to use:

1. To add new pages, follow the same steps you used earlier for working with the template. Be sure to name your files (they will be empty until you edit them later), and save them in the My Webs folder.

2. In the main page, highlight the placeholder text where you would like to add the link, and rename the link as is appropriate for your needs.

3. Open the Insert menu, then click Hyperlink. The Create Hyperlink dialog box appears.

4. Select the page to which you want to link by clicking its name. Click OK.

Continue adding links until you have added all the links you require. Save the page so your changes are updated. When you have finished (or whenever you want to see how your page will look online), you can click the Preview tab. Alternatively, if you prefer to see your page in an actual Web browser, open the File menu, then click Preview in Browser.

Of course, there are many other modifications and additions you can make to this document, but you are off to a great start.

Creating a hyperlink to another page on your site

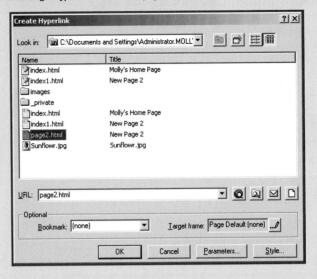

The final results: a simple but attractive home page, shown here in Netscape

WEB DESIGN TIPS

No matter what kind of content your Web page or site contains, you want it to look great. You also want the visitors to your Web site to find your content easy to read and navigate. You can accomplish these goals and avoid common Web design pitfalls by following these tips:

◆ Use bold and italic sparingly; these effects actually make text harder to read. Use bold and italic for emphasis only.

◆ Be sure to properly align body text. Centered body text (that is, paragraphs of body text centered between the margins, usually with "ragged" left and right edges) is very hard to read. It is better to adjust your margins than to center body text. You can center headers, footers, and accent text.

Alignment can make a big difference in the readability of your body text. Compare the centered body text to the properly aligned text.

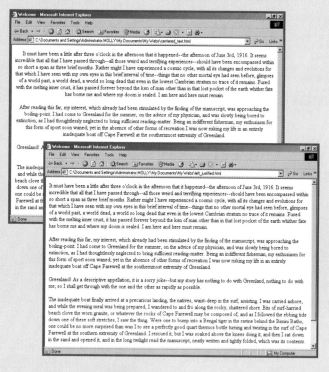

Your page may be hard to read if your page's background and body text do not work together.

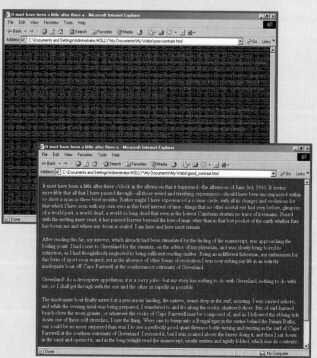

◆ Use a plain background that will not interfere with your text. Don't use complicated backgrounds (such as patterns or textures). Plain backgrounds are almost always best with any text.

◆ Use contrasting colors for backgrounds, text, and links. The higher the contrast, the better the readability. White text on a yellow background is just annoying.

◆ Keep body text at its default size.

◆ Look carefully at your page. Is there anything on it that is unnecessary? If so, get rid of it!

◆ Unless you update your pages regularly, do not post the date on which the page was last updated, and do not put time-sensitive information on it. If you are offering Christmas greetings to your visitors in July, for example, they will think your whole site is stale!

◆ Never put your home address or home phone number on a Web page, and always think carefully before putting very personal information on a page.

FINDING A HOST FOR YOUR WEB SITE

Once your page or site is ready to go, you will want to publish it online. This means finding a "host"—a person or company with a server computer that stores Web pages. A wide range of Web hosting options are available.

If you already have an account with an Internet Service Provider (ISP), you may have some free Web space available as part of your account. Check with your provider to see if this is true, and if so, ask how to access your area on the ISP's Web server.

If your ISP does not provide Web space, there are plenty of other hosting options. The most popular options for enthusiasts are free hosting services and low-cost services.

Free Hosting Services

Free services can be a terrific option if you are just starting out. The big problem with using a free service, however, is that you may have no control over the advertisements that the service uses. This means your site might display pop-up advertisements (which "pop up" in a small browser window) or banner ads (which appear as part of your page, in the form of a banner). This is the price you pay for the free hosting.

Some free hosting services include:

◆ **Free Servers.** This service offers ad-supported free Web hosting. If you upgrade to Free Servers' premium pay service, you can get rid of the advertising. For information, visit **http://www.freeservers.com/**.

◆ **FortuneCity.** Another service with ad-supported free home page publishing. There are low-cost and flex options as well, should you decide to upgrade. Visit **http://www. fortunecity.com/** for information.

◆ **AngelFire.** Particularly popular among young Web designers, AngelFire offers a variety of services including ways to connect to other home pages with similar interests. The service is free if you accept the display of advertisements on your page, and low-cost options are also available. To learn more, visit **http://www.angelfire.com/**.

Fee-Based Hosting Services

When you pay for hosting services, you can expect to receive other services along with storage for your Web site. Some fee-based hosts provide e-mail accounts, or even the ability to host your own domain name (such as www.yourname.com/). Your choice of service depends on what you want to do and how much you can afford. Some pay services include the following:

◆ **Hosting.Com.** This company offers a wide range of services to meet all kinds of needs, from beginning to high-end professional. For information, visit **http://www.hosting.com/**.

◆ **Cedant Web Hosting.** Cedant provides a variety of services, ranging from low to medium cost. To learn more, visit **http://www.cedant.com/**.

◆ **TopHosts.com.** This portal site can help you find the best hosting service for you. Visit **http://www.tophosts.com/**.

Once you have a host, the next step is to publish your site.

Publishing Web content with FrontPage

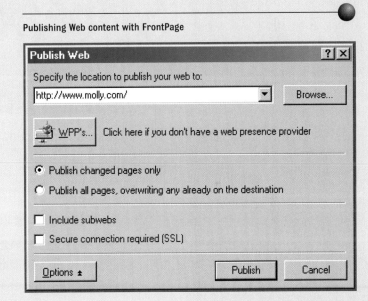

PUBLISHING YOUR SITE

With your log-on information to your Web host at the ready, you are prepared to publish.

Publishing your pages to a Web server requires you to have some form of file transfer software. If you create your site in FrontPage, open the File menu, then click Publish Web. A set of steps will appear, telling you how to publish your Web content to your host's server.

If you decide not to use FrontPage, or if you want to use a different means of transferring files, you need to use FTP client software. This type of program uses the File Transfer Protocol (FTP) to transfer your files over the Internet to the host's computer. (FTP is discussed in greater detail in Unit 8, "The Internet and Online Resources.") Two very popular FTP client programs are WS_FTP (**http://www.wsftp.com/**) and CuteFTP (**http://www.cuteftp. com/**).

Application Software: Word Processors and Spreadsheets

UNIT CONTENTS

This unit contains the following sections:

Section 9A: Word Processing and Desktop Publishing Software

- ► Word Processing Programs and Their Uses
- ► The Word Processor's Interface
- ► Entering and Editing Text
- ► Formatting Text
- ► Special Features of Word Processing Software
- ► Desktop Publishing Software

Section 9B: Spreadsheet Software

- ► Spreadsheet Programs and Their Uses
- ► The Spreadsheet's Interface
- ► Entering Data in a Worksheet
- ► Editing and Formatting a Worksheet
- ► Adding Charts
- ► Analyzing Data in a Spreadsheet

The Interactive Browser Edition CD-ROM provides additional labs and activities to apply concepts from this unit.

Word Processing and Desktop Publishing Software

OVERVIEW:
The Importance of Documents in Our World

Every day, millions of people use word processing software to create and edit memos, letters, reports, and many other kinds of documents. In fact, it has been estimated that more than 90 percent of all personal computers have a word processor installed.

If this fact comes as a surprise, consider the number of documents that surround you.

Newspapers, magazines, letters, and advertisements crowd your mailbox each day. You read books for school and for pleasure. Businesses, government agencies, schools, and individuals create untold numbers of documents for a myriad of purposes. On desktops around the world, printers spit out tons of documents every week. Probably, just as many documents are created but never printed.

If you have not had any experience yet with productivity software, a word processor is an ideal place to start. Modern word processors are easy to use and require no special skills to master. A word processor will familiarize you with many common tools. You may find little or no personal use for other types of applications, but you may find your word processor to be an application that is essential for personal use.

OBJECTIVES

- Identify three basic word processing tools that simplify document editing.
- Explain what is meant by "selecting" parts of a document.
- Identify five special features commonly found in modern word processors.
- Distinguish desktop publishing software from word processing software.

RETURN

DELETE

WORD PROCESSING PROGRAMS AND THEIR USES

Word processing software (also called a word processor) is an application that provides extensive tools for creating all kinds of text-based documents, as shown in Figures 9A.1 through 9A.3. Word processors are not limited to working with text. Word processors enable you to add images to your documents and design documents that look like products of a professional print shop. Using a word processor, you can create long documents with separate chapters, a table of contents, an index, and other features.

A word processor can enhance documents in other ways; you can embed sounds, video clips, and animations into them. You can link different documents together—for example, link a chart from a spreadsheet into a word processing report—to create complex documents that update themselves automatically. Word processors can even create documents for publishing on the World Wide Web, complete with hyperlinked text and graphics.

Figure 9A.1
This simple birthday card was created in a word processing program. It features colors, rotated text, and graphics.

Figure 9A.2
Word processors are used frequently to create business letters and resumes. The formatting can be simple (as demonstrated by the cover letter) or more elaborate (as in the resume).

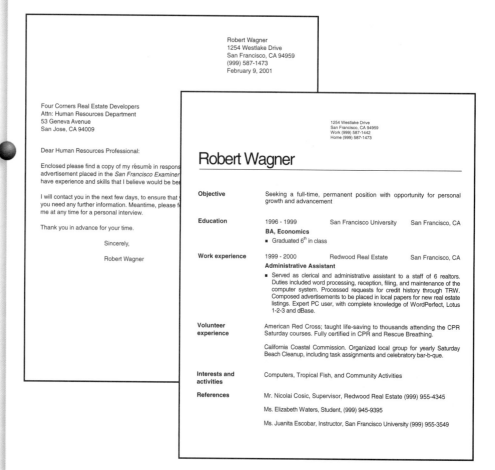

NORTON ONLINE

Visit **www.norton.glencoe.com** for more information on **word processing software.**

THE WORD PROCESSOR'S INTERFACE

The word processor's main editing window displays a document and several tools, as illustrated in Figure 9A.4. In addition to a **document area** (or **document window**), which is where you view the document, a word processor provides several sets of tools, including:

◆ A **menu bar,** which displays titles of menus (lists of commands and options).

◆ **Toolbars,** which display buttons that represent frequently used commands.

◆ **Rulers,** which show you the positions of text, tabs, margins, indents, and other elements on the page.

◆ **Scroll bars,** which let you scroll through a document that is too large to fit inside the document area.

◆ A **status bar,** which displays information related to your position in the document, the page count, and the status of keyboard keys.

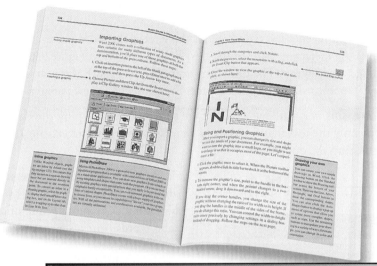

Figure 9A.3
Word processors allow you to create long, highly complex documents that are ready to send to a commercial printer.

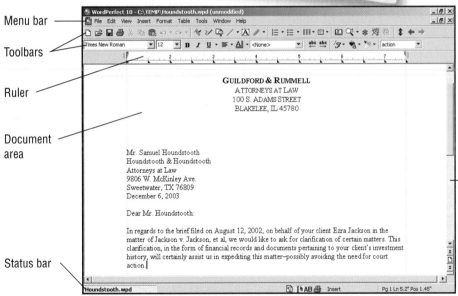

Menu bar

Toolbars

Ruler

Document area

Status bar

Scroll bar

Figure 9A.4
WordPerfect's interface features tools that are commonly found in word processing programs.

ENTERING AND EDITING TEXT

You create a document by typing on the keyboard—a process known as entering text. In a new document, the program places a blinking insertion point (also called a cursor) in the upper left corner of the document window. As you type, the insertion point advances across the screen, showing you where the next character will be placed.

Figure 9A.5
Word wrap

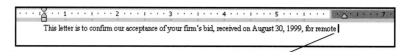

When the insertion point reaches the end of a line...

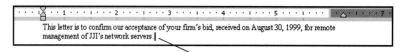

...it automatically moves down to the next line.

When your text reaches the right edge of the screen, the word processor automatically moves the insertion point to the next line, as shown in Figure 9A.5. This feature is called **word wrap.** The only time you need to press Enter is at the end of a paragraph. (In a word processor, you press Enter to start a new paragraph.)

Word processing software lets you change text without retyping the entire page; you retype only the text that needs to be changed. Changing an existing document is called **editing** the document.

The word processor's real beauty is its ability to work with blocks of text. A **block** is a contiguous group of characters, words, lines, sentences, or paragraphs in your document that you mark for editing. To mark text for editing, you select the text to be edited. You can select text by using the mouse, the keyboard, or both. When you select text, it changes color—becoming **highlighted,** as shown in Figure 9A.6—to indicate that it is selected.

flow, or a burst of waves, the reservoir cushions the banks from changing forces. A UPS is like a reservoir for electricity. As your electricity fluctuates, the UPS absorbs and supplements the flow.

To fully appreciate how helpful a UPS is, take the water analogy one step further and think of the plumbing in your home. If someone is drawing water when you start a shower, the other person notices a drop in the water pressure and you notice that the water pressure isn't as high as it should be. Then, if someone else flushes a toilet, you can expect the flow of cold water to momentarily drop even more. When the toilet finishes filling up, you can expect a sudden return of the cold water. And, when the original person drawing water stops, you notice a sudden increase in water pressure. Once you're through fiddling with the faucets, you appreciate how nice a personal reservoir could be. The electricity in your home works much the same way, so a UPS goes a long way to even out the flow as various appliances are turned on an off.

What Are the Most Common Electrical Problems?
Electrical problems come in all types, from the nearly harmless minor fluctuation in the voltage level, to

Figure 9A.6
The paragraph that appears as white text against a black background is highlighted. The user has selected the text for editing or formatting.

You can erase an entire selected block by pressing the Delete key or by typing other text over the selected block. You can change the formatting of the selection by making it bold or underlined, for example, or by changing the font or font size. To **deselect** a selected block of text, click the mouse anywhere on the screen or press any arrow key. The text is displayed again as it normally would be.

You also can copy or move a block of selected text from one part of the document to another, or even from one document to another. In a word processor, moving text is as easy as dragging the block to a new location, a technique called drag-and-drop editing. The same effect can be accomplished by cutting or copying the block to the Clipboard, and then pasting it to a new location.

FORMATTING TEXT

Most word processing features are used to **format** the document. The process of formatting a document includes controlling the appearance of text, the layout of text on the page, and the use of pictures and other graphic elements. Most formatting features fall into one of three categories: character formats, paragraph formats, and document formats.

Character Formats

Character formatting includes settings that control the attributes of individual text characters, such as:

◆ **Fonts.** The term **font** refers to the characteristics of the letters, symbols, and punctuation marks in your document. Fonts have names like Times New Roman, Helvetica, and Palatino (see Figure 9A.7). In addition to those that come with the operating system, most word processors provide at least a handful of built-in fonts.

◆ **Type size.** A font is measured in **points,** as shown in Figure 9A.8. One point equals $\frac{1}{72}$ of an inch, so 72 points equal one inch, 36 points equal $\frac{1}{2}$ inch, and so forth. A common font size used in business documents is 12-point type. Characters are measured from the top of the tallest letters (such as *T* and *P*) to the bottom of letters that descend below the baseline (such as *g* and *p*). Word processors let you work with type sizes from as little as 8 points to as large as 72 points.

◆ **Type style.** In addition to the font and type size, the appearance of characters can be controlled with **type styles** (which are often referred to as attributes or effects). The most common styles used in documents are bold, italic, and underlining, as shown in Figure 9A.9. Less commonly used style attributes include strikethrough, superscript, subscript, small caps, and others.

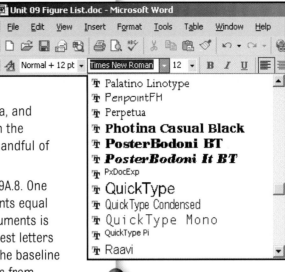

Figure 9A.7
Your computer may have dozens or even hundreds of fonts installed. Programs like Microsoft Word show you what a font looks like before you select it.

This is 10 point Times type.

This is 12 point Times type.

This is 14 point Times type.

This is 16 point Times type.

This is 18 point Times type.

Figure 9A.8
Type sizes

You can make your text **bold.**

You can use *italics*, too.

Underlining is an old standby.

Sometimes you can use ~~strike through.~~

You can also use SMALL CAPS VS. LARGE CAPS.

Figure 9A.9
Type styles

Paragraph Formats

In word processing, the word *paragraph* has a slightly different meaning than it does traditionally. Word processing software creates a **paragraph** each time you press the Enter key. A group of sentences is a paragraph, but a two-word heading (like the one above this paragraph) is defined as a paragraph, as well. **Paragraph formatting** includes settings applied only to one or more entire paragraphs, such as:

◆ **Line spacing.** The amount of space between each line of text in a paragraph is called **line spacing.** Lines can be single-spaced, double-spaced, or set for an amount of spacing between the lines that you select.

◆ **Paragraph spacing.** The amount of space between each paragraph is called **paragraph spacing.** Word processing software lets you place extra space before or after each paragraph.

◆ **Indents.** **Indents** determine how close each line of a paragraph comes to the margins. In some documents, lines of body text may reach all the way to the left and right margins, but quoted material may be indented one inch from each margin. You can set indents so they affect every line of text in a paragraph, at the right edge, the left edge, or both edges. A common style of indent is applied only to the first line of a paragraph, moving its first character several spaces—usually 5 spaces—in from the left margin. You also can create a reverse effect, called a hanging indent, which leaves the paragraph's first line flush with the left margin but indents the following lines.

Figure 9A.10

The vertical dotted lines represent the left and right margins on the page. Notice how the different paragraph alignments adjust the text in relation to the margins.

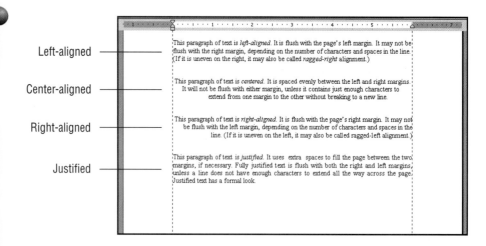

◆ **Alignment.** **Alignment** refers to the orientation of the lines of a paragraph with respect to the margins. There are four alignment options—left, right, center, and justified (or full justification)—as shown in Figure 9A.10.

◆ **Tab stops.** The keyboard's Tab key moves the insertion point forward (to the right) until it encounters a **tab stop** (or just a **tab**), inserting a fixed amount of space in the line. A tab stop is a position, both on screen and in the document, usually measured from the left margin of the document. By default, most word processors place tab stops in increments of one-half inch across the width of the page. However, you can set tabs at any point between the page's right and left margins. Most word processors allow you to change or remove the tab stops by displaying a ruler across the top or bottom of the screen that shows where tab stop positions are set. Tabs are most often used to align columns of text accurately or to create tables; word processors provide at least four different types of tab stops so that you can align columns in different ways. For example, in Figure 9A.11, the columns are separated by tab spacing (rather than by spaces inserted with the space bar). The first column is aligned along the left margin of the page, the second column is aligned by a left-aligned tab stop, the third by a centered tab stop, the fourth by a right-aligned tab stop, and the fifth by a decimal tab stop.

Left-aligned	Centered	Right-aligned	Decimal-aligned

Today's Purchases

Department	Part Code	Description	Quantity	Cost
Purchasing	44HF35	Disks	50	$12.50
Marketing	KD4323	Pens	2000	$50.25
Research	D387567	Test Tubes	1200	$2500.00
Admin.	DFG776	Binder Clips	100	$50.00
Research	DGK473	Gloves	500	$32.00
Day Care	H483JGH	Diapers	100	$50.00

Figure 9A.11

Four kinds of tab stops

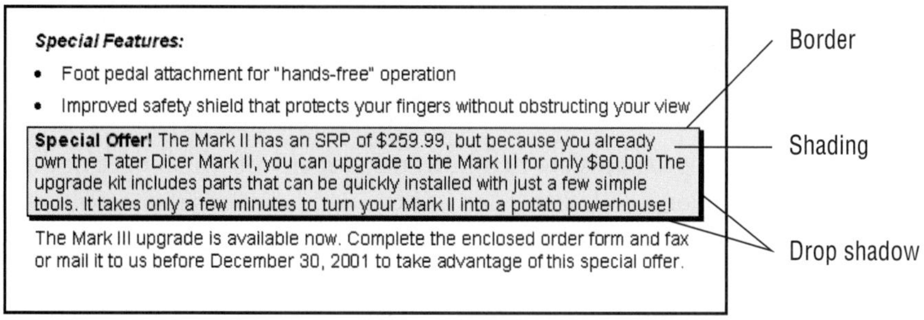

Special Features:
- Foot pedal attachment for "hands-free" operation
- Improved safety shield that protects your fingers without obstructing your view

Special Offer! The Mark II has an SRP of $259.99, but because you already own the Tater Dicer Mark II, you can upgrade to the Mark III for only $80.00! The upgrade kit includes parts that can be quickly installed with just a few simple tools. It takes only a few minutes to turn your Mark II into a potato powerhouse!

The Mark III upgrade is available now. Complete the enclosed order form and fax or mail it to us before December 30, 2001 to take advantage of this special offer.

Border
Shading
Drop shadow

Figure 9A.12
This paragraph is formatted with a border, shading, and a drop shadow.

◆ **Borders and shading.** Paragraphs can be formatted with borders or shading (see Figure 9A.12). A **border** is a line that is drawn on one or more sides of a paragraph. **Shading** consists of a pattern or color that is displayed as a background to the text in a paragraph. A drop shadow is a partial shadow around a bordered paragraph, which creates the illusion that the paragraph is "floating" above the page.

Document Formats

Document formats include the size of the page, its orientation, and headers or footers. Word processing software also lets you apply special formats, such as columns, to documents. You also can divide a document into sections and give each section its own unique format. Standard document formats include:

◆ **Margins.** **Margins** are the white borders around the edge of the page. Every document has top, bottom, left, and right margins, and all four margins can be the same or different.

◆ **Page size.** Normally, documents are set up to fit on 8½- by 11-inch paper, a standard known as letter-size paper. You can set up a word processor document for other standard sizes, such as legal size (8½- by 14-inch paper). You can also set up a document to fit custom paper sizes.

◆ **Orientation.** Document dimensions are also determined by the orientation of the paper. By default, documents are set up with **portrait orientation** (or tall orientation), where the document is taller than it is wide. You also can switch to **landscape orientation** (or wide orientation), in which the paper is turned on its side, as shown in Figure 9A.13.

◆ **Headers and footers.** Long documents generally include headers, footers, or both. **Headers** and **footers** are lines of text that run along the top and bottom of every page. For example, the footers in this book include the unit number or the unit title (depending on whether they are located on a left page or a right page, respectively) and the page number. There are no headers.

◆ **Columns.** **Columns** are effective formats for certain types of documents. Newsletters, for example, are often laid out in a two- or three-column format to make them easy to read.

◆ **Sections.** Word processors also allow you to divide a document into **sections** and apply a different format to each section. In Figure 9A.14, the document's top section is a heading followed by page-width text. The second section is a three-column format.

Figure 9A.13
A document in landscape orientation

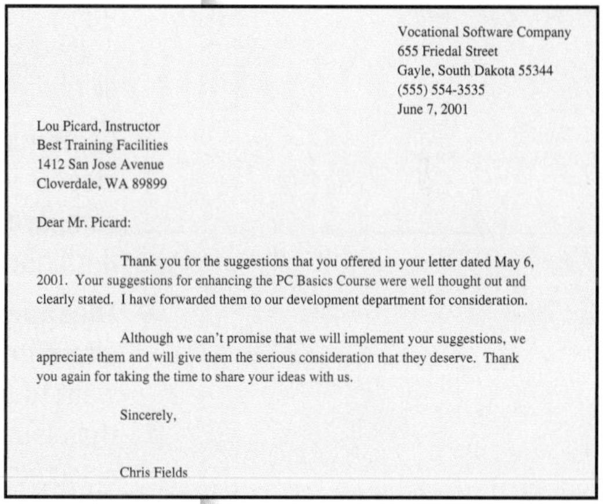

Figure 9A.14
A two-section document, with different document formats in each section

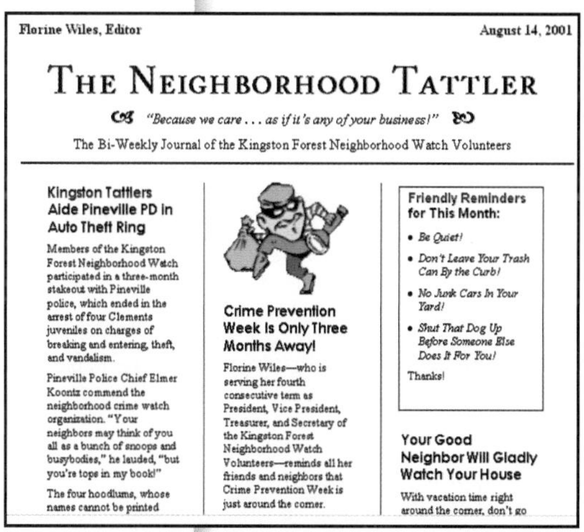

SPECIAL FEATURES OF WORD PROCESSING SOFTWARE

All word processing programs are rich in features, many of which have nothing to do with text editing or formatting. Such utilities add functions that are almost like adding new software programs to your word processor.

Language Tools

A word processor cannot make you a good writer, but it can help. Many word processors feature language tools that can help you find errors in your spelling and grammar; they also may have tools to help you find just the right word or avoid overusing certain words. These tools include the following:

◆ **Spell Checkers.** If your word processor has a **spell checker,** you can enable it to catch spelling mistakes as you type or use it to review an entire document for spelling errors. A spell checker matches each word in a document against a built-in dictionary containing standard spellings. If the utility encounters a word that has no match in the dictionary, it lets you know. A good spell checker will provide options for replacing the word, ignoring it, or adding it to the spelling dictionary (see Figure 9A.15).

◆ **Grammar Checkers.** **Grammar checkers** work like spell checkers, but they inspect your document for grammatical problems. A grammar checker compares each sentence to a set of standard grammatical rules, notifies you if it finds a potential problem, and provides grammatically correct options.

◆ **Thesaurus.** An electronic **thesaurus** is just like a printed one—a source of alternative words. Suppose you think you are using a word incorrectly, or you want to find a different word with a similar meaning. You can select a word, then launch the thesaurus. A good thesaurus will display a definition of the selected word and a list of possible replacements.

Tables

Although tabs can be used to set up rows and columns of information in a document, word processors provide features that let you create **tables** in just a few steps. The size of a table is limited only by the amount of page space that can be devoted to it, and tables can be formatted in dozens of ways. Tables typically are set up with a header row across the top to describe the contents of each column. Many tables also include a special first column that describes the contents of each row.

Tables also are useful for arranging images (such as clip art or photographs) on a page and for arranging images and text in interesting ways. In fact, many professional document designers use tables as a quick and easy way to create customized page layouts, when standard text-control tools do not provide enough flexibility.

Figure 9A.15

Checking spelling in a document in Lotus WordPro

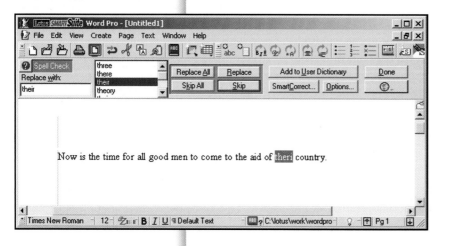

Mail Merge

A **mail merge** is the process of combining a form letter with the contents of a database—usually a name and address list—so that each copy of the letter has one entry from the database printed on it. The mail merge feature makes it easy to send the same letter to a list of different people with the correct name and address printed on each letter.

Adding Graphics and Sounds

With a word processor, you easily can add graphic images—photos, drawings, or clip art—to your documents. You set the cursor where you want the graphic to appear, tell the word processing program that you want to insert a graphic, and then locate the graphic file. After the graphic has been imported, you can move, size, crop, and add borders to it. You can even adjust the alignment so that your text flows around the picture.

You can embed sound files in your documents in much the same way that you embed a graphic file. The only difference is that an icon appears in the document (see Figure 9A.16). Clicking the icon plays the sound file, if the PC has a sound card and speakers. Although sound files are of no value in printed documents, they can be useful in documents that are distributed electronically—on disk, online, or across a network.

Templates

Templates are predesigned documents that are blank except for preset margins, fonts, paragraph formats, headings, rules, graphics, headers, or footers (see Figure 9A.17). You can open a document template, type your text into it, save it, and print the finished document. When you use a template, you do not have to manually format complex documents.

Internet-Related Features

Since 1994, thousands of companies and individuals have created electronic documents that can be accessed on the part of the Internet known as the World Wide Web. These documents are known as Web pages. To create a page for the Web, you need to format the page with special codes that explain how the page will appear and behave in a Web browser (a program like Netscape Navigator, for example). These special codes are part of a page-description language called Hypertext Markup Language, or HTML.

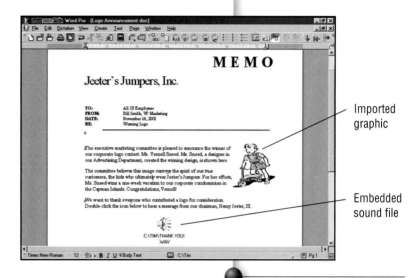

Imported graphic

Embedded sound file

Figure 9A.16
Documents can contain both graphics and sounds.

Figure 9A.17
Predesigned templates make it easy to create professional documents, from fax cover sheets to newsletters. Here, a Microsoft Word template is being used to create business cards.

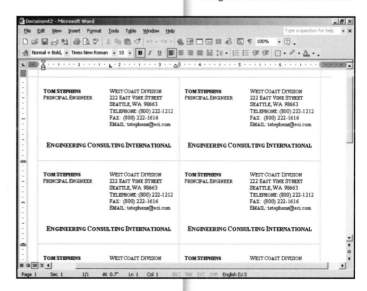

Figure 9A.18

This is a document coded with HTML tags; the document also contains style information (called a style sheet), and tags in Extensible Markup Language (XML). This document was created in Word's editing window like any normal document. Here, the document is being viewed in the Microsoft Script Editor, an application that Word uses to create Web pages. Word provides tools for designing Web pages and creating hyperlinks. The tags were inserted by the word processor.

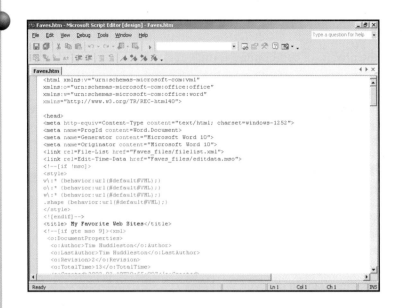

Many word processors can convert standard text documents into the HTML format for you. The resulting Web page contains the original text and is formatted with HTML tags so that headings, body text, lists, and other elements will appear in a standard Web format. An example of a document coded with HTML is shown in Figure 9A.18. The resulting page, as it appears in a Web browser, is shown in Figure 9A.19.

Word processors are not the only programs that can convert documents into Web pages. Almost any new version of a spreadsheet, presentation, or database program can convert a user's files into HTML format.

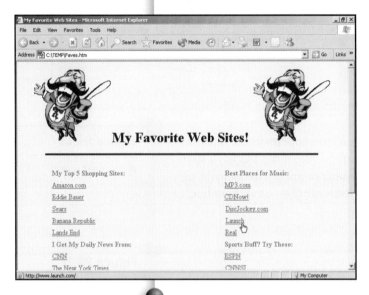

Figure 9A.19

The HTML document viewed in a browser

Many new programs also provide HTML templates. These templates function just like normal word processing templates, which you learned about earlier in this unit. HTML document templates provide predesigned navigation tools: places where the user can insert hyperlinks, frames, and many other features found in well-designed Web pages.

Self Check

Complete each statement by filling in the blank(s).

1. A(n) _____ is an application that provides tools for creating text-based documents.

2. Changing an existing document is called _____ the document.

3. _____ determine how close each line of a paragraph comes to the margins.

Norton Notebook

MANAGING THE SMALL OR HOME OFFICE

Because resources are so limited for the small-business owner, application suites and a new breed of financial software are making it easy to run a small office/home office (SOHO). Instead of relying on outside accountants, marketers, designers, and other consultants, many SOHO workers can do many nontraditional chores—as well as their normal work—by using sophisticated software packages. These applications help small business owners solve various problems without making a large educational or monetary investment.

Application suites such as Microsoft Office, Corel's WordPerfect Office, and Lotus's SmartSuite include the following types of programs:

◆ **Word Processor.** Most word processors include templates that give documents a clean, professional look and help the user with spelling, grammar, and word choices. Word processors greatly simplify mass mailings and can print envelopes, brochures, and other complex documents. For SOHO workers who want to design their own Web pages, a word processor may be the only tool they need.

◆ **Spreadsheet.** Spreadsheets help managers tackle crucial financial tasks. The resulting files can be imported into many financial or accounting programs and can be useful to an accountant or consultant.

◆ **Database.** These packages enable the small-business owner to track products, orders, shipments, customers, and much more. When used as part of an application suite, the database program can provide much of the data required for invoices, receipts, form letters, and other mission-critical documents.

◆ **Presentation.** These programs help the user quickly create impressive slide shows. Color graphics, animation, and concise text can help persuade clients and close sales.

◆ **E-Mail, Contact, and Schedule Management.** Even in a small office, time is valuable, and people cannot afford to confuse schedules. Programs like Microsoft Outlook and Lotus Organizer help people (individually and in groups) manage and coordinate their schedules, set appointments, and manage contacts. These programs offer e-mail software, making it even easier to send a message to someone from the contact list.

The specialty software market for small businesses is growing rapidly. Here are three examples of the types of special business-oriented programs targeted at small businesses:

◆ **Financial.** These inexpensive—yet powerful—packages can track inventories, billings, expenses, and much more. Many popular financial programs allow users to write checks and manage their bank account balances. They also can help users categorize income and expenses and do tax planning.

◆ **Business Planning.** New business-planning programs provide templates to help the users create business plans and customize documents by industry, product type, or market type. These programs can help the aspiring business owner find investors.

◆ **Tax Planning and Preparation.** Tax software enables business owners to prepare their own taxes without using an accountant or consultant. The user plugs in the numbers; the software does the rest.

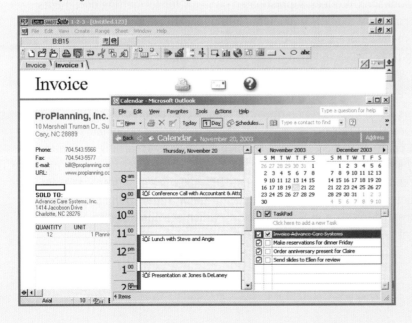

Small-business owners can use a wide range of software programs to simplify everything from sales to accounting.

DESKTOP PUBLISHING SOFTWARE

The introduction of **desktop publishing (DTP) software** revolutionized the publishing and design industries, giving ordinary users the power to produce professional-quality documents and publications. Popular DTP software packages include Adobe PageMaker, QuarkXPress, and Adobe FrameMaker, among others.

Before DTP software, producing publications of any kind was a complex process involving multiple people with different skills. DTP software enabled one person to perform all the required tasks—design, layout, typesetting, placement of graphics, and more—and create a document that was ready to be printed.

Word processors now feature many capabilities once found only in DTP software (graphics importing, font controls, and many others), and most users find that their word processor more than satisfies their daily desktop publishing and page layout requirements. However, because DTP software is designed specifically to produce complex, multicolor, printer-ready documents, it is the better choice for professional document design. A sampling of the advanced document-design features found in DTP software includes the following:

Figure 9A.20
Kerning can be especially important in headlines.

SUSPECT VANISHES
West-Side Police Lose James in Corn Field

SUSPECT VANISHES
West-Side Police Lose James in Corn Field

With kerning, these letters were moved closer together.

◆ **Type Controls.** Because spacing is often a concern in page layout, DTP software enables the user to control **kerning** (the spacing between individual letters, as shown in Figure 9A.20) and **tracking** (a general setting for character spacing for entire blocks of text). DTP software also provides nearly infinite control of **leading** (pronounced LED-ding), which is a typesetting term for line spacing.

◆ **Graphics Controls.** DTP software gives the user direct control over the exact placement of graphics on the page, the wrapping of text around the graphic, and the use of borders or shading with graphics. This book provides many excellent examples of the graphics capabilities of DTP software.

◆ **Page Layout and Document Controls.** Because DTP software was designed for the publisher, it offers sophisticated controls for formatting documents and coordinating multiple documents in a publication. Magazines, for example, contain many different documents, with some laid out in different styles. A common page layout control in DTP software is called **master pages**—special pages that are set aside for defining elements that are common to all pages in the document, such as page numbers, headers, headings, rules, and more.

◆ **Prepress Controls.** Perhaps the most unique characteristics of DTP software are prepress controls—that is, its capability to prepare documents for the printing press. DTP enables the user to specify colors according to printing industry standards, such as Pantone and TruMatch, so that the printer can understand precisely what colors to use. DTP software also prepares color separations for documents printed in color. **Color separations** are separate pages created for each of the four colors, which are combined to give the illusion of full color on the printed page.

At Issue

Who Really Owns the Software on Your PC?

Most people know that software can be very expensive. But even though you pay a lot for software, you do not necessarily *own* the programs on your PC. What happens, then, when you pay for a piece of software? Very few developers grant you actual ownership of a program, even after you "purchase" it. Instead of buying the software itself, you really pay for a license that grants you permission to install and use the software.

Why a License?

A license is an agreement between you and the software's maker. Under most software license agreements, the developer grants you a few rights to the program, but keeps all remaining rights.

Most licenses allow the user to install the program on a single computer, and to make one backup copy of the installation disk(s). If you want to install the software on a different computer, the agreement may state that you must uninstall it from the first computer. If you install the program on multiple PCs or make multiple duplicates of it, you may be violating the terms of the license. If the software developer catches you, it can take the software away from you and even press charges under applicable laws.

Software developers have good reasons for licensing software instead of selling it outright:

◆ **Piracy.** Software piracy, which costs developers billions of dollars every year, is the act of copying software without the developer's consent and without paying the developer, then selling or giving away the copies. If you install the program on multiple computers at the same time, that is piracy too. By licensing their products and maintaining some ownership of them, however, developers can take action against pirates.

◆ **Modifications**. Most license agreements state that you cannot make modifications to a program's source code. If developers allowed this, it would be an easy matter for others to make changes to a program, then try to claim the modified program as their own.

But even though the developer keeps most rights to a program, you still have some rights, too. If the program does not perform as you expected, you have the right to return or exchange it. You also should be able to expect reasonable customer support from the developer.

Where Will I Find the License?

The license agreement and its terms may be printed on the software's packaging; when you open the package and install the program, you are bound by the license's terms. But many developers are adding the agreement to the software installation process. This means that when you install the program, the agreement appears on the screen. You then click a button to indicate whether you accept or decline the agreement. If you accept, the installation continues. If you decline, the installation aborts.

If you do not accept the license agreement, you may be able to return the software. (Note, however, that many stores may not accept opened software packages for a refund, although you may be able to exchange it for a store credit or a different program.) If you accept a license agreement, however, you should honor its terms.

A software license agreement. This agreement appears on the screen when you install the program. You can accept or decline the agreement.

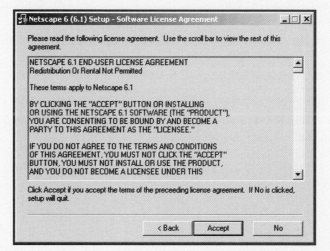

SUMMARY

- A word processor provides tools for creating, editing, and formatting text-based documents.

- In a typical word processor interface, you will find a document area, menu bar, toolbars, rulers, scroll bars, and a status bar.

- In the document window, a blinking insertion point shows you where characters will be placed as you type.

- To perform most kinds of editing or formatting on text, you first must select the text; any editing or formatting commands you issue are applied to all the selected text.

- Character formats include fonts, type size, and type styles.

- Paragraph formats include line and paragraph spacing, indents and alignment, borders, and shading.

- Document formats include margins, page size and orientation, headers, and footers.

- Word processors enable you to add graphics and sound files to your documents.

- You can use a spell checker, grammar checker, and thesaurus to improve the language of a word-processed document.

- Using mail merge, you can combine a form letter with contents from an address database and create a separate copy of the letter for each person in the database.

- Templates are predesigned documents. They simplify document design, enabling you to create professional-looking documents simply by typing your text.

- Word processing programs can create documents in HTML format, which are ready to be published as pages on the World Wide Web.

- Desktop publishing (DTP) software is specialized for designing and laying out long or complex documents. Documents created in DTP software are ready to be sent to a professional printer.

KEY TERMS

alignment, *322*
block, *320*
border, *323*
character formatting, *321*
color separation, *328*
column, *323*
deselect, *320*
desktop publishing (DTP)
    software, *328*
document area, *318*
document format, *323*
document window, *318*
edit, *320*

font, *321*
footer, *323*
format, *320*
grammar checker, *324*
header, *323*
highlight, *320*
indent, *322*
kerning, *328*
landscape orientation, *323*
leading, *328*
line spacing, *321*
mail merge, *325*
margin, *323*

master page, *328*
menu bar, *319*
paragraph formatting, *321*
paragraph spacing, *322*
paragraph, *321*
point, *321*
portrait orientation, *323*
ruler, *319*
scroll bar, *319*
section, *323*
shading, *323*
spell checker, *324*
status bar, *319*

tab stop, *322*
tab, *322*
table, *324*
template, *325*
thesaurus, *324*
toolbar, *319*
tracking, *328*
type style, *321*
word processing
    software, *318*
word processor, *318*
word wrap, *320*

KEY TERM QUIZ

Complete each statement by writing one of the terms listed under Key Terms in each blank.

1. Word processors enable you to perform three basic types of formatting: _____ , _____ , and _____ .

2. In a long document, a(n) _____ can be added at the bottom of the page to display page numbers or other information.

3. _____ are the white borders around the edge of the page, where text is not allowed to be typed.

4. You can divide a document into _____ and apply a different format to each.

5. _____ makes it easy to send the same letter to many people with the correct name and address printed on each letter.

SECTION QUIZ

True/False

Answer the following questions by circling True or False.

True   False   1. Word processing programs can work only with text.

True   False   2. As you enter text in a word processor, you do not need to press Enter at the end of a line, unless you want to start a new paragraph.

True   False   3. To mark text for editing, you select it.

True   False   4. If you want to create a Web page, you must use a special HTML program, not a word processor.

True   False   5. In a document, the left and right margins must always be the same.

Multiple Choice

Circle the word or phrase that best completes each statement.

1. Most word processors feature one or more _____ , which provide tools that resemble buttons.
   A. menu bars   **B.** toolbars   **C.** status bars

2. Word processors feature built-in language tools, such as _____ .
   A. spell checkers   **B.** grammar checkers   **C.** both A and B

3. On the screen, selected text is _____ .
   A. highlighted   **B.** deleted   **C.** neither A nor B

4. A(n) _____ is a position, on screen and in a document, measured from the left margin.
   A. tab stop   **B.** Backspace   **C.** insertion point

5. Newsletters are commonly laid out in a _____ format.
   A. tabular   **B.** tabbed   **C.** column

REVIEW QUESTIONS

In your own words, briefly answer the following questions.

1. In a word processor, what makes a block of text?

2. How does a spell checker work?

3. What happens when you press Enter in a word processor?

4. What is the advantage of using a word processor's templates?

5. What are tab stops?

SECTION LABS

Complete the following exercise as directed by your instructor.

1. Practice some basic formatting:

   A. In your word processor's document area, type a few lines of text, allowing the lines to wrap when they reach the right edge of the screen. Press Enter, and type a new paragraph. Create several more paragraphs. (If you have trouble thinking of text to type, just copy a few paragraphs of text from this book.)

   B. Using the mouse, select a word. (Double-click the word, or drag the mouse pointer across it.) Click the Bold tool. Then deselect the word by pressing an arrow key on the keyboard. Select the word again, and click the Bold tool to turn off the effect.

   C. Select different words, lines, and paragraphs, and practice using other tools, such as a Font tool, a Font size tool, Italic, and Underline.

   D. Select an entire paragraph, and use the alignment tools to change its alignment. Deselect the paragraph when you are done.

   E. Select two or more paragraphs, and indent them from both the left and right margins.

   F. Close the program by clicking the Close button (the button marked with an **X** on the title bar). If the program prompts you to save the file, choose No.

Spreadsheet Software

OVERVIEW:
Crunching Data and
Presenting the Results

We live in a world that is run "by the numbers." It seems that we must work with more numerical data and financial information each day. Corporations track profits and losses, accountants manage huge balance sheets, and people balance their checkbook registers or try to maintain a household budget.

Whether their task is big or small, people commonly use spreadsheet programs to juggle all those numbers. When someone is "crunching the numbers," that person probably is using a spreadsheet.

As you will learn in this section, spreadsheets are amazing applications that can hold large amounts of numerical data arranged in rows and columns. A typical spreadsheet program provides all sorts of tools for arranging data, performing calculations, generating charts, and creating reports.

OBJECTIVES

- Define and differentiate the terms *worksheet* and *spreadsheet*.
- Identify four types of data that can be entered in a worksheet.
- Explain how cell addresses are used in spreadsheet programs.
- Explain what a formula is and how formulas can be used in spreadsheet programs.
- List three types of data-analysis tools commonly found in spreadsheets and describe their use.

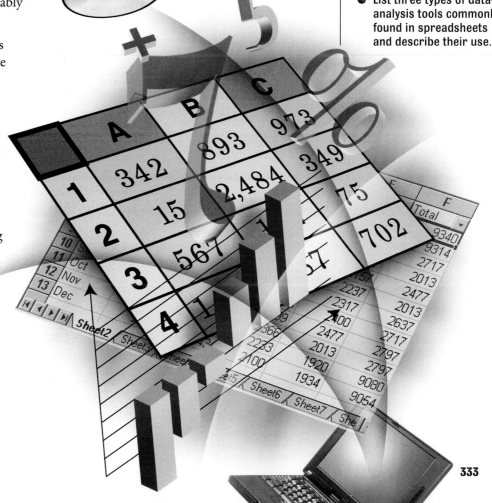

SPREADSHEET PROGRAMS AND THEIR USES

A **spreadsheet** program is a software tool for entering, calculating, manipulating, and analyzing sets of numbers. Spreadsheets have a wide range of uses—from family budgets to corporate earnings statements. As shown in Figure 9B.1, you can set up a spreadsheet to show information in numerous ways, such as the traditional row-and-column format (the format used in ledger books) or a slick report with headings and charts.

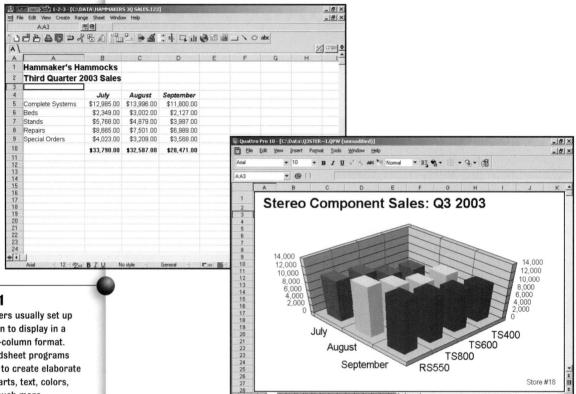

Figure 9B.1

Spreadsheet users usually set up their information to display in a classic row-and-column format. However, spreadsheet programs also enable you to create elaborate reports with charts, text, colors, graphics, and much more.

THE SPREADSHEET'S INTERFACE

Like a word processing program, a spreadsheet program lets you work in a main document area (also called a document window), which displays your data and various tools. In a spreadsheet program, you actually work in a document called a **worksheet** (or sheet, as it is also called), and you can collect related worksheets in a **workbook** (which is called a notebook in some programs). Worksheets can be named, and a workbook can contain as many individual worksheets as your system's resources will allow.

A typical spreadsheet interface also provides a menu bar, toolbars, and a special **formula bar,** where you can create or edit data and formulas in the worksheet. Scroll bars help you navigate a large worksheet, and at the bottom of the window, a status bar tells you specific information about the worksheet.

An empty worksheet (one without any data) looks like a grid of rows and columns. The intersection of any column and row is called a **cell,** as shown in Figure 9B.2. You interact with a spreadsheet primarily by entering data into individual cells. A typical worksheet contains thousands of individual cells.

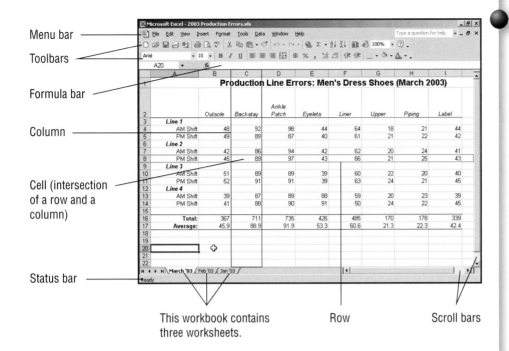

Menu bar
Toolbars
Formula bar
Column
Cell (intersection of a row and a column)
Status bar

This workbook contains three worksheets.
Row
Scroll bars

Figure 9B.2

Microsoft Excel's interface features tools common to nearly all spreadsheet programs.

Early spreadsheet programs provided only one worksheet at a time. Unlike current workbooks, which provide multiple sheets, earlier programs could support only one worksheet per file. Now programs provide **3-D worksheets,** which are like a pad of worksheets (see Figure 9B.3). This feature lets you perform calculations in one worksheet, but your calculations also can use data from a different worksheet in the same workbook, or from worksheets in other workbooks.

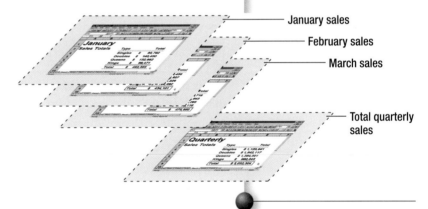

January sales
February sales
March sales
Total quarterly sales

Figure 9B.3

3-D worksheets let you perform calculations that include data from different sheets. For example, you can create three worksheets, each containing sales data for a different month. A fourth worksheet is used to create totals for the quarter.

ENTERING DATA IN A WORKSHEET

A worksheet's cells can hold several types of data, including labels (ordinary text), values (numbers), dates, and formulas (statements that perform calculations). Cells also can hold graphics, audio files, and video or animation files. To the spreadsheet program, each type of data has a particular use and is handled in a unique manner.

Entering data in a worksheet is simple. Using the mouse or arrow keys, you select a cell to make it active. The active cell is indicated by a **cell pointer,** a rectangle that makes the active cell's borders look bold (see Figure 9B.4).

To navigate the worksheet, you need to understand its system of **cell addresses.** All spreadsheets use row and column identifiers as the basis for their cell addresses. If you are working in the cell where column B intersects with row 3, for example, then the active cell's address is B3.

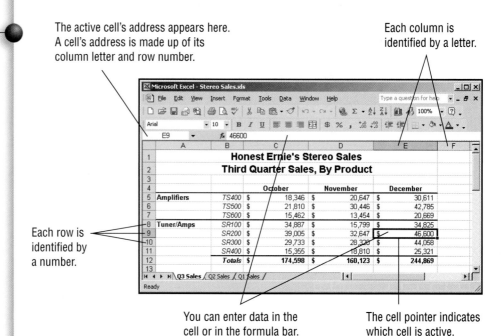

The active cell's address appears here.
A cell's address is made up of its
column letter and row number.

Each column is
identified by a letter.

Each row is
identified by
a number.

You can enter data in the
cell or in the formula bar.

The cell pointer indicates
which cell is active.

When you have selected a cell, you simply type the data into it. When a cell is active, you also can type its data into the formula bar. The formula bar is handy, because it displays much more data than the cell can. If a cell already contains data, you can edit it in the formula bar.

You also can use the spreadsheet's Cut, Copy, and Paste features to duplicate and move data to various parts of the worksheet. These features work among the different sheets in a workbook, from one workbook to another, and between the spreadsheet and other applications.

Labels

Worksheets can contain text—called **labels** (names for data values)—as well as values and formulas. In spreadsheets, text usually is used to identify a value or series of values (as in a row or column heading) or to describe the contents of a specific cell (such as a total). Labels help you make sense of a worksheet's contents (see Figure 9B.5). It is important to remember that values and formulas can be used in calculations, but labels cannot.

These labels are
column headings
that describe the
contents of the
cells below them.

These labels identify
the data in the cells
to their right.

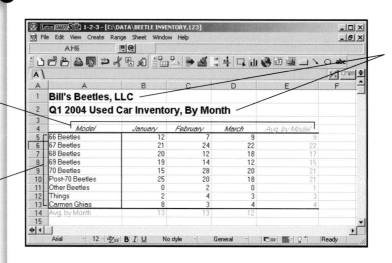

These labels are
used as titles
for the sheet.

Values

In a spreadsheet, a **value** is any number you enter or any number that results from a computation. You might enter a series of values in a column so that you can total them. Or you might enter several different numbers that are part of an elaborate calculation. Spreadsheets can work with whole numbers, decimals, negative numbers, currency, and other types of values, including scientific notation.

Dates

Dates are a necessary part of most worksheets, and spreadsheet programs can work with date information in many ways. A date may be added to a worksheet simply to indicate when it was created. Spreadsheets also can use dates in performing calculations, as when calculating late payments on a loan. If the spreadsheet knows the payment's due date, it can calculate late fees based on that date.

Formulas

The power of the spreadsheet lies in **formulas,** which calculate numbers based on values or formulas in other cells. You can create many kinds of formulas manually to do basic arithmetic operations, calculus or trigonometric operations, and so on.

Spreadsheets make it simple to perform calculations on a set of numbers. Suppose, for example, that the manager of a real estate office wants to calculate the commissions paid to agents over a specific time period. Figures 9B.6 and 9B.7 show a simple formula that takes the total sales for each agent and calculates the commission for that total. If any part of the formula (either the sales total or the commission percentage) changes, the formula can automatically recalculate the resulting commission.

NORTON
ONLINE

Visit **www.norton.glencoe.com** for more information on **formulas.**

Figure 9B.6
An example of a formula used to calculate simple percentages

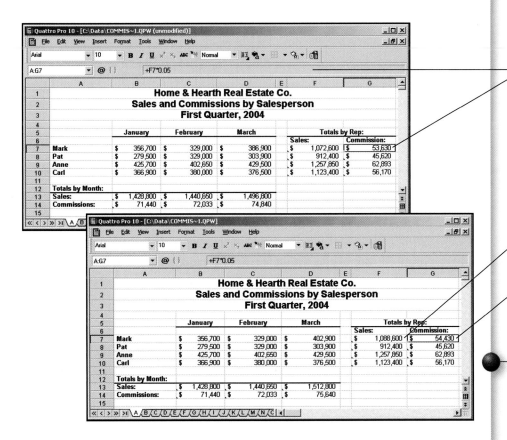

This cell contains a simple formula which multiplies total sales by a commission percentage. Notice that the cell displays the results of the formula, rather than the formula itself.

When this agent's sales total changes...

...the commission is automatically recalculated.

Figure 9B.7
Spreadsheet formulas can recalculate automatically if any of their base data changes.

Cell References and Ranges

Formulas typically refer to the values in other cells throughout the worksheet. To reduce time and errors, you can use a cell reference in formulas. A **cell reference** tells the formula to look up the contents of the referenced cell; this feature saves you the trouble of typing the referenced cell's contents into the formula. If the referenced cell's contents change, the change is reflected automatically in the formula that refers to the cell.

The most common method is to refer to the cell by its address, such as A1, B10, or Y254. Therefore, if you want to add the values in cells B13 and C16, your formula might look like this: =B13+C16. A cell reference can refer to one or more cells in the same worksheet, in a different worksheet from the same workbook, or in a different workbook. Sophisticated worksheets that draw data from many different sources may use dozens or even hundreds of formulas containing cell references.

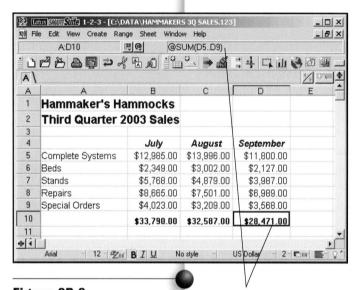

Figure 9B.8

An example of the SUM function in a Lotus 1-2-3 worksheet

This cell contains a SUM function, which adds the values in the cells above it.

If your formula uses cells that are contiguous, you can refer to all the cells at once as a **range** (also called a block). For example, in Excel, the formula =SUM(B4,C4,D4) can be written =SUM(B4:D4). (The SUM function calculates the total of the values in a specified range of cells.) Ranges can consist of a group of cells in a column, a row, or even a group that includes several rows and columns. For example, a range of B3:D14 includes the whole block that has B3 as the upper left corner and D14 as the lower right corner.

You can even give names to cells or cell ranges, instead of using their row and column addresses. After you assign a name to a cell, you can include the name, rather than the cell address, in formulas. The formula =SUM(B4,C4,D4) could appear as =SUM (April_Income, May_Income, June_Income). This makes the formula much more comprehensible, because words convey more meaning than cell addresses.

Functions

Spreadsheets come with many built-in formulas, called **functions,** that perform specialized calculations automatically. You can include these functions in your own formulas. Some functions are simple, such as the COUNT function, which counts how many values are in a range of cells. Many functions are complex. You may not know the mathematical equations for a loan payment or the depreciation of an asset using the double declining balance method. By using spreadsheet functions, however, you can arrive at the answer.

You add **arguments** within the parentheses of the function. Arguments are the values (often cell references) that the function uses in its operation. The number and type of arguments used depend on the function.

The most commonly used function is the SUM function (see Figure 9B.8), which adds a list of numbers to get a total. In the following formula, the SUM function's argument is a range: @SUM(D5..D9). This formula adds the values in the five cells that make up the range D5 through D9.

PRODUCTIVITY Tip

Automating Your Work with Macros

Although you may think your favorite software program saves you a great deal of time and energy, it probably could save you a great deal more if you used its most powerful tools—macros.

What Is a Macro?

Simply put, a macro is a list of commands, keystrokes, or other actions that has been saved and given a name. When you create a macro, you record a series of actions. When you replay the macro, it repeats those actions for you. You can use macros to automate nearly any task that requires multiple steps—no matter how many steps are involved.

Many commercial applications support macros, and some even feature an array of built-in, predefined macros that you can use right away or customize to suit your own work style. These applications usually allow you to create your own macros to automate tasks that you perform frequently or that require several steps (making them difficult to do manually).

Creating a Macro

Suppose, for example, that you are using a word processor to clean up a collection of old documents, which were keyed by someone who always inserted two blank spaces after every period. Today, it is more common to insert only one blank space after a period. One of your tasks is to eliminate all the extra blank spaces from the documents. To make this change to a document, you can scan through the document one line at a time, replacing the extra spaces as you find them. Or you can use the word processor's Find and Replace commands to automate the process. This function can search the document; when it finds a period followed by two spaces, it replaces them with a period followed by one space. Manually running the Find/Replace feature, however, can still take a lot of time.

If your word processor supports macros, you can create a new macro that does the job for you. Just open one of the documents, start the word processor's macro-recording feature, and manually perform the Find/Replace process while the recorder runs. You then can save the macro, give it a name (such as "Period_and_One_Space"), and assign it to a shortcut

Editing a macro with Visual Basic for Applications, in Microsoft Word

key (such as Alt+1) or a toolbar button, depending on your program's macro capabilities. Afterward, you can run the macro with the click of a mouse or by pressing a simple key combination, instead of manually repeating all the steps yourself.

Macros can be as simple or as complex as necessary, and you can create macros for nearly any task. In a spreadsheet, for example, you might create a macro that selects a column of data, applies a specific format, sorts the data, and inserts a function (like SUM) at the bottom. In a graphics program, you might create a macro that opens a group of image files, sizes them and adjusts their color settings, and prints them out on individual sheets, each identified by its file name. A macro can even include other macros, enabling you to perform multiple tasks at one time.

In fact, macros have become so popular and powerful that many productivity applications feature built-in programming languages that you can use to create macros. These languages enable advanced users to incorporate real programming functions (such as variables and loops) into their macros to create "programs within programs." Microsoft Office's programs, for example, support an advanced macro language called Visual Basic for Applications (VBA). The programs in Lotus SmartSuite support LotusScript, and Corel's WordPerfect Office suite supports a language called PerfectScript.

Complete each statement by filling in the blank(s).

1. A(n) _____ is a software tool for entering, calculating, manipulating, and analyzing numbers.

2. In a worksheet, the active cell is indicated by a(n) _____ .

3. A(n) _____ is any number that you enter or any number that results from a calculation.

EDITING AND FORMATTING A WORKSHEET

After a worksheet has been created, anything in it can be edited. Like word processors, spreadsheet programs are extremely accommodating when you want to make changes. To change a label or a date, you simply select its cell and make the desired changes. You can manually edit any part of a formula or function, simply by selecting its cell and making your changes in the formula bar.

Spreadsheet programs make it easy to move, copy, or delete the contents of cells. You also can insert or delete rows and columns. You can add new sheets to a workbook file or delete worksheets you no longer need.

Spreadsheet programs offer numerous formats specifically for numbers. Numbers can appear as dollars and cents, percentages, dates, times, and fractions. They can be shown with or without commas, decimal points, and so forth. In addition to number formats, spreadsheets offer a choice of fonts and type styles, shadowed borders, and more. You also can create special effects by adding graphics, such as clip art, to your worksheets.

Figure 9B.9
A worksheet containing data about stereo sales

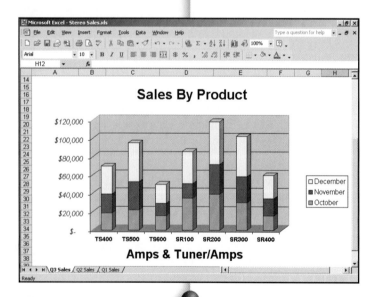

Figure 9B.10
The data from Figure 9B.9, summarized in a chart

ADDING CHARTS

A popular feature of spreadsheet software is the ability to generate **charts** based on numeric data. Charts make data easier to understand—for example, when presenting data to an audience. You often will see charts in business presentations, yet you rarely will see the worksheets used to create the charts.

The worksheet in Figure 9B.9 lists the total sales of various stereo components over a three-month period. Making quick conclusions based on this data is difficult. You must look carefully and do some mental arithmetic to determine which products sold best and which month had the best sales. But when the information is displayed in a chart, as in Figure 9B.10, you can see easily which products have performed best and which month had the best sales results.

With spreadsheets, creating a chart is simple. The one in Figure 9B.10 was created with just a few mouse clicks. Select the data you want to chart, select a chart type (bar chart, line chart, pie chart, or scatter chart, for example), and set the desired chart options. After the chart is created, you can continue to adjust its appearance using a set of special chart tools.

ANALYZING DATA IN A SPREADSHEET

You can use a worksheet to analyze data. Most spreadsheet programs enable you to use three useful techniques:

◆ **What-if analysis** is the process of using a spreadsheet to test how alternative scenarios affect numeric results. All spreadsheets allow you to do simple what-if analyses. You easily can change one part of a formula or a cell that it refers to and see how that change affects the rest of the worksheet. A more sophisticated type of what-if analysis is a table that automatically calculates the results based on any number of assumptions. Figure 9B.11 shows such a table; it calculates the monthly mortgage payment for several possible interest rates.

B7	= =PMT(B4/12,B5*12,-B3)				
	A	B	C	D	E	F
1	Mortgage Payment Examples				
2				Other Possible Interest Rates	
3	Total Mortgage:	125000			
4	Interest Rate:	8.25%		7.50%	$1,158.77
5	Years Paid:	15		7.75%	$1,176.59
6				8.00%	$1,194.57
7	Monthly Payment:	$1,212.68		8.25%	$1,212.68
8				8.50%	$1,230.92
9					

Figure 9B.11
Monthly mortgage payments based on different interest rates

What-if analysis is such an important tool that spreadsheets offer yet another way to do it. You can create several scenarios or versions of the same spreadsheet, each one containing different assumptions reflected in its formulas. In the mortgage loan example, you can create a best-case scenario that assumes you will find a house for $100,000 and an interest rate of 7.5%. Your worst-case scenario might be a house for $150,000 and an interest rate of 9%. Then you can create a report summarizing the different scenarios.

◆ **Goal seeking** finds values for one or more cells that make the result of a formula equal to a value you specify. In Figure 9B.12, cell B7 is the result of the Payment (PMT) formula. In this case, you know the maximum monthly payment you can afford is $1,200, so you want cell B7 to be your starting point. The bank is offering an interest rate of 8.25% over 15 years. The total mortgage, cell B3, can be calculated from the monthly payment, years paid, and interest rate.

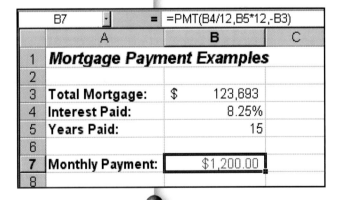

B7	= =PMT(B4/12,B5*12,-B3)	
	A	B	C
1	Mortgage Payment Examples		
2			
3	Total Mortgage:	$ 123,693	
4	Interest Paid:	8.25%	
5	Years Paid:	15	
6			
7	Monthly Payment:	$1,200.00	
8			

Figure 9B.12
The result of a goal-seeking operation

◆ **Sorting** is another data-analysis tool. When you sort data, you arrange it in a specific manner based on certain criteria, such as by date, dollar amount, or alphabetically. After data is sorted, it may be easier to perform calculations on the results.

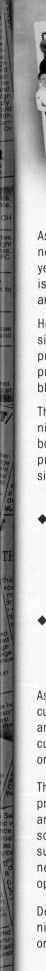

COMPUTERS
in your career

Help Desk and Technical Support Specialists

As long as people have been using computers, they have needed help with them. This fact has not changed for years, and it probably never will change. That is why there is an ongoing demand for qualified help desk workers and technical support specialists.

Help desk and technical support specialists perform a similar function. That is, they help people use their computers and software. Their jobs may involve explaining procedures, doing on-the-spot training, and troubleshooting.

The differences between a help desk worker and a technical support worker are basically in name only—they both have the same goal of helping others use their computers. Generally, however, these two types of professionals work in different environments:

◆ Help desk professionals usually are employed by a company to help its other employees with the computer systems they use at work. Suppose, for example, that you work for a large retailer and use its specialized order management or customer relationship management (CRM) software. If you need help using the program, you can call the company's internal help desk to ask for assistance. In many cases, the help desk representative will try to help you over the phone. If necessary, he or she may actually come to your desk and try to help you in person.

◆ Technical support specialists usually are employed by a company to help its customers use the products they have purchased from the company. If you have ever had trouble with a computer program and called the manufacturer for help, then you probably spoke with a technical support specialist.

As described here, a help desk worker assists internal customers—that is, workers within his or her company—and a technical support specialist works with external customers—that is, people who buy products from his or her company.

The qualifications for help desk and technical support professionals cover a wide range. This is because there are so many kinds of products (including hardware, software, networking, and others) that need to be supported. In general, however, any such professional needs a strong understanding of computer concepts, operating systems, and standard applications.

Depending on his or her employer, the help desk/technical support worker may need specialized training in one or more areas.

For example, a help desk worker may need additional training to assist other employees with special tools they must use. This is especially important in large corporations that use highly customized software or proprietary programs that have been developed specifically for the company's use. In such cases, help desk workers are often the first line of assistance for frustrated users, and they must have a thorough knowledge of the operation of these programs.

The same applies to technical support personnel. They must be experts in the products their own company produces, and they must have access to detailed product documentation and procedural instructions in order to assist frustrated customers. In most cases, these workers get product training directly from the developers or engineers who design the product.

SUMMARY

- Spreadsheet programs provide tools for working with numerical data.

- In addition to standard interface components, a spreadsheet also provides a formula bar where you can enter, view, and edit data.

- In a spreadsheet program, you work in a worksheet. Worksheets can be collected into groups called workbooks.

- A worksheet contains a series of columns and rows. Each row-and-column intersection is called a cell. Cells contain the data in the worksheet.

- Each cell is identified by a cell address, which is the combination of the cell's column letter and row number.

- You can enter text, values, dates, and formulas in the cells of a worksheet.

- Formulas are used to perform calculations in the worksheet. Formulas can use cell references to use data in other cells.

- A function is a predefined formula provided by the spreadsheet program.

- You can select a contiguous group of cells, called a range, for formatting or editing.

- Values and dates can be formatted in numerous ways.

- Spreadsheet programs provide charting tools that enable you to create graphical representations of your data. To create a chart, select the data to be charted, select a chart type, and set the desired chart options. The spreadsheet program creates the chart for you.

- Spreadsheets are useful for analyzing your data. Analysis can help you reach a desired numeric result. A what-if analysis lets you test different scenarios to see how each affects the results of a calculation. Goal seeking and sorting are other common data analysis tools found in spreadsheets.

KEY TERMS

3-D worksheet, *335*
argument, *338*
cell, *334*
cell address, *335*
cell pointer, *335*
cell reference, *338*
chart, *340*

formula, *337*
formula bar, *334*
function, *338*
goal seeking, *341*
label, *336*
range, *338*
sorting, *341*

spreadsheet, *334*
value, *337*
what-if analysis, *341*
workbook, *334*
worksheet, *334*

KEY TERM QUIZ

Complete each statement by writing one of the terms listed under Key Terms in each blank.

1. _____ are like a pad of worksheets.

2. A column letter and a row number combine to form a(n) _____ .

3. A(n) _____ shows you which cell is active in a worksheet.

4. _____ are built-in formulas that perform specialized calculations automatically.

5. When you _____ data, you arrange it in a specific manner.

SECTION QUIZ

True/False

Answer the following questions by circling True or False.

True	False	**1.** A spreadsheet and a worksheet are different names for the same item.
True	False	**2.** You can edit worksheet data directly in a cell or in the formula bar.
True	False	**3.** A label is any number that you enter or any number that results from a computation.
True	False	**4.** A range is a group of contiguous cells.
True	False	**5.** After adding data to a worksheet, you must load it into a database program if you want to analyze the data.

Multiple Choice

Circle the word or phrase that best completes each statement.

1. To navigate a worksheet, you should understand its system of _____ .
   A. cell addresses   **B.** spreadsheets   **C.** neither A nor B

2. _____ can help you make sense of a worksheet's contents.
   A. Cell pointers   **B.** Labels   **C.** Cell references

3. A _____ can calculate numbers based on values or formulas in other cells.
   A. chart   **B.** cell reference   **C.** formula

4. _____ are the values that a function uses in its operation.
   A. Arguments   **B.** Formulas   **C.** Subroutines

5. In _____ , you use a spreadsheet to test how alternative scenarios affect numeric results.
   A. what-if analysis   **B.** sorting   **C.** either A or B

REVIEW QUESTIONS

In your own words, briefly answer the following questions.

1. What is the difference between a spreadsheet and a worksheet?

2. Name the four kinds of data you can enter in a worksheet.

3. What do formulas do?

4. What is the advantage of using charts?

5. Describe the purpose of goal seeking in a spreadsheet program.

SECTION LABS

Complete the following exercise as directed by your instructor.

1. Practice using a worksheet:

   A. In your worksheet's document area, type numbers in cells A1 through A5.

   B. Using the mouse, select all the values in this range. (Click in cell A1. Then drag the mouse pointer down through cell A5.)

   C. Click in cell A6 and type =SUM(A1:A5). Press Enter. The total of the values in cells A1 to A5 should appear in cell A6. If it does not, ask your instructor for help.

   D. Click in cell A3, and press Delete. The value in the cell disappears, and the total in cell A6 changes.

   E. Issue the Undo command. (There should be an Undo tool on the toolbar. If not, ask your instructor for assistance.) The value is returned to cell A3, and the total in cell A6 updates once more.

   F. Click in cell B6 and type =A6*0.05. Press Enter. The formula's result appears in cell B6.

   G. Close the spreadsheet program by clicking the Close button. If the program prompts you to save the worksheet, choose No.

UNIT PROJECTS

UNIT LABS

Complete the following exercises using a computer in your classroom, lab, or home.

1. **Get Charted.** Spreadsheet programs make it easy to create charts and provide lots of options for doing so. Take the following steps:

    A. Launch your spreadsheet program. A blank worksheet appears.

    B. In cells B1 through D1, type the words **January, February,** and **March.** You will chart the sales figures of these months.

    C. In cells A2 through A4, type the words **Widgits, Whatsits,** and **Whosits.** You will chart the sales figures of these products.

    D. In cells B2 through D4, type numerical values representing the monthly sales of each product. Then select cells A1 through D4.

    E. Issue your spreadsheet's Chart command. It will provide you with instructions for picking a chart type and chart options.

    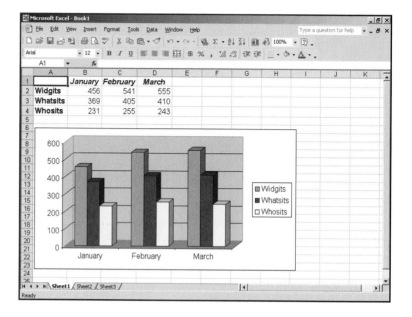

    When you are done, your spreadsheet should display a chart. Close the spreadsheet program without saving the worksheet.

2. **Copy and Paste.** You can create a document in one application that contains data from a different application. Create a document now, using your word processor and spreadsheet. Take the following steps:

    A. Launch your word processor and your spreadsheet. Each program will open in its own window. Switch to the word processor so that it becomes the active application.

    B. Type three short paragraphs of text, pressing Enter after each one. Move the insertion point to the beginning of the third paragraph, and press Enter to create a blank paragraph. Press the up arrow button to move the insertion point to the blank paragraph.

    C. Switch to the spreadsheet program. Fill cells A1 through D5 with data of any kind. Now select the entire range.

    D. Issue the Copy command in your spreadsheet program. The cells' data is copied.

    E. Switch to the word processor, and issue the Paste command. The data from the spreadsheet program appears in the word processor's document.

    F. In the word processor, select the spreadsheet's data and see what changes you can make to it. For example, can you format it, type over it, or delete it?

    G. Close both applications without saving either document.

3. Find Some Fonts. The Internet is a good place to find and acquire fonts. Some fonts can be downloaded from various Web sites at no cost. Other fonts can be purchased over the Web. Visit these Web sites and study the available fonts, but do not download any fonts without your instructor's permission.

- Font Mania—**http://www.webfxmall.com/fonts/index1.html**
- Microsoft Typography—**http://www.microsoft.com/typography/default.asp**
- CNet—**http://www.cnet.com/** (Use the Search tool to search on the term "fonts.")
- ZDNet—**http://www.zdnet.com/** (Use the Search tool to search on the term "fonts.")

DISCUSSION QUESTIONS

As directed by your instructor, discuss the following questions in class or in groups.

1. Do you think that using a spell checker and a grammar checker for all your final documents is a sufficient substitute for proofreading? Explain your answer.

2. What basic feature of spreadsheet software provides the real power behind its calculation capabilities? Describe one operation that demonstrates this capability.

RESEARCH AND REPORT

Using your own choice of resources (such as the Internet, books, magazines, and newspaper articles), research and write a short paper discussing one of the following topics.

- The ways word processing software is used in business
- The ways spreadsheet programs are used in business
- The impact today's standard productivity applications have had in the workplace

When you are finished, proofread and print your paper, and give it to your instructor.

ETHICAL ISSUES

Word processors and spreadsheets have made tools such as typewriters and ledger books obsolete. But like any powerful tool, they can be used and abused. With this thought in mind, discuss the following questions in class.

1. Word processors make it easy to create documents and to copy documents created by others. Many people download others' writings and research from the Internet and disks and then use the documents as their own. Would you use this tactic, say, to create a term paper for school? Do you think it is legally or morally right?

2. Spreadsheets give us fast access to numerical data and analysis. Some say that this access is partly to blame for our "numbers-oriented society," in which companies are run by numbers, with little apparent regard for issues like product quality, customer satisfaction, or loyalty to employees. Do you agree?

UNIT 10

Application Software: Presentation Programs and Databases

UNIT CONTENTS

This unit contains the following sections:

Section 10A: Presentation Programs

- ▸ Presentation Program Basics
- ▸ Integrating Multiple Data Sources in a Presentation
- ▸ Presenting Slide Shows

Section 10B: Database Management Systems

- ▸ Databases and Database Management Systems
- ▸ Working With a Database

The Interactive Browser Edition CD-ROM provides additional labs and activities to apply concepts from this unit.

Presentation Programs

OVERVIEW:
Sharing Ideas and Information

If you have ever attended a seminar or lecture that included slides or overhead transparencies that were projected on a wall screen or displayed on a computer screen or video monitor, then you probably have seen the product of a modern presentation program. Presentation programs enable the user to create and edit colorful, compelling presentations that can be displayed in various ways and used to support any type of discussion.

Presentation programs are used to produce a series of **slides**—single-screen images that contain a combination of text, numbers, and graphics (such as charts, clip art, or pictures), often on a colorful background. Slides can be simple or sophisticated. Depending on your needs, you can turn a basic slide show into a multimedia event by using the built-in features of many presentation programs.

Presentation software is an important tool for anyone who must present information to a group. Sales and marketing professionals, for example, maintain several "stock" presentations that they can customize for different clients or products. Managers use slides to present information to employees, such as lists of benefits and responsibilities explained during new-hire orientation. Teachers and trainers commonly rely on slides in the classroom to serve as a roadmap for discussion.

OBJECTIVES

- Identify four interface elements found in most presentation programs.
- Describe the process of creating a presentation.
- Name three media sources that might be used in a multimedia presentation.
- List at least three ways that slides can be presented from a presentation program.

PRESENTATION PROGRAM BASICS

Before the first PC-based presentation programs were developed, creating a presentation could be a tedious and time-consuming ordeal. To start, you needed to create all the contents for your slides, which could entail handwriting the text or drawing graphics for each slide, then taking the materials to a professional print shop for typesetting. Creating the actual slides or overhead transparencies was a separate process, which could be as simple as using a photocopier or another specialized mechanical duplicating device to print the content onto transparency sheets, or hiring a photographer to create 35-mm slides of the content. The result was a set of slides or a set of transparencies that could be used repeatedly (see Figure 10A.1)—but which could never be changed without going through the entire process again.

Figure 10A.1
The principles behind presentations have not changed, but the process for creating presentations has changed radically.

The process changed for the better, however, with the advent of computerized tools that were designed specifically to aid in creating slides. **Presentation programs** provide powerful design tools that make it easy for anyone to outline, create, edit, arrange, and display complex slide presentations. Functions—such as drag-and-drop, cut, copy, and paste—that are used in presentation programs also are found in most desktop applications; thus, presentation programs are as familiar and comfortable to use as your favorite word processor.

The Presentation Program's Interface

The typical presentation program displays a slide in a large document window and provides a wide array of tools for designing and editing slides. Presentation programs provide many of the features found in word processors (for working with text), spreadsheets (for creating charts), and paint programs (for creating and editing simple graphics). You can add elements to the slide simply by typing, making menu or toolbar choices, and dragging. As you work on the slide, you see exactly how it will look when it is shown to an audience.

Figure 10A.2
Interface features of Microsoft PowerPoint, a popular presentation program

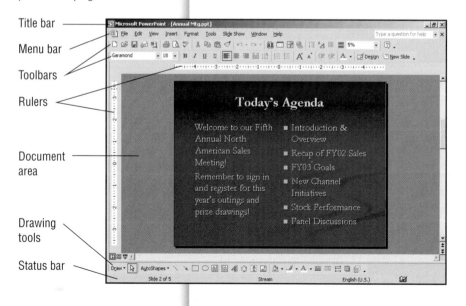

Title bar

Menu bar

Toolbars

Rulers

Document area

Drawing tools

Status bar

Figure 10A.2 shows a slide designed in Microsoft Power Point, a popular presentation program. Note that the status bar says that the presentation contains five slides. A presentation can contain a single slide or hundreds. Most presentation programs let you save a set of slides as a group in one file so that you can open the related slides and work with them together.

A windowed presentation program includes a menu bar, one or more toolbars (for managing files, formatting, drawing, and doing other tasks), rulers, slide-viewing or navigation buttons that let you move from one slide to another, a status bar, and other tools.

Visit **www.norton.glencoe.com** for more information on **presentation programs**.

Creating a Presentation

Creating a presentation is simple; just choose the type of slide you want to create, and then start adding the content. A complete presentation usually includes multiple slides arranged in a logical order. As you go, you can insert new slides anywhere, copy slides from other presentations, and reorder the slides.

You can create slides from scratch (starting with a blank slide), but it is easier and faster to work with one of the presentation program's many templates. Like a template in a word processor, a presentation template is a predesigned document that already has coordinating fonts, a layout, and a background. Your presentation program should provide dozens of built-in templates, as shown in Figure 10A.3.

Figure 10A.3
Choosing a presentation template in PowerPoint

In preview mode, you can see how a template looks before you use it.

Figure 10A.4
Choosing a slide type in Lotus Freelance Graphics

After you select a template, you can quickly assemble a presentation by creating individual slides. To create a slide, you can choose a slide type, as shown in Figure 10A.4. Presentation programs provide several types of slides that can hold varying combinations of titles, text, charts, and graphics. You can choose a different type for each slide in your presentation, if you want.

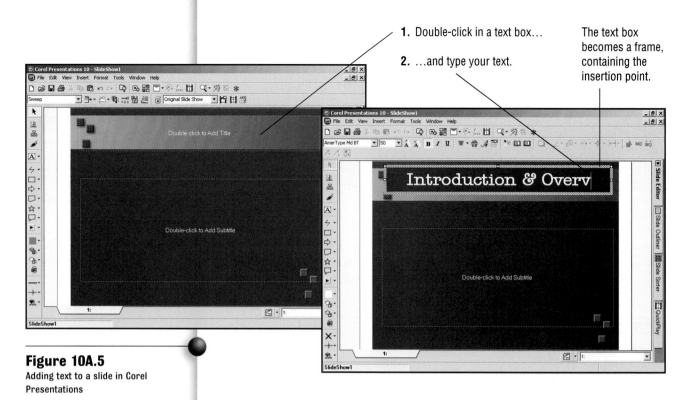

1. Double-click in a text box...

2. ...and type your text.

The text box becomes a frame, containing the insertion point.

Figure 10A.5
Adding text to a slide in Corel Presentations

After you select a slide type, the blank slide appears in the document window, ready for you to add text, charts, or graphics. The program provides special **text boxes** and **frames** (special resizable boxes for text and graphical elements) to contain specific types of content. These special boxes often contain instructions telling you exactly what to do. To add text to a text box, simply click in the box at the place where you want to insert text, and then type your text, as shown in Figure 10A.5. The text is formatted automatically, but you can easily reformat the text later, using many of the same formatting options that are available in word processors.

Adding charts, tables, clip art, or other graphics is nearly as easy (see Figure 10A.6). When you choose a slide type that contains a chart or a table, for example, you can create the chart or the table in a separate window, and then insert it in the slide.

Figure 10A.6
Creating a chart in PowerPoint

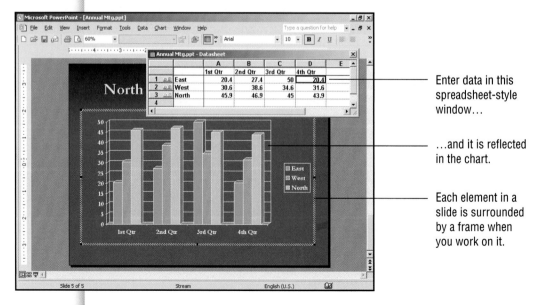

Enter data in this spreadsheet-style window...

...and it is reflected in the chart.

Each element in a slide is surrounded by a frame when you work on it.

To insert clip art or another type of graphic in a slide, you can select an image from your software's collection of graphics (as shown in Figure 10A.7) or import an image file, such as a scanned photograph or clip art. There also are many sources of free, downloadable clip art images on the World Wide Web. Built-in paint tools also enable you to draw simple graphics and add them to your slides. (These tools are handy if you want to add callouts to specific elements of a slide.)

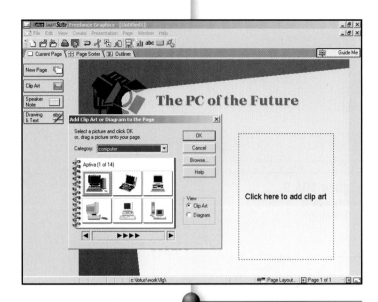

Formatting Slides

Because presentation programs are similar to a combination of word processor, spreadsheet, and paint programs, you easily can format slides in many ways, including:

◆ **Formatting Text.** Formatting text in a presentation program is just like formatting text in a word processor. Text in slides is usually in the form of titles, headings, and lists. Although a text box can hold multiple paragraphs, the paragraphs themselves are usually quite short. Most often, these paragraphs are formatted as bullets. To format text, you select it, and then apply formats by using the toolbars or menu options.

◆ **Resizing Frames.** When you add a chart or graphic to a slide, you may need to resize the chart or graphic to allow better spacing for other elements on the slide. Sometimes it is necessary to resize text boxes, too, if you type more or less text than the box can hold by default. Resizing is easy using frames that surround most of the elements in a slide. To resize a frame, click it;

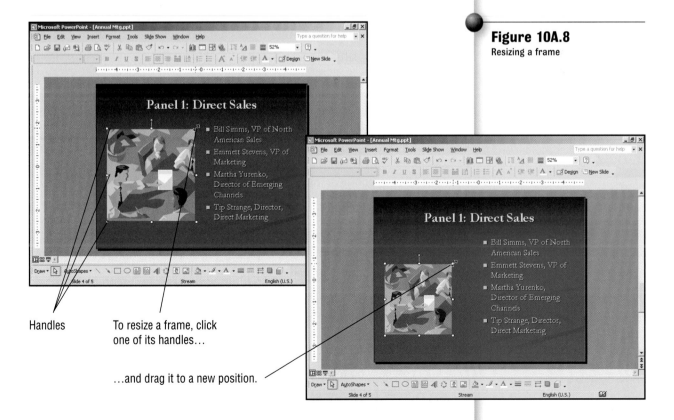

Handles

To resize a frame, click one of its handles…

…and drag it to a new position.

several **handles** will appear around it, as shown in Figure 10A.8. Handles are small boxes (usually white or black in color) that you can drag to resize the frame.

◆ **Adding Colors.** Adding color enables you to create a wide range of moods for your presentations; therefore, it is important to choose colors carefully. You also should make sure that the slides' colors complement one another and that they do not make text difficult to read (see Figure 10A.9).

Figure 10A.9
Setting a color scheme for a presentation

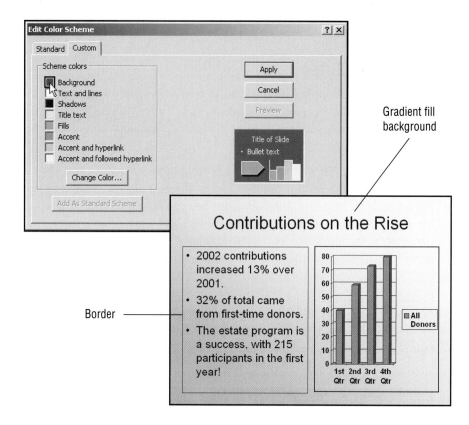

Figure 10A.10
Borders and backgrounds can make a dull presentation more appealing.

◆ **Adding a Background or Shading.** You can add depth to a plain presentation by giving it a shaded background and by placing borders around certain elements. Borders separate different elements and help hold the viewer's attention on individual parts of the slide. Shaded backgrounds provide depth and can make static information appear dynamic. A **gradient fill,** as shown in Figure 10A.10, changes color as it moves from one part of the slide to another. This effect can almost make the slide appear as if it is in motion.

Special Features of Presentation Programs

In addition to the quick creation of dynamic and detailed slides, a presentation program can help you make your presentations lively and engaging (a dynamic presentation will encourage your audience to pay attention and participate). Some special features found in presentation programs include the following:

◆ **Outlining.** Like any document with more than one part, a good presentation should be outlined (organized so information flows logically). An outlining tool enables you to organize your slides' contents as you create them by rearranging them and viewing them in order (see Figure 10A.11).

Visit **www.norton.glencoe.com** for more information on **adding graphics and audio files to a presentation.**

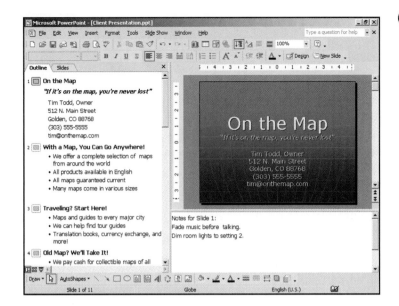

Figure 10A.11
Viewing a presentation's outline in PowerPoint

◆ **Annotations.** Speakers often prepare a set of notes (called **annotations**) to accompany their slides. Using a presentation program, you can prepare notes for each slide as you create your presentation. You can set up notes so they are visible only to you, or you can print them with or without the actual slide.

◆ **Animation.** You can use animation tools to make text pop up or crawl onto the screen, or to make slides "build" themselves by adding individual pieces of text that appear as you introduce them to the audience. You also can create animated **transitions,** a special effect that causes slides to blend together when you switch from one slide to the next. Popular transitions include the "fade" (where the first slide fades out and the next slowly appears) and the "blind" (where the first slide seems to disappear behind a closing Venetian blind, and the next slide appears as the blind reopens).

◆ **Sound and Video.** Slide presentations can be full-fledged multimedia events. You can embed a sound or video object into a slide, then play the object by double-clicking its icon during a presentation. All the multimedia objects can be played directly from the computer, if you have the appropriate sound and video display hardware.

◆ **Other Embedded Objects.** You can embed different types of objects, such as links to Web pages or other applications, in a slide in a presentation. When you click a link to a Web page, the Web page opens in a browser window; if you click the link to another application, the other application launches.

Complete each statement by filling in the blank(s).

1. A(n) _____ is a single-screen image that contains text and images, often on a colorful background.

2. A presentation _____ is a predesigned document with fonts, a layout, and a background.

3. You can resize a frame by dragging one of its _____ .

PRODUCTIVITY Tip

Putting Your Presentations Online

Viewing traditional presentations requires everyone to be in the same room at the same time in order to watch the slides being shown on a big screen or a monitor. If a person cannot attend the presentation at its scheduled time, the meeting will need to be rescheduled, or that person will have to view the slides separately. Either solution, however, means a hassle for everyone involved.

With the presentation programs and networking technologies that are available today, however, your audience members do not need to be in the same room—or the same country—to view your slides. They do not even have to view them at the same time. By publishing a presentation in HTML format, and then posting it on the Internet or an intranet, you can enable your audience to view your presentation whenever they want, as often as they want. Using the latest Web broadcasting features of presentation software, you can schedule an online broadcast of your presentation.

Converting to HTML

Like word processors and other types of applications, presentation programs let you save your slides in HTML format for use as Web pages. While this process is not the best technique for creating a personal home page, it is an easy way to make a presentation available online.

Suppose, for example, that you are giving a presentation, but some people cannot attend. By converting the presentation to HTML format and posting it on the Internet or an intranet, you make the presentation available for those persons to view online.

New presentation programs feature a "Save As HTML" or "Save As Web Page" command. When you issue this command, the program does all the work for you, converting each slide into a separate Web page. If you like, the software can embed navigation tools (such as forward and back buttons), hyperlinks, and other multimedia elements into

an HTML presentation. The finished product is ready to be viewed in a Web browser.

Broadcasting a Presentation

If you use PowerPoint and Outlook XP, you can do more than just convert a presentation to HTML format. Using these programs and the Internet, you can actually schedule an online broadcast of your presentation. To do this, you use Outlook to send invitations to the people you want to see the slides, telling them when the broadcast will occur and providing a Web address for the presentation.

Audience members visit the address at the same time, and you can begin the broadcast. If everyone has the right multimedia hardware and software, you can run your presentation online and provide a narration for others to hear. When you combine these capabilities with Internet-based conferencing software (such as Microsoft's NetMeeting), you can run a completely interactive presentation, in which the audience can speak and ask questions.

Viewing a presentation online and in HTML format. The presentation features navigation buttons and links. The viewer can zoom in or out on each slide, see the speaker's notes, and perform other actions.

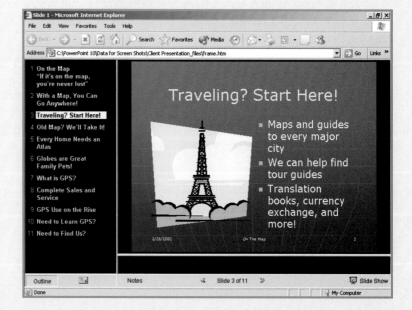

INTEGRATING MULTIPLE DATA SOURCES IN A PRESENTATION

In the days of manual presentations, a slide show typically contained two elements: the slides themselves and the speaker's voice. Adding other types of data required the data to be incorporated separately, played on cue, and perfectly timed. Also, the presenter may have been required to use other types of hardware—such as a tape player or VCR—during the presentation. If the separate media type (like a videotape) was viewed separately from the slides, it distracted the audience and created a potential stumbling block for the presenter.

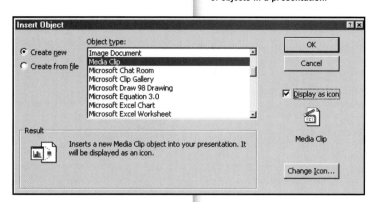

Figure 10A.12
You can embed different types of objects in a presentation.

Today's presentation programs enable you to incorporate many different types of media into a slide show. If you present the slides directly from the PC—instead of having them printed and placing them on a slide or overhead projector—you can actually embed different media objects, such as audio files, QuickTime movies, or animation in your slides (see Figure 10A.12). The objects can play without interrupting the flow of the presentation to use additional hardware, such as a tape player or VCR.

A media type can be any file that you store on the computer's disk. For example, it is possible to embed a link to a Word document, a Web page, an audio clip, or a full-motion video clip into a slide.

Figure 10A.13 shows a slide as it appears in "slide show" mode on a computer screen. In other words, this screen shows how the audience would see the slide in a presentation. In the slide's lower left corner, a small icon indicates that a sound file has been embedded as an audio object. When you click the icon, the sound file plays directly from the PC's disk.

Figure 10A.13
Using an audio clip in a slide

This icon represents an embedded media object. Click it, and a sound file plays.

PRESENTING SLIDE SHOWS

As mentioned earlier, presentations once required the use of a projector (slide or overhead) and a hard-copy version of the content, either on 35-mm slides or overhead transparencies. The presenter had to display each slide manually in a preset order. Jumping to a slide out of sequence meant quickly finding the right slide, pulling it, displaying it, and getting the presentation back on track. This tactic could be difficult if the presenter had to deal with a large group of slides or an impatient audience.

Thanks to presentation programs, you can present your slides directly from the computer's disk, along with any audio or video files that you embed in your slides. Your audience can view slides in several ways:

Figure 10A.14
You can get the best results from your slide shows if you present them directly from the PC's disk, using a display device that is appropriate for the audience and room size.

◆ **On the PC's Screen.** If you are presenting slides to a few people, your PC's monitor might be adequate for an informal slide show. Of course, the larger the monitor, the better your audience can see the slides. Also, note that flat-panel monitors are not well suited for this purpose because of their limited viewing angle. If you want to show slides to more than three or four people at a time, consider a different display method.

◆ **On a Large-Format Monitor.** Large-format CRT and gas plasma monitors can display your slides at the proper resolution and in a large enough format for a sizable audience to view comfortably. These devices are expensive and more difficult to transport than a standard monitor, but they may be the best solution for some presentation settings (see Figure 10A.14).

◆ **On a Television Screen.** Using a **PC-to-TV converter,** you can connect your computer to a standard television and view the PC's video output on the television monitor. While this solution may sound convenient, many compatibility issues must be considered (not all converters work with all televisions, for example), and televisions do not display images at the same resolution as a PC monitor. As a result, image quality may suffer when a PC-to-TV converter is used.

◆ **From a Digital Projector.** Portable, high-resolution digital projectors are expensive, but they can display slides to a large audience. These projectors plug into one of the PC's ports and accept the system's video output. New-generation projectors can display crisp images in only semidarkened rooms, and a projector displays the image at the same resolution as the PC's monitor.

Regardless of the method you use to project your slides, navigating a slide show is a simple process. You can move from one slide to the next by clicking the mouse button or pressing Enter. Or you can automate the presentation by setting a display time for each slide. Presentation programs make it easy to take slides out of sequence or rearrange slides during a presentation. You can even use the program's drawing tools to draw on a slide while it is being displayed.

NORTON
ONLINE

Visit www.norton.glencoe.com for more information on **tools for delivering a presentation.**

At Issue

Death by PowerPoint

Poorly designed presentations. Unprepared presenters. Slides with too much text. Slides with too little text. Too many slides for the time allotted. Too few slides that actually say something meaningful. Distracting animations. Annoying sound effects.

Legions of business professionals endure bad presentations every day, in a ritual referred to as "death by PowerPoint." In fact, the problem of ineffective presentations has become so bad that some managers have banned slide shows altogether.

It is easy to see why bad presentations are a plague on the business world. Presentation programs such as PowerPoint and Freelance Graphics put powerful design tools into the hands of everyday users—but they do not turn their presenters into designers. Many people make poor design choices by trying to stuff as many "cool tricks" into their slides as they can, by preparing too many slides, or by failing to prepare themselves to act as a narrator. Their presentations, while often complex, fail to accomplish the intended objectives and end up wasting their audience's time.

Subjecting an audience to "death by PowerPoint" can lead to severe consequences. Many business deals—sales, contract signings, hirings, and others—depend on the information presented in a slide show. If the presenter does not get it right, the deal can go right out the window.

How can you make sure that your presentations are not a painful ordeal for the audience? Professional presenters advise that you stick to a few basic design principles:

◆ **Keep it short and simple.** You should plan on each slide being on the screen for no more than two or three minutes. So, if your presentation is supposed to last 20 minutes, allow for a maximum of eight to ten slides. Each slide should focus on one unique topic and have no more than three to five bullet points.

◆ **Be consistent.** Use the same design and color scheme—and no more than two or three fonts—throughout the presentation. Make sure your text is worded consistently; if you use sentence fragments on one slide, use them on all slides.

◆ **Do not go overboard.** Animations, sound effects, and hyperlinks are cool, but they get annoying quickly. Use them only when needed for emphasis or when you want to be able to grab the viewers' attention.

◆ **Practice, practice, practice.** If you do not rehearse your presentation, your audience will know you are not well prepared. Rehearse as often as necessary to get your timing right and to make sure you can narrate the slides without a hitch. For best results, you may wish to have some colleagues review your rehearsals.

◆ **Remember: Timing is everything.** Presentation programs have a built-in timing feature that you can use to determine how long your slides are going to be on the screen. Use the timer as you rehearse.

◆ **Allow for audience reaction and interaction.** If your topic is interesting, and your presentation is crisp, your audience is more likely to respond. Your viewers may ask questions or even make comments. Be prepared by allowing some time for impromptu "Q-and-A" sessions during the presentation.

For a busy executive, nothing is worse than being stuck in a bad presentation.

SUMMARY

- Presentation programs enable you to create a series of slides that can be used to support a discussion.

- A presentation can be saved as a single file—containing one slide or many slides—that are used together.

- Slides can include different types of text, charts, tables, and graphics.

- Most presentation programs provide templates, which are predesigned slides.

- Slides can be formatted with different fonts, colors, backgrounds, and borders. Using frames, you can resize many of the elements in a slide.

- Presentation programs provide several special features that enable you to add annotations to your slide show, create animations within slides, convert a slide to an HTML document, and more.

- You can add different media types, such as audio or video files, to your slides.

- An efficient way to present a slide show is to display the slides directly from the PC's disk. This technique enables you to present slides out of order, or even mark slides as they appear on the screen.

- Depending on the size of your audience and room, you can display slides on the PC's monitor, project them onto a screen, or connect the PC to a television or larger display.

- You can move from one slide to the next manually, or you can automate the presentation so that each slide appears on screen for a set amount of time before being replaced by the next slide.

- You can print your slides and present them using a slide projector or overhead projector.

- If you present your slide show directly from your PC's disk (and if the system is connected to a suitable video and audio output device), you can present its multimedia elements.

KEY TERMS

annotation, *355*

frame, *352*

gradient fill, *354*

handle, *354*

PC-to-TV converter, *358*

presentation program, *350*

slide, *349*

text box, *352*

transition, *355*

KEY TERM QUIZ

Complete each statement by writing one of the terms listed under Key Terms in each blank.

1. A(n) _____ enables you to create colorful slides.

2. A(n) _____ is designed to hold text content in a slide.

3. To resize a frame, you can drag one of its _____ .

4. You can prepare a set of notes, called _____ , to accompany your slides.

5. Using a(n) _____ , you can connect your computer to a television.

SECTION QUIZ

True/False

Answer the following questions by circling True or False.

True   False   **1.** Before you can display a presentation, you must print it out and convert the hard copy into transparencies for use on a projector.

True   False   **2.** As you create a slide presentation, you can rearrange slides in any order.

True   False   **3.** To resize a frame, click it and drag its outline.

True   False   **4.** Annotations are notes that accompany slides in a presentation.

True   False   **5.** If you display a presentation from disk, you can show it only on your PC's monitor.

Multiple Choice

Circle the word or phrase that best completes each statement.

1. You use a presentation program to produce a series of _____ .
   A. objects   **B.** frames   **C.** slides

2. A presentation _____ is a predesigned document, with fonts, a layout, and a background.
   A. format   **B.** template   **C.** program

3. When you add text to a slide, you insert it in a _____ .
   A. text box   **B.** handle   **C.** chart

4. A _____ changes color as it moves from one part of the slide to another.
   A. background   **B.** border   **C.** gradient fill

5. A(n) _____ is a special effect that causes slides to blend together when you switch from one slide to the next.
   A. annotation   **B.** video   **C.** transition

REVIEW QUESTIONS

In your own words, briefly answer the following questions.

1. Before presentation programs were used, how were slide shows commonly created?

2. How do you add text in a text box when creating a slide?

3. What effect can you use to make a slide appear as if it were in motion?

4. What can you do with a slide if you save it in HTML format?

5. List four ways you can display a slide show to an audience.

SECTION LABS

Complete the following exercises as directed by your instructor.

1. Explore your presentation program's interface. When you launch the program, it will open with a new, blank slide ready for you to design, or by giving you options for the type of slide you want to create. Review the program's interface closely and identify the title bar, menu bar, toolbars, rulers, scroll bars, status bar, and other tools.

2. Follow your instructor's directions to view the list of templates provided by your presentation program. Review the templates and their basic appearance. Now, list the template you would choose if you had to give the following types of presentations:

Presentation	Template
Lecture on the Civil War	_____
Motivational Speech	_____
Pitch to prospective investors	_____
Orientation for new employees	_____

Database Management Systems

OVERVIEW:
The Mother of All Computer Applications

People need data, so we create all kinds of lists to store and organize it. A grocery list, a phone book, a library's card catalog, and an instructor's list of students are all organized lists of data. Likewise, computers need to store and manage lists of data, and this is the reason for the computerized database. In fact, many early attempts to build and program computers grew out of a need to manage large lists of data.

Today's computers are much more complex than early computers, but they still need an organized data source, and this need applies to just about every type of computer program. For example, a word processor maintains several databases— a dictionary of words for the spell checker and thesaurus, a list of available fonts, user preferences, data for mail merges, and other types of data.

Practically every application—even if it has nothing to do with words or organized lists—has grown from earlier programs that stored and processed data. Large commercial applications (such as facilities management or sales support software) may look very different from a common word processor, but there is still a database at the heart of each operation. In short, you can think of the database as the mother of all computer applications.

OBJECTIVES

- Define the terms *database* and *database management system* (DBMS).
- List at least three tasks that a DBMS enables users to do.
- Differentiate between flat-file databases and relational databases.
- List three steps needed to create a database.
- Explain the purpose of filters and forms.
- List three examples of query languages.

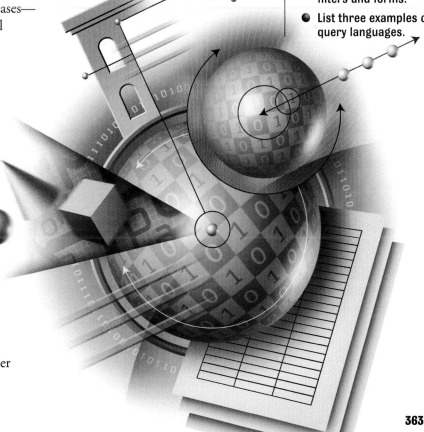

DATABASES AND DATABASE MANAGEMENT SYSTEMS

To make large collections of data useful, people and organizations use computers and an efficient data management system. Like a warehouse, a **database** is a collection of related data or facts. A **database management system (DBMS)** is a software tool that allows people to store, access, and process data or facts into useful information.

Database management is one of the primary reasons people use computers. Many large companies and organizations rely heavily on a commercial or custom DBMS to handle immense data resources. Often, a DBMS is custom-programmed to fit the exact needs of a company; it may be designed to run on a large mainframe computer system or a large client-server network.

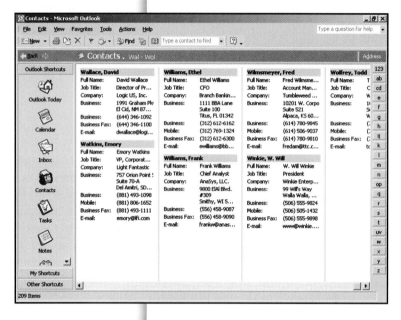

Personal computers have brought database management to the desktops of individuals in businesses and homes. Although the casual computer user may not need an inventory-tracking system, home users utilize commercial DBMS products to maintain address lists of friends and business contacts, manage household purchases and budgets, organize music CD and video libraries, and store data for home businesses.

These types of software usually are not referred to as database or database management programs; instead, they are called personal information managers, personal organizers, and other names. Behind their interfaces, however, these PC programs have the heart of a database management system. For example, Figure 10B.1 shows Microsoft Outlook, a popular personal information manager that uses databases. With applications such as Outlook, you can store and manage your schedules, e-mail addresses, news sources, and other types of information.

A dedicated DBMS makes it possible to do many routine tasks that otherwise would be tedious and time-consuming without a computer. For example, a DBMS can:

◆ Sort thousands of addresses by ZIP Code.

◆ Find all records of people who live in a certain state.

◆ Print a list of selected records, such as all real estate listings that closed escrow last month.

◆ Invoice a customer's new car lease, adjust the dealership's inventory, and update the service department's mailing list merely by entering the data for a single sales transaction.

In other words, a DBMS not only stores information—it allows users to find that information easily. The DBMS can sift easily through thousands or even millions of pieces of data, returning only the data you need.

The Database

A database contains a collection of related items or facts arranged in a specific structure. The most obvious example of a noncomputerized database is a telephone directory. Telephone companies use electronic database programs to produce their printed phone books. Sometimes you will see a specialized phone book that is sorted not only by last name, but by other items, such as phone number or street address. These books are easy to produce, because the telephone company's electronic database can sort and organize the data in many different ways. (You learned about sorting in the discussion of spreadsheet programs in Unit 9.)

Before learning more about the powers of electronic databases, you need to learn how data is organized within a database and some of the more common DBMS terms. You also need to know that, while there are some standard and accepted database terms, the terms are not always used or used correctly. To help you visualize how a database stores data, think about a typical address book like the one shown in Figure 10B.2.

Three of the most important terms to know about databases are:

◆ **Fields.** Notice in Figure 10B.2 that each piece of information in the address book is stored in its own location, called a **field.** For example, each entry has a field for First Name and another field for Last Name, as well as fields for Address, City, State, ZIP Code, and Phone Number. Each unique type of information is stored in its own field.

◆ **Records.** One full set of fields—that is, all the related information about one person or object—is called a **record.** Therefore, all the information for the first person is record 1, all the information for the second person is record 2, and so on.

◆ **Tables.** A complete collection of records makes a **table.**

Figure 10B.2

Data is stored in tables. A table is divided into records, and each record is divided into fields.

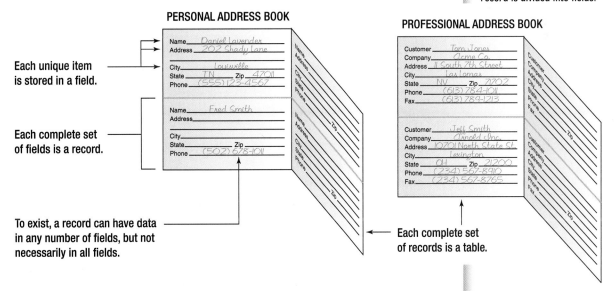

PERSONAL ADDRESS BOOK

Each unique item is stored in a field.

Each complete set of fields is a record.

To exist, a record can have data in any number of fields, but not necessarily in all fields.

PROFESSIONAL ADDRESS BOOK

Each complete set of records is a table.

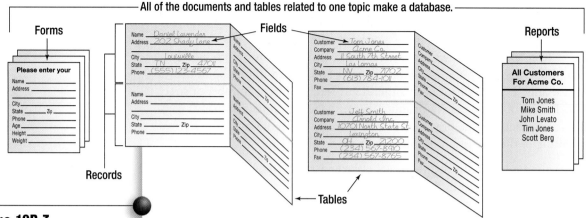

All of the documents and tables related to one topic make a database.

Forms

Fields

Reports

Records

Tables

Figure 10B.3

A database consists of tables and all the supporting documents.

Once you have a structure for storing data, you can enter and view data, create reports, and perform other tasks with the data. For example, you might create a customer report that lists customers by ZIP Code. These extra tools, along with the tables, combine to form a database, as shown in Figure 10B.3.

Now that you have a better understanding of database terms, you can begin exploring an electronic database. Figure 10B.4 shows a customer information table as it appears in the popular PC database application, Lotus Approach.

Notice that the table arrangement consists of a set number of named columns (fields) and an arbitrary number of unnamed rows (records). The table organizes each record's data by the same set of fields, but the table can store any number of records. For example, if you are storing employee data, theoretically, you can have an unlimited number of employees. However, there are a finite number of "facts" or fields about each employee. The only limit is the storage capability of the disk. Each record in the table does not necessarily have data in every field. For a record to exist, however, it must have data in at least one field. For example, a record for

Figure 10B.4

A customer information table in Lotus Approach

Field name

Field

Record

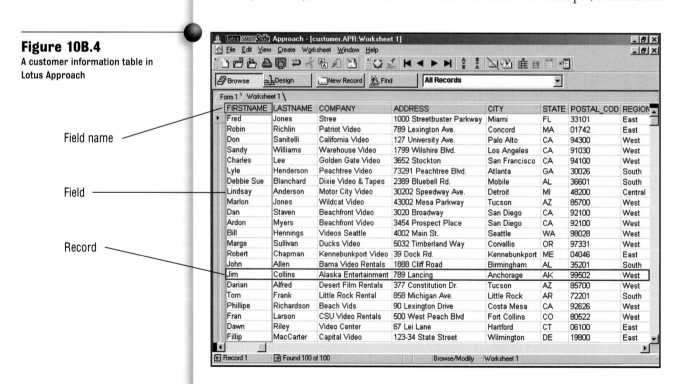

an employee must include the person's name. The employee's name is not an optional fact about an employee; it will always be present in the record for each employee. A record may or may not include the person's home phone number or date of birth; these types of data may be considered optional facts about an employee, and therefore may not always be included in the record.

The order of fields in a table strictly defines the location of data in every record. For example, a phone number field must contain a record's phone number—it cannot contain a person's name or ZIP Code. Similarly, the set of fields in any one table provides a sensible definition of the database for those who must access its data. For instance, you would expect to find the part number for a radiator in an inventory of auto parts, but you should not expect to view an employee's payroll record in the same table.

Flat-File and Relational Database Structures

Many early database applications and some current low-end applications access and manipulate only one table at a time. These applications store each table in its own file. When dealing with such databases, there is no reason to use the term *table,* because the table and the database are one and the same. Very often, the table is simply called a file or just "the database."

To be more precise, however, a database file that consists of a single data table is called a **flat-file** (or sequential file) **database.** Flat-file databases are useful for certain single-user or small-group situations, especially for maintaining lists such as address lists or inventories. Data that is stored, managed, and manipulated in a spreadsheet is similar to a flat-file database. (Notice that the table in Figure 10B.4 looks like a spreadsheet. If this table were stored by itself or not associated with any other database tables, it would be a flat-file database.)

Although they are easy to learn and use, flat-file database systems can be difficult to maintain, and they are limited in power. When numerous files exist (one for each table or related document), there is often a lot of data redundancy, which increases the chance for errors, wastes time, and uses excess storage space. Adding, deleting, or editing any field requires that you make the same changes in every file that contains the same field.

In a **relational database**—a database made up of a set of tables—a common field existing in any two tables creates a relationship between the tables. As shown in Figure 10B.5, a Customer ID Number field in both the Customers table and the Orders table links the two tables, while a Product ID field links the Orders and Products tables.

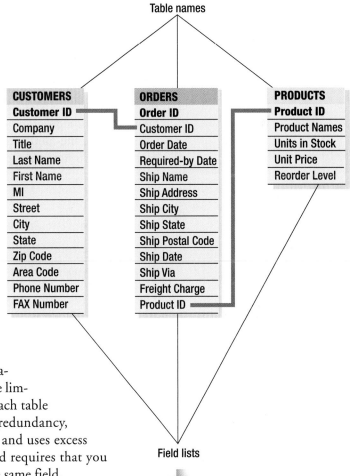

Figure 10B.5
Linked fields in relational database tables

The relational database structure is easily the most prevalent in today's business organizations. In a business, a typical relational database likely would contain data tables, such as the following:

◆ Customer information

◆ Employee information

◆ Vendor information

◆ Order information

◆ Inventory information

Multiple tables in this kind of database make it possible to handle many data management tasks, for example:

◆ The customer, order, and inventory tables can be linked to process orders and billing.

◆ The vendor and inventory tables can be linked to maintain and track inventory levels.

◆ The order and employee tables can be linked to control scheduling.

The DBMS

As you have seen, a database is basically a collection of data. A database management system is a program, or collection of programs, that allows any number of users to access and modify the data in a database. A DBMS also provides tools that enable users to construct special requests (called queries) to find specific records in the database.

Data management tasks fall into one of three general categories:

◆ Entering data into the database

◆ Sorting the data—that is, arranging or reordering the database's records

◆ Obtaining subsets of the data

The last type of data-management task—finding records—is extremely important. Because database files can grow very large (many gigabytes—millions of records—on large systems), finding data quickly is not a trivial matter. A DBMS, especially when it is running on powerful hardware, can find any speck of data in an enormous database in minutes, sometimes even in seconds or fractions of a second.

Equally important, a DBMS provides the means for multiple users to access and share data in the same database by way of networked computer systems.

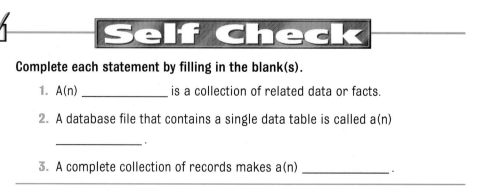

Complete each statement by filling in the blank(s).

1. A(n) _____ is a collection of related data or facts.

2. A database file that contains a single data table is called a(n) _____ .

3. A complete collection of records makes a(n) _____ .

Norton Notebook

DATA WAREHOUSES, PART II

In Part I of this discussion (in Unit 5), you learned that many companies use large storage systems to create data warehouses that can store enormous amounts of data. The hardware portion of the data warehouse may be a mainframe system or a RAID disk array, providing gigabytes or terabytes of storage space.

On the software side are the DBMS and tools that enable users to add and work with data in the database, converting it into useful information. The process of searching and sorting data to find relationships within it is called data mining, and it is possible only with the proper tools and approach to managing large volumes of data.

Many corporate data warehouses are based on large-scale enterprise DBMS software packages. These applications—developed by companies such as IBM, Oracle, and Sybase—can manage relational databases with hundreds of unique tables and millions of individual records. An enterprise-level DBMS provides programming-style tools that allow database managers or developers to create customized forms and reports and to set up queries to find the tiniest, most unique pieces of data in the system.

Because these systems are network-enabled, they provide data access to users in wide-ranging locations. Users in remote offices can access the centralized data warehouse from their location and work with data in real time, using a network connection or the Internet.

You may have accessed a data warehouse without even realizing it. For example, if you have ever visited the Federal Express Web site (**http://www.fedex.com/**) and tracked the location of a package, then you have tapped into the company's database. By using Web-enabled tools to create forms that customers can use in their Web browser, Federal Express (and many other companies) provides its clients with a simplified "front end" into its database.

Such forms enable you to create a database query, such as "What is the status of the package whose tracking number is 812371566015?" The DBMS can (with the use of internal indexes) sift through the millions of records stored in the database and return the one record related to your package, within seconds. The result of the query is the package's current location in the system and its

anticipated delivery date and time—or news that the package has already been delivered. These forms accept only certain types of input and therefore enable you to view only the data from a given set of fields for a single record. This limitation provides you the information you need without jeopardizing the security of the database.

An important step in making all the data useful is called data scrubbing. Data scrubbing or data validation is the process of safeguarding against erroneous data or duplicate data. In the case of Federal Express's database, for example, imagine the problems that could result if multiple packages were assigned the same tracking number. A data-scrubbing procedure prevents this mishap from occurring.

Data scrubbing can be handled in many ways. During the data-entry process, for example, the DBMS may refuse to accept data that does not conform to a certain format, that is not spelled in a specific way, or that is duplicated in a different record. Masks also may be applied, for instance, to ensure that all customer IDs, ZIP Codes, and telephone numbers are formatted in the same manner. This safeguard guarantees consistency throughout the database.

The results of a package-tracking query at the Federal Express Web site

WORKING WITH A DATABASE

The DBMS interface presents the user with data and the tools required to work with the data. You work with the interface's tools to perform data management functions:

◆ Creating tables   ◆ Viewing records

◆ Sorting records   ◆ Creating queries

◆ Generating reports

Creating Database Tables

The first step in building any database is to create one or more tables. As you know, tables hold the raw data that the DBMS will work with. To create a new database, you first must determine what kind of data will be stored in each table. In other words, you must define the table's fields with a three-step process:

1. Name the field.   **2.** Specify the field type.   **3.** Specify the field size.

Understanding Field Types

When naming the field, indicate as briefly as possible what the field contains. Figure 10B.6 shows a database table with clearly named fields.

Specifying the field type requires knowledge of what kind of data the DBMS can understand. Most modern database systems can work with seven predefined field types. Figure 10B.7 shows examples of each of these field types.

Figure 10B.6
Clearly named fields in a database table

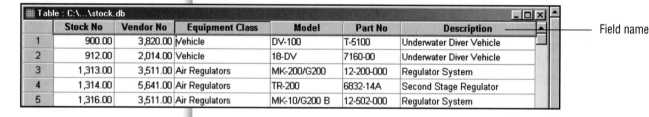

Field name

Text fields (also called character fields or alphanumeric fields) accept any string of alphanumeric characters that are not used in calculations. Such an entry might be a person's name, a company's name, an address, a phone number, or any other textual data. Text fields also typically store entries consisting of numbers, such as phone numbers or ZIP Codes not used in calculations.

Numeric fields store purely numeric data. The numbers in a numeric field might represent currency, percentages, statistics, quantities, or any other value that can be (but is not necessarily) used in calculations. The data itself is stored in the table strictly as a numeric value, even though the DBMS can display the value with formatting characters such as dollar or percent signs, decimal points, or commas.

A **date field** or **time field** stores date or time entries. This field type converts a date or time entry into a numeric value, just as dates and times are stored internally as serial numbers in spreadsheet cells. In most database systems, a date value represents the number of days that have elapsed since a specific start date. When you enter a date in a date field, the DBMS accepts your input, displays it in the format of a date (such as 9/9/2003), and converts it to a number (such as 37873) that it stores in the database. Date and time fields typically include automatic error-checking features. For instance, date fields can verify a date's accuracy and account for the extra day in a leap year. Date and time fields are handy for calculating elapsed time periods, such as finding records for invoices 31 days overdue.

Logical fields (also called Boolean fields) store one of only two possible values. You can apply almost any description for the data (yes or no, true or false, on or off, and so forth). For example, a Catalog field in a Customer table can tell a customer service representative whether a customer has ordered a new catalog (Yes) or not (No).

Binary fields store binary objects, or BLOBs. A **BLOB (Binary Large OBject)** can be a graphic image file such as clip art, a photograph, a screen image, a graphic, or formatted text. A BLOB also can be an audio file, video clip, or other object, as shown in Figure 10B.8.

Figure 10B.7
Field types

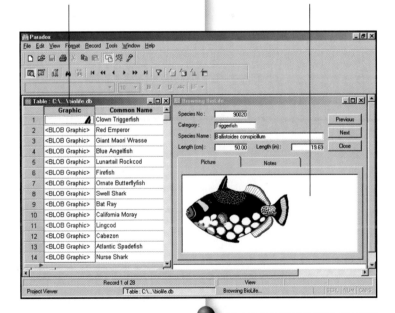

Memo field

In some DBMSs, **counter fields** (sometimes called autonumber fields) store a unique numeric value that the DBMS assigns to each record. Because it is possible for two records to have identical data in some tables (such as two employees with the same name), a counter field ensures that every record will have a completely unique identification. Counter fields also may be used for creating records that number sequentially, such as invoices.

Because most field types have fixed lengths that restrict the number of characters in an entry, **memo fields** (also called description fields) provide fields for entering notes or comments of any length.

Entering Data in a Table

After the table has been set up, data can be entered. In most cases, entering data is a matter of typing characters at the keyboard. Entering data in a database table is much like entering data in a spreadsheet program. The process can have more pitfalls than you might expect, however, especially if it is being carried out by someone other than the user who set up the tables. For example, the DBMS might not handle a number correctly if the user enters it with a dollar sign—even though the number will be displayed as a dollar amount. If the data is entered with an inconsistent mix of upper- and lowercase letters, the DBMS may not be able to sort the data or locate specific records.

Figure 10B.8
Binary fields allow graphics and other nontext items to be stored in a database.

Most DBMSs allow you to create a data entry **form** to make data entry easier (see Figure 10B.9). A form is a custom view of the table that typically shows one record at a time and includes special controls and labels that make data entry less confusing. For example, you can include controls that automatically move the insertion point to the next field when the typist presses the Enter or Tab key, or you can convert all the input into capital letters to maintain data consistency. You can even direct input into multiple tables, which makes it easier for a typist who does not know about the underlying structure of the DBMS and database tables.

Understandable labels / Form

Filtered column

The techniques you can employ to control data entry have different names and different capabilities, depending on the specific DBMS product. Some products call these controls **masks;** others call them **pictures** or **field formats.** Regardless of the name, the device accepts only valid characters and controls the entry's display format. For example, you can set up a State field so that a state's two-letter code appears uppercase (TN), no matter how the data is typed (tn, Tn, tN, or TN). A phone number field's entry can be controlled in a similar manner, so that even if the user types only the phone number's ten digits, it will appear with the area code enclosed in parentheses, a space, and a hyphen following the prefix—for example, (818) 555-1234.

Viewing Records

The way data appears on screen contributes to how well users can work with it. You already have seen examples of data presented in two-dimensional, worksheet-style tables. With many DBMS products, the table view (sometimes called the datasheet view) is what you use to create a database table and to modify field specifications. This view is also suitable for viewing lists of records that you group together in some meaningful way, such as all customers who live in the same city.

Sometimes viewing the entire table is unwieldy because there are too many entries. **Filters** are a DBMS feature for displaying a selected list or subset of records from a table. The visible records satisfy a condition that the user sets. It is called a filter, because it tells the DBMS to display those records that satisfy the condition while hiding—or filtering out—those that do not. For example, you can create a filter that displays only those records that have the data "Gold" in the Status field, as shown in Figure 10B.10.

Figure 10B.10

When you view a data table in datasheet view, you can see all records and fields at the same time—or as many as will fit on the screen.

As shown in Figure 10B.11, a DBMS also allows you to create forms for viewing records. These forms are similar in design to those used in data entry, but they are used to display existing data instead of receiving new data. By using forms, you can create simple, easily understood views of your data that show just one record at a time. You also can create complex forms that display related information from multiple tables.

Figure 10B.11
The form lets the user work with information for a single record.

Sorting Records

One of the most powerful features of a DBMS is its ability to sort a table of data, either for a printed report or for display on the screen. Sorting arranges records according to the contents of one or more fields. For example, in a table of products, you can sort records into numerical order by product ID or into alphabetical order by product name. To obtain the list sorted by product name, you define the condition for the Product Name field that tells the DBMS to rearrange the records in alphabetical order for this data (see Figure 10B.12). You can sort the same list on another field, such as Supplier, as shown in Figure 10B.13.

Figure 10B.12
Records arranged alphabetically by product name

Here, the records are sorted according to entries in this field.

Now the records are sorted according to entries in this field.

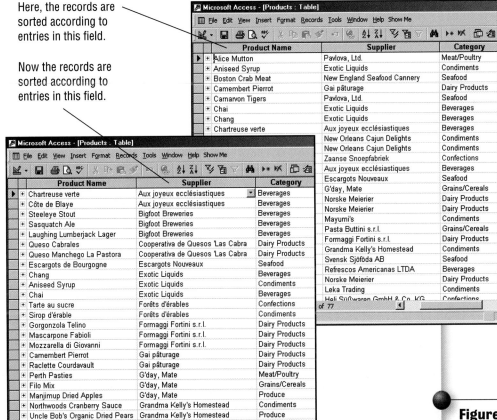

Figure 10B.13
The records have now been arranged alphabetically according to the contents of the Supplier field.

When sorting records, one important consideration is determining the sort order. An ascending sort order arranges records in alphabetical order (from A to Z), numerical order (from 0 to 9), or chronological order (from 1/1/1900 to 12/31/1999). For example, if you base an ascending sort on a Last Name field, the records will be arranged in alphabetical order by last name. Conversely, a descending sort order arranges records in the opposite order—that is, from Z to A, or from 9 to 0.

Querying a Database

In a manner similar to entering sort conditions, you can enter expressions or criteria that:

◆ Allow the DBMS to locate records.

◆ Establish relationships or links between tables to update records.

◆ List a subset of records.

◆ Perform calculations.

◆ Delete obsolete records.

◆ Perform other data management tasks.

Any of these types of requests is called a **query,** a user-constructed statement that describes data and sets criteria so that the DBMS can gather the desired data and construct specific information. In other words, a query is a more powerful type of filter that can gather information from multiple tables in a relational database.

For example, a sales manager might create a query to list orders by quarter. The query can include field names such as CUSTOMER and CITY from a Customers table, and ORDER DATE from an Orders table. To obtain the desired information, the query requires the specific data or criteria that will isolate those records (orders received during a given period) from all the records in both tables. In this case, the sales manager includes a range of dates during which the orders would ship.

Some database systems provide special windows or forms for creating queries. Generally, such a window or form provides an area for selecting the tables the query will work with and columns for entering the field names where the query will obtain or manipulate data.

Because nearly all databases are designed and built using accepted terms and structures, it should be possible to generate a single language that can, in theory, query any database. If such a language were developed, a user who knew the language could query any database, regardless of who created the database or what software was used in the creation. Mainframe database developers created the Structured English QUEry Language (SEQUEL) in the mid-1970s to solve this dilemma. SEQUEL, and its later variant **SQL,** are English-like query languages that allow the user to query a database without knowing much about the underlying database structure (see Figure 10B.14).

NORTON
ONLINE

Visit www.norton.glencoe.com for more information on **database query languages.**

Figure 10B.14
This SQL query opens the Employees table and extracts a list of all employees whose hire date is after 01/01/1993.

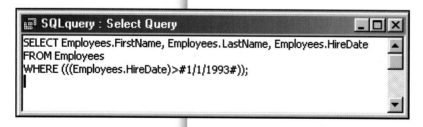

Figure 10B.15
An Xbase query to generate a list of employees hired after 01/01/1993

Because SQL is such a powerful tool, some PC-based database management systems now enable users to perform SQL queries. Because each DBMS application has its own special features, however, developers have a tendency to create "dialects" of SQL that do not quite meet the standard for a universal database querying language. Sometimes the developers add commands; other times they limit the commands or some of the command options. Nevertheless, SQL is useful, and you may see it from time to time, especially if you are using a relational DBMS such as Oracle or DB2, or a more recent PC-based DBMS such as Microsoft Access.

Figure 10B.16
A QBE query to generate a list of employees hired after 01/01/1993

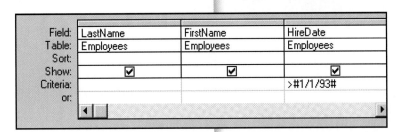

In addition to SQL, PC-based databases sometimes use a query/programming language called **Xbase** (see Figure 10B.15). Xbase is a generic query language derived from the query/programming language used in the Dbase family of database products developed by Ashton Tate. Like SQL, Xbase is somewhat English-like, but it is more complicated, because its commands cover the full range of database activities, not just queries. As with SQL, software developers have a tendency to create dialects of Xbase to suit their software's needs, so each version of Xbase may be a little different from its peers.

For those users who prefer a graphic interface when querying a database, some programs provide an interface, like a form or a grid, that collects the facts about a query from the user and composes the SQL or query statements behind the scenes. This feature allows a user to **query by example (QBE)** or to perform "intuitive" queries. With QBE, you specify the search criteria by typing values or expressions into the fields of a QBE form or grid (see Figure 10B.16).

Whether a DBMS uses SQL, Xbase, or QBE—or offers all three—the results of a query are always the same (see Figure 10B.17).

Figure 10B.17
The results of the SQL, Xbase, or QBE query showing a list of employees hired after 01/01/1993

Figure 10B.18
This polished-looking summary is a relatively simple database report.

Generating Reports

Not all DBMS operations have to occur on screen. Just as forms can be based on queries, so can reports. A **report** is printed information that, like a query result, is assembled by gathering data based on user-supplied criteria. In fact, report generators in most DBMSs create reports from queries.

Reports can range from simple lists of records to customized formats for specific purposes, such as invoices. Report generators can use selected data and criteria to carry out automated mathematical calculations as the report is printed. For example, relevant data can be used to calculate subtotals and totals for invoices or sales summaries. Reports are also similar to forms, because their layout can be customized with objects representing fields and other controls, as shown in Figure 10B.18.

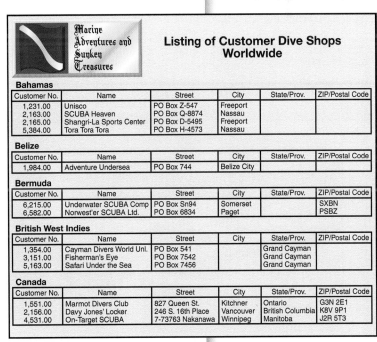

COMPUTERS
in your career

Database-Related Jobs

Database technologies touch the work lives of millions of people each day. You do not have to be a database expert, however, to work with a database management system. As described in this unit, many people work with databases every day without even realizing it.

◆ **Secretaries, Clerks, Data-Entry Specialists, and Telemarketers.** Most computer users do not work with a true DBMS on a daily basis. Instead, most work with a front-end program, such as a contact management, order-entry, or accounts payable/receivable system, that acts as an intermediary between the user and the actual database.

◆ **Help Desk and Product Support Specialists.** Persons who work at call centers or help desks interact with large databases of product and customer information and continuously add and edit information about customer complaints, problems, and suggestions. By drawing from the information stored in a help desk's database, product designers can find unpopular features in their products and fix those problems in new versions.

◆ **Software Engineers.** Software engineering is one of the fastest growing careers in the computer industry. Some commercially developed software uses a DBMS to store the data relevant to that software. Software engineers design, develop, and test these applications. Other software engineers design, develop, and test the DBMS application itself.

◆ **Database Programmers and Developers.** The demand for experienced database professionals is high, especially for high-end users who can develop forms and set up complex relational databases. Database developers create custom tools for corporate databases, create special front ends and order-entry tools, generate complicated queries, develop report-generation macros, and more. These developers are skilled in programming languages such as COBOL, Visual Basic, Java, and C, as well as database query languages such as SQL. They are familiar with powerful databases such as Sybase, DB2, Oracle, and others.

◆ **Database Administrators.** Database administrators typically lay out, design, and construct corporate databases using the DBMS software. After the corporate databases are constructed, database administrators are called upon to develop backup, load, and unload strategies. They often are involved with altering the database based on system enhancements and upgrades to the DBMS software.

◆ **System Analysts.** Many organizations hire system analysts to review and update the operation of their enterprise applications. The analyst must be well-versed in database concepts and terminology and must understand how the organization uses its DBMS and data tables to store, retrieve, and manage data. Analysts frequently assist managers in designing queries and reports that draw data from the database or in creating forms that make data input easier or more efficient.

SUMMARY

- A database is a repository for collections of related data or facts.

- A database management system (DBMS) is a software tool that enables many users to add, view, and work with the data in a database.

- Flat-file databases are two-dimensional tables of fields and records. They cannot form relationships with other tables.

- Relational databases are powerful because they can form relationships among different tables.

- To create a database, you first must set up its tables and define the types of fields each table will contain.

- A DBMS provides tools that can validate data as it is entered, thus ensuring that the data is in the correct format.

- Forms are custom screens for displaying and entering data that can be associated with database tables and queries.

- Filters let you browse through selected records that meet a set of criteria.

- Sorting arranges records in a table according to specific criteria.

- Queries are user-constructed statements that set conditions for selecting and manipulating data.

- Reports are user-generated sets of data usually printed as a document.

KEY TERMS

binary field, *371*
binary large object (BLOB), *371*
counter field, *371*
database management
   system (DBMS), *364*
database, *364*
date field, *370*
field format, *372*
field, *365*

filter, *372*
flat-file database, *367*
form, *372*
logical field, *371*
mask, *372*
memo field, *371*
numeric field, *370*
picture, *372*
query by example (QBE), *375*

query, *374*
record, *365*
relational database, *367*
report, *375*
SQL, *374*
table, *365*
text field, *370*
time field, *370*
Xbase, *375*

KEY TERM QUIZ

Complete each statement by writing one of the terms listed under Key Terms in each blank.

1. In a database table, each row represents a(n) _____ .

2. In a record, it is not necessary for every _____ to contain data.

3. A(n) _____ field stores a unique numeric value that the DBMS assigns for every record.

4. A(n) _____ displays a selected list or subset of records from a table.

5. You can create printed _____ from the data in a database.

SECTION QUIZ

True/False

Answer the following questions by circling True or False.

True	False	**1.** A database is a software tool that allows users to store, access, and process data or facts into useful information.
True	False	**2.** A record is a full set of fields about one person or object.
True	False	**3.** Once the structure of a database is established, you can place any type of information you want into any field.
True	False	**4.** A flat-file database uses only one data table.
True	False	**5.** To create a new database, you first must define its fields.

Multiple Choice

Circle the word or phrase that best completes each statement.

1. A _____ is an example of a database.
   A. telephone book   **B.** video library   **C.** both A and B

2. A _____ is a complete collection of records.
   A. table   **B.** field   **C.** DBMS

3. A _____ database is made up of a set of tables where a common field in any two tables creates a relationship between the tables.
   A. flat-file   **B.** large   **C.** relational

4. A(n) _____ can store an object, such as a picture, rather than text or numeric data.
   A. counter field   **B.** binary field   **C.** logical field

5. A _____ tells the DBMS to display records that satisfy a condition, while hiding those that do not.
   A. form   **B.** filter   **C.** report

REVIEW QUESTIONS

In your own words, briefly answer the following questions.

1. What is the difference between a database and a database management system?

2. In a database table, what does each column represent?

3. What is a form?

4. What is a filter?

5. What is a query?

SECTION LABS

Complete the following exercises as directed by your instructor.

1. Determine whether a database management program is installed on your computer. If you have an application suite (such as Lotus SmartSuite) installed, a database application may be installed as part of the suite. Otherwise, a stand-alone DBMS package may be installed. Locate your DBMS and launch it. What steps must you take to start the program?

2. Create a sample database by using a database application, a spreadsheet program, or your word processor's table feature.

   A. Launch the program.

   B. Set up the following field names: Last Name, First Name, Street Address, City, State, ZIP Code, and Phone Number. If you are using a database program, you may need to specify whether these fields should be text, numeric, or other types of fields.

   C. Enter data in each field for six people. When you are finished, save the new file to disk. Name it My First Database. Then close the program.

UNIT PROJECTS

UNIT LABS

1. **Create a Presentation.** This exercise assumes that you have a presentation program installed on your computer. If you do, launch the program (with your instructor's help, if necessary) and create a single slide. Use a template to design the slide, and choose a slide format that provides a title and a text box. Make the slide about yourself, as if you were going to use it to introduce yourself to a group of people during a presentation.

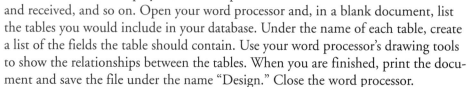

2. **Design a Database.** You can create an outline for a database by using a word processor. Imagine that you own a small business that sells gourmet coffees. You want to create a database system to store information about products, vendors, customers, employees, accounts paid and received, and so on. Open your word processor and, in a blank document, list the tables you would include in your database. Under the name of each table, create a list of the fields the table should contain. Use your word processor's drawing tools to show the relationships between the tables. When you are finished, print the document and save the file under the name "Design." Close the word processor.

3. **Which Presentation Program Is Right for You?** Visit the following Web sites and gather information about the presentation programs offered by these vendors:

   Microsoft PowerPoint—**http://www.microsoft. com/office/powerpoint/**

   Corel Presentations—**http://www.corel.com/**

   Lotus Freelance Graphics—**http://www.lotus. com/home.nsf/welcome/freelance/**

   Harvard Graphics—**http://www. harvardgraphics.com/**

   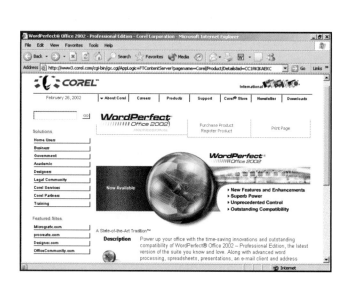

   When you are done, launch Notepad and write a one-page paper summarizing your findings and explaining which presentation program you would purchase. Give your reasons for choosing that program. Print the paper and give a copy to your instructor.

4. **Discover Enterprise Databases.** Several PC-based database management products are available, but if you work for a large corporation, chances are you will use an enterprise application based on a large-scale DBMS. Visit the following Web sites for information about some of these enterprise-level database programs:

   IBM DB2—**http://www.software.ibm.com/data/db2/**

   Oracle—**http://www.oracle.com/**

Microsoft SQL Server—**http://www.microsoft.com/sql/default.asp**

Sybase—**http://www.sybase.com/**

DISCUSSION QUESTIONS

As directed by your instructor, discuss the following questions in class or in groups.

1. Suppose that you were asked to give a presentation on a subject you understand well. To support your presentation, you must prepare a twenty-minute slide show using presentation software. Describe the slide presentation you would create. How many slides would you use? How would you organize them? What types of content would you use in each? What features of the presentation program would you use to enhance the presentation?

2. Describe a scenario in which a large organization might use a database management system. What types of tables would the organization's database contain? What kinds of relationships would exist among the tables? What types of forms would be needed, and by what users? What types of queries and reports would managers want to run on this database?

RESEARCH AND REPORT

Using your own choice of resources (such as the Internet, books, magazines, and newspaper articles), research and write a short paper discussing one of the following topics.

- Basic design principles you should follow when creating a slide show
- SQL and its uses in business
- The advantages of relational databases, compared to flat-file databases

When you are finished, proofread and print your paper, and give it to your instructor.

ETHICAL ISSUES

Businesses and governments now maintain huge databases filled with information about individuals. With this thought in mind, discuss the following questions in class.

1. You submit information about yourself whenever you apply for a credit card, subscribe to a magazine, or register a product that you have purchased. Should businesses and government agencies be allowed to keep this data permanently? How much information should they be allowed to collect about individuals? Do you feel the practice of maintaining personal data is wrong or should be illegal? Why or why not?

2. Credit agencies and banks commonly sell information about their customers, which then is used to create direct-marketing lists. Some people feel that banks and credit agencies thus profit by selling individuals' private information, leading to an erosion of personal privacy. Do you share this view? Why or why not?

Computing *Keynotes*

Professional Certification Programs

When computers first came to the American workplace—and for many years afterward—very few corporate computer users specialized in any one area of technology. The workforce was roughly divided into two groups:

1. End users, who were expected to know very little beyond the basic operation of the programs they used.

2. "Computer guys," people with a broad general knowledge of computers, who could install systems, troubleshoot problems, and perhaps even manage a network.

Today, however, the world of information technology (IT) has evolved into many specialized areas of processes and applications. You would be hard-pressed to go into any medium-size or large company and find a single "computer guy" who is in charge of running the entire system. This evolution has created many different, highly specialized jobs for IT professionals. Depending on the company and the type of business it does, you can find people filling dozens of varied and equally important IT-related jobs. Each of these jobs requires a unique kind of training and special skills.

With so many people involved in specialized roles, employers now face a difficult question. That is, how do you verify someone's skills to make sure that he or she is right for the job? While a four-year or two-year degree is important, many companies now look for computing professionals who have completed an IT certification program.

Certifications have become an extremely important type of credential in today's IT-oriented workplace. Whether you complete a certification program by itself or as part of your college or vocational training, your IT certification proves that you have received specialized training in a specific area of computing technology. By demonstrating that you have the skills required for a certain job, a certification differentiates you from other job seekers in a crowded and competitive marketplace. Certification can improve your chances of getting the job you want, earning promotions, and increasing your earnings.

TYPES OF COMPUTER CERTIFICATIONS

If you are interested in an IT-related career, you can choose from a multitude of computer certification programs. You may have heard of certifications from such companies as Microsoft and Novell, but they are just the tip of the iceberg; many manufacturers—such as IBM, Cisco Systems, Citrix, and others—offer certifications related to their particular products.

In addition to product-specific certifications, there are also vendor-independent certifications that are sponsored by various professional groups. One of the more popular vendor-independent certifications is the A+ Service Technician certification. This certification does not come from any single manufacturer, but it is overseen by the Computer Technology Industry Association (CompTIA), and it covers a variety of products and technologies.

Many independent training companies also offer certification programs. One example is Prosoft, a training company that sponsors the Certified Internet Webmaster (CIW) certification.

The following sections describe some of the various certifications that apply to information technology. While this list is not complete, it should give you an idea of the many kinds of certifications that are available.

Application Certifications

An application certification is basically what the name implies: a certification that proves your knowledge of a certain program or application. Two popular application certification programs are:

◆ The **Microsoft Office User Specialist (MOUS)** program certifies your skill as a user of the applications in the Microsoft Office suite of programs, including Word, Excel, PowerPoint, Access, and Outlook. Certifications are available for Office versions 97, 2000, and XP. You can earn three types of certification—Master, Expert, or Core—in any or all of the Office programs. Special MOUS certificates are available for expert-level Office users who want to work as trainers. To earn a MOUS certification, you must pass a set of core- or expert-level examinations. For details on the MOUS certification program, visit **http://www.microsoft.com/traincert/mcp/mous/default.asp.**

◆ The **Corel Certification** program offers certifications for users of Corel products, including the most recent versions of CorelDRAW and WordPerfect. Corel offers three types of certification: Proficient, Expert, and Instructor. To earn a certification, you must pass an examination, which can be taken online. For more information, visit the Corel home page at **http://www.corel. com/** and click the Training link.

The home page of the MOUS certification program

Programming and Application Development Certifications

Programming or application development certifications prove your ability to work within a particular development environment. To earn one of these certifications, you must pass examinations that test your product knowledge, your understanding of the actual development environment or language on which the product is based, and your ability to use the product to develop a custom solution.

◆ One of the more popular application development certifications is the **Microsoft Certified Solution Developer (MCSD)** program. This certification is for programmers who design and implement custom business solutions with Microsoft development platforms, such as VisualBasic and Visual C++. To qualify, you must pass three core exams and one elective exam. The core exams consist of an application development test, a distributed development test, and a solutions architecture test. You also must pass one elective, which you can choose from a list of options. The elective topics range from data warehousing to implementing e-commerce solutions. For more information on the MCSD program visit **http://www.microsoft.com/traincert/mcp/mcsd/default.asp.**

The home page of the MCSD certification program

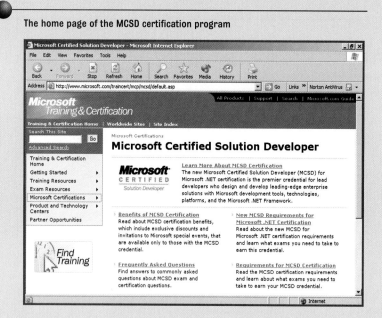

◆ The **Certified Lotus Professional (CLP)—Collaborative Solutions Application Developer** program is also a vendor-specific certification, which verifies your expertise in the use of Lotus application development tools. This certification focuses on knowledge of products such as Sametime, Domino.doc, Discovery Server, and Lotus Workflow. This relatively new certification track has certain initial requirements. Candidates must hold a Certified Lotus Specialist designation, and they also must be able to pass three separate exams: Developing Applications Using Lotus Workflow, Developing Web Applications in Same-time 2, and Domino.Doc 3.0 Customization. For more information, visit **http://www.lotus.com/home.nsf/welcome/certification.**

The home page of the Lotus CLP certification program

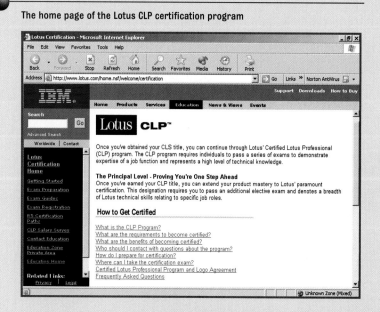

Networking and Operating System Certifications

Networking and operating system certifications prove your ability to implement, manage, and administer certain operating systems and network operating systems.

◆ A **Microsoft Certified Systems Engineer (MCSE)** certificate proves that you are skilled with the Microsoft suite of network server and operating system products, including programs such as Windows NT 4.0, Windows 2000 Server, and Windows XP and .NET Server. To earn an MCSE certification, you must pass four core exams, one design exam, and two electives. The four core exams test for knowledge of a particular operating system. The core exams cover such topics as installing, configuring, and administering the operating system, as well as understanding the network infrastructure and the corresponding directory services component. Candidates can choose from an extensive list of electives, which includes examinations on SQL Server, Internet Security and Acceleration (ISA) Server, Exchange Server, and Clustering Services. For more information, visit **http://www.microsoft. com/traincert/mcp/mcse/default.asp.**

◆ The **Certified Novell Engineer (CNE)** program verifies your knowledge of Novell's network server products— including Netware, IntraNetware, and GroupWise—as well as your ability to plan, implement, configure, and administer these products. For NetWare version 6, you must pass three core exams: Networking Technologies, Service and Support, and Desktop Management with ZENWorks for Desktops 3. You also must pass one elective exam; you can choose an elective such as Internet security, network management, or integrating Windows NT with Netware. For more information on Novell's certification programs, visit **http://www.novell. com/education/certinfo/.**

◆ The **Cisco Certified Network Administrator (CCNA)** certification verifies your ability to implement, configure, and operate local area and wide area network services, as well as dial-up services for small networks. To earn a CCNA certification, you need a good understanding of networking protocols, such as IP, IPX, RIP, Ethernet, and IGRP. Cisco offers two basic certification tracks in the CCNA program: basic and advanced. You must pass a single exam to earn a CCNA certification. To learn about Cisco's certification programs, visit **http://www.cisco.com/warp/public/10/wwtraining/certprog/.**

The home page of the MCSE certification program

The home page of Novell's certification programs

The home page of Cisco's certification programs

Entry-Level Certifications

These certifications qualify as entry-level because they typically require only six months of computing experience. These certifications have given hundreds of thousands of people the chance to enter a new area of employment, in spite of the fact that many of them have little computing experience. Two of the most popular entry-level certifications are:

◆ The **A+ Service Technician Certification** is a testing program sponsored by the Computer Technology Industry Association (CompTIA). It certifies the experience of entry-level computer service technicians on a wide range of hardware, software, and networking technologies. Through CompTIA, applicants can find resources to help prepare and register for exams and learn about hundreds of different certification programs. For more information on CompTIA and its certification programs, visit **http://www.comptia.com/** and click the Certification link.

◆ The **Network+ Certification** is an entry-level exam that focuses on the skills that would be needed by any general networking practitioner. It is considered entry-level because it measures the technical knowledge of networking professionals with 18 to 24 months of experience in the IT industry. The exam covers a wide range of vendor- and product-neutral networking technologies. This means that you don't have to be an expert in any single networking product to pass the exam. Many industry leaders were involved in the creation and development of Network+ certification, such as 3Com, IBM, Microsoft, and Novell. There is only one test to take and pass to become Network+ certified, so the program continues to grow in popularity for individuals looking to earn a certification for their entry-level general networking knowledge. You can learn about the Network+ certification program by visiting the CompTIA Web site at **http://www.comptia.com/,** clicking the Certification link, and then clicking the Network+ link.

Internet and Web Development Certifications

From the Internet's explosion has grown a host of different Web-related careers, such as Web development, Web administration, and Web security. There are certifications for all types of Web professionals. Two of the most popular Web-related certifications are:

The home page of CIW certification programs

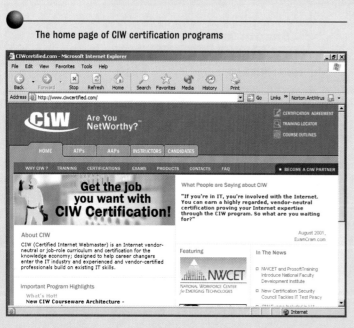

◆ The **Certified Internet Webmaster (CIW)** program offers vendor-neutral certifications, which help networking professionals use their existing IT skills to move into Internet-based technologies. The CIW program lets you follow different tracks, based on the skills you want to acquire. CIW tracks cover a range of professional roles, including application developer, e-commerce designer, enterprise developer, and internetworking and security professional. To learn more about CIW certification, visit **http://www.ciwcertified.com/.**

- The **Macromedia Certified Professional** designation qualifies candidates who are skilled at Web development and implementation using various Macromedia products. Macromedia offers certification on such products as Cold Fusion. You also can become a Certified Web Site Developer. The Cold Fusion exam focuses specifically on Web development using Cold Fusion and the ability to manage user sessions. The Certified Web Site Developer certification tests your knowledge of Web-related topics such as Web page design, Web page authoring, and technologies surrounding Web development. For complete information on Macromedia's certification programs, visit **http://www.macromedia.com/support/training/certified_professional_program/**.

The home page of Macromedia's certification programs

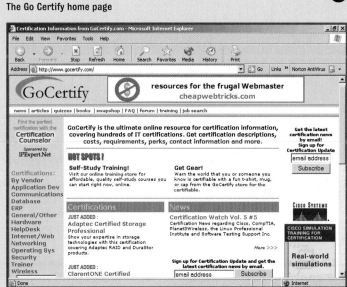

Certification Resources

If you are interested in earning one or more technology-related certifications, here are some Web sites that can provide helpful, general information:

- The **Go Certify** Web site offers information on a wide range of IT certifications. Certifications are grouped both by vendor and type. Go Certify provides information about each certification, such as the certification vendor, the skill level, the initial and continuing requirements, and the exam pricing. It is a great place to start when deciding on what certification to pursue. Visit **http://www.gocertify.com/**.

The Go Certify home page

- **Cert Cities** is an online subsidiary of *MCP Magazine*. It is completely devoted to news and new events that are happening in the world of IT certification. Within this site, you will find certification information, articles on different certifications, study tips, and reference material guides. It also publishes an annual salary survey of individuals who hold various certifications. Visit **http://www.certcities.com/**.

- **Certification Corner** offers study guides and testing materials for various certifications. Some are available for purchase, while others can be downloaded free of charge and used as study aids for various exams. The site also offers a free newsletter, articles, and commentary from knowledgeable people within the certification community, as well as a complete list of professional certification sites. Visit **http://www.certificationcorner.com/**.

UNIT 11

Graphics and Multimedia

UNIT CONTENTS

This unit contains the following sections:

The Interactive Browser Edition CD-ROM provides additional labs and activities to apply concepts from this unit.

388

Graphics and Graphics Software

OVERVIEW:
Graphics, Graphics Everywhere

You may not realize that many of the images you see are created on a computer. From postage stamps to magazine illustrations, from billboards to television programs, all kinds of graphics are created and edited using computers and graphics software. Graphics programs—and the designers who use them—have become so polished that it is often impossible to tell a photograph or hand-drawn illustration from a computer-generated graphic.

With the computer's capability to mimic traditional artists' media, graphics software allows artists to do with a computer what they once did with brushes, pencils, and darkroom equipment. Similarly, architects and engineers now do most of their design and rendering work on computers—although many were trained in traditional paper-based drafting methods. By using the computer, they produce designs and renderings that are highly accurate and visually pleasing.

Graphics software has advanced a great deal in a short time. In the early 1980s, most graphics programs were limited to drawing simple geometric outlines, usually in one color. Today, graphics software offers advanced drawing and painting tools and almost unlimited color control. You can see the products of these powerful tools everywhere you look. Their results can be subtle or stunning, obviously artificial, or amazingly lifelike.

OBJECTIVES

- Define the terms *bitmap* and *vector*, and differentiate these file types.
- List all the standard file formats for bitmap and vector images.
- Identify four ways to load graphic files onto a computer.
- List five types of graphics software and their uses.
- Name five graphic elements commonly found on Web pages.

TYPES OF GRAPHICS FILES

Computers can create many, many kinds of graphics—from simple line drawings to three-dimensional animations. But all graphics files fall into one of two basic categories. Graphics files are made up of either:

◆ A grid, called a **bitmap**, the cells of which are filled with one or more colors, as shown in Figure 11A.1. The individual cells in the grid can all be filled with the same color, or each cell can contain a different color. The term **raster** is sometimes used to describe bitmap images. Bitmap images also may be referred to as bitmapped images.

◆ A set of **vectors**, which are mathematical equations describing the size, shape, thickness, position, color, and fill of a closed graphical shape or of lines (see Figure 11A.2).

Some types of graphics programs work with bitmaps; others work with vectors. Each type of graphic file has its own advantages and disadvantages. Whether you use a bitmap- or vector-based program depends on what you are trying to do. For example, if you want to be able to retouch a photo, create seamless tiling textures for the Web or for 3-D surfaces, or create an image that looks like a painting, you will choose bitmap-based software (see Figure 11A.3).

Vector-based software is your best choice if you want the flexibility of resizing an image without degrading its sharpness, the ability to reposition elements easily in an image, or the ability to achieve an illustrative look, as when drawing with a pen or pencil.

Working With Bitmaps

When you use bitmap-based graphics software, you are using the computer to change the characteristics of the pixels that compose an image. Manipulating pixels can become complex. For example, an 8- by 10-inch, black-and-white image—if displayed at a typical screen resolution of 72 pixels per inch (ppi)—is a mosaic of 414,720 pixels, as shown in Figure 11A.4.

The computer must remember the precise location of each and every pixel as it is viewed, moved, or altered. If you decide that the same 8- by 10-inch piece of artwork must have up to 256 colors in its makeup (which is considered minimal with today's technology), then the computer must keep track of the 414,720 pixels multiplied by the 8 bits per pixel that are necessary to identify 256 different colors. In other words, the computer must keep track of 3,317,760 bits (see Figure 11A.5).

Working With Vectors

Strictly speaking, vectors are lines drawn from one point to another, as shown in Figure 11A.6. Vector-based software can use mathematical equations to define the thickness and color of a line, its pattern or fill, and other attributes. Although

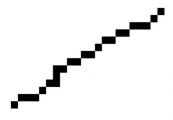

Figure 11A.3
This text has been generated with a bitmap-based paint program; the text is actually composed of tiny blocks, called pixels. The text is a simple bitmap image.

Congratulations!

a line on the screen is still displayed as a series of blocks (because that is how all monitors work), it is an equation to the computer. Thus, to move the line from location A to location B, the computer replaces the coordinates of location A with those of location B. This substitution saves the effort of calculating how to change the characteristics of thousands of individual pixels.

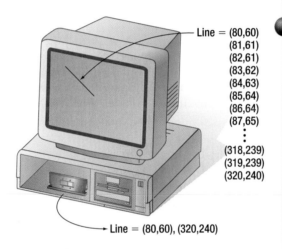

Line = (80,60)
(81,61)
(82,61)
(83,62)
(84,63)
(85,64)
(86,64)
(87,65)
⋮
(318,239)
(319,239)
(320,240)

Line = (80,60), (320,240)

File Formats and Compatibility Issues

Perhaps more than other types of computer-generated documents, graphics files require users to understand and work with different types of file formats. A **file format** is a standardized method of encoding data for storage. File formats are important, because they tell the program what kind of data is contained in the file and how the data is organized.

File formats may be proprietary or universal. The structure of a proprietary file format is under the sole control of the software developer who invented the format. Universal file formats are based on openly published specifications and are commonly used by many different programs and operating systems. For example, Adobe Photoshop, by default, saves images in its proprietary PSD format, but it also can save files in several universal formats, such as TIF, GIF, JPEG, PICT, and TGA. Word processing programs can read and save files in specific formats such as DOC or TXT (see Figure 11A.7).

NORTON
ONLINE

Visit **www.norton.glencoe.com** for more information on **graphic file formats.**

Figure 11A.7

When viewing files on your computer's disks, you can distinguish their formats in two ways. First, look at the extension (DOC, HTML, and others) at the end of each file's name, assuming your system is set to display file-name extensions. You also can tell by looking at the Type column in your operating system's file manager. Here you see a group of files in Windows Explorer.

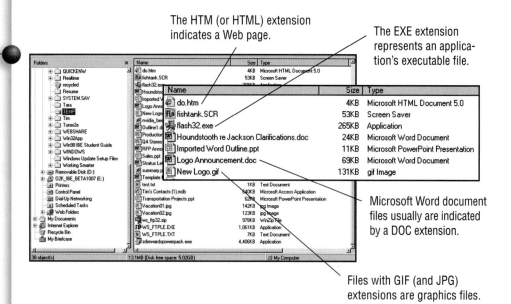

The HTM (or HTML) extension indicates a Web page.

The EXE extension represents an application's executable file.

Name	Size	Type
do.htm	4KB	Microsoft HTML Document 5.0
fishtank.SCR	53KB	Screen Saver
flash32.exe	265KB	Application
Houndstooth re Jackson Clarifications.doc	24KB	Microsoft Word Document
Imported Word Outline.ppt	11KB	Microsoft PowerPoint Presentation
Logo Announcement.doc	69KB	Microsoft Word Document
New Logo.gif	131KB	gif Image

Microsoft Word document files usually are indicated by a DOC extension.

Files with GIF (and JPG) extensions are graphics files.

Nearly all bitmap-based graphics programs can use any of the file formats listed in Table 11A.1. For this reason, these formats are said to be **compatible** with such programs. For example, most bitmap-based programs can open, read, and save files in GIF format and convert them to a different bitmap format, such as TIFF.

Most vector-based programs create and save files in a proprietary file format. These formats are either **incompatible** with (cannot be used by) other programs, or they are not totally supported by other programs. When they are not supported by other programs, import filters may be required in order to use these proprietary file

Table 11A.1	Standard Formats for Bitmap Graphics

Format	Description
BMP	(BitMaP) A graphics format native to Windows and OS/2, BMP is widely used on PCs for icons and wallpaper. Some Macintosh programs also can read BMP files. The BMP file format is not recommended for use with high-quality graphics images or photographs because it uses only 256 unique colors.
PICT	(PICTure) This is the native format defined by Apple for the Mac. It is widely used on Macs, but it is not usually used on PCs.
TIFF	(Tagged Image File Format) TIFF is a bitmap format, defined in 1986 by Microsoft and Aldus, that is widely used on both Macs and PCs. This format is usually the best to use when exchanging bitmap files that will be printed or edited further.
JPEG	(Joint Photographic Experts Group) JPEG is often abbreviated as JPG (pronounced JAY-peg). This bitmap format is common on the World Wide Web; it often is used for photos and other high-resolution (24-bit or millions of colors) images that will be viewed on screen.
GIF	(Graphic Interchange Format) Like JPEG images, GIF images often are found on World Wide Web pages. Unlike JPEG images, GIF images are reduced to 256 or fewer unique colors.
PNG	(Portable Network Graphics) This format was developed as an alternative to GIF and JPEG. PNG, like JPEG, can store color images in a small amount of space, but PNG files also can store transparency information the way GIF files do. The PNG format was designed mainly for use in Web pages.

formats. Import filters never work perfectly, because the program using the import filter will not have the exact features as the program that created the file. This lack of commonality has forced developers to create universal file formats, which enable users of one program to work with files created in other programs. Only a handful of common file formats, such as **DXF** (Data Exchange Format) and **IGES** (Initial Graphics Exchange Specification), exist for vector graphics. These universal formats should enable you to create a vector file in one program, such as AutoCAD, and use it in another program, such as CorelDRAW or Visio.

COPYRIGHT ISSUES

It is easy to acquire and manipulate images—so easy, in fact, that the popularity of computer graphics has brought the issue of copyright laws into the spotlight (see Figure 11A.8). Although clip art often is licensed for unlimited use, most pieces of artwork (drawings, backgrounds, buttons, animation, and photos) that you see in print or on the Internet are not licensed for use without permission. Instead, they are owned by the creator or publisher of the artwork. Artwork also may have been licensed for publication or displayed in a specific place for a limited number of times.

Adobe® FrameMaker® 5.5
Localization

Copyright 1986-1998 Adobe Systems Incorporated. All rights reserved.
345 Park Avenue, San Jose, CA 95110-2704, USA (408) 536-6000, www.adobe.com
Adobe, the Adobe logo, Acrobat, Acrobat Exchange, Adobe Type Manager, ATM, Display Postscript, Distiller, Frame, FrameMaker, FrameReader, FrameViewer, InstantView, PostScript, and SuperATM are trademarks of Adobe Systems Incorporated.
PANTONE ® and PANTONE CALIBRATED ™ are trademarks of Pantone, Inc.

Figure 11A.8
Many programs display a splash screen when started, to remind the user of copyright and trademark information. In programs that have not been registered, this type of window may be called a "nag screen" or a "beg screen," because it reminds the user that the software should be registered or paid for.

If you scan a photograph from a magazine, place it in your work, and sell it to someone else, you are infringing on a copyright, and you can be fined or prosecuted. This restriction applies even if you edit the image; making changes to someone else's work does not make you the owner. If you want to use an image you did not create solely on your own, and it is not part of a clip art package, you must contact the copyright holder for permission to use the copyrighted piece.

Self Check

Complete each statement by filling in the blank(s).

1. A(n) _Bitmap_ is a grid, the cells of which are filled with one or more colors.

2. Graphics files require users to understand and work with different _File formats_.

3. The _PNG_ file format was developed as an alternative to GIF and JPEG.

VISUAL ESSAY: GETTING IMAGES INTO YOUR COMPUTER

Nearly all graphics programs will let you create images from scratch by building simple lines and shapes into complex graphics. But artists and designers do not always start from scratch; they commonly begin with an existing image, and then edit or enhance it using graphics software. There are several ways to load images into a computer for editing. Three of the most common methods are by using scanners, digital cameras, and clip art. For full-motion video, digital camcorders are now easy and inexpensive enough for anyone to use.

A A scanner is a little bit like a photocopy machine; instead of copying the image to paper, it transfers the image directly into the computer. If the image is on paper or a slide, a scanner can convert it into a digital file that a computer can manipulate. A scanned image is usually a bitmap file, but software tools are available for translating these images into vector formats.

B Digital cameras store digitized images (in on-board flash memory and on removable media, such as a PC card, floppy disk, or disk cartridge) for transfer into a computer. The resulting file is generally a bitmap.

C The term **clip art** originated with large books filled with professionally created drawings and graphics that could be clipped from the pages and glued to a paper layout. Today, clip art provides an easy way to enhance digital documents. It is commonly available on CD-ROM, and it can easily be found online. Many programs also feature a selection of clip art. The variety of clip art is huge, ranging from simple line drawings and cartoons to lush paintings and photographs.

D **Digital video cameras** (also called **digital camcorders**) are becoming increasingly popular among home users and professional videographers. These cameras capture and store full-motion video on compact digital tapes. You can copy the tape's content onto a computer's disk for editing, and even save the video onto a compact disk or digital video disk. Full-motion video requires a great deal of storage space, but a new generation of software makes video editing easy and fun.

A

B

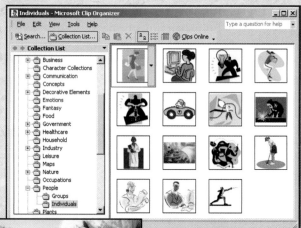

C

D

At Issue

Graphics Piracy on the Internet

One reason the World Wide Web has become so popular is its support of graphics in Web pages. By adding all sorts of images to HTML documents, Web designers make their sites more attractive and appealing to visitors. Similarly, Internet services such as FTP and newsgroups enable users to find, download, and exchange files of all types quickly, including graphics.

This easy access to images, however, also has created a cottage industry of graphics piracy, because some Internet users gather large quantities of images and distribute them online. The primary purpose of hundreds of Web sites and Usenet newsgroups is to provide users with a place to find, exchange—and sometimes even purchase—illegally obtained graphics.

The Internet provides a seemingly limitless number of pirated images, including clip art, electronic photographs, scanned artwork and photographs, video clips, and more. The subject matter of these images runs the gamut from family-oriented cartoons, to celebrity images, to pornography.

Although a small percentage of these online graphics are homemade (created by the person distributing them), the vast majority are illegally acquired by scanning or copying from digital sources. You easily can find images scanned directly from popular magazines, clips pirated from videotapes, and still images captured from television shows and movies.

The real problem is that pirates distribute these copyrighted graphics freely, ignoring the rights of the images' actual owners. Some pirates scan images from magazines, and then attempt to sell them over Web sites, through newsgroups, or on CD-ROM.

Ignorance Is No Excuse

Many graphics pirates take up this practice because they do not understand copyright laws or the possible consequences of their actions. They believe that once an image has been digitized, it enters the public domain—in other words, it is the property of no one and is free for anyone to use. Some graphics pirates believe that by making a small change to an image (such as adding a name or logo), they are making it their personal property. However, the pirates are wrong in both cases. Graphics are protected—in the United States, at least—by copyright laws that strictly limit the way graphics and images can be reused.

Staying Out of Trouble

Here are some steps you can take to make sure you are handling electronic graphics properly:

◆ **Consider the Source.** If you find images of any kind on a Web site or newsgroup, consider them suspect. If you need electronic images for a document of your own, especially if you want to sell the document, look for sources of license-free images (meaning you do not need to pay a license fee to use them) or be ready to pay a fee for an image from a legitimate source.

◆ **Get Proof and Permission.** Regardless of where you obtain an image, the distributor should be willing and able to provide proof of ownership of the image and to grant or deny permission to use it, regardless of whether a fee is involved. If you cannot obtain this type of documentation in writing (not over e-mail or on a Web page), then do not use the image.

Internet newsgroups are filled with pirated graphics.

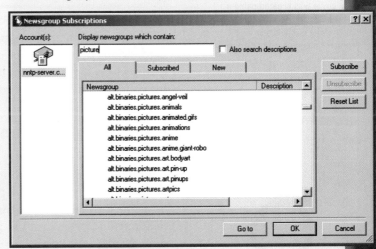

GRAPHICS SOFTWARE

Creating a digital image or manipulating an existing image can involve a complex array of processes. Since even the most sophisticated graphics program cannot perform all the operations that may be required for some types of graphics, designers frequently use more than one of the five major categories of graphics software to achieve their goals, including:

◆ Paint programs

◆ Photo-manipulation programs

◆ Draw programs

◆ Computer-Aided Design (CAD) programs

◆ 3-D modeling and animation programs

Of the five, the first two are bitmap-based paint programs; the rest are vector-based draw programs. This lesson will help you understand how artists use each type of program and why.

Paint Programs

Paint programs are bitmap-based graphics programs. You may be familiar already with a paint program, like Windows Paint, or you may have used similar bitmap-based tools in a word processor to draw simple shapes or lines in a document. Paint programs range from the very simple (with only a handful of tools) to the very complex, with tools that have names like paintbrush, pen, chalk, watercolors, airbrush, crayon, and eraser. Because paint programs keep track of each and every pixel placed on a screen, they also can perform tasks that are impossible with traditional artists' tools—for example, erasing a single pixel or creating instant copies of an image.

Paint programs lay down pixels in a process comparable to covering a floor with tiny mosaic tiles. Changing an image created with a paint program is like scraping tiles off the floor and replacing them with different tiles. For example, once you create a circle or make an electronic brush stroke, you can zoom in close enough to see the individual pixels that make up the image, as shown in Figure 11A.9. Then you can erase or tinker with the individual pixels, making minor adjustments until the image is exactly what you want.

Paint programs provide the tools for creating some spectacular effects. More sophisticated paint programs can make brush strokes that appear thick or thin, soft or hard, drippy or neat, opaque or transparent. Some programs allow you to change media with a mouse click, turning your paintbrush into chalk or a crayon or giving your smooth "canvas" a texture like rice paper or an eggshell (see Figure 11A.10).

Photo-Manipulation Programs

When scanners made it easy to transfer photographs to the computer at high resolution, a new class of software was needed to manipulate these images on the screen. Cousins to paint programs, **photo-manipulation programs** now take the place of a photographer's darkroom for many tasks. Because photo-manipulation programs (like paint programs) edit images at the pixel level, they can control precisely how a picture will look. They also are used to edit nonphotographic images and to create images from scratch. This is why some artists put

Visit **www.norton.glencoe.com** for more information on **paint and photo-manipulation programs.**

Figure 11A.9
This circle was created using a paint program. As you zoom in, making the circle larger on the screen, you can see the pixels that comprise it.

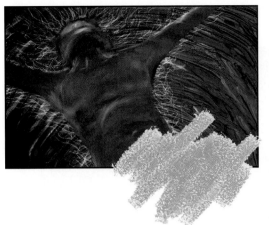

Figure 11A.10
Chalk, watercolors, and textures are a few of the effects available in sophisticated paint programs.

photo-manipulation programs in the same category as paint programs. The advent of photo-manipulation programs has caused an explosion in the use of computers for modifying images.

Although used most often for simple jobs—such as sharpening focus or adjusting contrast—photo-manipulation programs also are used to modify photographs in ways far beyond the scope of a traditional darkroom. The picture shown in Figure 11A.11, for example, obviously has been subjected to electronic manipulation.

Photo-manipulation programs can accomplish some amazing feats. After a photograph has been loaded into a computer— usually by scanning or from a digital camera or PhotoCD—the artist can change or enhance the photo, down to individual pixels, at will. For example, if a photo has dust spots or someone's eyes look red from a flash, the artist can draw the

Figure 11A.11
This image demonstrates how a photo-manipulation program can be used to combine two photos to create a striking effect.

right number of appropriately colored pixels delicately into the affected areas to correct the problem (see Figure 11A.12). Photo-manipulation programs are used frequently to correct color and brightness levels in photographs, to apply special effects, and to combine different parts of images seamlessly so that they look like a complete image.

Draw Programs

Draw programs are vector-based graphics programs that are well suited for work when accuracy and flexibility are as important as coloring and special effects. Although they do not possess the pixel-pushing capability of paint programs, draw programs can be used to create images with an "artsy" look, and so they have been adopted as the primary tool of many designers. You see the output of draw programs in everything from cereal box designs to television show credits.

NORTON
ONLINE

Visit **www.norton.glencoe.com** for more information on **draw programs**.

White lines come from scratches on the original film.

Using the airbrush tool, the artist can blend them into the background.

Figure 11A.12
Repairing a scratched image with an airbrush tool

Draw programs work by defining every line as a mathematical equation, or vector. They sometimes are referred to as object-oriented programs, because each item drawn—whether it is a line, square, rectangle, or circle—is treated as a separate and distinct object from all the others. (Some designers and draw programs use the term *entity* rather than *object,* but the concept is the same.) All objects created in modern draw programs consist of an outline and a fill. The fill can be nothing at all, a solid color, a vector pattern, a photo, or something else. For example, when you draw a square with a draw program, the computer remembers your drawing as a square of a fixed size at a specific location, that may or may not be filled—not as a bunch of pixels in the shape of a square.

Draw programs offer two big advantages over paint programs. First, when objects are created, they remain objects to the computer. After you draw a circle, you can move it intact by dragging it with the mouse—even if it has been covered with other shapes or lines—to another location. You can change the circle's shape, its size, or its color, or you can fill its interior with a color, a blend of colors, or a pattern (see figures 11A.13 and 11A.14). You can make these changes without affecting any other objects in the drawing.

Figure 11A.13
Simply by clicking and dragging in a draw program, you can change a circle into an oval. You can use similar techniques to change squares to rectangles and to modify other shapes.

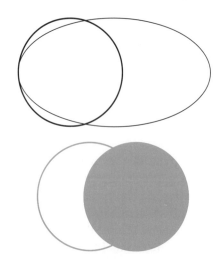

Another advantage draw programs have is the ability to resize images easily, without degrading their sharpness or focus, so that they match the size of the paper on which they will be printed. The software mathematically changes all the objects so they appear larger or smaller. Similarly, many draw programs can scale objects—increasing or reducing size by a certain factor or in relation to other objects in the drawing. With scaling, the resolution does not change, so there

Figure 11A.14
Because this circle was created with a draw program, it can be filled with a color (green, in this case), moved, and copied.

is no loss in the image's quality. Draw programs are described as resolution-independent; in other words, the image will look the same, no matter what its resolution.

Computer-Aided Design Programs

Computer-aided design (CAD), also called *computer-aided drafting* or *computer-aided drawing,* is the computerized version of the hand-drafting process that used to be done with a pencil and ruler on a drafting table. Over the last fifteen years, the drafting process has been almost completely computerized, because CAD programs have become easier to use and offer a wider array of features. CAD is used extensively in technical fields, such as architecture, and in mechanical, electrical, and industrial engineering. CAD software also is used in other design disciplines, such as textile and clothing design, product and package design.

Unlike drawings made using paint or drawing programs, CAD drawings are usually the basis for the actual building or manufacturing process of houses, engine gears, or electrical systems, for example. To satisfy the rigorous requirements of manufacturing, CAD programs provide a high degree of precision. If you want to draw a line that is 12.396754 inches long or a circle with a radius of 0.90746 centimeters, a CAD program can fulfill your needs. In fact, CAD programs are so precise, they can produce designs accurate to the micrometer—or one-millionth of a meter.

This accuracy also extends to the other end of the scale. Not only can you design the tiniest object in a CAD program, but you also can design the largest objects in full scale. In the CAD program's database, the measurements of each line are identical to their actual measurements in real life. Therefore, if you want to draw a full-scale, three-dimensional version of Earth, you can do it. (In fact, it has already been done, as shown in Figure 11A.15.)

NORTON
ONLINE

Visit **www.norton.glencoe.com** for more information on **CAD programs.**

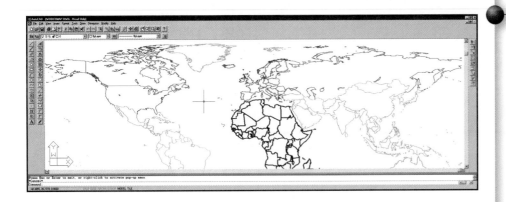

Figure 11A.15
You cannot tell from the computer screen, but in the AutoCAD database, this three-dimensional image of Earth is in full-scale. If you had a sheet of paper large enough, you could print this drawing, and it would be the same size as Earth.

The CAD world is largely responsible for the 3-D craze that has swept through the design industry since the early 1990s. Three-dimensional design started in CAD programs during the late 1980s as a way to allow designers to view their designs from all possible angles on screen. Today, most CAD programs provide different ways to design, display, animate, and print 3-D objects, called **models.** For example, **wireframe models** represent 3-D shapes by displaying their outlines and edges (see Figure 11A.16). Many CAD programs also work with **solid models,** which work by giving the user a representation of a block of solid material. The user then can use different operations (cutting, adding, combining, and so on) to shape the material and create a finished model. Once a model is finished, CAD programs can **render** the image, shading in the solid parts and creating output that looks almost real. Figure 11A.17 shows a rendered image of the wireframe model from Figure 11A.16. A solid model would look the same.

Figure 11A.16
A 3-D wireframe model

Figure 11A.17
A rendering of the 3-D wireframe model. If the model had been solid—rather than wireframe—the rendering would look almost the same.

3-D Modeling Programs

Whether you are aware of it or not, you are constantly exposed to elaborate 3-D imaging in movies, television, and print. Many of these images are now created with a special type of graphics software, called **3-D modeling software,** which enables users to create electronic models of three-dimensional objects without using CAD software. Fast workstations or PCs coupled with 3-D modeling programs can lend realism to even the most fantastic subjects.

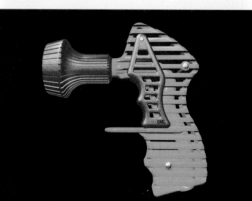

Figure 11A.18
This gear is an example of a CAD model rendered with surface modeling techniques.

Figure 11A.19
This CAD model of a spray nozzle for a hose was created using solid modeling techniques.

There are four different types of 3-D modeling programs, and each uses a different technique to create three-dimensional objects:

◆ **Surface modelers** build objects by stretching a surface—like a skin—over an underlying wireframe structure (see Figure 11A.18).

◆ **Solid modelers** use the same technique as surface modelers, but they also understand thickness and density (see Figure 11A.19). This capability can be important if you need to punch a hole through an electronic object.

◆ **Polygonal modelers** combine many tiny polygons to build objects—similar to the way one would build a geodesic dome out of many perfectly fitted triangles (see Figure 11A.20).

◆ **Spline-based modelers** build objects, either surface or solid, using mathematically defined curves that are rotated on an axis to form a 3-D shape.

Regardless of the method used to create them, 3-D objects can be modified to any shape using electronic tools, much like those used in woodworking. Wood can be cut, drilled, shaped, and sanded, using woodworking tools; similarly, objects created with a 3-D modeling program can be changed or molded by using computer tools. For example, holes can be drilled into computer-based 3-D objects, and corners can be made round or square by selecting the appropriate menu item. Three-dimensional objects also can be given realistic textures and patterns; they can be animated or made to fly through space.

Figure 11A.20
This model shows how polygonal modeling techniques can be used.

Animation

An outgrowth of the 3-D explosion is computer-based animation. Since the creation of filmmaking, animation was possible only through a painstaking process of hand-drawing a series of images (called cells), as shown in Figure 11A.21, and then filming them one by one. Each filmed image is called a **frame.** When the film is played back at high speed (usually around 30 frames per second for high-quality animation), the images blur together to create the illusion of motion on the screen. The process of manually creating a short animation—even just a few seconds' worth—can take weeks of labor.

Computer-generated imaging (CGI) has changed the world of animation in many ways. Although computer animation works on the same principles as traditional animation (a sequence of still images displayed in rapid succession), computer animators now have highly sophisticated tools that take the drudgery out of the animation process and allow them to create animation more quickly than ever. Computer animators also have the advantage of being able to display their animations on the computer screen or output them to CD-ROM, videotape, or film.

An added bonus of computer animation is the ability to animate three-dimensional characters and create **photorealistic** scenes. (The computer-generated image looks so realistic that it could be mistaken for a photograph of a real-life object.) These capabilities make computer-generated characters difficult to distinguish from real ones. Some examples are the dinosaur in *Godzilla,* the space ships in *Galaxy Quest,* and the eerie landscapes of *The Matrix.* Using computers and special animation software, artists and designers can create many types of

Figure 11A.21
Images from a traditional, manually drawn animation. Although computers speed up the animation process tremendously, they still work on the same idea: Generate hundreds or thousands of individual images, and then display them in rapid succession to create the illusion of motion.

   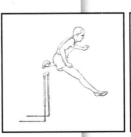 

Figure 11A.22
Computer-generated animation is often so lifelike that it is hard to distinguish from the real thing.

animation, from simple perspective changes to complex full-motion scenes that incorporate animated characters with real-life actors and sound (see Figure 11A.22).

Computers are routinely used in several kinds of animation:

◆ **The Fly-By.** In a **fly-by,** the designer sets up an exterior view of a three-dimensional model, which may be of a human-made structure (like a building or a stadium) or a natural one (such as a canyon or a storm). The view is provided by one of the software "cameras" in the CAD or 3-D software. The designer then plots a motion path for the camera—that is, a line along which the camera travels. The designer then sets the camera in motion; as the camera travels along its path, the software captures still images (frames) of the scene as if it were being recorded by a real camera. The motion path may take the camera around, over, or through the building, providing a "flying" effect or bird's-eye view. An example is shown in Figure 11A.23.

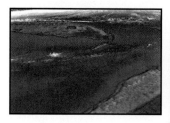 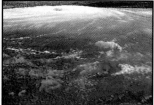 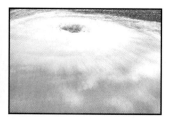 

Figure 11A.23
A 3-D fly-by can provide a bird's-eye view of a scene.

◆ **The Walk-Through.** A **walk-through** operates on the same principle as a fly-by, but it is used to capture moving interior shots of a building or scene. If you ever play a video game in which you control a character's movements through a 3-D scene, you are controlling a walk-through.

◆ **Character Animation.** **Character animation** is the art of creating a character (such as a person, an animal, or even a nonorganic item, such as a box or a car) and making it move in a lifelike manner. The basic techniques of character animation have not changed much from the drawing board to the computer. The process still involves drawing the character in a sequence of positions—one position per frame of film, and each one at a slightly more advanced position than the preceding one—until the entire movement is achieved. If a character must walk from point A to point B, for example, the designer starts by drawing the character at the starting point, and then again at the ending point of the walk (see Figure 11A.24). These two points are called the **keyframes,** because they represent the most important focal points in the action. Next, the designer creates all the frames that show the character moving between points A and B; these frames are called **tweens** (short for between, because these frames are positioned between the keyframes).

Figure 11A.24
This animation cycle shows the beginning and ending keyframes and some of the tweens that fall between them.

   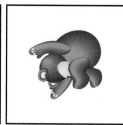 

GRAPHICS AND THE WORLD WIDE WEB

The World Wide Web has aroused interest in computer graphics, because nearly anyone can create and post a Web page. By using basic paint and draw software, it is easy to create or edit graphics for use on a Web page. Such graphics include simple items like bullets and horizontal rules, more complicated images such as logos, and complex artwork and photographs. After spending any amount of time surfing the Web, you may agree that graphic elements truly enhance the viewing experience, and that they make even a simple page look elegant (see Figure 11A.25).

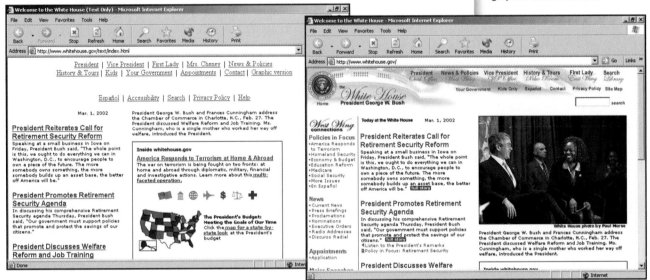

Figure 11A.25
Graphics can make nearly any Web page easier to use, or simply more appealing visually. On the left is a text-only version of the White House home page. On the right is the graphics-enabled version.

Although a Web page might look like one big graphic, most pages are actually collections of graphics and text elements, combined by the browser according to HTML tags embedded in the page's content. If any navigation buttons, icons, bullets, bars, or images appear on the page, they are separate graphics files that are being displayed at the same time. When a designer creates a Web page, he or she usually begins by adding the text elements to an HTML-format file. By surrounding the text elements with special codes—called HTML tags—the designer can cause different pieces of text to be displayed in different ways by the Web browser. Tags tell the browser what information to display—including graphics—and how to display it, as shown in Figure 11A.26.

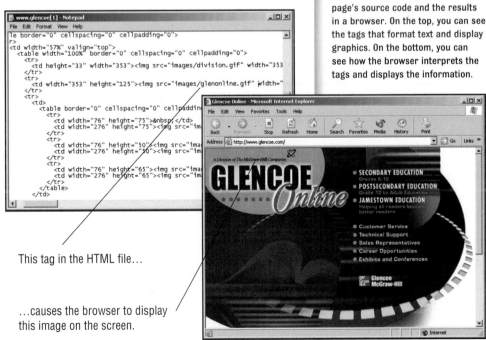

This tag in the HTML file…

…causes the browser to display this image on the screen.

Figure 11A.26
These two screens show a Web page's source code and the results in a browser. On the top, you can see the tags that format text and display graphics. On the bottom, you can see how the browser interprets the tags and displays the information.

Whenever your browser encounters a graphic in a Web page, the browser must download the graphic file from the Web server to your disk, and then display it on screen. If the file is large, or if the page contains many graphics, download time can be annoyingly slow. Therefore, Web designers have adopted a few standards to ensure that their pages download as quickly as possible from the server to the user's disk:

◆ **Resolution.** Web graphics are typically saved and displayed at a resolution of 72 pixels per inch (ppi)—although it is possible to save pictures at a much higher resolution—because monitors have a fixed display resolution of 72 ppi. As Figure 11A.27 demonstrates, higher-resolution settings do not necessarily improve the appearance of an image when it is displayed on a standard monitor. Higher-resolution images also require more storage space and take longer to download to the user's computer.

◆ **Color Depth.** Although most computer screens can display colors of up to 24 or even 32 bits (called true color), the files that take advantage of these color settings can be large. Generally, Web designers use only two file formats—GIF and JPEG—which have specific color settings and specific uses. The maximum color depth for a GIF file is 8 bits, or 256 colors. JPG images are always 24-bit images that can display millions of colors.

◆ **Image Size.** Although it is possible to save images that are larger than the user's display space, Web designers avoid this practice. When a Web page requires large graphics, designers try to ensure that the image is not so large that it will run off the edge of the user's screen at 800 × 600 screen resolution.

To maintain compatibility with the visitor's browser, designers create Web-page graphics in two file formats: GIF and JPG. Although just about any graphics file format can be used on a Web page, browsers support only the GIF, JPG, and PNG file formats without requiring the use of special plug-in software. Generally, browsers can open and view images in GIF, JPG, and PNG formats directly in the browser window, although PNG-format images are not commonly used. (For descriptions of various file formats, refer back to Table 11A.1 on page 392.)

Figure 11A.27

These three images were saved at different resolutions: 72 ppi, 144 ppi, and 244 ppi, from left to right. Note that the quality of the image does not improve much with the change in resolution.

PRODUCTIVITY Tip

Drawing Tools for Everyone

A popular piece of computing wisdom tells us this: "Having a word processor does not make you a writer." Similarly, owning some graphics software cannot make you an artist, but it cannot hurt, especially if you need to create graphics for reports, Web pages, or other projects. Even if you have no artistic skills, you can create effective graphics with basic, inexpensive (or free) software. Paint and draw programs have become so sophisticated and simple to use that you really do not need to be an artist to achieve professional-looking results.

If your graphics needs are simple, start by trying some inexpensive shareware programs. You can obtain a shareware program for free, initially, and can easily download one from Web sites such as **www.download. com/ and www.shareware.com/.** If you decide to keep the program after trying it, register your copy and pay the fee required by the developer. With some practice, you may be ready to try a full-featured commercial program.

For simple drawings (such as plain geometric shapes and line drawings), start with Windows Paint, which comes with every copy of Windows. You also can find basic drawing tools in word processing programs. If your needs are more complex, try the shareware version of a paint program such as LView (available at **www.lview. com/**) or PaintShop Pro (available at **www.jasc.com/**). Such programs offer the following features:

- ◆ **Rich Drawing Tools.** Many inexpensive programs provide a wide array of drawing tools, including brushes, chalk, pencils, airbrushes, and more.

- ◆ **Photo-Manipulation Features.** If you can save your scanned photos or digital pictures to a common file format (such as JPEG or TIFF), you can edit them, change color settings, make contrast and brightness corrections, and hide flaws.

- ◆ **Support for Multiple File Formats.** Even shareware paint programs support most commonly used file formats, such as JPEG, PCX, TIFF, and many others.

If you need to create more accurate, easily scalable drawings and want an illustrated "look" to your work, then you should get a draw program. Instead of spending several hundred dollars for a draw package, try a low-cost program such as CorelXARA (available from online vendors such as **www.i-us-com/** or **www.corel.com/**), Visio,

Shareware versions of products like PaintShop Pro are popular, because they provide professional-quality features at low cost.

or an older version of CorelDRAW. You can also download trial versions of powerful draw programs like Adobe Illustrator (at **www.adobe.com/**) and CorelDRAW (at **www.corel.com/**). Unlike shareware products, trial products may have some disabled features, or they may expire after a certain time. These programs are packed with features, such as the following:

- ◆ **Drag-and-Drop Editing.** You can move, copy, reshape, scale, and distort shapes, simply by clicking and dragging. This capability eliminates the need to navigate menus and provides instant results.

- ◆ **High Resolution and Color Depth.** Even inexpensive draw programs can save files at high resolutions and in 16 million colors.

- ◆ **Sophisticated Text Handling.** Most draw programs provide outstanding text features, allowing you to create special text effects, shows, 3-D text, and more. Because text is made of vectors, edges are clean when viewed on the screen and in print.

Low-cost and shareware CAD and 3-D modeling programs are available. If you are just beginning to experiment with computer graphics, however, you may want to delay installing or purchasing such programs. Start with the basics, and work your way up. You will be amazed at the results you can get with a little practice and patience.

SUMMARY

- Graphics files fall into one of two basic types: bitmap and vector.

- Bitmap graphics define images as a grid of cells, with each cell filled with a color. Vectors define objects in a drawing by using mathematical equations to pinpoint their location and other features.

- A file format is a means of encoding data for storage. Many different file formats are used with graphics.

- Not all file formats work in all programs, a problem called incompatibility. To solve this problem, developers have created universal file formats that are compatible across various software applications.

- There are several ways to get existing images into a computer for editing. The most popular are by using scanners, digital cameras, digital video cameras, and clip art.

- Copyright laws govern the way images can be reused and distributed; thus, the laws protect the rights of the images' owner(s).

- Paint programs work with bitmap images and manage the individual pixels that make up an image.

- Paint programs include various tools. They can be used to add special effects to an image.

- Photo-manipulation programs work with bitmap images. They are widely used to edit digitized photographs.

- Draw programs work with vectors; these programs give the designer a great deal of flexibility in editing an image. Objects created in a draw program can be altered easily and without loss of image quality.

- Computer-Aided Design (CAD) software is used in technical design fields to create models of objects that will be built or manufactured.

- Three-dimensional (3-D) modeling programs are used to create spectacular visual effects. Three-dimensional modeling programs work by creating objects via surface, solid, polygonal, or spline-based modeling.

- Computers are used to create animation for use in various fields, including games and movies. Fly-bys and walk-throughs are basic types of computer animation. Character animation is the art of creating a character and making it move in a lifelike manner.

- The GIF and JPEG image formats are the most widely used formats on the World Wide Web.

KEY TERMS

3-D modeling software, *400*
bitmap, *390*
BMP, *392*
character animation, *402*
clip art, *394*
compatible, *392*
computer-aided design (CAD), *399*
computer-generated
    imaging (CGI), *401*
digital video camera
    (digital camcorder), *394*
draw program, *397*
DXF, *393*

file format, *391*
fly-by, *402*
frame, *401*
GIF, *392*
IGES, *393*
incompatible, *392*
JPEG, *392*
keyframe, *402*
model, *399*
paint program, *396*
photo-manipulation program, *396*
photorealistic, *401*
PICT, *392*

PNG, *392*
polygonal modeler, *400*
raster, *390*
render, *400*
solid model, *399*
solid modeler, *400*
spline-based modeler, *401*
surface modeler, *400*
TIFF, *392*
tween, *402*
vector, *390*
walk-through, *402*
wireframe model, *399*

KEY TERM QUIZ

Complete each statement by writing one of the terms listed under Key Terms in each blank.

1. Paint and photo-manipulation programs work with _bitmap_ images.

2. Someone with no artistic training can use _____ as an easy way to start or enhance digital artwork.

3. If a file format and program do not work together, they are said to be _incompatible_

4. If a computer-generated object looks like a photograph of a real object, it is said to be _photorealistic_

5. With CAD programs, you can create various types of _____ to represent 3-D objects. _models_

SECTION QUIZ

True/False

Answer the following questions by circling True or False.

True ~~False~~   **1.** Vector images use groups of dots to define entities.

~~True~~ False   **2.** A typical screen resolution is 72 pixels per inch.

~~True~~ False   **3.** Draw programs are sometimes called object-oriented programs.

~~True~~ False   **4.** A spline-based modeler uses curves rotated on an axis to form 3-D shapes.

True ~~False~~   **5.** A fly-by can be used to depict an interior scene, while an exterior scene can be depicted by a walk-through.

Multiple Choice

Circle the word or phrase that best completes each statement.

1. A _____ image is a grid, the cells of which are filled with color.
   A. bitmap   **B.** vector   **C.** workstation

2. A file format is _____ .
   A. proprietary   **B.** compatible   **C.** a standardized method of encoding data for storage

3. A(n) _____ can convert a printed image into digital format.
   A. photocopier   **B.** digital camera   **C.** scanner

4. _____ programs edit images at the pixel level.
   A. Paint   **B.** Photo-manipulation   **C.** Both A and B

5. A Web designer can use _____ to tell a browser to display an image.
   A. HTML tags   **B.** resolution   **C.** both A and B

REVIEW QUESTIONS

In your own words, briefly answer the following questions.

1. Name the two primary categories of graphics files.

2. List four popular methods you can use to get digital images into a computer.

3. What is the origin of the term *clip art*?

4. Name the four types of 3-D modelers described in this unit.

5. What is character animation?

SECTION LABS

Complete the following exercises as directed by your instructor.

1. If your computer came with Windows installed, it may have one or more graphics programs, such as Windows Paint, Microsoft Image Composer, or some other program. Check your Programs menu for programs that might be used for graphics. If the product's name does not make its use clear, ask your instructor for help. List the graphics programs installed on your system.

2. Launch Windows Paint, and draw a picture. Windows Paint is a basic bitmap-based paint program that is almost always installed with Windows. To launch the program, click the Start button, open the Programs (or All Programs) menu, point to Accessories, and click Paint. Experiment with the program's drawing tools to create a simple image. Print and save the image, if your instructor approves, and then close Paint.

Understanding Multimedia

OVERVIEW:
Bringing Content to Life

As technology improves, computer users become more and more demanding. In an era of high-speed communications, we want to receive information immediately, and we want to be able to see it in different ways at the same time. This demand explains why television news channels commonly feature text that crawls across the bottom of the screen while an announcer talks and videotaped images roll. It explains why Web sites now feature graphics, animation, and sound in addition to text and hyperlinks.

Simple, one-dimensional content is no longer acceptable to most of us. Information, lessons, games, and shopping are more appealing to us and are capable of holding our attention longer if we can approach and arrange them in different ways, even on a whim. These demands and technological advances have worked hand in hand to propel the art and science of multimedia to new levels, resulting in products that weave together text, graphics, animation, audio, and video.

When we use these products—whether a Web-based encyclopedia or a CD-ROM video game—we are doing more than working with a computer program. We are experiencing a multimedia event. Today's multimedia products appeal to multiple senses at one time and respond to our changing needs with ever-increasing speed.

OBJECTIVES

- Define the terms *multimedia*, *interactivity*, and *new media*.
- Describe the six phases of the multimedia design process.
- List three technologies that support full-motion video in multimedia products.
- Identify one technology that supports streaming audio and video on the Web.

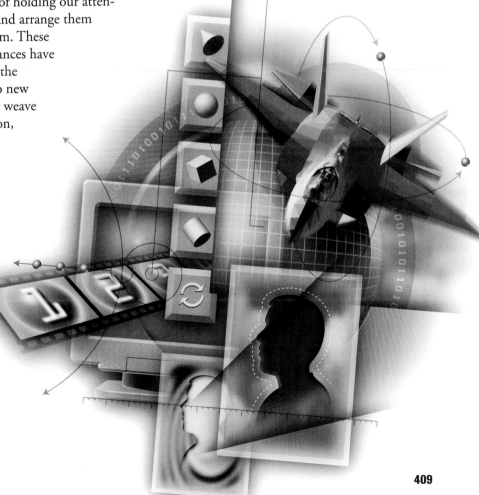

409

MULTIMEDIA, INTERACTIVITY, AND NEW MEDIA DEFINED

For much of history, information was presented via a single, unique medium. In this context, a medium is simply a way of conveying information. Sound, such as the human voice, is one type of medium; for centuries before written language came into widespread use, speech was the primary way of exchanging information (see Figure 11B.1). Eventually, people began telling stories (and leaving a record of their lives) through drawings and paintings, such as the famous cave paintings found in the Ardèche region of France.

The creation of written language gave people yet another medium for expressing their thoughts. Today, people commonly use speech, sounds, music, text, graphics, animation, and video to convey information. These are all different types of media (the term *media* is the plural of *medium*), and each traditionally has been used to present certain types of information.

Multiple Media = Multimedia

Long ago, people discovered that messages are more effective (that is, the audience understands and remembers them more easily) when they are presented through a combination of different media. This combination is what is meant by the term **multimedia**—using more than one type of medium at the same time.

In practice, you can say that even the simplest speech-and-text presentation is a multimedia event, because it uses more than one unique medium to deliver a message (see Figure 11B.2). As an example, consider teachers who use a chalkboard in the classroom so they can use written text to support a spoken lecture. At a more advanced level, people use movies and television to combine multiple types of media (sound, video, animation, still graphics, and text) to create different kinds of messages that inform or entertain in unique and meaningful ways.

Figure 11B.1
Speech is the most basic and universal medium for communicating thoughts and ideas. After centuries of practice, people find speech a natural and effective way to communicate.

NORTON ONLINE

Visit www.norton.glencoe.com for more information on **the basics of multimedia and interactivity.**

Interactivity: Just Add Users

The computer has taken multimedia to an even higher level by enabling us to use many different media simultaneously. A printed encyclopedia, for example, is basically pages of text and pictures. In a multimedia version, however, the encyclopedia's pictures can move, a narrator's recorded voice can provide the text, and the user can move around the Web site at will by clicking hypertext links and using navigational tools. By combining different types of media to present the message, the encyclopedia's developer improves the chances that users will understand and remember the information.

Of course, the same point can be made about television programming, because it uses various media at the same time. Computer technologies, however, enable PC-based multimedia products to go one step further. Because the computer can accept input from the user, it can host **interactive** multimedia events, involving the user unlike any book, movie, or television program.

Figure 11B.2
It does not take much to create a basic multimedia event. Simply by using text to underscore the important points of a spoken message, you incorporate two unique media. The number of media types used is not important, as long as the author has complete control of each medium, and the presenter delivers the message in a clear and engaging way.

Interactivity has been defined in many ways, but in the realm of multimedia, the term means that the user and the program respond to one another; the program continually provides the user with a range of choices that the user selects to direct the flow of the program. This level of interactivity is the primary difference between computer-based multimedia programs and other kinds of multimedia events. Most television programs, for example, require the viewer only to sit and observe (see Figure 11B.3). Computers, however, make it possible to create interactive media, which enable people to respond to—and even control—what they see and hear. By using the PC to control the program, the user can make choices, move freely from one part of the content to another and, in some cases, customize the content to suit a specific purpose.

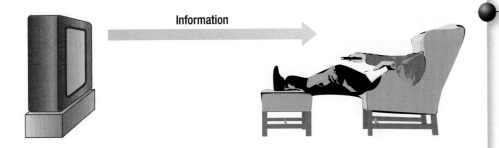

Information

Figure 11B.3
Television provides multimedia, but usually only with one-way communication. Although the viewer can select different programs to watch, television does not yet provide the level of interactivity currently available in computer-based interactive media products.

By accepting input from the user, interactive media create a **feedback loop,** which generally works as follows:

1. To start the loop, the user launches the interactive media program and chooses the content.

2. The program responds by displaying the content with choices (navigation tools, links to other topics, controls for displaying different types of content, and so on) for the user.

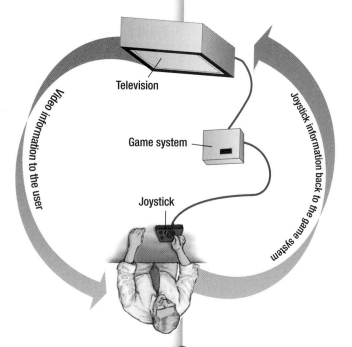

Television

Game system

Joystick

Video information to the user

Joystick information back to the game system

3. The user responds by making a choice, such as moving to a different place in the program or selecting different content.

4. The program responds to the user's selection and usually presents a new set of options for the user.

5. The process continues—sometimes at a rapid and complex pace, as in the case of many computer games—until the user stops the program (see Figure 11B.4).

Interactive media programs are effective (and successful) because they provide this give-and-take with the user. You will find this level of interactivity in practically any popular multimedia product, whether the program is a video game, a CD-based reference tool, an electronic test bank, or a shopping site on the Web (see Figure 11B.5).

The New Media

Interactivity involves more than just a computer and a mouse. The **new media** (a term encompassing all types of interactive multimedia technologies) bring together different communication technologies, such as cable TV, telephone lines, private networks, the Internet, and others. The new media are created by a convergence of many types of technology, enabling individuals and large groups to communicate and convey information using computers and communications systems.

At the core of new media is a concept known as **digital convergence.** Computers are used to create all kinds of digital content, from plain text to video. All these types of digital information can travel to the consumer along the same path—perhaps via a CD-ROM disk, a cable TV wire, or a satellite transmission. Rather than delivering movies on film or videotape, music on tapes or compact disks, and

Figure 11B.4

Interactive media with feedback loop. By choosing options continually and using the joystick to guide the action on-screen, the user can control the flow of the program's content.

Figure 11B.5

Because they provide the user with different types of content and options for navigating and displaying that content, computer-based games and references are highly interactive.

books on the printed page, different kinds of content now can reach the computer or cable TV box in the same way. Thus, a variety of content comes together, converging into one digital stream.

To the user, this technology means that multimedia content can be stored and delivered in several ways. As you use your PC, multimedia content may come from a compact disk, a DVD, your hard disk, the Internet, or an online service. If you use the television reception features of Windows, you also may receive such content in the form of television broadcasts delivered to your desktop. If you use a service such as WebTV, you can enjoy broadcast programming and Internet content simultaneously.

Depending on the technologies used, some multimedia events are strictly stand-alone, single-user applications, such as a reference book or a training program on CD-ROM. Others can involve more than one user. Examples are multiplayer games that can be accessed over a local area network or the Internet, video conferences that enable participants to see one another and share data in real time over a telephone line or a satellite connection, or interactive television shows that accept viewer input through a Web site or a chatroom.

NORTON
ONLINE

Visit www.norton.glencoe.com for more information on **new media and digital convergence.**

INFORMATION IN LAYERS AND DIMENSIONS

Multimedia developers continually look for ways to make their products more appealing to users, whether the product is a fast-paced action game, a tutorial on disk, or an e-commerce Web site. A basic strategy in multimedia development is to provide information that is layered and multidimensional. This requirement may mean giving the user multiple pieces of information simultaneously—such as a rotating 3-D image of a motor, an audio description of its function, and pop-up text boxes that provide more information when the user points at certain parts of the graphic. In a multidimensional presentation, the user has the option of experiencing the information from different perspectives; for example, one user may prefer to see only an animated demonstration of a landscaping project, while another may prefer to read a text description.

One way to make plain text and pictures inviting to an audience is to add time-based content, such as audio, cartoon animation, and video. It is important, however, that the added media do more than merely mimic the static text and graphics content. It would be boring indeed to watch a video of someone reading a passage of text that appears on the screen. But if the text is a scene from *Hamlet,* and the video displays that same scene with Sir Laurence Olivier's film portrayal, then the video enlivens the printed text.

More educational materials, including textbooks and encyclopedias, are being developed into multimedia products (see Figure 11B.6). These products use sound, animation, and video clips to make the content "come alive."

A focus on the content of a multimedia program or presentation is essential. The content is what the consumer pays for or what the audience comes to see. For example, the first feature-length

Figure 11B.6
Interactive textbooks on compact disks or Web sites can offer multimedia content to enhance the learning process.

computer-animated film, *Toy Story*, would have had limited appeal if its technical wizardry was its only attraction. But because it also had an appealing story and strong character development, the film attracted children and adults alike. Likewise, live-action films using computer animation and graphics to enhance or create objects or environments on the screen—such as the dream sequences in *The Matrix*—would have limited appeal if the story were flat.

Hypermedia: User-Directed Navigation

A major challenge accompanies the large volume of multimedia content that arrives via a compact disk, DVD, Web site, or online service: finding your way through the text, pictures, and other media available in the presentation. This challenge is where the interactivity component comes into play. The user is responsible for deciding where and when to go to a particular place within the collection of data.

Wending your way through electronic information is commonly called **navigation.** The content's developer is responsible for providing the user with on-screen aids to navigate. In software that mimics the old format of books, the navigation aid might be a simple palette of left- and right-facing arrow icons to navigate backward or forward one page. Because authors of digital content are not bound by the physical constraints of pages, they also can provide buttons that allow you to jump to locations outside the normal, linear sequence (see Figure 11B.7).

The term **hypermedia** has been coined to describe the environment that allows users to click on one type of media to navigate to the same or other type of media. You have probably encountered various types of hypermedia tools if you have spent any time surfing the Web or using disk-based multimedia products. In a Web page devoted to The Beatles, for example, clicking on a photo of the band might bring up a page containing biographies of the band members. A click on such a link may automatically connect you to a related item on a computer in another country— and it appears on your screen as if it were coming from your own hard disk (see Figure 11B.8).

Hypermedia also can exist on a smaller scale. For example, Figure 11B.9 shows a screen from the Help system in Microsoft Word that utilizes hypermedia. In this Help window, notice that some words are highlighted, indicating that they are

NORTON
ONLINE

Visit **www.norton.glencoe.com** for more information on **hypermedia**.

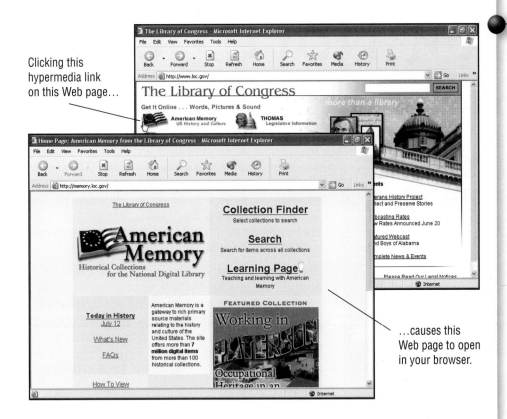

Clicking this hypermedia link on this Web page…

…causes this Web page to open in your browser.

Figure 11B.8

In any Web page, clicking a hyperlinked word or image opens a new Web page in your browser window. The first and second pages may be on the same Web server, or they may be on different servers many miles apart. The purpose of hypermedia links is to make information of all kinds, and in all locations, appear as a seamless whole, so that accessing different types of information becomes as simple as flipping through the pages of a magazine.

hyperlinks. Clicking a link may display a pop-up window, which provides a definition of a term or a list of additional links. Other links may open separate Help windows, providing helpful information on a different topic.

Even though hypermedia links often can be helpful, sometimes it is undesirable to let the user wander off to other locations, perhaps never to return. Some content must continue to exist in a linear fashion, at least for part of the time. Steps in a tutorial or a carefully crafted story, for example, must be told in an unalterable sequence for accuracy or the most dramatic impact.

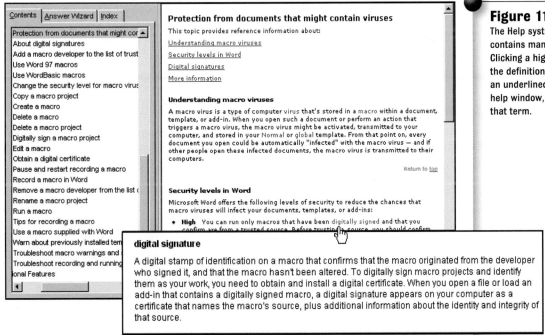

Figure 11B.9

The Help system in Microsoft Word contains many hypertext links. Clicking a highlighted term displays the definition for that word. Clicking an underlined term opens a new help window, with information about that term.

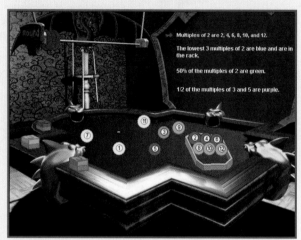

Norton Notebook

MULTIMEDIA IN EDUCATION AND TRAINING

Multimedia learning products prove that children can have fun and master basic skills while working in a game-like environment.

Education has embraced new media technologies and is one of the first and best consumers of multimedia products. In today's schools, multimedia computers are an integral part of many classrooms, and they bring a new level of interactivity to learning.

The CD-ROM-based encyclopedia is probably the most obvious example of an interactive multimedia application in education. If students must write a report on a region of Africa, they can read about its history and geography and, with the click of the mouse button, see video clips of the hustle and bustle of a city or hear audio clips of African languages and music. The information comes to life, and students may even have the software tools to produce their reports in the form of a multimedia presentation.

Even young children can engage in serious learning while having fun, and CD- and Internet-based multimedia products are at the forefront of this movement. Using animated characters to lead the way, multimedia games such as Reader Rabbit, MathBlaster, JumpStart, and other programs help young students master basic skills in an enjoyable interactive environment that provides personalized feedback.

It may seem odd that media such as animation, sound, and video would play a role in business, but there is an unstoppable trend toward enlisting these media in many business activities. Companies use new media technologies in many ways to perform internal tasks more efficiently and to reach customers more effectively.

For example, training is a never-ending task in large corporations, especially as companies expect their employees to master the latest computer technologies. As a replacement for—or supplement to—classroom training, many companies have developed customized interactive training materials. These materials fall into a category of products called computer-based training (CBT).

Corporations invest millions of dollars to develop custom CBT courses dealing with various issues, such as company policies, computer systems, and customer relations. Many companies use custom CBT products to keep sales representatives up-to-date about constantly changing products, services, and price structures—information that is essential to successful sales and account management.

CBT courseware is provided most commonly on compact disk, which is convenient for workers in the field or remote offices. These products can include audio and video content as well as text; the products can even provide real-time testing and evaluation to ensure that the user has mastered the concepts or skills being taught. Many CBT products feature an animated narrator, who leads the user through the course one topic at a time. The user can follow the course linearly, or skip from topic to topic at will. These products also may feature links to Web sites that provide more detailed information and updates on many topics. This type of content can be provided entirely over the Internet or a corporate intranet, using streaming audio and video technologies at the server end, and browser and plug-in technologies at the user's PC.

CBT products are popular training methods in corporations, used to teach employees about products, company policies, and more.

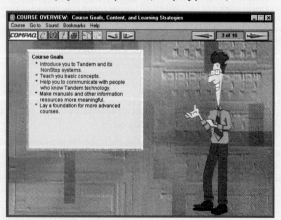

VISUAL ESSAY: CREATING NEW MEDIA CONTENT

To capture and hold the user's attention and to remain competitive with other products, a multimedia program must provide three features:

◆ Information, action, or a story line that compels the user to interact with the program.

◆ A wide assortment of cleverly and seamlessly interwoven media types.

◆ Flexibility in navigation, thus enabling the user to move around at will or even redirect the flow of content.

As a result, creating effective multimedia can be a challenging process. To cover all the bases, a multimedia development team usually includes people with various skills who adhere to a complex but well-defined development process.

A

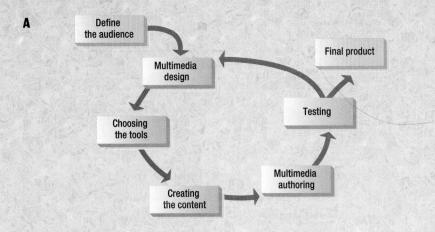

B

☐ What specific interest will the product fulfill, and what type of person has this interest?

☐ What assumptions can be made about the audience?

☐ What do users expect to gain by using this program?

☐ How much time will users want to spend exploring this content?

☐ What media will best deliver the message to this user?

☐ What method or methods (CD-Rom, DVD, Internet, intranet) will be used to distribute this product?

☐ Will a typical audience member be able to access this product easily, using the prescribed distribution method?

C

A The multimedia development process involves several distinct steps for achieving a final product. After defining the audience (Step 1), the development team begins to outline the basic structure of the product by creating a storyboard (Step 2). This helps designers decide what specific kinds of content need to be created; this knowledge is essential in the next phase of the process, which involves selecting the tools that will be used (Step 3). After that, the actual content can be created (Step 4); then the different media components can be combined in a phase called multimedia authoring (Step 5). After rigorous testing (Step 6), the product is ready to be released.

B Step 1: Define the audience. Because a multimedia program can offer so much in the way of content and can be developed in so many different ways, its creators must understand the audience. In other words, who will use the product? This issue is the most essential aspect that developers must tackle, and it is discussed in detail long before actual development work begins. To define the audience for their product, developers ask questions such as those shown here.

C Step 2: Design and storyboarding. Planning the overall design is often the longest part of the development process. A common way to start is by composing an outline of the sequences and blocks of information that will appear on the screen. This is the time to determine how much information—text, graphics, links—will be presented on each screen and to establish a navigation method for the user. When a program includes lots of animation and different scenes, the best design aid is the **storyboard**. Used for all kinds of productions, the storyboard consists of sketches of the scenes and action.

Steps 3 and 4: Choosing tools and creating content. Multimedia includes different kinds of content, so it involves many types of software. Creating text requires a word processor; digital images require graphics software; video requires a video-capture program and editing software; and sound requires its own editing software. HTML is commonly used in interactive multimedia programs, so HTML editors are important tools in the developer's arsenal. Similarly, products such as Macromedia's Shockwave—which helps developers incorporate interactive animation into multimedia products and Web pages—are increasingly common in content development. All this software is used to generate the content.

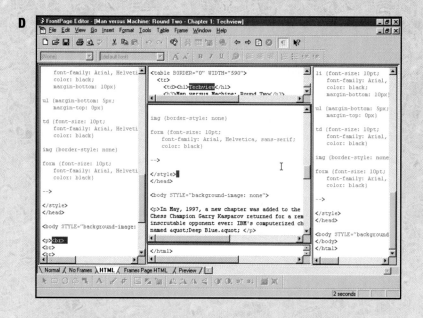

Step 5: Multimedia authoring. When the content is ready, it must be assembled in a process called **multimedia authoring.** This process requires still another type of software—such as Macromedia Director—that can understand all the different types of media, combine them, control the sequences in which they appear, and create navigational tools and an interface for the user.

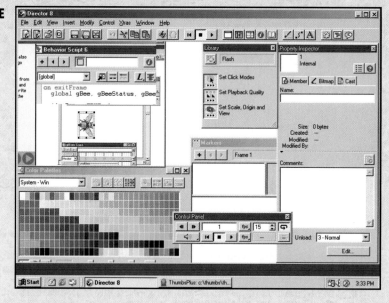

Step 6: Testing. It is vital that the program be tested by the people who ultimately will use it. With this testing, the programmer can locate any flaws and repair them before releasing the finished product. If the product does not perform as expected during testing, it may be returned to an earlier phase in the development cycle for repairs or improvements.

Complete each statement by filling in the blank(s).

1. The level of _interactivity_ differentiates computer-based multimedia programs and other kinds of multimedia events.

2. New media are created by a(n) _Convergence_ of many types of technology.

3. _Hypermedia_ is the concept behind the hyperlinks found in World Wide Web pages.

TECHNOLOGIES THAT SUPPORT NEW MEDIA

Since the first PC-based multimedia products appeared, developers and programmers have worked ceaselessly to create new technologies that will allow graphics, audio, video, and user feedback to work more seamlessly. As a result, dozens of specialized file formats, audio/video platforms, and programming techniques have become available.

Today's most sophisticated multimedia products incorporate any number of these technologies, resulting in smoother animation, audio and video streams that flow without interruption, and a heightened level of interactivity. These technologies are used in products of all kinds, from games to Web sites, and they are found in both CD-ROM-based and Web-based multimedia events.

The following sections provide a brief introduction to a few of the technologies commonly used to support multimedia products. It is not important to understand the details or operation of these technologies; however, you should be aware of their existence and the impact they can have on your multimedia experience. You also should be aware that some of the technologies require special software to function properly on your system.

MPEG and JPEG

Even though a modern multimedia PC is capable of displaying multimedia content, other factors must be considered by the multimedia developer. Perhaps the most important is the issue of data compression.

High-quality digital video requires that millions of bits be transmitted to the monitor every second. Remember, the monitor is attached to a video controller, which assigns 24 bits to each pixel on a full-color monitor. Monitors display a grid of pixels that measures at least 640 × 480, and full-motion video requires at least fifteen image frames per second. If you multiply all these numbers, you get the number of bits it takes to display digital video.

It does not matter whether the information comes from a CD-ROM and is being displayed on a monitor, or whether it comes through a cable box and is being displayed by the television. The components of the system usually are not capable of transmitting, processing, and displaying the digital information fast enough. The capacity for data transmission is known as bandwidth. Somewhere in a computer system, there is almost always a bottleneck in the bandwidth. When it comes to video, one potential solution is data compression.

Data compression typically uses mathematical analyses of digital source material to strip away unnecessary bits of data prior to sending it across the wire. This process is called **encoding**, and it results in much smaller image files than would be possible if they were not encoded. At the receiving end (for example, inside a modern cable TV converter or direct-broadcast satellite receiver), the compressed file undergoes a **decoding** process, and the missing bits are quickly reinserted to produce a copy that is extremely close to the original in quality and detail. Special hardware or software may be required to decode compressed files of certain types.

Among the most common multimedia compression schemes currently being used are JPEG (as you saw in Section 11A), which is commonly used for high-resolution still images, and **MPEG** (pronounced EM-peg, for Motion Picture Experts Group), which is used for full-motion video files (see Figure 11B.10). Each scheme is sponsored by an industry consortium whose goal is to achieve high rates of compression and industry-wide agreement on standards.

To play MPEG-format audio or video files, you need an MPEG-compliant player. Several MPEG-compliant players are available, many of which can be downloaded from various sources on the Internet.

Figure 11B.10

Many of the most colorful, high-resolution images on Web pages are JPEG-format graphics. MPEG compression allows high-quality video and audio to be viewed on the computer screen, whether the source is a compact disk or the Internet.

Figure 11B.11
Apple's QuickTime Player is commonly used on the Internet to play music videos, movie trailers, and other streaming video or audio files.

QuickTime and QuickTime VR

The **QuickTime** multimedia file format, which was developed for use on Apple computers, allows users to play high-quality audio and video files on the desktop. To play QuickTime-format files on your desktop, you need either the Apple QuickTime Player or a QuickTime plug-in that will work with your browser. (The plug-in will enable the browser to play QuickTime content directly in the browser window.) The QuickTime Player supports a wide variety of multimedia file formats, including MPEG, AVI, and others (see Figure 11B.11).

An adaptation of the QuickTime format, called **QuickTime VR,** enables developers to create virtual reality-like environments from flat, two-dimensional images. By stitching together a series of images (such as a series of photographs creating a panoramic view of an entire room or the interior of a car), QuickTime VR can be used to create immersive environments that look and feel a lot like artificial 3-D environments created by expensive VR workstations. You can view QuickTime VR movies in the QuickTime Player or in a Web browser that includes the QuickTime plug-in, as shown in Figure 11B.12.

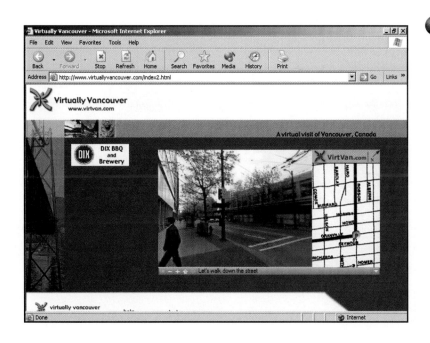

Figure 11B.12
Using QuickTime VR movies, the Virtually Vancouver Web site enables you to navigate up and down any street of Vancouver, British Columbia.

Video for Windows (AVI Format)

The **Video for Windows** format was developed by Microsoft as a way to store compressed audio and video information. Video for Windows files use the file-name extension **AVI,** which stands for *audio-video interleave.* AVI-format files do not provide the resolution or speed available from MPEG, QuickTime, and other audio-video formats. Because AVI files require no special hardware or software, they can be played on any Windows computer. AVI is seldom used in high-quality multimedia products, but it is commonly found on Web sites.

Windows Media Formats

Microsoft's Windows Media Player is one of the most popular media players around. It comes installed with Windows, is continuously updated with new features, and is free. Increasingly, file types supported by this player are becoming universal; many multimedia and Web page developers incorporate these formats into their products, knowing that the user will probably have Windows Media Player already, and so will be able to view or hear the files with no problem. In fact, other media players now also support these file types, so you may not even need to use Windows Media Player to view them, if you prefer to use another player. Similarly, Windows Media Player supports file formats used by some other media players, as well.

RealAudio and RealVideo

RealNetworks first released the RealAudio Player in 1995, and the program quickly became the standard for playing streaming audio over the Internet. Now called the RealOne Player, the product incorporates **RealVideo** and **RealAudio** technologies and can play streaming audio and video broadcast from a Web site.

As you learned in Unit 8, "The Internet and Online Resources," the terms *streaming audio* and *streaming video* refer to technologies that enable high-quality audio and video data to be transmitted over an Internet connection. Streaming capabilities are essential to many types of multimedia Web sites, such as the CNN and Weather Channel sites, which broadcast their programming live over the Internet

Figure 11B.13
Using RealPlayer technology, Web sites such as CNN Headline News Online can broadcast television programming over the World Wide Web.

Figure 11B.14
Using Shockwave content, developers can create interactive games—like this online arcade game—which can be played live on the Web.

(see Figure 11B.13). By using RealNetworks' technologies, artists such as Jimmy Buffet, the Rolling Stones, and others provide music and videos over the Web and can broadcast live concerts online. (The quality of the streaming audio and video depends on the speed of your Internet connection and the processing power of your PC.)

Shockwave and Flash

Macromedia Corp. created a stir in 1997 with the release of its Shockwave plug-in, and soon thereafter with its newer Flash animation plug-in. **Shockwave** and **Flash** are part of a suite of products that allows developers to add multimedia content (such as audio, video, and animation) to Web pages. Web designers can create multimedia content and compress it into a file that can be displayed directly in a Web page. Even though the Shockwave and/or Flash plug-ins are required to view this special interactive content, the material appears in the browser window, not in a separate window.

One advantage that Shockwave and Flash offer to Web designers is their ability to accept user input. For instance, you may be able to click on or roll your mouse pointer over a Shockwave animation to redirect the animation, cause a different event to occur, or initiate a hypertext jump. Because Shockwave supports user interaction, it can be used to develop online games, puzzles, and other types of fun interactive content (see Figure 11B.14).

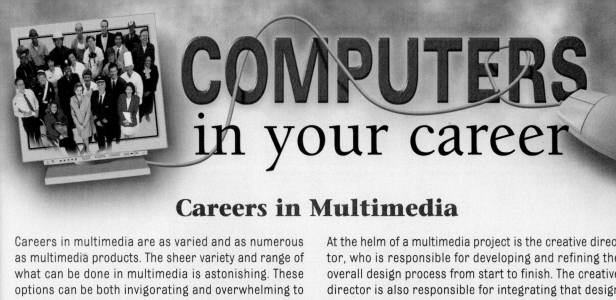

COMPUTERS
in your career

Careers in Multimedia

Careers in multimedia are as varied and as numerous as multimedia products. The sheer variety and range of what can be done in multimedia is astonishing. These options can be both invigorating and overwhelming to the multimedia professional. How is the volume of work involved in a multimedia product accomplished? Usually by a team.

At the helm of a multimedia project is the creative director, who is responsible for developing and refining the overall design process from start to finish. The creative director is also responsible for integrating that design process into the developmental process of the company. The team members of a multimedia project usually include some or all of the following:

◆ **Art Director.** He or she directs the creation of all art for the project. This work involves a variety of original media, which are changed to digital form for manipulation on the modern artist's "canvas," the computer.

◆ **Technical Lead.** He or she ensures that the technological process of a project works and that it accommodates all project components and media.

◆ **Interface Designer.** The interface designer directs the development of the user interface for a product, which includes not only what users see, but also what they hear and touch.

◆ **Instructional Designer.** This team member designs the instructional system for the product, which determines how material is taught, if the product is educational.

◆ **Visual Designer.** He or she creates the various art forms, usually within a specialized area such as graphic design, calligraphy, illustration, photography, image manipulation, packaging, or typesetting.

◆ **Interactive Scriptwriter.** The scriptwriter weaves the project's content among various media and forms of interactivity. A multimedia scriptwriter is both a writer and an interactive designer.

◆ **Animator.** Animators used to create their finished work by photographing models and sculptures or hand-drawn and painted pictures. Today, animators have a wealth of specialized 2-D and 3-D software at their disposal, which not only enables them to create animation more quickly, but also produce effects that could not be created manually.

◆ **Sound Producer.** As a manager, creative artist, and programmer, a sound producer designs and produces all the audio in a product, including musical scores, vocals, voice-overs, and sound effects. The producer makes sure that each sound interacts correctly with all the other media.

◆ **Videographer.** This professional creates the video footage that interfaces with the interactive technology of the product. Video is often the most complex, time-consuming, and resource-demanding medium to create.

◆ **Programmer/Software Designer.** He or she designs and creates the underlying software that runs a multimedia program and carries out the user's commands.

424

SUMMARY

- A medium is a way of communicating information, such as speech or text. Multimedia is the use of more than one unique medium at a time.

- Multimedia programs are described as interactive if they accept input from the user and enable the user to direct the flow of information or action in the program.

- The term new media is used to describe the combination of multimedia programming and communications technologies that enable multimedia to be distributed in different ways (such as on disk, via the Internet, or over television).

- Effective multimedia programming provides information that is layered and multidimensional.

- In layered multimedia, multiple types of information may be presented simultaneously. In multidimensional programming, the user can approach information in different ways, such as a text-only description or an animated demonstration.

- Navigation is the act of moving through electronic information. Multimedia products typically provide the user with a set of navigation tools.

- Hypermedia is commonly used in multimedia products. When the user chooses a hypermedia link, the program moves to a different piece of information, possibly represented by a different type of media.

- The process of creating a multimedia product usually results from the effort of a group of professionals who follow a multistep process.

- The development process involves defining the audience, designing the product, choosing development tools, creating content, multimedia authoring, and testing.

- Multimedia developers must gain a detailed understanding of the audience who will use the final product to make sure it will succeed.

- Using basic tools such as outlines and storyboards, designers lay out and organize the content and flow of the information for their products.

- Because a multimedia product can use so many types of media, designers use a wide variety of tools to create individual components, ranging from text editors to video editors.

- After the individual components of a multimedia product are created, the developer uses sophisticated multimedia authoring tools to assemble them into a single working program.

- A wide range of new technologies has been created to support multimedia on CD-ROM and the Internet. These technologies enable developers to create sophisticated content using almost any type of medium and allow the end user to play the content in a seamless manner.

- The MPEG, AVI, and QuickTime formats are just a few technologies that allow full-motion video files to be compressed and played back on a PC, whether from a CD or an Internet connection.

- The RealAudio and RealVideo formats are the current standard for streaming audio and video played over an Internet connection.

- Formats such as Macromedia's Shockwave allow developers to create entertaining, colorful animation that not only displays directly within a browser, but also accepts input from the user.

KEY TERMS

AVI, *422*
decode, *420*
digital convergence, *412*
encode, *420*
feedback loop, *411*
Flash, *423*
hypermedia, *414*

interactive, *410*
interactivity, *411*
MPEG, *420*
multimedia authoring, *418*
multimedia, *410*
navigation, *414*
new media, *412*

QuickTime VR, *421*
QuickTime, *421*
RealAudio, *422*
RealVideo, *422*
Shockwave, *423*
storyboard, *417*
Video for Windows, *422*

KEY TERM QUIZ

Complete each statement by writing one of the terms listed under Key Terms in each blank.

1. By accepting input from the user, interactive multimedia create a(n) *feedback loop*

2. Wending your way through electronic information is commonly called *navigation*

3. A(n) *storyboard* consists of sketches of the scenes and action that will be organized into a multimedia program.

4. The *MPEG* format is commonly used for high-resolution, moving images in multimedia products and Web sites.

5. Because they require no special hardware or software *AVI* -format files can be played on any Windows computer.

SECTION QUIZ

True/False

Answer the following questions by circling True or False.

True   False   **1.** A medium is simply a means of conveying information.

True   *False*   **2.** Digital convergence is the practice of using individual technologies in distinct, separate ways.

True   False   **3.** A computer program's help system may provide examples of hypermedia.

True   False   **4.** The multimedia development process usually involves the efforts of a group of people.

True   *False*   **5.** Video files generally are not compressed before they are included in a multimedia product.

Multiple Choice

Circle the word or phrase that best completes each statement.

1. The practice of using more than one type of medium at the same time is called _____ .
   A. interactivity　　**B.** multimedia　　**C.** a computer game

2. In a _____ , the user and program respond to one another.
   A. feedback loop　　**B.** TV program　　**C.** new media

3. To start the process of creating a new multimedia product, the developer must identify the product's
   _____ .
   A. audience　　　**B.** price　　　**C.** multimedia authoring tools

4. The term _____ refers to high-quality audio and video data transferred over an Internet connection.
   A. compression　　**B.** streaming　　**C.** multimedia

5. In multimedia programs and Web sites, the _____ format is commonly used for high-resolution still images, such as photographs.
   A. MPEG　　　**B.** AVI　　　**C.** JPEG

REVIEW QUESTIONS

In your own words, briefly answer the following questions.

1. What does the term *interactive media* mean?

2. Briefly describe what is meant by *digital convergence*.

3. List the basic steps involved in developing a multimedia product.

4. Why is data compression such an important issue for multimedia developers?

5. Explain how hypermedia links allow a user to navigate through digital content without necessarily following a linear sequence.

SECTION LABS

Complete the following exercises as directed by your instructor.

1. Is any multimedia software installed on your system? Click the Start button; then open and inspect your Programs menu. Look for programs like Windows Media Player, QuickTime Player, RealOne Player (or RealPlayer), and others. Are there any games or reference products installed?

2. If your school's computer lab or library has multimedia products on CD-ROM, check one out and use it. What type of application did you select? Determine what types of media it uses. What sorts of navigational tools does it provide? How easy is the product to use? Does it serve its purpose? Write a one-page report on the product, and summarize its strengths and flaws.

UNIT PROJECTS

UNIT LABS

Complete the following exercises using a computer in your classroom, lab, or home.

1. **Check your settings.** The way your PC displays graphics depends a great deal on your monitor's settings. You can check your settings and change them if you need better graphics performance. In this exercise, you will learn how to check monitor settings, but do not change them without your instructor's permission. Take the following steps:

   A. Right-click your Windows desktop. When the shortcut menu appears, click Properties to open the Display Properties dialog box. Click the Settings tab.

   B. Your system's color and resolution settings appear in the Settings tab. Write them down.

   C. To see the other available color settings for your system, click the Colors drop-down arrow. (This tool may be labeled Color quality, depending on which version of Windows you use.) Review the settings, and write them down. Is your system set to the highest possible color setting? Click outside the list to close it without changing anything.

   D. To see the other available resolution settings for your monitor, drag the Screen area (or Screen resolution) slider control to the right and left. It should display the available settings. Return the slider to its original position.

   E. Click Cancel to close the Display Properties dialog box.

2. **Set your volume.** If your PC has a set of speakers, you can use Windows' volume control to set the volume, mute the speakers, and possibly configure special effects. Take the following steps:

   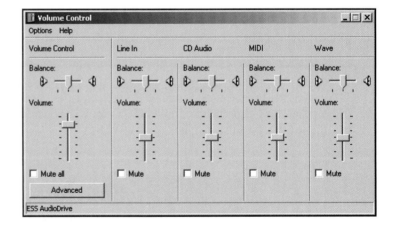

   A. On the Windows taskbar, double-click the speaker icon. The Volume Control dialog box appears. (If the speaker icon does not appear on your taskbar, ask your instructor for assistance.)

   B. Use the slider controls to set the volume and balance for your speakers. If you are not sure which setting to use, simply move all the available sliders to the middle position.

   C. Click the Advanced button to view any other options that may be available on your system. Check these settings, but do not change them.

3. **Check out some audio/video players.** As you learned in this unit, several audio and video players are available for use on the PC, and each provides a unique set of features in addition to supporting various multimedia file types. Visit these Web sites for information on a few players, but do not download any software without your instructor's permission:

Real Networks, Inc.—For information about the RealOne Player, visit **http://www.real.com/**

Microsoft Corp.—For information about Windows Media Player, visit **http://www.microsoft.com/windows/ windowsmedia/download/default.asp**

Apple Computer, Inc.—For information on the QuickTime player, visit **http://www.apple.com/quicktime/**

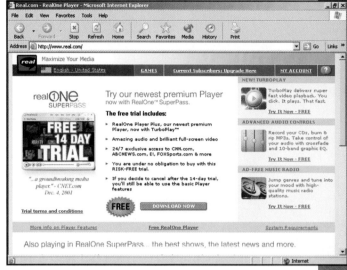

DISCUSSION QUESTIONS

As directed by your instructor, discuss the following questions in class or in groups.

1. In your opinion, what tools and techniques must today's designers know and understand to be successful?

2. You probably have been exposed to some examples of multimedia educational software. Describe the examples you have seen. What were the strengths and weaknesses of this software? What suggestions can you make for improving educational multimedia?

RESEARCH AND REPORT

Using your own choice of resources (such as the Internet, books, magazines, and newspaper articles), research and write a short paper discussing one of the following topics:

■ Copyright protection, as it applies to graphics

■ The use of multimedia programs in schools

■ The primary differences between today's most popular multimedia players, such as Windows Media Player, RealOne Player, and the QuickTime player

When you are finished, proofread and print your paper, and give it to your instructor.

ETHICAL ISSUES

Computers and graphics software provide powerful creative tools to artists and designers, but is there a downside to the explosion of computer graphics? With this question in mind, discuss the following issues in class.

1. Magazines commonly retouch photographs before printing them, especially on covers. In some cases, editors make the subjects look very different from what they look like in reality, and not always for the better. Should this type of retouching be regulated, or do you see it as a harmless practice? Support your position.

2. It is increasingly common to find copyrighted images being used on Web sites, distributed in newsgroups and chat rooms, and in other places. Often, these images are used without the knowledge or permission of their owner. Do you believe that once an image is digitized, it enters the public domain and no longer belongs to its creator? Support your position.

UNIT 12

Development of Information Systems

UNIT CONTENTS

This unit contains the following sections:

The Interactive Browser Edition CD-ROM provides additional labs and activities to apply concepts from this unit.

The Basics of Information Systems

OVERVIEW:
What Is an Information System?

In its most basic form, an **information system** is a mechanism that helps people collect, store, organize, and use information. The basic purpose of any information system is to help its users get a certain type of value from the information in the system, regardless of the type of information that is stored or the type of value desired. Information systems, therefore, can be designed to help people harness many kinds of information in countless ways. Ultimately, the information system is the computer's reason for being.

Information systems have become such a normal part of the modern business world that we do not notice them anymore. For example, do you realize that the process of making an ATM withdrawal is managed by a huge financial information system?

As you study information systems, remember that they not only help people store and retrieve data—they help people *use* information, whether that involves sorting lists, running a factory's computer-controlled machining system, printing reports, matching a single fingerprint against a national database of millions of prints, or tracking the locations of planes in the night sky.

OBJECTIVES

- Define the term *information system*.
- Name five types of information systems.
- Explain the purpose of each major type of information system.
- List at least six jobs that are part of an IS department.

THE PURPOSE OF INFORMATION SYSTEMS

Information systems consist of three basic components:

◆ The physical means for storing information, such as a file cabinet or hard disk. Depending on the organization's needs, a notebook may be enough to meet data storage requirements. For many businesses, however, data storage can be an enormous requirement that involves large computer systems with terabytes of disk space (see Figure 12A.1).

◆ The procedures for handling information to ensure its integrity. Regardless of the size of the information system, data-management rules must be followed to eliminate duplicate entries, validate the accuracy or format of data, and avoid the loss of important information.

◆ The rules regarding information's use and distribution. In any organization, data is meant to be used for specific purposes in order to achieve a desired result. For example, a sales organization will use its data to make decisions about prices, inventory, and account management. By establishing rules governing the use of its information, an organization preserves its resources, rather than wasting them on manipulating data in useless ways. To ensure the security of their mission-critical data, many organizations set rules that limit the information that can be made available to certain workers, enabling workers to access only the most appropriate types of information for their jobs. Different people require different information to perform their jobs. The rules of the system govern what information should be distributed to whom, at what time, and in what format.

Figure 12A.1
Computer storage systems often are compared to file cabinets, and for good reason: They give people a way to organize and store large amounts of information.

These basic components may seem simple, but a large information system can be very complicated. In addition to the three components listed above, it is important that the system has a means for distributing information to different users, whether it is a system of desk trays or a modern network. Most of today's information systems also include tools for sorting, categorizing, and analyzing information—further adding to their complexity, but also making them much more useful to people.

Imagine that you have agreed to maintain a list of 200 clients for a small, local flower shop. You start by buying 200 index cards. On each card, you write the name, address, and favorite flower of a client. When finished, you sort the cards alphabetically by the clients' last names. When a customer calls to order flowers, you write the type and quantity of flowers on that person's card.

Your choice of a card system (see Figure 12A.2) is understandable. For generations, card-based systems have been a popular type of database system. Commonly found in public libraries, card files also were widely used in many kinds of businesses. Despite the fact that they can be slow to set up and use, card catalogs provide a relatively intuitive way to organize information.

Figure 12A.2
For generations, card files have been a widely used (if somewhat inefficient) system for managing information. Most have been replaced by computerized systems.

This initial step of creating the card database, however, is not nearly as difficult as maintaining it. To provide timely and accurate information to the store's owner, you must update the list continually. Clients move away, and others change names or addresses. New clients must be added, and clients' preferences change. As a result, your cards quickly become covered with crossed-out information. You need to replace outdated cards, create new ones, and then sort them again. And this effort is required simply to keep track of customers!

Suppose, too, that you want to use the information on the cards to control inventory. Each day, you must order fresh flowers to make sure that the florist has the right amount and types of flowers in stock. To determine what kinds of flowers to order (and how many), you thumb through all the index cards daily to see which flowers are selling the most and the least.

Now consider the following scenario. Your manager agrees to invest in a computer system for the store. You create a database of information to track the activities of the business by setting up tables to store information about customers, products, suppliers, purchase orders, and more (see Figure 12A.3). You enter relevant information for each customer, including the name, address, and every floral arrangement purchased. When customers call and request information about their orders, you can tell them instantly what they ordered last year, where the arrangements were delivered, or what type of flowers an aunt who lives in another city prefers. This variety of information is possible because you can store different facts about each customer and order in the database (or information system) that you have created.

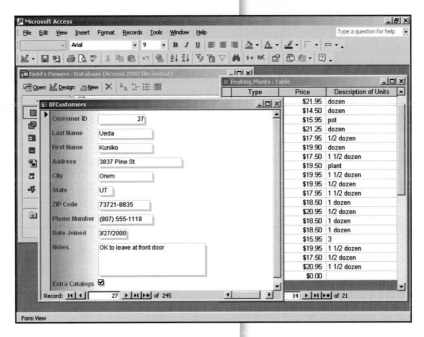

Figure 12A.3

A simple database can serve as the basis for a company's entire information system by providing information about customers, products, sales, inventory, revenues, and much more.

Using the information on sales and inventory, you create a report (that can be outputted each week) that will help the store's manager determine which flowers sold well that week. Eventually, you will have gathered enough information to predict how many flowers of each type to buy each month. As a result of the improved service, the customer base increases—as well as the volume of sales—until the store expands into three locations. The employees of the other stores enter data regarding the flowers sold, and you can continue to improve your trends analysis on flower preferences at different times of the year. In addition, you set up a system so that you can check on the availability of flowers at the different stores by checking the database.

Because you now have three locations, you want to enable your customers to shop at any store with equal convenience. This means that each store must have access to all the information in your database. To make your database available at every location, you can link the stores' computers together in a wide area network. Now your information system has grown to include a database system that contains customer information and a computer network that allows all stores to access the data when needed.

TYPES OF INFORMATION SYSTEMS

As more business functions have been automated, information systems have become increasingly specialized. One of a company's systems, for example, may be designed to help users gather and store sales orders. Another system may be designed to help managers analyze data. These specialized systems can operate alone, or they can be combined to create a larger system that performs different functions for different people.

Office Automation Systems

An **office automation system** uses computers and/or networks to perform various operations, such as word processing, accounting, document management, or communications. Office automation systems are designed to manage information and—more importantly—to help users handle certain information-related tasks more efficiently. In large organizations, simple tasks such as project scheduling, record keeping, and correspondence can become extremely time-consuming and labor-intensive. By using office automation tools, however, workers at all levels can spend less time and effort on mundane tasks, allowing time for handling more mission-critical jobs, such as planning, designing, and selling. For this reason, nearly any complete information system has an office automation component.

Office automation systems can be built from **off-the-shelf applications.** A good example is Microsoft Office—a suite of programs that includes a word processor, a spreadsheet program, a presentation program, and a database management system, as well as other tools. The programs can be used interchangeably to facilitate office tasks (see Figure 12A.4).

Transaction Processing Systems

A **transaction** is a complete event, which may occur as a series of many steps, such as taking an order from a customer. Although you may conduct business transactions frequently, you may have never considered the steps that make up a typical transaction. All of these steps can be processed through an information system. A system that handles the processing and tracking of transactions is called a **transaction processing system (TPS).**

Figure 12A.4
Companies often automate standard tasks, such as the creation of correspondence or invoices. Here, a worker is using Microsoft Excel to create an invoice based on an existing template and information from a customer database.

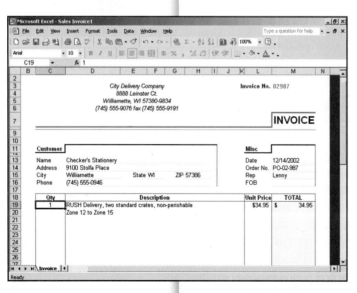

Consider the process for ordering a product from a catalog by telephone. The transaction typically begins when a customer service representative collects information about you, such as your name, address, credit card number, and the items you want to purchase. The customer service representative may enter the data into a database through an on-screen form, which ensures that the data is saved in the appropriate data tables. On the other hand, if you order or purchase a product in person, a sales clerk might "swipe" your credit card through a card reader and enter other information about you into a point-of-sales (POS) system. Either way, the critical data must be entered into the information system before the transaction's steps can be completed.

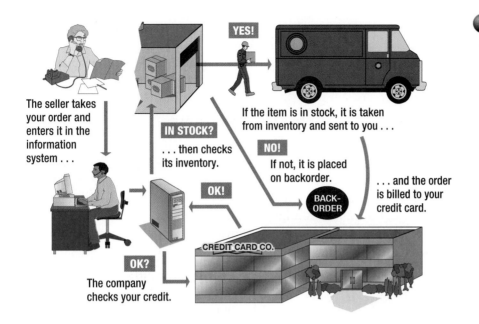

The seller takes your order and enters it in the information system . . .

IN STOCK? . . . then checks its inventory.

OK!

OK?

The company checks your credit.

YES!

If the item is in stock, it is taken from inventory and sent to you . . .

NO! If not, it is placed on backorder.

BACK-ORDER

. . . and the order is billed to your credit card.

CREDIT CARD CO.

Figure 12A.5
A simple example of a transaction processing system. In this case, your order information is used to manage the processes of inventory control, shipping, billing and payment, and more.

NORTON ONLINE

Visit www.norton.glencoe.com for more information on **transaction processing systems and decision support systems.**

After taking your order, the company verifies your credit card information, checks its inventory to determine whether the items are available, "picks" the items from inventory, ships them to you, and bills your credit card. At each step, the order must be passed to the appropriate department (see Figure 12A.5).

It is important that the right people review the data at the appropriate times. Suppose, for example, that an item you order is out of stock. In a well-designed system, a customer service representative receives an alert about this information and notifies you, giving you the option of placing the item on backorder and ensuring that your credit card will not be billed until the item is actually shipped to you. If you receive a product and want to return it, the information from your order also is used to process the return, so you do not need to restart the process with the vendor.

Decision Support Systems

A **decision support system (DSS)** is a special application that collects and reports certain types of business data, which can help managers make better decisions (see Figure 12A.6). Business managers often use decision support systems to access and analyze data in the company's transaction processing system. In addition, these systems can include or access other types of data, such as stock market reports or data about competitors. By compiling this kind of data, the decision support system can generate specific reports that managers can use in making mission-critical decisions.

Decision support systems are useful tools, because they give managers highly tailored, highly structured data about specific issues. Many decision support systems are spreadsheet or database applications that have been customized for a certain business. These powerful systems can import and analyze data in various formats, such as flat database tables or

Figure 12A.6
A simple example of a decision support system

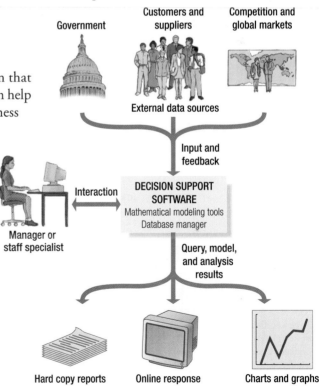

Government

Customers and suppliers

Competition and global markets

External data sources

Input and feedback

Manager or staff specialist

Interaction

DECISION SUPPORT SOFTWARE
Mathematical modeling tools
Database manager

Query, model, and analysis results

Hard copy reports

Online response

Charts and graphs

spreadsheets, two-dimensional charts, or multidimensional "cubes" (meaning that several types of data and their interrelationships can be graphically shown). They can quickly generate reports based on existing data, and they can update those reports instantly as data changes.

Management Information Systems

Within any business, workers at different levels need access to the same type of information, but they may need to view the information in different ways. At a call center, for example, a supervisor may need to see a daily report detailing the number of calls received, the types of requests made, and the production levels of individual staff members. A midlevel manager, such as a branch manager, may need to see only a monthly summary of this data shown in comparison to previous months, with a running total or average.

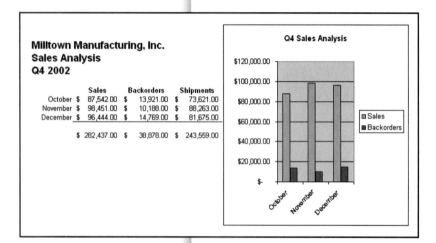

Managers at different levels also may need very different types of data. A senior manager, such as a vice president of finance or a chief financial officer, could be responsible for a company's financial performance; he or she would view the company's financial information (usually in detail) regularly. But a front-line manager who oversees daily production may receive little or no financial data, except when it specifically affects his or her area of responsibility.

A **management information system (MIS)** is a set of software tools that enables managers to gather, organize, and evaluate information about a workgroup, a department, or an entire organization. These systems meet the needs of three different categories of managers—executives, middle managers, and front-line managers—by producing different kinds of reports drawn from the organization's database. An efficient management information system summarizes vast amounts of business data into information that is useful to each type of manager (see Figure 12A.7).

Figure 12A.7

Management information systems generate reports for managers at different levels.

Expert Systems

An **expert system** performs tasks that normally would be done by a human, such as medical diagnoses or loan approvals. After analyzing the relevant data, some expert systems recommend a course of action, which a person then can consider taking. For example, a diagnostic system might review a patient's symptoms and medical history and then suggest a diagnosis and possible treatments. A doctor then can consider the system's recommendations before treating the patient.

Some expert systems are empowered to make decisions and take actions. An example is an expert system that monitors inventory levels for a grocery store chain. When the system determines that inventory of a product falls below a given level, it automatically can order a new shipment of the product from a supplier. Another good example is the type of expert system used in air traffic control. If the system detects that two aircraft are on a collision course or are flying too near one another, it can issue a warning without human intervention.

An expert system requires a large collection of human expertise in a specific area. This information is entered into a highly detailed database, called a **knowledge base,** which is refined as new information becomes available. A program called an **inference engine** then examines a user's request in light of that knowledge base and selects the most appropriate response or range of possible responses (see Figure 12A.8).

If you have ever used the World Wide Web to get technical support for a computer product, then you may have used an expert system. In the example shown in Figure 12A.9, you can specify the problem, and the system quickly finds one or more possible solutions. This type of Web-based system raises customer satisfaction by providing fast, accurate help at any time. It also helps the company manage costs by reducing the number of telephone inquiries from customers. Figure 12A.9 shows the Microsoft Windows 2000 Server Online Documentation, which is a good example of a well-structured knowledge base that allows users to search for information or get questions answered.

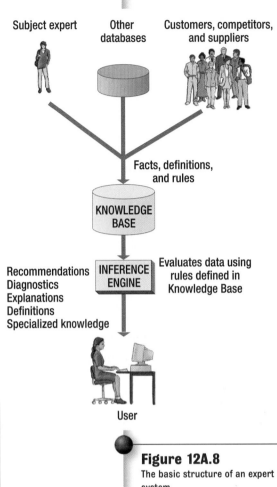

Figure 12A.8
The basic structure of an expert system

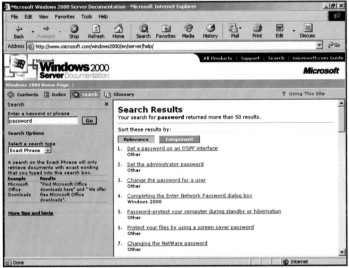

Figure 12A.9
The Microsoft Windows 2000 Server Online Documentation knowledge base

Self Check

Complete each statement by filling in the blank(s).

1. In an information system, the procedures for handling information help ensure its _____ .

2. By using _____ tools, workers reduce the time and effort spent on some tasks.

3. A(n) _____ system provides different types of information for different types of managers.

Norton Notebook

THE KNOWLEDGE WORKER

As you will see in this unit, there are plenty of career opportunities for people who want to work directly in an information systems department. Beyond those specialized careers, however, many other professions have been changed because of information systems. People in these jobs (many of which are not technical in nature) work differently than they did before; the tools and skills required by these jobs have changed dramatically, thanks to the growing use of information systems. These people are the knowledge workers, and their ranks have increased by untold numbers in the past decade.

What Is a Knowledge Worker?

The term *knowledge worker* dates back to the mid-1990s when—thanks to the proliferation of the Internet, corporate networks, and computerized information systems—people began sharing information on an unprecedented scale. As more people and organizations became connected and exchanged data electronically, many experts saw a great societal shift occurring. We were moving, they said, from the "information age" to the "knowledge age."

The knowledge worker, therefore, was any person whose work involved the use or development of knowledge of any kind. The knowledge worker's tasks might include researching, verifying, analyzing, organizing, storing, distributing, or selling knowledge. Although this may sound like a specialized field of endeavor, it really is not, because any type of information may be considered knowledge, especially if it can be used in any way within a business. Therefore, a knowledge worker might be anyone from a financial strategist who uses expert systems for economic forecasts, to a technical writer who amasses information about a particular program for use in the product's documentation.

As a result, *knowledge worker* has become a catch-all term, referring to any worker whose job involves the processing of information, whether it includes mission-critical reports or involves a simple appointment book.

Even though the term knowledge worker has been diluted by overuse, it does not diminish the knowledge worker's role in the enterprise, especially when the knowledge at hand has real value. For example, consider the demographic data used by companies to market their products or services, or the financial information crucial to helping a business overcome its accumulated debt. When analyzed and used properly, such knowledge can mean the difference between success and failure. For this reason, knowledge workers of all types should recognize the potential value of the information they handle and treat it accordingly.

Becoming an Effective Knowledge Worker

Regardless of your actual job title, your employability increases if you can prove your skills as an effective knowledge worker. Here are some tips:

◆ **Master your organization's knowledge management tools.** The actual tools vary from one organization to another, but they often include file management; word processing, database, and spreadsheet applications; and analytical tools.

◆ **Develop your information-finding skills.** You may not be expected to know everything, but you will be respected for your ability to find information quickly and effectively. Practice using information-finding tools such as Internet search engines, reference books, and others that apply to your profession.

◆ **Prove your trustworthiness.** Knowledge can include trade secrets, market feedback, contracts, licenses, and other types of proprietary information. Employers expect their workers not to share this information with anyone who should not see it, so keep private information confidential.

Internet search engines such as Google can be valuable for any knowledge worker who needs to find information on the Internet. Google can perform basic or advanced searches, making it a good choice for many kinds of information-seeking tasks.

THE INFORMATION SYSTEMS DEPARTMENT

Over the years, as large companies began automating tasks with computers and information systems, a new type of department was created to service those rapidly growing and changing systems. Initially, these departments—and the people who worked in them—were isolated from the rest of a company's operations. These specialized departments were in charge of creating the systems (typically using the corporate mainframe or minicomputers) that collected data from the operations level and turning the data into information for managers.

Eventually, however, the rise of the PC and PC-based networks changed these departments and the systems they serviced. As people other than managers became information workers, the **Information Systems (IS) department** started serving entire organizations, becoming an integral part of the business operation.

The size of a company's IS department usually is relative to the company's size. In very large companies, these departments may employ hundreds or even thousands of people. The names of these departments vary, as well as their size. The organization chart of one company may include an Information Systems (IS) department, while another company may use the name Management Information Systems (MIS) or Information Technology (IT). In this discussion, the department responsible for creating and maintaining information systems in a company is called the IS department.

The Role of the IS Department

You might imagine that the IS department's role is mainly technical—installing software, troubleshooting PCs, and so on. This description is true, but only to an extent. Modern IS departments are involved in their company's business in many ways and at many levels; after all, an IS department is responsible for providing technical resources and generating the information that the business needs to run effectively and efficiently.

In fact, IS personnel can be found in almost every part of an organization, from the production floor, where technicians install and maintain hardware and software, to the boardroom, where IS managers work with executives to plan enterprise-wide systems (see Figure 12A.10). The IS department's role, therefore, has many facets and affects almost everyone in an organization.

NORTON
ONLINE

Visit **www.norton.glencoe.com** for more information on the **role of IS departments in businesses.**

Figure 12A.10
Today's IS professionals are integrated throughout the organization, from the production line to the boardroom. IS workers are involved in a company's daily operations and in its long-term decision making.

Some of the primary responsibilities of a typical IS department include the following:

◆ **System design and planning.** As you will see in Section 12B, "Building Information Systems," IS experts follow a set of procedures when creating a new information system or modifying an existing one. As part of the process, the IS team considers current and future information needs, ways the system can support the organization's basic mission, and ways the system can be used to benefit workers.

◆ **Information generation.** To ensure that workers and managers get the exact information they need (and can input information easily), the IS team carefully plans and develops the types of forms and reports that must be generated from the system. These reports sift through data, generate specific types of information, and then present the information in a predetermined way. For example, a company may provide sales managers with a range of reports on unit sales, revenue by product, territory sales figures, and the performance of individual account managers (see Figure 12A.11).

◆ **Custom reporting.** Occasionally, special information needs arise in an organization, such as when a company decides to go public (by offering shares of its stock for sale to the public) or when expansion is imminent. At these times, the IS staff may be called on to create unique, highly customized reports from the data in the company's transaction processing system.

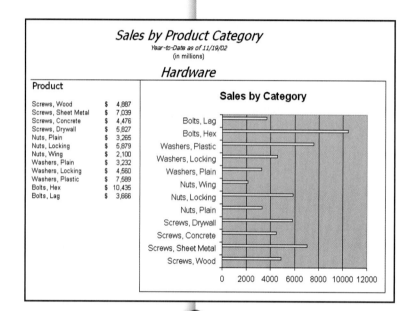

Figure 12A.11
IS departments usually are responsible for creating reports—like this sales report—using data from the organization's information system.

◆ **Hardware and software installation and maintenance.** As you would expect, the IS department provides hardware and software to any worker who needs them, and it also maintains the systems to ensure good performance. This part of the job includes installing and upgrading, troubleshooting, fixing problems, and even training workers in the use of their computerized systems.

◆ **Cost control.** In most companies, the IS department is considered a cost center—that is, a portion of the business that costs money to run but generates little or no direct revenues. Even so, the IS department plays an important role in an organization's financial picture by providing essential information to management, assisting in important decisions, and ensuring that systems run as efficiently as possible. IS departments also are charged with running in the most cost-effective manner possible, thus avoiding a drain on the organization's overall budget.

◆ **Help desk support.** In many organizations, users need ongoing help long after a new system (or part of a system) has been put into use. Many IS departments operate a **help desk,** a team of technical experts that helps the company's workers solve problems with or master the use of the information system. In many organizations, the help desk operates as a call center—an office staffed by experts who can assist workers with many kinds of problems (see Figure 12A.12). When a worker has a question or a problem with some aspect of the information system, he or she can call someone at the help desk, who can give assistance over the phone or come to the caller's aid in person. A growing number of companies now use Web-based help desk support. In this kind of system, a user logs on and describes a problem or asks a question. The system can respond in two ways—by generating possible answers from a knowledge base, or by notifying a technical support person who can give assistance.

A well-structured IS department also understands the mission of the organization and works to support that mission in the most direct manner possible. For this reason, IS departments are no longer isolated from the rest of the company, and they are becoming increasingly integrated in the day-to-day operations of organizations. Seasoned IS professionals know that they are not simply working with computers; they help the organization achieve its goals by providing the information and technical resources that each worker needs to accomplish his or her individual objectives.

Figure 12A.12
Corporate help desks can be responsible for assisting hundreds or thousands of users in the organization.

The Roles of an IS Department's Members

Building and supporting computer systems is complex work and can require the skills of many different professionals. For this reason, and because IS workers can be involved in many areas of an organization, a well-staffed IS department may include many different people working in various roles.

However, even a very large IS department may not employ individuals in all these different roles. Companies often hire other companies or individuals to provide specialized skills. This approach, in which freelance workers or outside companies are hired as contractors to do specific jobs, is called **outsourcing.** In addition, a single IS employee may provide more than one skill set, especially in a small company. A technical writer, for example, may be able to develop the help system for a program, and a systems analyst may undertake a programming role in a project.

IS Managers

Many IS departments are large enough to require their own management team, which may extend all the way to the senior level. Top-level IS managers may be involved in running the business, with status similar to that of a director or vice president. In large companies, the IS department often is led by a **chief information officer (CIO),** who works at the same level as the chief operating officer (COO) and chief financial officer (CFO) in making large-scale decisions and plans. Such managers typically have a broad background in IS technology, networking, and computer systems. Many also have a business background, or at least have a detailed understanding of the organization's mission and operations.

Computer Scientists

Computer scientists study the theory of computers by undertaking research, developing new computer designs, and attempting to achieve the next technological leap in the industry. Within academia, computer scientists take on projects such

Figure 12A.13

Technical analysts spend much of their time interviewing and listening to users.

as designing new hardware or developing new programming languages. They also work on multidisciplinary projects, such as artificial intelligence. In private industry, computer scientists apply theory, develop specialized languages, and design knowledge-based systems, such as the expert systems you read about earlier.

Technical Analysts

Technical analysts (also called systems analysts) look for solutions when an information system needs to be updated, modified, or revamped. After users or managers identify a need, analysts discuss the usability, business, scientific, or engineering problems with them (see Figure 12A.13). Technical analysts define the goals and issues of the information system. With the goals and issues defined, analysts sometimes work with computer scientists to start designing solutions. They must provide enough detail in the design so that other members of the project team can perform the work.

System Programmers

System programmers create computer programs, either as commercial products or as part of a company's information system. In some IS projects, programmers modify existing programs, consult on application design, or provide post-development support. Programmers also may be asked to create an entire application from scratch. Due to the complexity of information systems, this work usually is performed in teams, with each team responsible for specific components of the program.

Figure 12A.14

Online help authors use products such as RoboHelp to develop complete online help systems. The resulting system enables the end user to search for information on specific topics, view demonstrations, link to information on the Web or intranet, and more.

Technical Writers and Online Help Authors

Technical writers must organize and create the instructional manuals—called **documentation**—that will teach users how to operate various pieces of the information system. In the past, documentation was distributed on paper. Now, much of the information on systems is provided electronically, in online help systems (see Figure 12A.14). Many technical writers have shifted their skills from producing printed documentation to creating content for online help systems. Some organizations, however, use **online help authors** to develop these complex systems of tutorials and instructional information.

Procurement Specialists

Hardware or software **procurement specialists** (also known as purchasing agents) choose suppliers for system components and negotiate the terms for purchasing or leasing those items. Companies rely on agents because information systems are created from various components, including hardware and software. Because some percentage of these components will be bought rather than built from scratch,

IS departments need purchasing agents to bring all the pieces together within a certain time frame.

Security Administrators

Security is a sensitive issue in many organizations, especially those with networks that are connected to the Internet and thus may be susceptible to hacking. These organizations may hire one or more **security administrators**—specialists who are charged with ensuring the system's security. A security administrator may oversee the design, installation, and maintenance of the organization's firewall. These specialists also may implement the organization's strategy for password protection, remote user access to the network, user access rights to specific disks or files, and so on.

Trainers

Trainers prepare users to accept a new information system even before it is put in place. Users should be comfortable with a system before they start working with it. Through classes and one-to-one teaching sessions, trainers give users the opportunity to explore the new system, ask questions, and practice common tasks (see Figure 12A.15). Because users may forget a procedure they learned in a training class or encounter problems they cannot solve, IS personnel also provide ongoing support for users.

System or Network Administrators

System administrators or **network administrators** (sometimes called system managers or network managers) keep an information system up and running. PC-based LANs require full-time attention and maintenance to prevent system failures; even short amounts of "downtime" (periods when a system is inoperative) can be extremely costly to a business. In organizations with multiple LANs, WANs, bridges, and gateways to other systems, the network administrator may have a staff of technicians, analysts, and programmers. Network administrators handle a wide range of duties, such as controlling unauthorized access, protecting data integrity, maintaining backups, and recovering data after a disaster, such as a network-wide power outage or damage to one or more of a network's servers.

Figure 12A.15
Trainers may teach corporate users in computer-equipped classrooms or labs similar to those found on college campuses.

E-commerce Specialists

E-commerce specialists develop and implement procedures for businesses that need to conduct business online. They are charged with setting up a company's online infrastructure—a process that can include transferring some of the company's processes from a traditional framework to a completely computerized one. E-commerce specialists are primarily concerned with e-commerce strategy and planning, as well as building the necessary administrative infrastructure.

Database Specialists

Because many information systems are built around a central database, IS departments typically have at least one person who understands the database at a detailed level. **Database specialists**—sometimes called database administrators (DBAs)—may perform various essential functions, such as designing and building data tables, forms, queries, and reports used throughout the organization. Database specialists have mastered the query language used by the organization's system (such as SQL) and often possess programming skills, in addition to database-management expertise.

Hardware Maintenance Technicians

Hardware maintenance technicians maintain the hardware components of an information system. One of the most common problems for which technicians are called is a paper jam in a printer. Other problems, however, can be far more serious. Often, technicians are required for upgrading PCs with new peripherals, diagnosing problems with PCs and servers, scanning PCs for viruses, and maintaining the network (see Figure 12A.16).

Figure 12A.16

Hardware maintenance technicians install new devices and locate and solve problems in electronic equipment. Their offices often are full of circuit boards, computer parts, and testing devices.

PRODUCTIVITY Tip

Understanding Online Help Systems

For several reasons, online help systems have almost completely replaced printed manuals for many types of computer products. First, they are cheaper to produce than printed materials. Second, they can be updated and distributed much more quickly. Third, they can be interactive and intuitive, making them far more instructive and easier to use than any printed manual.

Online help can take several forms, which can be used in any combination:

◆ **Electronic documents.** An electronic document is a computer-based version of a printed manual. It may be included with software, even when no printed manuals are provided. Such documents look like printed books but are used on-screen, using a viewer such as Adobe's Acrobat Reader. Electronic documents may feature hyperlinked index and contents entries, as well as hyperlinked cross-references. You can click a heading, page number, or reference to jump to the desired section. Electronic documents also may feature search tools, bookmarking tools, and other helpful resources.

◆ **Application help systems.** Most software applications feature an online help system installed with the product. Windows-based application help systems use a standard interface; after you learn how to use one help system, you can use another with ease. Application help systems can include audio, animation, video-based demonstrations, links to Internet resources, and much more.

◆ **Web help.** Newer-generation help systems can be used over the World Wide Web or a corporate intranet through a standard Web browser. The advantage of Web help is that it is centralized—located on a single server—instead of being stored on each user's system. This enables administrators to update the information quickly.

◆ **FAQs.** Many companies post electronic documents containing frequently asked questions (FAQs) on their Web or intranet sites, on newsgroups, and on bulletin boards. As their name implies, FAQs provide

Most computer products, especially those sold to consumers, feature extensive online help systems.

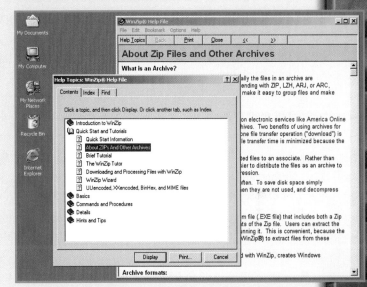

answers to the most commonly asked questions about a product, and a FAQ may be the first place to look when you have a problem with a product.

◆ **Knowledge bases.** As described elsewhere in this unit, knowledge bases can help you find information and technical support online. You can find many knowledge bases at the Web sites of companies that produce software and hardware products. To use a knowledge base, type a question or a term into the site's search box. The knowledge base then will provide you with one or more possible solutions to your problem.

◆ **E-Mail support.** Some software companies provide technical support via e-mail. You compose an e-mail message describing your question or problem, and submit it to the manufacturer. You receive a response within twenty-four hours, in most cases. Depending on the nature of your problem, you may receive a standard document or a customized response from a technical support person.

SUMMARY

- An information system includes a means of storing information, procedures for handling information, and rules that govern the delivery of information to people in the organization.

- Traditional information systems were manual and required users to manage each detail of information. An example is a card-based system, such as a card catalog in a library.

- All information systems, regardless of their type, serve the same purpose, which is to help users get value from their information.

- Office automation systems automate routine office tasks, such as correspondence and invoicing.

- Transaction processing systems not only store information about individual events, but also provide information that is useful in running an organization.

- Management information systems produce reports for different types of managers.

- Decision support systems can produce highly detailed, custom reports based on the information in an organization's transaction processing system and data from other sources. These reports can assists managers in making decisions.

- Expert systems include, in a knowledge base, the knowledge of human experts in a particular subject area. They analyze requests from users in developing a course of action.

- A well-structured IS department not only supports an organization's information systems, but also supports the organization's overall mission.

- A large IS department can include many people in a wide variety of roles, including IS managers, computer scientists, technology analysts, and others.

KEY TERMS

chief information officer (CIO), *441*
computer scientist, *441*
database specialist, *444*
decision support system (DSS), *435*
documentation, *442*
e-commerce specialist, *444*
expert system, *436*
hardware maintenance
   technician, *444*
help desk, *440*
inference engine, *437*

information system, *431*
Information Systems (IS)
   department, *439*
knowledge base, *437*
management information
   system (MIS), *436*
network administrator, *443*
office automation system, *434*
off-the-shelf application, *434*
online help author, *442*
outsource, *441*

procurement specialist, *442*
security administrator, *443*
system administrator, *443*
system programmer, *442*
technical analyst, *442*
technical writer, *442*
trainer, *443*
transaction processing
   system (TPS), *434*
transaction, *434*

KEY TERM QUIZ

Complete each statement by writing one of the terms listed under Key Terms in each blank.

1. Many office automation systems can be built from _____ , like those found in any computer store.

2. Managers commonly use _____ systems to assist in the decision-making process.

3. A(n) _____ analyzes data and produces a recommended course of action.

4. In many organizations, a(n) _____ is responsible for creating and maintaining information systems.

5. _____ (also called _____), are responsible for keeping an information system up and running.

SECTION QUIZ

True/False

Answer the following questions by circling True or False.

True	False	**1.** A factory's computer-controlled machining system would not be an example of an information system.
True	False	**2.** Although old-fashioned, a card-based system (like a library card catalog) provides a relatively intuitive way to organize information.
True	False	**3.** Most office automation systems must be built from customized software applications.
True	False	**4.** Buying a product over the Internet is an example of a transaction.
True	False	**5.** IS departments usually are isolated from other parts of the organization, and they focus exclusively on technical issues.

Multiple Choice

Circle the word or phrase that best completes each statement.

1. Many organizations set _____ that limit the information that is available to certain workers.
   A. rules   **B.** help systems   **C.** information systems

2. A(n) _____ is a complete event, such as processing an order from a customer.
   A. system   **B.** transaction   **C.** neither A nor B

3. Management information systems create different types of _____ for different types of managers in an organization.
   A. information   **B.** transactions   **C.** reports

4. An IS department understands and supports its organization's _____ .
   A. managers   **B.** mission   **C.** cost centers

5. _____ think of possible solutions when an information system needs to be updated, modified, or revamped.
   A. Computer scientists   **B.** Chief information officers   **C.** Technical analysts

REVIEW QUESTIONS

In your own words, briefly answer the following questions.

1. What is an information system?

2. What are the three basic components of an information system?

3. What is the basic purpose of any information system?

4. Why do organizations use office automation systems?

5. What is a transaction?

SECTION LABS

Complete the following exercises as directed by your instructor.

1. Determine what kinds of information systems are in place at your school. You may need to interview members of the school's IS department, or your instructor may divide the class into groups and assign each group to investigate the systems used in different departments in the school. What types of services does each system provide to its users?

2. Find out which types of IS employees work in your town. Pick a business or organization in your town and make an appointment to talk to its IS manager. Who works in that organization's IS department? Does the staff include managers, technology analysts, database specialists, programmers, or other types of specialists? Find out exactly what functions each person performs and how the organization benefits from each person's work.

Building Information Systems

OVERVIEW:
The Importance of
Well-Built Information Systems

As you learned in Section 12A, "The Basics of Information Systems," a well-designed information system can be an important factor in an organization's success. The system not only provides mission-critical information to its users, but enables users to input information quickly and efficiently.

In any organization, crucial decisions may be based on the reports produced by an information system. For this reason, developers must ensure that the system works accurately and leaves out no details as it sorts, queries, and analyzes its data. Customer satisfaction also may rely on an information system's performance, as is the case when support technicians use an expert system to help customers solve problems.

To create effective information systems, corporations will spend millions of dollars on development in a process that can take months and involve input from dozens or even hundreds of people. Along the way, IS professionals analyze the organization, its internal processes, the needs of its employees and customers, technologies already in place, and much more. All these factors are crucial to understanding the business and how an information system will help it achieve its goals. The following sections offer a brief introduction to the process that IS professionals follow in developing information systems—a process called the systems development life cycle.

OBJECTIVES

- Define the term *systems development life cycle (SDLC)*.
- Identify the five phases in the SDLC.
- Name some of the IS professionals involved in each phase of the SDLC.
- Describe four ways an organization can convert from an old information system to a new one.

THE SYSTEMS DEVELOPMENT LIFE CYCLE

To help create successful information systems, the **systems development life cycle (SDLC)** was developed. SDLC is an organized way to build an information system. As Figure 12B.1 illustrates, the SDLC is a series of five phases:

1. Needs analysis 2. Systems design 3. Development
4. Implementation 5. Maintenance

Together, the phases are called a life cycle, because they cover the entire "life" of an information system.

Phase 1: Needs Analysis

During the **needs analysis phase,** the first phase of the SDLC, the development team focuses on completing three tasks:

◆ Defining the problem and deciding whether to proceed

◆ Analyzing the current system in depth and developing possible solutions to the problem

◆ Selecting the best solution and defining its function

Phase 1 begins when the organization identifies a need, which can be met by creating a new information system or modifying the existing one. Users may complain, for example, that the current system is too difficult to use or that it does not meet some business requirement. Simple procedures may require too many steps, or the system may crash repeatedly and lose data (see Figure 12B.2). A manager may approach the IS department and request a report that is not currently produced by the system.

Technology analysts then begin a preliminary investigation, talking with users and the managers of the departments that are to be affected. The first challenge is to define the problem accurately. In many situations, the actual problem may not be the one that was reported initially to the team. Rather, it may be only a symptom of a different, underlying problem. Thus, accurately defining the problem is crucial to moving on with subsequent phases of the project.

Figure 12B.1
The systems development life cycle

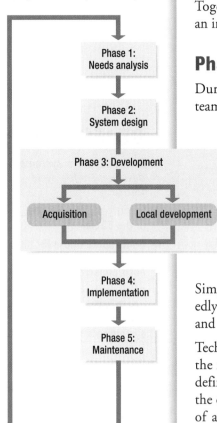

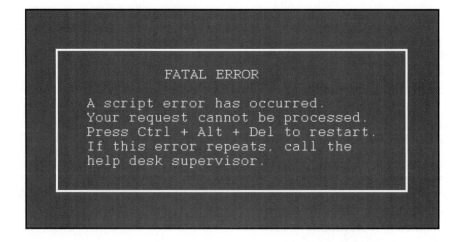

Figure 12B.2
If users see a lot of messages like this, there may be a problem with the system that needs attention from the IS department.

When the problem is defined, the IS department can decide whether to start the project (the "go/no go" decision). When a decision to proceed is made,

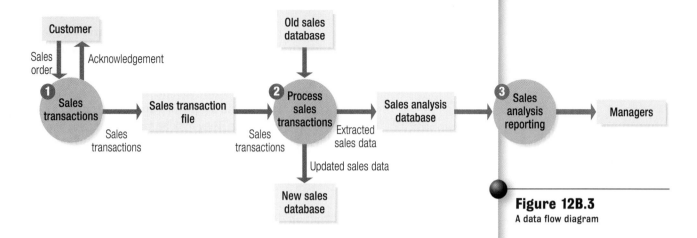

Figure 12B.3
A data flow diagram

technology analysts begin a thorough investigation of the current system and its limitations. They work with the people directly involved with the problem to document how it can be solved.

Analysts can document a problem or an entire system in several different ways. Some analysts use **data flow diagrams,** which show the flow of data through a system, as shown in Figure 12B.3. Analysts also may use **structured English**—

Figure 12B.4
Structured English

a method that uses English terms and phrases to describe events, actions, and alternative actions that can occur within the system, as shown in Figure 12B.4. Another option is to present the actions taken under different conditions in a **decision tree,** which graphically illustrates the events and actions that can occur in the system, as shown in Figure 12B.5.

> If item is received and
> > the invoice date is over 30 days old
> > > If supplier is on payment hold status
> > > > indicate status on invoice
> > > > issue pending/future payment transaction
> > >
> > > Else issue payment voucher transaction
> >
> > Else calculate payment date
> > > issue pending/future payment transaction
>
> Else issue invoiced/not received transaction

At the end of phase 1, the team recommends a solution. The analysts use information they have already gathered from system users to determine which features must be included in the solution (what reports should be generated, in what form they will be outputted, and what special tools are needed). Throughout the needs analysis phase, the team remains focused on what the system must do, not on how the features will be implemented.

Phase 2: Systems Design

During the **systems design phase,** the project team tackles the "how" of the selected solution. For example, a database application must be able to accept data from users and store it in a database. These are general functions, but how will the team implement them? How many input screens are necessary, for example, and what will they look like? What kind of menu options must be available? What kind of database will the system use?

NORTON
ONLINE

Visit **www.norton.glencoe.com** for more information on **information systems development.**

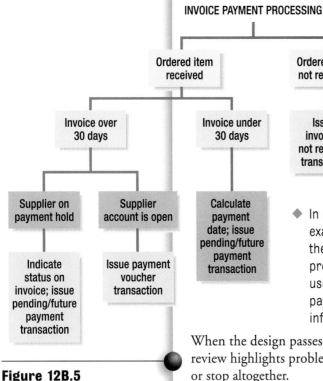

Figure 12B.5
A decision tree

The analysts and programmers involved at this point often use a combination of top-down and bottom-up designs to answer these questions:

- In **top-down design,** team members start with the big picture and move to the details. They look at major functions that the system must provide and break these down into smaller and smaller activities. Each of these activities then will be programmed in the next phase of the SDLC.

- In **bottom-up design,** the team starts with the details (for example, the reports to be produced by the system) and then moves to the big picture (the major functions or processes). This approach is particularly appropriate when users have specific requirements for output—for example, payroll checks, which must contain certain pieces of information.

When the design passes inspection, development begins. Sometimes, however, a review highlights problems with the design, and the team must return to analysis or stop altogether.

Many tools are available to help teams through the steps of system design. Most of these tools also can be used during the development phase (phase 3) or even during analysis (phase 1). Many teams, use working models called **prototypes** to explore the look and feel of screens with users. They also use special software applications for creating these prototypes quickly, as well as for building diagrams, writing code, and managing the development effort. These applications fall into the category of **computer-aided software engineering (CASE) tools.** In other words, computer software is used to develop other computer software more quickly and reliably.

Phase 3: Development

During the **development phase,** programmers play the key role, creating or customizing the software for the various parts of the system. There are two alternative paths through phase 3: the acquisition path or the local development path.

- **Acquisition.** As early as phase 1, the team may decide that some or all of the necessary system components are available as off-the-shelf hardware or software and may decide to acquire, rather than develop, these components. Buying off-the-shelf components means that the system can be built faster and cheaper than if every component is developed from scratch. Another advantage of acquired components is that they already have been tested and proven reliable, although they may need to be customized to fit into the overall information system.

- **Local development.** When an off-the-shelf solution is not available or will not work with other parts of the system, the project team may need to develop a solution themselves. On the software side, this means writing program code from scratch or making changes to existing software in the system. On the hardware side, it may mean physically constructing a portion of the information system, typically using purchased components.

In many cases, project teams buy some components and develop others. Thus, they follow both acquisition and local development paths at the same time through the SDLC (see Figure 12B.6).

Figure 12B.6

These parts are created or acquired during phase 3.

SOFTWARE DEVELOPMENT	SYSTEM AND USER DOCUMENTATION	PURCHASED COMPONENTS
Prototyping CASE tools Programming Unit testing Test planning System testing Purchased software integration	**Technical documentation** Database structures Menu systems User views Data and process flows **User documentation** System manuals Training materials	**Hardware components** Purchase vs. lease decisions RFP/RFQ processes Integration testing **Software components** Outsourcing Integration programming Integration testing

SYSTEM DEVELOPMENT PHASE

During this phase, technical writers and/or online help authors work with the project team to produce the technical documentation and online help for the system. Testing is also an integral part of phases 3 and 4 (development and implementation). The typical approach to testing is to move from an individual component to the system as a whole. The team tests each component separately (unit testing) and then tests the components of the system with each other (system testing). Errors are corrected, the necessary changes are made, and the tests are then run again. The next step is installation testing, when the system is installed in a test environment and tested with other applications used by the business. Finally, acceptance testing is done; the end users test the installed system to make sure that it meets their criteria.

Self Check

Complete each statement by filling in the blank(s).

1. The _____ is an organized way to build an information system.

2. _____ begins when a need is identified for a new or modified information system.

3. During the systems design phase, the project team may take either the _____ or _____ approach to design.

Phase 4: Implementation

In the **implementation phase,** the project team installs the hardware and software in the user environment. The users start using the system to perform work, rather than just to provide feedback on the system's development.

The process of moving from the old system to the new is called **conversion.** IS professionals must handle this process carefully to avoid losing or corrupting data or frustrating users trying to perform their work.

At Issue

Protecting Intellectual Property

Because people now use computers to exchange information with unprecedented freedom, organizations are faced with the growing problem of keeping proprietary and/or confidential information safe.

What Is Intellectual Property?

The term "intellectual property" can be defined in different ways, and many experts take differing views of it as a concept. But in very simple terms, intellectual property can be described as any creative, original work that could be protected under an applicable law, such as copyright or trademark law.

For instance, if you write a novel and you can prove that it is your own original creation, you may consider it your intellectual property. If you copyright the work, your rights of ownership are protected by law.

But many businesses have claimed other kinds of items as intellectual property, insisting that those items be afforded protection under law, whether or not they are actually copyrighted, trademarked, or patented. Many items, including software programs, source code, the contents of corporate databases, trade secrets, internal policies, official correspondence, and other kinds of corporate documents may be considered the intellectual property of their creators, it has been argued.

Whether you agree with such arguments or not, companies today are taking measures to secure their intellectual properties.

Companies may regard many kinds of information as intellectual property, whether it can be copyrighted or not, and take steps to safeguard it.

How Is Intellectual Property Threatened?

A few years ago, companies worried they might lose their trade secrets to corporate spies who might raid their trash dumpsters or steal files or computers. They also worried about unhappy employees who might sell sensitive information to competitors. Those concerns are still real, but today's networked corporations have other, more pressing worries. These threats include:

◆ **Internal threats.** If an unhappy employee e-mails a secret formula to a competitor or posts a customer list on a Web site, a company's very existence could be threatened.

◆ **Hackers.** Malicious hackers continually try to invade corporate networks to destroy or steal sensitive data, such as lists of customer names and credit card numbers.

◆ **Reverse engineering.** In this process, software or another type of product is dismantled in order to figure out how it works. This is why software developers keep their source code secret, so no one can reverse engineer the product and then use that information to create a competing product.

◆ **Viruses.** If a company does not guard its network against viruses, huge losses can result from data destruction and reduced productivity.

Protecting Intellectual Property

In today's workplace, companies use two techniques to protect intellectual assets:

◆ **Technology.** IS professionals are considered the first line of defense against threats to intellectual property. Data is protected by using virus scanners, firewalls, proxy servers, filters, password-protection systems, regular data backups, and much more.

◆ **Policies.** Many companies require employees to agree to strict policies, and discipline, fire, or sue workers who fail to follow the rules. Such policies may govern the use of computers and networks, e-mail, use of the Internet, and the handling of documents or trade secrets.

As shown in Figure 12B.7, there are several different ways to convert a department or an organization, including the following:

◆ **Direct conversion.** All users stop using the old system at the same time and then begin using the new. This option is fast, but it can be disruptive; pressure on support personnel can be excessive.

◆ **Parallel conversion.** Users continue to use the old system, while an increasing amount of data is processed through the new system. The outputs from the two systems are compared; if they agree, the switch is made. This option is useful for additional live testing of the new system, but it is fairly tricky, because both systems are operating at the same time.

◆ **Phased conversion.** Users start using the new system, component by component. This option works only for systems that can be compartmentalized.

◆ **Pilot conversion.** Personnel in a single pilot site use the new system, and then the entire organization makes the switch. Although this approach may take more time than the other three, it gives support personnel the opportunity to test user response to the system thoroughly. The support team then will be better prepared when many people make the conversion.

Trainers and support personnel play a significant role during the conversion. Training courses usually involve classroom-style lectures, hands-on sessions with sample data, and computer-based training that users can work with on their own time.

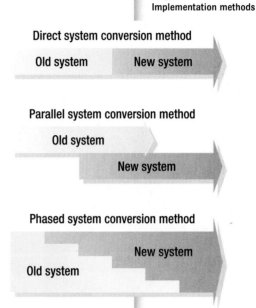

Figure 12B.7
Implementation methods

Phase 5: Maintenance

After the information systems are implemented, IS professionals continue to provide support during the **maintenance phase.** They monitor various indices of system performance, such as response time, to ensure that the system is performing as intended. They also respond to changes in users' requirements. These changes occur for various reasons. As users work with the system on a daily basis, they may recognize instances where a small change in the system would allow them to work more efficiently. In addition, management may request changes due to a change in state or federal regulations of the industry.

Errors in the system also are corrected during phase 5. Systems are often installed in a user environment with known programming or design errors. Typically, these errors have been identified as noncritical or not important enough to delay installation. Programmers have lists of such errors to correct during the maintenance phase. In addition, daily use of the system may highlight more serious errors for the programmers to fix.

Changes, or upgrades, to the system are made regularly during the remaining life of the system. At some point, however, making patch repairs to the system may not meet user requirements—particularly if radical changes have been made since the system was installed. The IS professionals or managers in a user department might then begin calling for a major modification or new system. At this point, the SDLC has come full circle, and the analysis phase begins again.

COMPUTERS
in your career

IS Professionals

As you have seen in this unit, there are many different careers in information systems technology. However, a thorough knowledge of computers may not be enough to land a dream job in an IS department, although it is a good start. To improve your prospects, you should consider getting some specialized training in the area of technology that most interests you. Some areas of specialized training include the following:

◆ **Network administration certification.** The network is an essential part of any information system, and many companies prefer to hire networking professionals who have earned certification in specific network technologies. For example, Novell and Microsoft offer certification programs for their network operating systems and other network-related products. One of Microsoft's more popular certification programs is their Microsoft Certified Systems Engineer (MCSE) program. Novell offers several certification programs, such as the Certified Novell Administrator (CNA) or the Certified Novell Engineer (CNE). Certification is also available for networking hardware, such as cabling, bridges, routers, and gateways. There are various certification levels available, from basic LAN administration to enterprise-wide development and management. In terms of hardware certifications, the A+ Hardware examination is a good first start in terms of basic help desk and support certifications. If you do not want to go through the rigors of a proprietary certification, such as the MCSE or CNA programs, you may prefer a vendor-neutral networking certification, such as CompTIA's Network+ program.

◆ **Software programming.** Software is a key component in any information system, and the demand for programmers continues to rise. Qualified programmers have training in current development languages, such as Java, C++, VisualBasic, and others. Because so many organizations depend on customized database systems, database-related skills (such as a knowledge of SQL and database structure) are considered essential to any programmer's résumé.

◆ **Database administration.** A database management system is at the heart of any corporate IS department, and database programmers and developers are constantly in demand. If you are interested in database management, you may be advised to study as many different DBMS applications as you can (such as Oracle, Sybase, Microsoft SQL Server, and others) and master the use of database querying tools, as well as the creation of forms and reports. Exposure to standard programming languages—such as C++, VisualBasic, and Java—also can help ensure your success in database development.

◆ **PC hardware and electronics.** Hardware maintenance technicians are always in demand, and their value increases as they learn more about new technologies. If a career in hardware maintenance appeals to you, consider studying electronics, as well as PC technologies. A counterpart of the hardware maintenance technician is the configuration specialist, who focuses on customizing hardware to meet special needs. This person is essential for keeping the business on the cutting edge of technology. These professionals have expertise not just in PC and electronics, but also in telecommunications and networking.

To ensure your long-term success in IS, remember that information systems are part of a complete business and are not simply an entity unto themselves. Successful IS managers often study business in addition to technology, earning advanced degrees, such as a master of business administration (MBA). With business expertise, the IS professional can better understand the relation of the IS department to the company and work more intelligently toward building information systems that help the company achieve its all-important business goals.

456

SUMMARY

- The systems development life cycle (SDLC) is an organized method for building an information system.

- The SDLC includes five phases: needs analysis, systems design, development, implementation, and maintenance.

- The needs analysis phase includes: (1) defining the problem and deciding whether to proceed with the project; (2) analyzing the current system; and (3) selecting a solution.

- During system design, the project team decides how the solution will work.

- During development, programmers create or customize software for the system.

- During implementation, the hardware and software are installed in the user environment.

- The process of moving from an old system to a new one is called conversion. The project team may follow four different conversion methods: direct, parallel, phased, and pilot.

- During the maintenance phase, IS professionals provide ongoing training and support to the system's users. Fixes or improvements to the system are made during its remaining life.

KEY TERMS

bottom-up design, *452*

computer-aided software engineering (CASE) tool, *452*

conversion, *453*

data flow diagram, *451*

decision tree, *451*

development phase, *452*

implementation phase, *453*

maintenance phase, *455*

needs analysis phase, *450*

prototype, *452*

structured English, *451*

systems design phase, *451*

systems development life cycle (SDLC), *450*

top-down design, *452*

KEY TERM QUIZ

Complete each statement by writing one of the terms listed under Key Terms in each blank.

1. The abbreviation SDLC stands for _____ .

2. During the _____ phase of the SDLC, the project team determines "how" a solution will work.

3. In _____ , the IS team starts with the big picture and moves to the details.

4. Programmers play the key role in the _____ phase of the SDLC.

5. The final phase of the SDLC is called the _____ phase.

SECTION QUIZ

True/False

Answer the following questions by circling True or False.

True   False   1. In the needs analysis phase of the SDLC, the first challenge is to accurately define any problems that might exist in the information system.

True   False   2. In the systems design phase, designers decide what the system must do.

True   False   3. If off-the-shelf products can be used, the development phase of the SDLC can be skipped.

True   False   4. Testing takes place during the development and implementation phases of the SDLC.

True   False   5. In a pilot conversion, users start using the new information system component by component.

Multiple Choice

Circle the word or phrase that best completes each statement.

1. During needs analysis, the development team must _____ .
   A. define the problem   **B.** implement the system   **C.** neither A nor B

2. By using _____ , developers can verbally describe the events, actions, and alternative actions that can occur within an information system.
   A. data flow diagrams   **B.** structured English   **C.** prototypes

3. In _____ , developers look at major system functions and break them into smaller activities.
   A. top-down design   **B.** bottom-up design   **C.** both A and B

4. When programmers take the _____ path, they elect to create system components.
   A. acquisition   **B.** maintenance   **C.** local development

5. The process of moving from an old system to a new one is called _____ .
   A. implementation   **B.** conversion   **C.** system design

REVIEW QUESTIONS

In your own words, briefly answer the following questions.

1. Why is it so important that information systems be well designed and structured?

2. What is the main focus of the systems design phase of the SDLC?

3. Describe the differences between top-down and bottom-up design.

4. What is the difference between the acquisition path and the local development path, in the development phase of the SDLC?

5. What are the four types of conversion methods that may be used in the implementation phase of the SDLC?

SECTION LABS

Complete the following exercises as directed by your instructor.

1. Using a sheet of paper, draw a decision tree that shows the actions and alternatives (such as order input, customer support, billing, and so on) that can occur in one portion of a transaction processing system. Your instructor may divide the class into groups and ask each group to design a tree for a specific part of the system.

2. Create some user documentation. Open a word processor, write a single paragraph of text on any subject, and then format the text. Now create a one-page document that explains the process of creating and formatting that paragraph. Write the documentation for someone who has never used a word processor. Be sure to include numbered steps, and explain the procedure in detail.

UNIT PROJECTS

UNIT LABS

Complete the following exercises using a computer in your classroom, lab, or home.

1. **Create Your Own IS Department.** Suppose that your city has just been granted an NFL expansion team. The team's owner is in the process of building a new stadium and hiring office staff; the team owner has hired you to be the organization's CIO. Your first task is to determine the types of information systems the team will need, and then you must hire IS professionals to build and maintain those systems. Follow these steps:

   A. Using two pieces of paper, map the information systems you think will be needed.

   B. List the IS department positions you want to fill.

   C. Describe the role you want each IS staff member to play.

   When you are finished with your diagrams and lists, share them with the class. Be prepared to support your design and hiring decisions.

2. **Chart the Flow.** On a piece of paper (or several pieces, if necessary), create a data flow diagram that maps the flow of data for a transaction processing system for a business that sells tickets to events, such as concerts or ball games.

3. **Get a Job.** Visit the following Web sites and see if you can find job listings for IS professionals, such as technology analysts, network administrators, or technical writers:

   - NationJob Network—**http://www.nationjob.com/**
   - Monster.com—**http://www.monster.com/**
   - EDP Professionals—**http://www.misjobs.com/**

4. **Search for Knowledge.** The Microsoft Knowledge Base is an excellent example of an online expert system. You can use it to obtain technical support and answer questions about any Microsoft product. Access the Microsoft Knowledge Base:

   A. Visit the Microsoft Web site at **http://www.microsoft.com/**

   B. Click the Support link, and then click the Knowledge Base link.

   C. When the Knowledge Base page appears, click the drop-down arrow next to the Search box and select a product, such as Internet Explorer or a version of Windows.

   D. Click in the For solutions containing box, and type a term that relates to the product you selected. For example, if you selected Windows XP as the product, you could type **security** in this box to find documents pertaining to security features and known security problems in Windows XP.

E. Click the Search now link. If the knowledge base contains any documents that match your search criteria, they are listed in the window. Click a link to view a document.

F. Once you get the hang of using the knowledge base, search for information on at least two more products.

DISCUSSION QUESTIONS

As directed by your instructor, discuss the following questions in class or in groups.

1. Suppose that you run a manufacturing facility that produces automotive parts. Discuss the types of information that would be important to the operation of the plant. What kind of information system or systems would you want to use at the facility?

2. Discuss the issues addressed during the needs analysis phase of the SDLC for a new hospital. What are the biggest challenges during this phase?

RESEARCH AND REPORT

Using your own choice of resources (such as the Internet, books, magazines, and newspaper articles), research and write a short paper discussing one of the following topics:

- Ownership of data on a corporate network. (For example, if you receive an e-mail message at work, who owns that message?)

- What type of information system is used by online retailers, such as amazon.com or orbitz.com? How do these retailers make use of their information systems?

- Pick one of the IS department jobs listed earlier in this unit, and do a more in-depth analysis of it. What is the salary range for that position? What kind of educational background is required for such a job?

When you are finished, proofread and print your paper, and give it to your instructor.

ETHICAL ISSUES

Information systems can make it easier for workers at many levels to access information within an organization. With this thought in mind, discuss the following questions in class.

1. In some organizations, managers insist that certain classes of employees be prevented from accessing some types of information, such as financial data. In your view, is this practice fair? Why or why not? What business reasons would managers have for limiting access to certain types of information?

2. You have become tired of your job so, while at work, you use a company PC and printer to create a new resume and cover letter. You store these files on the company's network, and they are found by a manager, who threatens to fire you for your actions. Is the manager correct in following this course of action? Support your views on this issue.

The History of Microcomputers

IN THE BEGINNING

In 1971, Dr. Ted Hoff puts together all the elements of a computer processor on a single silicon chip slightly larger than one square inch. The result of his efforts is the Intel 4004, the world's first commercially available micro-processor. The chip is a 4-bit computer containing 2,300 transistors (invented in 1948) that can perform 60,000 instructions per second. Designed for use in a calculator, it sells for $200. Intel sells more than 100,000 calculators based on the 4004 chip. Almost overnight, the chip finds thousands of applications, paving the way for today's computer-oriented world and for the mass production of computer chips now containing millions of transistors.

1975

The first commercially available micro-computer, the Altair 880, is the first machine to be called a "personal computer." It has 64 KB of memory and an open 100-line bus structure. Selling for about $400, the Altair 880 comes in a kit to be assembled by the user.

Two young college students, Paul Allen and Bill Gates, unveil the BASIC language interpreter for the Altair computer. During summer vacation, the pair form a company called Microsoft, which eventually grows into one of the largest software companies in the world.

At Bell Labs, Brian Kernighan and Dennis Ritchie develop the C pro-gramming language, which quickly becomes the most popular professional application development language.

1976

Steve Wozniak and Steve Jobs build the Apple I computer. It is less powerful than the Altair, but also less expensive and less complicated. Users must con-nect their own keyboard and video display, and they have the option of mounting the

computer's motherboard in any container they choose— whether a metal case, a wooden box, or a briefcase. Jobs and Wozniak form the Apple Computer Company together on April Fool's Day, naming it after their favorite snack food.

1977

The Apple II computer is unveiled. It comes already assembled in a case, with a built-in keyboard. Users must plug in their own TVs for monitors. Fully assembled microcomputers hit the general market, with Radio Shack, Commodore, and Apple all selling models. Sales are slow, because neither businesses nor the general public know exactly what to do with these new machines.

Datapoint Corporation announces Attached Resource Computing Network (ARCnet), the first commercial LAN technology intended for use with microcomputer applications.

1978

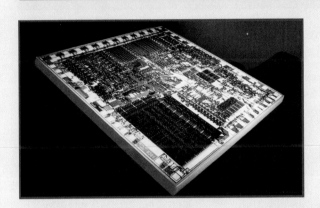

Intel releases the 8086 microprocessor, a 16-bit chip that sets a new standard for power, capacity, and speed in microprocessors.

Epson announces the MX-80 dot-matrix printer, coupling high performance with a relatively low price. (Epson from Japan sets up operations in the U.S. in 1975 as Epson America, Inc. and becomes one of the first of many foreign companies to contribute to the growth of the PC industry.)

1979

Intel introduces the 8088 microprocessor, featuring 16-bit internal architecture and an 8-bit external bus.

Motorola introduces the 68000 chip, used in early Macintosh computers.

Software Arts, Inc. releases VisiCalc, the first commercial spreadsheet program for personal computers. VisiCalc is generally credited as being the program that paved the way for the personal computer in the business world.

Bob Metcalf, the developer of Ethernet, forms 3Com Corp. to develop Ethernet-based networking products. Ethernet eventually evolves into the world's most widely used network system.

MicroPro International introduces WordStar, the first commercially successful word processing program for IBM-compatible microcomputers.

Appendix A   463

1980

IBM chooses Microsoft (co-founded by Bill Gates and Paul Allen) to provide the operating system for its upcoming PC. Microsoft purchases a program developed by Seattle Computer Products called Q-DOS (for Quick and Dirty Operating System), and modifies it to run on IBM hardware.

Lotus Development Corporation unveils the Lotus 1-2-3 integrated spreadsheet program, combining spreadsheet, graphics, and database features in one package.

Bell Laboratories invents the Bellmac-32, the first single-chip microprocessor with 32-bit internal architecture and a 32-bit data bus.

1981

IBM introduces the IBM-PC, with a 4.77 MHz Intel 8088 CPU, 16 KB of memory, a keyboard, a monitor, one or two 5.25-inch floppy drives, and a price tag of $2,495.

Hayes Microcomputer Products, Inc., introduces the SmartModem 300, which quickly becomes the industry standard.

Xerox unveils the Xerox Star computer. Its high price eventually dooms the computer to commercial failure, but its features inspire a whole new direction in computer design. Its "little box on wheels" (the first mouse) can execute commands on screen (the first graphical user interface).

1982

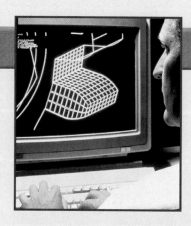

Intel releases the 80286, a 16-bit microprocessor.

AutoCAD, a program for designing 2-D and 3-D objects, is released. AutoCAD will go on to revolutionize the architecture and engineering industries.

Work begins on the development of TCP/IP. The term *Internet* is used for the first time to describe the worldwide network of networks that is emerging from the ARPANET.

1983

Time magazine features the computer as the 1982 "Machine of the Year," acknowledging the computer's new role in society.

Apple introduces the Lisa, the first commercial computer with a purely graphical operating system and a mouse. The industry is excited, but Lisa's $10,000 price tag discourages buyers.

IBM unveils the IBM-PC XT, essentially a PC with a hard disk

and more memory. The XT can store programs and data on its built-in 10 MB hard disk.

The first version of C++ programming language is developed, allowing programs to be written in reusable, independent pieces, called objects.

The Compaq Portable is released, the first successful 100 percent PC-compatible clone. Despite its hefty 28 pounds, it becomes one

of the first computers to be lugged through airports.

1984

Adobe Systems releases its PostScript system, allowing printers to produce crisp print in a

number of typefaces, as well as elaborate graphic images.

Apple introduces the "user-friendly" Macintosh microcomputer.

IBM ships the IBM-PC AT, a 6 MHz computer using the Intel

80286 processor, which sets the standard for personal computers running DOS.

IBM introduces its Token Ring networking system. Reliable and redundant, it can send packets at 4 Mbps; several years later, it speeds up to16 Mbps.

Satellite Software International introduces the WordPerfect word processing program.

1985

Intel releases the 80386 processor (also called the 386), a 32-bit processor that can address more than 4 billion bytes of memory. It performs ten times faster than the 80286.

Aldus releases PageMaker for the Macintosh, the first desktop publishing software for microcomputers. Coupled with Apple's LaserWriter printer and Adobe's PostScript system, PageMaker ushers in the era of desktop publishing.

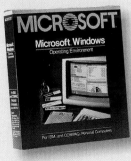

Microsoft announces the Windows 1.0 operating environment, featuring the first graphical user interface for PCs.

Hewlett-Packard introduces the Laser Jet laser printer, featuring 300 dpi resolution.

1986

IBM delivers the PC Convertible, IBM's first laptop computer and the first Intel-based computer with a 3.5-inch floppy disk drive.

Microsoft sells its first public stock for $21 per share, raising $61 million in the initial public offering.

The First International Conference on CD-ROM technology, hosted by Microsoft, is held in Seattle. Compact disks are seen as the storage medium of the future for computer users.

1987

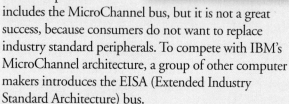

IBM unveils the new PS/2 line of computers, featuring a 20-MHz 80386 processor at its top end. This product line includes the MicroChannel bus, but it is not a great success, because consumers do not want to replace industry standard peripherals. To compete with IBM's MicroChannel architecture, a group of other computer makers introduces the EISA (Extended Industry Standard Architecture) bus.

IBM introduces its Video Graphics Array (VGA) monitor, which offers 256 colors at 320 × 200 resolution and 16 colors at 640 × 480.

The Macintosh II computer, aimed at the desktop publishing market, is introduced by Apple Computer. It features an SVGA monitor. Apple also releases HyperCard, a programming language for the Macintosh based on the metaphor of a stack of index cards to represent a program—a kind of visual programming language.

Motorola unveils its 68030 microprocessor.

Novell introduces its network operating system, called NetWare.

1988

IBM and Microsoft ship OS/2 1.0, the first multi-tasking desktop operating system. High price, a steep learning curve, and incompatibility with existing PCs contribute to its lack of market share.

Apple Computer files the single biggest lawsuit in the computer industry against Microsoft and Hewlett-Packard, claiming copyright infringement of its operating system and graphical user interface.

Hewlett-Packard introduces the first popular ink jet printer, the HP Deskjet.

Steve Jobs' new company, NeXT, Inc., unveils the NeXT computer, featuring a 25-MHz Motorola 68030 processor. The NeXT is the first computer to use object-oriented programming in its operating system and an optical drive, rather than a floppy drive.

Apple introduces the Apple CD SC, a CD-ROM storage device allowing access to up to 650 MB of data.

A virus called the "Internet Worm" is released on the Internet, disabling about ten percent of all Internet host computers.

1989

Intel releases the 80486 chip (also called the 486), the world's first one-million-transistor microprocessor. The 486 integrates a 386 CPU and math coprocessor onto the same chip.

Tim Berners-Lee develops software around the hypertext concept, enabling users to click on a word or phrase in a document and jump either to another location within the document or to another file. This software provides the foundation for the development of the World Wide Web, and it is the basis for the first Web browsers.

The World Wide Web is created at CERN, the European Particle Physics Laboratory in Geneva, Switzerland, for use by scientific researchers.

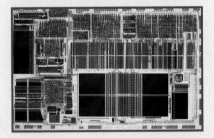

Microsoft's Word for Windows introduction begins the "Microsoft Office" suite adoption by millions of users. Word for DOS had been the second-highest-selling word processing package behind WordPerfect.

1990

Microsoft releases Windows 3.0, shipping 1 million copies in four months.

A multimedia PC specification setting the minimum hardware requirements for sound and graphics components of a PC is announced at the Microsoft Multimedia Developers' Conference.

The National Science Foundation Network (NSFNET) replaces ARPANET as the backbone of the Internet.

Motorola announces its 32-bit microprocessor, the 68040, incorporating 1.2 million transistors.

1991

Apple Computer launches the PowerBook series of battery-powered portable computers.

Apple, IBM, and Motorola sign a cooperative agreement to design and produce RISC-based chips, integrate the Mac OS into IBM's enterprise systems, produce a new object-oriented operating system, and develop common multimedia standards. The result is the PowerPC microprocessor.

1992

With an estimated 25 million users, the Internet becomes the world's largest electronic mail network.

In Apple Computer's five-year copyright infringement lawsuit, Judge Vaughn Walker rules in favor of defendants Microsoft and Hewlett-Packard, finding that the graphical user interface in dispute is not covered under Apple's copyrights.

Microsoft ships the Windows 3.1 operating environment, including improved memory management and TrueType fonts.

IBM introduces its ThinkPad laptop computer.

1993

Mosaic, a point-and-click graphical Web browser, is developed at the National Center for Supercomputing Applications (NCSA), making the Internet accessible to those outside the scientific community.

Intel, mixing elements of its 486 design with new processes, features, and technology, delivers the long-awaited Pentium processor. It offers users more than 3.1 million transistors.

Apple Computer expands its entire product line, adding the Macintosh Color Classic, Macintosh LC III, Macintosh Centris 610 and 650, Macintosh Quadra 800, and the PowerBooks 165c and 180c.

Apple introduces the Newton MessagePad at the Macworld convention, selling 50,000 units in the first ten weeks.

Microsoft ships the Windows NT operating system.

IBM ships its first RISC-based RS/6000 workstation, featuring the PowerPC 601 chip developed jointly by Motorola, Apple, and IBM.

1994

Apple introduces the Power Macintosh line of microcomputers based on the PowerPC chip. This line introduces RISC to the desktop market. RISC was previously available only on high-end workstations.

Netscape Communications releases the Netscape Navigator program, a World Wide Web browser based on the Mosaic standard, but with more advanced features.

CompuServe, America Online, and Prodigy add Internet access to their services.

After two million Pentium-based PCs hit the market, a flaw in the chip's floating-point unit is found by Dr. Thomas Nicely.

Linus Torvalds releases Linux, a freeware version of UNIX created by a worldwide collaboration of programmers who shared their work over the Internet.

Intel releases the Pentium Pro microprocessor.

Motorola releases the PowerPC 604 chip, developed jointly with Apple and IBM.

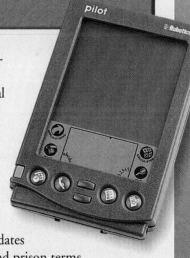

Microsoft releases its Windows 95 operating system with a massive marketing campaign, including prime-time TV commercials. Seven million copies are sold the first month, with sales reaching 26 million by year's end.

Netscape Communications captures more than 80 percent of the World Wide Web browser market, going from a start-up to a $2.9 billion company in one year.

A group of developers at Sun Microsystems create the Java development language. Because it enables programmers to develop applications that will run on any platform, Java is seen as the future of operating systems, applications, and the World Wide Web.

Power Computing ships the first-ever Macintosh clones, the Power 100 series with a PowerPC 601 processor.

Intel announces the 200 MHz Pentium processor.

U.S. Robotics releases the Pilot, a personal digital assistant that quickly gains enormous popularity because of its rich features and ease of use.

Microsoft adds Internet connection capability to its Windows 95 operating system.

Several vendors introduce Virtual Reality Modeling Language (VRML) authoring tools that provide simple interfaces and drag-and-drop editing features to create three-dimensional worlds with color, texture, motion video, and sound on the Web.

Congress enacts the Communications Decency Act as part of the Telecommunications Act of 1996. The act mandates fines of up to $100,000 and prison terms for transmission of any "comment, request, suggestion, proposal, image or other communication which is obscene, lewd, lascivious, filthy, or indecent" over the Internet. The day the law is passed, millions of Web page backgrounds turn black in protest. The law is immediately challenged on Constitutional grounds, ultimately deemed unconstitutional, and repealed.

VRML WORLDS BY JEFF HARRINGTON

1997

Intel announces MMX technology, which increases the multimedia capabilities of a micro-processor. Also, Intel announces the Pentium II microprocessor. It has speeds of up to 333 MHz and introduces a new design in packaging, the Single Edge Contact (SEC) cartridge. It has more than 7.5 million transistors.

AMD and Cyrix step up efforts to compete with Intel for the

$1,000-and-less PC market. Their competing processors are used by PC makers such as Dell, Compaq, Gateway, and even IBM.

The U.S. Justice Department charges Microsoft with an antitrust lawsuit, claiming Microsoft practiced anticompetitive behavior by forcing PC makers to bundle its Internet Explorer Web browser with Windows 95.

Netscape Communications and Microsoft release new versions of their Web browser. Netscape's Communicator 4 and Microsoft's Internet Explorer 4 provide a full suite of Internet tools, including Web browser, newsreader, HTML

editor, conferencing program, and e-mail application.

Digital Video Disk (DVD) technology is introduced. Capable of storing computer, audio, and video data, a single DVD disk can hold an entire movie. DVD is seen as the storage technology for the future, ultimately replacing standard CD-ROM technology in PC and home entertainment systems.

1998

Microsoft releases the Windows 98 operating system. Seen mainly as an upgrade to Windows 95, Windows 98 is more reliable and less susceptible to crashes. It also offers improved Internet-related features, including a built-in copy of the Internet Explorer Web browser.

The Department of Justice expands its actions against Microsoft, attempting to block the release of Windows 98 unless Microsoft agrees to remove the Internet Explorer browser from the operating system. Microsoft fights back and a lengthy trial begins in federal court, as the government attempts to prove that

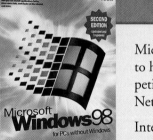

Microsoft is trying to hold back competitors such as Netscape.

Intel releases two new versions of its popular Pentium II chip. The Pentium II Celeron offers slower performance than the standard PII, but it is aimed at the $1,000-and-less PC market, which quickly embraces the chip. At the high end, the Pentium II Xeon is designed for use in high-performance workstations and server systems, and it is priced accordingly. Both chips boost Intel's market share, reaching deeper into more vertical markets.

Apple Computer releases the colorful iMac, an all-in-one system geared to a youthful market. The small, lightweight system features the new G3 processor, which outperforms Pentium II–based PCs in many respects. The iMac uses only USB connections, forcing many users to purchase adapters for system peripherals, and the computer does not include a floppy disk drive.

1999

Intel unveils the Pentium III processor, which features 9.5 million transistors. Although the Pentium III's performance is not vastly superior to the Pentium II, it features enhancements that take greater advantage of graphically rich applications and Web sites. A more powerful version of the chip (named Xeon) also is released, for use in higher-end workstations and network server systems.

With its Athlon microprocessor, Advanced Micro Devices finally releases a Pentium-class chip that outperforms the Pentium III processor. The advance is seen as a boon for the lower-price computer market, which relies heavily on chips from Intel's competitors.

Apple Computer introduces updated versions of its popular iMac computer, including a laptop version, as well as the new G4 system. The G4's performance is rated at 1 gigaflop, meaning the system can perform more than one billion floating point operations per second.

The world braces for January 1, 2000, as fears of the "Millennium Bug" come to a head. Airlines, government agencies, financial institutions, utilities, and PC owners scramble to make their systems "Y2K-compliant." Some people panic, afraid that basic services will cease operation when the year changes from 1999 to 2000.

2000

Shortly after the New Year, computer experts and government officials around the world announce that no major damage resulted from the millennium date change. People were concerned that major problems would occur when computer clocks rolled over from 1999 to 2000. Immediately, a global debate began to rage: Had the entire "Y2K bug" been a hoax created by the computer industry as a way to reap huge profits from people's fears? Industry leaders defended their approach to the Y2K issue, stating that years of planning and preventive measures had helped the world avoid a global computer-driven catastrophe, which could have brought the planet's economy to a stand-still.

Microsoft introduces Windows 2000 on February 17. It is the biggest commercial software project ever attempted and also is one of the largest engineering projects of the century, involving 5,345 full-time participants, over half of them engineers. The final product includes almost 30 million lines of code.

On March 6, Advanced Micro Devices (AMD) announces the shipment of a 1 GHz version of the Athlon processor, which will be used in PCs manufactured by Compaq and Gateway. It is the first 1 GHz processor to be commercially available to the consumer PC market. Within days, Intel Corp. announces the release of a 1 GHz version of the Pentium III processor.

In April, U.S. District Judge Thomas Penfield Jackson rules that Microsoft is guilty of taking advantage of its monopoly in operating systems to hurt competitors and leverage better deals with its business partners.

Intel releases the long-awaited Itanium processor—a hybrid CISC/RISC chip with more than 25 million transistors. The chip is designed for use in high-end workstations and server computers.

Microsoft releases the Windows XP operating system, with versions for home computers and business desktops. The XP version of Microsoft Office is also unveiled.

After suffering years of losses to digital music pirates, the Recording Industry Association of America (RIAA) files lawsuits against purveyors of MP3 technology—most notably Napster, an online service that enables users to share MP3-format files freely across the Internet. The suits effectively shut down Napster, but do not stop individuals and other file-sharing services from exchanging illegally copied music files.

Several versions of recordable DVD disks and drives hit the market. Users instantly adopt the devices to store digitized home movies and software, but movie pirates soon begin copying and distributing movies on DVD.

After several years of explosive growth, the "dot-com" revolution goes into sudden reverse. As thousands of Web-based companies go out of business (giving rise to the phrase "dot-bomb"), tens of thousands of workers lose their jobs, shareholders suffer billions of dollars in losses, and the world's financial markets learn a valuable lesson.

Technology takes an important new role in society after the United States is attacked by terrorists on September 11, 2001.

Government agencies, the military, and airlines place a new emphasis on security, recruiting new high-tech methods to monitor travellers and inspect people and baggage for dangerous items. Almost immediately, billions of dollars are invested in the development of new bomb-detection technologies and the creation of a huge, multinational database that can allow airlines to track the movements of passengers through the flight system.

Due to the high cost of flying and concerns about security, many American businesses drastically reduce business travel. Increasingly, companies rely on technologies such as video-conferencing, teleconferencing, and online document sharing to work with partners and customers.

After a year of devastating shake-outs, the dot-com world begins to pick itself up again. The new breed of online entrepreneur bases companies on sound business practices, rather than the glamour of simply being "new economy." Investments in new online ventures slow to a trickle, enabling only those companies with the best ideas and a real promise of profits to flourish.

The wireless networking boom continues, with an emphasis on enabling handheld computers and telephones to access the Internet via wireless connections. Products such as digital two-way pagers, wireless phones, and combination telephone/PDAs sell at unprecedented levels.

Self Check
Answers

Section 1A, page 10
1. computer
2. memory
3. disk drive

Section 1B, page 25
1. network
2. ARPANET
3. No single person or group

Section 2A, page 50
1. QWERTY
2. Shift
3. scan code

Section 2B, page 67
1. Pen-based computers
2. joysticks, game pads
3. Optical character recognition (OCR)

Section 3A, page 88
1. Monochrome
2. electron gun
3. viewing angle

Section 3B, page 102
1. resolution
2. print head
3. Daisy wheel

Section 4A, page 121
1. transistors
2. binary number system
3. Unicode

Section 4B, page 136
1. microprocessor
2. Advanced Micro Devices (AMD)
3. Motorola

Section 5A, page 163
1. storage media
2. electromagnets
3. cluster

Section 5B, page 177
1. milliseconds
2. File compression
3. data transfer rate

Section 6A, page 194
1. desktop
2. Start button
3. task switching

Section 6B, page 211
1. graphical user interfaces
2. Macintosh OS
3. operating environment

Section 7A, page 242
1. network server (or server)
2. Electronic mail (or e-mail)
3. peer-to-peer network

Section 7B, page 257
1. modulator-demodulator
2. bits per second (bps)
3. uploading

Section 8A, page 277
1. IP address
2. hyperlinks (or links)
3. plug-in *or* helper

Section 8B, page 297
1. remote terminal
2. digital subscriber line
3. cable modem

Section 9A, page 326
1. word processor
2. editing
3. Indents

Section 9B, page 340
1. spreadsheet
2. cell pointer
3. value

Section 10A, page 355
1. slide
2. template
3. handles

Section 10B, page 368
1. database
2. flat-file database
3. table

Section 11A, page 393
1. bitmap
2. file formats
3. PNG

Section 11B, page 419
1. interactivity
2. convergence
3. Hypermedia

Section 12A, page 437
1. integrity
2. office automation
3. management information system (MIS)

Section 12B, page 453
1. systems development life cycle (SDLC)
2. Needs analysis
3. top-down, bottom-up

GLOSSARY

3-D modeling software Graphics software used to create electronic models of three-dimensional objects. Types of 3-D modeling software include surface, solid, polygonal, and spline-based modelers.

3-D worksheet In a spreadsheet program, a workbook that contains multiple individual worksheets. The user can "layer" the sheets and perform calculations that include data from any or all sheets.

3GL See *third-generation language.*

4GL See *fourth-generation language.*

5GL See *fifth-generation language.*

A

Accelerated Graphics Port (AGP) A bus standard that incorporates a special architecture that allows the video card to access the system's RAM directly, greatly speeding up graphics performance. Most new computers feature AGP graphics capabilities, in addition to a PCI system bus and an expansion bus.

access point A device that enables one or more computers to connect to a wireless network topology.

accelerator card A circuit board that fits into an expansion slot and enhances the processing speed of the CPU.

activate (1) To initiate a command or load a program into memory and begin using it. (2) To *choose;* for example, you can activate a resource by choosing its icon, toolbar button, or file name.

active matrix LCD A liquid crystal display (LCD) technology that assigns a transistor to each pixel in a flat-panel monitor, improving display quality and eliminating the "submarining" effect produced by some types of flat-panel monitors. Also called a *thin-film transistor (TFT)* display.

active window On the computer screen, the window in which the user's next action will occur. The active window's title bar is highlighted, while the title bars of inactive windows appear dimmed.

adapter See *expansion board.*

address bus A set of wires connecting the computer's CPU and RAM, across which memory addresses are transmitted. The number of wires in the bus determines the amount of memory that can be addressed at any one time.

Advanced Micro Devices (AMD) A chip manufacturer that makes processors for PC-compatible computers. AMD initially focused on chips for lower-price, lower-performance systems, but later became a major manufacturer of high-performance processors for the PC market.

AGP See *Accelerated Graphics Port.*

alignment The orientation of the lines of a paragraph with respect to the margins. In word processors, alignment options include left, right, center, and justified.

alphanumeric field See *text field.*

alphanumeric keys On a computer keyboard, the keys that include the letters of the alphabet, numerals, and commonly used symbols.

ALU See *arithmetic logic unit.*

AMD See *Advanced Micro Devices.*

American Standard Code for Information Interchange See *ASCII.*

annotation In presentation programs, a feature that enables the user to embed notes in individual slides. The notes can be made visible only to the presenter, or they can be printed out for distribution to the audience.

anonymous FTP archives FTP sites with files available to the general public. The user types the word "anonymous" as the account name in order to access the files.

antivirus utility A program that scans a computer's disks and memory for viruses: when it detects viruses, it removes them. Some antivirus programs can help the user recover data and program files that have been damaged by a virus and can actively scan files as they are being copied from a disk or downloaded from the Internet.

application server A network server that hosts shared application files, enabling multiple users to use a network version of a software program. Generally, an application server also performs some or all of the processing tasks required by users of the application.

application software Any computer program used to create or process data, such as text documents, spreadsheets, graphics, and so on. Examples include database management software, desktop publishing programs, presentation programs, spreadsheet programs, and word processing programs.

architecture The design of any part of a computer system, or of an entire system, including software and hardware. The design of a microprocessor's circuits, for example, is called its architecture.

archive file A file that stores one or more compressed files, which have been shrunk by a data-compression program.

arithmetic logic unit (ALU) The component of the CPU that handles arithmetic and logical functions. Instructions are passed from memory to the ALU.

arithmetic operation One of two types of operations a computer can perform, which are handled by the arithmetic logic unit (ALU). Arithmetic operations include addition, subtraction, multiplication, and division. See also *logical operation.*

ARPANET Acronym for *Advanced Research Projects Agency Network.* An early network developed by the Department of Defense to connect computers at universities and defense contractors. This network eventually became part of the Internet.

article A message posted to an Internet newsgroup. A series of related articles and responses is called a *thread.*

ASCII An eight-bit binary code developed by the American National Standards Institute (ANSI) to represent symbolic, numeric, and alphanumeric characters. The ASCII character set is the most commonly used character set in PCs.

Asynchronous Transfer Mode (ATM) A network protocol designed to send voice, video, and data transmissions over a single network. ATM provides different kinds of connections and bandwidth on demand, depending on the type of data being transmitted.

autonumber field See *counter field.*

average access time The average amount of time a storage or memory device requires to locate a piece of data. For storage devices, average access time is usually measured in milliseconds (ms). Average time is measured in nanoseconds (ns) in memory devices. Also called *seek time.*

AVI Acronym for *audio-video interleave.* AVI is a file format supported by Microsoft's Video for Windows standard.

B

backbone The central structure of a network, which connects other elements of the network and handles the major traffic.

back up To create a duplicate set of program or data files in case the originals become damaged. (A duplicate file made for this purpose is called a *backup* file.) Files can be backed up individually, by entire folders, and by entire drives. Backups can be made to many types of storage media, such as diskettes, optical disks, or tape. Verb—two words ("I am going to back up the files on the server."); noun or adjective—one word ("He used a backup utility to make a backup of that file.")

backup utility A program that enables the user to copy one or more files from a hard disk to another storage medium (such as a floppy disk, tape, or compact disk) for safekeeping or use in case the original files become damaged or lost.

bandwidth The amount of data that can be transmitted over a network at any given time. Bandwidth may be measured in bits per second (bps) or in hertz (Hz).

bar code A pattern of bars printed on a product or its packaging. A device called a *bar code reader* can scan a bar code and convert its pattern into numeric digits. After the bar code reader has converted a bar code image into a number, it transfers that number to a computer, just as though the number had been typed on a keyboard.

bar code reader An input device that converts a pattern of printed bars (called a *bar code*) into a number that a computer can read. A beam of light reflected off the bar code into a light-sensitive detector identifies the bar code and converts the bar patterns into numeric digits, which can be transferred to a computer. Bar code readers are commonly used in retail stores.

binary field A database field that stores binary objects (such as clip art, photographs, screen images, formatted text, sound objects, and video clips) or OLE objects (such as charts or worksheets created with a spreadsheet or word processor).

binary large object (BLOB) (1) A graphic image file, such as clip art, a photograph, a screen image, formatted text, a sound object, or a video clip. (2) An OLE object, such as a chart or worksheet created with a spreadsheet or word processor; frequently used with object-oriented databases.

binary number system A system for representing the two possible states of electrical switches, which are on and off. (The binary number system is also known as *base 2*.) The binary number system gets its name from the fact that it includes only two numbers: 0 and 1. In computer storage and memory systems, the numeral 0 represents off, and a 1 represents on.

bit The smallest unit of data that can be used by a computer, represented by a 1 or a 0.

bitmap A binary representation of an image in which each part of the image, such as a pixel, is represented by one or more bits in a coordinate system. Also called a *raster*.

bits per second (bps) A measure of data transmission speed. This unit may be used to measure the data transmission rate of a specific device—such as a modem or disk drive—or for the components of a network. May be modified as kilobits per second (Kbps), megabits per second (Mbps), or gigabits per second (Gbps).

BLOB See *binary large object*.

block A contiguous series of characters, words, sentences, or paragraphs in a word processing document. This term is also sometimes used to describe a range of cells in a spreadsheet. Once a block of text or cells has been selected, the user can perform many different actions on it, such as moving, formatting, or deleting.

BMP Abbreviation for *bitmap*. BMP is a graphic-file format native to Windows and OS/2. BMP is widely used on PCs for icons and wallpaper.

board See *expansion board*.

Boolean field See *logical field*.

Boolean operator Special words—such as AND, OR, and NOT—which can be used to modify a keyword search in a Web-based search engine. These operators are commonly used in standard database queries.

boot To start a computer. The term comes from the expression "pulling oneself up by one's own bootstraps."

boot sector The portion of a disk that contains the master boot record—a program that runs when the computer is first started, and which determines whether the disk has the basic operating system components required to run successfully.

border A paragraph format that displays a line on any side of a block. This type of formatting is often used to distinguish the block from regular text. Borders are generally applied to an entire paragraph or group of paragraphs. Also called *rule*.

bottom-up design A design method in which system details are developed first, followed by major functions or processes.

bps See *bits per second*.

bridge A device that connects two LANs and controls data flow between them.

browser See *Web browser*.

bus The path between components of a computer or nodes of a network. The bus's width determines the speed at which data is transmitted. When used alone, the term commonly refers to a computer's data bus.

bus topology A network topology in which all network nodes and peripheral devices are attached to a single conduit.

byte The amount of memory required to store a single character. A byte is comprised of eight bits.

C

cache memory High-speed memory that resides between the CPU and RAM in a computer. Cache memory stores data and instructions that the CPU is likely to need next. The CPU can retrieve data or instructions more quickly from cache than it can from RAM or a disk.

CAD See *computer-aided design*.

campus area network (CAN) A larger version of a *local area network (LAN)*, usually used to connect adjacent buildings such as those found on college campuses.

CAN See *campus area network*.

card See *expansion board*.

CASE See *computer-aided software engineering*.

cathode ray tube (CRT) A type of monitor that uses a vacuum tube as a display screen. CRTs are most commonly used with desktop computers.

CD See *compact disk*.

CD-R See *CD-Recordable drive*.

CD-Recordable (CD-R) drive An optical disk drive that enables the user to create customized CD-ROM disks. Data that has been written to a CD-R disk cannot be changed (overwritten). CD-R disks can be read by any CD-ROM drive. CD-R drives are commonly used to create backup copies of program or data files, or to create duplicates of existing compact disks.

CD-ReWritable (CD-RW) drive An optical disk drive that enables the user to create customized CD-ROM disks. Unlike a CD-R disk, a CD-RW disk's data can be overwritten, meaning the data can be updated after it has been placed on the disk.

CD-ROM See *compact disk, read-only memory*.

CD-ROM drive An optical disk drive, which enables a computer to read data from a compact disk. Using a standard CD-ROM drive and compact disk, the computer can only read data from the disk and cannot write data to the disk.

CD-RW See *CD-ReWritable drive*.

cell In a spreadsheet or database table, the intersection of a row and column, forming a box into which the user enters numbers, formulas, or text. The term also is used to refer to the individual blocks in a table created in a word processing program.

cell address In a spreadsheet, an identifier that indicates the location of a cell in a worksheet. The address is composed of the cell's row and column locations. For example, if the cell is located at the intersection of column B and row 3, then its cell address is B3.

cell pointer A square enclosing one cell of a spreadsheet, identifying that cell as the active cell. The user positions the cell pointer in a worksheet by clicking the cell or by using the cursor movement keys on the keyboard.

cell reference The address of a spreadsheet cell used in a formula.

central processing unit (CPU) The computer's primary processing device, which interprets and executes program instructions and manages the functions of input, output, and storage devices. In personal computers, the CPU is composed of a control unit, an arithmetic logic unit, built-in memory, and supporting circuitry such as a dedicated math processor. The CPU may reside on a single chip on the computer's motherboard or on a larger card inserted into a special slot on the motherboard. In larger computers, the CPU may reside on several circuit boards.

channel Discussion group where chat users convene to discuss a topic.

character animation The process of animating a character—such as a drawing of a person, animal, or some other organic or inorganic object—to create the illusion of movement.

character field See *text field*.

character formatting In a word processor, settings that control the attributes of individual text characters, such as font, type size, type style, and color.

characters per second (cps) A measure of the speed of impact printers, such as dot matrix printers.

chart A graphic representation of numeric data. Also called a *graph*.

chat One of the services available to users of the Internet and some online services. Using special chat software or Web-based chatting tools, users can exchange messages with one another in real time.

chief information officer (CIO) In a large company, an executive manager who heads the Information Systems (IS) department.

choose See *activate*.

CIO See *chief information officer*.

circuit board A rigid rectangular card—consisting of chips and electronic circuitry—that ties the processor to other hardware. In a personal computer, the primary circuit board (to which all components are attached) is called the *motherboard*.

CISC See *Complex Instruction Set Computing*.

click To select an object or command on the computer screen (for example, from a menu, toolbar, or dialog box) by pointing to the object and then pressing and releasing the primary mouse button once.

client An application program on a user's computer that requests information from another computer, such as a network server or Web host, over a network or the Internet. The term may also be used to refer to the computer itself, as it requests services via a network.

client/server A hierarchical network strategy in which the processing is shared by a server and numerous clients. In this type of network, clients provide the user interface, run applications, and request services from the server. The server contributes storage, printing, and some or all processing services.

clip art Predrawn or photographed graphic images, which are available for use by anyone. Some clip art is available through licensing, some through purchase, and some for free.

Clipboard A holding area maintained by the operating system in memory. The Clipboard is used for storing text, graphics, sound, video or other data that has been copied or cut from a document. After data has been placed in the Clipboard, it can be inserted from the Clipboard into other documents, in the same application or in a different application.

clock cycle In a processor, the amount of time required to turn a transistor off and back on again. Also called a *tick*. A processor can execute an instruction in a given number of clock cycles, so as a computer's clock speed (the number of clock cycles it generates per second)

increases, so does the number of instructions it can carry out each second.

clock speed A measure of a processor's operating speed, currently measured in megahertz (MHz, or millions of cycles per second) or gigahertz (GHz, or billions of cycles per second). A computer's operating speed is based on the number of clock cycles, or ticks, it generates per second. For example, if a computer's clock speed is 800 MHz, it "ticks" 800 million times per second.

cluster On a magnetic disk (such as a hard disk) a group of sectors that are treated as a single data-storage unit. The number of sectors per disk can vary, depending on the type of disk and the manner in which it is formatted.

coaxial cable (coax) A cable composed of a single conductive wire wrapped in a conductive wire mesh shield with an insulator in between.

code The instructions or statements that are the basis of a computer program.

color monitor A computer monitor whose screen can display data in color. A color monitor's capabilities are based on a variety of factors. Current high-resolution color monitors can display more than 16 million colors, but they can also be set to display as few as 16 colors or varying shades of gray.

color separation A process used to prepare full-color pages for printing. This process creates a separate page for each color found in the image. During printing, the separations are combined to produce a single image that includes all the required colors.

column (1) A vertically arranged series of cells in a spreadsheet or database table, named with a letter or combination of letters. (2) In word processing, a document-formatting technique in which the page is divided into vertical sections, like a newspaper's columns.

command An instruction issued to the computer. The user can issue commands, usually by choosing from a menu, clicking an on-screen tool or icon, or pressing a combination of keys. Application programs and the operating system also issue commands to the computer.

command-line interface A user interface that enables the user to interact with the software by typing strings of characters at a prompt.

command prompt See *prompt*.

communications device An input/output device used to connect one computer to another to share hardware and information. This family of devices includes modems and network interface cards.

compact disk (CD) A type of optical storage device, identical to audio CDs. The type of CD used in computers is called Compact Disk Read-Only Memory (CD-ROM). As the device's name implies, you cannot change the information on the disk, just as you cannot record over an audio CD. Standard compact disks can store either 650 MB or 700 MB of computer data, or 70 minutes or 80 minutes of audio data.

compact disk read-only memory (CD-ROM) The most common type of optical storage medium. In CD-ROM, data is written in a series of lands and pits on the surface of a compact disk (CD), which can be read by a laser in a CD-ROM drive.

compatible Describes the capability of one type of hardware, software, or data file to work with another. See also *incompatible*.

Complex Instruction Set Computing (CISC) Describes a type of processor designed to handle large and comprehensive instruction sets. CISC processors are commonly used in IBM-compatible PCs.

computer An electronic device used to process data, converting the data into information that is useful to people.

computer-aided design (CAD) Software used to create complex two- or three-dimensional models of buildings and products, including architectural, engineering, and mechanical designs.

computer-aided software engineering (CASE) Software used to develop information systems. CASE automates the analysis, design, programming, and documentation tasks.

computer-generated imaging (CGI) The process of using powerful computers and special graphics, animation, and compositing software to create digital special effects or unique images. CGI is frequently used in filmmaking, game design, animation, and multimedia design.

computer scientist A person who studies computer theory and researches and develops new techniques in computer design and programming.

computer system A four-part system that consists of hardware, software, data, and a user.

configure To adapt a computer to a specific need by selecting from a range of hardware or software options. Configuration may include installing new or replacement hardware or software, or changing settings in existing hardware or software.

context menu In the Windows 95 and later operating systems, a brief menu that appears when the user right-clicks certain items. The menu contains commands that apply specifically to the item that was right-clicked. Also called a *shortcut menu*.

control unit The component of the CPU that contains the instruction set. The control unit directs the flow of data throughout the computer system. See also *instruction set*.

conversion The process of replacing an existing system with an updated or improved version. Information systems (IS) professionals may use one or more different conversion methods when changing an organization's system.

cookie A special file that stores personal information, such as credit card data. Web sites create cookies and store them on the user's computer.

cooperative multitasking A method by which programs share the CPU with one another. In a cooperative multitasking environment, each running program periodically checks with the operating system to see whether another program needs the CPU and, if so, relinquishes control of the CPU to the next program.

Copy An application command that makes a duplicate of data selected from a document and stores it in the Clipboard without removing the data from the original document. The data then can be used in other documents and other applications.

counter field A database field that stores a unique incrementing numeric value (such as an invoice number) that the DBMS automatically assigns to each new record. Also called *autonumber field*.

cps See *characters per second*.

CPU See *central processing unit*.

CRT See *cathode ray tube*.

cursor A graphic symbol on the screen that indicates where the next keystroke or command will appear when entered. Also called the *insertion point*.

cursor-movement keys On a computer keyboard, the keys that direct the movement of the on-screen cursor or insertion point, including the up, down, left, and right arrows, and the Home, End, Page Up, and Page Down keys.

Cut An application command that removes data selected from a document and stores it in the Clipboard. The data is no longer a part of the original document. While in the Clipboard, the data can be used in other documents or applications.

cylinder A vertical stack of tracks, one track on each side of each platter of a hard disk.

D

data Raw facts, numbers, letters, or symbols that the computer processes into meaningful information.

data area The part of the disk that remains free to store information after the logical formatting process has created the boot sector, file allocation table (FAT), and root folder.

data bus An electrical path composed of parallel wires that connect the CPU, memory, and other hardware on the motherboard. The number of wires determines the amount of data that can be transferred across the bus at one time.

data communications The electronic transfer of data between computers.

data compression The process of reducing data volume and increasing data-transfer rates by using mathematical algorithms to analyze groups of bits and encode repeating sequences of data.

data compression utility A program that reduces the volume of data by manipulating the way the data is stored.

Data Exchange Format (DXF) A universal file format for use with vector graphics.

data flow diagram A method of documenting how data moves through a system, including input, processing, and output.

data transfer rate The rate at which a data storage device can transfer data to another device; expressed as either bits per second (bps) or bytes per second (Bps). Also called *throughput*.

database A collection of related data organized with a specific structure.

database administrator See *database specialist*.

database management system (DBMS) A computer program used to manage the storage, organization, processing, and retrieval of data in a database.

database specialist In an information systems (IS) department, the person responsible for designing and building tables, forms, queries, and reports in the database. Also known as a *database administrator*.

date field A database field that stores a date.

DBMS See *database management system*.

debugging The process of tracking down and correcting errors (called *bugs*) in a software program.

decimal number system The system that uses 10 digits to represent numbers; also called *base 10*.

decision support system A specialized application used to collect and report certain types of business data, which can be used to aid managers in the decision-making process.

decision tree A graphical representation of the events and actions that can occur in a program or information system under different conditions.

decoding (1) In a machine cycle, the step in which the control unit breaks down a command into instructions that correspond to the CPU's instruction set. (2) During file compression, the process of reinserting bits stripped away during encoding.

dedicated media Media (such as cables or wireless links) that are specifically set up for use in a network.

density A measure of the quality of a magnetic disk's surface. The higher a disk's density, the more data the disk can store.

description field See *memo field*.

deselect The opposite of *select*. In many applications, the user can select, or highlight, blocks of text or objects for editing. By clicking the mouse in a different location or pressing a cursor-movement key, the user removes the highlighting and the text or objects are no longer selected.

desktop In a computer operating system, a graphical workspace in which all of the computer's available resources (such as files, programs, printers, Internet tools, and utilities) can be easily accessed by the user. In such systems, the desktop is a colored background on which the user sees small pictures, called icons. The user accesses various resources by choosing icons on the desktop.

desktop publishing (DTP) Software used to enhance standard word processing documents. DTP software creates professional-quality documents and publications using design, typesetting, and paste-up features.

development phase Phase 3 of the systems development life cycle, in which programmers create or customize software to fit the needs of an organization, technical documentation is prepared, and software testing is begun.

device Any electronic component attached to or part of a computer; hardware.

dialog box A special-purpose window that appears when the user issues certain commands in a program or graphical operating system. A dialog box gets its name from the "dialog" it conducts with the user as the program seeks the information it needs to perform a task.

digital The use of the numerals 1 and 0 (digits) to express data in a computer. The computer recognizes the numeral 1 as an "on" state of a transistor, whereas a 0 represents an "off" state.

digital camcorder See *digital video camera*.

digital camera A camera that converts light intensities into digital data. Digital cameras are used to record images that can be viewed and edited on a computer.

digital convergence The process of combining multiple digital media types (such as text, graphics, video, and sound) into a single multimedia product.

digital light processing (DLP) A technology used in some types of digital projectors to project bright, crisp images. DLP devices use a special microchip, called a digital micromirror device, which uses mirrors to control the image display. DLP projectors can display clear images in normal lighting conditions.

digital light projector An output device that can project a computer's display onto a screen or wall. Also called *LCD projector*.

Digital Subscriber Line (DSL) A form of digital telephone service used to transmit voice and data signals. There are several varieties of DSL technology, which include Asymmetrical DSL, High bit-rate DSL, and others.

digital video camera A camera that converts light intensities into digital data, but which is used to capture moving images. Most digital video cameras store their data on high-capacity tape. Many digital video cameras can also capture still images, like standard digital cameras. Digital video can be viewed and edited on a computer and transferred to another medium, such as standard video tape or optical disk. Also called *digital camcorder*.

digital video disk (DVD) A high-density optical medium capable of storing a full-length movie on a single disk the size of a standard compact disk (CD). Unlike a standard CD, which stores data on only one side, a DVD-format disk stores data on both sides. Using compression technologies and very fine data areas on the disk's surface, newer-generation DVDs can store several gigabytes of data.

Digital Video Disk-RAM (DVD-RAM) The newest optical technology to reach consumers, a sophisticated type of optical device that allows users to record, erase, and re-record data on a special disk. Using video editing software, you can record your own digitized videos onto a DVD-RAM disk, then play them back in any DVD player. (However, special encoding makes it impossible to copy movies from commercial DVD onto a DVD-RAM disk.) DVD-RAM drives can read DVDs, DVD-R disks, CD-R disks, CD-RW disks, and standard CDs.

digitize To convert an image or a sound into a series of binary numbers (1s and 0s), which can be stored in a computer.

DIMM See *Dual In-Line Memory Module*.

directory See *folder*.

disk A storage medium commonly used in computers. Two types of disks are used: magnetic disks, which store data as charged particles on the disk's surface; and optical disks, which use lasers to read data embossed on the disk in a series of lands and pits.

disk cartridge A removable magnetic storage medium that features a high-density disk enclosed in a plastic cartridge. Such cartridges generally provide greater storage capacities than standard floppy disks; some offer even higher capacities than many hard disks.

disk controller A device that connects a disk drive to the computer's bus, enabling the drive to exchange data with other devices.

disk defragmenter A utility program that locates the pieces of fragmented files saved in noncontiguous sectors on a magnetic disk, and rearranges them so they are stored in contiguous sectors. Defragmenting a disk can improve its performance because the operating system can locate data more efficiently.

disk drive A storage device that holds, spins, reads data from, and writes data to a disk.

disk management utility A program that assists the user in maintaining a computer's magnetic disks to ensure optimal performance.

diskette A removable magnetic disk, encased in a plastic sleeve. Also called *floppy disk* or *floppy*.

diskette drive A device that holds a removable floppy disk when in use; read/write heads read and write data to the diskette.

display adapter See *video controller*.

distributed computing A system configuration in which two or more computers in a network share applications, storage, and processing power. Also called *distributed processing*.

distributed processing See *distributed computing*.

DLL See *dynamic link library file*.

DLP See *digital light processing*.

DNS See *domain name system*.

docking station A base into which a portable computer can be inserted, essentially converting the portable computer into a desktop system. A docking station may provide connections to a full-size monitor, keyboard, and mouse, as well as additional devices like speakers or a digital video camera.

document A computer file consisting of a compilation of one or more kinds of data. There are many types including text documents, spreadsheets, graphics files, and so on. A document, which a user can open and use, is different from a program file, which is required by a software program to operate.

document area In many software applications, the portion of the program's interface in which the active document appears. In this part of the interface, the user can work directly with the document and its contents. Also called *document window*.

document formats In productivity applications, settings that affect the appearance of the entire document, such as page size, page orientation, and the presence of headers or footers.

document window See *document area*.

documentation Sets of printed or online manuals intended for people who use or support an information system.

domain A name given to a computer and its peripherals connected to the Internet, which identifies the type of organization using the computer. Examples of domain names are .com for commercial enterprises and .edu for schools. Also called *top-level domain*.

domain name system (DNS) A naming system used for computers on the Internet. This system provides an individual name (representing the organization using the computer) and a domain name, which classifies the type of organization.

dot matrix printer A type of impact printer that creates characters on a page by using small pins to strike an inked ribbon, pressing ink onto the paper. The arrangement of pins in the print head creates a matrix of dots—hence the device's name.

dot pitch The distance between phosphor dots on a monitor. The highest-resolution monitors have the smallest dot pitch.

dots per inch (dpi) A measure of resolution commonly applied to printers, scanners, and other devices that input or output text or images. The more dots per inch, the higher the resolution. For example, if a printer has a resolution of 600 dpi, it can print 600 dots across and 600 down in a one-inch square, for a total of 360,000 dots in one square inch.

double-click To select an object or activate a command on the screen by pointing to an object (such as an icon) and pressing and releasing the mouse button twice in quick succession.

Double Data Rate SDRAM (DDR SDRAM) A new, faster version of standard synchronous dynamic RAM (SDRAM), commonly used in today's computers.

download To retrieve a file from a remote computer. The opposite of *upload*.

drag To move an object on the screen by pointing to the object, pressing the primary mouse button, and holding down the button while dragging the object to a new location.

drag and drop To move text or graphics from one part of the document to another by selecting the desired information, pressing and holding down the primary mouse button, dragging the selection to a new location, and releasing the mouse button. Also called *drag-and-drop editing*.

DRAM See *dynamic RAM*.

draw program A graphics program that uses vectors to create an image. Mathematical equations describe each line, shape, and pattern, allowing the user to manipulate all elements of the graphic separately.

driver A small program that accepts requests for action from the operating system and causes a device, such as a printer, to execute the requests.

dpi See *dots per inch*.

DSL See *Digital Subscriber Line*.

DTP See *desktop publishing*.

Dual In-Line Memory Module (DIMM) One type of circuit board containing RAM chips.

dual-scan LCD An improved passive matrix technology for flat-panel monitors in which pixels are scanned twice as often, reducing the effects of blurry graphics and submarining (an effect that occurs when the mouse pointer blurs or disappears when it is moved).

DVD See *digital video disk*.

DVD-R See *DVD-Recordable*.

DVD-RAM See *Digital Video Disk-RAM*.

DVD-Recordable (DVD-R) An optical disk drive that can record data onto the surface of a special, recordable DVD disk. Once data has been written to the disk, it cannot be overwritten.

DXF See *Data Exchange Format*.

dye-sub (dye-sublimation) printer A printer that produces photographic-quality images by using a heat source to evaporate colored inks from a ribbon, transferring the color to specially coated paper.

dynamic RAM (DRAM) The most common type of RAM used in personal computers. While dynamic RAM is less expensive than static RAM (SRAM), it must be recharged with electricity many times each second in order to retain its contents.

E

EBCDIC Acronym for *Extended Binary Coded Decimal Interchange Code*. An eight-bit binary code developed by IBM to represent symbols and numeric and alphanumeric characters; most commonly used on IBM mainframe computers.

e-commerce See *electronic commerce*.

e-commerce specialist In an Information Systems (IS) department, a professional responsible for designing, implementing, and maintaining a company's systems for conducting business transactions over a network or the Internet.

edit To make modifications to an existing document file.

electronic commerce The practice of conducting business transactions online, such as selling products from a World Wide Web site. The process often involves the customer's providing personal or credit card information online, presenting special security concerns. Also called *e-commerce*.

electronic mail A system for exchanging written, voice, and video messages through a computer network. Also called *e-mail*.

e-mail address An address that identifies an individual user of an electronic mail system, enabling the person to send and receive e-mail messages. The e-mail address consists of a user name, the "at" symbol (@), and the DNS address.

e-mail program (or e-mail client) Software that lets you create, send, and receive e-mail messages.

embedded operating system A computer operating system that is built into the circuitry of an electronic device—unlike a PC's operating system, which resides on a magnetic disk. Embedded operating systems are typically found in devices such as PDAs.

EMF See *electromagnetic field*.

encoding The process of stripping away unneeded bits of digital source material, resulting in the transmission of smaller files.

Enhanced Integrated Drive Electronics (EIDE) An enhanced version of the IDE interface.

error-correction protocol A standard for correcting errors that occur when static interferes with data transmitted via modems over telephone lines.

Ethernet The most common network protocol.

execute To load and carry out a program or a specific set of instructions. Executing is also called *running*.

execution cycle The second portion of the machine cycle, which is the series of steps a CPU takes when executing an instruction. During the execution cycle, the CPU actually carries out the instruction by converting it into microcode. In some cases, the CPU may be required to store the results of an instruction in memory; if so, this occurs during the execution cycle.

expansion board A device that enables the user to configure or customize a computer to perform specific tasks or to enhance performance. An expansion board—also called a *card*, *adapter*, or *board*—contains a special set of chips and circuitry that add functionality to the computer. An expansion board may be installed to add fax/modem capabilities to the computer, for example, or to provide sound or video-editing capabilities.

expansion slot The area of the motherboard into which expansion boards are inserted, connecting them to the PC's bus.

expert system An information system in which decision-making processes are automated. A highly detailed database is accessed by an inference engine, which is capable of forming an intelligent response to a query.

extension point A device that allows a greater number of users to access a wireless network.

external modem A communications device used to modulate data signals. This type of device is described as "external" because it is housed outside the computer and connected to the computer through a serial port and to the telephone system with a standard telephone jack.

extract To uncompress one or more compressed files that have been stored together in an archive file.

extranet A network connection that enables external users to access a portion of an organization's internal network, usually via an Internet connection. External users have access to specific parts of the internal network but are forbidden to access other areas, which are protected by firewalls.

FAQ See *frequently asked questions.*

Fast Ethernet A networking technology, also called 100Base-T, that uses the same network cabling scheme as Ethernet but uses different network interface cards to achieve data transfer speeds of up to 100 Mbps.

FAT See *file allocation table.*

fax modem A modem that can emulate a fax machine.

feedback loop In interactive multimedia products, the interaction that occurs between the user and the program. As the user responds to the program by making choices and the program responds to the user by changing its behavior, a two-way "loop" of interaction takes place.

fetching The first step of the CPU's instruction cycle, during which the control unit retrieves (or fetches) a command or data from the computer's memory.

fiber-optic cable A thin strand of glass wrapped in a protective coating. Fiber-optic cable transfers data by means of pulsating beams of light.

field The smallest unit of data in a database; used to group each piece or item of data into a specific category. Fields are arranged in a column and titled by the user.

field format See *mask.*

file A set of related computer data (used by a person) or program instructions (used by an application or operating system) that has been given a name.

file allocation table (FAT) In a diskette or hard disk, a log created during the logical formatting process that records the location of each file and the status of each sector on the disk.

file compression See *data compression.*

file compression utility See *data compression utility.*

file format A standardized method of encoding data for storage.

file server The central computer of a network; used for shared storage. A server may store software applications, databases, and data files for the network's users. Depending on the way a server is used, it may also be called a *network server, application server,* or *server.*

file server network A hierarchical network strategy in which the server is used to store and forward files to the nodes. Each node runs its own applications.

file transfer The process of sending a file from one computer to another by modem or across a network. See also *download* and *upload.*

file transfer protocol (FTP) A set of rules that dictates the format in which data is sent from one computer to another.

filter A DBMS tool that enables the user to establish conditions for selecting and displaying a subset of records that meet those criteria.

firewall An antipiracy method for protecting networks. A firewall permits access to public sections of the network while protecting proprietary areas.

FireWire See *IEEE 1394.*

flat-file database A database file consisting of a single data table, which is not linked to any other tables.

flat-panel display A thin, lightweight monitor used in laptop and notebook computers. Most flat-panel displays use LCD technology.

floppy See *diskette.*

floppy disk See *diskette.*

fluorescent multi-layer disk, read-only memory (FMD-ROM) A new type of optical technology that uses special fluorescent material in the reflective surface of the disk. FMD-ROM disks can contain ten or more data layers (compared to two layers in the highest-capacity DVD-ROM disks). A single FMD-ROM disk can store up to 140 GB of data. FMD-ROM drives can read standard CD-ROM and DVD-ROM disks.

fly-by A specially rendered animation, created in a CAD or 3-D graphics program, that creates the illusion that the viewer is moving past, around, or over an object such as a building.

folder A tool for organizing data stored on a disk. A folder contains a list of files and other folders stored on the disk. A disk can hold many folders, which can in turn store many files and other folders. Also called a *directory.*

font A family of alphanumeric characters, symbols, and punctuation marks that share the same design. Modern applications provide many different fonts and enable users to use different fonts in the same document. Also called a *typeface.*

footer A recurring line or paragraph of text appearing at the bottom of each page in a document. Footers often include page numbers, the document's title, the name of the current chapter, or other information.

form A custom screen created in a database management system (DBMS) for displaying and entering data related to a single database record.

format (1) As relating to magnetic storage devices, the layout of tracks and sectors in which data is stored. (2) In productivity applications, a setting that affects the appearance of a document or part of a document.

formatting (1) The process of magnetically mapping a disk with a series of tracks and sectors where data will be stored. Also called *initializing.* (2) The process of applying formatting options (such as character or paragraph formats) to a document.

formula A mathematical equation within a cell of a spreadsheet. To identify it and distinguish it from other spreadsheet entries, a formula begins with a special symbol, such as a plus sign or an equal sign.

formula bar In spreadsheet programs, a special text box that displays the active cell's address and the data or formula entered in that cell. The user may be able to enter or edit data or formulas in this box.

fragmentation Describes the state of a file that has been broken into sections that are stored on noncontiguous sectors of a disk.

frame (1) In networking, a small block of data to be transmitted over a network. A frame includes an identifying header and the actual data to be sent. Also called a *packet.* (2) In animation, a single still image that, when viewed with many other images in rapid succession, creates the illusion of motion. (3) In many software applications, a special tool that enables the user to place an object—such as a text box or an image from a separate file—in a document. The frame surrounds the object in the document, enabling the user to position and resize the object as needed.

frequently asked questions (FAQs) A document routinely developed by a newsgroup; it lists questions most commonly asked in the newsgroup, along with their answers. FAQs help a newsgroup's members avoid the repeated posting of the same information to the group.

FTP client software Programs that enable users to download files from an FTP site.

FTP server A computer used to store FTP sites, many containing thousands of individual programs and files.

FTP site A collection of files stored on an FTP server from which users can copy files from and to their own computer.

full-duplex The ability to send and receive data simultaneously over a common data path or communications link.

function keys The part of the keyboard that can be used to quickly activate commands; designated F1, F2, and so on.

game controller A specialized type of input device that enables the user to interact with computer games. Two popular types of game controllers are game pads and joysticks.

game pad A type of game controller that usually provides two sets of controls—one for each hand. These devices are extremely flexible and are used to control a wide variety of game systems.

gateway A computer system that can translate one network protocol into another so that data can be transmitted between two dissimilar networks.

GB See *gigabyte*.

GHz See *gigahertz*.

GIF Acronym for *graphics interchange format*. A graphics file format supported by many graphics programs. GIF files are commonly used in Web pages.

Gigabit Ethernet The newest addition to Ethernet technology; capable of transferring 10 Gb of data per second. Gigabit Ethernet can also carry about 900 video signals at once, at about 1.5 MB per second of digital video.

gigabyte (GB) Equivalent to approximately one billion bytes; a typical measurement of data storage.

gigahertz (GHz) Equivalent to one billion cycles per second; a common measure of processor clock speed.

goal seeking A data-analysis process that begins with a conclusion and calculates the values that will lead to the desired outcome, such as figuring a mortgage amount based on an affordable monthly payment.

gradient fill In presentation or graphics software, an option in which the color changes as you go from one side of the object to another.

grammar checker A language tool built into many productivity applications, especially word processors. The program checks the grammar in a document by comparing its wording to a dictionary of accepted grammatical rules. The program reports any phrases or sentences that violate a rule and may suggest improvements or allow the user to ignore the rule.

graph See *chart*.

graphical user interface (GUI) A user interface in which actions are initiated when the user selects an icon, a toolbar button, or an option from a pull-down menu with the mouse or other pointing device. GUIs also represent documents, programs, and devices on screen as graphical elements that the user can use by clicking or dragging.

grayscale monitor A monitor that displays up to 256 shades of gray, ranging from white to black.

groupware Application software that enables multiple users on a network to cooperate on projects. Groupware suites usually include scheduling and calendar software, e-mail, and document-management tools.

GUI See *graphical user interface*.

H

half-duplex The ability to send or receive data—but not both simultaneously—over a common data path or communications link.

handheld personal computer A personal computer that is small enough to be held in one hand. Also called *palmtop computer*.

handle In many productivity applications, a specialized portion of a frame, which enables the user to drag the frame to resize it.

hard disk A nonremovable magnetic storage device included in most PCs. A stack of aluminum platters, each coated with iron oxide, enclosed in a hard disk drive.

hard disk drive (or hard drive) A device that consists of the hard disk platters, a spindle on which the platters spin, a read/write head for each side of each platter, and a sealed chamber that encloses the disks and spindle. Many hard disk drives also include the drive controller, although the controller is a separate unit on some hard disk drives.

hardware The physical components of a computer, including processor and memory chips, input/output devices, tapes, disks, modems, and cables.

hardware maintenance technician In an IS department, a worker responsible for maintaining and repairing hardware components used in the information system.

head crash Describes the results when a read/write head makes contact with the surface of a spinning hard disk. The contact can damage the disk's surface and even destroy the read/write head.

header (1) The initial part of a data packet being transmitted across a network. The header contains information about the type of data in the payload, the source and destination of the data, and a sequence number so that data from multiple packets can be reassembled at the receiving computer in the proper order. See *frame*. (2) A recurring line or paragraph of text appearing at the top of each page in a document. Headers often include page numbers, the document's title, the name of the current chapter, or other information.

help desk Within a company, a team of technical experts that helps the company's employees solve problems with or master the use of the information system.

helper application A program that must be added to your browser in order to play special content files—especially those with multimedia content—in real time. Also called *plug-in application*.

hertz (Hz) The frequency of electrical vibrations, or cycles, per second.

hierarchical file system A structured file organization system in which the root directory (also called a folder) may contain other directories, which in turn contain files.

high-capacity floppy disk A small, removable disk that resembles a standard diskette, but provides much higher data storage capacity. Typically, high-capacity floppy disks have data densities of 100 MB or greater.

highlight To select a block of text or cells for editing. Selected text is highlighted—displayed in a different color from the remaining text in a document.

HLP See *help file*.

holographic memory A futuristic type of storage device that stores enormous amounts of data within the structure of a crystal; it uses special lasers to read and write data.

home page An organization's principal Web page, which may provide links to other Web pages having additional information.

host A computer that provides services to other computers that connect to it. Host computers provide file transfer, communications services, and access to the Internet's high-speed data lines.

hot-swappable hard disk A magnetic storage device similar to a removable hard disk. A removable box encloses the disk, drive, and read/write heads in a sealed container. This type of hard disk can be added to or removed from a server without shutting down the server.

HTML See *Hypertext Markup Language*.

HTML tag A code used to format documents in Hypertext Markup Language (HTML) format.

HTTP See *Hypertext Transfer Protocol*.

hub In a network, a device that connects nodes and servers together at a central point.

hyperlink See *hypertext link*.

hypermedia Text, graphics, video, and sound linked and accessible in a hypertext format.

hypertext A software technology that provides fast and flexible access to information. The user can jump to a topic by selecting it on screen; used to create Web pages and help screens.

hypertext link A word, icon, or other object that when clicked jumps to another location on the document or another Web page. Also called *hyperlink* or *link*.

hypertext markup language (HTML) A page-description language used on the World Wide Web that defines the hypertext links between documents.

hypertext transfer protocol (HTTP) A set of file transfer rules used on the World Wide Web; it controls the way information is shared.

Hz See *hertz*.

I

I/O See *input/output*.

icon A graphical screen element that executes one or more commands when clicked with a mouse or other pointing device.

IEEE 1394 An expansion bus technology that supports data-transfer rates of up to 400 Mbps. Also called *FireWire*.

IGES See *Initial Graphics Exchange Specifications*.

image scanner An input device that digitizes printed images. Sensors determine the intensity of light reflected from the page, and the light intensities are converted to digital data that can be viewed and manipulated by the computer. Sometimes called simply a *scanner*.

impact printer A type of printer that creates images by striking an inked ribbon, pressing ink from the ribbon onto a piece of paper. Examples of impact printers are dot-matrix printers and line printers.

implementation phase Phase 4 of the systems development life cycle. In this phase new software and hardware are installed in the user environment, training is offered, and system testing is completed.

incompatible The opposite of *compatible*. Describes the inability of one type of hardware, software, or data file to work with another.

indent The distance between the beginning or end of a line of text and the left or right margin, whichever is closer.

Industry Standard Architecture (ISA) A PC bus standard developed by IBM, extending the bus to 16 bits. An ISA bus can access 8-bit and 16-bit devices.

inference engine Software used with an expert system to examine data with respect to the knowledge base and to select an appropriate response.

information system A mechanism that helps people collect, store, organize, and use information. An information system does not necessarily include computers; however, a computer is an important part of an information system.

Information Systems (IS) department The people in an organization responsible for designing, developing, implementing, and maintaining the systems necessary to manage information for all levels of the organization.

initializing See *formatting*.

Initial Graphics Exchange Specifications (IGES) One of a few universal file formats for vector graphics.

ink jet printer A type of nonimpact printer that produces images by spraying ink onto the page.

input device Computer hardware that accepts data and instructions from the user. Examples of input devices include the keyboard, mouse, joystick, pen, trackball, scanner, bar code reader, microphone, and touch screen.

input/output (I/O) Communications between the user and the computer or between hardware components that result in the transfer of data.

input/output (I/O) device A device that performs both input and output functions. Modems and network interface cards are examples of input/output devices.

insertion point See *cursor*.

instant messenger Chat software that enables users to set up buddy lists and open a window to "chat" when anyone on the list is online.

instruction A command that the computer must execute so that a specific action can be carried out.

instruction cycle The first portion of the machine cycle, which is the series of steps a CPU takes when executing an instruction. During the instruction cycle, the CPU's control unit fetches a command or data from the computer's memory, enabling the CPU to execute an instruction. The control unit then decodes the command so it can be executed.

instruction set Machine language instructions that define all the operations a CPU can perform.

integrated pointing device A pointing device built into the computer's keyboard; consists of a small joystick positioned near the middle of the keyboard, typically between the *g* and *h* keys. The joystick is controlled with either forefinger. Two buttons that perform the same function as mouse buttons are just beneath the spacebar and are pressed with the thumb. One type of integrated pointing device, developed by IBM, is called *TrackPoint*.

integrated services digital network (ISDN) A digital telecommunications standard that replaces analog transmissions and transmits voice, video, and data.

Intel A leading manufacturer of microprocessors. Intel invented the first microprocessor, which was used in electronic calculators. Intel's product line includes the *x*86 processors and the Pentium processor family.

intelligent smart card A type of smart card that contains its own processor and memory.

interactive Refers to software products that can react and respond to commands issued by the user or choices made by the user.

interactivity In multimedia, a system in which the user and program respond to one another. The program gives the user choices, which the user selects to direct the program.

interface See *user interface*.

internal modem A communications device used to modulate data signals. This type of modem is described as "internal" because it is a circuit board that is plugged into one of the computer's expansion slots.

Internet Originally, a link between ARPANET, NSFnet, and other networks. Today, a worldwide network of networks.

Internet protocol (IP) address A unique four-part numeric address assigned to each computer on the Internet, containing routing information to identify its location. Each of the four parts is a number between 0 and 255.

Internet relay chat (IRC) A multiuser system made up of channels that people join for exchanging messages either publicly or privately. Messages are exchanged in real-time, meaning the messages are transmitted to other users on the channel as they are typed in.

Internet service provider (ISP) An intermediary service between the Internet backbone and the user, providing easy and relatively inexpensive access to shell accounts, direct TCP/IP connections, and high-speed access through dedicated data circuits.

internetworking The process of connecting separate networks together.

interrupt request (IRQ) A signal sent by the operating system to the CPU, requesting processing time for a specific task.

intranet An internal network whose interface and accessibility are modeled after an Internet-based Web site. Only internal users are allowed to access information or resources on the intranet; if connected to an external network or the Internet, the intranet's resources are protected from outside access by firewalls.

IP address See *Internet Protocol address*.

IRC See *Internet Relay Chat*.

IRIS printer A type of ink jet printer that sprays the ink on paper mounted on a spinning drum. Such printers can produce images with a resolution of 1,800 dots per inch.

IRQ See *interrupt request*.

IS Department See *Information Systems department*.

ISA See *Industry Standard Architecture*.

ISDN See *Integrated Services Digital Network.*

ISP See *Internet service provider.*

Java A programming language, used for creating cross-platform programs. Java enables Web page designers to include small applications (called *applets*) in Web pages.

Java applet A Java-based program included in a Web page.

Joint Photographic Experts Group (JPEG) format A bitmap file format commonly used to display photographic images.

joystick An input device used to control the movement of on-screen components; typically used in video games.

JPEG See *Joint Photographic Experts Group format.*

KB See *kilobyte.*

kerning A text-editing feature that adjusts the distance between individual letters in a word to make that word easier to read.

keyboard The most common input device, used to enter letters, numbers, symbols, punctuation, and commands into the computer. Computer keyboards typically include numeric, alphanumeric, cursor-movement, modifier, and function keys, as well as other special keys.

keyboard buffer A part of memory that receives and stores the scan codes from the keyboard controller until the program can accept them.

keyboard controller A chip within the keyboard or the computer that receives the keystroke and generates the scan code.

keyboarding Touch typing using a computer keyboard.

keyframe In animation, the primary frame in a motion sequence, such as the starting or stopping point in a walk cycle.

keyword A term or phrase used as the basis for a search when looking for information on the World Wide Web.

kilobyte (KB) Equivalent to 1,024 bytes; a common measure of data storage.

knowledge base A highly specialized database used with an expert system to intelligently produce solutions.

label Descriptive text used in a spreadsheet cell to describe the data in a column or row.

LAN See *local area network.*

land A flat area on the metal surface of a CD-ROM that reflects the laser light into the sensor of an optical disk drive. See also *pit.*

landscape orientation A document format in which the text is printed parallel to the widest edges of the page; the opposite of *portrait orientation.*

laptop computer See *notebook computer.*

laser printer A quiet, fast printer that produces high-quality output. A laser beam focused on an electrostatic drum creates an image to which powdered toner adheres, and that image is transferred to paper.

LCD monitor See *liquid crystal display monitor.*

leading In desktop publishing, the amount of space between lines in a document. DTP software enables the user to adjust this spacing precisely to make text easier to read. (Pronounced LED-ding.)

Level-1 (L1) cache A type of cache memory built directly into the microprocessor. Also called *on-board cache.*

Level-2 (L2) cache A type of cache memory that is external to the microprocessor, but is positioned between the CPU and RAM. Also called *external cache.*

line spacing The distance between lines of text in a document. The most common examples include single-spaced and double-spaced.

link See *hypertext link.*

Linux A freely available version of the UNIX operating system. Developed by a worldwide cooperative of programmers in the 1990s, Linux is a feature-rich, 32-bit, multi-user, multiprocessor operating system that runs on virtually any hardware platform.

liquid crystal display (LCD) monitor A flat-panel monitor on which an image is created when the liquid crystal becomes charged; used primarily in notebook computers.

listserv An e-mail server that contains a list of names and enables users to communicate with others on the list in an ongoing discussion.

local area network (LAN) A system of PCs located relatively near to one another and connected by wire or a wireless link. A LAN permits simultaneous access to data and resources, enhances personal communication, and simplifies backup procedures.

local bus An internal system bus that runs between components on the motherboard.

logical field A database field that stores only one of two values: yes or no, true or false, on or off, and so on. Also called a *Boolean field.*

logical formatting An operating system function in which tracks and sectors are mapped on the surface of a disk. This mapping creates the master boot record, FAT, root folder (also called the *root directory*), and the data area. Also called *soft formatting* and *low-level formatting.*

logical operation One of the two types of operations a computer can perform. Logical operations usually involve making a comparison, such as determining whether two values are equal. See also *arithmetic operation.*

low-level formatting See *logical formatting.*

machine cycle The complete series of steps a CPU takes in executing an instruction. A machine cycle itself can be broken down into two smaller cycles: the instruction cycle and the execution cycle.

Macintosh operating system (Mac OS) The operating system that runs on machines built by Apple Computer. The Mac OS was the first commercially available operating system to use a graphical user interface, to utilize Plug and Play hardware compatibility, to feature built-in networking, and to support common user access.

magnetic disk A round, flat disk covered with a magnetic material (such as iron oxide), the most commonly used storage medium. Data is written magnetically on the disk and can be recorded over and over. The magnetic disk is the basic component of the diskette and hard disk.

magnetic storage A storage technology in which data is recorded when iron particles are polarized on a magnetic storage medium.

mail merge The process of combining a text document, such as a letter, with the contents of a database, such as an address list; commonly used to produce form letters.

mail server In an e-mail system, the server on which messages received from the post office server are stored until the recipients access their mailboxes and retrieve the messages.

mainframe computer A large, multiuser computer system designed to handle massive amounts of input, output, and storage. A mainframe is usually composed of one or more powerful CPUs connected to many input/output devices, called terminals, or to personal computers. Mainframe systems are typically used in businesses requiring the maintenance of huge databases or simultaneous processing of multiple complex tasks.

maintenance phase Phase 5 of the systems development life cycle. In this phase the new system is monitored, errors are corrected, and minor adjustments are made to improve system performance.

management information system (MIS) A set of software tools that enables managers to gather, organize, and evaluate information about a workgroup, department, or an entire organization. These systems meet the needs of three different categories of managers—executives, middle managers, and front-line managers—by producing a range of standardized reports drawn from the organization's database. A good management information system summarizes vast amounts of business data into information that is useful to each type of manager.

margin The space between the edge of a page and the main body of the document. Text cannot be entered within the margin.

mask In a database management system (DBMS), a technique for controlling data entry to ensure that data entered into any field adheres to a specific format. For example, in a database that contains a Telephone Number field, a field format can be set to ensure that each number is entered in the format (555) 555-5555. Also called a *field format* or *picture*.

massively parallel processing (MPP) A processing architecture that uses hundreds or thousands of microprocessors in one computer to perform complex processes quickly.

master boot record A small program that runs when a computer is started. This program determines whether the disk contains the basic components of an operating system necessary to run successfully. If the boot record determines that the required files are present and the disk has a valid format, it transfers control to one of the operating system programs, which continues the process of starting up.

master page A special page created in desktop publishing software that contains elements common to all the pages in the document, such as page numbers, headers and footers, ruling lines, margin features, special graphics, and layout guides.

mb See *megabit*.

MB See *megabyte*.

Mbps See *megabits per second*.

MBps See *megabytes per second*.

media The plural form of the word *medium*. See *medium*.

medium (1) In storage technology, a medium is material used to store data, such as the magnetic coating on a disk or tape, or the metallic platter in a compact disk. (2) In networking, a medium is a means of conveying a signal across the network, such as a cable. (3) In multimedia, a medium is a single means of conveying a message, such as text or video.

megabit (mb) Equivalent to approximately one million bits. A common measure of data transfer speeds.

megabits per second (mbps) Equivalent to one million bits of data per second.

megabyte (MB) Equivalent to approximately one million bytes. A common measure of data storage capacity.

megabytes per second (MBps) Equivalent to one million bytes of data per second.

megahertz (MHz) Equivalent to millions of cycles per second. A common measure of clock speed.

memo field A database field that stores text information of variable length. Also called *description field*.

memory A collection of chips on the motherboard, or on a circuit board attached to the motherboard, where all computer processing and program instructions are stored while in use. The computer's memory enables the CPU to retrieve data quickly for processing.

memory address A number used by the CPU to locate each piece of data in memory.

menu A list of commands or functions displayed on screen for selection by the user.

menu bar A graphical screen element—located above the document area of an application window—that displays a list of the types of commands available to the user. When the user selects an option from the menu bar, a list appears, displaying the commands related to that menu option.

mesh topology An expensive, redundant cabling scheme for local area networks, in which each node is connected to every other node by a unique cable.

metasearch engine A Web-based search engine that compiles the search results from several other engines, allowing for a wider range of results.

method See *member function*.

metropolitan area network (MAN) A larger version of a local area network (LAN); it can be used to connect computer systems in buildings in the same town or city.

MHz See *megahertz*.

microcode Code that details the individual tasks the computer must perform to complete each instruction in the instruction set.

microcomputer See *personal computer (PC)*.

micron A unit of measure equivalent to one-millionth of a meter.

microphone An input device used to digitally record audio data, such as the human voice. Many productivity applications can accept input via a microphone, enabling the user to dictate text or issue commands orally.

microprocessor Integrated circuits on one or more chips that make up the computer's CPU. Microprocessors are composed of silicon or other material etched with many tiny electronic circuits.

millions of instructions per second (MIPS) A common unit of measure when gauging the performance of a computer's processor.

MIDI See *Musical Instrument Digital Interface*.

millisecond (ms) Equivalent to one thousandth of a second; used to measure access time of storage devices such as hard disks. See also *nanosecond*.

minicomputer A midsize, multiuser computer capable of handling more input and output than a PC but with less processing power and storage than a mainframe. Also called a *midrange computer*.

MIS See *management information system*.

model A three-dimensional image that represents a real or imagined object or character; created using special computer software programs, including surface modelers, solid modelers, spline-based modelers, and others.

modem Abbreviation for *modulator/demodulator*. An input/output device that allows computers to communicate through telephone lines. A modem converts outgoing digital data into analog signals that can be transmitted over phone lines and converts incoming analog signals into digital data that can be processed by the computer.

moderator An overseer of a newsgroup; a person who sorts through articles before posting them to the World Wide Web and removes inappropriate ones.

modifier keys Keyboard keys that are used in conjunction with other keys to execute a command. The IBM-PC keyboard includes Shift, Ctrl, and Alt modifier keys.

monitor A display screen used to provide computer output to the user. Examples include the cathode ray tube (CRT) monitor, flat-panel monitor, and liquid crystal display (LCD).

monochrome monitor A monitor that displays only one color (such as green or amber) against a contrasting background.

motherboard The main circuit board of the computer; it contains the CPU, memory, expansion slots, bus, and video controller. Also called the *system board*.

Motorola A manufacturer of computer chips, most notably microprocessors and communications chips; the maker of processors used in Macintosh computers.

mouse An input device operated by rolling its ball across a flat surface. The mouse is used to control the on-screen pointer by pointing and clicking, double-clicking, or dragging objects on the screen.

MP See *multiprocessing*.

MPEG A multimedia data compression standard used to compress full-motion video. Stands for *Moving Pictures Experts Group*.

MPP See *massively parallel processing*.

ms See *millisecond*.

MS-DOS Acronym for *Microsoft-Disk Operating System*. The command-line interface operating system developed by Microsoft for PCs. IBM selected DOS as the standard for early IBM and IBM-compatible machines.

multimedia Elements of text, graphics, animation, video, and sound combined for presentation to the consumer.

multimedia authoring An application that enables the user to combine text, graphics, animation, video, and sound documents developed with other software packages to create a multimedia product.

multiprocessing (MP) See *parallel processing*.

multitasking The capability of an operating system to load multiple programs into memory at one time and to perform two or more processes concurrently, such as printing a document while editing another.

Musical Instrument Digital Interface (MIDI) A specialized category of input/output devices used in the creation, recording, editing, and performance of music.

N

nanosecond (ns) One-billionth of a second. A common unit of measure for the average access time of memory devices.

navigation The process of moving through a software program, a multimedia product, or a Web site.

needs analysis phase Phase 1 of the systems development life cycle. In this phase needs are defined, the current system is analyzed, alternative solutions are developed, and the best solution and its functions are selected.

network (1) A system of interconnected computers that communicate with one another and share applications, data, and hardware components. (2) The act of connecting computers together in order to permit the transfer of data and programs between users.

network administrator See *system administrator*.

network computer (NC) A specialized computer that provides basic input/output capabilities to a user on a network. Some types of NCs provide storage and processing capabilities, but other types include only a keyboard, mouse, and monitor. The latter category of network computer utilizes the network server for processing and storage.

network interface card (NIC) A circuit board that controls the exchange of data over a network.

network news transfer protocol (NNTP) A set of rules that enable news servers to exchange articles with other news servers.

network operating system (NOS) A group of programs that manage the resources on a network.

network protocol A set of standards used for network communications.

network server See *file server*.

network version An application program especially designed to work within a network environment. Users access the software from a shared storage device.

new media A term encompassing all types of interactive multimedia technologies.

news A public bulletin board service on the Internet; organized into discussion groups representing specific topics of interest.

news server A host computer that exchanges articles with other Internet servers.

newsgroup An electronic storage space where users can post messages to other users, carry on extended conversations, and trade information.

newsreader A software program that enables the user to post and read articles in an Internet newsgroup.

NIC See *network interface card*.

node An individual computer that is connected to a network.

non-impact printer A type of printer that creates images on paper without striking the page in any way. Two common examples are ink jet printers, which spray tiny droplets of ink onto the page, and laser printers, which use heat to adhere particles of toner to specific points on the page.

nonvolatile The tendency for memory to retain data even when the computer is turned off (as is the case with ROM).

NNTP See *network news transfer protocol*.

NNTP server Another name for news servers using the network news transfer protocol.

NOS See *network operating system*.

notebook computer A small, portable computer with an attached flat screen; typically powered by battery or AC and weighing less than 10 pounds. Notebook computers commonly provide most of the same features found in full-size desktop computers, including a color monitor, a fast processor, a modem, and adequate RAM and storage for business-class software applications. Also called *laptop computer*.

ns See *nanosecond*.

NSFnet Acronym for *National Science Foundation Network*. A network developed by the National Science Foundation (NSF) to accommodate the many users attempting to access the five academic research centers created by the NSF.

numeric field A database field that stores numeric characters.

numeric keypad The part of a keyboard that looks and works like a calculator keypad; it has 10 digits and mathematical operators.

O

object embedding The process of integrating a copy of data from one application into another, as from a spreadsheet to a word processor. The data retains the formatting applied to it in the original application, but its relationship with the original file is destroyed.

object linking The process of integrating a copy of data from one application into another so that the data retains a link to the original document. Thereafter, a change in the original document also appears in the linked data in the second application.

Object Linking and Embedding (OLE) A Windows feature that combines object embedding and linking functions. OLE allows the user to construct a document containing data from a single point in time or one in which the data is constantly updated.

OCR See *optical character recognition*.

office automation system A system designed to manage information efficiently in areas such as word processing, accounting, document management, or communications.

off-the-shelf application A software product that is packaged and available for sale; installed as-is in some system designs.

OLE See *Object Linking and Embedding*.

online (1) The state of being connected to, served by, or available through a networked computer system or the Internet. For example, when a user is browsing the World Wide Web, that person's computer is said to be online. (2) Describes any computer-related device that is turned on and connected, such as a printer or modem that is in use or ready for use.

online help author In an Information Systems (IS) department, the person who develops the organization and structure of online documentation, such as Help systems or tutorials. The online help author may also act as a technical writer, creating the content for such online systems.

online service A telecommunications service that supplies e-mail and information search tools.

OOP See *object-oriented programming*.

operating environment An intuitive graphical user interface that overlays the operating system but does not replace it. Microsoft Windows 3.*x* is an example.

operating system (OS) The master control program that provides an interface for a user to communicate with the computer; it manages hardware devices, manages and maintains disk file systems, and supports application programs.

optical character recognition (OCR) Technology that enables a computer to translate optically scanned data into character codes, which can then be edited.

optical drive A storage device that writes data to and reads data from an optical storage medium, such as a compact disk.

optical mouse A pointing device that tracks its location (and the pointer's location on the screen) by using a beam of light, such as a laser, bounced off a reflective surface.

optical storage Refers to storage systems that use light beams to read data from the surface of an optical disk. Data is stored as a series of lands and pits on the disk's reflective surface. Generally speaking, optical storage systems provide higher storage capacities than typical magnetic storage systems, but they operate at slower speeds.

OS See *operating system*.

OS/2 Warp A single-user, multitasking operating system with a point-and-click interface developed to exploit the multitasking capabilities of post-8086 computers.

output device A hardware component, such as a monitor or printer, that returns processed data to the user.

outsourcing Using outside expertise to accomplish a task, such as hiring a freelance writer to produce user documentation.

P

packet A small block of data transmitted over a network, which includes an identifying header and the actual data to be sent. Also called a *frame*.

pages per minute (ppm) A common measure for printer output speed. Consumer-grade laser printers, for example, typically can print from 6 to 10 pages per minute depending on whether text or graphics are being printed. See also *characters per second*.

paint program A graphics program that creates images as bitmaps, or a mosaic of pixels.

palmtop computer See *handheld computer*.

paragraph In a word processing program, any series of letters, words, or sentences followed by a hard return. (A hard return is created by pressing the Enter key.)

paragraph format A setting that affects the appearance of one or more entire paragraphs, such as line spacing, paragraph spacing, indents, alignment, tab stops, borders, and shading.

paragraph spacing The amount of blank space between two paragraphs in a document. Typically, this spacing is equivalent to one line of text.

parallel interface A channel through which eight or more data bits can flow simultaneously, such as a computer bus. A parallel interface is commonly used to connect printers to the computer; also called a parallel port.

parallel processing The use of multiple processors to run a program. By harnessing multiple processors, which share the processing workload, the system can handle a much greater flow of data, complete more tasks in a shorter period of time, and deal with the demands of many input and output devices. Also called *multiprocessing (MP)* or *symmetric multiprocessing (SMP)*.

passive matrix LCD Liquid crystal display technology used for flat-panel monitors; it relies on a grid of transistors arranged by rows and columns. In a passive matrix LCD, the color displayed by each pixel is determined by the electricity coming from the transistors at the end of the row and the top of the column.

Paste An application command that copies data from the Clipboard and places it in the document at the position of the insertion point. Data in the Clipboard can be pasted into multiple places in one document, multiple documents, and documents in different applications.

payload In a packet, the actual data being transmitted across a network or over telephone lines. Also refers to the executable portion of a computer virus or the output produced by a virus.

PC See *personal computer*.

PC Card A specialized expansion card the size of a credit card; it fits into a computer and is used to connect new components.

PCI See *Peripheral Component Interconnect*.

PC video camera A small video camera that connects to a special video card on a PC. When used with videoconferencing software, a PC video camera enables users to capture full-motion video images, save them to disk, edit them, and transmit them to other users across a network or the Internet.

PC-to-TV converter A hardware device that converts a computer's digital video signals into analog signals for display on a standard television screen.

PDA See *personal digital assistant*.

peer-to-peer (P2P) network A network environment in which all nodes on the network have equal access to at least some of the resources on all other nodes.

pen An input device that allows the user to write directly on or point at a special pad or the screen of a pen-based computer, such as a PDA. Also called *stylus*.

Peripheral Component Interconnect (PCI) A PC bus standard developed by Intel; it supplies a high-speed data path between the CPU and peripheral devices.

personal computer (PC) The most common type of computer found in an office, classroom, or home. The PC is designed to fit on a desk and be used by one person at a time; also called a microcomputer.

personal digital assistant (PDA) A very small portable computer designed to be held in one hand; used to perform specific tasks, such as creating limited spreadsheets or storing phone numbers.

photo printer A special color printer used for outputting photo-quality images. These printers are typically used to print images captured with a digital camera or an image scanner.

PhotoCD A special optical disk technology, developed by Kodak, for digitizing and storing standard film-based photographs.

photo-manipulation program A multimedia software tool used to make modifications, including adjusting contrast and sharpness, to scanned photographic images.

photorealistic Describes computer-generated images that are lifelike in appearance and not obviously models.

PICT Abbreviation for *picture*. A graphics file format developed for and commonly used on the Macintosh platform, but seldom used on the PC platform.

picture See *field format*.

pipelining A technique that enables a processor to execute more instructions in a given time. In pipelining, the control unit begins executing a new instruction before the current instruction is completed.

pit A depressed area on the metal surface of a compact disk or digital video disk that scatters laser light. Also see *land*.

pixel Contraction of *picture element*. One or more dots that express a portion of an image on a computer screen.

plain old telephone system (POTS) Refers to the standard, existing system of telephone lines that has been in use for decades in the United States. The system includes millions of miles of copper wiring and thousands of switching stations, which ensure that analog telephone signals are routed to their intended destination. This system is now also commonly used to transmit digital data between computers; however, the data must be converted from digital form to analog form before entering the telephone line, then reconverted back to digital form when it reaches the destination computer. This conversion is handled at the computer by a device called a modem.

plotter An output device used to create large-format hard copy; generally used with CAD and design systems.

Plug and Play An operating system feature that enables the user to add hardware devices to the computer without performing technically difficult configuration procedures.

plug-in application See *helper application*.

PNG Acronym for *portable network graphics*. A graphics file format developed as an alternative to GIF and JPEG. The PNG format was designed mainly for use in World Wide Web pages.

point (1) A standard unit used in measuring fonts. One point equals .02 inch in height. (2) To move the mouse pointer around the screen by manipulating the mouse or another type of pointing device.

pointer An on-screen object used to select text; access menus; move files; and interact with programs, files, or data represented graphically on the screen.

point-to-point protocol (PPP) A communications protocol used for linking a computer directly to the Internet.

pointing device A device that enables the user to freely move an on-screen pointer and to select text, menu options, icons, and other on-screen objects. Two popular types of pointing devices are mice and trackballs.

polarized The condition of a magnetic bar with ends having opposite magnetic polarity.

polygonal modeler A 3-D modeling program that builds images using an array of miniature polygons.

POP See *Post Office Protocol*.

POP server A server computer on an e-mail system that manages the flow of e-mail messages and attachments, using the post office protocol.

port (1) A socket on the back of the computer used to connect external devices to the computer. (2) To transfer a software application from one platform to another.

portrait orientation A document format in which the text is printed parallel to the narrowest edges of the page; the opposite of *landscape orientation*.

posting Publishing a document on the Internet by using one of its services, such as news, FTP, or the World Wide Web.

post office protocol (POP) A networking protocol used by e-mail servers to manage the sending and receiving of e-mail messages and attachments.

POTS See *plain old telephone system*.

PPP See *Point to Point Protocol*.

preemptive multitasking A multitasking environment in which the OS prioritizes system and application processes and performs them in the most efficient order. The OS can preempt a low-priority task to start a more critical one.

presentation program Software that enables the user to create professional-quality images, called slides, that can be shown as part of a presentation. Slides can be presented in any number of ways, but they are typically displayed on a large screen or video monitor while the presenter speaks to the audience.

printer An output device that produces a hard copy on paper. Two types are impact and nonimpact.

print head In impact printers, a device that strikes an inked ribbon, pressing ink onto the paper to create characters or graphics.

print job A single request made by a user on a network for printing services to be performed by a networked printer. A print job can include one or multiple documents.

processing A complex procedure by which a computer transforms raw data into useful information.

processor See *central processing unit (CPU)*.

procurement specialist In an Information Systems (IS) department, a professional who is responsible for acquiring hardware, software, or services from outside vendors. Also called *purchasing agent*.

program (1) A set of instructions or code to be executed by the CPU; designed to help users solve problems or perform tasks. Also called software. (2) To create a computer program. The process of computer programming is also called software development.

programmer The person responsible for creating a computer program, including writing new code and analyzing and modifying existing code.

prompt In a command-line interface, the on-screen location where the user types commands. A prompt usually provides a blinking cursor to indicate where commands can be typed. Also called a *command prompt*.

protocol A set of rules and procedures that determine how a computer system receives and transmits data.

purchasing agent See *procurement specialist*.

Q

QBE See *Query by Example*.

query In a database management system (DBMS), a search question that instructs the program to locate records that meet specific criteria.

Query by Example (QBE) In a database management system (DBMS), a tool that accepts a query from a user and then creates the SQL code to locate data requested by the query. QBE enables the user to query a database without understanding SQL.

QuickTime A multimedia playback standard that enables the user to play high-quality audio and video content on the desktop; developed for use with Macintosh computers.

QuickTime VR A "virtual reality" version of the QuickTime file format; it enables multimedia developers to create virtual-reality-like environments from flat, two-dimensional images.

R

Rambus Dynamic RAM (RDRAM) A newer and faster version of dynamic RAM (DRAM), commonly used in today's newer computer systems.

Rambus in-line memory module (RIMM) A special circuit board, used to house Rambus Dynamic RAM (RDRAM).

random access memory (RAM) A computer's volatile or temporary memory, which exists as chips on the motherboard near the CPU. RAM stores data and programs while they are being used and requires a power source to maintain its integrity.

range In a spreadsheet, a rectangular group of contiguous cells.

raster See *bitmap*.

read-only access A type of security right, which a network administrator can assign to a user of the network. If a user has read-only access to a given file on the network server, the user is allowed to open and view the file but is not permitted to make changes to the file or save the file back to its original location. Depending on the right's configuration, the user may be able to make a copy of the file.

read-only memory (ROM) A permanent, or nonvolatile, memory chip used to store instructions and data, including the computer's startup instructions.

read/write access A type of security right, which a network administrator can assign to a user of the network. If a user has read/write access to a given file on the network server, the user is allowed to not only open and view the file but also is permitted to make changes to the file and save the file back to its original location.

read/write head The magnetic device within the disk drive that reads, records, and erases data on the disk's surface. A read/write head contains an electromagnet that alters the polarity of magnetic particles on the storage medium. Most disk drives have one read/write head for each side of each disk in the drive.

RealAudio A standard for playing streaming audio broadcast over the Internet.

RealOne Player A program used for playing streaming audio and video content downloaded from Web servers or a disk.

RealVideo A standard for playing streaming video broadcast over the Internet.

record A database row composed of related fields; a collection of records makes up the database.

Reduced Instruction Set Computing (RISC) Refers to a type of microprocessor design that uses a simplified instruction set; it uses fewer instructions of constant size, each of which can be executed quickly.

refresh rate The number of times per second that each pixel on the computer screen is scanned; measured in hertz (Hz).

register High-speed memory locations built directly into the ALU and used to hold instructions and data currently being processed.

relational database A database structure capable of linking tables; a collection of tables that share at least one common field.

remote terminal connection An Internet connection in which the TCP/IP programs and protocols run on a UNIX host computer. The local computer exchanges data and commands in ASCII format.

removable hard drive A magnetic storage device that combines the speed and capacity of a hard disk with the portability of a diskette. A removable box encloses the disk, drive, and read/write heads in a sealed container that can be moved from computer to computer.

render To create an image of an object as it actually appears.

repeat rate A keyboard setting that determines how how rapidly the character is typed and how long an alphanumeric key must be held down before the character will be repeated.

report A database product that displays data to satisfy a specific set of search criteria presented in a predefined layout, which is designed by the user.

resolution The degree of sharpness of an image, determined by the number of pixels on a screen; expressed as a matrix.

right-click To use the right mouse button of a two-button mouse to select an object or command on the screen.

ring topology A network topology in which network nodes are connected in a circular configuration. Each node examines the data sent through the ring and passes on data not addressed to it.

RISC See *Reduced Instruction Set Computing*.

ROM See *read-only memory*.

root folder The top-level folder on a disk. This primary folder contains all other folders and subfolders stored on the disk. Also called the *root directory*, or sometimes just the *root*.

router A computer device that stores the addressing information of each computer on each LAN or WAN; it uses this information to transfer data along the most efficient path between nodes of a LAN or WAN.

rule See *border*.

ruler An on-screen tool in a word processor's document window. The ruler shows the position of lines, tab stops, margins, and other parts of the document.

run See *execute*.

S

scan code A code—generated by the keyboard controller—that tells the keyboard buffer which key has been pressed.

scanner See *image scanner*.

screen saver A utility program that displays moving images on the screen if no input is received for several minutes; originally developed to prevent an image from being burned into the screen.

scroll To move through an entire document in relation to the document window in order to see parts of the document not currently visible on screen.

scroll bar A vertical or horizontal bar displayed along the side or bottom of a document window, which enables the user to scroll horizontally or vertically through a document by clicking an arrow or dragging a box within the scroll bar.

SCSI See *Small Computer System Interface*.

SDLC See *systems development life cycle*.

search engine A Web site that uses powerful data-searching techniques to help the user locate Web sites containing specific types of content or information.

section A user-defined portion of a document, which can have its own unique formatting.

sector A segment or division of a track on a disk.

Secure HTTP (S-HTTP) An Internet protocol used to encrypt individual pieces of data transmitted between a user's computer and a Web server, making the data unusable to anyone who does not have a key to the encryption method.

secure sockets layer (SSL) An Internet protocol that can be used to encrypt any amount of data sent over the Internet between a client computer and a host computer.

secure Web page A Web page that uses one or more encryption technologies to encode data received from and sent to the user.

security administrator In an Information Systems (IS) department, a manager charged with overseeing the security of the network and data stored on it. A security manager may oversee the organization's firewall, password strategies, and the handling of other security-related issues.

seek time See *average access time*.

select (1) To highlight a block of text (in a word processor) or range (in a spreadsheet), so the user can perform one or more editing operations on it. (2) To click once on an icon.

serial interface A channel through which data bits flow one at a time. Serial interfaces are used primarily to connect a mouse or a communications device to the computer. Also called a serial port.

serial line interface protocol (SLIP) A method for linking a computer directly to the Internet by using a phone line connected to a serial communications port.

server See *file server*.

shading A paragraph format that displays a pattern or color as a background to the text. Shading may be used to emphasize a block of text.

shadow mask In a cathode ray tube (CRT) monitor, a fine mesh made of metal, fitted to the shape and size of the screen. The holes in the shadow mask's mesh are used to align the electron beams to ensure that they strike the correct phosphor dot. In most shadow masks, these holes are arranged in triangles.

shell account A type of Internet access used by remote terminal connections; it operates from a host computer running UNIX or a similar operating system.

Shockwave A plug-in application that allows interactive animations and audio to play directly in a Web browser window.

shortcut menu See *context menu*.

S-HTTP See *Secure HTTP*.

SIMM See *Single In-Line Memory Module*.

Single In-Line Memory Module (SIMM) One type of circuit board containing memory chips.

site license An agreement in which an organization purchases the right to use a program on a limited number of machines. The total cost is less than would be required if individual copies of the software were purchased for all users.

slide An individual graphic that is part of a presentation. Slides are created and edited in presentation programs.

SLIP See *serial line interface protocol*.

Small Computer System Interface (SCSI) A high-speed interface that extends the bus outside the computer, permitting the addition of more peripheral devices than normally could be connected using the available expansion slots.

smart card A plastic card—about the same size as a standard credit card—that contains a small chip that stores data. Using a special device, called a smart card reader, the user can read data from the card, add new data, or revise existing data.

smart card reader A device that can read data from or write data to a smart card.

SMP See *symmetric multiprocessing*.

soft formatting See *logical formatting*.

software See *program*.

solid model A 3-D model created in a solid modeling program; it appears to be a solid object rather than a frame or polygon-based object.

solid modeler A 3-D modeling program that depicts an object as a solid block of material, which the user shapes by adding and subtracting material or joining with other objects.

sort To arrange database records in a particular order—such as alphabetical, numerical, or chronological order—according to the contents of one or more fields.

sort order The order in which database records are sorted, either ascending or descending.

sound card An expansion card that records and plays back sound by translating the analog signal from a microphone into a digitized form that the computer can store and process, and then translating the data back into analog signals or sound.

spawn To launch a program from within another program. For example, to allow the user to view streaming multimedia content, a Web browser may spawn a second application, such as the QuickTime Player.

speech recognition An input technology that can translate human speech into text. Some speech-recognition systems enable the user to navigate application programs and issue commands by voice control, as well as to create documents by dictating text; also called voice recognition.

spell checker A language tool built into many types of productivity applications. A spelling checker can review any or all words in a document and compare each one to a dictionary of accepted spellings. If the checker encounters a word that appears to be misspelled, it notifies the user and provides alternative spellings; the user can accept the change, add the word to the dictionary, or ignore the spelling.

spline-based modeler A 3-D modeling program that builds objects using mathematically defined curves.

spoof To distribute unrequested e-mail messages while concealing the sender's identity. In spoofing, the spoofer's message identifies the sender as someone else or shows no sender's identity at all. This method protects the spoofer from retaliation from those who receive unwanted messages. See also *spam*.

spooling The process of queuing multiple print jobs that have been sent to a networked printer. Print jobs are temporarily stored while they await their turn to be printed.

spreadsheet A grid of columns and rows used for recording and evaluating numbers. Spreadsheets are used primarily for financial analysis, record keeping, and management, as well as to create reports and presentations.

SQL See *Structured Query Language*.

SRAM See *static RAM*.

SSL See *Secure Sockets Layer*.

star topology A network topology in which network nodes connect to a central hub through which all data is routed.

Start button A Windows 95/98/2000/NT/XP screen element—found on the taskbar—that displays the Start menu when selected.

Start menu A menu in the Windows 95/98/2000/NT/XP operating systems; the user can open the Start menu by clicking the Start button; the Start menu provides tools to locate documents, find help, change system settings, and run programs.

static RAM (SRAM) A type of random access memory (RAM) sometimes used in personal computers. Static RAM chips do not need to be refreshed (recharged with electricity) as often as dynamic RAM, another commonly used type of memory. As a result, SRAM can hold its contents longer than dynamic RAM. SRAM is also very fast, supporting access times of around 10 nanoseconds.

status bar An on-screen element that appears at the bottom of an application window and displays the current status of various parts of the current document or application, such as page number, text entry mode, and so on.

storage The portion of the computer that holds data or programs while they are not being used. Storage media include magnetic or optical disks, tape, and cartridges.

storage device The hardware components that write data to and read data from storage media. For example, a diskette is a type of storage medium, whereas a diskette drive is a storage device.

storage media The physical components or materials on which data is stored. Diskettes and compact disks are examples of storage media.

storing The second step of the CPU's execution cycle.

storyboard A production tool that consists of sketches of scenes and actions that map a sequence of events in a multimedia program.

streaming audio/video Multimedia content that is sent to the user's desktop in a continuous "stream" from a Web server. Because audio and video files are large, streaming content is sent to the user's disk in pieces; the first piece is temporarily buffered (stored on disk), then played as the next piece is stored and buffered.

structured English A programming design tool and a method of documenting a system using plain English terms and phrases to describe events, actions, and alternative actions that can occur.

Structured Query Language (SQL) The standard query language used for searching and selecting records and fields in a relational database.

stylus See *pen*.

subdomain A division of a domain name system (DNS) address that specifies a particular level or area of an organization, such as a department or a branch office.

submarining In older passive matrix LCD displays, a problem caused by the monitor's inability to refresh itself fast enough. One characteristic of submarining is the disappearance of the mouse pointer when it moves across the screen.

subscribe To select a newsgroup so the user can regularly participate in its discussions. After subscribing to a newsgroup in a newsreader program, the program automatically downloads an updated list of articles when it is launched.

supercomputer The largest, fastest, and most powerful type of computer. Supercomputers are often used for scientific and engineering applications and for processing complex models that use very large data sets.

supervisor access In a network environment, a type of access right granted only to users with management-level status. Users with supervisor access rights usually can access any drive or file on the network, with the ability to edit, copy, move, or delete any file.

surface modeler A 3-D modeling program that depicts an object as an outer layer (a surface) stretched over a wire frame.

Super VGA (SVGA) An IBM video display standard capable of displaying resolutions up to 1024 × 768 pixels, with 16 million colors.

swap in To load essential parts of a program into memory as required for use.

swap out To unload, or remove, nonessential parts of a program from memory to make room for needed parts.

Synchronous Dynamic RAM (SDRAM) A type of RAM that delivers bursts of data at very high speeds (up to 100 MHz), providing more data to the CPU at a given time than older RAM technologies.

symmetric multiprocessing (SMP) See *parallel processing.*

system administrator In an information systems (IS) department, the person responsible for ensuring a system's security, protecting data integrity, performing routine maintenance, and recovering lost data. Also called a *network administrator.*

system board See *motherboard.*

system call A feature built into an application program that requests a service from the operating system, as when a word processing program requests the use of the printer to print a document.

system clock The computer's internal clock, which is used to time processing operations. The clock's time intervals are based on the constant, unchanging vibrations of molecules in a quartz crystal; currently measured in megahertz (MHz).

system operator (sysop) In an online discussion group, the person who monitors the discussion.

system software A computer program that controls the system hardware and interacts with application software. The designation includes the operating system and the network operating system.

systems analyst In an Information Systems (IS) department, the individual who analyzes and designs software systems.

systems design phase Phase 2 of the systems development life cycle. In this phase the project team researches and develops alternative ways to meet an organization's computing needs.

systems development life cycle (SDLC) A formal methodology and process for the needs analysis, system design, development, implementation, and maintenance of an information system.

T

T1 A communications line that represents a higher level of the ISDN standard service and supplies a bandwidth of 1.544 Mbps.

T3 A communications line capable of transmitting a total of 44.736 Mbps.

tab stop A preset position in a document to which the cursor moves when the Tab key is pressed.

table A grid of data, set up in rows and columns.

tablet PC A newer type of portable PC, similar in size to a notebook PC; it allows the user to input data and commands with a pen rather than a standard keyboard or pointing device.

tape drive A magnetic storage device that reads and writes data to the surface of a magnetic tape. Tape drives are generally used for backing up data or restoring the data of a hard disk.

task switching The process of moving from one open window to another.

taskbar A Windows 95/98/2000/NT/XP screen element—displayed on the desktop—which includes the Start button and lists the programs currently running on the computer.

TB See *terabyte.*

TCP/IP See *Transmission Control Protocol/Internet Protocol.*

technical analyst In an Information Systems (IS) department, a specialist who looks for solutions when an information system needs to be updated, modified, or revamped. After users or managers identify a need, the analyst discusses the usability, business, scientific, or engineering problems with them.

technical writer In an Information Systems (IS) department, the person who documents the system, from the technical details needed by system managers to the procedural instructions designed for the end users.

telecommute To work at home or on the road and have access to a work computer via telecommunications equipment, such as modems and fax machines.

telecommuter A person who works at home or on the road and requires access to a work computer via telecommunications equipment, such as modems and fax machines.

teleconference A live, real-time communications session involving two or more people in different locations, using computers and telecommunications equipment.

Telnet An Internet service that provides a transparent window between the user's computer and a distant host system.

template A preformatted document used to quickly create a standard document, such as a memo or report.

temporary (TEMP) file A file created by an operating system or application, which is needed only temporarily. Such files are usually del489 eted from the disk when they are no longer required.

terabyte Equivalent to one trillion bytes of data; a measure of storage capacity.

terminal An input/output device connected to a multiuser computer, such as a mainframe.

text box In word processing and presentation software, a special frame that enables the user to contain text in a rectangular area. The user can size and position the text box like a frame by dragging the box or one of its handles. Also see *frame.*

text code A standard system in which numbers represent the letters of the alphabet, punctuation marks, and other symbols. A text code enables programmers to use combinations of numbers to represent individual pieces of data. EBCDIC, ASCII, and Unicode are examples of text code systems.

text field A database field that stores a string of alphanumeric characters; also called *alphanumeric field* or *character field.*

TFT See *thin-film transistor.*

thermal-wax printer A printer that produces high-quality images by using a heat source to evaporate colored wax from a ribbon, which adheres to the paper.

thesaurus A text editing tool that lists alternative words with similar meanings.

thin-film transistor (TFT) See *active matrix LCD.*

thread A series of related articles and responses about a specific subject, posted in a newsgroup.

throughput See *data-transfer rate.*

TIFF Acronym for *tagged image file format.* A graphics file format widely used on both PCs and Macintosh computers. Commonly used when exchanging bitmap files that will be printed or edited, the TIFF format can faithfully store images that contain up to 16.7 million colors without any loss of image quality.

time field A database field that stores a time.

title bar An on-screen element displayed at the top of every window that identifies the window contents. Dragging the title bar changes the position of the window on the screen.

token In a network using ring topology, any piece of data that is being transferred across the network. Each node examines the data and passes it along until it reaches its destination.

Token Ring IBM's network protocol, based on a ring topology in which linked computers pass an electronic token containing addressing information to facilitate data transfer.

toner A substance composed of tiny particles of charged ink, which is used in laser printers. The ink particles stick to charged areas of a drum and are transferred to paper with pressure and heat.

toolbar In application software, an on-screen element appearing just below the menu bar. The toolbar contains multiple tools, which are graphic icons (called buttons) representing specific actions the user can perform. To initiate an action, the user clicks the appropriate button.

top-down design A systems design method in which the major functions or processes are developed first, followed by the details.

top-level domain See *domain*.

topology The physical layout of wires that connect the computers in a network; includes bus, star, ring, and mesh.

touch pad See *trackpad*.

touch screen An input/output device that accepts input directly from the monitor. To activate commands, the user touches words, graphical icons, or symbols displayed on screen.

track An area used for storing data on a formatted disk. During the disk-formatting process, the operating system creates a set of magnetic concentric circles on the disk: these are the tracks. These tracks are then divided into sectors, with each sector able to hold a given amount of data. By using this system to store data, the operating system can quickly determine where data is located on the disk. Different types of disks can hold different numbers of tracks.

trackball An input device that functions like an upside-down mouse, consisting of a stationary casing containing a movable ball that is operated by hand. Trackballs are used frequently with laptop computers.

tracking The letter spacing within blocks of text. Adjusting this spacing can make text easier to read.

trackpad A stationary pointing device that the user operates by moving a finger across a small, touch-sensitive surface. Trackpads are often built into portable computers. Also called a *touchpad*.

TrackPoint See *integrated pointing device*.

trainer In an IS department, the person responsible for teaching users how to use a new system, whether hardware, software, procedures, or a combination thereof.

transaction A series of steps required to complete an event, such as taking an order or preparing a time sheet.

transaction processing system A type of information system that handles the processing and tracking of transactions.

transistor An electronic switch within the CPU that exists in two states, conductive (on) or nonconductive (off). The resulting combinations are used to create the binary code that is the basis for machine language.

transition In a presentation program, an animation-like effect applied when switching from one slide to the next during a presentation.

Transmission Control Protocol/Internet Protocol (TCP/IP) The set of commands and timing specifications used by the Internet to connect dissimilar systems and to control the flow of information.

tween Abbreviation for "in-between." In animation, tweens are the frames that depict a character's or object's motion between keyframes.

twisted-pair cable Cable used in network connections. Twisted-pair cable consists of copper strands, individually shrouded in plastic, twisted around each other in pairs and bound together in a layer of plastic insulation; also called unshielded twisted-pair (UTP) wire. Twisted-pair wire encased in a metal sheath is called shielded twisted-pair (STP) wire.

typeface See *font*.

type style An attribute applied to a text character, such as underlining, italic, and bold, among others. Most application programs provide a wide variety of type styles, which the user can freely apply to text anywhere in a document.

U

UART See *Universal Asynchronous Receiver Transmitter*.

Unicode Worldwide Character Standard A character set that provides 16 bits to represent each symbol, resulting in 65,536 different characters or symbols, enough for all the languages of the world. The Unicode character set includes all the characters from the ASCII character set.

Uniform Resource Locator (URL) An Internet address used with HTTP in the format *type://address/path*.

uninstall To remove an installed program from a computer's disk.

Universal Asynchronous Receiver Transmitter (UART) A chip that converts parallel data from the bus into serial data that can flow through a serial cable, and vice versa.

Universal Serial Bus (USB) A new expansion bus technology that currently enables the user to connect 127 different devices into a single port.

UNIX A 32-bit, fully multitasking, multithreading operating system developed by Bell Labs in the 1970s. A powerful, highly scalable operating system, UNIX (and variants of it) is used to operate supercomputers, mainframes, minicomputers, and powerful PCs and workstations. UNIX generally features a command-line interface, although some variants of UNIX feature a graphical operating environment, as well.

uploading Sending a file to a remote computer. The opposite of *downloading*.

URL See *Uniform Resource Locator*.

USB See *Universal Serial Bus*.

user The person who inputs and analyzes data using a computer.

user interface The on-screen elements that enable the user to interact with the software.

utility A software program that may be used to enhance the functionality of an operating system. Examples of utility software are disk defragmenters and screen savers.

V

value A numerical entry in a spreadsheet—representing currency, a percentage, a date, a time, a fraction, and so on—which can be used in formulas.

vector A mathematical equation that describes the position of a line.

Video Graphics Array (VGA) An IBM video display standard capable of displaying resolutions of 640 × 480, with 16 colors.

video capture card A specialized expansion board that enables the user to connect video devices—such as VCRs and camcorders—to the PC. This enables the user to transfer images from the video equipment to the PC, and vice versa. Many video cards enable the user to edit digitized video and to record the edited images on videotape.

videoconference A live, real-time video communications session involving two or more people using computers, video cameras, telecommunications and videoconferencing software.

video controller A circuit board attached to the motherboard that contains the memory and other circuitry necessary to send information to the monitor for display on screen. This controller determines the refresh rate, resolution, and number of colors that can be displayed. Also called the *display adapter*.

Video for Windows An audio/visual standard developed by Microsoft as a way to store and display compressed audio and video information.

video RAM (VRAM) Memory on the video controller (sometimes called *dual-ported memory*) that can send a screen of data to the monitor while receiving the next data set.

viewing angle The widest angle from which a display monitor's image can be seen clearly. Generally speaking, cathode ray tube (CRT) monitors provide a wider viewing angle than liquid crystal display (LCD) monitors do.

voice recognition See *speech recognition*.

volatile The tendency for memory to lose data when the computer is turned off, as is the case with RAM.

VRAM See *video RAM*.

W

walk-through A specially rendered animation, created in a CAD or 3-D graphics program, which creates the illusion that the viewer is moving through an object, such as a building.

WAN See *wide area network*.

Web browser A program that enables the user to view Web pages, navigate Web sites, and move from one Web site to another. Also called *browser*.

Webmaster A person or group responsible for designing and maintaining a Web site.

Web page A document developed using HTML and found on the World Wide Web. Web pages contain information about a particular subject with links to related Web pages and other resources.

Web server An Internet host computer that may store thousands of Web sites.

Web site A collection of related Web pages.

what-if analysis A data analysis process used to test how alternative scenarios affect numeric results.

wide area network (WAN) A computer network that spans a wide geographical area.

window An area on the computer screen in which an application or document is viewed and accessed.

Windows A family of operating system products developed and produced by Microsoft Corp. The vast majority of personal computers run Windows, with versions including Windows 3.*x*, 95, 98, NT, 2000, and XP. Windows versions 3.*x* and earlier were actually operating environments—graphical interfaces that ran on top of the DOS operating system. In versions 95 and later, Windows is a full-fledged operating system.

Winsock Windows Sockets; a standard network interface that makes it possible to mix and match application programs from more than one developer to communicate across the Internet.

wireframe model A CAD tool that represents 3-D shapes by displaying their outlines and edges.

wireless topology A network topology used for wireless networks, whose nodes are not connected by cables or wires.

word processing software Software used to create and edit text documents such as letters, memos, reports, and publications. Also called a word processor.

word size The size of the registers in the CPU, which determines the amount of data the computer can work with at any given time. Larger word sizes lead to faster processing; common word sizes include 16 bits, 32 bits, and 64 bits.

word wrap A word processing feature that computes the length of each line of text as the text is entered.

workbook A data file created with spreadsheet software, containing multiple worksheets.

worksheet The data file created with spreadsheet software.

workstation A fast, powerful microcomputer used for scientific applications, graphics, CAD, CAE, and other complex applications. Workstations are usually based on RISC technology and operated by some version of UNIX, although an increasing number of Intel/Windows-based workstations are coming into popular use.

World Wide Web (the Web or WWW) An Internet service developed to incorporate footnotes, figures, and cross-references into online hypertext documents.

write access In a network environment, an access right granted to some users. Users with this type of access right can open, edit, and save files on the network.

X, Y, Z

Xbase A generic database language used to construct queries. Xbase is similar to SQL, but more complex because its commands cover the full range of database activities beyond querying.

Microsoft Windows .NET Enterprise Server
(network operating system), 216–217
Microsoft Windows NT (operating system),
210–211
Microsoft Windows NT Server (network
operating system), 211, 247
Microsoft Windows NT Workstation (operating
system), 210–211
Microsoft Windows XP, 216, 247
Microsoft Windows XP Home Edition, 247, 261
MIDI (Musical Instrument Digital Interface),
140–141
mid-range computers (minicomputers), 15
millions of instructions per second (MIPS), 119
milliseconds (ms), 175
minicomputers (mid-range computers), 15
Mobile Information Server (server of Windows
.NET Enterprise Server), 217
modeling programs, 400–401
models, 399–401
modems (modulator-demodulators), 9, 253, 293
cable, 260, 294–295
choosing, 254–255
transmission technologies for, 257–260
uses for, 255, 257
modifier keys, 45
monitoring software, 243
monitors, 8, 80–90
comparing, 85–86
CRT (cathode ray tube) monitors, 80, 81–82
flat-panel monitors, 82–84
large-format monitors, 358
other types, 84
for slide presentations, 358
monochrome monitors, 80
Mosaic (Web browser), 274
motherboards, 5–6
Motorola processors, 136
mouse devices, 7, 52–56
history of, 68
using, xxvi
variants of, 55–56
mouse button configurations, 55
mouse keys, 57
MPEG compression, 419–420
MP3 (MPEG Layer 3; audio compression
standard), 92
MS-DOS (Microsoft Disk Operating System),
207–208
required for Windows 3.x operating
environments, 209
Windows operating systems and, 210, 213
mulitmedia, 409–424
authoring, 12, 418
careers in, 424
in education and training, 416
hypermedia in, 414–415
interactivity in, 410–412
layering information, 413–415, 417–418
MP3 (MPEG Layer 3; audio compression
standard) for, 92
new media and, 412–413, 417–418, 419–423
in presentation programs,
multimedia authoring applications, 12, 418
multimedia developers, 302
multiprocessing (MP; parallel processing), 138
multitasking, 196
music
MIDI Musical Instrument Digital Interface,
140–141
MP3 (MPEG Layer 3; audio compression
standard), 92

Musical Instrument Digital Interface (MIDI),
140–141

nanoseconds (ns), 175
Napster, 92
National Center for Supercomputing
Applications (NCSA), 274
National Science Foundation (NSF), 24
navigation, 414
needs analysis phase in information systems,
450–451
NetBEUI, 238
netiquette, 287
Netscape Navigator, 274
NetWare (network operating system), 247
network administrator certification, 456
network administrators, 262, 443, 456
network backbones, 24
network card, 256
network interface card (NIC), 245
network news transfer protocol (NNTP), 280
network operating systems (NOSs), 246–247
network sales, 144
network servers, 232
network versions of software, 234–235
networking, 198, 231, 252
careers in, 262
networks
campus area networks (CAN), 240
client/server networks, 241–242
firewalls to control access to, 297–298
home networks, 260–261
intranets and extranets, 298
local area networks (LANs), 101, 237–239, 293
media for, 253–255, 257–260
metropolitan area networks (MANs), 240
network software, 246–247
network technologies, 246
network topology, 244–245
peer-to-peer networks, 242
server-based networks, 240–241
structure of networks, 237–242
uses of, 232–237
wide area networks (WANs), 240
workstations on, 15, 16
new media, 412–413
careers in, 424
creating content in, 417–418
MP3 (MPEG Layer 3; audio compression
standard) for, 92
technologies that support, 419–423
See also multimedia
news, on Internet, 280–281
newsgroups, 193, 280, 281
newsreader, 280
news server, 280
NNTP (network news transfer protocol), 280
nodes, in networks, 240
nonimpact printers, 98, 100–102
nonvolatile memory, 120
notebook (laptop) computers, 16
Novell NetWare (network operating system), 247
NSFnet, 24
numbers
data represented as, 114
spreadsheet software for calculating,
333–334
numeric fields, 370
numeric keypad, 46

Object Linking and Embedding (OLE), 195–196
office automation systems, 434
off-the-shelf applications, 434
OLE (Object Linking and Embedding), 195–196
online
accounts, 300
broadcast of presentations, 356
etiquette, 287
presentations, 356
security, 248, 297–298, 300–301
services, 284, 445
technical assistance, 193
See also Internet; World Wide Web
online help architects, 218
online help systems, 445
online help writers, 442
Open VMS (version of UNIX), 206
operating systems (OSs), 12, 157–158, 189, 212
changing, 201
data found on disks by, 157
DOS, 207–208
embedded operating systems, 217
file management by, 196–197
hardware management by, 197–198
Linux, 214–215
Macintosh, 208
multitasking by, 196
network operating systems, 246–247
NET Server, 247
OS/2 Warp, 210
running programs under, 194–196
storage space needed by, 151
UNIX, 206
user interfaces for, 190–192
utility software used with, 199–200
Windows, 205, 212
Windows .NET Enterprise server, 216–217
Windows NT, 210–211
Windows 3.x, 209
Windows 9x, 213–214
Windows 95, 213
Windows 98a, 214
Windows 2000, 215, 247
Windows CE, 217
Windows for Workgroups, 209
Windows ME, 214
Windows .NET Enterprise Server, 216–217
Windows NT, 210–211
Windows NT Server, 211, 247
Windows NT Workstation, 210–211
Windows XP, 216, 247, 261
optical character recognition (OCR), 65–66
optical drives, 9
optical input devices, 64–66
optical mouse, 52
optical storage devices, 152, 165
CD-ROM, 165–167
DVD-ROM, 167
recordable optical technologies, 168
orientation pages, 323
OS/2 Warp (operating system), 210
outlining features, in presentation programs, 354
Outlook XP (presentation program), 356
output devices, 7, 8–9
digital light projectors, 90
monitors, 80–90
printers, 96–105
sound systems, 90–92
See also input devices

rulers, 319
running programs, 12, 194–196

S

scan codes, 49
scanners, 8, 65–66, 394
scanning disks, 180
screen readers, 57
screen savers, 200
scroll bars, 319
SCSI (Small Computer System Interface), 140, 181
search engines, 30, 32–35
sections, 323
sectors, 156
secure HTTP (S-HTTP) protocol, 301
secure sockets layer (SSL), 301
secure Web pages, 300–301
security
    for e-commerce, 300–301
    firewalls to control access to networks, 248, 297–298
security administrators, 443
seek time, 175
SerialKey device support, 57
serial interface, 139
serial line interface protocol (SLIP), 139, 292
serial ports, 139, 142
Server Standard Edition (version of Windows 2000), 215
server-based networks, 240–241
service accounts, 256
shading
    in documents, 323
    in slides, 354
    in CAD (computer aided design) programs, 400
shadow masks, 82
SharePoint Portal Server (server of Windows .NET Enterprise Server), 217
shell accounts, 292
Shockwave (Macromedia program), 418, 423
shortcut key, 47
shortcut menus, 191
SIMMs (single in-line memory modules), 124
simultaneous access, 232–235
single in-line memory modules (SIMMs), 124
site licenses, 234
site-specific search tools, 35
64-bit processors, 134
slides and slide shows, 349
    creating, in presentation programs, formatting, 353–354
    presenting slide shows, 358
small business owners, 327
Small Computer System Interface (SCSI) standard, 140, 181
smart card readers, 169
smart cards, 48, 169
soft (logical; low-level) formatting, 157
software, 4, 12–14
    accessibility features for, 57
    application software, 12
    for backing up data, 164
    computer-aided software engineering, 452
    for data compression, 176
    documentation for, 218, 442, 445
    financial software, 327
    keyboard shortcuts for, 51
    licensing of, 329
    Linux support for, 214
    network software, 246–247

operating systems, 12
    for the small or home office, 327
    utility software, 199–200
    See also application software; computer programming; operating systems
software designers, 424
software engineers, 376
software programming, 456. See also computer programming
software sales, 144
Solaris (version of UNIX), 206
solid models, 399, 400
Sony Corp. (firm), 162
sorting data, 341
sound
    in presentation programs, 355
    in word processing programs, 325
sound cards, 91
sound producers , 424
sound systems, 90–92
spam, 287
spawn, 277
special-purpose keys, 47–48
specialty keyboards, 49
speech recognition systems, 57, 67, 69
spell checkers, 324
spline-based modelers, 401
spooling, 235
spreadsheet software, 12, 13, 327, 333
    analyzing data with, 341
    editing and formatting worksheets, 340
    entering data in worksheets, 335–338
    generating charts with, 340–341
    user interfaces for, 334–335
    uses of, 334
SQL (Structured English QUEry Language; SEQUEL), 374–375
SQL Server (server of Windows .NET Enterprise Server), 217
Stanford Research Institute (SRI), 68
star network topology, 244
start button, 190
start key, 47
start menu, 190
static RAM (SRAM), 121
status bars, in word processing software, 319
sticky keys, 57
storage, 9–10
    data warehouses for, 170, 369
storage devices, 151
    average access time for, 175
    backing up data on, 164
    categorizing, 152–153
    data transfer rates for, 177
    data warehouses, 170, 369
    emerging storage technologies, 169
    file compression on, 176
    magnetic, 154–163
    optical, 165–168
    speed of, 174
storage media, 152
    diskettes (floppy disks), 152, 159–160
    See also magnetic disks
storing, 119
storyboarding, 417
streaming audio, 276
streaming video, 276
structured English, 451
Structured English QUEry Language (SEQUEL; SQL), 374
StuffIT (compression utility), 176, 177

stylus (pen), 62
subdomains, on Internet, 271–272
submarining, 83
Sun Microsystems, Inc., 136
Super VGA (SVGA) display standard, 86
supercomputers, 15
SuperDisks, 162
SVGA (Super VGA) display standard, 86
supervisor access, 234
surface modelers, 400
surveillance software, 243
swap in, 123
swap out, 123
symmetrical multiprocessing (SMP; parallel processing), 138, 170
synchronous DRAM (SDRAM), 121
systems development life cycle (SDLC), 450–453
system administrators, 443
system calls, 194
system clock, 124–125
system operator (sysop), 284
system programmers, 442
system software, 12
systems analysts, 376
systems design phase, 451–452

T

T1 service, 259
T3 service, 259
table plotters, 105
tables
    in databases, 370–374, 365–367
    in relational databases, 367–368
    in word processing software, 324
tablet PC, 17
tape drives, 9, 163
taskbar, 190
task switching, 191
TCP/IP (Transmission Control Protocol/Internet Protocol), 238, 270, 292
technical analysts, 442
technical illustrators, 218
technical leads, 424
technical support, 193
technical support specialists, 342
technical writers, 218, 442
telecommunications. See cellular phones; data communications
telecommunications sales, 144
telecommuters, 256, 297, 299
telecommuting, 256
teleconferencing, 236–237
telemarketers, 376
telephone lines, 253, 256
    analog, 253–255, 257
    digital, 257–260
television
    and multimedia, 411, 413
    PC-to-TV converter, 358
Telnet, 281–282
templates
    for slides, in presentation programs, 352, 353
    Web templates, 285
    in word processing software, 325, 326
temporary (temp) files, 179
terabyte (TB), 7
terminals, 15

IMAGE CREDITS

All Table of Contents and section opener illustrations created by tom white.images.

PHOTO CREDITS:

Abbreviation Key: IBM = Courtesy International Business Machines Corporation. Unauthorized use not permitted.

Feature Article Headers: *Computers in Your Career* Comstock; *Productivity Tip, At Issue, Computing Keynotes* PhotoDisc.

Cover (c)Jim Karageorge/Getty Images; **iv** Aaron Haupt; **v** (bl)Liaison Agency, (br)NASA/Roger Ressmeyer/CORBIS, (c)U.S. Department of Defense Camera Combat Center, (cl)SuperStock, (cr)Dan Nelken/Liaison Agency, (tr)1999/Dan Abrams; **xxiii** Aaron Haupt; **xxiv** Aaron Haupt; **xxv** Amanita Pictures; **5** Aaron Haupt; **6** Courtesy Intel Corporation; **7** Kingston; **8** (b)Amanita Pictures, (t)IBM; **9** (b)Mark Steinmetz, (l)Courtesy Sony, (tr)IBM; **10** (bl)Mark Burnett, (tl)Mark Burnett, (tr)Aaron Haupt; **11** (b)Gary Gladstone/Getty Images, (t)Henry Sims/Getty Images; **15** (b)Hewlett Packard, (l)John Connell/IndexStock, (t)Courtesy Cray Inc.; **16** (b)IBM, (bc)IBM, (t)Sun Microsystems, (tcl)IBM, (tcr)IBM; **17** (b)Reuters New Media Inc./CORBIS, (c)Courtesy Nokia, (t)Compaq; **18** Mark Romanelli/ Getty Images; **23** Bettmann/CORBIS; **24** Gary Buss/Getty Images; **36** Joe Baraban/CORBIS Stock Market; **47** Aaron Haupt; **48** (b)Compaq, (t)Matt Meadows; **49** Aaron Haupt; **52** (t)Compaq; **54** Matt Meadows; **55** (b)Aaron Haupt; **56** (b)IBM, (t)Compaq; **62** (b)United Parcel Service, (c)Aaron Haupt, (t)Michael Keller/CORBIS Stock Market; **63** (b)Jose Luis Peleaz/ CORBIS Stock Market, (t)Bob Daemmrich/The Image Works; **64** (b) Federal Express, (c)IBM, (t)Matt Meadows; **65** (t)Mak-1; **66** (b)William Taufic/CORBIS Stock Market; **68** The Bootstrap Institute; **69** Roger Ball/CORBIS Stock Market; **70** (b)Sony, (t)B. Busco/Getty Images; **71** Digital Stock; **72** Richard T. Nowitz/CORBIS; **80** (c)IBM, (l)SGI, (r)IBM; **81** (tl)Sony; **83** Courtesy Hewlett-Packard; **84** IBM; **85** (t)Applied Optical Company; **88** Doug Martin; **89** (l)Compaq, (r)SGI; **90** Courtesy Hewlett-Packard; **91** Sony; **97** (b)Courtesy EPSON, (t)Aaron Haupt; **98** Courtesy Hewlett-Packard; **99** Aaron Haupt; **100** Aaron Haupt; **101** Courtesy Hewlett-Packard; **103** SuperStock; **104** (b)Courtesy Hewlett-Packard, (t)Courtesy KODAK; **105** Courtesy Hewlett-Packard; **106** David Kelly Crow/PhotoEdit; **121** Doug Martin; **122** Masterfile Productions/ Masterfile; **124** Newer Technology; **133** (l)Tony Freeman/PhotoEdit, **133** (l) Courtesy Intel Corporation, (t)Courtesy Motorola; **134** Courtesy Intel Corporation; **135** (b)AMD, (cl)Courtesy Intel Corporation, (cr)Courtesy Intel Corporation, (tc)Courtesy Intel Corporation, (tl)Courtesy Intel Corporation, (tr)Courtesy Intel Corporation; **136** (b)Matt Meadows, (t)Courtesy Motorola; **137** (b)Courtesy Rich La Salle/Index Stock; **138** Compaq; **141** (b)3Com, (t)Mark Burnett; **142** Mark Burnett; **143** (b)Mark Burnett, (tl)Mark Burnett, (tr)Aaron Haupt; **144** Chabruken/Getty Images; **152** (c)IBM, (l)Amanita Pictures, (r)Mark Burnett; **153** (b)Courtesy Hewlett-Packard, (bc)Sony, (t)Maxtor, (tc)Courtesy Iomega; **154** (t)Aaron Haupt; **162** Courtesy Iomega; **163** (b)Courtesy Kingston, (t)Courtesy Hewlett-Packard; **167** (bl)Mark Burnett, (br)Sony, (t)Matt Meadows; **168** (b)IBM, (t)Mark Burnett; **169** Hitachi; **181** Sun Microsystems; **182** Burgum Boorman/Getty Images; **217** Palm; **218** (t)Aaron Haupt; **224** (br)Courtesy Hewlett-Packard, (t)Doug Martin; **243** Jose Luis Pelaez Inc./CORBIS Stock Market; **245** Aaron Haupt; **247** Aaron Haupt; **248** Courtesy Symantec; **253** Jon Feingersh/CORBIS Stock Market; **254** Aaron Haupt; **255** (c)Hayes Microcomputer Products, Inc., (t)3Com; **256** Michael Keller/CORBIS Stock Market; **265** Everybook Inc.; **293** 3Com; **294** (b)3Com, (t)Matthew Borkoski/Index Stock; **298** John Henley/CORBIS Stock Market, Chuck Keeler/Stone; **310** (t)Doug Martin, Tom McCarthy/ SKA; **311** (b)D. Sarraute/Getty Images, (t)Property of AT&T Archives. Reprinted with permission of AT&T; **320** (b)Doug Martin; **324** IBM; **342** Charles Gupton/CORBIS Stock Market; **350** (t)Michael Rosenfeld/ Getty Images; **358** Mark Burnett; **359** Aaron Haupt; **374** Kreber Studios; **376** Charles Gupton/CORBIS Stock Market; **391** Walt Disney/Kobel; **394** (b)Ghislain & Marie David de Lossy/Getty Images, (tl)Doug Martin, (tr)Amanita Pictures; **397** (b)Larry Hamill, (tl)Fractal, (tr)Corel; **398** Glencoe; **402** (b)Glencoe, (t)1997 Universal Photo by David James/ MPTV; **410** Aaron Haupt; **411** (tl)Aaron Haupt, (tr)LWA-DANN TARDIF/ CORBIS Stock Market; **432** (b)Michael S. Yamashita/CORBIS, (t)Lawrence Manning/CORBIS; **438** Charles Gupton/CORBIS Stock Market; **439** (bl)Sun Microsystems, (r)Aaron Haupt; **441** MTPA Stock/Masterfile; **442** (t)Sun Microsystems; **443** SuperStock; **444** Mark Burnett; **454** Charles Gupton/ CORBIS Stock Market; **456** Lee White/CORBIS; **462** (b)The Computer Museum, Boston, (c)The Computer Museum, Boston, (t)Courtesy Intel Corporation; **463** (c)Courtesy Intel Corporation, (tr)Apple Corp.; **464** (bl) Courtesy Hewlett-Packard, (cl)IBM, (cr)Apple Corp., (tc)Used with permission of Lotus Development Corp., (tl)Microsoft Corporation; **465** (bl)Microsoft Corporation, (br)Courtesy Hewlett-Packard, (cl)Apple Corp., (cr)IBM, (t)Compaq; **466** (bl)Shahn Kermani/Getty Images News Services, (cl)IBM, (cr)Apple Corp., (tl)IBM, (tr)Courtesy PhotoDisk, all rights reserved; **467** (b)Apple Corp., (tc)Courtesy Intel Corporation, (tr)Donna Coveny/MIT News Office, (cr)IBM; **468** (b)Apple Corp., (cl)Courtesy Intel Corporation, (cr)Courtesy Motorola, (tr)IBM; **469** (b)Amanita Pictures, (c)Power Computing, (tcr)Courtesy Intel Corporation, (tl)Microsoft Corporation, (tr)Courtesy Motorola; **470** (b)Aaron Haupt, (bl)Amanita Pictures, (cr)Amanita Pictures, (t)Courtesy Intel Corporation; **471** (tl)Courtesy Intel Corporation, (tr)Aaron Haupt, (cl)Amanita Pictures, (cr)Courtesy Intel Corporation, (b)AMD; **472** (bl)Steve Chenn/CORBIS, (br)Courtesy Handspring, (c)AP/Wide World Photos, (t)Aaron Haupt.

SCREEN CAPTURE CREDITS:

Abbreviation Key: COREL = Screen shots are copyright ©Corel Corporation and Corel Corporation Limited. All rights reserved. Corel, WordPerfect, Quattro, Presentations, and Paradox are trademarks or registered trademarks of Corel Corporation or Corel Corporation Limited. Reprinted by permission. **LOTUS** = Screen Captures ©2001 Lotus Development Corporation. Used with permission of Lotus Development Corporation. **MS** = Screen shot reprinted by permission from Microsoft Corporation. **NET** = Netscape Communicator browser window ©1999 Netscape Communications Corporation. Used with permission. **REAL** = ©RealNetworks and/or its licensors, 1995–1999, All rights reserved. RealNetworks, RealAudio, RealPlayer, WebActive, and the RN logo are registered trademarks of RealNetworks.

4 (b)MS; **13** (t)MS, (b)Adobe; **14** (t)Lotus, (tc)MS, (bc)NET, (b)MS; **26** M-W.com; **27** (t)MS, (b)MSN; **28** (b)Adobe, (c)NBA.com, (t)Whitehouse. gov; **29** (t)MS, (b)MSN; **30** (b)Looksmart.com, (t)MS; **31** (b)Looksmart. com, (c)Looksmart.com, (t)Excite.com; **32** Lycos.com; **34** Google.com; **35** (b)ZDnet.com, (t)Mamma.com; **40** MS; **41** Ultrabrowser.com; **52** (b) NET; **55** (t)MS; **67** (b)MS; **76** MS; **80** (b)MS; **81** (tr)Cartoonnetwork.com; **92** REAL; **110** MS; **155** (bl)Iomega, (br)MS; **158** (t)MS; **164** Backup.com; **165** REAL; **175** Seagate Technology, Inc.; **176** Winzip Computing, Inc.; **178** Rollingstone.com; **179** MS; **180** MS; **186** MS; **190** MS; **191** (tc)MS, (bc)LOTUS, (b)LOTUS, (t)MS; **192–195** MS; **196** C/Net.com & NET; **197** MS; **199** (b)Winzip Computing, Inc., (c)MS; **200** (b)MS, (c)PowerQuest Corporation, (t)MS; **201** MS; **206** UNIX; **208** Apple Corp.; **209** MS; **210** Falon Networking; **211–214** MS; **215** (b)MS, (t)X-CD-Roast; **216** MS; **218** Roxio; **222** MS; **223** Linuxplanet.com; **228** (b)AMD, (t)Courtesy Intel Corporation; **229** Compaq; **236** MS; **237** (b)MS, (t)NET; **261** MS; **266** (b) 2Wire, Inc., Reprinted with permission. All rights reserved., (t)MS; **267** Ivisit.com; **273** MS; **274** (l)MS, (r)NET; **275** (b)CIA.gov; **276** Whitehouse. gov; **277** (b)MS, (t)Weather.com; **278** MSN.com; **279** MS; **281–282** MS; **283** (b)MSN.com, (t)NET; **284** (b)MS, (t)AOL.com; **286** (t to b)MS; **287** Earthlink.com; **293** MS; **295** MS; **296** (b)Mail.com, (t)Terra Lycos Network; **299** MS; **300** (b)PCConnection.com, (t)Amazon.com; **301** (t) Buy.com; **306** (t)Webmonkey is a registered service mark and/or trademark of Wired Ventures Inc., a Lycos Company. All Rights Reserved., (b)MS; **308** MS; **310** Pspbook.com; **311–315** MS; **319** MS; **321** MS; **322** (b) COREL, (t)MS; **323** (c)MS, (t)Footmouse.com; **324** LOTUS; **325** (b)MS, (t)LOTUS; **326** (b)MS, (t)MS; **327** LOTUS; **329** NET; **334** (cl)LOTUS, (cr)MS; **335** MS; **336** (b)LOTUS, (t)MS; **337** COREL; **338** LOTUS; **339** MS; **340** MS; **341** LOTUS; **346** MS; **350** (b)MS; **351** (b)MS, (c)LOTUS; **352** (b)MS, (t)COREL; **353** (bl)MS, (br)MS, (t)LOTUS; **354–357** MS; **364** MS; **366** (b) LOTUS; **369** FedEx.com; **370–371** MS; **372** (b)LOTUS, (t)MS; **373** (b)MS, (c)MS, (t)LOTUS; **374** MS; **375** MS; **380** (b)COREL, (t)LOTUS; **381** Sybase.com; **383** MS; **384** (b)MS & LOTUS, (t)MS; **385** (b)MS & Cisco.com, (c)MS & Novell.com, (t)MS; **386** MS & ciwcertified.com; **387** (b)Gocertify.co, (t)Courtesy Macromedia; **392** MS; **393** Adobe; **394** (t)MS, (c)MS; **401** Adobe; **403** (bl)MS, (br)MS, (tl)Whitehouse.gov, (tr)Whitehouse.gov; **405** MS & screenshots used by permission of JASC Software; **412** MS; **413** NET; **414** NET & REAL; **415** (t)LOC.gov, (b)MS; **416** Compaq; **417** Power Production Software. All Rights Reserved.; **418** (c)Courtesy Macromedia, (t)MS; **420** (b)MS, (c)Apple Corp.; **421** (b)MS & Virtually VancouVR. All Rights Reserved., (t)MS & Courtesy MTV; **422** REAL; **423** AtomShockwave Corp.; **428** MS; **429** REAL; **433–434** MS; **437** (c)MS; **438** Google.com; **442** (b)Courtesy eHelp Corporation; **445** Winzip Computing, Inc.; **460** (b)Monster.com; (t)NationJob.com; **461** MS; **467** MS; **468** (bc)AOL.